Nicky Epstein's
KNITTING
FOR YOUR HOME

ABCDEFGHIJKLMN
OPQRSTUVWXYZ
1234567890

MARY AND JOHN SMITH
AUGUST 3 1999

Nicky Epstein's
KNITTING
FOR YOUR HOME
Afghans, Pillows, and Accents

Photographs by Jack Deutsch

The Taunton Press

Publisher: Jim Childs
Acquisitions Editor: Jolynn Gower
Assistant Editor: Sarah Coe
Technical Editor: Carla Patrick Scott
Copy Editor: Nancy N. Bailey
Cover Designer: Lynne Phillips
Interior Designer: Stephen Hughes
Layout Artist: Susie Yannes
Photographer: Jack Deutsch
Illustrator: Rosalie Vaccaro

Taunton
BOOKS & VIDEOS
for fellow enthusiasts

Printed in the United States of America
10 9 8 7 6 5 4 3 2 1

The Taunton Press, Inc., 63 South Main Street, PO Box 5506, Newtown, CT 06470-5506
e-mail: tp@taunton.com

Distributed by Publishers Group West

Library of Congress Cataloging-in-Publication Data
Epstein, Nicky.
    Nicky Epstein's Knitting for Your Home
        p.   cm.
    ISBN 1-56158-294-8
        1. Knitting—Patterns. 2. Afghans (Coverlets). 3. Pillows.
        I. Title: Knitting for Your Home. II. Title.
    TT825.E49   2000
    746.43'20437—dc21   99-089552

To Michael Anthony DeFazio, with love

Acknowledgments

This book could not have been completed without the assistance of many accomplished people, who contributed countless hours of dedicated work.

The following knitters were invaluable to me for their great skill and enthusiastic support: Jean Bloodgood, Shelly Charney, Sue Colistra, Eileen Curry, Tonya Ford, Nancy Henderson, Janet Imdorf, Arnetta Kenny, Michella Leary-Bova, Daphne McIntyre, Margarita Mejia, Julie Sabella, Jessica Saddler, Jacqueline Smyth, Mary Spagnuolo, and Dianne Weitzul.

Thank you to Carla Scott for her technical editing, diligence, and professionalism. Thanks to Elizabeth Berry, Gilda Malone, and Elke Doctorman.

Special thanks to Vincent Caputo for always being there for me with an artistic eye.

I would also like to extend my appreciation to the yarn companies for their generosity and their beautiful yarns, and to JHB Buttons, Fiber Fantasy for the useful blockers, and Fairfield Processing who graciously supplied all the pillow forms.

My sincere gratitude to the needlecraft editors who have always been so generous in encouraging and promoting my designs and books.

Thank you to the staff at The Taunton Press who have been patient and helpful in the preparation and completion of this book and to Jack Deutsch for the centrally focused photography.

Last, thanks to my husband, Howard, for not shooting me during the preparation of this book.

Contents

Introduction

Home accessories that are hand-knit with love and care often become heirlooms and family treasures. They are always a source of pride and joy. This "Unicorn in the Garden" sweater was my first design and the one that launched my career. When a knit piece is as special as this one is to me, it can always be framed as artwork. When I give a hand-knit gift to someone special, I always say "There is a kiss in every stitch!"

The collection of knit accessories in *Nicky Epstein's Knitting for Your Home* includes an array of both easy and challenging projects. I have tried to create designs that I hope will appeal to many tastes as well as to knitting skill levels from beginner to advanced.

The afghans, pillows, and home accents vary in complexity and incorporate an extensive selection of knitting techniques. Sun Visions, Textural Leaf, Provence, Cables and Cables, Tapestry, Zodiac, and Diamond Lace Floral are just a few examples of the different styles that you will encounter in this book.

I have also included some easy, fun, and quick-to-knit unusual small decorative items for the home such as felted apples, velvet pears, a gold leaf photo frame, and three lamp shades.

You will find a variety of two color and multi-color intarsia, fair isle, fair isle using the circular steeking method, duplicate stitch colorwork motifs, counterpanes, cables, arans, lace, mosaic, embroidery, appliqué pieces, three-dimensional, and special fringing and tassel techniques.

Yarn colors and styles are changed yearly by yarn companies, so don't be discouraged if some of them aren't available when you choose a project to knit. I encourage you to use your own taste and judgement when substituting yarns and consult your yarn shop for advice.

Each design includes a brief description that gives you an idea of the style of knitting techniques incorporated and prepares you for the excitement that lies ahead. I hope you'll like the variety of pieces and will try several of the classic and new techniques. You can create original pieces that will grace your home or serve as special gifts in our new century.

Happy knitting for your home!
Nicky

Abbondanza Afghan and Fruit Basket Pillow

Intermediate

Abbondanza *means "abundance" in Italian. This beautiful afghan is worked in wool panels that are connected with an easy lace pattern. The motifs are worked in duplicate stitch using chenille, creating a rich and elegant look. The matching fruit basket pillow is worked in the same style as the afghan.*

AFGHAN

FINISHED AFGHAN SIZE

Approx 54 in./137 cm wide ×
67 in./170 cm long (without fringe)

MATERIALS

Anny Blatt "No 5" (100% wool,
1¼ oz./50 g skeins, each approx
110 yds./100 m)
30 skeins #383 black (MC)
Anny Blatt "Velours" (100% acrylic,
1¼ oz./50 g skeins, each approx
110 yds./100 m)
6 skeins #298 kraft (A)
2 skeins #235 grenat (B)
1 skein each #617 verdi (C), #534
  sanguine (D), #363 mousse (E), #020
  automne (F), #507 rouge (G), #213
  fuchsia (H), #193 emaux (I) and #160
  daim (J), and #407 or (K)
Alternate colorway: "No 5" #093
  celedon (MC); "Velours" #160 daim
  (A), #534 sanguine (B)
One pair size 7 US (4.5 mm) knitting
  needles OR SIZE REQUIRED TO
  OBTAIN GIVEN GAUGE
Crochet hook for fringe
Tapestry needle
Sewing thread to match A

GAUGE

20 sts and 28 rows = 4 in./10 cm over St
  st and MC, using size 7 US (4.5 mm)
  needles.
TO SAVE TIME, TAKE TIME TO
CHECK GAUGE.

Instructions

St St Panels (make 5)

With MC, cast on 47 sts and work in St
st for 471 rows, or until piece measures
approx 67 in./170 cm from beg. Bind
off.

Lace Panels (make 4)

With MC, cast on 8 sts.
Row 1 (RS): K2, yo, ssk, k2tog, yo, k2.
Row 2: Purl. Rep last two rows until
piece measures 67 in./170 cm from beg.
Bind off.

FINISHING

Block panels lightly. With A, duplicate
stitch seven frames (63 rows) foll chart
(see p. 6 and 7) on each panel, beg the
first frame on the 7th row from cast-on
edge and leaving three MC rows
between each frame, with the 7th frame
ending six rows below the bound-off
edge. Duplicate st fruit and leaf charts
inside of frames (see placement diagram
on p. 8). With C, embroider a double-
daisy-stitch bow between each frame
(see p. 8) Sew lace strips between each
panel. Weave two strands H through
eyelets on lace panel, and stitch at
each end.

Fringe

Cut four strands MC 8 in./20.5 cm long
for each fringe. With crochet hook,
attach fringe evenly along cast-on and
bound-off edge. Trim fringe evenly.

Tassels (make 28)

Cut a piece of cardboard 4 in./10 cm wide × 4½ in./12 cm long. With MC, wrap yarn around the length of cardboard 24 times. Cut a piece of yarn about 10 in./25.5 cm long, and thread onto a tapestry needle. Insert needle under all strands at upper edge of cardboard. Pull tightly and knot securely around strands. Cut yarn loops at lower edge of cardboard. With H, cut a piece of yarn 12 in./30.5 cm long. Wrap this piece four times, 1½ in./4 cm below top knot, to form tassel neck. Thread ends onto tapestry needle, and pull to center of tassel. Attach a tassel between every 7th and 8th fringe.

Color Key

- • kraft (A)
- grenat (B)
- verdi (C)
- sanguine (D)
- mousse (E)
- automne (F)
- rouge (G)
- fuchsia (H)
- emaux (I)
- daim (J)
- or (K)
- ⟋ stem stitch

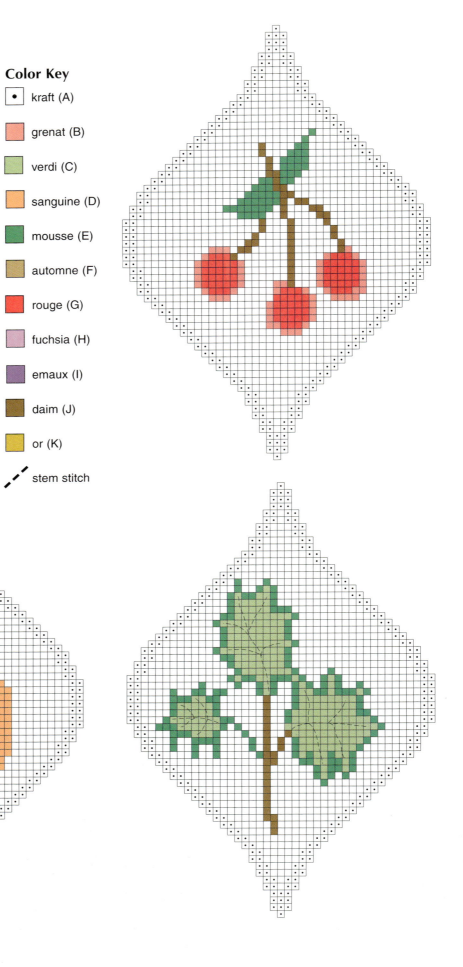

Abbondanza Placement Diagram

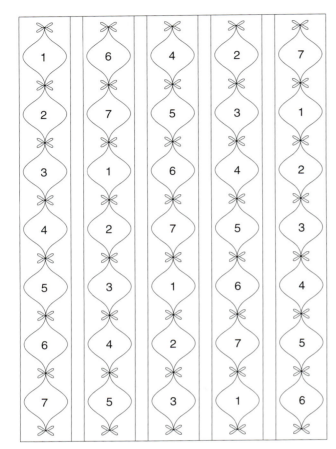

1. Red cherries
2. Orange
3. Green leaves
4. Purple grapes
5. Red apple
6. Yellow pear
7. Purple plum

Double Daisy Bow

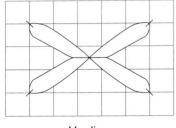

Verdi

FRUIT BASKET PILLOW

FINISHED PILLOW SIZE
Approx 20 in./50.5 cm square

MATERIALS
Anny Blatt "No 5" (100% wool, 1¼ oz./50 g skeins, each approx 110 yds./100 m)

Six skeins #383 black (MC)

Anny Blatt "Velours" (100% acrylic, 1¼ oz./50 g skeins, each approx 110 yds./100 m)

One skein each #298 kraft (A), #235 grenat (B), #617 verdi (C), #534 sanguine (D), #363 mousse (E), #020 automne (F), #507 rouge (G), #213 fuchsia (H), #193 emaux (I), #160 daim (J), #407 or (K), and #225 garance (L)

Alternate colorway: "No 5" #093 celedon (MC); "Velours" #160 daim (A), #534 sanguine (B)

One 20-in./50.5-cm-square pillow form

One pair size 7 US (4.5 mm) knitting needles OR SIZE REQUIRED TO OBTAIN GIVEN GAUGE

Crochet hook for fringe

Tapestry needle

Matching sewing thread for #160 daim (J)

GAUGE

20 sts and 28 rows = 4 in./10 cm over St st and MC, using size 7 US (4.5 mm) needles.

TO SAVE TIME, TAKE TIME TO CHECK GAUGE.

Instructions

Front

With MC, cast on 93 sts, and work in St st for 133 rows. Bind off.

Back

Work same as Front.

FINISHING

Embroider fruit basket using duplicate st, centering motif foll Fruit Basket Chart on this page. Block lightly. Sew top and sides of front and back tog, leaving bottom edge open. Insert pillow form and sew opening. With two strands A, make four twisted cords 20 in./50.5 cm long, or to fit one side, and sew to four seams with matching thread. Make four wrapped tassels same as for afghan, wrapping yarn 34 times instead of 24 times. *Note:* Necks for pillow tassels are knitted. With H, cast on 12 sts and k 1 row. Bind off knitwise on next row. Sew to neck (1½ in./4 cm down from top knot) of each tassel. Sew one tassel to each corner.

Color Key

black (MC)	mousse (E)
kraft (A)	automne (F)
grenat (B)	rouge (G)
verdi (C)	fuchsia (H)
sanguine (D)	emaux (I)

daim (J)
or (K)
garance (L)
stem stitch

Angel Afghan

Angel blocks, star blocks, and small diamonds are crocheted together to make this heavenly afghan. A duplicate stitch along with embroidery and a connecting crochet stitch are the techniques used. The border is a bold rib stitch, and the four corners are adorned by four wrapped tassels with knitted gold necks. An alternate version with a white background is shown.

FINISHED SIZE
Approx 48 in./122 cm × 62 in./157.5 cm

MATERIALS
JCA/Reynolds "Paterna" (100% wool, 1¾ oz./50 g skeins, each approx 110 yds./100 m)
13 skeins #707 navy (MC)
6 skeins #439 dark gold (CC)
1 skein each #994 peach (A), #10 ecru (B)
For Angel I:
1 skein each #431 yellow (C), #214 medium pink (D), #478 light pink (E)
For Angel II:
1 skein each #847 rust (C), #329 medium teal (D), #730 light teal (E)
For Angel III:
1 skein each #472 tan (C), #627 medium purple (D), #636 light purple (E)
JCA/Reynolds "Cloisonne" (metallic yarn, each approx 20 yds./18 m)
Three cards gold metallic (F)
One pair size 8 US (5 mm) knitting needles OR SIZE REQUIRED TO OBTAIN GIVEN GAUGE
Size 8 US (5 mm) circular needle for border
Tapestry needle
Size 6/G US (4.5 mm) crochet hook

GAUGE
20 sts and 28 rows = 4 in./10 cm over St st, using size 8 US (5 mm) needles.
TO SAVE TIME, TAKE TIME TO CHECK GAUGE.

Instructions

Blocks (make 12)
With MC, cast on 43 sts. Working in St st, inc 1 st each side every RS row

Color Key

- ■ navy (MC)
- ■ dark gold (CC)
- □ peach (A)
- □ ecru (B)
- ■ gold metallic (F)

Angel

- ◌ (C)
- ■ (D)
- □ (E)

Star Block Chart 1

90
85
80
75
70
65
60
55
50
45
40
35
30
25
20
15
10
5

---

10 times—63 sts. Work even until piece measures 10 in./25.5 cm from beg, end with a WS row. Dec 1 st each side every RS row 10 times, end with a WS row—43 sts. Bind off.

Whole Diamonds (make 6)

With CC, cast on 1 st.

Next row (RS): K into front, back and front of st—3 sts.

Next row: Purl. Cont in St st, inc 1 st each side every RS row 8 times, end with a WS row—19 sts. Dec 1 st each side every RS row 8 times, end with a WS row—3 sts. SK2P. Bind off.

Horizontal Half-Diamonds (make 4)

Work as for whole diamonds until all increases have been worked, end with a WS row—19 sts. Bind off.

Right Vertical Half-Diamonds (make 3)

With CC, cast on 1 st.

Next row (RS): K into front and back of st—2 sts.

Next row: Purl. Cont in St st, inc 1 st at end of every RS row 7 times, end with a WS row—9 sts. Dec 1 st at end of every RS row 7 times, end with a WS row—2 sts. K2tog. Fasten off.

Left Vertical Half-Diamonds (make 3)

Work as for right vertical half-diamonds, reversing all shaping by working incs and decs at beg of RS row.

Corners (make 4)

Make first two corners as follows: With CC, cast on 1 st.

Next row (RS): K into front and back of st—2 sts.

Next row: Purl. Cont in St st, inc 1 st at end of every RS row 7 times, end with a WS row—9 sts. Bind off.

Make last two corners as follows: With CC, cast on 1 st.

Next row (RS): Knit into front and back of st—2 sts.

Next row: Purl. Cont in St st, inc 1 st at beg of every RS row 7 times, end with a WS—9 sts. Bind off.

EMBROIDERY

Duplicate st six blocks, foll Star Block Chart 1. Duplicate st six blocks, foll Angel Block Chart 2, making two of each color version (see Materials for Angels I, II, and III). Duplicate st each whole diamond, foll Chart 3.

Angel Block Chart 2

Chart 3

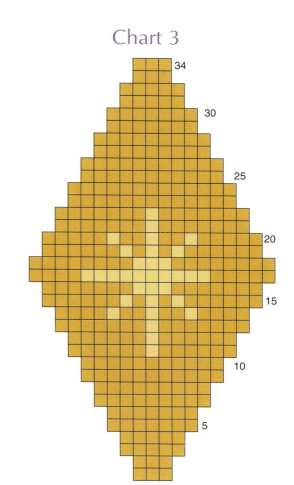

Embroider eyes with straight st, using C. Embroider accents on wings with straight st, using F. Embroider belt ties with stem stitch, using F, then add a French knot at the end of each tie.

FINISHING

Angel and Star Block Edging

With RS facing and CC, work sc evenly around each block, making sure that the work lies flat, as foll: 41 sc across each long edge and 9 sc across each shaped edge, working 3 sc in each corner. Join rnd with a sl st in first sc. Fasten off.

Diamond and Corner Edging

Work 1 rnd sc evenly around each diamond and corner, working 3 sc in each corner, making sure that work lie flat. With CC, whipstitch pieces tog from WS. Referring to photo for placement

of different color angels and star blocks, sew side edges of three blocks tog to form four rows. Sew rows tog adding whole and half diamonds and corners as you go.

Top and Bottom Borders

With RS facing, circular needle, and CC, pick up and k 179 sts evenly spaced across top edge.

Row 1 (WS): P1, *k3, p3; rep from *, end k3, p1.

Row 2: K1,* p3, k3; rep from *, end p3, k1.

Cont in k3, p3 rib as established, inc 1 st each side every RS row 4 times— 187 sts. Bind off loosely in ribbing. Work in same way across bottom edge.

Side Borders

Work as for top and bottom borders, picking up 191 sts. Sew mitered corner edges tog.

Tassels (make 4)

Wrap CC 80 times around a 5½ in./ 14 cm length of cardboard. Thread tapestry needle with a double strand of CC. Run needle under tassel strands at top of cardboard. Tie tight at top, then cut strands at bottom of cardboard. With F, cast on 17 sts. K 1 row. Bind off on next row. Wrap around neck and sew to tassel 1 in./2.5 cm from top. Fasten off securely. Sew a tassel to each corner.

Felted Apple

Knit an apple a day to keep the therapist away! Or knit a whole bushel. The trick to getting the right size is to knit approximately a third size larger than you want the finished apple to be. It shrinks to size when felted. Two skeins of Paterna make five apples. Make a basket of these and felt them together.

FINISHED SIZE

Approx circumference 13 in./33 cm (after felting)

MATERIALS

JCA/Reynolds "Paterna" (100% wool, 1¾ oz./50 g skeins, each approx 110 yds./100 m)

Red apple: One skein #808 red, small amount #121 brown and #922 green

Green apple: One skein #914 green, small amount #439 gold

One pair knitting needles and one set double-pointed needles, each size 8 US (5 mm) OR SIZE REQUIRED TO OBTAIN GIVEN GAUGE

Poly-Fil stuffing

Long tapestry needle

Liquid laundry detergent

GAUGE

20 sts and 28 rows = 4 in./10 cm over St st, using size 8 US (5 mm) needles.

TO SAVE TIME, TAKE TIME TO CHECK GAUGE.

Instructions

Cast on 12 sts.

Row 1 (RS): K1, *k in front and back of next st; rep from * to end—23 sts.

Row 2 and all WS rows, except Rows 34 and 36: Purl.

Row 3: Rep Row 1—45 sts.

Row 5: Knit.

Row 7: *K5, m1; rep from *, end k5—53 sts.

Rows 9–26: Work even in St st.

Row 27: *K3, k2tog; rep from * to end—43 sts. End K3.

Row 29: Knit.

Row 31: *K2, k2tog; rep from *, end k3—33 sts.

Row 33: *K1, k2tog; rep from * to end—22 sts.

Row 34: P1, *p2tog; rep from *, end p1—12 sts.

Row 35: K1, *k2tog; rep from *, end k1—7 sts.

Row 36: P1, *p2tog; rep from * to end—4 sts.

Stem

With dpn and stem color, k2tog, k2—3 sts. *Slide sts back to beg of needle and k3; rep from * until stem measures 1½ in./4 cm. Work SK2P. Fasten off, leaving a long length for sewing.

Sew back seam of apple using mattress st, leaving bottom open.

Leaf

Foll the instructions on p. 143.

Felting

Agitate apple in hot/cold water cycle with laundry detergent for half an hour. Press out water with a towel. Stuff apple with Poly-Fil, and sew bottom closed. Thread long length of yarn through top to bottom, pull tightly and knot; shape apple. Wash in machine on hot/cold cycle with laundry detergent three or four times until apple is completely felted. *Note:* Complete felting takes three or four wash cycles.

Bear

Soft and cuddly, this bear is easy three-dimensional knitting.
It is made of a yarn appropriately called "Teddy." The hardest part
of this project is finding the fish to put on your pole.

SIZE

Approx. 20 in./50.5 cm high and as fat
as you like

MATERIALS

Stahl Wolle/Tahki "Teddy" (56% wool,
37% acrylic, 7% polymide, 1¼ oz./
50 g skeins, each approx 59 yds./55 m)
Three skeins #5227 tan (A)
Small amount #5212 brown (B)
"Hobby" (40% wool, 60% acrylic,
1¼ oz./50 g skeins, each approx
135 yd./125 m)
One skein #4829 jade (C)
"Hobby Kids" (40% wool, 60% acrylic,
1¼ oz./50 g skeins, each approx
135 yd./125 m)
One skein #4663 red multi (D)
Alternate colorway: "Teddy" #5212
brown (A) and #5227 tan (B)
One pair each size 4 US and 10 US
(3.5 mm and 6 mm) knitting needles
OR SIZE REQUIRED TO
OBTAIN GIVEN GAUGE
Size D/3 (3 mm) crochet hook
Two 6¼-in. (15.5-cm)-diameter circles
of brown fabric
Sew-on animal eyes and nose

Poly-Fil stuffing
Small amount weighted stuffing pellets
6-in./15-cm twig
String

GAUGE

28 sts and 32 rows = 4 in./10 cm over
rev St st with A, using larger needles.
TO SAVE TIME, TAKE TIME TO
CHECK GAUGE.

Instructions

Body

With larger needles and A, cast on 53
sts. Work in rev St st for 12 in./30.5 cm,
end with a RS row.

Head Shaping

Next row: K1, k2tog across, end k2—
28 sts. Work even for 1½ in./4 cm, inc
7 sts evenly spaced across last row—
35 sts. Work even until head measures
5 in./12.5 cm.
   Next row: K1, *k2tog; rep from * to
end—18 sts.
   Next row: *P2tog; rep from * to
end—9 sts.
   Next row: K1, *k2tog; rep from * to
end. Cut yarn, leaving a long end. Draw
end through rem sts, gather tightly tog,
and fasten off.

Ears

Outer ear (make 2)

With larger needles and A, cast on 9 sts.
Work in rev St st for 1 in./2.5 cm, end
with a RS row.
   Next row: K2 tog, k5, k2tog—7 sts.
   Next row: P2tog, p3, p2tog—5 sts.
   Next row: K2tog, k1, k2tog—3 sts.
Bind off.

Ear lining (make 2)

With larger needles and B, cast on 7 sts.
Work in rev St st for 1 in./2.5 cm, end
with a RS row.
   Next row: K2 tog, k3, k2tog—5 sts.
   Next row: P2tog, p1, p2tog—3 sts.
Bind off. Sew pairs of ears tog.

Tail

With larger needles and A, cast on 7 sts.
Work in rev St st for 1 in./2.5 cm, end
with a RS row.
   Next row: K2 tog, k3, k2tog—5 sts.
   Next row: P2tog, p1, p2tog—3 sts. K
1 row.
   Next row: SK2P. Fasten off. Fold tail
and sew side seam.

FINISHING

Note: Use smooth yarn for sewing.

Sew back seam. Stuff head first, inserting a small ball of Poly-Fil stuffing for nose. Foll manufacturer's directions, attach eyes and nose. With B, foll photo, embroider stem st mouth. Sew on ears. Stuff body. Whipstitch one fabric circle to open end of body. Whipstitch rem circle over first, leaving a small opening. Roll scrap piece of paper into a funnel shape and use to fill space between circles with a small amount of stuffing pellets. Finish sewing closed. With B, foll photo, backstitch outlines of arm and leg, working through bear body. Work straight st claws on paws. Sew on tail.

Scarf

With smaller needles and C, cast on 22 sts. Work in St st for 6 rows. Change to D and work 2 rows. Cont working in St st and Stripe Pat as established until piece measures 25 in./63.5 cm from beg. Bind off. Fold scarf in half lengthwise and sew seam. Cut 28 2½ in./6 cm lengths of D. Knot two lengths at a time, 7 times across each end of scarf for fringe. Trim ends evenly. Tie scarf around bear's neck.

Fishin' Pole

Tie string to one end of twig and a small fish to the end of the string, if you like. Poke twig into bear's body to secure.

Cables and Cables Afghan and Pillow

Intermediate

Like working cables? This afghan is for you. It uses a cable pattern stitch with knit cable "twisted fringe." A small and large cable combination is worked in panels that alternate the cable pattern stitches. The unusual cable fringe is unraveled, then each fringe is twisted and steamed to hold the twist.

AFGHAN

FINISHED AFGHAN SIZE

Approx 45 in./114 cm wide × 64 in./ 162 cm long

MATERIALS

Brown Sheep "Lambs Pride Superwash Bulky" (100% wool, 3½ oz./100 g skeins, each approx 110 yds./100 m)

15 skeins #M76 misty blue

Alternate colorways: #M77 blue magic, #M08 wild oak, or #M86 almond blossom

One pair size 10½ US (6.5 mm) knitting needles OR SIZE REQUIRED TO OBTAIN GIVEN GAUGE

Cable needle

Tapestry needle

GAUGES

16 sts and 20 rows = 4 in./10 cm over St st, using size 10½ US (7 mm) needles.

18 sts and 20 rows = 4 in./10 cm over Cable Panel #1, using size 10½ US (7 mm) needles.

TO SAVE TIME, TAKE TIME TO CHECK GAUGES.

STITCH GLOSSARY

4-st BC: Sl 2 sts to cn and hold at back of work, k2, k2 from cn.

12-st BC: Sl 6 sts to cn and hold at back of work, k6, k6 from cn.

PATTERN STITCHES

Cable Panel #1
(multiple of 6 sts plus 2)

Row 1 (RS): P2, *4-st BC, p2; rep from * to end.

Rows 2 and 4: K2, *p4, k2; rep from * to end.

Row 3: P2, *k4, p2; rep from * to end.

Rep Rows 1–4 for Cable Panel #1.

Cable Panel #2 (over 12 sts)

Row 1 (RS): K3, p1, k4, p1, k3.

Row 2 and all WS rows: K the knit sts and p the purl sts.

Rows 3, 7, and 11: Rep Row 1.

Rows 5 and 9: K3, p1, 4-st BC, p1, k3.

Rows 13, 15, 17, and 19: Knit.

Row 21: 12-st BC.

Rows 23, 25, and 27: Knit.

Row 28: Rep Row 2.

Rep Rows 1–28 for Cable Panel #2.

Cable Panel #3 (over 16 sts)

Rows 1, 3, and 5 (RS): P2, k12, p2.

Row 2 and all WS rows: K the knit sts and p the purl sts.

Row 7: P2, 12-st BC, p2.

Rows 9, 11, and 13: P2, k12, p2.

Rows 15, 17, 21, and 25: P2, k3, p1, k4, p1, k3, p2.

Rows 19 and 23: P2, k3, p1, 4-st BC, p1, k3, p2.

Row 27: P2, k12, p2.

Row 28: Rep Row 2.

Rep Rows 1–28 for Cable Panel #3.

Cable Panel #4 (over 40 sts)

Row 1 (RS): [K3, p1, 4-st BC, p1, k3, p2] twice, k3, p1, 4-st BC, p1, k3.

Rows 2 and 4: K the knit sts and p the purl sts.

Row 3: [K3, p1, k4, p1, k3, p2] twice, k3, p1, k4, p1, k3.

Rep Rows 1–4 for Cable Panel #4.

Instructions

Right Panel

Cast on 62 sts. Foundation row (WS): K2, p4, k2, p3, k1, p4, k1, p3, k2, p12, k2, p3, k1, p4, k1, p3, k2, [p4, k2] twice.

Beg pats—Row 1 (RS): Work Cable Panel #1 over 14 sts, Cable Panel #2 over 12 sts, Cable Panel #3 over 16 sts, Cable Panel #2 over 12 sts, Cable Panel #1 over 8 sts. Cont in pats as established for a total of 96 rows. Next row (RS): Cont Cable Panel #1 over 14 sts, work Cable Panel #4 over 40 sts, cont Cable Panel #1 over 8 sts. Cont in pats as established for a total of 96 rows. Rep 96 rows between *'s. Bind off.

Center Panel

Cast on 56 sts. Foundation row (WS): K2, p4, k2, p3, [k1, p4, k1, p3, k2, p3] twice, k1, p4, k1, p3, k2, p4, k2. *Beg pats—Row 1 (RS): Work Cable Panel #1 over 8 sts, Cable Panel #4 over 40 sts, Cable Panel #1 over 8 sts. Cont in pats as established for a total of 96 rows.* Next row (RS): Work Cable Panel #1 over 8 sts, Cable Panel #2 over 12 sts, Cable Panel #3 over 16 sts, Cable Panel #2 over 12 sts, Cable Panel #1 over 8 sts. Cont in pats as established for a total of 96 rows. Rep 96 rows between *'s. Bind off.

Left Panel

Work same as Right Panel.

FINISHING

Block lightly. Sew panels tog.

Cable Fringe (make 2)

Cast on 14 sts.

Row 1 (RS): K1, p2, k4, p2, k5.

Rows 2 and 4: K the knit sts and p the purl sts.

Row 3: K1, p2, 4-st BC, p2, k5. Rep Rows 1–4 until piece measures the width of one short side of afghan, end with a WS row. Bind off first 8 sts, tie off 9th st, unravel rem 5 sts for fringe. Sew to ends of afghan. Using a long tapestry needle, twist and steam each fringe.

Tip: If you don't choose to twist the fringe, you may just leave it looped or cut it evenly.

PILLOW

FINISHED PILLOW SIZE

Approx 18 in./45.5 cm square

MATERIALS

Brown Sheep "Lamb's Pride Superwash Bulky" (100% wool, 3½ oz./100 g skeins, each approx 110 yds./100 m)

Three skeins #M76 misty blue

One 18-in./45-cm-square pillow form

One pair size 10½ US (7 mm) knitting needles OR SIZE REQUIRED TO OBTAIN GIVEN GAUGE

Cable needle

One button

Tapestry needle

GAUGES

16 sts and 20 rows = 4 in./10 cm over St st, using size 10½ US (7 mm) needles.

18 sts and 20 rows = 4 in./10 cm over Cable Panel #1, using size 10½ US (7 mm) needles.

TO SAVE TIME, TAKE TIME TO CHECK GAUGES.

Instructions

Cast on 82 sts. Foundation row (WS): P1, *k2, p4; rep from *, end k2, p1. Beg pat—Next row (RS): K1, work in Cable Panel #1 over 80 sts, k1. Cont in pats as established until piece measures 39 in./99 cm from beg, end with a pat Row 2.

Shape flap: Bind off 7 sts at beg of next 2 rows. Work 2 rows even. Bind off 6 sts at beg of next 2 rows. Work 2 rows even. Rep last 4 rows until there are 8 sts. Bind off rem sts on last RS row.

Cable fringe: Work same as afghan until piece fits along flap. Complete same as afghan. Sew fringe along flap.

FINISHING

Block lightly. Fold knitted pillow cover around pillow form, with shaped flap overlapped to the front. Sew side seams. Sew a button in center point of flap.

By the Sea Afghan

By the sea, by the sea, by the beautiful sea. Made up of intarsia blocks, this afghan is sprinkled with seashore motifs on solid basketweave blocks. The blocks are sewn together and then embroidered with a whipstitch. The entire afghan is edged with garter stitch in a contrasting color.

FINISHED SIZE

Approx 42 in./106 cm wide × 64 in./ 162 cm long

MATERIALS

JCA/Reynolds "Saucy" (100% cotton, 3½ oz./100 g skeins, each approx 185 yds./169 m)

Ten skeins #817 ecru (A)

Three skeins #71 teal (B)

One skein each #395 mauve (C), #901 corn (D), #820 tan (E), and #654 lavender (F)

One pair each size 5 US and 6 US (3.75 mm and 4 mm) knitting needles OR SIZE REQUIRED TO OBTAIN GIVEN GAUGE

Bobbins

Tapestry needle

GAUGE

20 sts and 28 rows = 4 in./10 cm over St st, using size 6 US (4 mm) needles. TO SAVE TIME, TAKE TIME TO CHECK GAUGE.

Notes: Use a separate bobbin of yarn for each block of color.

When changing colors, twist yarn to prevent holes.

Work first row of each new color in St st, then cont in garter st, seed st, or rib st, as required.

PATTERN STITCHES

Basketweave Stitch (multiple of 6 sts plus 3 sts)

Rows 1 and 3 (RS): K3, *p3, k3; rep from * to end.

Row 2 and all WS rows: K the knit sts and p the purl sts.

Rows 5 and 7: P3, *k3; p3; rep from * to end.

Row 8: Rep Row 2.

Rep Rows 1–8 for basketweave st.

Instructions

Ecru Block (make 12)

With larger needles and A, cast on 49 sts. Beg pat.

Row 1 (RS): K2, work basketweave st to last 2 sts, k2.

Cont in pat as established, keeping first and last 2 sts in St st until 68 rows have been worked from beg. Bind off.

Motif Block (make 2 of each motif)

With larger needles and A, cast on 46 sts. Work in St st and chart pat (see pp. 24 to 25) for 68 rows. Bind off.

FINISHING

Block pieces. With B, embroider details on butterfly fish and sundial shell in stem st. Foll placement diagram (see p. 25), alternate basketweave blocks with motif blocks to make six strips of four blocks each. Sew strips tog. With B, embroider whipstitch over horizontal and vertical seams.

Top and Bottom Borders

With RS facing, smaller needles, and B, pick up and k 183 sts along top edge of afghan. Work in garter st for 9 rows, inc 1 st each side every other row—191 sts. Bind off. Work in same way along bottom edge.

Side Borders

With RS facing, smaller needles, and B, pick up and k 312 sts along each side edge. Work in garter st for 9 rows, inc 1 st each side every other row—320 sts. Bind off. Sew mitered corners tog.

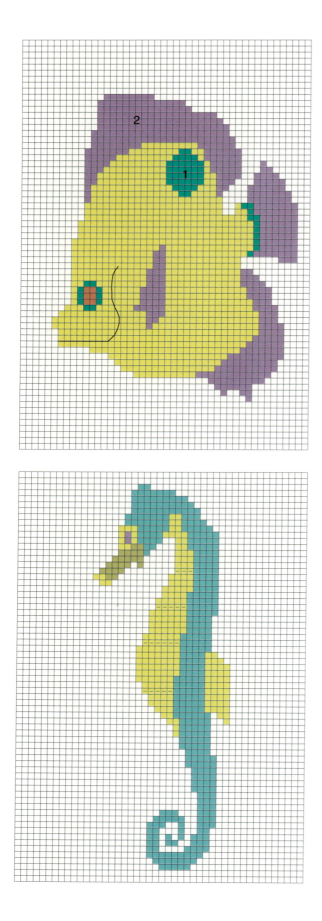

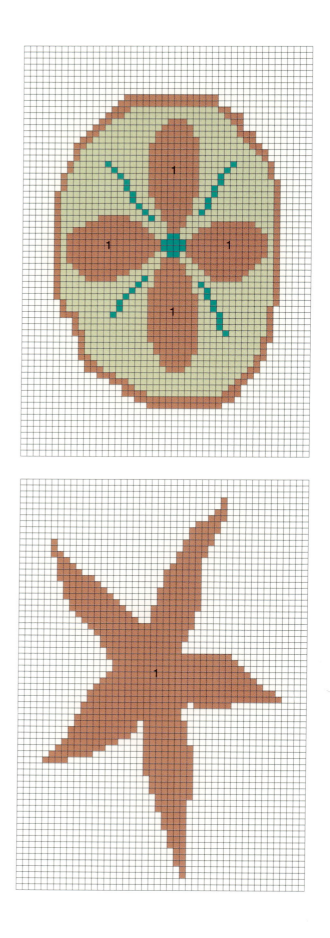

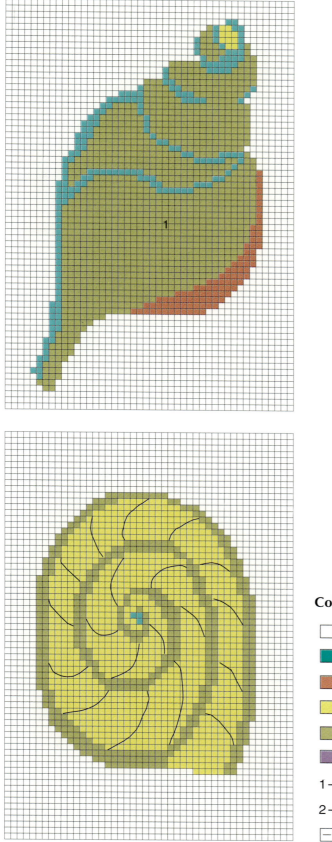

By the Sea Placement Diagram

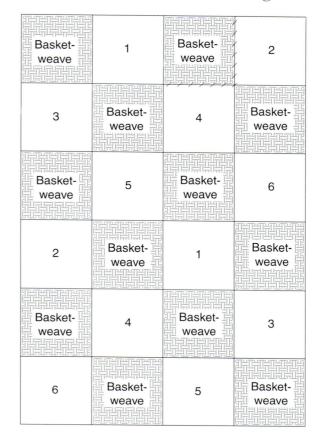

1. Butterfly fish
2. Sand dollar
3. Tulip shell
4. Sea horse
5. Starfish
6. Sundial shell

Color Key

☐ ecru (A)

■ teal (B)

■ mauve (C)

■ corn (D)

■ tan (E)

■ lavender (F)

1 — seed st

2 — K1, p1 rib

─ K on WS

Cables and Berries Afghan

Intermediate

Juicy berries done in appliquéd patchwork combine with a cable pattern stitch to create this afghan. The background is knit in one piece using a cable stitch. The patches are reverse stockinette stitch with appliqués sewn onto each one. A picot border is sewn around each block before it is sewn to the afghan background.

FINISHED SIZE

Approx 50 in./127 cm wide × 65 in./165 cm long

MATERIALS

Brown Sheep "Lamb's Pride Superwash" (100% wool, 3½ oz./100 g skeins, each approx 110 yds./100 m)

23 skeins #SW18 lichen (MC)

1 skein each #63 midnight pine (A), #55 plum crazy (B), #96 purple haze (C), #34 rose quartz (D), #43 romantic ruby (E), #27 mysterious fuchsia (F)

One size 10½ US (6.5 mm) circular knitting needle and 1 pair size 9 US (5.5 mm) knitting needles OR SIZE REQUIRED TO OBTAIN GIVEN GAUGE

Cable needle

Tapestry needle

GAUGE

17 sts and 17 rows = 4 in./10 cm over Cable Pat, using size 10½ US (6.5 mm) needles.

TO SAVE TIME, TAKE TIME TO CHECK GAUGE.

STITCH GLOSSARY

RT: Sk next st, k 2nd st in front of first st, k first st, and drop both sts from needle.

8-st BC: Sl 4 sts to cn and hold at back of work, k1, p2, k1; then k1, p2, k1 from cn.

PATTERN STITCHES

Cable Pattern
(multiple of 18 sts plus 14)

Foundation row (WS): P1, k2, *p1, k2, p2, k2, p1, [k2, p2] twice, k2; rep from * to last 11 sts, end p1, k2, p2, k2, p1, k2, p1.

Rows 1, 5, and 9: K1, p2, *k1, p2, k2, p2, k1, [p2, k2] twice, p2; rep from * to last 11 sts, end k1, p2, k2, p2, k1, p2, k1.

Row 2 and all WS rows: K the knit sts and p the purl sts.

Rows 3 and 7: K1, p2, *k1, p2, k2, p2, k1, p2, [RT, p2] twice; rep from * to last 11 sts, end k1, p2, k2, p2, k1, p2, k1.

Row 11: K1, p2, *8-st BC, p2, [RT, p2] twice; rep from * to last 11 sts, end 8-st BC, p2, k1.

Row 12: Rep Row 2.

Rep Rows 1–12 for Cable Pat.

Instructions

With MC, cast on 212 sts. Work back and forth in Cable Pat for approx 63 in./160 cm, end with pat row 9. Bind off.

Patches (make 10)

With MC, cast on 30 sts and work in St st for 8 in./20.5 cm. Bind off.

Make two patches of each berry. Foll diagram (see p. 28) for berry and patch placements.

Note: All berries are worked with smaller needles.

Cables and Berries Placement Diagram

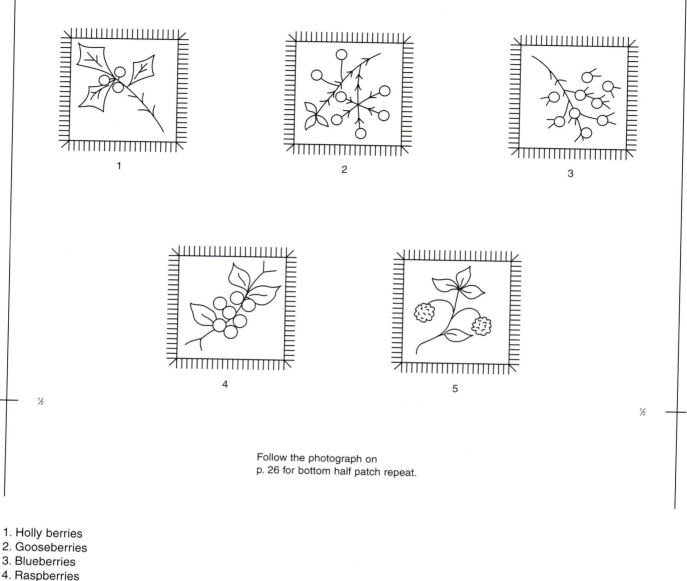

½   ½

Follow the photograph on
p. 26 for bottom half patch repeat.

1. Holly berries
2. Gooseberries
3. Blueberries
4. Raspberries
5. Mulberries

1. Holly Berries (make 3)

With E, cast on 1 st. K into front, back, front, and back of st to make 4 sts in one. P 1 row, k 1 row, p 1 row.

Next row: K2tog twice.

Next row: P2tog. Tie off.

Leaves (make 3)

With A, cast on 5 sts.

Row 1: K2, yo, k1, yo, k2.

Rows 2, 4, 6, and 10: Purl.

Row 3: K3, yo, k1, yo, k3—9 sts.

Row 5: K4, yo, k1, yo, k4—11 sts.

Row 7: Bind off 3 sts, k1, yo, k1, yo, k5.

Row 8: Bind off 3 sts, p6.

Row 9: K3, yo, k1, yo, k3.

Row 11: Bind off 3 sts, k5.

Row 12: Bind off 3 sts, p2.

Row 13: SK2P. Tie off.

Tie berries to p side of patch, foll diagram (above).

Stem

With A, work stem st, foll diagram. Sew on leaves.

2. Gooseberries (make 7)

With B, cast on 11 sts. K 1 row. Pass the last 10 sts, one at a time, over the first st. Tie off. Sew ends tog and tie in place. With A, work stem, foll diagram. Add three leaves, using daisy st.

3. Blueberries (make 9)

With C, cast on 1 st. K into front, back, front, back, and front of st to make 5 sts in one. P 1 row, k 1 row, p 1 row.

Next row: K2tog, k1, k2tog—3 sts. P 1 row.

Next row: SK2P. Tie off. Tie berries in a cluster to p side of patch, foll diagram.

Stem

With two strands A, work stem st, foll diagram. With single strand A, make two single daisy sts above each berry.

4. Raspberries (make 7)

With D, cast on 1 st. K into front, back, front, back, and front of st to make 5 sts in one.

Next row: [K1, p1] twice, k1. Rep last row for seed st for 5 rows.

Next row: K2tog, k1, k2tog.

Next row: SK2P. Tie off. Tie berries to p side of patch, foll diagram.

Leaves (make 3)

With A, cast on 5 sts.

Row 1 (RS): K2, yo, k1, yo, K2—7 sts.

Row 2 and all WS rows: Purl.

Row 3: SSK, k3, k2tog—5 sts.

Row 5: SSK, k1, k2tog—3 sts.

Row 7: SK2P. Tie off last st.

Stem

With A, work stem st, foll diagram. Sew on leaves.

5. Mulberries (make 2)

With F, cast on 1 st. K into front, back, front, back, and front of st to make 5 sts in one.

Next row: [K1, p1] twice, k1. Rep last row for seed st for 5 rows.

Next row: K2tog, k1, k2tog.

Next row: SK2P. Tie off. Sew berries to p side of patch, foll diagram.

Leaves (make 4)

With A, cast on 5 sts.

Row 1: K2, yo, k1, yo, k2—7 sts.

Row 2 and all WS rows: Purl.

Row 3: K3, yo, k1, yo, k3—9 sts.

Dec Row 5: SSK, k to last 2 sts, k2tog.

Rep dec row every RS row until 3 sts rem. SK2P and tie off.

Stem

With two strands A, work stem st, foll diagram. Sew on leaves.

Sew berries flat to p side of patch, foll diagram.

Borders (make 10, 1 for each patch)

With MC, cast on 5 sts, *bind off 4 sts, sl rem st from RH needle to LH needle, cast on 4 sts; rep from * until piece fits around one patch. Bind off all sts. Sew around patch.

FINISHING

Sew patches to background, foll diagram.

Work border in same way for cast-on and bound-off edge of afghan. Sew border to top and bottom edge of afghan.

Counterpane Afghan and Pillow

Counterpane blocks and solid blocks with floral appliqués combine to make this creamy white afghan. Double-knit tassels are sewn to each garter-stitch-bordered point. My matching pillow uses the counterpane block with four tassels sewn to the corners. If you like, you can also use the floral block to make the pillow.

AFGHAN

FINISHED AFGHAN SIZE

Approx 50 in./127 cm wide × 66 in./168 cm long (from point to point)

MATERIALS

Coats and Clarks "Soft" (100% Acrilan acrylic, 3½ oz./100 g skeins, each approx 230 yds./210 m)

15 skeins #1602 aran

One pair size 8 US (5 mm) knitting needles OR SIZE REQUIRED TO OBTAIN GIVEN GAUGE

Size 6 US (4 mm) circular needle

Stitch markers

12 large 1-in./2.5-cm cotton balls

GAUGES

20 sts and 28 rows = 4 in./10 cm over St st, using size 8 US (5 mm) needles.

One panel = 5½ in./14 cm from longest (bound-off) edge to point, using size 8 US (5 mm) needles.

TO SAVE TIME, TAKE TIME TO CHECK GAUGES.

Note: The main part of the square is made in four panels, which are then sewn tog.

Instructions

Counterpane Panel (make 48, which are sewn tog to make 12 squares)

Cast on 2 sts.

Row 1 (RS): K1, yo, k1.

Row 2: K1, p to last st, k1.

Row 3: [K1, yo] twice, k1.

Row 4: K1, p to last st, k1.

Row 5: [K1, yo] 4 times, k1.

Row 6: K1, p to last st, k1.

Row 7: K1, yo, p1, k2, yo, k1, yo, k2, p1, yo, k1.

Row 8: K1, p1, k1, p7, k1, p1, k1.

Row 9: K1, yo, p2, k3, yo, k1, yo, k3, p2, yo, k1.

Row 10: K1, p1, k2, p9, k2, p1, k1.

Row 11: K1, yo, p3, k4, yo, k1, yo, k4, p3, yo, k1.

Row 12: K1, p1, k3, p11, k3, p1, k1.

Row 13: K1, yo, p4, k5, yo, k1, yo, k5, p4, yo, k1.

Row 14: K1, p1, k4, p13, k4, p1, k1.

Row 15: K1, yo, p5, k6, yo, k1, yo, k6, p5, yo, k1.

Row 16: K1, p1, k5, p15, k5, p1, k1.

Row 17: K1, yo, p6, yb, SKP, k11, k2tog, p6, yo, k1.

Row 18: K1, p1, k6, p13, k6, p1, k1.

Row 19: K1, yo, p7, yb, SKP, k9, k2tog, p7, yo, k1.

Row 20: K1, p1, k7, p11, k7, p1, k1.

Row 21: K1, yo, p8, yb, SKP, k7, k2tog, p8, yo, k1.

Row 22: K1, p1, k8, p9, k8, p1, k1.

Row 23: K1, yo, p9, yb, SKP, k5, k2tog, p9, yo, k1.

Row 24: K1, p1, k9, p7, k9, p1, k1.

Row 25: K1, yo, p10, yb, SKP, k3, k2tog, p10, yo, k1.

Row 26: K1, p1, k10, p5, k10, p1, k1.

Row 27: K1, yo, p11, yb, SKP, k1, k2tog, p11, yo, k1.

Row 28: K1, p1, k11, p3, k11, p1, k1.

Row 29: K1, yo, p12, yb, SK2P, p12, yo, k1.

Row 30: K1, p to last st, k1.

Row 31: K2tog, k to last 2 sts, k2tog.

Row 32: Rep Row 30.

Row 33: *K2tog, yo; rep from * to last 3 sts, k3tog.

Row 34: Knit.

Row 35: Rep Row 31.

Rep Rows 30–35 three times more, then Rows 30 and 31 once more.

P3tog and tie off.

Stockinette Blocks (make 6)

Cast on 55 sts, and work in St st for 11 in./28 cm (approx 77 rows). Bind off.

Stockinette Half-Blocks (make 6)

Work three half-blocks as foll:

Cast on 55 sts.

Rows 1 and 5: K1, k2tog, k to end.

Rows 2 and 4: P to last 3 sts, p2tog, p1.

Row 3: Knit.

Row 6: Purl.

Rep last 6 rows 11 times more, then rep Rows 1–3 once more.

Row 76: K2tog twice, k1.

Row 77: P3tog. Tie off.

Work three half-blocks as foll:

Cast on 55 sts.

Rows 1 and 5: K to last 3 sts, SSK, k1.

Rows 2 and 4: P1, SSP, p to end.

Row 3: Knit.

Row 6: Purl.

Rep last 6 rows 11 times more, then rep Rows 1–3 once more.

Row 76: SSK twice, k1.

Row 77: P3tog. Tie off.

Large 6-Point Scallop Flower (make 6) (see photo at right)

Cast on 68 sts.

Row 1: Purl.

Row 2: K2, *k1 and sl back to LH needle, lift the next 8 sts one at a time over the knit st and off needle, [yo] twice, and k the first st again, k2; rep from * to end.

Row 3: P1, *p2tog, drop one loop of double yo of previous row, [k in front, back, front, back, and front] in rem loop, p1; rep from * to last st, p1—38 sts.

Row 4 (RS): Knit.

Rows 5 and 7: Purl.

Row 6: K5, *SK2P, k3; rep from *, end SK2P—26 sts.

Row 8: *K2tog; rep from * to end—13 sts.

Row 9: P1, *p2tog; rep from * to end—7 sts. Pass the first 6 sts over the last st. Tie off.

Small 5-Point Scallop Flower (make 12)

Cast on 57 sts.

Row 1: Purl.

Row 2: K2, *k1 and sl back to LH needle, lift the next 8 sts one at a time over the knit st and off needle, [yo] twice, and k the first st again, k2; rep from * to end.

Row 3: P1, *p2tog, drop one loop of double yo of previous row, [k in front, back, front, back and front] in rem loop, p1; rep from * to last st, p1—32 sts.

Row 4 (RS): Knit.

Row 5: Purl.

Row 6: *K2tog; rep from * to end—16 sts.

Row 7: *P2tog; rep from * to end—8 sts. Pass the first 7 sts over the last st. Tie off.

3-Point Half-Flower (make 12)

Cast on 35 sts.

Row 1: Purl.

Row 2: K2, *k1 and sl back to LH needle, lift the next 8 sts one at a time over the knit st and off needle, [yo] twice, and k the first st again, k2; rep from * to end.

Row 3: K1, *p2tog, drop one loop of double yo of previous row, [k in front, back, front, back and front] in rem loop, p1; rep from * to last st, k1.

Row 4 (RS): *K2tog, p2tog; rep from * to end—10 sts.

Rows 5–11: Cont in k1, p1 rib for 7 rows.

Row 12: *K2tog; rep from * to end— 5 sts.

Row 13: P1, *p2tog; rep from * to end—3 sts.

Row 14: SK2P. Tie off.

Bobble (make 54)

Bobbles are made separately and tied onto background. Cast on 1 st.

Row 1: [K in front, then back of st] twice, k in front of same st again to make 5 sts in one st, turn.

Rows 2 and 4: Purl, turn.

Row 3: Knit, turn.

Row 5: K2tog, k1, k2tog.

Row 6: P3tog. Tie off last st.

Leaf (make 36)

Medium leaf

Cast on 5 sts.

Row 1 (RS): K2, yo, k1, yo, k2—7 sts.
Row 2 and all WS rows: Purl.
Row 3: K3, yo, k1, yo, k3—9 sts.
Row 5: K4, yo, k1, yo, k4—11 sts.
Row 7: SSK, k7, k2tog—9 sts.
Row 9: SSK, k5, k2tog—7 sts.
Row 11: SSK, k3, k2tog—5 sts.
Row 13: SSK, k1, k2tog—3 sts.
Row 15: SK2P. Tie off last st.

Double-Knitted Tassels (make 6)

Cast on 20 sts. Work in garter st for 24 rows. Bind off 12 sts. Sew seam, gather and pull tightly at top edge. *Insert one large cotton ball. Gather at base of ball and tie securely. Rep from * once. Unravel rem 8 sts for fringe. Cut and trim fringe evenly.

Bands (make 12)

Cast on 13 sts. Bind off 13 sts. Sew bands at base of each cotton ball.

FINISHING

Foll diagram below, sew large, small, half-flowers and leaves to St st blocks. Tie one bobble to center of larger flower. Tie three bobbles on either side of floral arrangement. Work stem st at base of bobbles. *Sew four counterpane panels into a square, and tie a bobble to the center of each. Sew square to appliquéd St st block and half-blocks; rep from * until all pieces are sewn tog.

Top and bottom edge

With WS facing and smaller needle, *pick up 55 sts along one side of counterpane panel, pick up 55 sts along other side of counterpane point; rep from * twice more—330 sts.

Counterpane Floral Placement Diagram

Row 1: K2tog, *k53, [inc 1, k1, inc 1] in next st, k53, sl 2 knitwise, k1, pass 2 slipped st over k st; rep from *, end last rep k2tog.

Row 2: Knit.

Rows 3–14: Rep last 2 rows 6 times more (7 garter ridges). Bind off. Rep these 14 rows along other end of afghan.

Side edge

With WS facing and smaller needle, pick up 7 sts in garter st trim, *1 st in counterpane point, 55 sts along side of half-block; rep from * twice more, 1 st in counterpane point, and 7 sts in garter st trim—183 sts.

Row 1: K1, k2tog, k to last 3 sts, SSK, k1.

Row 2: Knit.

Rows 3–14: Rep last 2 rows 6 times more (7 garter ridges)—169 sts. Bind off. Rep these 14 rows along other side of afghan. Sew ends of garter edges tog.

Attach tassels to end of points. Weave in all ends.

PILLOW

FINISHED PILLOW SIZE
Approx 14 in./35.5 cm square

MATERIALS
Coats and Clarks "Soft" (100% Acrilan acrylic, 3½ oz./100 g skeins, each approx 230 yds./210 m)
One skein #1602 aran
One pair size 8 US (5 mm) knitting needles OR SIZE REQUIRED TO OBTAIN GIVEN GAUGE
Size 6 US (4 mm) circular needle
Stitch markers
Four large 1-in./2.5-cm cotton balls
One 14-in./35.5-cm-square pillow form

GAUGES
20 sts and 28 rows = 4 in./10 cm over St st, using size 8 US (5 mm) needles.
One panel = 5½ in./14 cm from longest (bound-off) edge to point, using size 8 US (5 mm) needles.
TO SAVE TIME, TAKE TIME TO CHECK GAUGES.

Instructions

Front and Back
Make two counterpane squares as for afghan.

Top and bottom edge: Pick up 55 sts, and work incs same as afghan edge.

Side edge: Pick up 55 sts, and work incs same as afghan.

FINISHING
Sew corners tog. Sew three sides of front and back tog, leaving bottom edge open. Insert pillow form, and sew opening. Make four tassels, and sew one tassel to each corner.

Country Animal Pillows

How ya gonna keep 'em down on the farm after they've seen "Pareee"?
These delightful country animal pillows will brighten any decor.

FINISHED PILLOW SIZE
Approx 15 in./38 cm in diameter

MOO-MOO PILLOW

Moo-Moo's eating a daisy and couldn't be more content. Add a bell around her neck if you are afraid she will get lost. The body is spiral knit with the spots knit in. No two cows are alike so make your own cow spot coloring. I've used a novelty fur yarn to make Moo-Moo.

Notes: When working the spots, use a separate skein of yarn for each large block of color. Work black spots as desired (see the photo for inspiration).

When changing colors, twist yarns to prevent holes.

MATERIALS

Lion Brand "Thick and Quick Chenille" (98% acrylic, 2% rayon, 6 oz./170g skeins, each approx 185 yds./169 m)
One skein each #098 antique white (A) and #153 black (B)
Small amount of pink worsted-weight yarn
One pair knitting needles and one set double-pointed needles, each size 11 US (8 mm) OR SIZE REQUIRED TO OBTAIN GIVEN GAUGE
Poly-Fil stuffing
One 15-in./38-cm-round pillow form
Fabric for backing
Two 15-mm eyes
Purchased daisy (optional)

GAUGE

8 sts and 10 rows = 4 in./10 cm over St st, using size 11 US (8 mm) needles.
TO SAVE TIME, TAKE TIME TO CHECK GAUGE.

Instructions

Front

With straight needles and A, cast on 104 sts. K 1 row on RS. Working spots as desired, cont as foll:

Next dec row (WS): P5, p3tog, [p10, p3tog] 7 times, p5—88 sts. K 1 row.

Next dec row (WS): P5, p2tog, [p9, p2tog] 7 times, p4—80 sts. K 1 row.

Next dec row (WS): P4, p2tog, [p8, p2tog] 7 times, p4—72 sts. K 1 row.

Cont in this way, dec 8 sts every other row, until 16 sts rem, end with a RS row.

Next row: P2tog across row—8 sts.

Cut yarn, leaving a long end. Draw end through rem sts, pull tog tightly, and secure. Sew seam.

Cow Nose and Mouth

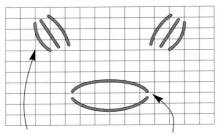

3 straight   2 long stitches
stitches

Head

With straight needles and A, cast on
10 sts. P 1 row, inc 5 sts evenly spaced
across.

Next row: K, inc 8 sts evenly
spaced—23 sts. P 1 row.

Next row: K, inc 12 sts evenly spaced
and work first 11 sts with B, next 13 sts
with A and last 11 sts with B—35 sts.

Next row: P, dec 2 sts evenly on each
B section. K 1 row.

Next row: P, dec 2 sts evenly on each
B section, 2 sts on A section.

Next row: K, dec 2 sts evenly on each
B section. P 1 row.

Next row: K, dec 1 st on each B section, 1 st on A section. P 1 row.

Next row: K, dec 2 sts evenly on A
section. Work 3 rows even.

Next row: K, dec 1 st on A section.
With B, work 5 rows even. Bind off,
working k2tog while binding off.

Ears

With straight needles and B, cast on
8 sts. K 1 row. Cont in St st, dec 1 st at
beg of every row, until 2 sts rem. Tie
off. Pleat ear at cast-on edge, and tack
folds tog.

Tail

Braid three double strands of black,
leaving loop at bottom, and knot.

FINISHING

Embroider cow nose and mouth. Stuff
and sew head. Sew on ears. Sew chosen
backing approx halfway around. Stuff
and sew opening. Sew on tail.

MEOW KITTY PILLOW

Meow Kitty had a little mouse hanging
from its mouth, but it is gone now.
Meow uses the same techniques as
Moo-Moo.

Note: When working spots, use a separate skein of yarn for each large block
of color. Work white spots as desired
(see the photo below for inspiration).
When changing colors, twist yarns to
prevent holes.

MATERIALS

Lion Brand "Thick and Quick
   Chenille" (98% acrylic, 2% rayon,
   6 oz./170 g skeins, each approx
   185 yds./169 m)

One skein each #124 khaki (A) and #098
   antique white (B)

Small amount light pink worsted-weight
   yarn

One pair knitting needles and one set
   double-pointed needles, each size
   11 US (8 mm) OR SIZE REQUIRED
   TO OBTAIN GIVEN GAUGE

Poly-Fil stuffing

One 15-in./38-cm-round pillow form

Fabric for backing

Two 18-mm eyes

GAUGE

8 sts and 10 rows = 4 in./10 cm over St
   st, using size 11 US (8 mm) needles.
   TO SAVE TIME, TAKE TIME TO
   CHECK GAUGE.

Instructions

Front

With straight needles and A, cast on
104 sts. K 1 row on RS. Working spots
as desired, cont as foll:

Cat Nose and Mouth

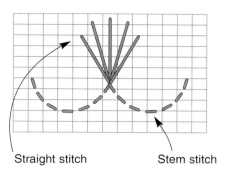

Straight stitch   Stem stitch

Next dec row (WS): P5, p3tog, [p10, p3tog] 7 times, p5—88 sts. K 1 row.

Next dec row (WS): P5, p2tog, [p9, p2tog] 7 times, p4—80 sts. K 1 row.

Next dec row (WS): P4, p2tog, [p8, p2tog] 7 times, p4—72 sts. K 1 row.

Cont in this way, dec 8 sts every other row, until 16 sts rem, end with a RS row.

Next row: P2tog across row—8 sts.

Cut yarn, leaving a long end. Draw end through rem sts, pull tog tightly, and secure. Sew seam.

Head

With dpn and A, cast on 6 sts. Divide sts evenly over three needles. Join, placing marker for beg of rnd. K 1 rnd.

Next rnd: Inc 1 st in each st—12 sts. K 1 rnd.

Next rnd: *K1, inc 1 in next st; rep from * around. K 1 rnd.

Next rnd: *K2, inc 1 in next st; rep from * around. K 1 rnd.

Cont in this way to work inc rnd every other rnd, working 1 more st between incs every inc rnd, until there are 60 sts. K 2 rnds. Bind off, working k2tog while binding off.

Ears

With straight needles and A, cast on 6 sts. K 1 row. Cont in St st, dec 1 st at beg of every row, until 1 st rem. Tie off.

Tail

With straight needles and B, cast on 3 sts. Work in St st, inc 1 st each side every other row 3 times—9 sts. Work 5 rows even. Change to A, and work even until piece measures 15 in./38 cm from beg. Bind off. Sew seam, stuffing lightly as you sew.

FINISHING

Embroider cat nose and mouth. Stuff and sew head. Sew on ears. Sew chosen backing approx halfway around. Stuff and sew opening. Sew on tail.

BAA-BAA PILLOW

Yards of scalloped edging is sewn to a round knit background. The head is dimensional and oh, when it looks at you with those eyelashes, you have to have it! Baa-Baa is made with 100% wool. This is one baa you shouldn't have any other way. The eyes and eyelashes are purchased.

MATERIALS

JCA/Reynolds "Candide" (100% wool, 3½ oz./100 g skeins, each approx 170 yds./153 m)

Four skeins #100 gray (MC), One skein #50 black (A)

Small amount #65 pink (B)

One pair knitting needles, one set double-pointed needles, and one circular needle, each size 7 US (4.5 mm) OR SIZE REQUIRED TO OBTAIN GIVEN GAUGE

One 15-in./38-cm-round pillow form

Purchased animal eyelashes and 15-mm eyes

Small amount of Poly-Fil stuffing

Fabric for backing

Tapestry needle

Sheep Nose and Mouth

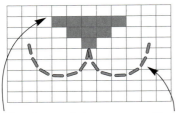

Duplicate stitch　　　　Stem stitch

GAUGE
18 sts and 22 rows = 4 in./10 cm over St st, using size 7 US (4.5 mm) needles.
TO SAVE TIME, TAKE TIME TO CHECK GAUGE.

Instructions

Front
With straight needles and MC, cast on 52 sts.

Row 1 (RS): Knit.

Row 2 and all WS rows: Purl.

Row 3: K6, *M1, k5; rep from * to last st, k1—61 sts.

Row 5: K5, *M1, k6; rep from * to last st, k1—70 sts.

Cont in this way to inc 9 sts every 4th row 4 times, every 6th row 7 times—169 sts.

Bind off loosely. Sew seam. Gather center of pillow tog, and tack closed.

Optional: If you choose to knit the back, work same as for front.

Scallops (make 7 strips)
With straight needles and MC, cast on 90 (134, 178, 222, 266, 310, 354) sts.

Row 1: Purl.

Row 2: K2, *k1 and sl this st back onto left needle, lift the next 8 sts one at a time over the knit st and off the needle, [yo] twice, and k the first st again, k2; rep from * to end.

Row 3: K1, *p2tog, drop 1 loop of double yo of previous row, ([k in front, back] twice, front) in rem yo, p1; rep from * to last st, k1.

Rows 4–6: Knit. Bind off.

Beg at bottom edge, sew first strip around pillow front along first dec rnd so that bottom of first scallop just meets the outer edge of pillow. Sew each succeeding scallop strip along dec rnds so that the bottom edge just meets the top edge of previous strip.

Head
With straight needles and A, cast on 20 sts. Work in St st, inc 1 st at beg of every row 12 times—32 sts. Work evenly until piece measures 9 in./23 cm from beg, ending with a RS row.

Row 1 (WS): P1, *p2tog, p3; rep from * to last st, p1—26 sts.

Rows 2 and 4: Knit.

Row 3: P2, *p2tog; rep from * to last 2 sts, p2—15 sts.

Row 5: P1, *p2tog; rep from * to end—8 sts. Cut yarn leaving long end. With tapestry needle, thread end through rem sts on needle. Gather up and fasten securely.

Top Knot
With straight needles and MC, cast on 46 sts. Work scallop pattern. Set aside.

Ears
With straight needles and A, cast on 5 sts. K1 row. Cont in St st, inc 1 st at beg of every row 11 times—16 sts. Work 10 more rows in St st. Bind off.

FINISHING
Sew head to center of pillow top with chin resting on bottom center. Stuff head with Poly-Fil stuffing. Sew on ears. Embroider sheep nose and mouth. Sew chosen backing approx halfway around. Insert pillow form. Finish sewing backing. Sew on eyelashes.

OINK-OINK PILLOW
Oink-Oink's body is worked in wool with converging cables. The face is dimensional and, of course, there's a curly-Q tail.

MATERIALS
JCA/Reynolds "Candide" (100% wool, 3½ oz./100 g skeins, each approx 170 yds./153 m)

Four skeins #65 pink (MC)

Small amount light pink worsted-weight yarn for nose and mouth

One pair knitting needles, one set double-pointed needles, and one circular needle, each size 7 US (4.5 mm) OR SIZE REQUIRED TO OBTAIN GIVEN GAUGE

One 15-in./38-cm-round pillow form

Purchased animal eyelashes and 15-mm eyes

Small amount of Poly-Fil stuffing

Fabric for backing

Tapestry needle

GAUGE
18 sts and 22 rows = 4 in./10 cm over St st, using size 7 US (4.5 mm) needles.
TO SAVE TIME, TAKE TIME TO CHECK GAUGE.

Instructions

Cable Pattern (multiple of 17 sts)
Rnd 1 (RS): *K4, p13; rep from * around.

Rnds 2, 4, 5, and 6: K the knit sts and p the purl sts.

Rnd 3: *Sl 2 sts to cn and hold to front of work, k2, k2 from cn (4-st FC), p13; rep from * around.

Rep Rnds 1–6 for Cable Pat.

Front
With circular needle and MC, cast on 170 sts. Join, being careful not to twist sts. Place marker for beg of rnd. Work in Cable Pat for 6 rnds.

Pig Nostrils and Mouth

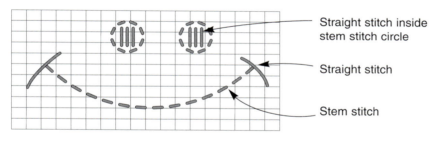

Straight stitch inside
stem stitch circle

Straight stitch

Stem stitch

Note: Change to dpn when there are not enough sts to fit on circular needle.

Rnd 7: *K4, p11, p2tog; rep from * around—160 sts.

Rnds 8–12: Work even in pat, working p12 instead of 13 between cables.

Rnd 13: *K4, p2tog, p10; rep from * around—150 sts.

Rnds 14–18: Work even in pat, working p11 between cables.

Cont in this way to dec 10 sts every 6th rnd until 50 sts rem, end with a pat rnd 6.

Next rnd: *K3, ssk; rep from * around—40 sts. K 1 rnd.

Next rnd: *4-st FC; rep from * around. K 1 rnd.

Next rnd: *K2tog; rep from * around—20 sts.

Cut yarn, leaving a long end. With tapestry needle, thread end through rem sts. Gather up and fasten securely.

Optional: If you choose to knit the back, work same as front.

Head

With dpn and MC, cast on 8 sts. Divide sts evenly over three needles. Join, placing marker for beg of rnd.

Rnd 1: Knit.

Note: Cont to k all sts through back loop.

Rnd 2 and all even rnds: Knit.

Rnd 3: Inc 1 st in each st—16 sts.

Rnd 5: *K1, inc 1; rep from * around—24 sts.

Rnd 7: *K2, inc 1; rep from * around—32 sts.

Cont in this way to inc 8 sts every other rnd, working 1 more st between inc every inc rnd, until piece measures 4 in./10 cm from center. Work 4 rnds even. Bind off, working k2tog while binding off. Cut yarn leaving a long end. Use end to slightly gather outside edge of head, pulling last 4 rnds to back. Stitch center sts tog.

Nose

Work same as Head until there are 32 sts. Bind off. Gather center sts, and loosely gather outside edge.

Ears

With straight needles, cast on 15 sts. Work in St st, dec 1 st each side every 4th row 3 times, then 1 st at beg of every row until 3 sts rem. Cut yarn. With tapestry needle, thread end through rem sts on needle, and fasten securely.

Tail

With straight needles, cast on 40 sts.

Row 1: Knit into front, back, and front of each st. Bind off purlwise.

FINISHING

Embroider nostrils and mouth with light pink. Stuff nose, and sew to head. Stuff head, and then sew to body. Sew on ears. Sew on tail. Sew chosen backing approx halfway around. Insert pillow form. Finish sewing backing. Sew on eyelashes, foll instructions on package for eyes.

Daisy Stitch Afghan and Bolster Pillow

Intermediate

Daisy stitches give a fresh look to an afghan and pillow with a cabled pattern stitch. The background of the afghan is knit in strips, and then the daisy stitches are embroidered on. The fringe is knit with a cable pattern stitch and "extra" knit stitches that are later unraveled to make the fringe.

AFGHAN

FINISHED AFGHAN SIZE
Approx 60 in./152 cm long × 72 in./ 183 cm wide

MATERIALS
Manos del Uruguay (distributed by Design Source) "700 Tex" (100% wool, 3½ oz./100 g skeins, each approx 137 yds./127m)

27 skeins #49 henna

Alternate colorways: #29 steel, #26 rosin, or #35 uranium

One pair size 10 US (6 mm) knitting needles OR SIZE REQUIRED TO OBTAIN GIVEN GAUGE

Cable needle

Stitch markers

GAUGE
18 sts and 26½ rows = 4 in./10 cm over Cable Pat, using size 10 US (6 mm) needles.

TO SAVE TIME, TAKE TIME TO CHECK GAUGE.

STITCH GLOSSARY
4-st FC: Sl 2 sts to cn and hold at front of work, k2, k2 from cn.

4-st BC: Sl 2 sts to cn and hold at back of work, k2, k2 from cn.

3-st FPC: Sl 2 sts to cn and hold at front of work, p1, k2 from cn.

3-st BPC: Sl 1 st to cn and hold at back of work, k2, p1 from cn.

Cluster 4: Worked on WS, sl 4 wyib, bring yarn to front, sl same 4 sts back to LH needle, bring yarn to back, sl 4 wyib again.

PATTERN STITCHES

**Daisy Stitch Cable Panel
(multiple of 16 sts plus 14)**

Row 1 (RS): P3, *4-st FC, 4-st BC, p8; rep from *, end last rep p3.

Rows 2 and 4: K3, *p8, k8; rep from *, end last rep k3.

Row 3: P3, *k8, p8; rep from *, end last rep p3.

Rows 5–9: Rep Rows 1–4, then Row 1 again.

Row 10: K3, *p2, Cluster 4, p2, k8; rep from *, end last rep k3.

Row 11: P2, *3-st BPC, p4, 3-st FPC, p6; rep from *, end last rep p2.

Row 12: K2, *p2, k6; rep from *, end last rep p2.

Row 13: P1, *3-st BPC, p6, 3-st FPC, p4; rep from *, end last rep p1.

Row 14: K1, p2, *k8, p2, cluster 4, p2; rep from *, end k8, p2, k1.

Row 15: P1, k2, *p8, 4-st FC, 4-st BC; rep from *, end p8, k2, p1.

Rows 16 and 18: K1, p2, *k8, p8; rep from *, end k8, p2, k1.

Row 17: P1, k2, *p8, k8; rep from *, end p8, k2, p1.

Rows 19–23: Rep Rows 15–18, then Row 15 again.

Row 24: Rep Row 14.

Row 25: P1, *3-st FPC, p6, 3-st BPC, p4; rep from *, end last rep p1.

Row 26: Rep Row 12.

Row 27: P2, *3-st FPC, p4, 3-st BPC, p6; rep from *, end last rep p2.

Row 28: Rep Row 10.

Rep Rows 1–28 for Daisy St Cable Panel.

Cable Edge (over 10 sts)

Row 1 (RS): P1, 4-st FC, 4-st BC, p1.

Rows 2 and 4: K1, p8, k1.

Row 3: P1, k8, p1.

Rep Rows 1–4 for Cable Edge.

Instructions

Panel 1

Cast on 66 sts.

Foundation row (WS): K1, p8, k1, pm, k3, p8, [k8, p8] twice, k3, pm, k1, p8, k1.

Beg pats—Row 1 (RS): Work Cable Edge over 10 sts, sl marker, work Daisy St Cable Panel over 46 sts, sl marker, work cable edge over 10 sts. Cont in pats as established until 28 rows of Daisy St Cable Panel have been worked 13 times, then work 2 rows more. Piece measures approx 64 in./140 cm from beg. Bind off.

Panels 2, 3, 4, 5

Cast on 57 sts.

Foundation row (WS): K1, p8, k1, pm, k3, p8, [k8, p8] twice, k3, pm, k1.

Beg pats—Row 1 (RS): P1, sl marker, work Daisy St Cable Panel over 46 sts, sl marker, work cable edge over 10 sts. Cont in pats as established until same number of rows as Panel 1. Bind off.

Fringe Borders (make 2)

Cast on 19 sts.

Foundation row (WS): P7, pm, k1, p8, k1, pm, k2. Beg pats—Row 1 (RS): P2, sl marker, work Cable Edge over 10 sts, sl marker, k7. Cont in pat as established until piece measures the width of one short side, end with a WS row. Bind off first 11 sts, tie off 12th st, unravel rem 7 sts for loop fringe.

FINISHING

Block lightly. Sew panels tog right to left 1, 2, 3, 4, and 5. Embroider daisy st flowers (6 loops) in center of rev St st sections. Sew borders to cast-on and bound-off edges.

BOLSTER PILLOW

FINISHED PILLOW SIZE

Approx. 5 in./12.5 cm × 14 in./35.5 cm

MATERIALS

Manos del Uruguay (distributed by Design Source) "700 Tex" (100% wool, 3½ oz./100 g skeins, each approx 137 yds./127m)

Two skeins #49 henna or alternate colorway shown on p. 41.

One pair size 10 US (6 mm) knitting needles OR SIZE REQUIRED TO OBTAIN GIVEN GAUGE

Cable needle (cn)

Stitch markers

One 5-in./12.5-cm × 14-in./35.5-cm bolster pillow form

GAUGE

18 sts and 26½ rows = 4 in./10 cm over Cable Pat, using size 10 US (6 mm) needles.

TO SAVE TIME, TAKE TIME TO CHECK GAUGE.

Instructions

Cast on 80 sts.

Foundation row (WS): P7, pm, k1, p8, k1, pm, k3, p8, [k8, p8] twice, k3, pm, k1, p8, k1, pm, p7.

Beg pats—Row 1 (RS): K7, sl marker, work Cable Edge over 10 sts, sl marker, work Daisy St Cable Panel over 46 sts, sl marker, work Cable Edge over 10 sts, sl marker, k7. Cont in pats as established until until 28 rows of Daisy St Cable Panel have been worked 4 times, then work Rows 1–8 once more. Next row (RS): Sl first 7 sts off needle for loop fringe, bind off next 65 sts, tie off next st, sl last 7 sts off needle for loop fringe.

End Pieces (make 2)

Cast on 80 sts. K 1 row, p 1 row. Next dec row (RS): *Sl 1 knitwise, k2tog, psso (SK2P), k13; rep from * to end—70 sts. P 1 row. Next row: *SK2P, k11; rep from * to end—60 sts. P 1 row. Cont in this way to dec 10 sts every RS row, until 10 sts rem. K2tog across last RS row. Fasten off.

FINISHING

Block lightly. Sew cast-on and bound-off edges of main piece tog. Sew one end piece in place. Insert pillow form, and sew on other end piece. Unravel fringe on each side.

Diamond Lace Floral Afghan

Intermediate

Embellished with embroidered flowers and woven ribbon, this delicate afghan is knit in a diamond lace pattern. The afghan is worked in five panels with six eyelet-connecting panels that are laced with ribbon. A knitted fringe adds a unique border.

FINISHED AFGHAN SIZE

Approx 52 in./132 cm wide ×
66 in./168 cm long (without fringe)

MATERIALS

Tahki "Cotton Classic" (100% cotton,
1¾ oz./50 g skeins, each approx
108 yds./99 m)
26 skeins #3752 light green (MC)
One skein each #3934 lilac, #3942
orchid, #3534 yellow, and #3754
medium sage green for embroidery
Size 5 US (3.75 mm) circular knitting
needle OR SIZE REQUIRED TO
OBTAIN GIVEN GAUGE
80 yds./73 m Offray Ribbon, single face
satin, ¼ in./0.5 cm wide, in #464
delphinium

GAUGE

55 sts = 8½ in./21.5 cm and 44 rows =
6 in./15 cm over Diamond Lace
Panel, using size 5 US (3.75 mm)
needles.
TO SAVE TIME, TAKE TIME TO
CHECK GAUGE.

PATTERN STITCHES

Eyelet Panel (over 10 sts)
Row 1 (RS): K1, k2tog, yo, k4, yo, SSK,
k1.

Row 2: Purl, including yo's.
Rep Rows 1 and 2 for Eyelet Panel.

Diamond Lace Panel (over 45 sts)
Row 1 (RS): K1, [yo, SSK] twice, k2,
yo, SSK, yo, k3tog, yo, k1; rep
between *'s once more, k1, rep between
*'s once, k1, rep between *'s twice, k1,
[k2tog, yo] twice, k1.

Row 2 and all WS rows: Purl, including yo's.

Row 3: K2, [yo, SSK] twice, k2, *yo,
SK2P, yo, k3*; rep between *'s once
more, k1, rep between *'s once, k1, rep
between *'s once, yo, SK2P, yo, k2,
[k2tog, yo] twice, k2.

Row 5: K3, [yo, SSK] twice, *k3, yo,
SSK, yo, SK2P, yo, k3*; [k2tog, yo]
twice, k1, [yo, SSK] twice, rep between
*'s once, [k2tog, yo] twice, k3.

Row 7: K4, [yo, SSK] twice, *k3, yo,
SK2P, yo, k3*; [k2tog, yo] twice, k3, [yo,
SSK] twice, rep between *'s once,
[k2tog, yo] twice, k4.

Row 9: K5, [yo, SSK] twice, k7,
[k2tog, yo] twice, k5, [yo, SSK] twice,
k7, [k2tog, yo] twice, k5.

Row 11: K6, [yo, SSK] twice, k5,
[k2tog, yo] twice, k7, [yo, SSK] twice,
k5, [k2tog, yo] twice, k6.

Row 13: K7, [yo, SSK] twice, k3,
[k2tog, yo] twice, k9, [yo, SSK] twice,
k3, [k2tog, yo] twice, k7.

Row 15: K8, [yo, SSK] twice, k1,
[k2tog, yo] twice, k11, [yo, SSK] twice,
k1, [k2tog, yo] twice, k8.

Row 17: K9, *yo, SSK, yo, SK2P,
yo, k2tog, yo*; rep between *'s
once, k9.

Row 19: K10, *k2tog, yo, k1, yo,
SSK*, k15; rep between *'s once, k10.

Row 21: K9, *k2tog, yo, k3, yo, SSK*,
k13; rep between *'s once, k9.

Row 23: K10, *yo, SSK, yo, k3tog,
yo*, k15; rep between *'s once, k10.

Row 25: K11, *yo, SK2P, yo*, k17;
rep between *'s once, k11.

Row 27: K8, *[k2tog, yo] twice, k1,
[yo, SSK] twice*, k11; rep between *'s
once, k8.

Row 29: K7, *[k2tog, yo] twice, k3,
[yo, SSK] twice*, k9; rep between *'s
once, k7.

Row 31: K6, *[k2tog, yo] twice, k5,
[yo, SSK] twice*, k7; rep between *'s
once, k6.

Row 33: K5, *[k2tog, yo] twice, k7,
[yo, SSK] twice*, k5; rep between *'s
once, k5.

Row 35: K4, *[k2tog, yo] twice, k9, [yo, SSK] twice*, k3; rep between *'s once, k4.

Row 37: K3, *[k2tog, yo] twice, k3, k2tog, yo, k1, yo, SSK, k3, [yo, SSK] twice*, k1; rep between *'s once, k3.

Row 39: K2, [k2tog, yo] twice, *k3, k2tog, yo, k3, yo, SSK, k3*, yo, SSK, yo, SK2P, yo, k2tog, yo; rep between *'s once, [yo, SSK] twice, k2.

Row 41: K1, [k2tog, yo] twice, k2, k2tog, yo, k1, yo, SSK, yo, k3tog, yo, k1, yo, k3, k3tog, yo, k1, yo, SK2P, k3, yo, k1, yo, SSK, yo, k3tog, yo, k1, yo, SSK, k2, [yo, SSK] twice, k1.

Row 43: K1, SSK, yo, k3, k2tog, yo, k3, yo, SK2P, yo, k3, yo, k1, k3tog, yo, k3, yo, SK2P, k1, yo, k3, yo, SK2P, yo, k3, yo, SSK, k3, yo k2tog, k1.

Row 44: Purl.

Rep Rows 1–44 for Diamond Lace Panel.

Instructions

With MC, cast on 287 sts.

Beg Pats

Next row (RS): K1 (selvage st), [work 10 sts Eyelet Panel, 45 sts Diamond Lace Panel] 5 times, work 10 sts Eyelet Panel, k1 (selvage st). Cont in pats as established until 44 rows of Diamond Lace Panel have been worked 11 times and piece measures approx 66 in./ 168 cm from beg. Bind off.

Fringe Border
Note: Slip all sts knitwise.

Cast on 12 sts.

Row 1: Sl 1, k11, turn.

Row 2: K7, yo, k1, [yo, k2tog] twice—13 sts.

Row 3: Sl 1, k3, p1, k8.

Row 4: K7, yo, k2, [yo, k2tog] twice—14 sts.

Row 5: Sl 1, k3, p2, k8.

Row 6: K7, yo, k3, [yo, k2tog] twice—15 sts.

Row 7: Sl 1, k3, p3, k8.

Row 8: K7, yo, k4, [yo, k2tog] twice—16 sts.

Row 9: Sl 1, k3, p4, k8.

Row 10: K7, yo, k5, [yo, k2tog] twice—17 sts.

Row 11: Sl 1, k3, p5, k8.

Row 12: K7, yo, k6, [yo, k2tog] twice—18 sts.

Row 13: Sl 1, k3, p6, k8.

Row 14: K7, yo, k7, [yo, k2tog] twice—19 sts.

Row 15: Sl 1, k3, p7, k8.

Row 16: K7, yo, k8, [yo, k2tog] twice—20 sts.

Row 17: Sl 1, k3, p8, k8.

Row 18: K7, yo, k2tog, k7, [yo, k2tog] twice.

Row 19: Sl 1, k3, p6, p2tog, k8—19 sts.

Row 20: K7, yo, k2tog, k6, [yo, k2tog] twice.

Row 21: Sl 1, k3, p5, p2tog, k8—18 sts.

Row 22: K7, yo, k2tog, k5, [yo, k2tog] twice.

Row 23: Sl 1, k3, p4, p2tog, k8—17 sts.

Row 24: K7, yo, k2tog, k4, [yo, k2tog] twice.

Row 25: Sl 1, k3, p3, p2tog, k8—16 sts.

Row 26: K7, yo, k2tog, k3, [yo, k2tog] twice.

Row 27: Sl 1, k3, p2, p2tog, k8—15 sts.

Row 28: K7, yo, k2tog, k2, [yo, k2tog] twice.

Row 29: Sl 1, k3, p1, p2tog, k8—14 sts.

Row 30: K7, k2tog, k1, [yo, k2tog] twice—13 sts.

Row 31: Sl 1, k3, p2tog, k7—12 sts.

Row 32: K7, k1, [yo, k2tog] twice.

Rep Rows 1–32 until straight edge measures width of cast-on edge, ending with a RS row. Bind off first 6 sts, pull end through last bind-off st. Sl rem sts off LH needle. Unravel first 6 sts on every row to make fringe. Sew straight edge to cast-on edge. Work in same way for bound-off edge.

FINISHING
Block lightly. With contrasting colors, embroider daisy sts in center of St st diamonds (see photo on the facing page for colors). Weave ribbon through eyelets of Eyelet Panel.

Diamond Drapes Afghan and Pillow

Intermediate

This classic afghan and pillow combination is knit using a wrapped pattern stitch, seed stitch, and rib stitch with knit rib fringe. The afghan is worked in panels, then sewn together to form the background. The fringe is knit in rib stitch with extra stitches that unravel to become fringe.

AFGHAN

FINISHED AFGHAN SIZE

Approx 46 in./117 cm wide × 56 in./ 142 cm long

MATERIALS

Rowan Yarns "Magpie" (100% wool, 3½ oz./100 g skeins, each approx 155 yds./141 m)

19 skeins #450 dapple

Alternate colorways shown: #309 cork and #608 sea lord

One pair size 8 US (5 mm) knitting needles OR SIZE REQUIRED TO OBTAIN GIVEN GAUGE

Cable needle

GAUGES

16 sts and 24 rows = 4 in./10 cm over Moss St, using size 8 US (5 mm) needles.

44 sts = 8½ in./21.5 cm over Diamond Panel, using size 8 US (5 mm) needles.

TO SAVE TIME, TAKE TIME TO CHECK GAUGES.

PATTERN STITCHES

Slip Stitch Rib (over 12 sts)

Note: Sl all sts purlwise wyib.

Row 1 (RS): P2, [k1, sl 1, k1, p2] twice.

Row 2: K2, [p3, k2] twice.

Rep rows 1 and 2 for sl st rib.

Moss Stitch (over 8 sts)

Rows 1 and 2: [K1, p1] 4 times.

Rows 3 and 4: [P1, k1] 4 times.

Rep Rows 1–4 for Moss St.

Diamond Panel (over 44 sts)

Row 1 (RS): [P2, k2] 3 times, p2, *M1, p1, M1, p2, [k2, p2] 3 times; rep from * to end.

Row 2: [K2, p2] 3 times, k2, *p1, k1, p1, k2, [p2, k2] 3 times; rep from * to end.

Row 3: [P2, k2] 3 times, p2, *M1, p1, k1, p1, M1, p2, [k2, k2] 3 times; rep from * to end.

Row 4: [K2, p2] 3 times, k2, *[p1, k1] twice, p1, k2, [p2, k2] 3 times; rep from * to end.

Row 5: [P2, k2] 3 times, p2, *M1, [p1, k1] twice, p1, M1, p2, [k2, k2] 3 times; rep from * to end.

Row 6: [K2, p2] 3 times, k2, *[p1, k1] 3 times, p1, k2, [p2, k2] 3 times; rep from * to end.

Row 7: [P2, k2] 3 times, p2, *M1, [p1, k1] 3 times, p1, M1, p2, [k2, k2] 3 times; rep from * to end.

Row 8: [K2, p2] 3 times, k2, *[p1, k1] 4 times, p1, k2, [p2, k2] 3 times; rep from * to end.

Row 9: [P2, k2] 3 times, p2, *M1, [p1, k1] 4 times, p1, M1, p2, [k2, k2] 3 time; rep from * to end.

Row 10: *K1, k in front and back of next st, sl 10 wyib, pass the first of the 10 slipped sts over the other 9 sts, k2, [p1, k1] 5 times, p1; rep from *, end k1, k in front and back of next st, sl 10, pass first sl st over the other 9, k2.

Row 11: [P2, k2] 3 times, p2, *SSK, [p1, k1] 3 times, p1, k2tog, p2, [k2, p2] 3 times; rep from * to end.

Row 12: [K2, p2] 3 times, k2, *[p1, k1] 4 times, p1, k2, [p2, k2] 3 times; rep from * to end.

Row 13: [P2, k2] 3 times, p2, *SSK, [p1, k1] twice, p1, k2tog, p2, [k2, p2] 3 times; rep from * to end.

Row 14: [K2, p2] 3 times, k2, *[p1, k1] 3 times, p1, k2, [p2, k2] 3 times; rep from * to end.

Row 15: [P2, k2] 3 times, p2, *SSK, p1, k1, p1, k2tog, p2, [k2, p2] 3 times; rep from * to end.

Row 16: [K2, p2] 3 times, k2, *[p1, k1] twice, p1, k2, [p2, k2] 3 times; rep from * to end.

Row 17: [P2, k2] 3 times, p2, *SSK, p1, k2tog, p2, [k2, p2] 3 times; rep from * to end.

Row 18: [K2, p2] 3 times, k2, *p1, k1, p1, k2, [p2, k2] 3 times; rep from * to end.

Row 19: [P2, k2] 3 times, p2, *SK2P, p2, [k2, p2] 3 times; rep from * to end.

Row 20: [K2, p2] 3 times, k2, *p1, k2, [p2, k2] 3 times; rep from * to end.

Rep Rows 1–20 for Diamond Panel.

Instructions

Left Panel

Cast on 73 sts.

Foundation row (WS): K2, [p3, k2] twice, [k1, p1] 4 times, [k2, p2] 3 times, k2, *p1, k2, [p2, k2] 3 times; rep from * once more, [k1, p1] 4 times, p1 (edge st).

Beg pats—Row 1 (RS): K1, work Moss St over 8 sts, work Diamond Panel over 44 sts, work Moss St over 8 sts, work sl st rib over last 12 sts. Cont in pats as established, working edge st in St st, until piece measures approx 58 in./147 cm from beg, end with Diamond Panel Row 20. Bind off.

Center Panel

Cast on 86 sts.

Foundation row (WS): P1 (edge st), k2, [p3, k2] twice, [k1, p1] 4 times, [k2, p2] 3 times, k2, *p1, k2, [p2, k2] 3 times; rep from * once more, [k1, p1] 4 times, k2, [p3, k2] twice, p1 (edge st).

Beg pats—Row 1 (RS): K1, work sl st rib over 12 sts, Moss St over 8 sts, work Diamond Panel over 44 sts, work Moss St over 8 sts, work sl st rib over last 12 sts, k1. Cont in pats as established until same number of rows as left panel. Bind off.

Right Panel

Cast on 73 sts.

Foundation row (WS): P1 (edge st), [k1, p1] 4 times, [k2, p2] 3 times, k2, *p1, k2, [p2, k2] 3 times; rep from * once more, [k1, p1] 4 times, k2, [p3, k2] twice.

Beg pats—Row 1 (RS): Work sl st rib over 12 sts, Moss St over 8 sts, work Diamond Panel over 44 sts, work Moss St over 8 sts, k1. Cont in pats as established until same number of rows as left panel. Bind off.

Fringe Borders (make 2)

Note: Slip all sts purlwise wyib.

Cast on 18 sts.

Row 1 (WS): [K2, p3] twice, k8.

Row 2: P8, [k1, sl 1, k1, p2] twice.

Rep Rows 1 and 2 until piece measures the width of one short side, end with a RS row. Bind off first 9 sts, tie off 10th st, unravel rem 8 sts for fringe. Cut fringe evenly.

FINISHING

Block lightly. Sew panels tog. Sew border to cast-on and bound-off edges.

PILLOW

FINISHED PILLOW SIZE

Approx 18 in./45.5 cm square

MATERIALS

Rowan Yarns "Magpie" (100% wool, 3½ oz./100 g skeins, each approx 155 yds./141 m)

Three skeins #450 dapple

Alternate colorways: #309 cork and #608 sea lord

One 18-in./45.5-cm-square pillow form

One pair size 8 US (5 mm) knitting needles OR SIZE REQUIRED TO OBTAIN GIVEN GAUGE

Cable needle

GAUGES

16 sts and 24 rows = 4 in./10 cm over
   Moss St, using size 8 US (5 mm)
   needles.
44 sts = 8½ in./21.5 cm over Diamond
   Panel, using size 8 US (5 mm)
   needles.
TO SAVE TIME, TAKE TIME TO
CHECK GAUGES.

Instructions

Cast on 86 sts and work pats same as
Center Panel on afghan until piece
measures 42 in./106 cm from beg.
Bind off.

Fringe Border

Note: Slip all sts purlwise wyib.
   Cast on 18 sts.
   Row 1 (WS): [K2, p3] twice, k8.
   Row 2: P8, [k1, sl 1, k1, p2] twice.
   Rep Rows 1 and 2 until piece

measures 18 in./45.5 cm from beg, end
with a RS row. Bind off first 9 sts, tie off
10th st, unravel rem 8 sts for fringe. Cut
fringe evenly.

FINISHING

Block lightly. Sew fringe border along
cast-on edge. Place knitted pillow over
pillow form, overlapping 6 in./15 cm
with the fringe border to front (see
photo above). Sew side seams.

Flowered Fur Pillow

Easy

The gorgeous yarn makes this pillow special and is worth the splurge.
To get the same results, you need one skein of "Fluff" and one skein
of "Charmeuse" ribbon, both made by the Great Adirondack Yarn Company.
Use a few matching beads in the center of the flowers.

FINISHED SIZE
Approx 16 in./41 cm

MATERIALS
Great Adirondack "Fluff" (100% rayon, each skein approx 82 yds./74 m)

One skein iris (MC) each if knitting the front and the back

Great Adirondack "Charmeuse" (100% rayon, each skein approx 70 yds./ 64 m)

One skein iris (CC)

One pair each size 8 US and 15 US (5 mm and 10 mm) knitting needles OR SIZE REQUIRED TO OBTAIN GIVEN GAUGE

One 16-in./41-cm-square pillow form, or purchased pillow

Matching beads for center (optional)

GAUGE
11 sts = 4 in./10 cm over St st, using size 15 US (10 mm) needles.

TO SAVE TIME, TAKE TIME TO CHECK GAUGE.

STITCH GLOSSARY
Loop st: Insert needles in next st, wrap yarn over needle as if to knit, then wrap yarn over two fingers of left hand twice, then over needle again; draw three

loops on needle through the st and place them on LH needle; k the three loops tog through the back.

Instructions

Front
With larger needles and MC, cast on 43 sts and work in garter st for 16 in./ 41 cm. Bind off.

Back
Work same as front.

Flower (make 2)
With smaller needles and CC, cast on 41 sts. Work in loop st as foll:

Rows 1 and 3 (RS): Knit.

Row 2: K1, *work loop st, k1; rep from * to end.

Row 4: K2, *work loop st, k1; rep from *, end last rep k2.

Next dec row (RS): [K2tog, k2] 10 times, k1—31 sts.

Work Rows 2–4 as before.

Next dec row (RS): [K2tog, k2] 7 times, k2tog, k1—23 sts.

Work Row 2.

Next dec row (RS): K1, [k2tog] 11 times—12 sts.

P2tog across next row. Tie off rem 6 sts. Sew beads to center of flowers if desired.

FINISHING
Block lightly. Sew three sides of front and back together, leaving bottom edge open. Insert pillow form and sew opening, or sew front to purchased pillow. Sew flowers to upper right corner at an angle (see photo on the facing page).

Gentleman's Sampler Afghan and Pillow

Intermediate

Based on the colors used in traditional British tweeds, this gentleman's sampler afghan and pillow are sure to delight that special man. With all the different styles used, this is an excellent project to practice your knitting. Choose any of your favorite four blocks to make the coordinating pillow.

AFGHAN

FINISHED AFGHAN SIZE

Approx 53½ in./136 cm wide × 71 in./180 cm long

MATERIALS

Unger/JCA "Darby" (52% wool, 48% acrylic, 1¾ oz./50 g skeins, each approx 96 yds./87 m)

Eight skeins #12 blue (A)

Seven skeins each #01 taupe (B) and #09 burgundy (C)

Six skeins each #06 gold (D) and #05 rust (E)

Five skeins each #04 brown (F) and #10 dark gray (G)

One pair knitting needles and two double-pointed needles, each size 6 US (4 mm) OR SIZE REQUIRED TO OBTAIN GIVEN GAUGE

Cable needle

Buttons from JHB International:

Five ⅝ in. #92190 "Button up" (for houndstooth)

Twelve ¾ in. #62100 "Surrey" (for check pattern)

Five ⅞ in. #50150 "Woodstock" (for welt rib)

Five ⅞ in. #10579 "Lizard Like" (for cable and seed st pocket)

GAUGE

20 sts and 24 rows = 4 in./10 cm over St st, using size 6 US (4 mm) needles.

Each square measures 8¾ in./22 cm after blocking.

TO SAVE TIME, TAKE TIME TO CHECK GAUGE.

Notes: Squares are made separately, then sewn tog foll placement diagram.

Work first and last st of every row in St st for selvage sts.

STITCH GLOSSARY

Left twist (LT): Sk next st and p into back of 2nd st, then k skipped st through front, sl both sts from needle.

Right twist (RT): Sk next st and k 2nd st, then p skipped st, sl both sts from needle.

4-st FC: Sl 2 sts to cn and hold to front of work, k2, k2 from cn.

4-st BC: Sl 2 sts to cn and hold to back of work, k2, k2 from cn.

6-st FC: Sl 3 sts to cn and hold to front of work, k3, k3 from cn.

6-st BC: Sl 3 sts to cn and hold to back of work, k3, k3 from cn.

Seed stitch

Row 1: *K1, p1; rep from * to end.

Row 2: K the purl sts and p the knit sts.

Rep Row 2 for seed st.

Instructions

1. Plaited Cables Square (make 5)

With C, cast on 51 sts. K 1 row on RS.

Row 1 and all WS rows: P1, K2, *p9, k1, p1, k1; rep from *, end last rep p9, k2, p1.

Rows 2 and 6: K1, p2, *k9, p1, k1, p1; rep from *, end last rep k9, p2, k1.

Row 4: K1, p2, *6-st FC, k3, p1, k1, p1; rep from *, end last rep p2, k1.

Row 8: K1, p2, *k3, 6-st BC, p1, k1, p1; rep from *, end last rep p2, k1.

Rep Rows 1–8 until piece measures 8¾ in./22 cm from beg, end with a pat row 2 or 6. Bind off.

2. Diamond Cluster Square (make 5)

With A, cast on 41 sts.

Row 1 (WS): P4, *k4, p1, k4, p3; rep from *, end last rep p4.

Row 2: K3, *LT, p3, k1, p3, RT, k1; rep from *, end k3.

Row 3: P3, *k1, p1, [k3, p1] twice, k1, p1; rep from *, end p2.

Row 4: K3, *p1, LT, p2, k1, p2, RT, p1, k1; rep from *, end k3.

Row 5: P3, *k2, p1; rep from *, end p3.

Row 6: K3, *p2, LT, p1, k1, p1, RT, p2, k1; rep from *, end k3.

Row 7: P3, *k3, [p1, k1] twice, p1, k3, p1; rep from *, end p3.

Row 8: K3, *p3, LT, k1, RT, p3, k1; rep from *, end k3.

Row 9: P3, *k4, p3, k4, p1; rep from *, end p3.

Row 10: K3, *p4, k next 3 sts and transfer these 3 to dpn, then wrap yarn 4 times around these sts under dpn in a counterclockwise direction, then return the 3 sts to RH needle (cluster 3), p4, k1; rep from *, end k3.

Rows 11, 13, 15, 17, and 19: Rep Rows 9, 7, 5, 3, and 1.

Row 12: K3, *p3, RT, k1, LT, p3, k1; rep from *, end k3.

Row 14: K3, *p2, RT, p1, k1, p1, LT, p2, k1; rep from *, end k3.

Row 16: K3, *p1, RT, p2, k1, p2, LT, p1, k1; rep from *, end k3.

Row 18: K3, *RT, p3, k1, p3, LT, k1; rep from *, end k3.

Row 20: K4, *p4, k1, p4, cluster 3; rep from *, end p4, k1, p4, k4.

Rep Rows 1–20 until piece measures 8¾ in./22 cm from beg, end with a pat row 16. Bind off.

3. Houndstooth Square (make 5)

With G, cast on 42 sts.

Row 1 (RS): K across row as foll: 2 G, *1B, 3G; rep from * to last 4 sts, 1B, 3G.

Row 2: P across row as foll: 1B, *3B, 1G; rep from *, end 2G.

Row 3: K across row as foll: 1B, *3B, 1G; rep from *, end 2G.

Row 4: P across row as foll: 2G, *1B, 3G; rep from *, to last 4 sts, 1B, 3G.

Rep Rows 1–4 until piece measures 8¾ in./22 cm from beg. Bind off with G.

Frog: With B, cast on 7 sts and work in k1, p1 rib for 4 in./10 cm. Bind off. Sew to square, with cast-on edge 1 in./2.5 cm from RH side and one long side 5 in./12.5 cm from lower edge. Sew a button in center of frog.

4. Hourglass Cables Square (make 5)

With B, cast on 49 sts.

Row 1 (and all WS rows): [P1, k1] twice, *p3, k1, p1, k1; rep from *, end p1.

Row 2: K1, p1, k1 in row below (k1-b), p1, * 4-st FC, 4-st BC, p 1, k1-b, p1; rep from *, end k1.

Row 4: K1, p1, k1-b, p1, *k8, p1, k1-b, p1; rep from *, end k1.

Row 6: K1, p1, k1-b, p1, *4-st BC, 4-st FC, p1, k1-b, p1; rep from *, end k1.

Row 8: Rep Row 4.

Rep Rows 1–8 until piece measures 8¾ in./22 cm from beg, end with a pat row 6. Bind off.

5. Vertical Cables Square (make 5)

With F, cast on 50 sts.

Rows 1, 3 and 5 (WS): P1, *k2, p4, k2, p2; rep from *, end last rep k2, p1.

Row 2: K1, *p2, 4-st FC, p2, wyib insert needle purlwise into first st on LH needle, k 2nd st in front lp then k first st through back lp (twist 2); rep from *, end last rep p2, k1.

Row 4: P3, k4, p2, *twist 2, p2, k4, p2; rep from *, end p3.

Row 6: Rep Row 4.

Rep Rows 1–6 until piece measures 8¾ in./22 cm from beg, end with a pat row 2. Bind off.

6. Dice Check Pattern Square (make 4)

With A, cast on 46 sts.

Row 1 (WS): With A, purl.

Row 2: With B, k1, sl 1 wyib, *k2, sl 2 wyib; rep from *, end k2, sl 1, k1.

Row 3: With B, p1, sl 1 wyif, *p2, sl 2 wyif; rep from *, end p2, sl 1, p1.

Row 4: With A, knit.

Row 5: With G, p2, *sl 2 wyif, p2; rep from * to end.

Row 6: With G, k2, *sl 2 wyib, k2; rep from * to end.

Rep Rows 1–6 until piece measures 8¾ in./22 cm from beg, end with a WS row. Bind off with A.

Button rib

With RS facing and G, pick up and k 45 sts along center of square and work in k1, p1 rib for 1 in./2.5 cm. Bind off in rib. Sew three buttons evenly spaced along rib.

7. Argyle Square (make 4)

Note: If desired, diagonal lines can be worked in duplicate st after piece is knit.

With A, cast on 43 sts. Work in St st for 2 rows, then work in chart pat (see facing page as foll): 1 selvage st, work 10-st rep 4 times, then work first st once more, 1 selvage st. Cont as established for 42 rows. With A, k 1 row, p 1 row. Bind off.

8. Welt Rib Square (make 5)

With D, cast on 44 sts.

Rows 1 and 3 (WS): P1, k2, *p6, k2; rep from *, end p1.

Row 2: K1, p2, *[k2tog, do not drop sts from needle, k the first st again and drop both sts from needle] twice, p2; rep from *, end k1.

Row 4: K1, p2, *k1, rep between [ ]'s of row 2 twice, k1, p2; rep from *, end k1.

Argyle Chart

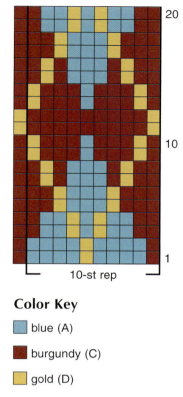

20

10

1

10-st rep

Color Key

■ blue (A)

■ burgundy (C)

■ gold (D)

Rep Rows 1–4 until piece measures 8¾ in./22 cm from beg, end with a WS row. Bind off.

9. Cable and Seed Square (make 5)
With E, cast on 43 sts.

Row 1 and all WS rows: [P1, k1] twice, p6, 7 sts in seed st, p9, 7 sts seed st, p6, [k1, p1] twice.

Row 2: [K1, p1] twice, 6-st FC, seed st over 7 sts, k2, k2tog, yo, k1, yo, SKP, k2, seed st over 7 sts, 6-st FC, [p1, k1] twice.

Row 4: [K1, p1] twice, k6, seed st over 7 sts, k1, k2tog, yo, k3, yo, SKP, k1, seed st over 7 sts, k6, [p1, k1] twice.

Row 6: [K1, p1] twice, k6, seed st over 7 sts, k2tog, yo, k5, yo, SKP, seed st over 7 sts, k6, [p1, k1] twice.

Fair Isle Chart

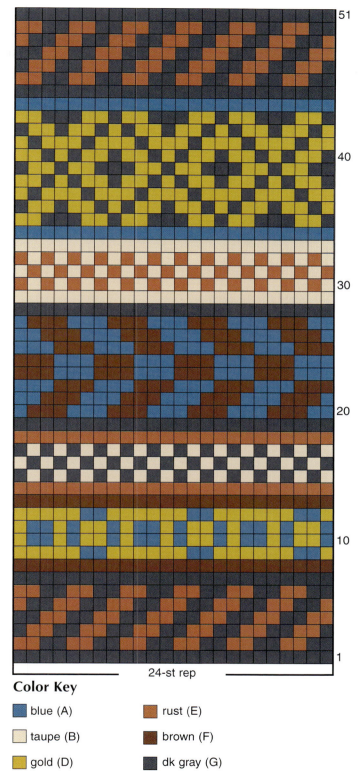

51

40

30

20

10

1

24-st rep

Color Key

■ blue (A)

■ taupe (B)

■ gold (D)

■ rust (E)

■ brown (F)

■ dk gray (G)

Row 8: [K1, p1] twice, 6-st FC, seed st over 7 sts, k1, yo, SKP, k3, k2tog, yo, k1, seed st over 7 sts, 6-st FC, [p1, k1] twice.

Row 10: [K1, p1] twice, k6, seed st over 7 sts, k2, yo, SKP, k1, k2tog, yo, k2, seed st over 7 sts, k6, [p1, k1] twice.

Row 12: [K1, p1] twice, k6, seed st over 7 sts, k3, yo, SK2P, yo, k3, seed st over 7 sts, k6, [p1, k1] twice.

Rows 13–24: Rep Rows 1–12, but omit cable twists on Row 8.

Rep Rows 1–24 until piece measures 8¾ in./22 cm from beg, end with a pat row 12. Bind off.

Pocket flap

With E, cast on 41 sts. Work in seed st for 1 in./2.5 cm. Dec 1 st each side every row until there are 3 sts. SK2P and fasten off. Sew pocket flap to top of square.

10. Fair Isle Square (make 5)

With G, cast on 46 sts.

Next row (RS): K1 G, work 44 sts of Fair Isle Chart on p. 55 as foll: Work 24-st rep once, then work first 20 sts once more, k1 G. Cont as established until all 51 rows of chart have been worked. Bind off with G.

FINISHING

Block lightly. Sew squares tog, foll placement diagram.

Top and Bottom Border

With RS facing and C, pick up and k 243 sts along top edge. Work in k3, p3 rib as foll: Next row (WS): K3, *p3, k3; rep from * to end. Next row: Cast on 1 st, p3, *k3, p3, rep from * to end, cast on 1 st. Rep last 2 rows (working inc sts into rib) once more.

Bind off purlwise on WS. Work in same way along bottom edge.

Side Borders

Work same as top and bottom border, picking up 339 sts. Sew corner edges tog.

Gentleman's Sampler Afghan Placement Diagram

5. Vertical cables	10. Fair Isle	9. Cable and seed	2. Diamond cluster	7. Argyle	8. Welt rib
6. Dice check	8. Welt rib	4. Hourglass ↔	3. Houndstooth	1. Plaited cables ↔	10. Fair Isle
7. Argyle	2. Diamond cluster	10. Fair Isle	9. Cable and seed	5. Vertical cables	4. Hourglass ↔
1. Plaited cables ↔	3. Houndstooth	8. Welt rib	4. Hourglass ↔	6. Dice check	1. Plaited cables ↔
9. Cable and seed	5. Vertical cables	7. Argyle	2. Diamond cluster	10. Fair Isle	9. Cable and seed
3. Houndstooth	8. Welt rib	1. Plaited cables ↔	6. Dice check	4. Hourglass ↔	3. Houndstooth
2. Diamond cluster	10. Fair Isle	9. Cable and seed	5. Vertical cables	8. Welt rib	7. Argyle
6. Dice check	5. Vertical cables	4. Hourglass ↔	3. Houndstooth	2. Diamond cluster	1. Plaited cables ↕

1. Plaited cables (5)
2. Diamond cluster (5)
3. Houndstooth (5)
4. Hourglass (5)
5. Vertical cables (5)
6. Dice check (4)
7. Argyle (4)
8. Welt rib (5)
9. Cable and seed (5)
10. Fair Isle (5)

PILLOW

FINISHED PILLOW SIZE

18 in./45.5 cm square

MATERIALS

One skein of desired colors (see p. 53) for each square for front of pillow and two skeins of one color for back of pillow (unless using fabric back or purchased pillow)

One pair knitting needles and two double-pointed needles, each size 6 US (4 mm) OR SIZE REQUIRED TO OBTAIN GIVEN GAUGE

Cable needle

One 18-in./45.5-cm-square pillow form, or purchased pillow

GAUGE

20 sts and 24 rows = 4 in./10 cm over St st, using size 6 US (4 mm) needles.

Each square measures 8¾ in./22 cm after blocking.

TO SAVE TIME, TAKE TIME TO CHECK GAUGE.

Instructions

Front

Choose any four squares from afghan, and sew tog to form pillow front.

Knitted Back

With back color, cast on 72 sts, and work in St st for18 in./45.5 cm. Bind off.

FINISHING

Sew top and two sides of front and back tog, leaving bottom open. Insert pillow form and sew opening closed.

Tip: Pillow can be backed with fabric, if desired. Cut fabric 19 in./48 cm square. Make a hem on all four sides, and sew to pillow front.

Golf Afghan and Golf Ball Pillow

Intermediate

Here's the perfect gift for your favorite golfer. Worked in one piece, the golf afghan is done in stockinette stitch with a duplicate stitched golfer in the center. An easy seed stitch border adds the finishing touch. What better accent for the afghan than a golf ball? This fun pillow uses the honeycomb stitch and is made in three pieces.

AFGHAN

FINISHED AFGHAN SIZE

Approx 40½ in./103 cm wide × 53 in./ 134.5 cm long

MATERIALS

Plymouth "Galway" (100% wool, 3½ oz./100 g, each skein approx 230 yds./210 m)

Seven skeins #711 brown (MC)

Three skeins #703 green (A)

Two skeins #705 blue (B)

One skein #710 burgundy (C)

Small amount #712 dark brown (D), #95 gold (E), #722 beige (F), and #01 off-white (G)

Size 7 US (4.5 mm) circular needle OR SIZE REQUIRED TO OBTAIN GIVEN GAUGE

GAUGE

20 sts and 28 rows = 4 in./10 cm over St st, using size 7 US (4.5 mm) needles.

TO SAVE TIME, TAKE TIME TO CHECK GAUGE.

PATTERN STITCHES

Seed Stitch

Row 1 (RS): *K1, p1; rep from * to end.

Row 2: K the purl sts and p the knit sts.

Rep Rows 1 and 2 for seed st.

Notes: Alternate blue and green diamonds (see photo on the facing page). Red diagonal lines are worked in duplicate st after piece is complete.

Golfer chart can be knit in or worked in duplicate st after piece is complete.

Work background of center diamond in brown.

When changing colors, twist yarns to prevent holes.

Instructions

With brown, cast on 199 sts. Work in seed st for 1½ in./4 cm.

Row 1 (RS): With brown, cont 7 sts in seed st, cont in St st over next 185 sts, as foll: Work 74-st rep of Chart 1 twice, work first 37 sts once more, with brown, cont seed st over last 7 sts. Cont as established until 104 rows of chart have been worked.

Next row (RS): Work 63 sts as established, work next 73 sts, foll Center Diamond Chart (see p. 61), work last 63 sts as established. Cont as established until 136 rows of chart have been worked. Then cont Diamond Pat, foll Chart 1 same as first half of afghan

(remember to alternate blue and green), until there are five complete brown diamonds. With brown, work in Seed st over all sts for 1½ in./4 cm. Bind off.

FINISHING

Duplicate st red diagonal lines as shown on chart and golfer if necessary. Weave in all ends. Block lightly.

PILLOW

Tip: Work inset first to learn Honeycomb Pat so it will be easier to work incs and decs into pat.

FINISHED PILLOW SIZE

Approx circumference 38 in./96.5 cm

Chart 1

72
70
60
50
40
30
20
10
1

74-st rep

MATERIALS

Four skeins #1 off-white Plymouth
"Calway"

One pair size 7 US (4.5 mm) knitting
needles OR SIZE REQUIRED TO
OBTAIN GIVEN GAUGE

Cable needle

Stitch markers

Poly-Fil stuffing

GAUGE

22 sts and 24 rows = 4 in./10 cm over
Honeycomb Pat , using size 7 US
(4.5 mm) needles.

TO SAVE TIME, TAKE TIME TO
CHECK GAUGE.

PATTERN STITCHES

**Honeycomb Pattern
(multiple of 8 sts, plus 2)**

Rows 1, 3, 7, and 9 (RS): Knit.

Row 2 and all WS rows: Purl.

Row 5: K1, *4-st FC (sl 2 sts to cn
and hold at front of work, k2, k2 from
cn), 4-st BC (sl 2 sts to cn and hold at
back of work, k2, k2 from cn); rep from
*, end k1.

Row 11: K1, *4-st BC, 4-st FC; rep
from *, end k1.

Row 12: Rep Row 2.

Rep Rows 1–12 for Honeycomb Pat.

Instructions

Inset

Cast on 18 sts. Work in Honeycomb
Pat for 41 in./104 cm. Bind off. Sew
bound-off and cast-on edges tog.

Back

Cast on 50 sts. Work in Honeycomb
Pat, inc 1 st each side (working incs at
1 st in from edge and into pat) every
other row 19 times—88 sts, end with a
WS row. Work even for 20 rows. Dec
1 st each side on next row, then every
other row until there are 50 sts.
Bind off.

Front

Work same as back.

FINISHING

Pin and sew front to inset. Pin and sew
back to inset, leaving a 3-in./7.5-cm
opening. Stuff pillow to form a ball.
Sew opening closed.

Center Diamond Chart

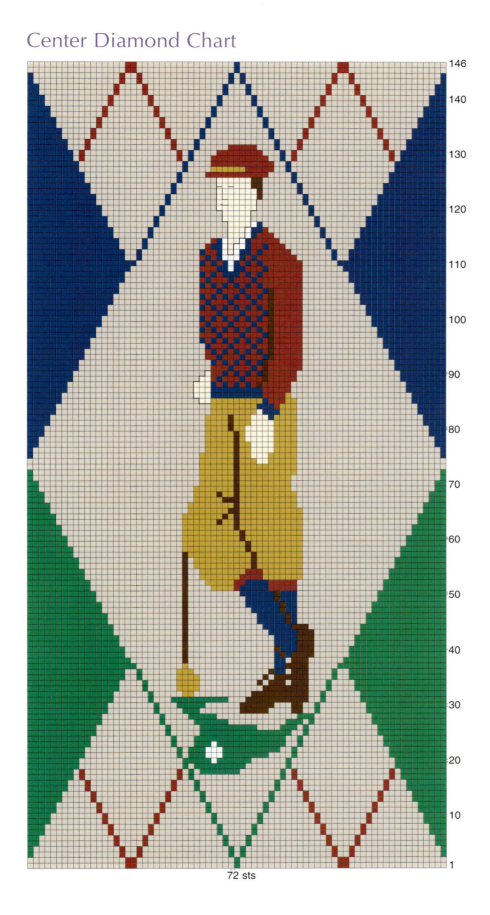

72 sts

Color Key

☐ brown (MC)

☐ green (A)

☐ blue (B)

☐ burgundy (C)

☐ dark brown (D)

☐ gold (E)

☐ beige (F)

☐ off-white (G)

Illusion Pillows

Easy

The special texture of these easy and elegant pillows is made by contrasting stripes of chenille yarn with stripes of ribbon yarn. A unique mock cord closure finishes each design. The diagonal-stripe square is knit from edge to edge, and the four corners are folded to the center. The envelope pillow uses the same stripe pattern and an even decrease on each side to shape the point.

FROG CLOSURE PILLOW

FINISHED SIZE
Approx 12 in./30.5 cm square

MATERIALS
Anny Blatt "Velours" (100% acrylic, 1¼ oz./50 g balls, each approx 110 yds./100 m)

Two balls #087 canard (A)
Anny Blatt "Victoria" (100% polyamide, 1¾oz/50 gram cones, each approx 110 yds./100 m)
One cone #439 petrole (B)
One 12-in./30.5-cm-square pillow form
One pair size 5 US (3.75 mm) knitting needles OR SIZE REQUIRED TO OBTAIN GIVEN GAUGE

Two size 4 US (3.5 mm) double-pointed needles for I-cord
Sewing thread to match color of I-cord

GAUGE
19 sts and 26 rows = 4 in./10 cm over St st, using size 5 US (3.75 mm) needles.
TO SAVE TIME, TAKE TIME TO CHECK GAUGE.

STRIPE PATTERN
*8 rows A, 4 rows B; rep from * (12 rows) for Stripe Pat.

Instructions
With size 5 US (3.75 mm) needles and A, cast on 77 sts. Work in St st and Stripe Pat for 32 in./81.5 cm. Bind off.

FINISHING
Block lightly. Place pillow form in center of square. Fold each corner point to center around pillow form, and sew four seams.

Frog Closure
Make two lengths of I-cord, one 14 in./35.5 cm and one 16 in./41 cm. Make frog, foll diagram on the opposite page. With matching sewing thread, sew in center of front of pillow.

ENVELOPE PILLOW

FINISHED SIZE
Approx 12 in./30.5 cm square

MATERIALS
Anny Blatt "Velours" (100% acrylic,
1¾ oz./50 g balls, each approx
110 yds./100 m)
Two balls #617 verdi (A)
One ball #353 miel (B)
One 12-in./30.5-cm-square pillow form
One pair size 5 US (3.75 mm) knitting
needles OR SIZE REQUIRED TO
OBTAIN GIVEN GAUGE
Two size 4 US (3.5 mm) double-pointed
needles for I-cord
Sewing thread to match color of I-cord

GAUGE
19 sts and 26 rows = 4 in./10 cm over St
st, using size 5 US (3.75 mm) needles.
TO SAVE TIME, TAKE TIME TO
CHECK GAUGE.

Instructions
With size 5 US (3.75 mm) needles and
A, cast on 77 sts. Work in St st and
Stripe Pat for 32 in./81.5 cm.

Flap
Cont in Stripe Pat, dec 1 st each side
every row until 1 st rem. Tie off.

FINISHING
Block lightly. Fold pillow cover over
pillow form, and sew two side seams.
Insert pillow form. Sew cast-on edge to
first dec row of flap, overlapping the
point.

Spiral Closure
With B, make one I-cord 8 in./20.5 cm
long and one 18 in./45.5 cm long. Sew
shorter cord to right side of flap. Work
rem cord in a spiral, and stitch to point
of flap.

Frog Closure

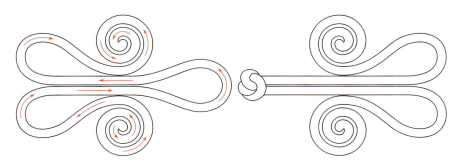

Begin by winding cord into a clockwise spiral. Make three loops to form the buttonhole, and then end with another clockwise spiral. Sew to center of pillow at an angle.

Spiral Closure

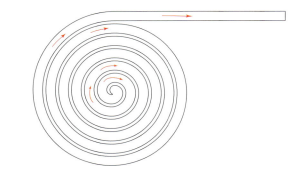

Begin at center, and wind cord clockwise to form spiral. Stitch cords together to hold shape. Continue to sew remaining cord to left side of pillow flap.

Game Room Ornaments

Intermediate

These whimsical ornaments are fun and easy to make. Each ornament is knit in two pieces, then sewn together and stuffed. Double twisted cords add the finishing touch.

MATERIALS

Rainbow Gallery "Ribbon Rays" (10–14 ct. metallic ribbon, 10 yd./9 m cards)

Two cards each #RR91 black (A), #RR81 gold (B), and #RR82 silver (C)

One pair size 5 US (3.75 mm) knitting needles OR SIZE REQUIRED TO OBTAIN GIVEN GAUGE

Poly-Fil stuffing

Matching thread

GAUGE

20 sts and 28 rows = 4 in./10 cm over St st , using size 5 US (3.75 mm) needles.

TO SAVE TIME, TAKE TIME TO CHECK GAUGE.

Diamond (make 2)

With C, cast on 3 sts

Row 1 (RS): Knit.

Row 2 and all WS rows, except Row 42: Purl.

Row 3: [K1, M1] twice, k1—5 sts.

Row 5: K1, M1, k3, M1, k1—7 sts.

Row 7: K1, M1, k5, M1, k1—9 sts.

Rows 9–22: Cont to inc 1 st each side every RS row—23 sts.

Row 23: K1, SSK, k to last 3 sts, k2tog, k1—21 sts.

Rows 25–39: Cont to dec 1 st each every RS row until 5 sts rem.

Row 41: Ssk, k1, k2tog—3 sts.

Row 42: P3tog. Tie off.

FINISHING

Sew two pieces tog, leaving a small opening. Stuff with Poly-Fil. Sew opening closed. Make a twisted cord (see Appendix C) to fit around ornament, leaving 6 in./15 cm for a 3-in./7.5-cm loop hanger. With sewing thread, beg at top, sew around seam. Fold rem cord, and attach to top for loop hanger.

Spade (make 2)

Left base

With A, cast on 5 sts.

Row 1 (RS): K1, M1, k3, M1, k1—7 sts.

Rows 2, 4, and 6: Purl.

Row 3: K1, M1, k5, M1, k1—9 sts.

Row 5: K1, M1, k7, M1, k1—11 sts.

Row 7: Knit.

Row 8: Purl. Cut yarn, leave sts on needle.

Stem

On same needle, cast on 9 sts.

Row 1: K1, SSK, k3, k2tog, k1—7 sts.

Rows 2 and 4: Purl.

Row 3: Knit.

Row 5: K1, SSK, k1, k2tog, k1—5 sts.

Rows 6–14: Work in St st. Cut yarn, leave sts on needle.

Right base

On same needle, cast on 5 sts.

Rows 1–8: Work same as left base. There are 27 sts total on needle.

Row 9 (joining row): K10, k2tog (last st of right base with first st of stem), k3, k2tog (last st of stem with first st of left base), k10—25 sts.

Row 10: Purl.

Rows 11–19: Work in St st.

Row 21 and all RS rows through Row 39: K1, SSK, k to last 3 sts, k2tog, k1—5 sts.

Row 20 and all WS rows: Purl.

Row 41: Ssk, k1, k2tog—3 sts.

Row 43: P3tog. Tie off last st.

FINISHING

Work same as Diamond.

Heart (make 2)

Top

With B, cast on 3 sts. With separate skein of yarn, cast on 3 more sts on same needle—6 sts in total.

Row 1 (RS): *[K1, M1] twice, k1; rep from * on 2nd set of sts—5 sts each set.

Row 2 and all WS rows: Purl.

Row 3: *K1, M1, k3, M1, k1; rep from * on 2nd set of sts—7 sts each set.

Rows 5–8: Cont to inc 1 st each side every RS row until there are 11 sts for each set.

Body

Row 9 (joining row): K1, M1, k9, k2tog, k9, M1, k1—23 sts. Cut 2nd yarn.

Rows 10–12: Work in St st.

Row 13: K1, SSK, k to last 3 sts, k2tog, k1.

Cont in this way to dec 1 st each side every RS row until there are 5 sts.

Row 31: K1, SK2P, k1—3 sts.

Row 32: Purl.

Row 33: SK2P. Tie off last st.

FINISHING

Work same as Diamond.

Club (make 2)

With A, cast on 5 sts.

Row 1 (RS): [K1, M1] 4 times, k1—9 sts.

Row 2 and all WS rows: Purl.

Row 3: [K1, M1] 8 times, k1—17 sts.

Rows 5 and 7: Knit.

Row 9: K7, sl 2 sts tog knitwise, k1, p2sso (DD), k7—15 sts.

Row 11: K6, DD, k6—13 sts.

Row 13: K5, DD, k5—11 sts.

Row 15: K4, DD, k4—9 sts.

Row 17: K3, DD, k3—7 sts.

Row 18: Purl. Leave sts on needle.

With same needle and new yarn, rep Rows 1–18 twice more—21 sts total on needle.

Row 19: K6, k2tog, k5, k2tog, k6—19 sts.

Rows 20 and 22: Purl.

Row 21: K1, [k2tog] 9 times—10 sts.

Row 23: [K2tog] 5 times—5 sts.

Rows 24–32: Work in St st.

Row 33: [K1, M1] twice, k1—9 sts.

Rows 34–36: Work in St st.

Bind off all sts knitwise.

FINISHING

Work same as Diamond.

Tip: Make a mix of several of these for next year's Christmas tree ornaments for card lovers or just make the hearts for Valentine's Day decorations or gifts.

Lamp Shades

Dress up your room with one of these wonderful lamp shades. A converging rib stitch is the background for each shade; different embellishment techniques make them unique. If you don't purchase a "self-sticking" shade, you can use a glue gun to tack the shade lightly, with glue on the top and bottom edges only.

FINISHED SIZE

To fit a shade 4 in./10 cm top × 6 in./ 15.5 cm bottom × 5 in./12.5 cm high

Tip: *To make a larger lamp shade, repeat the 24 rows until desired size is reached.*

GOODNIGHT ROSE LAMP SHADE

MATERIALS

Anny Blatt "Antique" (72% viscose, 28% polyester, ⅞ oz./25 g balls, each approx 50 yds./46 m)

Five balls #016 argent

One pair size 4 US (3.5 mm) knitting needles OR SIZE REQUIRED TO OBTAIN GIVEN GAUGE

Decorator lamp shade 4 in./10 cm top × 6 in./15 cm bottom × 5 in./12.5 cm high

Glue gun and glue sticks

GAUGE

22 sts and 25 rows = 4 in./10 cm over pat st, using size 4 US (3.5 mm) needles.

TO SAVE TIME, TAKE TIME TO CHECK GAUGE.

FINISHING

Sew roses evenly around bottom edge of shade. Sew back seam. Using a glue gun, carefully attach knitted piece to lamp shade on top edge and then on bottom edge.

FALLING LEAVES LAMP SHADE

MATERIALS

Tahki "Cotton Classic" (100% cotton, 1¾ oz./50 g skeins, each approx 108 yds./100 m)

One skein each #3203 tan (MC), #3462 claret red (A), #3568 gold (B), #3754 sea green (C), and #3248 brown (D)

One pair size 4 US (3.5 mm) knitting needles OR SIZE REQUIRED TO OBTAIN GIVEN GAUGE

Decorator lamp shade 4 in./10 cm top × 6 in./15 cm bottom × 5 in./ 12.5 cm high

Glue gun and glue sticks

GAUGE

22 sts and 25 rows = 4 in./10 cm over Pat st, using size 4 US (3.5 mm) needles.
TO SAVE TIME, TAKE TIME TO CHECK GAUGE.

Instructions

Work cover the same as Goodnight Rose.

Make two leaves each of the foll color combinations: Color 1 = A and Color 2 = C; Color 1 = B and Color 2 = C; Color 1 = A and Color 2 = B.

With Color 1, cast on 5 sts.

Row 1 (RS): K2, yo, k1, yo, k2—7 sts.

Row 2: With Color 1, purl.

Row 3: With Color 1, k3, yo, k1, yo, join Color 2 and k3—9 sts.

Row 4: With Color 2, p4; with Color 1, p5.

Row 5: With Color 1, k4, yo, k1, yo; with Color 2, k4—11 sts.

Instructions

Cast on 53 sts, and work in k1, p1 rib for 2 rows.

Row 1 (RS): K1, *p1, M1, k1; rep from * to end—79 sts.

Row 2: P1, *k2, p1; rep from * to end.

Cont in rib as established for 6 rows more.

Row 9: K1, *P2, M1, k1; rep from * to end—105 sts.

Row 10: K1, *k3, p1; rep from * to end.

Cont in rib as established for 12 rows more.

Row 23: K1, *p3, M1, k1; rep from * to end—131 sts.

Row 24: P1, *k4, p1; rep from * to end.

Cont in rib as established until length of lamp shade. Bind off purlwise on WS. Sew seam.

Roses (make 7)

Cast on 37 sts, leaving a long tail for seaming.

Row 1 (RS): K1, *p1, k1; rep from * to end.

Rows 2, 4, 6, and 8: K the knit sts and p the purl sts.

Row 3: K1, *p1, M1, k1; rep from * to end—55 sts.

Row 5: K1, *p2, M1, k1; rep from * to end—73 sts.

Row 7: K1, *p3, M1, k1; rep from * to end—91 sts.

Row 9: K1, *p4, M1, k1; rep from * to end—109 sts.

Bind off all sts purlwise on WS. Roll the ruffle st, and seam the cast-on edge to form a rose.

Row 6: With Color 2, p5; with Color 1, p6.

Row 7: With Color 1, bind off 3 sts, [k1, yo] twice; with Color 2, k5—10 sts.

Row 8: With Color 2, bind off 3 sts, p1; with Color 1, p5—7 sts.

Row 9: With Color 1, k3, [yo, k1] twice; with Color 2, k2—9 sts.

Row 10: With Color 2, p3; with Color 1, p6.

Row 11: With Color 1, k4, [yo, k1] twice; with Color 2, k3—11 sts.

Row 12: With Color 2, p4; with Color 1, p7.

Row 13: With Color 1, bind off 3 sts, [k1, yo] twice, k1; with Color 2, k4—10 sts.

Row 14: With Color 2, bind off 3 sts, p1; with Color 1, p5—7 sts.

Row 15: With Color 1, SSK, k2; with Color 2, k1, k2tog—5 sts.

Row 16: With Color 2, p3; with Color 1, p2.

Row 17: With Color 1, SSK; with Color 2, k1, k2tog—3 sts.

Row 18: With Color 2, p3.

Row 19: With Color 2, SK2P. Tie off last st.

Bobbles (make 6 each of A, B, C, and D)

Cast on 1 st.

Row 1: ([k in front and back] twice, k1) in same st—5 sts.

Rows 2 and 4: Purl.

Row 3: SSK, k3, k2tog—5 sts.

Row 5: SSK, k1, k2tog—3 sts.

Row 7: SK2P. Tie off last st.

FINISHING

Sew leaves to cover at opposite angles, alternating top and bottom. Sew bobbles to each purl st at bottom of cover, repeating A, B, C, and D. Sew back seam. Using a glue gun, carefully attach knitted piece to lamp shade on top edge and then on bottom edge.

BOUDOIR LAMP SHADE

MATERIALS

Anny Blatt "Victoria" (100% polyamide, 1¾ oz./50 g cones, each approx 110 yds./100 m)

One cone #235 grenat

1 yd./1 m of ¼ in./1 cm black velvet ribbon

1 yd./1 m of bead fringe

One pair size 4 US (3.5 mm) knitting needles OR SIZE REQUIRED TO OBTAIN GIVEN GAUGE

Decorator lamp shade 4 in./10 cm top × 6 in./15 cm bottom × 5 in./12.5 cm high

Glue gun and glue sticks

GAUGE

22 sts and 25 rows = 4 in./10 cm over Pat st, using size 4 US (3.5 mm) needles.

TO SAVE TIME, TAKE TIME TO CHECK GAUGE.

Instructions

Work cover same as Goodnight Rose Lamp Shade.

FINISHING

Weave velvet ribbon in and out of the holes made from increases at the top and middle of cover. Sew beaded fringe around the bottom of the shade. Using a glue gun, carefully attach knitted piece to lamp shade on top edge and then on bottom edge.

Harlequin Magic Afghan

Easy

The colors for this afghan were chosen to depict the essence of a harlequin, and the rhinestones add the magic. Stockinette stitch diamonds worked with ribbon yarn for the solid diamonds and novelty yarn for the multicolored diamonds make up this striking afghan. Knitted tassels adorn the bottom.

FINISHED AFGHAN SIZE

Approx 48 in./122 cm × 74 in./188 cm

MATERIALS

Trendsetter Yarns "Dune" (41% mohair, 12% viscose, 6% metallic, 30% acrylic, 11% nylon, 1¼ oz./50 g balls, each approx 90 yds./81 m)

11 balls #58 multi (A)

Trendsetter Yarns "Dolcino" (75% acrylic, 25% polyamide, 1¼ oz./50 g balls, each approx 99 yds./90 m)

6 balls each #106 teal (B) and #10 fuchsia (C)

3 balls each #30 purple (D) and #8 green (E)

One pair each size 8 US and 9 US (5 mm and 5.5 mm) knitting needles OR SIZE REQUIRED TO OBTAIN GIVEN GAUGE

Stitch markers

Matching sewing thread

Colored ½-in./1.5-cm rhinestones (optional)

Poly-Fil stuffing for tassels

GAUGE

16 sts and 24 rows = 4 in./10 cm over St st, using size 8 US (5 mm) needles for "Dune" and size 9 US (5.5 mm) needles for "Dolcino."

TO SAVE TIME, TAKE TIME TO CHECK GAUGE.

Note: Remember to use smaller needles with "Dune" yarns and larger needles with "Dolcino."

Instructions

Diamonds (make 25 with A, 8 with B, 8 with C, 4 with D, and 4 with E)

Cast on 1 st.

Row 1 (RS): K into front, back, and front of st—3 sts.

Row 2: Purl.

Row 3: K1, M1, k to last st, M1, k1.

Rep last 2 rows until there are 39 sts, end with a WS row. Place a marker each side of row.

Next row: K1, SKP, k to last 3 sts, k2tog, k1.

Next row: Purl.

Rep last 2 rows until there are 5 sts.

Next row: K1, SK2P, k1.

Next row: Sl 1, p2tog, psso. Tie off.

Left-Half Diamonds (make 2 with C, and 1 each with D and E)

Cast on 1 st.

Row 1 (RS): K into front and back of st—2 sts.

Row 2: Purl.

Row 3: K1, M1, k to end.

Rep last 2 rows until there are 24 sts, end with a WS row. Place a marker at beg of RS row.

Next row (RS): K1, SKP, k to end.

Next row: Purl.

Rep last 2 rows until there are 3 sts. SK2P. Tie off.

Right-Half Diamonds (make 2 with C and 1 each with D and E)

Cast on 1 st.

Row 1 (RS): K into front and back of st—2 sts.

Row 2: Purl.

Row 3: K to last st, M1, k1.

Harlequin Magic Afghan Placement Diagram

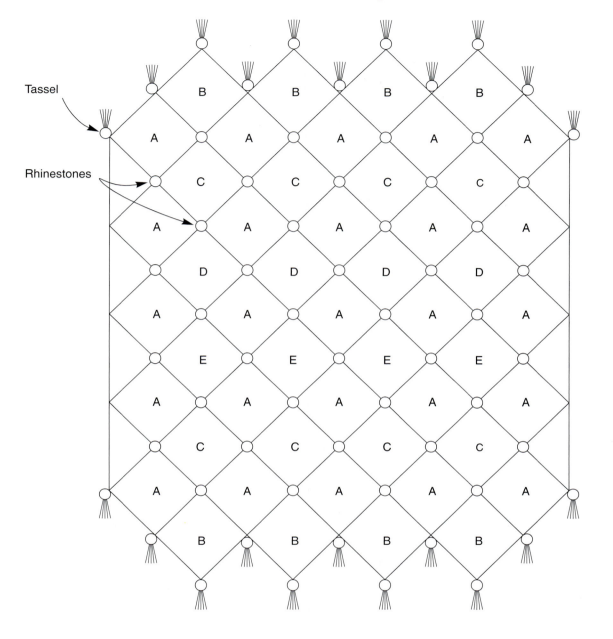

Tassel

Rhinestones

Rep last 2 rows until there are 24 sts, end with a WS row. Place a marker at end of RS row.

Next row (RS): K to last 3 sts, SKP, k1.

Next row: Purl.

Rep last 2 rows until there are 3 sts. SK2P. Tie off.

FINISHING

Using sewing thread, sew diamonds and half diamonds tog, foll placement diagram above. Sew rhinestones at each diamond point if desired.

Tassels (make 22)

With A, cast on 14 sts, and work in St st for 16 rows. On next RS row, bind off 7 sts, tie off 8th st. Sew bound-off sts to cast-on sts. Stuff with Poly-Fil stuffing. Unravel rem 6 sts.

Tassel band (make 24 B, 14 C, and 2 each D and E)

Cast on 8 sts. K and bind off at same time. Sew ends tog around base of skein. Sew to points of afghan as foll: left to right, 1 B, 2 C, 1 D, 3 C, 1 E, 2 C, 1 B.

Attach a tassel to each diamond point at top and bottom of afghan.

Prism Pillows

Easy

An easy stockinette and garter stitch combination looks luxurious in these three pillows made with novelty yarn. Keep in mind that each skein of yarn is hand-dyed so your pillows may not look exactly like mine. Each pillow uses one skein of "Cool Stuff," a multicolored and textured yarn, and one skein of "Bonbon," a solid ribbon yarn.

ROUND PILLOW

FINISHED SIZE

15 in./38 cm in diameter

MATERIALS

Prism "Bonbon" (100% rayon, 2 oz./
   57 g skeins, each approx 94 yds./86 m)
Prism "Cool Stuff"
   (cotton/viscose/nylon/poly/silk,
   6 oz.–8 oz. skeins, each approx
   300 yds./274 m)
One skein "Cool Stuff" terra-cotta (A)
   One skein "Bonbon" #102 rust (B)
One 15-in./38-cm-round pillow form
Two 1½-in./4-cm Styrofoam balls
One pair size 7 US (4.5 mm) knitting
   needles OR SIZE REQUIRED TO
   OBTAIN GIVEN GAUGE
½-yd./0.5-m matching fabric
   (optional)

GAUGE

16 sts and 22 rows = 4 in./10 cm over St
   st, using size 7 US (4.5 mm) needles.
TO SAVE TIME, TAKE TIME TO
   CHECK GAUGE.

Instructions

With A, cast on 52 sts.

Beg pat. *With A, beg with a k row, work in St st for 8 rows. Change to B and k 2 rows, p 1 row, k 1 row. Rep from * (12 rows) for pat 15 times more (192 rows in total). Bind off. Sew bound-off edge to cast-on edge.

FINISHING

Optional: Cut two 16-in./41-cm circles from fabric. With RS tog and using a ½-in./1.5-cm seam, stitch circles tog, leaving an opening to insert pillow form. Turn cover to RS. Insert pillow form, and slip st opening closed. By hand, gather one edge of knitted piece tog at center. Slip covered (or uncovered) pillow inside. Gather rem edge of knitted piece at opposite center.

Fringed Tassels (make 2)

With A, cast on 18 sts, and work in St st for 4 in./10 cm. Bind off 7 sts, tie off 8th st. Sew these 8 sts to corresponding 8 cast-on sts. Gather top edge and sew. Insert Styrofoam ball, and wrap a piece of yarn around tassel near base of ball to secure. Unravel rem 10 sts gently, one row at a time. Sew one tassel to center of pillow on front and one to back. With B, cast on 15 sts. K 3 rows. Bind off. Wrap around base of covered ball.

BLOCK PILLOW

FINISHED SIZE

16 in./41 cm square

MATERIALS

Prism "Bonbon" (100% rayon, 2 oz./
   57 g skeins, each approx 94 yds./86 m)
Prism "Wild Stuff" (mohair/wool/
   alpaca/silk/cotton/viscose/nylon,
   6 oz.–8 oz. skeins, each approx
   300 yds./274 m)
One skein "Bonbon" #312 blue (A)
One-half skein "Wild Stuff" ginger (B)
One 16-in./41-cm-square pillow form
One pair size 7 US (4.5 mm) knitting
   needles OR SIZE REQUIRED TO
   OBTAIN GIVEN GAUGE
½-yd./0.5-m matching fabric (optional)

16 sts and 22 rows = 4 in./10 cm over St
st, using size 7 US (4.5 mm) needles.
TO SAVE TIME, TAKE TIME TO
CHECK GAUGE.

Instructions

With B, cast on 68 sts. Work in St st for
4 in./10cm, end with a RS row.

Next row (WS): P18 B; p14 A; p16 B;
p20 A. Cont in St st, matching colors,
for 5 in./12.5 cm, end with a RS row.

Next row (WS): P18 B; p14 A; k36 B.
Cont in St st, matching colors, for
3½ in./9 cm, end with a RS row.

Next row (WS): P18 B; p with A to
end. Cont in St st, matching colors, for
2½ in./6 cm, end with a RS row.

Next row (WS): With B, p all sts.
Cont in St st with B only until piece
measures 16 in./41 cm from beg. Bind
off.

Fringe

With B, cast on 14 sts. Work in garter st
for 5½ in./14 cm. Bind off 5 sts, and tie
off 6th st; unravel rem 8 sts to make
looped fringe. Sew vertically to RS of
small A block (see photo on p. 72).

FINISHING

Sew knitted pillow front to fabric, leaving opening at lower edge. Insert pillow
form, and sew lower edge opening
closed. If using a purchased matching
pillow, sew knitted front piece onto pillow on all edges.

DIAGONAL PILLOW

FINISHED SIZE

16 in./41 cm square

MATERIALS

Prism "Bonbon" (100% rayon, 2 oz./
57 g skeins, each approx 94 yds./86 m)
Prism "Wild Stuff" (mohair/wool/
alpaca/silk/cotton/viscose/nylon,
6 oz.–8 oz. skeins, each approx
300 yds./274 m)
One skein "Bonbon" #310 sage (A)
One-half skein "Cool Stuff" sage
green (B)
One 16-in./41-cm-square pillow form
One pair size 7 US (4.5 mm) knitting
needles OR SIZE REQUIRED TO
OBTAIN GIVEN GAUGE
½-yd./0.5-m matching fabric (optional)

GAUGE

16 sts and 22 rows = 4 in./10 cm over St
st, using size 7 US (4.5 mm) needles.
TO SAVE TIME, TAKE TIME TO
CHECK GAUGE.

STRIPE PATTERN

*4 rows B, 4 rows A; rep from * (8 rows)
for Stripe Pat.

Instructions

With B, cast on 1 st. Work in Stripe Pat
as foll:

Inc Row 1 (RS): K in front, back and
front of st—3 sts.

Rows 2 and 4: Purl.

Inc Row 3: K in front and back of
first st, k to last st, k in front and back
of last st (2 sts inc'd). Rep Rows 3 and 4
until there are 81 sts. Mark each end of
last row.

Dec Row 1 (RS): SSK, k to last 2 sts,
k2tog (2 sts dec'd).

Row 2: Purl. Rep Rows 1 and 2 until
3 sts rem.

Next row: SK2P. Tie off.

Fringe

With 1 strand each of A and B held tog,
cast on 14 sts. Work in garter st for
6 in./15 cm. Bind off 5 sts, tie off the
6th st; unravel the rem 8 sts to make
looped fringe. Sew to center of pillow
on the diagonal.

FINISHING

Work same as for Block Pillow.

Mosaic Diamonds Afghan

The yarn used here makes the afghan lightweight and luxurious. The two-color classic mosaic stitch is used with a simple garter stitch border. The afghan is highlighted with two-color knit tassels that dress the top and bottom.

FINISHED SIZE

Approx 42 in./106 cm wide × 58 in./ 147 cm long

MATERIALS

Lion Brand "Alpaka" (30% alpaca, 30% wool, 40% acrylic, 1¾ oz./50 g skeins, each approx 107 yds./98 m)

12 skeins #152 oxford gray (A)

10 skeins #098 natural (B)

Alternate colorways:

#098 natural (A), #152 oxford gray (B)

#124 camel (A), #098 natural (B)

#098 natural (A), #149 silver gray (B)

Size 8 US (5 mm) circular knitting needle OR SIZE REQUIRED TO OBTAIN GIVEN GAUGE

Poly-Fil stuffing for tassels

GAUGE

17 sts and 30 rows = 4 in./10 cm over Stripe Pat, using size 8 US (5 mm) needles.

TO SAVE TIME, TAKE TIME TO CHECK GAUGE.

PATTERN STITCHES

Stripe Pattern

Rows 1 and 2: With A, knit.

Rows 3 and 4: With B, k 1 row, p 1 row.

Rep Rows 1–4 for Stripe Pat.

Mosaic Pattern
(multiple of 10 sts plus 1 st)

Note: On all RS rows, sl all sl-sts wyib; on all WS row, sl all sl-sts wyif.

Row 1 (RS): With B, k5, *sl 1, k9; rep from *, end sl 1, k5.

Rows 25 and 26: With B, rep Rows 9 and 10.

Rows 27 and 28: With A, rep Rows 7 and 8.

Rows 29 and 30: With B, rep Rows 5 and 6.

Rows 31 and 32: With A, rep Rows 3 and 4.

Rep Rows 1–32 for Mosaic Pat.

Instructions

With A, cast on 169 sts. K 4 rows.

Beg Mosaic Pat

Next row (RS): With A, k4; work Mosaic Pat over next 161 sts; with A, k4. Cont in pat as established, keeping first and last 4 sts in garter st with A, until 32 rows of Mosaic Pat have been work three times, then work Rows 1 and 2 once more. Work in Stripe Pat, keeping first and last sts in garter st before, for 50 rows. Rep between *s (148 rows) once, then work 98 rows in Mosaic Pat as before. K4 rows A. Bind off.

Tassels (make 36)

With A, cast on 14 sts. Work in Stripe Pat for 20 rows. Bind off 7 sts. Sew these 7 sts to cast-on edge. Stuff with Poly-Fil. Unravel rem 7 sts.

Tie

With A, cast on 10 sts, and k 2 rows. Bind off knitwise. Place around tassel neck, and sew the seam. Sew to edge around tassel to hold in place.

Sew 18 tassels along cast-on edge, with 1 at end of each diamond point and 1 in each corner. Sew the other 18 in the same way along bound-off edge of afghan.

Row 2: With B, p5, *sl 1, p9; rep from *, end sl 1, p5.

Row 3: With A, knit.

Row 4: With A, k4, *p3, k7; rep from *, end p3, k4.

Row 5: With B, k4, *sl 1, k1, sl 1, k7; rep from *, end last rep k4.

Row 6: With B, p4, *sl 1, k1, sl 1, p7; rep from *, end last rep p4.

Row 7: With A, knit.

Row 8: With A, k3, *p5, k5; rep from *, end p5, k3.

Row 9: With B, k3, *[sl 1, k1] twice, sl 1, k5; rep from *, end last rep k3.

Row 10: With B, p3, *[sl 1, k1] twice, sl 1, p5; rep from *, end last rep p3.

Row 11: With A, knit.

Row 12: With A, k2, *p7, k3; rep from *, end p7, k2.

Row 13: With B, k2, *[sl 1, k1] 3 times, sl 1, k3; rep from *, end last rep k2.

Row 14: With B, p2, *[sl 1, k1] 3 times, sl 1, p3; rep from *, end last rep p2.

Row 15: With A, knit.

Row 16: With A, purl.

Rows 17 and 18: With B, k1, *sl 1, k1; rep from * to end.

Rows 19 and 20: With A, rep Rows 15 and 16.

Rows 21 and 22: With B, rep Rows 13 and 14.

Rows 23 and 24: With A, rep Rows 11 and 12.

Mudcloth Afghan and Pillow

Advanced

Inspired by wonderful mudcloth fabrics, this afghan is worked in two main panels, then the center is connected and bordered with a wide garter stitch. I used three gold African masks for a little extra touch on the pillow, but there are many African beads and buttons on the market, so don't hesitate to add your own touches.

AFGHAN

FINISHED AFGHAN SIZE
Approx 46 in./117 cm wide × 64 in./162 cm long (without fringe)

MATERIALS
Patons "Decor" (75% acrylic, 25% wool, 3½ oz./100 g skeins, each approx 210 yds./192 m)
Nine skeins #1603 black (MC)
Seven skeins #1662 bronze (CC)
One pair size 8 US (5 mm) knitting needles OR SIZE REQUIRED TO OBTAIN CORRECT GAUGE
Tapestry needle

GAUGE
18 sts and 24 rows = 4 in./10 cm over St st, using size 8 US (5 mm) needles.
TO SAVE TIME, TAKE TIME TO CHECK GAUGE.

Instructions

Note: When working Chart 1, work Rows 1-134 of Chart 1a, Rows 135-262 of Chart 1b, and Rows 263-317 of Chart 1c. When working Chart 2, work Rows 1-134 of Chart 2a, Rows 135-265 of Chart 2b, and Rows 266-317 of Chart 2c.

Left Panel
With MC, cast on 91 sts. K1 row, p1 row. Work Chart 1 (pp. 80-82) to end. Bind off with MC.

Right Panel
With MC, cast on 91 sts. K1 row, p1 row. Work Chart 2 (pp. 80-82) to end. Bind off with MC.

Center Connecting Border
With RS of right panel facing, pick up and k 270 sts evenly along inside edge. Work in garter st for 2 in./5 cm. Bind off on RS. Sew bound-off edge to inside edge of left panel.

Top and Bottom Borders
With RS facing and MC, pick up and k 191 sts along cast-on edge. Work in garter st, inc 1 st each side every RS row 8 times—207 sts. Bind off on RS. Work in same way along bound-off edge.

Side Borders
With RS facing and MC, pick up and k 270 sts evenly along one side edge. Work same as top border until there are 286 sts. Bind off.

FINISHING
Sew corners tog. Work in all ends. Block lightly.

Fringe
With MC, make 4½-in./11.5-cm fringe. Using three strands for each fringe, attach 93 fringes evenly along bottom edge. Using 3 fringes, make a braid. Tie at bottom and cut (31 braids). Work in same way along top edge.

Chart 1a

Chart 2a

Chart 1b

Chart 2b

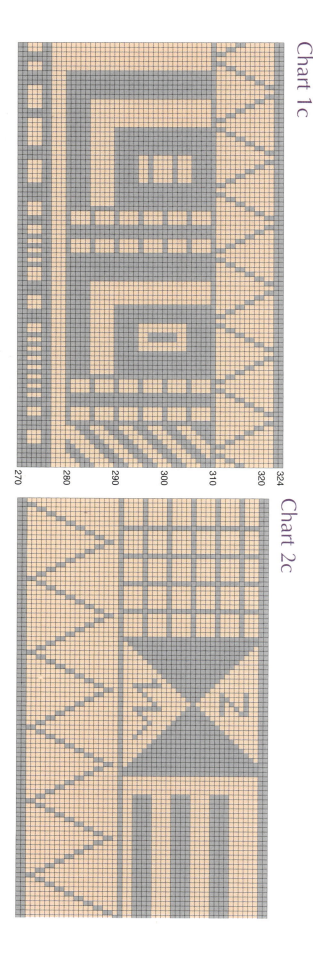

Chart 1c

270 280 290 300 310 320 324

Chart 2c

Color Key

	black (MC)
	bronze (CC)
·	knit on WS; purl on RS

PILLOW

FINISHED PILLOW SIZE

20 in./51 cm square

MATERIALS

Patons "Decor" (75% acrylic, 25% wool,
   3½ oz./100 g skeins, each approx
   210 yds./192 m)

Two skeins #1603 black (MC)

One skein #1662 bronze (CC)

One 20-in./51-cm-square pillow form

One pair size 8 US (5 mm) knitting needles OR SIZE REQUIRED TO
   OBTAIN CORRECT GAUGE

Tapestry needle

African mask ornaments (optional) (see
   photo above)

Instructions

Front

With MC, cast on 91 sts. Work 2 in./5 cm in garter stitch. Work 20 in./51 cm, foll photo above or your favorite section of the chart. With MC, work 2 in./5 cm in garter stitch. Bind off.

Back

With MC, cast on 91 sts, and work in St st and stripes as foll: *2 rows MC, 2 rows CC; rep from * until piece measures 20 in./51 cm. Bind off.

FINISHING

Sew front and back tog, leaving bottom edge open. Insert pillow form, and sew opening closed.

Fringe

With MC, make 4½-in./11.5-cm fringe. Using 3 strands for each fringe, attach 42 fringes evenly along one side edge. Using 3 fringes, make a braid. Tie at bottom and cut (14 braids). Work in same way along other side edge.

Pear

Easy

*Easy to do, these pears add an elegant touch to any decor.
Each skein of gold yarn makes three pears. Make multiple pears
and display them in a bowl, or add a loop and make Christmas tree
ornaments to give as gifts or to keep for your own decorating.*

FINISHED SIZE

Approx 5 in./12.5 cm in height

MATERIALS

Muench "Touch Me" (72% viscose,
   28% new wool, 1¾ oz./50 g balls,
   each approx 61 yds./56 m)
One ball each #3616 gold (A), #3617
   gray (B), and #3610 green (C)
One pair size 8 US (5 mm) knitting
   needles OR SIZE REQUIRED TO
   OBTAIN GIVEN GAUGE
Poly-Fil stuffing

GAUGE

16 sts and 24 rows = 4 in./10 cm over St
   st, using size 8 US (5 mm) needles.
TO SAVE TIME, TAKE TIME TO
   CHECK GAUGE.

Instructions

With A, cast on 7 sts. P 1 row.
   Row 1 (RS): K1, [m1, k1] 6 times—
13 sts.
   Row 2 and all WS rows: Purl.
   Row 3: K2, [m1, k1] 9 times, k2—
22 sts.
   Row 5: K1, [m1, k2] 10 times, k1—
32 sts.
   Rows 7, 9, 11, and 13: Knit.
   Row 15: K1, [k2tog] 15 times, k1—
17 sts.
   Rows 17, 19, 21, and 23: Knit.
   Row 25: K1, [k2tog] 8 times—9 sts.
   Sl rem sts over last st to bind off all
sts. Cut yarn and draw through last st.

Leaf (make one leaf each of B and C for each pear)

With B or C, cast on 6 sts.
   Row 1 (RS): K4, yf, sl 1, yb, turn.
   Row 2: Sl first st to RH needle, yb,
k3, k in front and back of last st, turn—
7 sts.

Rep Rows 1 and 2 until there are
9 sts. Rep Row 1 once more.
   Dec Row 1: Sl first st to RH needle,
yb, k4, turn.
   Dec Row 2: K2tog, k3, yf, sl 1, yb,
turn.
   Rep dec Rows 1 and 2 until there are
6 sts. Rep Row 1 once more. Bind off
5 sts—1 st. Leave st on needle to make
a stem.

Stem (for one leaf only)

Cable cast on 5 sts with 1 st on needle,
then bind off all 6 sts. Fasten off.

FINISHING

Sew back seam three-quarters of the
way, and fill with Poly-Fil to desired
firmness. Sew rem seam. Using one leaf
color, work an X at base of pear. Sew on
stem and leaves.

ABCDEFGHIJKLMN
OPQRSTUVWXYZ
1234567890

MARY AND JOHN SMITH
AUGUST 3 1999

Proposal Afghan

Give yourself plenty of time if you plan to give this labor of love as a wedding gift. Each row of this intarsia afghan is charted, and there are many colors. The afghan is worked in stockinette stitch in one piece from a chart. The lettering and some fine details are embroidered on after the piece is knit.

FINISHED SIZE

Approx 45 in./114 cm wide × 57 in./ 145 cm long

MATERIALS

Rowan Yarns "DK Tweed" (100% wool, 1¾ oz./50 g hanks, each approx 120 yds./110 m)

Six hanks #851 cricket (A)

Four hanks #850 wren (B)

Six hanks #852 seal (C)

Rowan Yarns "Designer DK Wool" (100% wool, 1¾ oz./50 g balls, each approx 114 yds./104 m)

One ball each #649 white (D), #625 dark gray (E), #693 sand (F), #640 medium green (G), #635 light medium olive (H), #685 forest green (I), #698 medium brown (J), #691 copper brown (K), #690 medium olive (L), #629 gray-blue (M), #665 light blue (N), #642 medium blue (O), #631 light orchid (P), #636 purple (Q), #670 rose (R), #694 mauve (S), #623 light maize (T)

Rowan Yarns "Kid Silk" (70% mohair, 30% silk, 0.8 oz./25 g balls, each approx 64 yds./59 m)

One ball each #969 cornflower (U) and #997 natural (V)

Size 6 US (4 mm) circular needle OR SIZE REQUIRED TO OBTAIN GIVEN GAUGE

Bobbins

Tapestry needle

Fabric for backing (optional)

GAUGE

20 sts and 26 rows = 4 in./10 cm over St st, using size 6 US (4 mm) needles.

TO SAVE TIME, TAKE TIME TO CHECK GAUGE.

Notes: Use a separate bobbin or length of yarn for each block of color. When changing colors, twist yarns to prevent holes. Use bobbins for large blocks of color and lengths of yarn for small color areas.

Instructions

With A, cast on 227 sts.

Next row (RS): K1, M1, k to last 2 sts, M1, k1. P 1 row. Rep last 2 rows twice more—239 sts. K 2 rows for turning ridge. Cont in St st, foll Charts 1 through 4, until all chart rows have been worked. Reverse Chart 1 for right side and Chart 4 for left side. With A, k 2 rows for turning ridge, then cont in St st as foll:

Next row (RS): K1, SSK, k to last 3 sts, k2tog, k1. P 1 row. Rep last 2 row twice more. Bind off.

Side Hems

With RS facing and A, pick up and k 285 sts evenly along one side edge. K 1 row on WS for turning ridge. Cont in St st, dec 1 st each side every RS row 3 times. Bind off loosely on last RS row. Work in same way along other side edge.

FINISHING

Weave in ends. Block lightly. Work embroidery, foll charts. Fold hems to WS and sew in place. Back with fabric if desired.

Chart 2

Chart 1

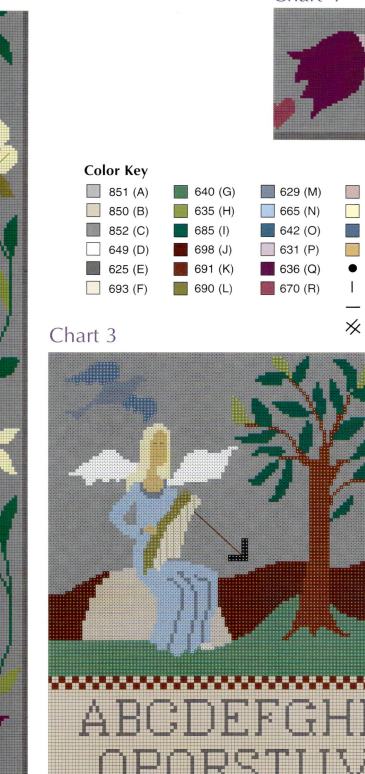

Chart 4

Color Key

■	851 (A)	■	640 (G)	■	629 (M)	■	694 (S)
■	850 (B)	■	635 (H)	■	665 (N)	■	623 (T)
■	852 (C)	■	685 (I)	■	642 (O)	■	969 (U)
☐	649 (D)	■	698 (J)	■	631 (P)	■	997 (V)
■	625 (E)	■	691 (K)	■	636 (Q)	●	French knot (with yarn color indicated)
■	693 (F)	■	690 (L)	■	670 (R)	I	Stem stitch (with yarn color indicated)

— Straight stitch (with yarn color indicated)

✕ Couching (with yarn color indicated)

Chart 3

Provence Afghan

Intermediate

The tiles and flowers of Provence, France, inspired this delightful afghan. Color blockwork and original appliquéd florals are worked in diagonal strips. The check motif is a seed and stockinette stitch combination. The floral motif appliqués are knit separately and then sewn to the six plain stockinette stitch blocks. The border is a two-colored textural pattern.

FINISHED SIZE

Approx 52 in./132 cm × 67 in./170 cm

MATERIALS

Muench/GGH "Samoa" (50% wool, 50% acrylic, 1¾ oz./50 g balls, each approx 105 yd./95 m)

12 balls #4 ecru (MC)

6 balls each #13 blue (A) and #5 maize (B)

3 balls #42 green (C)

1 ball each #38 light blue (D), #50 rose (E), and #148 light green (F)

One pair size 6 US (4 mm) knitting needles OR SIZE REQUIRED TO OBTAIN GIVEN GAUGE

Size 6 US (4 mm) circular needle

Two size 6 US (4 mm) double-pointed needles

Tapestry needle

GAUGE

19 sts and 26 rows = 4 in./10 cm St st, using size 6 US (4 mm) needles

TO SAVE TIME, TAKE TIME TO CHECK GAUGE.

Note: Afghan is knit in strips, beginning at lower right corner with MC triangle.

PATTERN STITCHES

Bobble

Cast on 1 st.

Row 1: ([k in front and back] twice, k1) in same st—5 sts.

Rows 2, 4, and 6: Purl.

Row 3: Knit.

Row 5: SSK, k1, k2tog—3 sts.

Row 7: SK2P. Tie off last st.

Seed Stitch (even number of sts)

Row 1 (RS): *K1, p1; rep from *.

Row 2: *P1, k1; rep from *.

Stockinette and Seed St Pattern Block (over 58 sts)

Setup Row 1: K5 B, [k12 CC, k12 MC] twice, join B, k5.

Setup Row 2: P5 B, *p12 MC, [p1, k1 CC] 6 times; rep from * once more, p5 B.

Cont in pats as established, beg with Row 1 of St St and Seed St pattern and working until there are 18 rows of pat completed.

Color block change row:

Setup Row 1: K5 B, [k12 MC, k12 CC] twice, k5 B.

Setup Row 2: P5 B, *[p1, k1 CC] 6 times, p12 MC; rep from * once more, p5 B.

Work as for first block with reverse colors and pats. Work until there are four blocks completed. Place sts on holder. Cut MC, CC, and B.

Diamonds

Bottom right quarter-diamond: With MC, cast on 2 sts.

Row 1: Knit in front and back of next 2 sts—4 sts.

Row 2: P1, inc 1, purl to last st, inc 1, p1—6 sts.

Row 3: K1, inc 1, knit to last st, inc 1, k1—8 sts.

Row 4: P1, inc 1, purl to last st, inc 1, p1—10 sts.

Row 5: Knit.

Row 6: P1, inc 1, purl to last st, inc 1, p1—12 sts.

Row 7: K1, inc 1, knit to last st, inc 1, k1—14 sts.

Row 8: P1, inc 1, purl to last st, inc 1, p1—16 sts.

Row 9: K1, inc 1, knit to last st, inc 1, k1—18 sts.

Row 10: Purl.

Row 11: K1, inc 1, knit to last st, inc 1, k1—20 sts.

Row 12: P1, inc 1, purl to last st, inc 1, p1—22 sts.

Row 13: Knit.

Row 14: P1, inc 1, purl to last st, inc 1, p1—24 sts.

Row 15: K1, inc 1, knit to last st, inc 1, k1—26 sts.

Row 16: P1, inc 1, purl to last st, inc 1, p1—28 sts.

Row 17: K1, inc 1, knit to last st, inc 1, k1—30 sts.

Row 18: Purl.

Rows 19–36: Rep Rows 3–18 once, then Rows 3 and 4—58 sts.

Work left half-diamond (inc version) as foll:

With MC, cast on 2 sts.

Row 1 (RS): K1, inc 1, knit to end—3 sts.

Row 2: P1, inc 1, purl to end—4 sts.

Row 3: Knit.

Row 4: P1, inc 1, purl to end—5 sts.

Row 5: Knit to last st, inc 1, k1—6 sts.

Row 6: Purl.

Rows 7–18: Rep Rows 1–6 twice.

Rows 19–22: Rep Rows 1 and 2 twice.

Rows 23–70: Rep Rows 1–22 twice then Rows 1–4 once more—53 sts.

Rows 71 and 72: K 1 row, p 1 row. Place sts on holder.

Work right half-diamond (inc version) as foll:

With MC, cast on 2 sts.

Row 1 (RS): K1, inc 1, knit to end—3 sts.

Row 2: Purl to last st, inc 1, p1—4 sts.

Row 3: Knit.

Row 4: Purl to last st, inc 1, p1—5 sts.

Row 5: K1, inc 1, knit to end—6 sts.

Row 6: Purl.

Rows 7–18: Rep Rows 1–6 twice.

Rows 19–22: Rep Rows 1 and 2 twice.

Rows 23–70: Rep Rows 1–22 twice then Rows 1–4 once more—53 sts.

Rows 71 and 72: K 1 row, p 1 row. Place sts on spare needle.

Work left half-diamond (dec version) with MC beg with 53 sts as foll:

Row 1 (RS): Knit to last 3 sts, k2tog, k1—52 sts.

Row 2: P1, p2tog, purl to end—51 sts.

Row 3: Knit.

Row 4: P1, p2tog, purl to end—50 sts.

Row 5: Knit to last 3sts, k2tog, k1—49 sts.

Row 6: Purl.

Rows 7–18: Rep Rows 1–6 twice.

Rows 19–22: Rep Rows 1 and 2 twice.

Rows 23–72: Rep Rows 1–22 twice then Rows 1–6 once more—1 st.

Cut yarn, thread needle, and draw through rem st.

Work right half-diamond (dec version) with MC beg with 53 sts as foll:

Row 1 (RS): K1, k2tog, knit to end—52 sts.

Row 2: Purl to last 3 sts, p2tog, p1—51 sts.

Row 3: Knit.

Row 4: Purl to last 3 sts, p2tog, p1—50 sts.

Row 5: K1, k2tog, knit to end—49 sts.

Row 6: Purl.

Rows 7–18: Rep Rows 1–6 twice.

Rows 19–22: Rep Rows 1 and 2 twice.

Rows 23–72: Rep Rows 1–22 twice then Rows 1–6 once more—1 st.

Cut yarn, thread needle, and draw through rem st.

Instructions

First strip: Work right and left half-diamond (inc version). Set aside. Work bottom right quarter-diamond. Cut MC, join B, work 6 rows St st. Work Stockinette and Seed st block in A and

MC—58 sts. Work in pats as established for 72 rows. Cut all colors. Leave on needle. Join B, work across 53 sts of right half-diamond on spare needle, 58 sts of pattern block, and 53 sts of left half-diamond on holder—164 sts. Work 6 rows St st.

Second strip: Work right and left half-diamond (inc version). Set aside. K5 B, 48-st pattern block in C and MC, k5 B, 48-st plain MC block, k5 B, 48-st pattern block in C and MC, k5 B—164 sts. Work in pats as established for 72 rows. Cut all colors. Leave on needle. Join B, work across 53 sts of right half-diamond on spare needle, 164 sts on needle, 53 sts of left half-diamond on holder—270 sts. Work 6 rows St st.

Third strip: Work right half-diamond (inc version). Set aside. [K5 B, 48-st pattern block in A and MC, k5 B, 48-st plain MC block] twice, k5 B, 48-st pattern block in A and MC, k5 B—270 sts. Work in pats as established for 72 rows. Cut all colors. Leave on needle. Join B, work across 53 sts of right half-diamond on spare needle, 270 sts on needle—323 sts. Work 6 rows St st.

Fourth strip: [Work k5 B, 48-st pattern block with C and MC, k5 B, 48-st plain MC block] twice, k5 B, 48-st pattern block with C and MC, k5 B, and 53-st left half-diamond (dec version) MC block—323 sts. Work in pats as established for 72 rows, dec on left diamond block as per instructions—270 sts. Join B, Work 6 rows St st.

Fifth strip: Work 53-st right half-diamond (dec version) MC block, k5 B, 48-st pattern block in A and MC, k5 B, 48-st plain MC block, k5 B, 48-st pattern block in A and MC, k5 B, and 53-st left half-diamond (dec version) MC block—270 sts. Work in pats as established, dec on left and right diamond block as per instructions—164 sts. Join B, Work 6 rows St st.

Sixth strip: Work 53-st right half-diamond (dec version) MC block, k5 B,

48-st pattern block in C and MC, k5 B, and 53-st left half-diamond (dec version) MC block—164 sts.

Work patterns as established, dec on left and right diamond block as per instructions—58 sts. Join B, k6 rows St st. Cut B.

Work top left quarter-diamond as foll:

Row 1: With MC, k58.

Row 2: P1, p2tog, purl to last 3 sts, p2tog, p1—56 sts.

Row 3: K1, k2tog, knit to last 3 sts, k2tog, k1—54 sts.

Row 4: P1, p2tog, purl to last 3 sts, p2tog, p1—52 sts.

Row 5: Knit.

Row 6: P1, p2tog, purl to last 3 sts, p2tog, p1—50 sts.

Row 7: K1, k2tog, knit to last 3 sts, k2tog, k1—48 sts.

Row 8: P1, p2tog, purl to last 3 sts, p2tog, p1—46 sts.

Row 9: K1, k2tog, knit to last 3 sts, k2tog, k1—44 sts.

Row 10: Purl.

Row 11: K1, k2tog, knit to last 3 sts, k2tog, k1—42 sts.

Row 12: P1, p2tog, purl to last 3 sts, p2tog, p1—40 sts.

Row 13: Knit.

Row 14: P1, p2tog, purl to last 3 sts, p2tog, p1—38 sts.

Row 15: K1, k2tog, knit to last 3 sts, k2tog, k1—36 sts.

Row 16: P1, p2tog, purl to last 3 sts, p2tog, p1—34 sts.

Row 17: K1, k2tog, knit to last 3 sts, k2tog, k1—32 sts.

Row 18: Purl.

Rows 19–36: Rep Rows 3–18 once, then Rows 3 and 4—2 sts. K2tog. Cut yarn, thread needle, and draw through rem st.

Work top right quarter-diamond as foll:

With MC, cast on 2 sts.

Row 1 (RS): K1, inc 1, knit to end—3 sts.

Row 2: Purl to last st, inc 1, p1—4 sts.

Row 3: Knit.

Row 4: Purl to last st, inc 1, p1—5 sts.

Row 5: K1, inc 1, knit to end—6 sts.

Row 6: Purl.

Rows 7–42: Rep these 6 rows 6 more times—30 sts.

Beg dec rows:

Row 1: K1, k2tog, knit to end—29 sts.

Row 2: Purl to last 3 sts, p2tog, p1—28 sts.

Row 3: Knit.

Row 4: Purl to last 3 sts, p2tog, p1—27 sts.

Row 5: K1, k2tog, knit to end—26 sts.

Row 6: Purl.

Rows 7–42: Rep these 6 rows 6 more times—2 sts. K2tog. Cut yarn, thread needle and draw through rem st.

Work bottom left quarter-diamond as foll:

With MC, cast on 2 sts.

Row 1 (RS): K1, inc 1, knit to end—3 sts.

Row 2: P1, inc 1, purl to end—4 sts.

Row 3: Knit.

Row 4: P1, inc 1, purl to end—5 sts.

Row 5: Knit to last st, inc 1, k1—6 sts.

Row 6: Purl.

Rows 7–42: Rep these 6 rows 6 more times—30 sts.

Beg dec rows:

Row 1: Knit to last 3 sts, k2tog, k1—29 sts.

Row 2: P1, p2tog, purl to end—28 sts.

Row 3: Knit.

Row 4: P1, p2tog, purl to end—27 sts.

Row 5: Knit to last 3 sts, k2tog, k1—26 sts.

Row 6: Purl.

Rows 7–42: Rep these 6 rows 6 more times—2 sts. K2tog. Cut yarn, thread needle and draw through rem st.

FINISHING

Sew bottom right half-diamond panels to adjacent color blocks. Sew top right and bottom left quarter-diamond panels in place. Stitch or appliqué motifs in center of plain diamonds following photo on p. 90.

Top and Bottom Edges

With WS facing and A, pick up 223 sts along top of afghan.

Row 1 (WS): *P1, k1; rep from *, end p1.

Row 2: K1, pm, inc 1 st, work seed st to last 2 sts, inc 1 st, pm, k1.

Row 3: Work even in seed st.

Row 4: K1, sl marker, inc 1 st, *K5 MC, work 1 st seed st with A; rep from * to last 2 sts, inc 1 st, sl marker, k1.

Row 5: Work 4 sts seed st with A, *p3 MC, work 3 sts seed st with A; rep from *, end 4 sts seed st with A.

Row 6: P1, inc 1 st, *work 3 sts seed st with A, k1 MC, 2 sts seed st with A; rep from * to last 2 sts, inc 1, p1.

Rows 7 and 9: Work all sts in seed st with A.

Row 8: Work seed st with A, inc 1 st each side as before—231 sts.

Row 10: With A, bind off knitwise on RS.

Work in same way along bottom edge.

Side Edges

With RS facing and A, pick up and k 281 sts evenly along each side edge. Work in seed st and inc 1 st each side (at 1 st in from edge) every RS row 4 times—289 sts. Bind off knitwise on last RS row. Sew mitered edges tog.

Provence Placement Diagram

1. Generic
2. Loop
3. Scallop
4. Canterbury
5. Ruffle picot
6. Friseur

FLOWER APPLIQUÉS

(foll diagram above for placement)

Medium Leaf (make 3)

Cast on 5 sts.

Row 1 (RS): K2, yo, k1, yo, k2—7 sts.
Row 2 and all WS rows: Purl.
Row 3: K3, yo, k1, k3—9 sts.
Row 5: K4, yo, k1, yo, k4—11 sts.
Row 7: SSK, k7, k2tog—9 sts.
Row 9: SSK, k5, k2tog—7 sts.

Row 11: SSK, k3, k2tog—5 sts.
Row 13: SSK, k1, k2tog—3 sts.
Row 15: SK2P. Tie off last st.

Small Leaf (make 4)

Cast on 5 sts.

Row 1 (RS): K2, yo, k1, yo, k2—7 sts.
Row 2 and all WS rows: Purl.
Row 3: K3, yo, k1, yo, k3—9 sts.
Row 5: SSK, k5, k2tog—7 sts.
Row 7: SSK, k3, k2tog—5 sts.
Row 9: SSK, k1, k2tog—3 sts.
Row 11: SK2P. Tie off last st.

Extra Small Leaf (make 9)

Cast on 5 sts.

Row 1 (RS): K2, yo, k1, yo, k2—7 sts.
Row 2, 4 and 6: Purl.
Row 3: SSK, k3, k2tog—5 sts.
Row 5: SSK, k1, k2tog—3 sts.
Row 7: SK2P. Tie off last st.

1. Generic Flower (make 1)

Flowers are worked from outer edge to center.

With A, cast on 57 sts.

Rows 1, 3, 5 and 7 (WS): Purl.
Row 2: K4, *yo, k1, yo, k2, SK2P, k2; rep from *, end yo, k1, yo, k4—59 sts.
Rows 4 and 6: K1, k2tog, k2, *yo, k1, yo, k1, SK2P, k2; rep from *, end yo, k1, yo, k1, SSK, k1. Cut A, join E.
Row 8: With E, k1, k2tog, *k1, SK2P; rep from *, end k1, SSK, k1—31 sts.
Row 9: P2, *p3tog, p1; rep from *, end p1—17 sts. Cut E, join B.
Row 10: With B, k1, *k2tog; rep from *—9 sts.

Cut yarn leaving a 12-in./30.5-cm end. With tapestry needle, thread end through rem sts on needle. Gather up and fasten securely. With C, make 6-in./15.5-cm I-cord and one medium and one small leaf.

2. Loop Flower (make 3)

With E, cast on 31 sts.

Rows 1 and 3 (RS): Knit.
Row 2: K1, *make loop (insert needle in next st, wrap yarn over needle as if to

k, then wrap yarn over two fingers of left hand, then over needle again; draw two loops on needle through the st and place them on LH needle; k the two loops tog through the back), k1; rep from * to end.

Row 4: K2, *make loop, k1; rep from * to last 2 sts, k2.

Rep Rows 1–4 once more.

Next row: K1, [k2tog] 14 times, k2—17 sts.

Next row: P1, [p2tog] 8 times. Tie off rem 9 sts tightly. Sew seam.

With F, make one 6-in./15.5-cm and two 2½-in./6.5-cm I-cords and three small leaves.

With B, make French knot in center of each flower.

3. Scallop Flower (make 3)
With A, cast on 57 sts.

Row 1 (RS): Purl.

Row 2: K2, *k1, sl this st back to LH needle, lift the next 8 sts on LH needle over this st and off needle, [yo] twice, k the first st again, k2; rep from * to end.

Row 3: K1, *p2tog, drop 1 loop of yo on previous row and [k1, k1tbl] twice in rem yo, p1; rep from * to last st, k1—37 sts. Cut A, join B.

Row 4: K1, [k2tog] 18 times—19 sts.

Row 5: P1, [p2tog] 9 times—10 sts. Tie off rem 10 sts tightly.

Make one more in same way, and one more reversing colors A and B.

With F, make French knots in center of each flower. With C, make one I-cord 5½ in./14 cm long, two 3 in./7.5 cm long, and three extra small leaves.

4. Canterbury Flower (make 1)
With D, cast on 35 sts.

Row 1 (RS): Purl.

Row 2: K2, *k1, sl this st back to LH needle, lift the next 8 sts on LH needle over this st. and off needle, [yo] twice, k the first st again, k2; rep from * to end.

Row 3: K1, *p2tog, drop 1 loop of yo on previous row and [k1, k1tbl] twice in rem yo, p1; rep from * to last st, k1—23 sts.

Row 4: Knit, dec 1 st at end of row—22 sts.

Row 5: *P2 D, p2 A; rep from *, end p2 D.

Rows 6 and 7: K 1 row, p 1 row, matching colors.

Row 8: [K2 D, k2tog A] 5 times, k2 D—17 sts.

Row 9: Purl, matching colors.

Row 10: [K2tog D, k1 A] 5 times, k2tog D—11 sts.

Rows 11 and 12: Work in k1, p1 rib, matching colors.

Row 13: With D, [k2tog] 5 times, k1—6 sts.

Rows 14–16: Work in St st.

Row 17: With dpn and F, k2tog across—3 sts. Cont to work rem 3 sts in I-cord for 7 in./17.5 cm. Tie off.

Make two more 3-st I-cords, each 3 in./7.5 cm long.

5. Ruffle Picot Flower (make 1)
With D, cast on 17 sts.

Row 1 (RS): K1, *p1, k1; rep from * to end.

Row 2 and all WS rows: K the knit sts and p the purl sts.

Row 3: K1, *p1, M1, k1; rep from * to end.

Row 5: K1, *p2, M1, k1; rep from * to end.

Row 7: K1, *p3, M1, k1; rep from * to end.

Row 9: K1, *p4, M1, k1; rep from * to end.

Row 11: K1, *p5, M1, k1; rep from * to end.

Work picot on RS with E as foll: Bind off 2 sts, *sl rem st from RH needle to LH needle, cast on 2 sts, bind off 4 sts; rep from * to end. Fasten off last st.

With F, make a 7½-in./19-cm I-cord and six extra small leaves. With B, make bobble for center of flower.

6. Friseur Flower (make 1)
With B, cast on 15 sts.

Rows 1, 2, 5, and 6: Knit.

Rows 3 and 7: Bind off 11 sts, k to end.

Row 4: K4, cast on 11 sts.

Rep Rows 4–7 eight times more. Bind off all sts on last row.

With C, make one 8-in./20.5-cm I-cord and two medium leaves. With MC, make bobble for center of flower. Fold each fringe in half counterclockwise when sewing to background.

Snowflake Afghan and Aran Pillow

This afghan will warm up any room on a cold snowy night. The snowflake afghan combines Aran and easy intarsia knitting. The bobbles are added after the piece is knitted. The pillow shown is a solid Aran block with a garter stitch border. You can also make the snowflake block into a pillow.

AFGHAN

FINISHED AFGHAN SIZE

Approx 54 in./137 cm wide × 72 in./183 cm long

MATERIALS

Cascade "Pastaza" (50% llama, 50% wool, 3½ oz./100 g skeins, each approx 132 yds./120 m)

12 skeins #006 light gray (A)

6 skeins #007 charcoal (B)

5 skeins #049 red (C)

One pair size 10 US (6 mm) knitting needles OR SIZE REQUIRED TO OBTAIN GIVEN GAUGE

Cable needle

Tapestry needle

GAUGE

14 sts and 20 rows = 4 in./10 cm over St st, using size 10 US (6 mm) needles. TO SAVE TIME, TAKE TIME TO CHECK GAUGE.

STITCH GLOSSARY

3-st BPC: Sl 1 st to cn and hold at back of work, k2, p1 from cn.

3-st FPC: Sl 2 sts to cn and hold at front of work, p1, k2 from cn.

4-st BC: Sl 2 sts to cn and hold at back of work, k2, k2 from cn.

4-st FC: Sl 2 sts to cn and hold at front of work, k2, k2 from cn.

9-st FC: Sl 5 sts to cn and hold at front of work, k4, sl p st from cn to LH needle and p it, k4 from cn.

12-st BC: Sl 8 sts to cn and hold at back of work, k4, sl 2nd 4 sts from cn to LH needle and k them, k4 from cn.

12-st FC: Sl 8 sts to cn and hold at front of work, k4, sl 2nd 4 sts from cn to LH needle and k them, k4 from cn.

Knot st: All in one st work [k1, p1] 3 times and k1 to make 7 sts in 1 st, pass the 2nd, 3rd, 4th, 5th, 6th, and 7th over the 1st for knot st.

PATTERN STITCHES

Cable Panel #1 (over 49 sts)

Row 1 (WS): [K2, p4] 4 times, k1, [p4, k2] 4 times.

Row 2: [P2, k4] 4 times, p1, [k4, p2] 4 times.

Rows 3, 5, 7, and 9: Rep Row 1.

Row 4: [P2, 4-st FC, p2, k4] twice, p1, [k4, p2, 4-st BC, p2] twice.

Row 6: Rep Row 2.

Row 8: P2, 4-st FC, p2, k4, p2, 4-st FC, p2, 9-st FC, p2, 4-st BC, p2, k4, p2, 4-st BC, p2.

Row 10: P2, k4, p2, *M1, [k4, p2] twice, k4, M1*, p1, rep between *'s once, p2, k4, p2.

Row 11: K2, p4, *k3, p4, [k2, p4] twice; rep from *, end k3, p4, k2.

Row 12: P2, 4-st FC, p3, M1, k4, p2tog, 4-st FC, p2tog, k4, M1, p3, M1, k4, p2tog, 4-st BC, p2tog, k4, M1, p3, 4-st BC, p2.

Row 13: P2, k4, p4, *[p4, k1] twice, p4*, k5; rep between *'s once, k4, p4, p2.

Row 14: P2, k4, p4, *M1, k3, SKP, k4, k2tog, k3, M1*, p5; rep between *'s once, p4, k4, p2.

Row 15: K2, p4, k5, p12, k7, p12, k5, p4, k2.

Row 16: P2, 4-st FC, p5, M1, k4, 4-st FC, k4, M1, p7, M1, k4, 4-st BC, k4, M1, p5, 4-st BC, p2.

Snowflake Chart

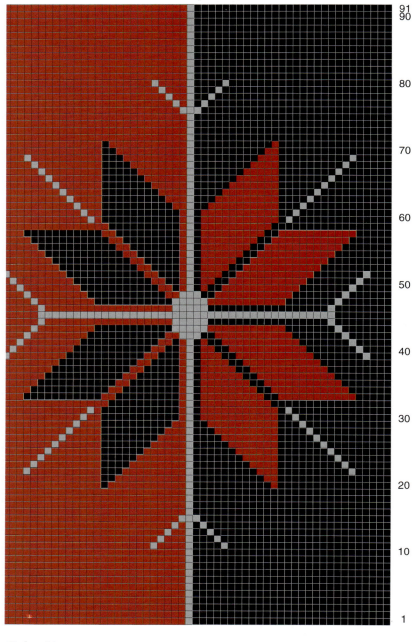

91
90

80

70

60

50

40

30

20

10

1

Color Key

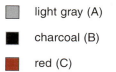

light gray (A)

charcoal (B)

red (C)

Row 17: K2, p4, k6, p12, k9, p12, k6, p4, k2.

Row 18: P2, k4, p6, 12-st BC, p9, 12-st FC, p6, k4, p2.

Rows 19, 21, 23, and 25: Rep Rows 17, 15, 13, and 11.

Row 20: P2, 4-st FC, p4, p2tog, k4, 4-st FC, k4, p2tog, p5, p2tog, k4, 4-st BC, k4, p2tog, p4, 4-st BC, p2.

Row 22: P2, k4, p3, *p2tog, [k4, M1] twice, k4, p2tog, p3; rep from *, end k4, p2.

Row 24: P2, 4-st FC, p2, p2tog, k4, M1, p1, 4-st FC, p1, M1, k4, p2tog, p1, p2tog, k4, M1, p1, 4-st BC, p1, M1, k4, p2tog, p2, 4-st BC, p2.

Row 26: P2, k4, p1, p2tog, *[k4, p2] twice, k4*, p3tog; rep between *'s once, p2tog, p1, k4, p2.

Row 27: Rep Row 3.

Row 28: Rep Row 8.

Rep Rows 1–28 for Cable Panel #1.

Cable Panel #2 (over 15 sts)

Rows 1, 3, 5, and 7 (WS): K5, p5, k5.

Row 2: P5, k2, knot st, k2, p5.

Row 4: P5, knot st, k3, knot st, p5.

Row 6: Rep Row 2.

Row 8: P4, 3-st BPC, p1, 3-st FPC, p4.

Row 9: K4, p2, k1, p1, k1, p2, k4.

Row 10: P3, 3-st BPC, k1, p1, k1, 3-st FPC, p3.

Row 11: K3, p3, k1, p1, k1, p3, k3.

Row 12: P2, 3-st BPC, [p1, k1] twice, p1, 3-st FPC, p2.

Row 13: K2, p2, [k1, p1] 3 times, k1, p2, k2.

Row 14: P2, k3, [p1, k1] twice, p1, k3, p2.

Rows 15, 17, and 19: Rep Rows 13, 11, and 9.

Row 16: P2, 3-st FPC, [p1, k1] twice, p1, 3-st BPC, p2.

Row 18: P3, 3-st FPC, k1, p1, k1, 3-st BPC, p3.

Row 20: P4, 3-st FPC, p1, 3-st BPC, p4.

Rep Rows 1-20 for Cable Panel #2.

Bobble

Cast on 1 st.

Row 1 (RS): [K in front and back] twice, then in front once more to make 5 sts in one st.

Rows 2 and 4: Purl.

Row 3: Knit.

Row 5: SSK, k1, k2tog—3 sts.

Row 6: P3 tog. Tie off last st.

Instructions

Aran Squares (make 6)

With A, cast on 85 sts.

Row 1 (WS): K3 (rev St st), pm, work Cable Panel #2 over 15 sts, pm, work Cable Panel #1 over 49 sts, pm, work Cable Panel #2 over 15 sts, k3 (rev St st). Cont in pats as established until piece measures 18 in./45.5 cm. Bind off.

Snowflake Squares (make 6)

Note: Diagonal lines are worked in duplicate st with A. Bobbles are made separately with A, then sewn to end of each diagonal line.

With C, cast on 29 sts; with B, cast on 29 sts. Work in St st and Snowflake Chart (on opposite page) for 91 rows. Bind off, matching colors.

FINISHING

Weave in all ends. Block lightly. Sew squares tog, three wide and four high, alternating cables and snowflakes.

Border

With RS facing and B, pick up and k 188 sts along bottom edge, and work in garter st for 5 rows, inc 1 st each side every RS row twice. Bind off. Work in same way along top edge. Work in same way along each side edge, picking up and k 264 sts. Sew mitered corners tog.

PILLOW

FINISHED PILLOW SIZE

18 in./45.5 cm square

MATERIALS

Cascade "Pastaza" (50% llama, 50% wool, 3½ oz./100 g skeins, each approx 132 yds./120 m)

Two skeins #006 light gray (A)

Two skeins #007 charcoal (B)

One 18-in./45-cm-square pillow form

One pair size 10 US (6 mm) knitting needles OR SIZE REQUIRED TO OBTAIN GIVEN GAUGE

Cable needle

Tapestry needle

Note: To save yarn costs and add interest, use A, B, and C yarn left over from the afghan to knit pillow back in alternating St st stripes.

GAUGE

14 sts and 20 rows = 4 in./10 cm over St st, using size 10 US (6 mm) needles.

TO SAVE TIME, TAKE TIME TO CHECK GAUGE.

Instructions

Front

Make one Aran Square (snowflake may also be used).

Border

With RS facing and B, pick up and k 72 sts along bottom edge and work in garter st for 5 rows, inc 1 st each side every RS row twice. Bind off. Work in same way along other three sides. Sew mitered corners tog.

Back

With any contrasting color, cast on sts and work in St st for 18 in./45.5 cm. Bind off.

FINISHING

Block lightly. Sew three sides of front and back tog, leaving bottom edge open. Insert pillow form, and sew opening closed.

SOS Shingles Pillow

The shingles on the front of this pillow make it an attractive and unusual project. Each shingle and half shingle is knit separately and then together from the bottom up in rows alternating the shingles. I have chosen to use a hand-dyed variegated yarn, which works up beautifully in the seed stitch.

Instructions

Front

Each shingle is worked separately. Cast on 9 sts for whole shingles and 5 sts for half shingles.

Rows 1–10: Work in seed st. This forms one shingle. Cut yarn.

Make five whole shingles and two half shingles for first row. Place on spare needle.

Work six whole shingles. Place on spare needle.

Cast on 57 sts and work 8 rows in St st.

Next row (RS): K1, beg with RS of half shingle on spare needle, then full shingle, place in front of background fabric, k tog 1 st from each needle across row. Rep four more whole shingles, end with one half shingle, k1. Work 7 rows St st.

Next row (RS): K2, beg with whole shingle and work six shingles tog with sts on needle, k1. Work 7 rows St st. Rep last 16 rows 3 times, end with first row of shingles.

Back

Cast on 56 sts, and work in St st for 16 in./41 cm. Bind off.

FINISHING

Block lightly. Sew three sides of front and back tog, leaving bottom edge open. Insert pillow form, and sew opening closed.

FINISHED PILLOW SIZE

Approx 16 in./41 cm square

MATERIALS

Schaefer Yarn "Celia" (99% merino wool, 1% nylon, 8 oz./ 230 g skeins, each approx 280 yds./252 m)

Two skeins Pebble

Two pairs size 9 US (5.5 mm) knitting needles OR SIZE REQUIRED TO OBTAIN GIVEN GAUGE

One 16-in./41-cm-square pillow form

GAUGE

13 sts and 15 rows = 4 in./10 cm over St st, using size 9 US (5.5 mm) needles.

TO SAVE TIME, TAKE TIME TO CHECK GAUGE.

PATTERN STITCHES

Seed Stitch

Row 1: *K1, p1; rep from *.

Row 2: K the purl sts and p the knit sts. Rep Row 2 for seed st.

Regal Tapestry Afghan and Pillow

Afghan: Expert

Pillow: Advanced

The Regal Tapestry afghan is a masterpiece combining intarsia and textured colorwork. If you've never done colorwork, this should not be your first project. The intarsia tapestry pear pillow is worked with a border showing a different colorway than the afghan.

AFGHAN

FINISHED AFGHAN SIZE

Approx 45 in./114 cm wide × 60 in./ 152 cm long

MATERIALS

Rowan Yarns "Designer DK Wool" (100% wool, 1¾ oz./50 g balls, each approx 114 yds./104 m)

20 balls #687 dark purple (MC)

1 ball each #649 cream (A), #623 pale yellow (B), #163 gray-beige (C), #685 forest green (J), #162 gray-green (K), #665 light blue (L), #629 gray-blue (M), #609 teal (N), #642 medium blue (O), #628 lilac (P), #634 grenadine (Q) #70 rosy peach (S), #630 mulberry (T), #691 copper brown (U), #618 copper (V), and #690 medium brown (W)

Rowan Yarns "DK Lightweight" (100% wool, 1¾ oz./50 g balls, each approx 154 yds./140 m)

1 ball each #13 gold (D), #72 antique gold (E), #616 gray-brown (F), #664 pale olive (G), #635 medium olive (H), #406 dark olive (I), and #26 pumpkin (R)

Size 7 US (4.5 mm) circular needle OR SIZE REQUIRED TO OBTAIN GIVEN GAUGE

Bobbins

GAUGE

20 sts and 26 rows = 4 in./10 cm over St st, using size 7 US (4.5 mm) needles.

TO SAVE TIME, TAKE TIME TO CHECK GAUGE.

Notes: Use a separate bobbin or length of yarn for each block of color.

When changing colors, twist yarns to prevent holes.

Instructions

Centerpiece

With MC, cast on 141 sts. Work in St st, foll Chart 1 through Row 148. Turn chart upside down and work in reverse from Row 148–Row 1. Bind off.

Top and Bottom Borders

With RS facing and MC, pick up and k 141 sts along cast-on edge. Work Chart 2 as foll: Work to center st, sk center st and work chart back in reverse. Cont in pat as established through chart Row 60, AT THE SAME TIME, inc 1 st each side every other row as shown on chart. P 1 row on RS for turning ridge. With MC, cont in St st, dec 1 st each side every other row for 1½ in./ 4 cm. Bind off.

Work in same way along bound-off edge.

Side Borders

With RS facing and MC, pick up and k 221 sts along one side edge. Work Chart 3 as foll: Work to center st, sk center st, and work chart back in reverse. Cont in pat as established through chart Row 59, AT THE SAME TIME, inc 1 st each side every other row as shown on chart. P 1 row on RS for turning ridge. With MC, cont in St st, dec 1 st each side every other row for 1½ in./4 cm. Bind off.

Work in same way along other side edge.

Chart 2

60
50
40
30
20
10
1

Chart 3

60
50
40
30
20
10
1

Color Key

- • cream (A)
- ○ pale yellow (B)
- + gray-beige (C)
- + gold (D)
- ~ antique gold (E)
- / gray-brown (F)
- / pale olive (G)
- ~ medium olive (H)
- + dark olive (I)
- / forest green (J)
- • gray-green (K)

- ~ light blue (L)
- • gray-blue (M)
- + teal (N)
- ~ medium blue (O)
- + lilac (P)
- deep purple (MC)
- • grenadine (Q)
- ~ pumpkin (R)
- + rosy peach (S)
- / mulberry (T)
- • copper brown (U)

- / copper (V)
- + medium brown (W)
- F French knot (with yarn color indicated)
- B bobble (with yarn color indicated)
- / straight stitch
- ∴ stem stitch

Chart 1

148
140
130
120
110
100
90
80
70
60
50
40
30
20
10
1

Bobbles

Cast on 1 st.

Row 1: K into front, back, front, back, and front of st to make 5 sts in one. P 1 row, k 1 row, p 1 row.

Row 5: Pass the 2nd, 3rd, 4th, and 5th st over the first st. Tie off.

FINISHING

Weave in ends. Block lightly. Work embroidery foll charts. Sew on bobbles foll chart. Turn all hems to WS at turning ridge, and sew in place.

PILLOW

Note: Pear motif is shown in photo. Any of the motifs on the afghan may be used to make a variety of beautiful pillows.

FINISHED PILLOW SIZE

Approx 16 in./41 cm × 20 in./51 cm

MATERIALS

Rowan Yarns "Designer DK Wool" (100% wool, 1¾ oz./50 g balls, each approx 114 yds./103 m)
Six balls #687 dark purple (MC)
One ball each #649 cream (A), #623 pale yellow (B), #691 copper brown (U), #690 medium brown (W)
Rowan Yarns "DK Lightweight" (100% wool, 1¾ oz./50 g balls, each approx 154 yds./140 m)
One ball each #162 gray-green (M), #72 antique gold (E), and #26 pumpkin (R)

Size 7 US (4.5 mm) circular needle OR SIZE REQUIRED TO OBTAIN GIVEN GAUGE
Bobbins
Poly-Fil stuffing

GAUGE

20 sts and 26 rows = 4 in./10 cm over St st, using size 7 US (4.5 mm) needles.
TO SAVE TIME, TAKE TIME TO CHECK GAUGE.

Instructions

Back

With MC, cast on 100 sts, and work in St st for 16 in./41 cm. Bind off.

Front

With MC, cast on 79 sts, and work in St st, working 13 rows of pillow borders.

Note: Pillow border is a color variation of the afghan border, which is represented by Charts 2 and 3.

Cont with MC, working pear motif from charts (see photo above for placement), until piece measures 14 in./35.5 cm from beg. Work 13 rows of the pillow borders. Bind off with MC.

Side Borders

With RS facing and MC, pick up and k 89 sts evenly along one side edge. Work 13 rows of the pillow borders. Bind off. Work in same way along other side edge.

FINISHING

Weave in ends. Block lightly. Sew front and back of pillow tog, leaving bottom edge open. Stuff with Poly-Fil, and sew opening closed.

Sun Visions Afghan and Pillow

Advanced

"You are the sunshine of my life" is what this afghan and pillow say! Appliqué knitting and duplicate stitch are used in the six large stockinette stitch blocks, bordered by a honeycomb cable pattern. The sun faces are worked in duplicate stitch, and each ray circumference is an unusual edging or edging combination.

AFGHAN

FINISHED AFGHAN SIZE

Approx 46 in./117 cm wide × 69 in./175 cm long

MATERIALS

Classic Elite "Provence" (100% Egyptian cotton, 125 g skeins, each approx 256 yds./234 m)

Nine skeins #2616 natural or #2613 black (MC)

Six skeins #2645 flaxen (A)

One skein #2637 mushroom (B)

One pair size 6 US (4 mm) needles OR SIZE REQUIRED TO OBTAIN GIVEN GAUGE

Two size 6 US (4 mm) double-pointed needles

Size 6 (4 mm) circular needle, 36 in./90 cm long

Tapestry needle

Cable needle

GAUGE

20 sts and 26 rows = 4 in./10 cm over St st, using size 6 US (4 mm) needles.

TO SAVE TIME, TAKE TIME TO CHECK GAUGE.

Instructions

Make six blocks with MC as foll:

Cast on 105 sts, and work in St st until piece measures 21 in./53.5 cm. Bind off.

Embroidery

Duplicate stitch face in center of each block, foll charts on pp. 108 to 110.

Tips: Use split yarn to sew on appliqués.

Round plates or bowls can be used to help make sunrays circular.

FACE FRAMES

Sunray 1

With A, cast on 13 sts.

Row 1 (WS): Sl 1, p1, p2tog, yo, k9.
Row 2: Sl 1, k8, yo, k2, k1 tbl, k1.
Row 3: Sl 1, p2, yo, p2tog, yo, k9.
Row 4: Sl 1, k8, yo, k2tog, yo, k2, k1 tbl, k1.
Row 5: Sl 1, p2, [yo, p2tog] twice, yo, k9.
Row 6: Sl 1, k8, [yo, k2tog] twice, yo, k2, k1 tbl, k1.

Row 7: Sl 1, p2, [yo, p2tog] 3 times, yo, k9.
Row 8: Sl 1, k8, [yo, k2tog] 3 times, yo, k2, k1 tbl, k1.
Row 9: Sl 1, p2, [yo, p2tog] 4 times, yo, k9.
Row 10: Bind off 8 sts, k10, k1 tbl, k1.

Rep Rows 1–10 for a total of 22 patterns. Bind off. Sew to cast-on edge to form a circle. Sew inner and outer edge to block around face. Embroider an elongated star at end of each point.

Sunray 2

Tube stitch

Cast on 5 sts.

Row 1 (RS): K1, [sl 1, k1] twice.
Row 2 and all WS rows: Sl 1, [p1, sl 1] twice.

Rep Rows 1 and 2 for tube st.

With A, make seven 11-in./28-cm lengths of tube st and seven 8-in./20.5-cm lengths of tube st. *Place one 11-in./28-cm tube, then one 8-in./20.5-cm tube on needle; rep from * six times more. With RS facing, cast on 1 st (edge st), [5 sts cord, cast on 5 sts] 14 times, cast on 1 st (edge st)—142 sts.

Sunray 1

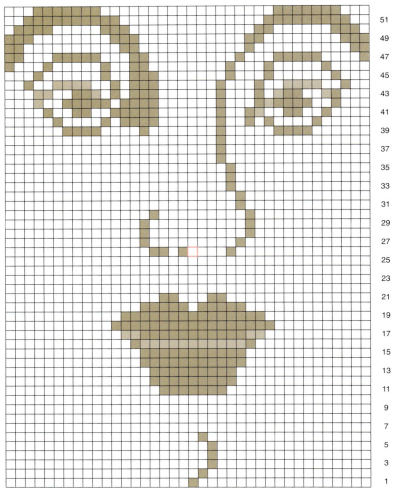

51
49
47
45
43
41
39
37
35
33
31
29
27
25
23
21
19
17
15
13
11
9
7
5
3
1

Sunray 2

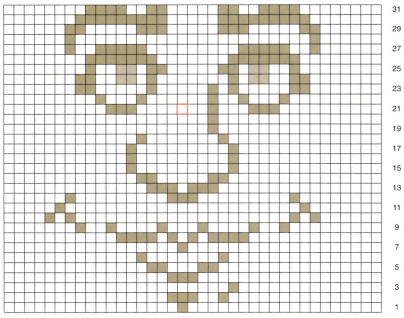

31
29
27
25
23
21
19
17
15
13
11
9
7
5
3
1

Color Key

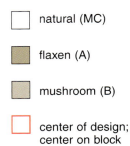

☐ natural (MC)

◼ flaxen (A)

◼ mushroom (B)

☐ center of design;
center on block

Row 1 (WS): P1, *k5, p5; rep from *, end p6.

Row 2: K1, *k5, p5; rep from *, end last rep k1.

Rep Rows 1 and 2 for 1 in./2.5 cm, ending on Row 1. Bind off on RS, and sew to cast-on edge to form a circle. Sew to block around face. Curl each tube st clockwise, and sew in place from front (see photo on p. 106).

Sunray 3

With A, cast on 23 sts.

Rows 1, 2, 5, and 6: Knit.

Rows 3 and 7: Bind off 19 sts, k to end.

Row 4: K4, using cable cast-on, cast on 19 sts.

Rep Rows 4–7 until there are 51 spokes. Bind off all sts on last row, and sew to cast-on edge. Sew to block around face at inner edge. Pin and sew each spoke from RS to form rays.

Sunray 4—Part 1

Note: Sl all sts purlwise.

Bobble (make 12)

With A, cast on 1 st.

Row 1: K into front and back of same st twice, then into front again—5 sts.

Rows 2 and 4: P5.

Row 3: K5.

Row 5: K5. With LH needle, pass the 2nd, 3rd, 4th, and 5th sts over the first st.

Sunray 3

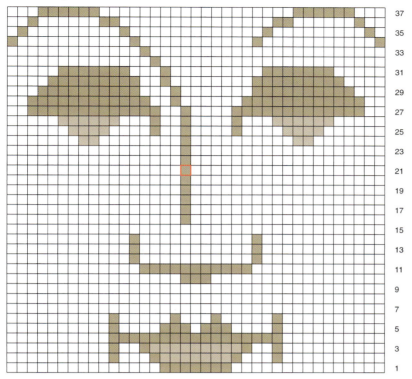

Sunray 4

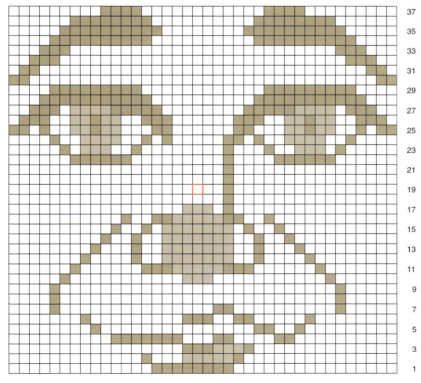

Part 2—Tube st with bobble

Rows 1–8: Work Rows 1 and 2 of tube st 4 times.

Row 9: K1, sl 1, make bobble as for Part 1, sl 1, k1.

Row 10: Rep Row 2 of tube st.

Rep Rows 1–10 for tube st with bobble, until there are 36 bobbles, end with Row 10. Bind off.

Part 3

With A, cast on 2 sts.

Row 1: K2.

Row 2: Yo, k2.

Row 3: Yo, k3.

Cont in this way, inc 1 st at beg of every row, until there are 18 sts. This forms one point. Cut yarn and leave finished point on needle. On the same needle, cast on 2 sts and work 2nd point. Cont in this way until there are 12 points on needle—216 sts.

Next row (WS): K8, [k2tog, k16] 11 times, k2tog, k8—204 sts. Bind off. Sew inner edge and points to block around face. Sew Part 2 inside of Part 3. Sew bobbles between each point.

Sunray 5

With A, cast on 1 st.

Note: Cast on all sts onto empty needle.

*Row 1 (RS): K into front and back of same st twice, then into front again—5 sts.

Row 2: Sl 1, p4.

Row 3: Sl 1, k4.

Rows 4–8: Rep Rows 2 and 3 twice, then work Row 2 once more.

Row 9: K2tog, k1, k2tog—3 sts.

Row 10: P3tog, turn. Fold bobble in half. Insert LH needle into cast-on st and k it tog with rem st of bobble—1 st.

Rep from * twice, leaving last st on needle.

Point

**Row 1 (RS): K into front, back and front of rem st of bobble—3 sts.

Row 2 and all WS rows: Purl.

Sunray 5

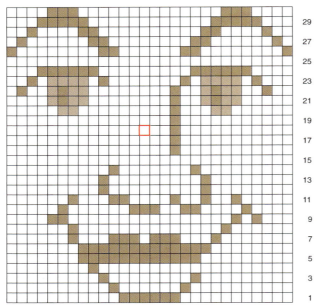

Sunray 6

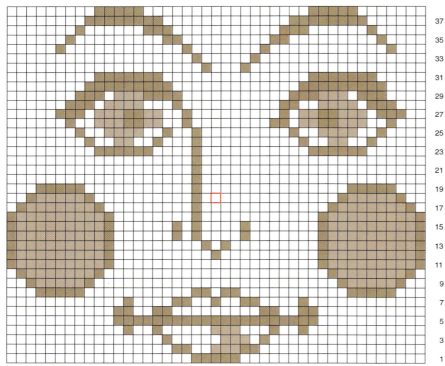

Row 3: K1, [yo, k1] twice.
Row 5: K2, yo, k1, yo, k2.
Row 7: K3, yo, k1, yo, k3.
Row 9: K4, yo, k1, yo, k4.
Row 11: K5, yo, k1, yo, k5.
Row 13: K6, yo, k1, yo, k6.
Row 15: K7, yo, k1, yo, k7.

Cut yarn. Make three bobbles and point (rep from **) 10 times more, but on the last point, leave sts on needle (187 sts). When all points are complete, p1 row, k1 row, p1 row. Work in k1, p1 rib for 1 in./2.5 cm. Bind off. Sew inner and outer edges to block around face.

Sunray 6

With A, cast on 40 sts.

Note: Cross all loops in front of each other when joining.

Row 1 (RS): K37, yo, k2tog, k1.
Row 2: Sl 1, p to end.
Row 3: Bind off 28 sts (1 spoke made), k8, yo, k2tog, k1.
Rows 4 and 8: Sl 1, k11.
Rows 5, 7, 9, and 11: K9, yo, k2tog, k1.
Rows 6 and 10: Sl 1, k2, p9.
Row 12: Sl 1, k11, cast on 28 sts (using cable cast on).
Row 13: K37, yo, k2tog, k1.
Row 14: Sl 1, k2, p to end.
Row 15: Bind off 28 sts (1 spoke made), k8, yo, k2tog, k1.
Row 16: Sl 1, k11.
Rows 17, 19, 21, and 23: K9, yo, k2tog, k1.
Row 18: Sl 1, k2, p9.
Row 20: Sl 1, k10, turn up end of the first spoke and k first thread of first bound-off st tog with last st on needle to make loop.
Row 22: Sl 1, k2, p8, k last thread of first bound-off st tog with last st on needle.

Rep Rows 12–23 for desired length, end with row 12—12 sts. Pick up 12 sts at cast-on edge. With 3rd needle and RS tog, k seam tog.

Cable Bands

Make one approx 67 in./170 cm long and four approx 21 in./53.5 cm long.

With MC, cast on 14 sts.

Row 1 (RS): K1, p2, k8, p2, k1.

Row 2 and all WS rows: K the knit sts and p the purl sts.

Row 3: K1, p2, sl next 2 sts to cn and hold to back, k2, k2 from cn (4-st BC), sl next 2 sts to cn and hold to front, k2, k2 from cn (4-st FC), p2, k1.

Row 5: Rep Row 1.

Row 7: K1, p2, 4-st FC, 4-st BC, p2, k1.

Row 8: Rep Row 2.

Rep Rows 1–8 for cable band until desired length. Bind off.

FINISHING

Sew a short cable band connecting Blocks 1 and 3, then 3 and 5 on left side, 2 and 4, then 4 and 6 on right side to make two panels. Sew long cable band to center of afghan, joining the two panels.

Outside border

With RS facing, circular needle, and B, pick up and k 208 sts along top of afghan. Row 1 (WS): Knit. Row 2: With eggshell, knit, inc 1 st each end of row. Rows 3–7: Rep Rows 1 and 2 twice, then Row 1 once more. Bind off all sts on RS. Work in same way along bottom of afghan. Work in same way along each side edge, picking up 372 sts.

PILLOW

FINISHED PILLOW SIZE

22 in./56 cm square

MATERIALS

Classic Elite "Provence" (100% Egyptian cotton, 125 g skeins, approx 256 yds./234 m)

Two skeins #2613 black (MC)

One skein #2645 flaxen (A)

Small amount #2637 mushroom (B)

One pair size 6 US (4 mm) knitting needles OR SIZE REQUIRED TO OBTAIN GIVEN GAUGE

Two size 6 (4 mm) double-pointed needles

Tapestry needle

Cable needle

22-in./56-cm-square pillow form

GAUGE

20 sts and 26 rows = 4 in./10 cm over St st, using size 6 US (4 mm) needles.

TO SAVE TIME, TAKE TIME TO CHECK GAUGE.

Instructions

Front

With MC, cast on 105 sts, and work in St st until piece measures 21 in./53.5 cm. Bind off. Work desired face on RS of piece.

Back

Work same as front, omitting face.

Cable Bands

Make two 18-in./45.5-cm and two 20-in./51-cm cable bands same as afghan using MC. Sew shorter bands to top and bottom of pillow. Sew longer bands to sides of pillow, including side of shorter band, leaving one side open. Insert pillow form, and sew opening closed.

Tea Time Lace Afghan and Pillow

Intermediate

You will want to use this pretty afghan and pillow combo all the time, not just at tea time. The Tea Time Lace afghan and pillow are made using a lace and solid stockinette stitch background with duplicate stitch motifs. The afghan is knit in one piece, and then the teacups and plaid are added with duplicate stitch.

AFGHAN

FINISHED AFGHAN SIZE

Approx 42 in./106 cm wide × 54 in./ 137 cm long

MATERIALS

JCA/Reynolds "Saucy" (100% cotton, 3½ oz./100 g balls, each approx 185 yds./169 m)

Ten balls #817 ecru (MC)

One ball each #71 light teal (A), #901 maize (B), #396 light dusty rose (C), #395 dusty rose (D), #74 teal (E), and #379 wine (F)

Size 7 US (4.5 mm) circular needle OR SIZE REQUIRED TO OBTAIN GIVEN GAUGE

Tapestry needle

GAUGE

20 sts and 26 rows = 4 in./10 cm over St st, using size 7 US (4.5 mm) needles. TO SAVE TIME, TAKE TIME TO CHECK GAUGE.

Tea Time Lace Afghan Placement Diagram

1	Plaid	2	Plaid
Plaid	3	Plaid	4
5	Plaid	1	Plaid
Plaid	2	Plaid	3
4	Plaid	5	Plaid

Plaid Chart

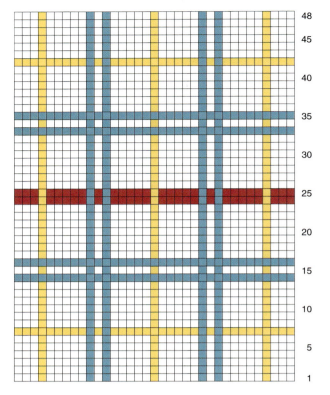

Teacup 1

Teacup 2

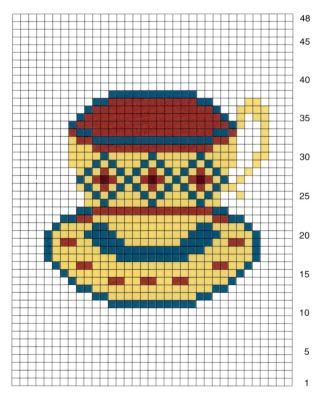

Teacup 3

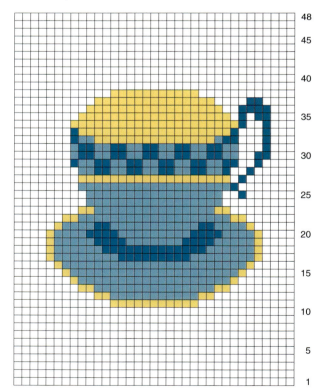

Teacup 4

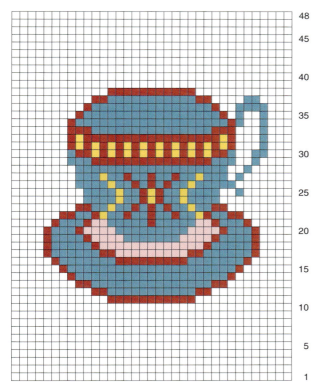

Teacup 5

Color Key

- ⬛ light teal (A)
- 🟨 maize (B)
- 🟫 light dusty rose (C)
- 🟥 dusty rose (D)
- ⬛ teal (E)
- ⬛ wine (F)

PATTERN STITCHES

Lace Pattern #1 (multiple of 8 sts plus 1)

Row 1 (RS): K1, *yo, k2, SK2P, k2, yo, k1; rep from * to end.

Rows 2, 4, and 6: Purl.

Row 3: K2, *yo, k1, SK2P, k1, yo, k3; rep from * to last 7 sts, yo, k1, SK2P, k1, yo, k2.

Row 5: K3, *yo, SK2P, yo, k5; rep from *, to last 6 sts, end yo, SK2P, yo, k3.

Rep Rows 1–6 for Lace Pat #1.

Lace Pattern #2 (worked over 9 sts)

Row 1 (RS): K2tog, k2, yo, k1, yo, k2, SSK.

Rows 2, 4, and 6: Purl.

Row 3: K2tog, k1, yo, k3, yo, k1, SSK.

Row 5: K2tog, yo, k5, yo, SSK.

Rep Rows 1–6 for Lace Pat #2.

Lace Pattern #3 (worked over 9 sts)

Row 1 (RS): K1, yo, k2, SK2P, k2, yo, k1.

Rows 2, 4, and 6: Purl.

Row 3: K2, yo, k1, SK2P, k1, yo, k2.

Row 5: K3, yo, SK2P, yo, k3.

Rep Rows 1–6 for Lace Pat #3.

Instructions

Note: Teacup and plaid motifs are worked in duplicate st on St st squares after piece is complete.

With MC, cast on 185 sts. Work in Lace Pat #1 for 12 rows.

Beg Panels

Row 1 (RS): [Work Lace Pat #3 over 9 sts, St st over 35 sts, Lace Pat #2 over 9 sts, St st over 35 sts] twice, work Lace Pat #3 over last 9 sts. Cont in pats as established for a total of 48 rows. Work Lace Pat #1 over all sts for 12 rows. Rep between *'s (60 rows) four more times. Bind off all sts.

FINISHING

Duplicate st Plaid Chart on every other St st square and teacup motifs on rem St st squares (see placement diagram on p. 113, or as desired). Weave in all ends. Block lightly.

PILLOW

FINISHED PILLOW SIZE

12 in./30.5 cm square

MATERIALS

JCA/Reynolds "Saucy" (100% cotton, 3½ oz./100 g balls, each approx 185 yds./169 m)

Two balls #817 ecru (MC)

Teacup colors, as desired

One pair size 7 US (4.5 mm) knitting needles OR SIZE REQUIRED TO OBTAIN GIVEN GAUGE

12-in./30.5-cm-square pillow form

Tapestry needle

Instructions

Front

With MC, cast on 59 sts. K 1 row, p 1 row. Work in Lace Pat #1 as foll: Next Row (RS): K1 (selvage st), work Lace Pat #1 over 57 sts, k1 (selvage st). Cont in pat as established for a total of 12 rows.

Beg Panel

Next row (RS): K1, work Lace Pat #3 over 9 sts, 39 sts St st, Lace Pat #3 over last 9 sts, k1. Cont in pats as established for a total of 48 rows. Work in Lace Pat

#1 and selvage sts over all sts as before for 12 rows. K 1 row, p 1 row. Bind off.

Back

With MC, cast on 52 sts. Work in St st for 12 in./30.5 cm. Bind off.

FINISHING

Embroider front St st square with a teacup motif of your choice. Sew front and back tog, leaving bottom edge open. Insert pillow form, and sew opening closed.

Patchwork Tree Afghan and Pillow

This set makes a lovely handmade gift with a small investment of time and money. The patchwork trees on the afghan are the perfect way to use up single balls of leftover yarns. The trees are then sewn by hand to a fabric background. The pillow is two trees sewn together with an inset and stuffed.

AFGHAN

FINISHED AFGHAN SIZE
Approx 42 in./106 cm × 57 in./145 cm

MATERIALS
Small amounts of tree-colored yarns in different textures and worsted weight

One pair size 8 US (5 mm) knitting needles OR SIZE REQUIRED TO OBTAIN GIVEN GAUGE

1¼ yd./1.75 m of 45-in./114-cm-wide, wide-wale corduroy (or fabric of choice) for afghan background

Sewing thread

Tapestry needle

Tip: This is a perfect chance to use one ball of each of your favorite yarns and colors. The more variety in color and textures, the better your trees will be. The yarn weights should be similar or you can change needle sizes to make the triangles the same size.

GAUGE
18 sts and 32 rows = 4 in./10 cm over garter st, using size 8 US (5 mm) needles.

TO SAVE TIME, TAKE TIME TO CHECK GAUGE.

Instructions

TREE

Triangles (make 16)
Cast on 23 sts and k 2 rows. K2tog at beg of every row until 1 st rem. Tie off.

Tip: To change the size of the pillow or afghan, triangles can easily be made larger or smaller by using more or fewer sts or simply by using more or fewer triangles.

Trunk
Cast on 11 sts, and work in garter st for 4½ in./11.5 cm. Bind off.

Sew triangles tog to form tree (see photo on p. 118). Sew trunk at base of tree.

FINISHING
Make six trees. Make a 1 in./2.5cm hem around all sides of fabric. With sewing thread, sew trees evenly spaced to fabric with two trees side by side stacked three trees high.

Border
Make 9 triangles each for top and bottom and 12 for each side. Sew cast-on edge of triangles to outside edge of fabric.

Pillow

FINISHED PILLOW SIZE

Approx. 18 in./45.5 cm high × 18 in./
45.5 cm at bottom of tree × 3 in./
7.5 cm deep

MATERIALS

Small amounts of tree-colored yarns in
different textures and worsted weight
One pair size 8 US (5mm) knitting nee-
dles OR SIZE REQUIRED TO
OBTAIN GIVEN GAUGE
Poly-Fil stuffing
Sewing thread
Tapestry needle

GAUGE

18 sts and 32 rows = 4 in./10 cm over
garter st, using size 8 US (5 mm)
needles.
TO SAVE TIME, TAKE TIME TO
CHECK GAUGE.

Instructions

Make two trees.

Inset

Cast on 26 sts, and work in rev St st for
approx 64 in./162 cm. Do not bind off.
Sew one long side of inset around outside edge of one tree, adjusting length if
necessary. Bind off 26 sts of inset. Sew
other side of inset to second tree, leaving a small opening for stuffing. Stuff
and sew opening closed.

Textural Leaf Afghan and Pillow

This afghan and pillow set uses a unique dimensional leaf fringe technique. The afghan is worked in rectangles with chenille, then the leaves are knit in cotton and sewn onto each rectangle. The leaf fringe is knit separately. For the pillow, choose the block of your choice and adorn it with a single leaf fringe at each corner.

AFGHAN

FINISHED AFGHAN SIZE

Approx 43 in./109 cm wide × 58 in./147 cm long

MATERIALS

Crystal Palace "Cotton Chenille" (100% cotton, 1¾ oz./50 g skeins, each approx 98 yds./89 m)

19 skeins #9024 dusty mauve (MC)

Crystal Palace "Breeze" (100% cotton, 1¾ oz./50 g skeins, each approx 110 yds./100 m)

7 skeins #9024 dusty mauve (CC)

Alternate colorways: #9008 blue dust, #3409 celadon, #7773 light salmon (see photo on p. 122)

One pair each size 5 US and 6 US (3.75 mm and 4 mm) knitting needles OR SIZE REQUIRED TO OBTAIN GIVEN GAUGE

Two size 5 (3.75 mm) double-pointed needles

Stitch holders

GAUGE

16 sts and 20 rows = 4 in./10 cm over St st, using size 6 US (4 mm) needles.

Each rectangle measures 14 in./35.5 cm × 9½ in./24.5 cm.

TO SAVE TIME, TAKE TIME TO CHECK GAUGE.

Notes: The main body of the afghan is worked in MC chenille. The leaves are made separately with size 5 US (3.75 mm) needles and CC cotton, and sewn on.

Rectangles are made separately and then sewn tog.

Work first and last st of every row in St st for selvage sts.

STITCH GLOSSARY

DD (Double Dec): Sl 2 sts tog knitwise, k1, pass 2 slipped sts over k1.

Instructions

Rectangle #1 (make 3)

Cast on 62 sts. K 1 row on RS.

Rows 1 and 3 (RS): K31, [p2, k2] 7 times, p2, k1.

Rows 2 and 4: K the knit sts and p the purl sts.

Rows 5 and 7: K31, [k2, p2] 7 times, k3.

Rows 6 and 8: K the knit sts and p the purl sts.

Rows 9–32: Rep Rows 1–8 three times.

Rows 33 and 35: K3, [p2, k2] 7 times, k to end.

Rows 34 and 36: K the knit sts and p the purl sts.

Rows 37 and 39: K1, p2, [k2, p2] 7 times, k to end.

Rows 38 and 40: K the knit sts and p the purl sts.

Rows 41–72: Rep Rows 33–40 three times.

Piece measures approx 9½ in./24.5 cm from beg. Bind off.

Elm leaf (make 2 for each rectangle)

Cast on 5 sts.

Row 1 (RS): K1, [sl 1, k1] twice.

Row 2 and all WS rows: Sl 1, [p1, sl 1] twice.

Rep Rows 1 and 2 for 1 in./2.5 cm, inc 1 st each side on last RS row—7 sts.

Beg leaf—Row 1 (RS): K3, yo, k1, yo, k3—9 sts.

Rows 2, 4, and 6: Purl.

Row 3: K4, yo, k1, yo, k4—11 sts.

Row 5: K5, yo, k1, yo, k5—13 sts.

Row 7: Bind off 3 sts, k2, yo, k1, yo, k6—12 sts.

Row 8: Bind off 3 sts, p8—9 sts.

Row 20: Bind off 3 sts, p6—7 sts.

Row 21: SSK, k3, k2tog—5 sts.

Rows 22 and 24: Purl.

Row 23: SSK, k1, k2tog—3 sts.

Row 25: SK2P.

Tie off.

Sew one leaf at an angle, in opposite directions, in center of each St st block.

Rectangle #2 (make 3)

Cast on 62 sts.

Row 1 (RS): Knit.

Row 2: Purl.

Rows 3 and 4: Knit.

Rows 5 and 6: Purl.

Rows 7–39: Rep Rows 1–6 five times then Rows 1 and 2 once.

Row 40 (WS): Cont 25 sts in ridge pat, p to end (35 sts in St st). Cont as established until piece measures 9½ in./24 cm from beg. Bind off.

Maple leaf (make 2 for each rectangle)

Note: Sl markers every row.

Cast on 5 sts.

Row 1 (RS): K1, [sl 1, k1] twice.

Row 2 and all WS rows: Sl 1, [p1, sl 1] twice.

Rep Rows 1 and 2 for 1 in./2.5cm, inc 1 st each side on last RS row—7 sts.

Beg Leaf—Preparation row (WS): P3, pm, sl 1 purlwise, pm, p3.

Row 1: K1, M1, k2, yo, k1, yo, k2, M1, k1—11 sts.

Rows 2, 4, 6, 8, 10 and 12: Purl, slipping 1 st between markers.

Row 3: K1, M1, k4, yo, k1, yo, k4, M1, k1—15 sts.

Row 5: K7, yo, k1, yo, k7—17 sts.

Row 7: K8, yo, k1, yo, k8—19 sts.

Row 9: K9, yo, k1, yo, k9—21 sts.

Row 11: Knit.

Row 13: [K7, M1] twice, k2, place last 5 sts on holder—18 sts.

Row 9: K4, yo, k1, yo, k4—11 sts.

Rows 10 and 12: Purl.

Row 11: K5, yo, k1, yo, k5—13 sts.

Row 13: Bind off 3 sts, k2, yo, k1, yo, k6—12 sts.

Row 14: Bind off 3 sts, p8—9 sts.

Row 15: K4, yo, k1, yo, k4—11 sts.

Rows 16 and 18: Purl.

Row 17: K5, yo, k1, yo, k5—13 sts.

Row 19: Bind off 3 sts, p9—10 sts.

Row 14: P13, place last 5 sts on holder—13 sts.

Center (worked on center 13 sts)

Row 15: Knit.

Rows 16, 18, 20, 22, 24, and 26: Purl.

Row 17: K1, SSK, k7, k2tog, k1—11 sts.

Row 19: K1, SSK, k5, k2tog, k1—9 sts.

Row 21: K1, SSK, k3, k2tog, k1—7 sts.

Row 23: K1, SSK, k1, k2tog, k1—5 sts.

Row 25: K1, SK2P, k1—3 sts.

Row 27: SK2P—1 st.

Tie off.

Right side (worked on first 5 sts)

Rows 14, 16, and 18: Purl.

Row 15: Knit.

Row 17: K1, SK2P, k1—3 sts.

Row 19: SK2P—1 st.

Tie off.

Left side (worked on rem 5 sts)

Rows 13 and 15: Knit.

Rows 14, 16, and 18: Purl.

Row 17: K1, SK2P, k1—3 sts.

Row 19: SK2P—1 st.

Tie off.

Sew leaves, side by side, in center of St st block.

Rectangle #3 (make 3)

Cast on 60 sts.

Row 1, 3, 5, and 7 (RS): K10, [k5, p1, k1, p1, k1, p1] 4 times, k10.

Rows 2, 4, 6, and 8: P10, [p1, k1, p1, k1, p6] 4 times, k10.

Rows 9, 11, 13, and 15: K10, [p1, k1, p1, k1, p1, k5] 4 times, k10.

Rows 10, 12, 14, and 16: P10, [p6, k1, p1, k1, p1] 4 times, p10.

Rep Rows 1–16 three times more. Piece measures approx 9½ in./24.5 cm from beg. Bind off.

Garter stitch leaf (make 10 for each rectangle)

Cast on 9 sts.

Rows 1, 3, and 5: K3, DD, k3—7 sts.

Rows 2 and 4: K1, M1, k2, p1, k2, M1, k1—9 sts.

Row 6: K3, p1, k3.

Row 7: K2, DD, k2—5 sts.

Row 8: K2, p1, k2.

Row 9: K1, DD, k1—3 sts.

Row 10: K1, p1, k1.

Row 11: DD—1 st. Tie off.

On RH St st panel, sew five leaves vertically, slanting to the right. On LH St st panel, sew five leaves vertically, slanting to the left.

Rectangle #4 (make 3)

Cast on 62 sts.

Row 1 (RS): K1, p4, [k4, p4] 7 times, k1.

Row 2: P1, [k4, p4] 7 times, k4, p1.

Rep Rows 1 and 2 until piece measures 9½ in./24.5 cm from beg. Bind off.

New leaf (make 6 for each rectangle)

Cast on 6 sts.

Row 1: K4, wyif, sl 1, wyib, turn.

Row 2: Sl 1 st to RH needle, wyib, k3, k in front and back of next st, turn—7 sts.

Rep Rows 1 and 2 until there are 15 sts. Work Row 1 once more.

Dec as foll:

Row 1: Sl 1 st to RH needle, wyib, k4, turn.

Row 2: K2tog, k3, wyif, sl 1, wyib, turn.

Rep dec Rows 1 and 2 until there are 6 sts. Then work Row 1 once more. Bind off 5 sts—1 st.

Short stem (make 4): Cast on 5 more sts, bind off 5 sts. Tie off.

Long stem (make 2): Cast on 30 more sts, bind off 30 sts. Tie off.

Sew short stem leaf on each side, 1 in./2.5 cm down from base of long stem leaf to form leaf branch. Make 2nd branch in same way. Sew branches to rectangle with stems facing center at an angle (see photo on p. 122).

Rectangle #5 (make 3)

Cast on 59 sts.

Row 1 (RS): K1, [k6, p1, k1, p1, k1] twice, k5, [k1, p1] 16 times, k1.

Row 2: P1, [p1, k1] 16 times, p5, [k1, p1, k1, p1, k1, p5] twice, p1.

Rep Rows 1 and 2 until piece measures 9½ in./24.5 cm from beg. Bind off.

Fan leaf (make 1 for each rectangle)

Cast on 5 sts.

Row 1 (RS): K1, [sl 1, k1] twice.

Row 2 and all WS rows: Sl 1, [p1, sl 1] twice.

Rep Rows 1 and 2 for 4½ in./11.5 cm.

Beg leaf—Row 1 (RS): *K1, M1; rep from * to end—9 sts.

Rows 2, 4, 6, and 8: Purl.

Row 3: Rep Row 1—17 sts.

Row 5: Rep Row 1—33 sts.

Row 7: Knit.

Rows 9–23: Work in St st, bind off 2 sts at beg of every row until 3 sts rem.

Row 24: Purl.

Row 25: SK2P.

Tie off.

Sew leaf to center of large seed st area.

Rectangle #6 (make 3)

Cast on 62 sts.

Row 1 (RS): K1, [k15, p15] twice, k1.

Row 2: K the knit sts and p the purl sts.

Rows 3–18: Rep Rows 1 and 2 eight times.

Row 19: K1, [p15, k15] twice, k1.

Row 20: K the knit sts and p the purl sts.

Rows 21–36: Rep Rows 19 and 20 eight times.

Rows 37–54: Rep Rows 1 and 2 nine times.

Piece measures approx 9½ in./24cm from beg. Bind off.

Aspen leaf (make 6 for each rectangle)

Cast on 5 sts.

Row 1 (RS): K1, [sl 1, k1] twice.

Row 2 and all WS rows: Sl 1, [p1, sl 1] twice.

Rep Rows 1 and 2 for 1 in./2.5 cm for stem.

Beg leaf–Row 1 (RS): K2, yo, k1, yo, k2—7 sts.

Row 2 and all WS rows: Purl.

Row 3: K3, yo, k1, yo, k3—9 sts.

Row 5: K4, yo, k1, yo, k4—11 sts.

Row 7: SSK, k7, k2tog—9 sts.

Row 9: SSK, k5, k2tog—7 sts.

Row 11: SSK, k3, k2tog—5 sts.

Row 13: SSK, k1, k2tog—3 sts.

Row 15: SK2P—1 st. Tie off.

Sew one leaf at an angle, in same direction, in center of each St st block.

FINISHING

Sew Rectangles #1, #2, and #3 tog horizontally for 1st row, then Rectangles #4, #5, and #6 tog horizontally for 2nd row. Sew 1st and 2nd rows tog for first set. Sew two more sets in same way to complete afghan.

Side Borders

With RS facing and MC, pick up and k 264 sts along one side edge. K 3 rows, inc 1 st each side on 2nd row. Bind off 266 sts. Work in same way along other side.

Top and Bottom Borders

With RS facing and MC, pick up and k 176 sts along top edge. Work same as side border, but bind off with CC. Work in same way along bottom edge.

Leaf Fringe

Front: Make 24 aspen leaves making stem 2½ in./6.5 cm instead of 1 in./2.5 cm (see Rectangle #6).

Back: Make 24 aspen leaves, omitting 1-in./2.5-cm stem.

Sew back leaf to front leaf with WS tog. Sew 12 leaf fringes evenly along top edge and 12 along bottom edge (approx 3 in./7.5 cm apart).

Pillow

FINISHED PILLOW SIZE

12 in./30.5 cm × 16 in./41 cm

MATERIALS

Crystal Palace "Cotton Chenille" (100% cotton, 1¼ oz./50 g skeins, each approx 98 yds./89 m)

Three skeins #9024 dusty mauve (MC)

Crystal Palace "Breeze" (100% cotton, 1¼ oz./50 g skeins, each approx 110 yds./100 m)

One skein #9024 dusty mauve (CC)

Alternate colorways: #9008 blue dust, #3409 celadon, #7773 light salmon

One pair each size 5 US and 6 US (3.75 mm and 4 mm) knitting needles OR SIZE REQUIRED TO OBTAIN GIVEN GAUGE

Two size 5 (3.75 mm) double-pointed needles

One 12-in./30.5-cm × 16-in./41-cm pillow form

Stitch holders

GAUGE

16 sts and 20 rows = 4 in./10 cm over St st using size 6 US (4 mm) needles.

Each rectangle measures 14 in./35.5 cm by 9½ in./24.5 cm.

TO SAVE TIME, TAKE TIME TO CHECK GAUGE.

Instructions

Chose one rectangle from afghan for front and one for back.

Side Borders

Work same as afghan, picking up 45 sts and inc to 47 sts.

Top and Bottom Borders

Work same as afghan, picking up 62 sts and inc to 64 sts.

FINISHING

Sew two sides and top of back and front tog, leaving bottom open. Insert pillow form and sew opening closed. Make four leaf fringes same as afghan, and sew one to each corner.

Zodiac Fair Isle Afghan and Pillow

Advanced

This cosmic duo came about because I wanted to do a traditional Fair Isle without it being too traditional. The afghan and pillow are made in the traditional Fair Isle technique using steek knitting. You may want to make the pillow first if you've never done Fair Isle knitting or steeking. Choose your own sign for the pillow.

AFGHAN

FINISHED AFGHAN SIZE

Approx 55½ in./141.5 cm wide × 75 in./190.5 cm long

MATERIALS

Harrisville Knitting Yarn "Highland Style" (100% wool, 3½ oz./100 g skeins, each approx 200 yds./183 m)

Seven skeins #33 midnight blue (MC)

Three skeins #29 royal (A)

Two skeins #45 pearl (B)

One skein each #14 woodsmoke (C), #7 tundra (D), #4 gold (E), #30 azure (F), #17 bermuda blue (G), #27 cornflower (H), #10 spruce (I), #13 peacock (J), #12 sea green (K), #24 periwinkle (L), #22 plum (M), #35 chianti (N), #40 topaz (O), #26 wedgewood (P), #20 purple haze (Q), #47 suede (R), #39 russet (S), #3 pumpkin (T), #5 yellow (U), #11 emerald (V), and #34 aster (W)

Sizes 7 US and 9 US (4.5 mm and 5.5 mm) circular needle, 32 in./81.5 cm OR SIZE REQUIRED TO OBTAIN GIVEN GAUGE

Stitch markers

Scissors

GAUGE

20 sts and 20 rows = 4 in./10 cm over St st, using size 9 US (5.5 mm) needles.

TO SAVE TIME, TAKE TIME TO CHECK GAUGE.

Note: Afghan is worked in the round, using the steek method, then cut lengthwise up the middle of the steek. To learn more about steeks, see Alice Starmore's *Book of Fair Isle Knitting* (The Taunton Press, 1988).

Chart 1

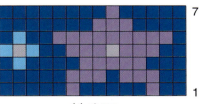

14-st rep

Instructions

Bottom Border

Tip: Approximately a 40-in./101.5-cm length of color makes one star. You can measure and cut yarn before starting border stars.

With smaller needles and A, cast on 249 sts. K 1 row, p 1 row.

Next row (RS): K1, M1, k to last st, M1, k1—251 sts. P 1 row. Rep last 2 rows 5 times—261 sts.

Picot row: K1, *yo, k2tog; rep from *, end k2. P 1 row, k 1 row. Change to MC and p 1 row.

Next row: K1, k2tog, k to last 3 sts, k2tog, k1—259 sts.

Next row: P5 MC, work 14-st rep of Chart 1 17 times, then work first 11 sts once more, p5 MC.

Next row: With MC, k1, k2tog, k2, cont Chart Pat to last 5 sts, with MC, k2, k2tog, k1—257 sts.

Rep last 2 rows twice more, then work 1 row even. With MC only, work dec row—249 sts. P 1 row.

Chart 2

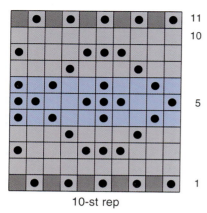

10-st rep

Chart 3—Aquarius

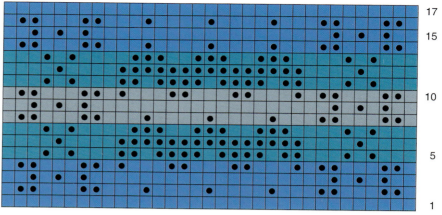

33 sts

Chart 4—Aries

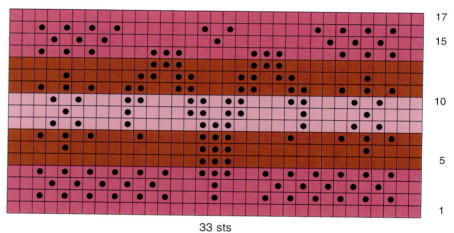

33 sts

Chart 5—Cancer

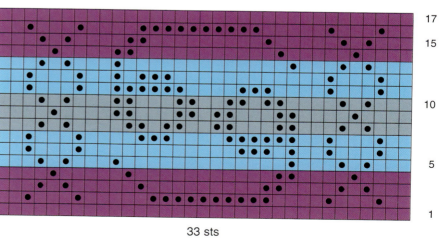

33 sts

Color Key

- ● midnight blue (MC)
- royal (A)
- pearl (B)
- woodsmoke (C)
- tundra (D)
- gold (E)
- azure (F)
- bermuda blue (G)
- cornflower (H)
- spruce (I)
- peacock (J)
- sea green (K)
- periwinkle (L)
- plum (M)
- chianti (N)
- topaz (O)
- wedgewood (P)
- purple haze (Q)
- suede (R)
- russet (S)
- pumpkin (T)
- yellow (U)
- emerald (V)
- aster (W)

Chart 6—Capricorn

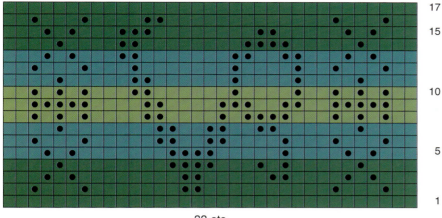

17
15

10

5

1

33 sts

Chart 7—Gemini

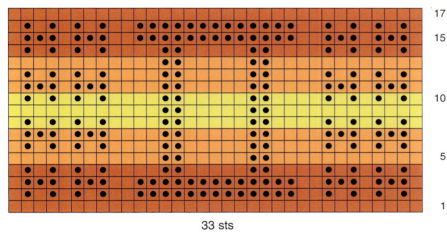

17
15

10

5

1

33 sts

Chart 8—Leo

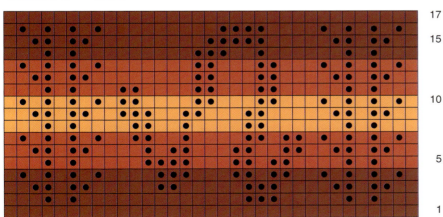

17
15

10

5

1

33 sts

Body

Change to larger needle. Join and beg working in the round, and work a knitted steek between the beg and end of each rnd as foll:

At the end of last row, place a marker. With MC, cast on 4 sts. Then with R and MC alternately, cast on 4 more sts—257 sts. Place a marker. Working in rnds of St st (k every rnd) beg Chart 2 on p. 128, changing colors in the middle of the steek as needed. Foll with Charts 3 through 14, alternating each with Chart 2. After Chart 14, work 11 rows of Chart 2.

Top Border

Bind off 8 steek sts, and resume working back and forth in rows with smaller needles as foll:

Row 1 (RS): With MC, knit. P 1 row.

Row 3: K1, M1, k to last st, M1, k1—251 sts.

Row 4: P1, work 14-st rep for Chart 1 (turn chart upside down and work Rows 15–1), 17 times, then work first 11 sts once more, p1.

Row 5: K1, M1, cont Chart 2 to last st, M1, k1—253 sts.

Rows 6–10: Cont in pat, inc 1 st each end of every RS row—257 sts.

Row 11: Rep Row 3—259 sts. P 1 row. Change to A.

Row 13: Rep Row 3—261 sts. P 1 row.

Row 15: K1, *yo, k2tog; rep from *, end k2. P 1 row.

Row 17: K1, k2tog, k to last 3 sts, k2tog, k1—259 sts.

Rows 18–28: Rep Rows 16 and 17—249 sts. Bind off all sts.

Side Border

With scissors, cut afghan lengthwise up the middle of the steek. With WS facing, MC, and smaller needles, pick up and k347 sts along length of afghan.

Foll pat for top border, inc sts from 347 to 359, then dec back to 347.

Work in same way along other side of afghan.

FINISHING

Weave in ends of star and diamond border design. Trim steek to 2 sts on each side. Stitch up mitered corners. Fold edges to WS at picot row, and with A, whipstitch in place. Block with hot iron and wet cloth.

PILLOW

FINISHED PILLOW SIZE

Approx 22 in./56 cm square

MATERIALS

Harrisville Knitting Yarn "Highland Style" (100% wool, 3½ oz./100 g skeins, each approx 200 yds./183 m)

One skein of each color for zodiac of your choice:

#33 midnight blue (MC), #29 royal (A), #45 pearl (B), #14 woodsmoke (C), #7 tundra (D), #4 gold (E), #30 azure (F), #17 bermuda blue (G), #27 cornflower (H), #10 spruce (I), #13 peacock (J), #12 sea green (K), #24 periwinkle (L), #22 plum (M), #35 chianti (N), #40 topaz (O), #26 wedgewood (P), #20 purple haze (Q), #47 suede (R), #39 russet (S), #3 pumpkin (T), #5 yellow (U), #11 emerald (V), and #34 aster (W)

Note: It takes 40 in./101.5 cm lengths of various colors for the Star Pattern (Chart 2).

Sizes 7 US and 9 US (4.5 mm and 5.5 mm) circular needle, 16 in./40 cm OR SIZE REQUIRED TO OBTAIN GIVEN GAUGE

Stitch markers

Scissors

One 22-in./56-cm-square pillow form

Chart 9—Libra

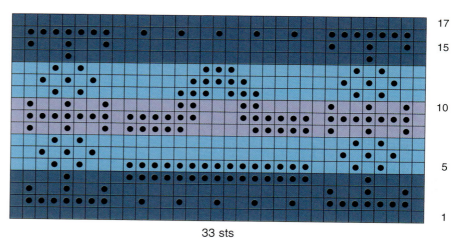

33 sts

Chart 10—Pisces

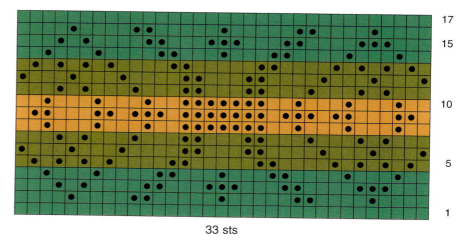

33 sts

Chart 11—Sagittarius

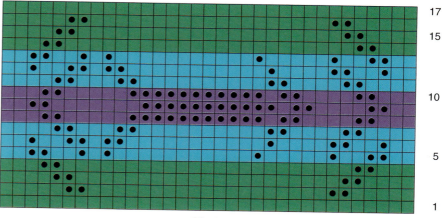

33 sts

Chart 12—Scorpio

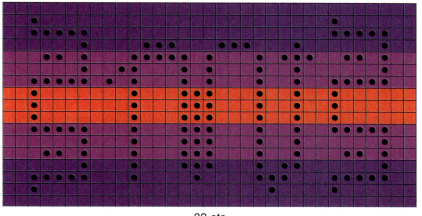

17
15

10

5

1

33 sts

Chart 13—Taurus

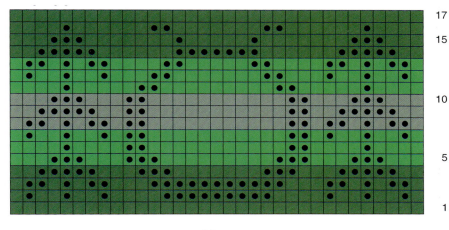

17
15

10

5

1

33 sts

Chart 14—Virgo

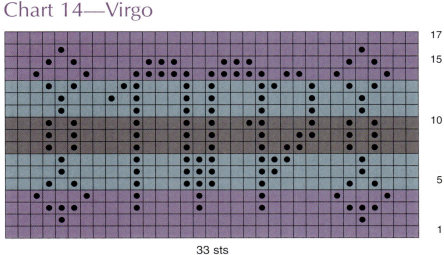

17
15

10

5

1

33 sts

GAUGE

20 sts and 20 rows = 4 in./10 cm over St
st, using size 9 US (5.5 mm) needles.
TO SAVE TIME, TAKE TIME TO
CHECK GAUGE.

Instructions

FRONT

Bottom Border

With smaller needles and A, cast on
93 sts. [K 1 row, p 1 row] twice.

Next picot row: K1, *yo, k2tog; rep
from *, end k2. P 1 row, k 1 row.
Change to MC and p 1 row.

Next row: K1, k2tog, k to last 3 sts,
k2tog, k1—91 sts.

Next row: P5 MC, work 14-st rep of
Chart 1 five times, then work first 11 sts
once more, p5 MC.

Next row: With MC, k1, k2tog, k2,
cont Chart Pat to last 5 sts, with MC,
k2, k2tog, k1—89 sts.

Rep last 2 rows twice more, then
work 1 row even. With MC only, work
dec row—83 sts. P 1 row.

Body

Change to larger needle. Join and beg
working in the round, and work a knitted steek between the beg and end of
each rnd as foll:

At the end of last row, place a marker.
With MC, cast on 4 sts. Then with R
and MC alternately, cast on 4 more
sts—89 sts. Place a marker. Working in
rnds of St st (k every rnd) beg Chart 2,
changing colors in the middle of the
steek as needed. Foll your choice of
three zodiac motifs, alternating each
with Chart 2. After third chart, work 11
rows of Chart 2.

Row 11: Rep Row 3—91 sts. P 1 row. Change to A.

Row 13: Rep Row 3—93 sts. P 1 row.

Row 15: K1, *yo, k2tog; rep from *, end k2. P 1 row, k 1 row, p 1 row. Bind off.

Side Border

With scissors, cut pillow lengthwise up the middle of the steek. With WS facing, MC and smaller needles, pick up and k95 sts along length one side edge. Foll pat for top border, working 14-st rep of Chart 2 six times, then first 11 sts once more, inc sts for mitered edges as before. Bind off.

Work in same way along other side of pillow.

BACK

With larger needles and MC, cast on 112 sts, and work in St st for 22 in./ 56 cm. Bind off.

FINISHING

Weave in ends of star and diamond border design. Trim steek to 2 sts on each side. Stitch up mitered corners. Fold edges to WS at picot row, and with A, whipstitch in place. Block with hot iron and wet cloth.

Sew back and front at cast-on edge of border on top and two sides. Insert pillow form, and sew bottom closed.

Top Border

Bind off 8 steek sts, and resume working back and forth in rows with smaller needles as foll:

Row 1 (RS): With MC, knit. P 1 row.

Row 3: K1, M1, k to last st, M1, k1—83 sts.

Row 4: P1, work 14-st rep for Chart 1 (turn chart upside down and work Rows 15–1) 5 times, then work first 11 sts once more, p1.

Row 5: K1, M1, cont Chart 2 to last st, M1, k1—85 sts.

Rows 6–10: Cont in pat, inc 1 st each end of every RS row—89 sts.

Royal Maze Afghan and Pillow

The rich jewel tones in this afghan and pillow are enhanced by a black border. The technique is easy colorwork, knit in one piece. The pillows are made using one color on the front and another color on the back. Choose your favorite colors for your pillow.

Tip: Chinchilla is beautiful yarn, but tricky to work with. Be sure to cast on and bind off with the same tension, and keep in mind that a dropped stitch is hard to find.

AFGHAN

FINISHED AFGHAN SIZE

Approx 44 in./112 cm wide × 52 in./ 132 cm long

MATERIALS

Berroco "Chinchilla" (100% rayon, 1¾ oz./50 g balls, each approx 77 yds./70.5 m)

Five balls #5334 black (MC)

Three balls #5420 petunia (A)

Two balls each #5371 evergreen (B), #5363 midnight (C), and #5533 provence green (D)

One ball each #5534 beaujolais (E), #5422 plum (F), #5356 teal (G), and #5532 auburn (H)

One pair size 9 US (5.5 mm) knitting needles OR SIZE REQUIRED TO OBTAIN GIVEN GAUGE

GAUGE

12 sts and 18 rows = 4 in./10 cm over St st, using size 9 US (5.5 mm) needles.

TO SAVE TIME, TAKE TIME TO CHECK GAUGE.

Notes: K first and last st of every row to keep edge from curling. Be sure to cast on and bind off with same tension.

Instructions

With MC, cast on 132 sts. Work in St st for 8 rows or 2 in./5 cm, end with a p row.

Beg Color Block Pat

Next row (RS): K6 MC, 40 B, 6 MC, 74 C, 6 MC. Cont in St st, matching colors, for 43 rows more.

Next row (RS): K6 MC, 40B, 86 MC. Cont matching colors for 7 rows more.

Next row (RS): K6 MC, 40B, 6 MC, 36 E, 6 MC, 32 A, 6 MC. Cont matching colors for 25 rows more.

Next row (RS): K6 MC, 40B, 48 MC, 32 A, 6 MC. Cont matching colors for 7 rows more.

Next row (RS): K6 MC, 40B, 6 MC, 36 F, 6 MC, 32 A, 6 MC. Cont matching colors for 25 rows more.

Next row (RS): K94 MC, 32 A, 6 MC. Cont matching colors for 7 rows more.

Next row (RS): K6 MC, 82 D, 6 MC, 32 A, 6 MC. Cont matching colors for 43 rows more.

Next row (RS): K94 MC, 32 A, 6 MC. Cont matching colors for 7 rows more.

Next row (RS): K6 MC, 38 H, 6 MC, 38 G, 6 MC, 32 A, 6 MC. Cont matching colors for 51 rows more.

Work 8 rows with MC only. Bind off.

FINISHING

Weave in ends.

Pillow

FINISHED PILLOW SIZE

Approx 16 in./41 cm square

MATERIALS

Berroco "Chinchilla" (100% rayon, 1¾ oz./50 g balls, each approx 77 yds./71 m)

One ball each #5334 black (MC) and desired contrast color

One 16-in./41-cm-square pillow form

One pair size 9 US (5.5 mm) knitting needles OR SIZE REQUIRED TO OBTAIN GIVEN GAUGE

GAUGE

12 sts and 18 rows = 4 in./10 cm over St st, using size 9 US (5.5 mm) needles.
TO SAVE TIME, TAKE TIME TO CHECK GAUGE.

Instructions

Front

With MC, cast on 50 sts and work in St st for 8 rows.

Next row (RS): K6 MC, 38 sts of a contrast color, 6 MC. Cont in St st, matching colors, for 51 rows more. With MC, work 8 rows over all sts. Bind off.

Back

Work same as Front.

FINISHING

Sew sides of front and back tog, leaving bottom edge open. Insert pillow form, and sew opening closed.

Doilies

When I hear the word doilies, I think of my grandmother and all the beautiful starched lace doilies in her home. Sadly, not many homes today use doilies, and I fear that many of the wonderful patterns will become extinct. The following patterns are not my original designs, but I want to include them to make sure the patterns are not lost.

BRIGHTON LACE DOILY OR PLACE MAT

This pattern was sent to me from Brighton, England. The pattern was called "Viennese Lace Luncheon Set," dated 1932. This piece can be used as a doily, a place mat, or a table runner. My sincere thanks to Nancy Henderson for translating the pattern into U.S. knitting language.

FINISHED SIZE
Approx 11 in./28 cm × 20 in./50.5 cm

MATERIALS
DMC "Cébélia 5" (100% cotton, 1¾ oz./50 g balls, each approx 142 yds./130 m)
Two balls ecru
Size 2 US (2.75 mm) circular needles, 12 in./30.5 cm, 16 in./41 cm, and 24 in./61 cm, OR SIZE REQUIRED TO OBTAIN GIVEN GAUGE
No. 10 (0.8 mm) steel crochet hook
Stitch markers

GAUGE
26 sts = 4 in./10 cm over St st, using size 2 US (2.75 mm) needles.
TO SAVE TIME, TAKE TIME TO CHECK GAUGE.

STITCH GLOSSARY (for all doilies)
SKP: Sl 1, k1, psso.
SK2P2: Sl 1, k2, pass sl st over k2.
SK2TP: Sl 1, k2tog, pass sl st over k2tog.
S2K2TP2: Sl 2, k2tog, pass 2 sl sts over k2tog.
S2K3TP2: Sl 2, k3tog, pass 2 sl sts over k3tog.
M3: K1, yo and k1 into front of st.
Inc 1: K in front and back of st.

Instructions

With 12 in./30.5 cm circular needle, loosely cast on 49 sts, pm, 4 sts, pm, 49 sts, pm, 4 sts, pm. Join, taking care not to twists sts. K 1 rnd.

Part A
Rnd 1: *Yo, k1 tbl, [yo, SKP] twice, k4, [yo, SKP] twice, [SK2P2, yo] 7 times, SK2P2, [k2tog, yo] twice, k4, k2tog, yo, k2tog, [yo, k1 tbl] 4 times; rep from * once more.

Rnd 2 and all even rnds: Knit.

Rnd 3: *[Yo, k1 tbl] 3 times, [yo, SKP] twice, k4, [yo, SKP] twice, [SK2P2, yo] 6 times, SK2P2, [k2tog, yo] twice, k4, k2tog, yo, k2tog, [yo, k1 tbl] 8 times; rep from * once more.

Rnd 5: *Yo, k2tog, k1, yo, k1 tbl, yo, k1, SKP, [yo, SKP] twice, k4, [yo, SKP] twice, [SK2P2, yo] 5 times, SK2P2, [k2tog, yo] twice, k4, k2tog, yo, k2tog, [yo, k2tog, k1, yo, k1 tbl, yo, k1, SKP, yo k1 tbl] twice; rep from * once more.

Rnd 7: *Yo, k2tog, k2, yo, k1 tbl, yo, k2, SKP, [yo, SKP] twice, k4, [yo, SKP] twice, [SK2P2, yo] 4 times, SK2P2, [k2tog, yo] twice, k4, k2tog, yo, k2tog, [yo, k2tog, k2, yo, k1 tbl, yo, k2, SKP, yo, k1 tbl] twice; rep from * once more.

Rnd 9: *Yo k2tog, k3, yo, k1 tbl, yo, k3, SKP, [yo, SKP] twice, k4, [yo, SKP] twice, [SK2P2, yo] 3 times, SK2P2, [k2tog, yo] twice, k4, k2tog, yo, k2tog, [yo, k2tog, k3, yo, k1 tbl, yo, k3, SKP, yo, k1 tbl] twice; rep from * once more.

Rnd 11: *+Yo, k2tog, k3, yo, k1, yo, k1 tbl, yo, k1, yo, k3, SKP+, [yo, SKP] twice, k4, [yo, SKP] twice, [SK2P2, yo] twice, SK2P2, [k2tog, yo] twice, k4, k2tog, yo, k2tog; [rep between +'s once, yo, k1 tbl] twice; rep from * once more.

Rnd 13: *+Yo, k2tog, yo, k4, yo, k5, yo, k4, yo, SKP+, [yo, SKP] twice, k4, [yo, SKP] twice, SK2P2, yo, SK2P2, [k2tog, yo] twice, k4, k2tog, yo, k2tog; [rep between +'s once, yo, k1 tbl] twice; rep from * once more.

Rnd 15: *+Yo, k2tog, yo, k1 tbl, yo, SKP, k3, yo, SKP, k1, k2tog, yo, k3, k2tog, yo, k1 tbl, yo, SKP+, [yo, SKP] twice, k4, [yo, SKP] twice, SK2P2, [k2tog, yo] twice, k4, k2tog, yo, k2tog; [rep between +'s once, yo, k1 tbl] twice; rep from * once more. Change to 16 in./41 cm circular needle.

Rnd 17: *+Yo, k2tog, k1, yo, k1 tbl, yo, k1, SKP, k3, yo, SK2P, yo, k3, k2tog, k1, yo, k1 tbl, yo, k1, SKP+, [yo, SKP] twice, k4, yo, SKP, yo, S2K2TP2, yo, k2tog, yo, k4, k2tog, yo, k2tog; [rep between +'s once, yo, k1 tbl] twice; rep from * once more.

Rnd 19: *+Yo, k2tog, k2, yo, k1 tbl, yo, k2, SKP, k7, k2tog, k2, yo, k1 tbl, yo, k2, SKP+, [yo, SKP] twice, k4, yo, SKP, k1, k2tog, yo, k4, k2tog, yo, k2tog; [rep between +'s once, yo, k1 tbl] twice; rep from * once more.

Rnd 21: *+Yo, k2tog, k3, yo, k1 tbl, yo, k3, SKP, k5, k2tog, k3, yo, k1 tbl, yo, k3, SKP+, [yo, SKP] twice, k4, yo, SK2TP, yo, k4, k2tog, yo, k2tog; [rep between +'s once, yo, k1 tbl] twice; rep from * once more.

Rnd 23: *+Yo, k2tog, k3, yo, k1, yo, k1 tbl, yo, k1, yo, k3, SKP, k3, k2tog, k3, yo, k1, yo, k1 tbl, yo, k1, yo, k3, SKP+, [yo, SKP] twice, k9, k2tog, yo, k2tog; [rep between +'s once, yo, k1 tbl] twice; rep from * once more.

Rnd 25: *+Yo, k2tog, yo, k4, yo, k5, yo, k4, S2K3TP2, k4, yo, k5, yo, k4, yo, SKP+, [yo, SKP] twice, k7, k2tog, yo, k2tog; [rep between +'s once, yo, k1 tbl] twice; rep from * once more.

Part B

Note: Change to 24-in./61-cm circular needle when needed.

Rnd 27: *+Yo, k2tog, [yo, k1 tbl, yo, SKP, k3, yo, SKP, k1, k2tog, yo, k3, k2tog] twice, yo, k1 tbl, yo, k1, SKP+, [yo, SKP] twice, k5, k2tog, yo, k2tog; [rep between +'s once, yo, k1 tbl] twice; rep from * once more.

Rnd 29: *+Yo, k2tog, k1, [yo, k1 tbl, yo, k1, SKP, k3, yo, SK2TP, yo, k3, k2tog, k1] twice, yo, k1 tbl, yo, k1, SKP+, [yo, SKP] twice, k3, k2tog, yo, k2tog; [rep between +'s once, yo, k1 tbl] twice; rep from * once more.

Rnd 31: *+Yo, k2tog, k2, [yo, k1 tbl, yo, k2, SKP, k7, k2tog, k2] twice, yo, k1 tbl, yo, k2, SKP+, [yo, SKP] twice, k1, k2tog, yo, k2tog; [rep between +'s once, yo, k1 tbl] twice; rep from * once more.

Rnd 33: *+Yo, k2tog, k3, [yo, k1 tbl, yo, k3, SKP, k5, k2tog, k3] twice, yo, k1 tbl, yo, k3, SKP+, yo, SKP, yo, SK2TP, yo, k2tog; [rep between +'s once, yo, k1 tbl] twice; rep from * once more.

Rnd 35: *+Yo, k2tog, k3, yo, k1, [yo, k1 tbl, yo, k1, yo, k3, SKP, k3, k2tog, k3, yo, k1] twice, yo, k1 tbl, yo, k1, yo, k3, SKP+, yo, SKP, k1, k2tog; [rep between +'s once, yo, k1 tbl] twice; rep from * once more.

Rnd 37: *Yo, k2tog, yo, k1, +k3, yo, k1, [k4, yo, k4, yo, S2K3TP2, yo, k4, yo, k1] twice, k4, yo, k3+, [SK2TP, yo] twice, SK2TP; [rep between +'s once, k1, yo, SKP, yo, k1 tbl, yo, k2tog, yo, k1; rep between +'s once, k1, yo, SKP, yo, k1 tbl; Rep from * once more.

Part C

Note: Rep between +'s 6 times for Sides 1 and 3 and 3 times for Sides 2 and 4. Markers for sides will move. Use markers for sts between +'s to make knitting easier.

Rnd 39—Preparation rnd: [*Yo, k1, +k2, yo, SKP, k3, yo, SKP, k1, k2tog, yo, k3, k2tog, yo, k1+, k2, yo, k1 tbl, pm; rep from * once, pm] twice.

Rnd 41: *Yo, k2tog, yo, +k1 tbl, [yo, SKP] twice, k3, yo, SK2TP, yo, k3, [k2tog, yo] twice+, k1 tbl, yo, SKP, yo, k1 tbl; rep from * for each side.

Rnd 43: *Yo, k2tog, yo, inc 1, +inc 1, k1, [yo, SKP] twice, k7, [k2tog, yo] twice, inc 1+, inc 1, k1, yo, SKP, yo, k1 tbl; rep from * for each side.

Rnd 45: *Yo, k2tog, yo, k2, inc 1, +inc 1, k3, [yo, SKP] twice, k5, [k2tog, yo] twice, k2, inc 1+, rep between +'s once, inc 1, k3, yo, SKP, yo, k1 tbl; rep from * for each side.

Rnd 47: *Yo, k2tog, yo, k4, inc 1, +inc 1, k5, [yo, SKP] twice, k3, [k2tog, yo] twice, k1, inc 1+, inc 1, k5, yo, SKP, yo, M3; rep from * for each side.

Rnd 48: Knit.

FINISHING

Edging

Note: Work each section between [ ]'s 4 times, rep between *'s 6 times for Sides 1 and 3 and 3 times for Sides 2 and 4.

With crochet hook, [sc 3 sts tog, ch 9, sc 4 sts tog, ch 9, *sc 5 sts tog, ch 9, sc 4 sts tog, ch 9, sc 3 sts tog, ch 7, sc 5 sts tog, ch 7, sc 3 sts tog, ch 9, sc 4 sts tog, ch 9 *, sc 5 sts tog, ch 9, sc 4 sts tog, ch 9, (sc 3 sts tog, ch 9) twice].

Sl st to first sc, and fasten off.

Fold in half lengthwise with RS facing. Working from WS, sl st corresponding sts tog from each side of cast-on edge, working loosely.

Stretch and block place mat.

HEART DOILY

Dear to my heart, this pattern belonged to my grandmother.

FINISHED SIZE

Approx 16 in./41 cm in diameter

MATERIALS

Crystal Palace Yarns "Baby Georgia"
   (100% mercerized cotton, 1.4 oz./40
   g balls, each approx 140 yds./126 m)
2 balls #6807 sea green
One set (4) size 1 US (2.25 mm)
   double-pointed needles OR SIZE
   REQUIRED TO OBTAIN GIVEN
   GAUGE
No. 12 (0.6 mm) steel crochet hook

GAUGE

32 sts = 4 in./10 cm over St st, using
   size 1 US (2.25 mm) needles.
TO SAVE TIME, TAKE TIME TO
   CHECK GAUGE.

Instructions

Cast on 12 sts. Divide sts evenly over 3
needles. Join and place marker for beg
of rnd.

Rnd 1: *Yo, k1; rep from * around.
Rnd 2 and all even rnds: Knit.
Rnd 3: *Yo, k2; rep from * around.
Rnd 5: *Yo, k1, k2tog; rep from *
around.
Rnd 7: *Yo, k3; rep from * around.
Rnd 9: *[Yo, k1] twice, k2tog; rep
from * around.
Rnd 11: *Yo, k1, yo, k2, k2tog; rep
from * around.
Rnd 13: *Yo, k1, yo, k3, k2tog; rep
from * around.
Rnd 15: *Yo, k1, yo, k4, k2tog; rep
from * around.
Rnd 17: *[Yo, k1] twice, yo, k4, k2tog;
rep from * around.
Rnd 19: *[Yo, k1] twice, yo, k6, k2tog;
rep from * around.
Rnd 21: *[Yo, k1] twice, yo, k8, k2tog;
rep from * around.

Rnd 23: *[Yo, k1] twice, yo, k10,
k2tog; rep from * around.
Rnd 25: *[Yo, k1] twice, yo, k12,
k2tog; rep from * around.
Rnd 27: *Yo, k1, yo, SKP, k13, k2tog;
rep from * around.
Rnd 29: *Yo, k1, [k1, p1] in next st,
k1, yo, SKP, k11, k2tog; rep from *
around.
Rnd 31: *Yo, k6, yo, SKP, k9, k2tog;
rep from * around.
Rnd 33: *Yo, k8, yo, SKP, k7, k2tog;
rep from * around.
Rnd 35: *Yo, k10, yo, SKP, k5, k2tog;
rep from * around.
Rnd 37: *Yo, SKP, k8, k2tog, yo, SKP,
k3, k2tog; rep from * around.
Rnd 39: *Yo, SKP, k8, k2tog, yo, SKP,
k1, k2tog; rep from * around.
Rnd 41: *Yo, k1, yo, SKP, k3, yo, k3,
k2tog, yo, k1, yo, SK2P; rep from *
around.
Rnd 43: *Yo, SK2P, yo, SKP, k2tog,
using the last 2 sts, sl the first st over
the 2nd st (X-st made), yo, k1, yo, SKP,
k2tog, X-st, yo, SK2P, yo, k1; rep from
* around.
Rnd 45: K first st onto the preceeding
needle, *yo, k3, yo, k1; rep from *
around.
Rnd 47: *Yo, SK2P, k3; rep from *
around.
Rnd 49: *Yo, k3, yo, SK2P; rep from *
around.
Rnd 50: Knit, inc 1 st at end of each
needle—55 sts on each needle.
Rnd 51: Knit.
Rnd 53: *Yo, k1, yo, SKP, k6, k2tog;
rep from * around.
Rnd 55: *Yo, k1, inc 1 in next st, k1,
yo, SKP, k4, k2tog; rep from * around.
Rnd 57: *Yo, k6, yo, SKP, k2, k2tog;
rep from * around.
Rnd 59: *Yo, k8, yo, SKP, k2tog; rep
from * around.
Rnd 61: *Yo, k10, yo, k2tog; rep from
* around.

Rnd 63: *Yo, SKP, k8, k2tog, yo, k1; rep from * around.

Rnd 65: K first st onto the preceding needle, *yo, SKP, k3, yo, k3, k2tog, yo, k3; rep from * around.

Rnd 67: *[Yo, k1, yo, SK2P, k2tog, X-st] twice, yo, k1, yo, SK2P; rep from * around.

Rnd 69: *K3, yo, k1, yo; rep from * around.

Rnd 71: *Yo, SK2P; rep from * around.

Rnd 72: Knit.

Rnd 74: *Sl 6 sts onto crochet hook, yo and pull through all 6 sts, ch 5, sl next 3 sts onto hook, yo and pull through all 3 sts, ch 5; rep from * around.

FINISHING

Stretch and block doily to 16 in./41 cm in diameter.

STAR DOILY

This project is based on a doily I purchased at a flea market many years ago. I added bead embellishment to the pattern.

FINISHED SIZE

Approx 10 in./25.5 cm in diameter

MATERIALS

Crystal Palace Yarns "Baby Georgia" (100% mercerized cotton, 1.4 oz./40 g balls, each approx 140 yds./126 m)
Two balls #6904 dark rose
One set (5) size 1 US (2.25 mm) double-pointed needles
Three circular needles, 12 in./30.5 cm, 16 in./41 cm, and 24 in./61 cm, OR SIZE REQUIRED TO OBTAIN GIVEN GAUGE
No. 10 (0.8 mm) steel crochet hook
Stitch markers
Eight beads #03248 from Bead Warehouse (optional)

GAUGE

32 sts = 4 in./10 cm over St st, using size 1 US (2.25 mm) needles.
TO SAVE TIME, TAKE TIME TO CHECK GAUGE.

Instructions

With dpn, cast on 4 sts. Divide sts evenly over four needles. Join and place marker for beg of rnd.

Rnd 1: Knit.

Rnd 2: K into front and back of each st—8 sts.

Rnds 3–5: Knit.

Rnd 6: K into front and back of each st—16 sts.

Rnds 7–10: Knit.

Rnd 11: *Yo twice, k1; rep from * around.

Rnd 12: *K1 in double yo, k1; rep from * around—32 sts.

Rnds 13–15: Knit.

Rnd 16: Rep Rnd 11.

Rnd 17: Rep Rnd 12—64 sts.

Rnds 18–21: Knit.

Rnd 22: *Yo twice, k2; rep from * around.

Rnd 23: *K1 in double yo, k2; rep from * around—96 sts.

Rnds 24–27: Knit.

Note: On Rnd 28, change to 12-in./30.5-cm circular needle, placing markers as indicated. Each section will move 2 sts to the right. The first 2 sts of rnd will be used twice as first 2 and last 2 sts.

Rnd 28: K2, pm, [(yo twice, k2) 12 times, pm] 3 times, (yo twice, k2) 12 times.

Rnd 29: Rep rnd 23—144 sts.

Rnds 30–33: Knit.

Rnd 34: *[K3, yo twice] 5 times, k3, pm; rep from * around. 8 sections.

Rnd 35: *[K3, k1 in double yo] 5 times, k3; rep from * around—184 sts. Change to 16-in./41-cm circular needle.

Rnd 36: *Yo, SKP, k21; rep from * around.

Rnd 37: *Yo, k1 tbl, yo, SKP, k18, k2tog; rep from * around.

Rnd 38: *Yo, k3, yo, SKP, k16, k2tog; rep from * around.

Rnd 39: *Yo, k5, yo, SKP, k14, k2tog; rep from * around.

Rnd 40: *Yo, k1, k2tog, yo, k1 tbl, yo, SKP, k1, yo, SKP, [k3, yo twice] 3 times, k3, k2tog; rep from * around.

Rnd 41: *Yo, k1, k2tog, yo, k1 tbl, k1, k1 tbl, yo, SKP, k1, yo, SKP, k2, k1 in double yo, [k3, k1 in double yo] twice, k2, k2tog; rep from * around—208 sts.

Rnd 42: *Yo, k1, k2tog, yo, k1 tbl, k3, k1 tbl, yo, SKP, k1, yo, SKP, k11, k2tog; rep from * around.

Rnd 43: *Yo, k1, k2tog, yo, k1 tbl, k5, k1 tbl, yo, SKP, k1, yo, SKP, k9, k2tog; rep from * around.

Rnd 44: *Yo, k1, k2tog, yo, k1 tbl, k7, k1 tbl, yo, SKP, k1, yo, SKP, k7, k2tog; rep from * around.

Rnd 45: *Yo, k1, k2tog, yo, k1 tbl, k9, k1 tbl, yo, SKP, k1, yo, SKP, k5, k2tog; rep from * around.

Rnd 46: *Yo, k1, k2tog, yo, k1 tbl, k11, k1 tbl, yo, SKP, k1, yo, SKP, k3, k2tog; rep from * around. Change to 24-in./61-cm circular needle.

Rnd 47: *Yo, k1, k2tog, yo, k1 tbl, k13, k1 tbl, yo, SKP, k1, yo, SKP, k1, k2tog; rep from * around.

Rnd 48: *Yo, k1, k2tog, yo, k1 tbl, k8, yo, k7, k1 tbl, yo, SKP, k1, yo, SK2TP; rep from * around—216 sts.

Rnd 49: *K1, k2tog, yo, k1 tbl, k18, k1 tbl, yo, SKP, k2; rep from * around.

Rnd 50: *K2tog, yo, k1 tbl, k9, yo, SKP, yo, k9, k1 tbl, yo, SKP, k1; rep from * around.

Note: On Rnd 51, the first st of each section will become the last st of previous section. Move markers as indicated. The first st of rnd will be last st also.

Rnd 51: K1, pm, *yo, k1 tbl, k23, k1 tbl, yo, sl 1, k last st tog with first st of next section, psso, pm; rep from *, end yo, k1 tbl, k23, k1 tbl, yo, SK2TP.

Rnd 52: *Yo twice, k1 tbl, k12, yo, SKP, k11, k1 tbl, yo twice, k1 tbl; rep from * around.

Rnd 53: *(P1, k1) in double yo, k27, (p1, k1) in double yo, k1; rep from * around—256 sts.

Rnds 54–59: Knit.

FINISHING

Edging

With crochet hook, *ch 5, sl next 2 sts to hook, yo, draw through these 2 sts, yo and through 2 loops on hook (sc 2 tog); rep from * around, join with sl st to first ch. Fasten off. Stretch and block doily to 10 in./25.5 cm in diameter. Sew a bead to each star point.

Leaf Photo Frame

Easy

The leaves are knit separately and glued to a photo frame.
Yes, it is okay to combine your glue gun with your knitting. Well, at least
to make this picture frame. Just be very careful not to overglue.

Tip: You may use any size and any shape frame.

MATERIALS

Rowan Yarns "Lurex" (75% viscose, 25% lurex, 0.8 oz./25 g skeins, each approx 59 yds./54 m)

Two skeins #842 gold

One pair size 5 US (3.75 mm) knitting needles OR SIZE REQUIRED TO OBTAIN GIVEN GAUGE

Any size photo frame (5 × 7 frame is shown)

Glue gun and glue sticks

GAUGE

20 sts and 24 rows = 4 in./10 cm over St st, using size 5 US (3.75 mm) needles.
TO SAVE TIME, TAKE TIME TO CHECK GAUGE.

Instructions

Leaf (make approx 20 for a 5 × 7 frame)

Cast on 5 sts.

Beg leaf—Row 1 (RS): K2, yo, k1, yo, k2—7 sts.

Row 2 and all WS rows: Purl.
Row 3: K3, yo, k1, yo, k3—9 sts.
Row 5: K4, yo, k1, yo, k4—11 sts.
Row 7: SSK, k7, k2tog—9 sts.
Row 9: SSK, k5, k2tog—7 sts.
Row 11: SSK, k3, k2tog—5 sts.
Row 13: SSK, k1, k2tog—3 sts.
Row 15: SK2P—1 st. Fasten off.

FINISHING

Using glue gun, glue each leaf separately, overlapping one another, to the frame. Angle a leaf at each corner.

Cable Leaf Place Mat and Pillow

Intermediate

*This place mat is knit in a leaf shape and accented with a cable border.
The veins of the leaf are embroidered in a contrasting yarn. You can make
your leaf place mats in one color or in a variety of colors. To make the pillow,
just sew two place mats together and stuff it with Poly-Fil.*

PLACE MAT

FINISHED PLACE MAT SIZE

Approx 13¾ in./35 cm × 22 3/4 in./
58 cm

MATERIALS

Classic Elite Yarns "Newport Cotton"
(100% cotton, 1¾ oz./50 g balls, each
approx 70 yds./64 m)
Two balls #2044 rust, #2053 claret,
#2081 olive, or #2068 gold for one
place mat
Small amount of a contrast color for
vein embroidery
One pair size 9 US (5.5 mm) knitting
needles OR SIZE REQUIRED TO
OBTAIN GIVEN GAUGE
Cable needle
Stitch markers

GAUGE

16 sts and 22 rows = 4 in./10 cm over St
st, using size 9 US (5.5 mm) needles.
TO SAVE TIME, TAKE TIME TO
CHECK GAUGE.

PATTERN STITCHES

4-st FC: Sl 2 sts to cn and hold to front,
k2, k2 from cn.
4-st BC: Sl 2 sts to cn and hold to
back, k2, k2 from cn.
DD (Double Dec): Sl 2 sts tog knitwise, k1, pass 2 slipped sts over k1.

Instructions

Cast on 9 sts.
Preparation row (WS): P4, k1, p4.
Rows 1 and 5: K4, p1, k4.
Rows 2, 4, and 6: K the knit sts and p
the purl sts.
Row 3: 4-st FC, p1, 4-st BC.
Rows 7–21: Rep Rows 1–6 twice,
then rep rows 1–3 once more.
Row 22: P4, pm, in next st work k1,
yo, k1, pm, p4—11 sts.
Note: Sl markers every row.
Row 23: K4, p in front and back of
next 2 sts, p1, k4—13 sts.
Row 24: P4, k in front and back of
next st, k to 2 sts before marker, k in
front and back of next st, k1, p4—15 sts.

Row 25: K4, p to marker, k4.
Row 26: P4, k in front and back of
next st, k to 2 sts before marker, k in
front and back of next st, k1, p4—17 sts.
Row 27: 4-st FC, p in front and back
of next st, p to 2 sts before marker, p in
front and back of next st, p1, 4-st BC—
19 sts.
Row 28: P4, k to marker, p4.
Row 29: K4, p in front and back of
next st, p to 2 sts before marker, p in
front and back of next st, p1, k4—21 sts.
Rows 30–61: Rep Rows 24–29, ending with Row 25—63 sts.
Rows 62–79: Work even in pat as
established, twisting cable on Rows 63,
69, and 75.
Row 80: P4, k2tog, k to 2 sts before
marker, SSK, p4.
Row 81: 4-st FC, p to marker,
4-st BC.
Row 82: Rep Row 80.
Row 83: K4, p to marker, k4.
Rows 84–124: Rep Rows 82 and 83,
twisting cable every 6th row, end with
Row 82—17 sts.

Row 125: K4, SSP, p to 2 sts before marker, p2tog, k4.

Row 126: P4, k2tog, k to 2 sts before marker, SSK, p4.

Row 127: Rep Row 125.

Row 128: P3, drop markers, k2tog, k1, SSK, p3.

Row 129: K3, DD, k3.

Row 130: P7.

Row 131: SSK, DD, k2tog.

Row 132: P3tog. Fasten off.

FINISHING

With contrast color, work stem st for veins (see photo above).

PILLOW

FINISHED PILLOW SIZE

Approx 13¾ in./35 cm x 22¾ in./58 cm

MATERIALS

Classic Elite Yarns "Newport Cotton" (100% cotton, 1¾ oz./50 g balls, each approx 70 yds./64 m)

Four balls of #2044 rust, #2053 claret, #2081 olive, or #2068 gold

Small amount of a contrast color for vein embroidery

Poly-Fil stuffing

One pair size 9 US (5.5 mm) knitting needles OR SIZE REQUIRED TO OBTAIN GIVEN GAUGE

Cable needle

Stitch markers

GAUGE

16 sts and 22 rows = 4 in./10 cm over St st, using size 9 US (5.5 mm) needles. TO SAVE TIME, TAKE TIME TO CHECK GAUGE.

Instructions

Make two leaf place mats. With wrong sides tog, beg at stem, and leaving cable edges free, sew two pieces tog inside of cable, leaving 5 in./12.5 cm open. Stuff pillow with Poly-Fil, and sew opening closed.

Appendix A: Knitting Abbreviations

approx	approximately			

approx — approximately

BC — back cable

beg — begin(ning)

cc — contrast color

ch — chain

cm — centimeter(s)

cn — cable needle

co — cast on

cont — continu(e)(ing)

DD — double dec: see individual pattern on means of working

dec — decreas(e)(ing)

dpn — double-pointed needles

FC — front cable

foll — follow(s)(ing)

inc — increas(e)(ing)

k — knit

k1tbl — knit in back of stitch

k2tog — knit 2 sts together

m — meter(s)

mb — make bobble; see specific pattern--bobbles vary

M1 — make one; lift running thread between st just made and next st and knit into the back of the thread

mm — millimeter(s)

oz. — ounce(s)

p — purl

pat — pattern

p2tog — purl 2 sts together

pm — place marker

psso — pass slipped stitch over

rem — remain(s)(ing)

rep — repeat(s)(ing)

rev — revers(e)(ing)

rnd — round

RS — right side(s)

RT — right twist

sc — single crochet

SK2P — sl 1, k2tog, pass sl st over k2 tog

SKP — sl 1, k1, psso

sk — skip

sl — slip

SSK — slip 1 st as if to knit, slip another st as if to knit, then knit these 2 sts together

SSP — sl 1 st as if to purl, sl another st as if to purl, then purl these two sts tog

st(s) — stitch(es)

St st — stockinette stitch

tbl — through back of loop(s)

tog — together

wyib — with yarn in back

wyif — with yarn in front

WS — wrong side(s)

yb — yarn to back

yd. — yard(s)

yf — yarn to front

yo — yarn over

yo2 — yarn over twice

* — repeat instructions after asterisk or between asterisks as many times as instructed

[ ] — repeat instructions inside brackets as many times as instructed

+ — repeat instructions after plus sign as many times as instructed

Appendix B: Stitch Glossary

Daisy Stitch

This stitch, also called single or detached chain stitch, is formed from chain stitches. Each chain stitch forms a petal, and when grouped, the petals form a flower.

Beginning each stitch at the same point on the knitted background, work six chain stitches to form a flower.

Daisy Stitch Bow

Work two daisy stitches opposite each other to form a bow.

Double Daisy Stitch

Work a flower out of daisy stitches, but make the stitches larger. Work second, smaller stitches in the center of each daisy stitch.

Duplicate Stitch

Duplicate stitch is an embroidery stitch used on stockinette stitch. It is called duplicate stitch because it duplicates the stitch below it. It is formed by retracing the path of the original stitch and thereby covering it. Connect the yarn at the right-hand side where the embroidered line is desired. From the back, place the needle at the base of the first stitch you want to cover. Pull toward the front. Pass the needle under the two loops of the same stitch, going from right to left. Pull through. Go back into the base of the same stitch from front to back. Place the needle into the base of the next stitch from the back, and repeat for as many stitches as desired.

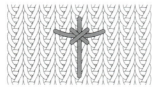

Elongated Star

First work a cross by bringing the threaded needle out at the base of the knitted stitch. Insert the needle in the base of the stitch the desired number of rows above. Work a horizontal stitch in same way. Work a cross-stitch on top.

Fly Stitch

*Bring threaded needle out from back to front at the upper left corner of a knitted stitch. Insert needle at upper right corner of the same stitch forming a loop and back out at the center of the same stitch, holding the loop below the tip of the needle as it comes out. Insert needle into center of stitch directly below. Repeat from *.

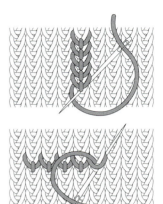

To work a vertical grouping, bring needle out again at upper left corner of the stitch directly below the one just covered and work in the same manner. To work a horizontal grouping, bring needle out at upper left corner of the stitch to the right of the one just covered.

French Knot

Work French knots singularly or in clusters to make flowers or flower centers.

Bring needle out of the knitted background from back to front, wrap yarn around needle one to three times and use your thumb to hold the yarn in place as you pull needle through the wraps into the background a short distance (one background thread) from where the thread first emerged.

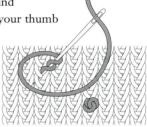

Jacobean Couching

Make long straight stitches parallel to each other and about ½ in./1.5 cm apart. Work another series of straight stitches on top of and at right angles to the previous ones. Then make a small couching stitch (a small straight stitch or cross-stitch) where the stitches cross each other.

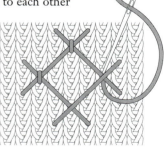

Mattress Stitch

With right sides together and the edges of the work side by side, make a join at the lower edge. Insert the needle between the first and second stitch, pick up one horizontal bar, and draw the thread through. *Insert the needle under two horizontal bars on the alternate side, and draw the thread through. Repeat from * for the seam.

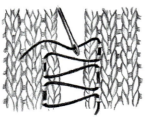

Stem Stitch

This stitch is excellent for flower stems and outlines. Bring threaded needle out from back to front at the center of a knitted stitch. *Insert the needle into the upper right edge of the next stitch to the right, and then out again at the center of the stitch below. Repeat from *, working regular, slightly slanted stitches.

Selvage Stitches

Selvage stitches, or edge stitches, are extra stitches used at the seams for sewing knit pieces together or for keeping an edge flat.

Straight Stitch

Straight stitches can be worked side by side or can radiate out from a center point. Avoid stitches that are too long, too loose, or too close together. *Bring threaded needle out from back to front at the base of the knitted stitch. Insert the needle at the top of the stitch(es) you want to cover. Repeat from *.

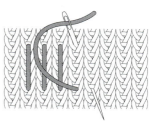

Whipstitch

Bring the threaded needle out from back to front at the center of a knitted stitch. Moving from left to right, *insert the needle over two knitted stitches and up two rows. Bring the needle back out through the center of the stitch two rows below. Repeat from *.

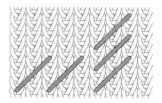

Appendix C: Finishing Techniques

Twisted Cord

Everybody's idea of a cord.

1. Cut several strands of yarn, three times the desired length of cord.

2. Knot the two ends, keeping the strands at an even tension.

3. Anchor one end on a door knob or hook and insert a knitting needle through the other.

4. Turn needle over and over, until the strands are well twisted.

5. Fold in half, keeping the cord taut to avoid tangling.

6. Knot the two ends together, let the cord twist, and even out the turns.

Braided Cord

Any cord, yarn, or string can be braided. For an ordinary, three-strand braid:

1. Cut three strands, or bunches of strands, 1½ times the desired length of cord.

2. Knot them at one end, and hook or pin this end.

3. Take left strand(s) over center strand, then right strand(s) securely over center strand, until strands run out.

4. Knot the strand ends.

Applied Fringe

Cut several strand of yarn (the more strands, the thicker the fringe) two times the desired fringe length, plus about 1 in./2.5 cm for knotting. Fold the yarn in half.

Insert a crochet hook into the edge of the knitted piece, catch the folded yarn, and pull it through the knitting.

Then use the hook to grasp the ends of the yarn group and pull them through the fold. Tighten to secure.

Tassel

Cut a piece of stiff cardboard the desired tassel length. Loop yarn around the cardboard the desired number of times (the more times, the fatter the tassel). Tie one end of the loops with a piece of yarn.

Slip the loops off the cardboard and tie another piece of yarn around the loops near the top, concealing the end in the tassel.

Cut the ends of the loops and trim, if desired.

Resources

Yarn

Anny Blatt
7796 Boardwalk Road
Brighton, MI 48116
(810) 486-6160

Berroco, Inc.
14 Elmdale Road
Uxbridge, MA 01569-0367
(508) 278-2527

Brown Sheep Co., Inc.
100662 County Road 16
Mitchell, NE 69357
(308) 635-2198

Cascade Yarn, Inc.
Suite 505
2401 Utah Avenue South
Seattle, WA 98134-1431
(416) 763-3628

Classic Elite
12 Perkins Street
Lowell, MA 01854
(978) 453-2837

Coats & Clark
Susan Bates
Suite 351
30 Patewood Drive
Greenville, SC 29615-3530
(864) 234-0331

Coats Paton
1001 Roselawn Avenue
Toronto, ON M6B 1B8
Canada
(416) 782-4481

Crystal Palace
3006 San Pablo Avenue
Berkeley, CA 94702-2428
(510) 548-9988

Design Source
Manos del Uruguay Yarns
P.O. Box 770
Medford, MA 02155
(781) 438-9631

The DMC Corporation
10 Port Kearny
South Kearny, NJ
07032-4688
(201) 589-0606

Great Adirondack Yarn Co.
950 County Highway 126
Amsterdam, NY 12010
(518) 843-3381

Harrisville Designs
Box 806
Center Village
Harrisville, NH 03450
(800) 338-9415

JCA, Inc.
35 Scales Lane
Townsend, MA 01469-1094
(508) 597-8794

Lion Brand Yarn Co.
34 W. 15th Street
New York, NY 10011-6815
(212) 243-8995

Muench Yarns
118 Ricardo Road
Mill Valley, CA 94941-2461
(415) 383-1005

The Plymouth Yarn Co.
P.O. Box 28
Bristol, PA 19007-0028
(215) 788-0459

Prism
2595 30th Avenue
St. Petersburg, FL 33713-2925
(813) 327-3100

Rainbow Gallery
7412 Fulton Avenue #5
North Hollywood, CA
91605-4126
(818) 982-6407

The Schaefer Yarn Co., Ltd.
3514 Kellys Corners Road
Interlaken, NY 14847
(800) 367-9276

Skacel
11612 S.E. 196th Street
Renton, WA 98058
(253) 854-2710

Spinrite, Inc.
320 Livingston Avenue
S.P.O. Box 40
Listowel, Ontario
N4W   3H3
Canada
(519) 291-3780

Tahki
11 Graphic Place
Moonhachie, NJ
07074-1106
(201) 807-0070

Trendsetter Yarns
16742 Stagg Street
Suite 104
Van Nuys, CA 91406-1641
(818) 780-5497

Westminster Fibers, Inc.
Rowan Yarns
5 Northern Boulevard
Amherst, NH 03031-2335
(603) 886-5041

Other Supplies

Bead Warehouse
4 Meadow Lake Drive
Mendon, UT 84325
(802) 775-3082
(Beads)

Craft King
P.O. Box 90637
Lakeland, FL 33804
(888) CRAFTY1
(Eyes and eyelashes for
    animals)

**Fairfield Processing
    Corporation**
88 Rose Hill
P.O. Drawer 1157
Danbury, CT 06813
(203) 744-2090
(Pillow forms)

**Fibers Fantasy Knitting
    Products**
6 Hunters Horn Court
Owings Mills, MD 21117
(410) 517-1020
(Blockers)

JHB International, Inc.
1955 S. Quince Street
Denver, CO 80231-3223
(303) 751-8100
(Buttons)

C. M. Offray and Son, Inc.
Chester, NJ 07930-0601
(908) 879-4700
(Offray ribbons)

Skacel Collection, Inc.
224 SW 12th Street
Renton, WA 98055-3155
(206) 255-3411
(Addi needles)

K1#C2 Solutions, Inc.
2220 Eastman Avenue #105
Ventura, CA 93003
(805) 676-1175 (fax)

Other Threads Books

Look for these and other Taunton Press titles at your local bookstore. You can order them direct by calling (800) 888-8286 or by visiting our website at www.taunton.com.
Call for a free catalog.

- The Art of Fabric Collage
- Beyond the Pattern
- A Close-Knit Family
- Couture Sewing Techniques
- Distinctive Details
- Embellishments A to Z
- 50 Heirloom Buttons to Make
- Fabric Savvy
- Family Album
- Fine Embellishment Techniques
- Fine Machine Sewing
- Fit and Fabric
- Fitting Solutions
- Fitting Your Figure
- Great Quilting Techniques
- Great Sewn Clothes
- Hand-Manipulated Stitches for Machine Knitters
- Jackets, Coats and Suits
- The Jean Moss Book of World Knits
- Just Pockets
- Kaffe's Classics
- The Knit Hat Book
- Knitted Sweater Style
- Knitting Bazaar
- Knitting Counterpanes

- Knitting Emporium
- Knitting Lace
- Knitting Tips & Trade Secrets
- Linen and Cotton
- Mosaics
- Quilts and Quilting
- Ribbon Knits
- Ribbon Trims
- Rudgyard Story
- Scarves to Make
- Sew the New Fleece
- Sewing Basics
- Sewing for Plus Sizes
- The Sewing Machine Guide
- Sewing Tips & Trade Secrets
- Shirtmaking
- Techniques for Casual Clothes

Sewing Companion Library:
- Easy Guide to Serging Fine Fabrics
- Easy Guide to Sewing Blouses
- Easy Guide to Sewing Jackets
- Easy Guide to Sewing Linings
- Easy Guide to Sewing Pants
- Easy Guide to Sewing Skirts
- Easy Guide to Sewing Tops and T-Shirts

AME ENGAGE™

Welcome to the fully integrated and interactive online learning hub for *Key Accounting Principles, Volume Two, Fourth Edition.*

Online & Interactive

AME Learning's integrated and interactive online learning hub, AME Engage™, contextualizes the study of accounting in a practical, hands-on online learning environment. Designed to personalize the learning experience and engage students *before* class, our multi-sensory online tutorials guide students through the key accounting concepts for each chapter. These tutorials help students to *learn by doing,* using a variety of effective learning tools ranging from gaming to interactive problem solving.

In order to encourage students to truly understand the concepts rather than simply rely on memorization, AME Engage™ features randomized algorithmic homework questions, allowing students to practice the same concept repeatedly at their own leisure. The "Take me to the text" online homework feature links each question to the relevant examples in the digital textbook, immediately providing students the help they need at any time and from anywhere. Instructors have full control over all resources in AME Engage™, and can therefore effectively tailor their online environment according to their own teaching style.

Unique PIN Code

If you purchased this book brand-new, the PIN Card (image to the right) is attached to the front cover. Open this to get your unique **PIN Code**, then follow the instructions to log in to AME Engage™.

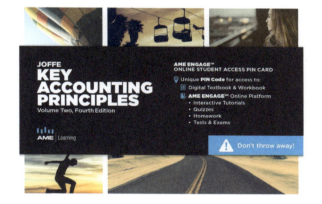

Don't have a PIN Card?

If you **did not** purchase this book brand-new, you will need to purchase your unique PIN Code at www.amelearning.com/store or contact your campus bookstore.

Instructor looking for access?

Please contact your AME Learning representative.

AME ENGAGE™

Welcome to the fully integrated and interactive online learning hub for
Key Accounting Principles, Volume Two, Fourth Edition.

The AME Learning™ Cycle

The AME Learning™ Cycle is an integrated learning method that puts a unique focus on pre-class **interactive tutorials**. These tutorials are seamlessly integrated with all other components of the program, and will allow students to not only better prepare for in-class work, but they will also help students to engage with difficult concepts while effectively leading to successful knowledge retention.

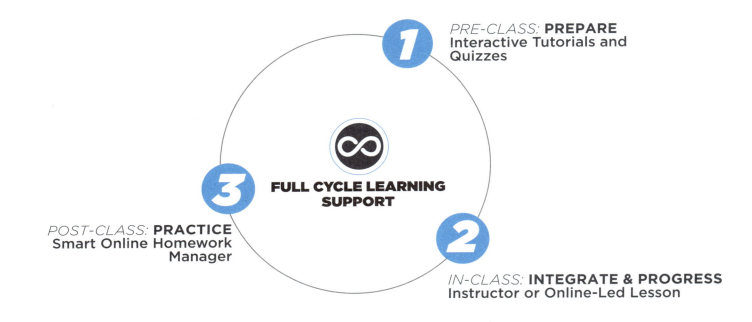

1 PRE-CLASS: **PREPARE**
Interactive Tutorials and Quizzes

FULL CYCLE LEARNING SUPPORT

2 IN-CLASS: **INTEGRATE & PROGRESS**
Instructor or Online-Led Lesson

3 POST-CLASS: **PRACTICE**
Smart Online Homework Manager

AME Engage: Features

⊕ Interactive Online Tutorials
Perform real-world accounting transactions with our innovative Accounting Map™.

▤ Online Homework Manager
Algorithmic homework questions, assignments, projects, cases, tests and quizzes.

Resource Library
Focus-in on key lesson objectives with Microsoft Excel™ worksheet templates and our vast PowerPoint™ library.

⊙ Digital Textbook
Practical explanations and examples seamlessly integrated with workbok and online tutorials.

ⓘ Digital Workbook
Hundreds of questions and cases perfectly integrated with textbook lessons and interactive tutorials.

KEY ACCOUNTING PRINCIPLES

Volume Two, Fourth Edition

Lead Author
Neville Joffe

Contributors and Reviewers

Bharat Aggarwal, BBA, MBA, CMA
Sheridan College

Maria Belanger, CPA, CA
Algonquin College

Ben Carnovale, BBA, MASc
Confederation College

Annette deWeerd, CMA, CGA, MBA
Northern Alberta Institute of Technology

Dave Hummel, CPA, CA
Conestoga College

Laurette Korman, MBA, CMA
Kwantlen Polytechnic University

Chris Leduc, CPA, CA
Cambrian College

Kayla Levesque, CPA, CA
Cambrian College

Sarah Magdalinski, CA, MPACC, BCOMM
Northern Alberta Institute of Technology

Penny Parker, MBA, CPA, CGA
Fanshawe College

Susan Rogers, CPA, CMA
Sheridan College

Ruby So, B. Comm, CA, CGA
Northern Alberta Institute of Technology

Textbook ISBN: 978-1-926751-31-3
Workbook ISBN: 978-1-926751-32-0

Key Accounting Principles, Volume 2, Fourth Edition
Author: Neville Joffe
Publisher: AME Learning Inc.
Content Contributors and Developmental Editors:
        Vicki Austin/Kobboon Chotruangprasert
Production Editors: Graeme Gomes/Melody Yousefian
Copy Editor: Nicola Balfour/Lisa McManus
Indexer: Elizabeth Walker
Typesetter: Paragon Prepress Inc.
Vice President and Publishing Manager: Linda Zhang
Cover Design: Sasha Moroz/Bram Wigzell
Online Course Design & Production: AME Multimedia Team

3 4 5 MCRL 19 18 17

This book is written to provide accurate information on the covered topics.
It is not meant to take the place of professional advice.

For more information contact:

AME Learning Inc.
410-1220 Sheppard Avenue East
Toronto, ON, Canada M2K 2S5
Phone: 416.479.0200
Toll-free: 1.888.401.3881
E-mail: info@amelearning.com
Visit our website at: www.amelearning.com

About the Author

Neville Joffe created the AME Learning System after spending more than 25 years leading and transforming teams in the manufacturing and distribution industries. His innovative style of management is characterized by a unique philosophy: bottom-line business success is dependent on the financial literacy of an organization's employees.

The truth of this philosophy first revealed itself when he helped to transition his 400 person company to sustainable profitability after a period of loss and decline. For the company and its employees, this newly acquired business acumen had opened a world of opportunity and prosperity.

This experience highlighted the importance of a financially literate employee base. From here, Neville sold his stake in the company and focused on fully developing and patenting the AME Accounting Map™ – a learning framework that borrowed from the ideas of Game Theory to create a multisensory toolkit for true learning, interaction and engagement. Neville took his system around the world, training internationally with corporate clients, government institutions and non-profit organizations.

After years of successfully training clients around the world, Neville set his eyes on the sector responsible for producing the employees that inevitably ended up in his training sessions: Education. Understanding that our colleges and universities were the front lines of training for the corporate world, Neville adapted his system to suit the needs of higher learning institutions. Since then, he has worked with practicing accounting professionals and educators to develop seven textbooks that accompany the AME Learning System for use in higher education institutions around the globe.

The AME Approach to Learning Accounting

AME utilizes a unique method to simplify accounting concepts, using step-by-step logic to ensure that the subject is extremely easy to understand. Accounting concepts are communicated using straightforward language and AME Accounting Maps™ that make potentially complex transactions simpler and easier to follow.

The AME Accounting Map™ is used throughout the textbook to show the impact of transactions on the financial statements. It is a visual representation of the balance sheet and income statement. The Accounting Map™ is also used in our interactive tutorials. Increases and decreases in values of specific items are clearly shown on the Map without needing to resort to technical accounting terminology.

The Accounting Map™

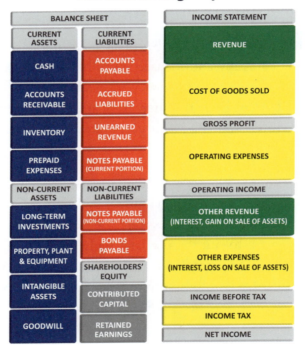

This textbook is part of a larger and blended program that is being used to teach the course. As an instructor it is recommended to follow these steps to ensure your students get the most out of the program.

1. Encourage students to use the interactive online tutorials before attending each class.

2. Use the PowerPoint™ presentations to provide visuals to assist with teaching the material.

3. Online quizzes are available to test student's comprehension of the material. Quizzes can be used either before or after class.

4. Online post-class homework questions are available to test student's ability to complete accounting problems. These should be used after class.

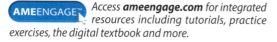 Access **ameengage.com** for integrated resources including tutorials, practice exercises, the digital textbook and more.

Every chapter has reminders for students to check their online course for additional resources to help explain the accounting topics.

The learning outcomes in each chapter are prepared using Bloom's taxonomy. In the textbook, each blue heading in the chapters is linked to at least one learning outcome. The learning outcomes are also linked to all the questions in the workbook.

Chapter 4
THE ACCOUNTING CYCLE: JOURNALS AND LEDGERS

LEARNING OUTCOMES

❶ Distinguish between debits and credits

❷ Describe the accounting cycle

❸ Explain how to analyze a transaction

❹ Record transactions in the general journal

❺ Post journal entries to the general ledger

❻ Prepare a trial balance

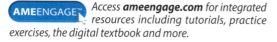 Access **ameengage.com** for integrated resources including tutorials, practice exercises, the digital textbook and more.

Transition to Debits and Credits

We have been using the terms increase and decrease to record transactions in T-accounts, but formal accounting requires the use of debits and credits. In the debit and credit system (unlike increases and decreases), a **debit** is always recorded on the left-hand side of an account and a **credit** is always recorded on the right-hand side. DR represents debits and CR represents credits.

Debit DR	Credit CR

Remember that debit and credit do not always mean increase or decrease. A credit means an entry on the right side of the account, and it may cause the account to increase or decrease, depending on the type of ac-

WORTH REPEATING

In accounting, there are always at least two parts to a transaction. For each transaction, the total value of debits equals

At the end of the chapter is a summary, highlighting key points for each learning outcome.

AMEENGAGE *Access **ameengage.com** for integrated resources including tutorials, practice exercises, the digital textbook and more.*

In Summary

Distinguish between debits and credits

- ⮞ Debits are recorded on the left side of an account and credits are recorded on the right side. For the accounting equation to be correct, the total value of the debits must equal the total value of the credits. This will ensure that the accounting equation stays in balance.

- ⮞ Assets, expenses, and owner's drawings increase with debits and decrease with credits. Liabilities, revenues, and owner's capital increase with credits and decrease with debits.

Describe the accounting cycle

- ⮞ The accounting cycle consists of the steps required to prepare financial statements. The cycle repeats every period.

Explain how to analyze a transaction

- ⮞ Analysis of transactions begins with source documents which indicate a transaction has occurred. The analysis helps to determine which accounts are affected, whether they are increasing or decreasing, and whether they are debited or credited.

Each chapter has a Review Exercise covering the major topics of the chapter. The Review Exercises are prepared so students can complete them and then compare their answers to the solutions. Solutions to the Review Exercises are in Appendix I of the textbook.

———— Review Exercise ————

Catherine Gordon is running her own proprietary business called CG Accounting. CG Accounting provides bookkeeping services to small and mid-sized companies. The company prepares financial statements on a monthly basis and had the following closing balances at the end of May 2016.

CG Accounting Balance Sheet As at May 31, 2016			
Assets		**Liabilities**	
Cash	$4,200	Accounts Payable	$2,300
Accounts Receivable	3,100	Unearned Revenue	600
Equipment	6,000	Bank Loan	4,000
		Total Liabilities	6,900
		Owner's Equity	
		Gordon, Capital	6,400
Total Assets	$13,300	**Total Liabilities & Owner's Equity**	$13,300

CG Accounting uses a variety of accounts and account numbers in its accounting records.

Account Description	Account #	Account Description	Account #
ASSETS		**REVENUE**	
Cash	101	Service Revenue	400
Accounts Receivable	105		
Prepaid Insurance	110	**EXPENSES**	
Equipment	120	Advertising Expense	500
Accumulated Depreciation	125	Bad Debt Expense	505
		Depreciation Expense	510
		Insurance Expense	515
LIABILITIES		Interest Expense	520
Accounts Payable	200	Maintenance Expense	525
Interest Payable	205	Office Supplies Expense	530
Unearned Revenue	210		

In addition to the Review Exercise solutions in the appendix, you will also find a handy chart to illustrate some key differences between ASPE and IFRS organized by chapter and topic.

Appendix III

ASPE VS IFRS

Chapter	Topic	Accounting Standards for Private Enterprises (ASPE)	International Financial Reporting Standards (IFRS)
	When to use	• Private organization (sole proprietorship, partnership, private corporations) • No plans to become public in the near future • ASPE also used by most competitors	• Public corporation or owned by a public company • Private organization intending to become public in the near future • IFRS already adopted by most competitors • Private enterprises adopting IFRS by choice for other reasons, such as, in anticipation of a bank's requirement for IFRS-based financial statements in loan application

The workbook is comprised of assessment and application questions.

- Assessment questions (AS) are designed to test theory and comprehension of topics.
- Application questions (AP) are split into Group A and Group B problems. These questions test the ability to perform the accounting functions, such as creating journal entries and financial statements.

Chapter 4

THE ACCOUNTING CYCLE: JOURNALS AND LEDGERS

LEARNING OUTCOMES

❶ Distinguish between debits and credits

❷ Describe the accounting cycle

❸ Explain how to analyze a transaction

❹ Record transactions in the general journal

❺ Post journal entries to the general ledger

❻ Prepare a trial balance

AMEENGAGE *Access ameengage.com for integrated resources including tutorials, practice exercises, the digital textbook and more.*

———————— **Assessment Questions** ————————

AS-1 (❶)

What does

A debit is

———————— **Application Questions Group A** ————————

AP-1A (❶ ❸)

Esteem Fitness provides fitness services for its customers. During June 2016, Esteem Fitness had the following transactions.

———————— **Application Questions Group B** ————————

AP-1B (❶ ❸)

Have-a-Bash is owned by Shelly Fisher and provides party planning services. During April 2016, Have-a-Bash had the following transactions.

Some additional segments

This textbook was designed to make your learning experience productive and engaging. To that end, we have added some segments to each chapter that highlight learning objectives.

A CLOSER LOOK

The *A Closer Look* segments are meant to closely examine a part of the chapter to broaden your understanding of an underlying concept. They may also include an example that applies the concepts being learned, in a way that is easy to understand and follow.

WORTH REPEATING

The *Worth Repeating* segments are meant to remind students of concepts in accounting already learned, and to highlight current concepts being taught that are "worth repeating."

IN THE REAL WORLD

The *In The Real World* segments are meant to provide applied examples of elements being learned. They are meant to put some of the concepts being learned in context and to drive home the point that eventually, accounting has to be done outside the classroom. We hope that these segments give you a sense of what "the real world" can be like for the accountant or business professional.

ASPE vs IFRS

The *ASPE vs IFRS* segments are meant to discuss differences in the treatment of the topic being covered in the chapter based on the two different *sets* of accounting standards. Not all topics will have a difference between the two.

Brief Table of Contents

Detailed Table of Contents

Chapter 4: Current Liabilities

Chapter 5: Partnerships

Chapter 6: Corporations: Contributed Capital and Dividends

Chapter 7: Corporations: The Financial Statements

Chapter 8: Non-Current Liabilities

Chapter 9: Investments

Chapter 10: The Statement of Cash Flows

Chapter 11: Financial Statement Analysis

Chapter 1

RECOGNITION AND MEASUREMENT

AMEENGAGE™ *Access ameengage.com for integrated resources including tutorials, practice exercises, the digital textbook and more.*

LEARNING OUTCOMES

❶ Explain the objective and list the key components of the conceptual framework of accounting

❷ Describe the fundamental and enhancing qualitative characteristics of financial information

❸ Explain the underlying assumptions and the concept of cost constraint in financial reporting

❹ List and describe the basic elements of financial statements

❺ List and apply the revenue and expense recognition criteria under IFRS

❻ Describe the three bases of measurement criteria under IFRS

The Conceptual Framework of Accounting

In previous accounting studies, you learned that the fundamental objective of accounting is to provide financial information that readers can use to make appropriate decisions. As illustrated in Figure 1.1, the users of financial information are divided into two categories.

1. Internal users—those who own and/or work in the organization
2. External users—those outside the organization, primarily existing or potential investors, creditors and lenders

FIGURE 1.1

The main objective of financial reporting is to accurately and completely communicate financial information to the users who provide resources to the organization. These external users want to ensure that their investment of resources is protected, and so they require information about the organization's economic resources and any claims on those resources. To meet this objective, the accounting profession created processes, standards and principles to provide guidance on how financial information should be reported.

The Accounting Standards Board (AcSB), which is the primary accounting standard-setting body in Canada, has decided that Canadian businesses must adhere to one of two sets of accounting standards when recording and reporting financial information. The first set of standards, which is used in many countries worldwide and that public enterprises in Canada must follow, are **International Financial Reporting Standards (IFRS)**. Private Canadian enterprises may also choose to follow IFRS, or they can follow the second set of standards, known as **Accounting Standards for Private Enterprises (ASPE)**.

Both ASPE and IFRS conform to an underlying **conceptual framework of accounting** that is based on fundamental economic concepts. This conceptual framework provides a common basis for those organizations responsible for setting accounting standards, so that there is little or no risk that identical activities or events might be interpreted differently. This chapter will focus primarily on the explanation and application of IFRS. The conceptual framework of accounting consists of these key components

- the objective of financial reporting
- qualitative characteristics of useful financial information
- underlying assumptions and principles defined by IFRS
- cost constraint on useful financial reporting
- elements of the financial statements

Figure 1.2 gives an overview of the components included in the conceptual framework of accounting. Next, the individual components that form this conceptual framework will be examined.

The Conceptual Framework of Accounting

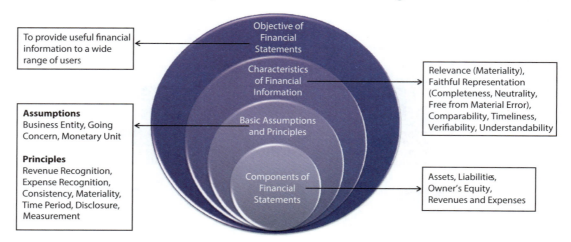

FIGURE 1.2

The Qualitative Characteristics of Financial Information

There are a number of important characteristics in the accounting framework, upon which accounting standards are based. The characteristics are referred to as *qualitative characteristics*, because they describe the qualities that make accounting information useful. In other words, accounting information must have these qualitative characteristics for financial reporting to achieve its main objective of accurately and completely communicating financial information to users. Qualitative characteristics are distinguished as two types: **fundamental qualitative characteristics** and **enhancing qualitative characteristics**.

Fundamental Qualitative Characteristics

IFRS defines two fundamental qualitative characteristics that are required to provide useful financial information.

- relevance
- faithful representation

Let us look at each of these characteristics in more detail.

Relevance

The characteristic of **relevance** is met when the information that may affect a user's decision is present in the financial statements. Information is relevant if it helps users predict future performance or improve previous predictions, or both. For example, if an investor wants to predict the future cash flows of a company, and the company deliberately avoided reporting a bank loan, the investor would not understand the company's debt correctly. Therefore, the investor would not be able to accurately predict the company's interest expenses and available cash flow. This means the balance of the bank loan is considered relevant financial information.

IFRS defines **materiality** as a component of relevance. Materiality is the ability of a piece of information to affect a user's decision. Information is material if its inclusion or omission could influence a user's decision. Information is immaterial if a user's decision would be unchanged with or without the piece of information. Usually, the dollar amount associated with a piece of financial information determines its materiality; the higher the dollar amount, the more material the information. Information that is material must be included in the financial statements.

Faithful Representation

Financial information must also be a **faithful representation** of the actual events that it describes. This means that the information must capture the true substance of a transaction, and must not be manipulated to throw off the users. To achieve faithful representation, information must be complete, neutral and free from material error.

Completeness of information refers to the inclusion of all details necessary to understand the true nature of an event. This is achieved by providing both the financial data and the accompanying notes in the financial statements, and is known as the principle of **full disclosure**. For example, suppose a company must repay a bank loan in five years, but the company does not indicate if payment is due in annual installments or as a lump sum. Without this detail, users cannot accurately predict the upcoming cash flows of the company.

Neutrality is achieved when information is free from bias. Bias occurs when the information is influenced by the interests of particular parties. For example, if a department manager reports just enough earnings for his department to ensure that he is eligible for a bonus, this information is not neutral.

Financial information almost always contains errors which arise from the use of estimates and certain accounting methods. For example, residual values are estimated for depreciation purposes and there are several different methods to account for inventory. To be **free from material error**, these estimates and assumptions must be based on the best available information and they must be reasonably justified.

Enhancing Qualitative Characteristics

IFRS defines four additional qualitative characteristics which enhance the usefulness of financial information by distinguishing more-useful information from less-useful information. These are very similar to certain qualitative characteristics defined under ASPE. The four enhancing qualitative characteristics are comparability, timeliness, verifiability and understandability.

Comparability means that the financial statements of a company must be prepared in a similar way year after year. The accounting policies used should be consistent to prevent misconceptions. This allows a comparison of the current year's performance to past years. By comparing yearly statements, users can identify trends in the company's financial position and performance. For example, an investor may be interested in observing the change in a company's debt balance from one year to the next to see if the company incurred additional debt or was able to pay off its creditors. Financial information should also be comparable across companies. This means that companies should disclose which accounting methods it uses for depreciation, inventory valuation and so on. This allows users to make a true comparison of different companies.

Timeliness refers to the promptness with which financial information is prepared. Information is timely if it is presented to users while it is still able to influence decisions. For instance, shareholders may prefer to receive monthly financial statements from a company to continually monitor the company's performance. If the business only prepares annual statements, the information may be available too late to make informed decisions.

Verifiability refers to the ability of financial information to be proven. Information is verifiable when two or more independent users would agree that it is accurate and can be relied upon. Paper trails are useful in creating verifiability for financial information. Receipts, invoices and purchase orders should all be kept so that dollar figures can be confirmed. For example, if a company records an expense transaction in its financial records, an invoice must be provided to back it up (i.e. the expense can be verified).

Understandability means that the financial information can be reasonably understood by its users if the users have knowledge of the business and a basic knowledge of accounting. To be understandable, companies often include notes in the financial statements to explain many of the numbers and terms, especially those that are based on company policy. For example, details of long-term debt such as the principal, interest rate and term would be outlined in the notes.

Figure 1.3 summarizes the qualitative characteristics of financial information.

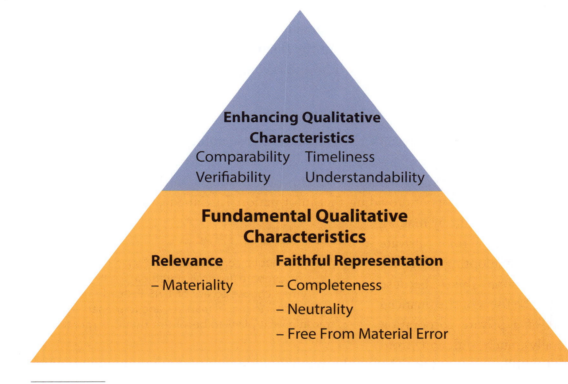

FIGURE 1.3

Underlying Assumptions and Cost Constraint in Financial Reporting

Underlying Assumptions

Financial statements of a business are assumed to contain information about transactions that only belong to the business organization, which is a separate economic entity from its owners or shareholders. The **concept of economic entity**, which refers to recording and reporting of business affairs separately from the owners' or shareholders' personal affairs, applies to all kinds of organizations, including sole proprietorships, partnerships and private and public corporations. Even if the business has only one owner, who is also the only worker within the company, the accounting and reporting for the business must be kept separate from the personal affairs of the owner or any other business. Users of the financial statements must be able to assume that the statements contain only items that pertain to the business.

The financial reporting process is based on an underlying **going concern assumption**, which assumes that the business will continue to operate into the foreseeable future. If an accountant deems that the business will not be able to continue operating into the foreseeable future, the company must disclose this information in notes to the financial statements. Also, the company's balance sheet must show the value for which assets such as plant, property, and equipment could be sold, known as the net realizable value of the assets.

The **monetary unit assumption** requires that accounting records be expressed in terms of money in a single currency such as Canadian dollars or euros. This allows accountants to assign monetary values to business events, and enables users of the financial statements to assume that the unit of measure used remains fairly constant over time and is comparable from period to period.

Cost Constraint

The conceptual accounting framework recognizes the considerable costs of providing the detailed information required by users of financial statements, and therefore applies the concept of **cost constraint**. Cost constraint ensures that the benefits of relevant and faithfully represented financial information exceed the costs of providing that information. In Canada, the AcSB has applied the concept of cost constraint by making ASPE available for private corporations and adopting IFRS for public corporations. This is because the needs of the users of the financial statements of a private corporation are generally much different from those of a public corporation. The primary users of the financial statements of a private enterprise are lenders such as banks, rather than equity investors for a public enterprise. ASPE is generally simple to adhere to and requires minimal disclosure by the organization. ASPE typically provides more accounting policy choices than IFRS. Simply stated, cost constraint is a standard based on benefits versus costs.

ASPE vs IFRS

All public corporations in Canada must follow IFRS to prepare financial statements. A private enterprise may choose to adopt IFRS instead of ASPE to gain more access to global markets, and to prepare for a smooth transition if it plans to become a public corporation in the future.

ASPE shares many of the same underlying assumptions and principles as IFRS already discussed in this chapter. ASPE and IFRS often differ in allowing certain reporting methods for specific situations, with IFRS typically requiring more disclosures. Another important distinction is that conservatism is an underlying principle in the framework for ASPE, but it does not appear anywhere in IFRS.

In addition, ASPE and IFRS sometimes use different terminologies for the same concept. For example, "cost constraint," which is the term used under IFRS, is called "benefit versus cost constraint" by ASPE.

Elements of the Financial Statements

Early in your accounting studies, you learned about the basic elements included in a company's financial statements: assets, liabilities, equity, revenue and expenses. Figure 1.4 summarizes these elements in preparation for discussing on the presentation of financial statements.

Element	Definition
Asset	Any item that is owned and controlled by a business and expected to provide a future economic benefit, such as cash, accounts receivable, inventory, land and machinery.
Liability	A debt or legal obligation that the business owes and must pay with an outflow of resources.
Equity	The owners' claim on the assets of a business, representing the assets remaining after deducting all liabilities.
Revenue	Income earned by a business, usually for products or services provided by the business.
Expense	A decrease in equity as a result of the costs of products or services used to produce revenue.

FIGURE 1.4

Financial Statements under ASPE and IFRS

One of the differences between ASPE and IFRS is the presentation of financial statements. For certain financial statements, the name and format under IFRS will look very different from what exists under ASPE. A complete set of financial statements under IFRS comprises the following (the corresponding name under ASPE is shown in parentheses).

1. Statement of Financial Position (Balance Sheet)
2. Statement of Comprehensive Income (Income Statement)
3. Statement of Changes in Equity (Statement of Owner's Equity)
4. Statement of Cash Flows (Cash Flow Statement)
5. Notes summarizing significant accounting policies and other explanatory information

Statement of Financial Position (Balance Sheet)

A balance sheet includes three main categories listed in order of: assets, liabilities and equity. Within assets and liabilities, ASPE lists items in the following order.

*   Assets: in sequence according to the level of liquidity (or how quickly they can be turned into cash, with the most liquid items being listed first)
*   Liabilities: in sequence according to the timing of payment (with payments that are due sooner being listed first)

Under IFRS, the name of the balance sheet is changed to **statement of financial position** and it often lists assets and liabilities in reverse liquidity order, with the three categories presented in the order of: assets, equity, liabilities. Within assets and liabilities, the order of items is reversed as follows

- Assets: non-current or long-term assets are presented before the current assets (the least liquid items are listed first)
- Liabilities: non-current or long-term liabilities are presented before the current liabilities (payments due later are listed first)

Statement of Comprehensive Income (Income Statement)

You have seen how the income statement is prepared under ASPE. Revenues are listed first, followed by expenses and net income. Under IFRS, the income statement is called the **statement of comprehensive income**. It lists revenue, expenses, and net income in the same way as ASPE, but it also has a category called other comprehensive income. Other comprehensive income will be covered later in this course.

Statement of Changes in Equity (Statement of Owner's Equity)

Under ASPE, for sole proprietorships, the statement of owner's equity is prepared using owner's capital. Additional investments and net income are added to the opening capital balance, and drawings are deducted, to arrive at the ending owner's capital.

Instead of owner's capital, corporations have a few equity accounts, including common shares and retained earnings. Private corporations using ASPE are required to report changes only to the retained earnings account in a statement of retained earnings. Under IFRS, the name of the statement is changed to the statement of changes in equity. IFRS requires that changes to all equity accounts (not just to the retained earnings account) be shown on a statement of changes in equity, which will be discussed in detail in a later chapter.

The terminology differences in this statement between that of a sole proprietorship and that of a corporation are shown in Figure 1.5. For simplicity, only the retained earnings section of the statement of changes in equity is illustrated for a corporation.

ABC Group (Sole Proprietorship) Statement of Owner's Equity For the Year Ended December 31, 2016		
Owner Capital January 1, 2016		$x
Add: Investment	$x	
Add: Net Income	x	x
Subtotal		x
Less: Smith, Drawings		x
Owner Capital December 31, 2016		$x

ABC Group (Corporation) Statement of Changes in Equity For the Year Ended December 31, 2016	
Retained Earnings January 1, 2016	$x
Add: Net Income	x
Subtotal	x
Less: Dividends	x
Retained Earnings December 31, 2016	$x

FIGURE 1.5

Statement of Cash Flows (Cash Flow Statement)

A statement of cash flows is the fourth and final financial statement required under IFRS. This statement simply lists the balance of cash at the beginning of the accounting period, followed by the items which caused changes to the balance of cash throughout the period. The balance of cash at the end of the period is shown at the very bottom of the statement. This format is identical to cash flow statement under ASPE.

The purpose of this statement is to inform users where cash was spent and where cash was generated during the period. The preparation of this statement will be covered later in this textbook.

Recognition of Financial Information

Both ASPE and IFRS rely on **accrual-based accounting**. This means that transactions must be recorded *when they occur,* not when cash is paid or received. **Recognition** is an accounting principle that entails including an item on the financial statements. For example, a company must record a maintenance expense at the time the maintenance is performed, even if the bill is not paid until the next month. Likewise, sales made on account must be recorded at the time at which goods or services are transferred, even though the customer will not pay until later.

One of the most common misstatements in accounting stems from improper recognition of a transaction. It is the most difficult concept for many people to grasp. To help resolve many of these issues, accounting standards have defined several criteria as guidelines to determine whether or not to recognize a transaction in the financial statements. Any event that meets all of the recognition criteria should be recorded in the financial statements.

Asset and Liability Recognition

The criteria for when to recognize an asset or liability involves not only known purchases and obligations, but also the likeliness of them. An **asset** is defined as any resource owned by a business that is expected to provide future economic benefits to the business. Notice that it does not have to be certain that an item will provide future benefits to the company for it to be recorded as an asset; it just has to be probable. For example, inventory is not guaranteed to sell. In fact, a portion of inventory is usually never sold due to breakage, theft and obsolescence. However, as long as it is probable that inventory will be sold, it is recorded as an asset.

Likewise, a **liability** is defined as any obligation of a business that is expected to be settled by using the economic resources of the business. Again, an item does not have to be certain to be recorded as a liability; it must be probable. For example, car dealerships offer warranties on the vehicles they sell. Customers do not always use these warranties, but it is probable that many customers will use them and the dealership is obligated to provide service under the warranty. Therefore, as long as it is probable that warranty service will be claimed, it must be recorded as a liability.

Revenue Recognition

Revenue can only be recorded (recognized) when goods are sold or when services are performed. Revenue recognition has become one of the most difficult concepts to understand because sales transactions are more complex now than they were in the past. Companies have also been accused of deliberately abusing the recognition of revenues in order to overstate or understate profits. As such, IFRS has identified several revenue recognition criteria for the sales of goods and services.

Sale of Goods

The following five revenue recognition criteria have been defined for the sale of goods. All criteria must be met before revenue may be recognized.

1. The significant risks and rewards of ownership have been transferred to the buyer.
2. The seller no longer controls or manages the goods sold.
3. The amount of revenue can be measured reliably (agreed upon by both the buyer and seller).
4. It is probable that the seller will collect the economic benefits associated with the transaction.
5. The costs related to the sale of goods can be measured reliably.

In a typical retail environment, these criteria are generally all met at the point of sale. For example, a customer that purchases groceries for cash immediately assumes the risks and rewards of ownership. The customer may consume the goods as (s)he wishes; the seller no longer controls them. At the point of sale, the customer has agreed to pay the specified price of the goods set by the seller and the economic benefit (cash) has already been transferred.

However, consider a customer who purchases furniture from a big box retailer. The retailer offers to deliver the goods within 10 business days from the sale. When can the seller recognize revenue for this sale? Even though the customer has already paid for the goods at the agreed-upon price, he has not yet received the risks and rewards of ownership. The customer cannot actually use and enjoy the furniture until it is delivered. Therefore, the seller must wait until the owner accepts and signs for the delivery before revenue can be recognized.

Now suppose the big box retailer purchases additional inventory from its supplier, but the inventory will not be shipped until next month. When can the supplier recognize the revenue? This depends on the shipping terms outlined in the sale. If the goods are shipped FOB shipping point, the buyer assumes the risks of ownership at the time the goods are loaded onto the truck and shipped out. In this case, the seller may recognize revenue on the shipping date. If instead the goods are shipped FOB destination, the seller must remain responsible for the goods until they arrive at their destination. In this case, the seller may recognize revenue on the delivery date.

Sometimes retailers will offer products such as furniture and appliances to customers for no money down and no payments for a specified period of time. This means that the products are transferred to the customer and the customer may use them for a period of time before they are required to pay for them. When can a retailer recognize revenue for these types of sales? Usually, these retailers perform credit checks on customers so that they can be reasonably sure that the customer will pay. All other recognition criteria are met when the goods are delivered to the customer, so these retailers do not have to wait until payments start to recognize the revenue.

Sale of Services

The following four revenue recognition criteria have been defined under IFRS for the sale of services. Notice the similarity to the criteria for the sale of goods. Again, all criteria must be met before revenue may be recognized.

1. The amount of revenue can be measured reliably (agreed upon by both the buyer and seller).
2. It is probable that the seller will collect the economic benefits associated with the transaction.
3. The stage of completion can be measured reliably.
4. The costs related to the sale can be measured reliably.

Most commonly, services are rendered over a short period of time and the customer pays an agreed-upon price to the seller. The seller generally recognizes revenue after the service has been completed and payment has been made or has been agreed to be paid. For example, a barber will cut a client's hair and recognize revenue after the customer is satisfied with the service.

However, the set of criteria does not state that the service must be completed in order for revenue to be recognized; only the stage of completion needs to be known. This means that a service company can recognize a percentage of revenue for a service that is partially completed. This is known as the **percentage-of-completion** method. This method is

ASPE vs IFRS

Under ASPE, companies are allowed to use the percentage-of-completion method as well as the completed-contract method. Under the completed-contract method, a company waits until the entire service has been completed and the contract fulfilled before any revenue or expenses are recognized. This method is not allowed under IFRS.

commonly used in the construction industry for projects that take years to complete.

For example, Ketch Construction signs a contract to build a condo building. Building is scheduled to begin on June 1, 2016 and is estimated to take two years to complete. Ketch Construction charges $500 million for the project and expects to incur $400 million in costs. How much revenue should be recognized in 2016? We must first determine the stage of completion at the end of 2016. Due to reasons such as weather or the complexity of the build, long-term construction projects are often not completed uniformly over time. Instead, the actual costs incurred in the year is divided by the total estimated costs for the project to calculate the percentage of completion.

$$\text{Percentage of Completion} = \frac{\text{Actual Costs Incurred in Current Year}}{\text{Total Estimated Project Costs}}$$

Suppose that the actual costs incurred by Ketch Construction for this project are $100 million in 2016, $280 million in 2017, and $20 million in 2018. After the percentage of completion is calculated for a given year, it is multiplied by the total revenue for the contract to calculate the amount of revenue to be recognized for that year. The calculations are performed in Figure 1.6.

Year	Actual Costs Incurred	Total Estimated Project Costs	Percentage of Completion	Total Revenue for Contract	Revenue Recognized
2016	$100 million	$400 million	25%	$500 million	$125 million
2017	280 million	400 million	70%	500 million	350 million
2018	20 million	400 million	5%	500 million	25 million
Total	$400 million		100%		$500 million

FIGURE 1.6

Therefore, Ketch Construction recognizes $125 million of revenue in 2016 for this project. It also incurs costs of $100 million, resulting in gross profit of $25 million in 2016.

The percentage-of-completion method relies on estimates. Estimates can be justified using historical data or industry analysis. If these figures cannot be estimated reliably, revenue may only be recognized to the extent that the costs are recoverable until the contract is completed.

Expense Recognition

Recall that expense recognition requires expenses to be recorded in the same period in which they were used to generate revenue. Expense recognition is closely tied to revenue recognition because there is often a direct association between incurring expenses and generating revenue. For example, the cost of goods sold is directly associated with sales revenue in a merchandising business. For these types of expenses, recognition should occur in the same period as the related revenue. This is referred to as matching revenues and expenses.

Other expenses may not be easily associated with generating revenue, such as utility or payroll expenses. These expenses are recognized in the period in which they are incurred. Remember that long-term assets are converted to expenses through depreciation. This is because the future economic benefits associated with these assets decrease over time. Other assets may also lose their ability to provide future economic benefits, and must also be converted to an expense in the current period. For example, inventory that becomes outdated and can no longer be sold for an amount higher than its cost must be written down as an expense.

Measurement of Financial Information

After it is determined that an item should be recorded, we must decide on the amount. **Measurement** is an action process that determines this amount. There are several different bases of measurement used under IFRS: historical cost, fair value and amortized cost.

The most common amount that items are recorded at on financial statements is their historical cost. The historical cost is the price actually paid, or the value of resources given up for the item. For example, a vehicle acquired in exchange for $20,000 cash has a historical cost of $20,000, even if the listing price of the vehicle was higher. If the vehicle was acquired in exchange for a combination of $8,000 cash and another vehicle worth $10,000, the historical cost of the new vehicle would be $18,000 ($8,000 + $10,000). Relating to the conceptual framework, historical cost is relevant and provides a faithful representation of the transaction. That is, there is evidence to support the historical cost of items.

Another common base of measurement is called **fair value**. Fair value is the price that would be received in exchange for an item in a transaction between independent parties. This is the amount of cash that could be collected if an asset were sold. In some cases, fair value provides more information to users because they are interested in the amount that could be received for certain items. As you will see later, certain investments are measured at fair value when they are held for the purposes of being sold within a short period of time for a gain. In other cases, fair value is used to value long-term assets. Under IFRS, companies have the option to use the **revaluation model** to value long-term assets. Suppose that the revaluation model is used to value the vehicle from the above example. The vehicle is listed at its fair value, less depreciation and impairment. If after five years the vehicle has a carrying amount of $15,000 but is revalued at a fair value of $10,000, the $5,000 difference must be accounted for as a loss.

The final measurement base allowed under IFRS is called **amortized cost.** This amount is most often used to value financial assets and liabilities such as bonds. Bonds will be covered in a later chapter using the amortized cost method.

Errors and Intentional Misuse of Recognition and Measurement Concepts

Revenue recognition can be a difficult concept to understand because of its complexities. It is almost impossible to find completely error-free accounting records in any size of business. That is why accountants have numerous checks and balances to catch and correct any errors in the accounting records. Sometimes companies are accused of deliberately abusing the recognition of revenues or expenses to overstate or understate their profits. A company's management may overstate its profits to attract investors or to meet shareholders' expectations. Or a company may intentionally understate its profits to avoid paying a high amount of tax. The following is a list of possible errors or intentional misuse of recognition and/or measurement concepts that result in overstating or understating elements of the financial statement.

- Incorrect recording of revenues or expenses, or failure to record revenues or expenses
- Recognizing revenues or expenses in the wrong accounting period
- Overstating or understating estimates for items such as returns, warranties or other allowances
- Overstating or understating accruals for revenues or expenses
- Using incorrect measurements for assets or liabilities

Users place significant trust in the accuracy of financial information when they are making business decisions. This is why the main objective of financial reporting is to accurately and completely communicate financial information to all the users who provide resources to the reporting entity. It also emphasizes the importance of a conceptual framework of accounting.

Access **ameengage.com** for integrated resources including tutorials, practice exercises, the digital textbook and more.

In Summary

Explain the objective and list the key components of the conceptual framework of accounting

⇨ The main objective of financial reporting is to accurately and completely communicate financial information to users providing resources to the reporting entity.

⇨ The conceptual framework of accounting is based on fundamental economic concepts that provide a common basis for those who set the standards.

⇨ The conceptual framework of accounting consists of the following key components: the objective of financial reporting, qualitative characteristics of financial information, underlying assumptions and principles, cost constraint on useful financial reporting and the elements of the financial statements.

Describe the fundamental and enhancing qualitative characteristics of financial information

⇨ Accounting standards are based on two types of qualitative characteristics: fundamental and enhancing qualitative characteristics.

⇨ The fundamental qualitative characteristics are relevance and faithful representation.

⇨ The enhancing qualitative characteristics are comparability, timeliness, verifiability and understandability.

Explain the underlying assumptions and the concept of cost constraint in financial reporting

⇨ The three underlying assumptions of the conceptual accounting framework are the concept of economic entity, the going concern assumption and the monetary unit assumption.

⇨ Cost constraint ensures that the benefits of providing financial information exceed the costs of providing that information.

⇨ Cost constraint is applied by making ASPE available for private corporations.

List and describe the basic elements of financial statements

⇨ The basic elements of financial statements are assets, liabilities, equity, revenues and expenses.

⇨ A complete set of financial statements under IFRS (ASPE equivalent shown in parentheses) comprises: statement of financial position (balance sheet), statement of comprehensive income (income statement), statement of changes in equity (statement of owners' equity), statement of cash flows (cash flow statement) and notes to the financial statements.

List and apply the revenue and expense recognition criteria under IFRS

- ➪ ASPE and IFRS rely on accrual-based accounting.
- ➪ IFRS has identified different revenue recognition criteria for sales of goods and sales of services.
- ➪ A service company can recognize a percentage of revenue for services partially completed; this is known as the percentage-of-completion method.
- ➪ Expense recognition is closely tied to revenue recognition when there is a direct association between incurring expenses and generating revenue.

Describe the three bases of measurement criteria under IFRS

- ➪ Measurement is the process of determining the amount at which an item will be recorded on the financial statements.
- ➪ The three bases of measurement criteria under IFRS are historical cost, fair value and the revaluation model.

Review Exercise 1

For each of the following individual financial reporting scenarios, list the most relevant components of the conceptual framework of accounting (the qualitative characteristic, assumption, principle, constraint, recognition criteria or measurement criteria). State whether the company has failed to apply any key component(s) of the conceptual framework. For each answer, explain your reasoning. Write your answers in the table provided.

a) Due to the complicated nature of mining operations, Golden Opportunity Mining Company has sophisticated accounting practices in estimating, accruing and recording closure and environmental liabilities and expenses. To meet the "understandability" characteristic of the conceptual framework, the company omitted the information about closure and environmental liabilities and expenses in its financial statements to avoid confusing statement users.

b) This year's net income of Ta Tao Company was a little lower than the target set at the beginning of the year. To meet the target, which will entitle the manager to receive a special bonus, the manager decided to recognize sales revenue of $3,000 as this year's revenue even though the merchandise will not be delivered until the beginning of next year. The amount of $3,000 is usually considered immaterial for Ta Tao Company.

c) Handelson Company has a large number of different suppliers that the company owes money to at the end of an accounting period. All amounts owed are due within the next accounting period. Because the cost of listing all the balances due to all suppliers would exceed the benefits of providing this information, Handelson simply reported the aggregate number of all amounts due to suppliers as Accounts Payable and reported it under the current liabilities section of the balance sheet.

d) GoJays Company hires a large number of workers temporarily for one month in December 2016 to help with the busy Christmas season. GoJays pays December wages to these temporary workers on January 5, 2017. The wages expenses are recorded in January 2017. GoJays has a December 31 year-end.

e) The owner of Mai Foodz Restaurant, which has been in operation for 20 years, intends to retire and close the restaurant in February 2017. To meet the "comparability" characteristic of the conceptual framework, the company's balance sheet as at December 31, 2016 reports property, plant and equipment at their net book value based on the depreciation calculation that is consistent with last year's calculation.

See Appendix I for answers.

	Relevant components of the conceptual framework	Violation? (Y/N)	Explanation
a)			
b)			
c)			
d)			
e)			

Review Exercise 2

Longcrane Construction signs a contract to build a resort. The construction is scheduled to begin on January 1, 2016 and is estimated to take four years to complete. Longcrane charges $875 million for the project and expects to incur $750 million in costs. It uses the percentage-of-completion method to recognize revenue. The actual costs incurred by Longcrane for this project are $150 million in 2016, $225 million in 2017, $300 million in 2018, and $75 million in 2019.

Calculate the percentage of completion, revenue recognized and gross profit for each year in the table provided below.

See Appendix I for answers.

Year	Costs Incurred	Percentage of Completion	Revenue Recognized	Gross Profit
Total				

Notes

Chapter 2
ACCOUNTING FOR RECEIVABLES

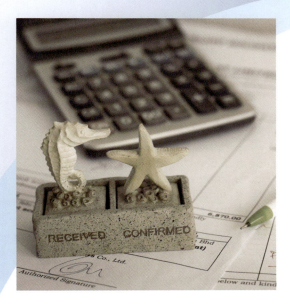

LEARNING OUTCOMES

❶ Explain the importance of accounts receivable

❷ Account for bad debt using the allowance method

❸ Estimate bad debt using income statement and balance sheet approaches

❹ Utilize reports, including the accounts receivable subledger, to manage accounts receivable information

❺ Calculate financial ratios pertaining to accounts receivable

❻ Apply controls relating to accounts receivable

❼ Record promissory notes and notes receivable

❽ Apply ethics relating to accounts receivable and notes receivable

 Access **ameengage.com** for integrated resources including tutorials, practice exercises, the digital textbook and more.

Accounts Receivable: An Introduction

You have been introduced to many common assets and liabilities on the balance sheet. You know their definitions and how to record them as debits and credits. However, there are more complex accounts and processes that companies use to account for them. These topics will be covered in depth as we explore the balance sheet in more detail. The first topic is accounts receivable, since it ranks immediately after cash and cash equivalents in terms of liquidity.

When customers purchase a product or service from a company, they often do so using payment terms. **Payment terms**, also known as credit terms, are a promise to pay for the product or service at a future date. In other words, the customers receive the product or service, but pay for it later—usually on credit terms established by the company. Accounts receivable represents the amounts customers owe as a result of the company exchanging goods or services in return for the promise to pay.

CURRENT ASSETS

CASH

➡ **ACCOUNTS RECEIVABLE**

FIGURE 2.1

Figure 2.1 highlights a portion of the current assets section of the classified balance sheet. Starting with cash and cash equivalents, as we move down the accounts, there is a decrease in liquidity. Accounts receivable is less liquid than cash because it takes some time for accounts receivable to be converted into cash through collection from customers. In addition, there is some risk that customers will not pay the amount they owe.

Nevertheless, accounts receivable is an integral part of doing business in a modern economy. Sales may be increased by allowing customers to pay at a later date since some customers may be unable to pay for their purchases immediately.

Many businesses have accounts receivable on their books, so it is important to know how to record and manage them. Throughout this chapter, we will look at how this is achieved.

Compared to cash and cash equivalents, accounts receivable requires more hands-on administration, because it involves debt collection and management of debtor information.

Cash is held in a bank account and the bank provides the account holder with a statement outlining the movement of the cash and the status of the account. Any changes to the account are authorized by the business (or account holder) with transactions such as deposits or withdrawals. However, the bank is responsible for handling the day-to-day administration of cash held in the account.

Administration of accounts receivable requires some basic information to be collected and managed. The information could include a debtor's company name, full address, contact information, what the company bought, the cost of the item bought, delivery and payment or credit terms.

Employees need to spend a significant amount of time on the day-to-day administration of accounts receivable. Even a business with a relatively small number of customers has many transactions to record and manage on a daily basis.

IN THE REAL WORLD

 One of the most prominent business trends of the past decade has been outsourcing, whereby one company hires another company to take over a certain business function — whether it is call centre duties or specialized manufacturing capabilities.

The accounts receivable department has not escaped this outsourcing trend. Accounts receivable may represent only a small percentage of a company's total assets; yet the administrative burdens associated with this asset can be overwhelming, and a company's resources in dealing with it are often inadequate.

To handle this challenge, companies have the option of hiring firms that specialize in taking over the accounts receivable function. Such specialists possess the technical hardware, expertise and experience to maximize this important asset.

Outsourcing accounts receivable offers certain advantages, especially for companies that don't have a good history of managing this asset. Outsourcing can

- improve a company's profitability by having the asset managed and controlled more efficiently;

- make a company's accounts receivable function more consistent, thereby making customers more satisfied;

- ensure financial reporting is more accurate; and

- allow a company to focus on its core business, while leaving some of the administrative duties to specialists.

Accounts receivable is an important asset for most companies. Leaving it in good hands is necessary for business success, and that may involve outsourcing the accounts.

Accounts receivable is considered a control account, since it is the sum total of all amounts owed by customers to the company and controls the accounts receivable subledgers. The subledgers are individual customer accounts to track the amounts each customer owes. For example, if the credit sales report in Figure 2.2 is the total credit sales for a company, the accounts receivable control account would show a balance equal to the total credit sales of $7,150. Each customer would have its own subledger account showing the balance owed. For example, Dunwoody Company has a balance owing of $200.

Credit Sales Report		
Customer Name	**Item Purchased**	**Price**
Archer Limited	Purchased 6 boxes of tiles	$1,000
Beta Company	Purchased 8 boxes of tiles	1,250
Cooper Inc.	Purchased a cord of timber	1,800
Dunwoody Company	Purchased spare parts	200
Archer Limited	Purchased a truck full of concrete	2,000
Beta Company	Purchased tools	900
	Total Credit Sales	**$7,150**

FIGURE 2.2

Having covered some basic accounting practices related to accounts receivable in previous courses, we will focus on more complex receivable-related accounting requirements in this chapter. You may recall that when a sale is made on account, it is recorded as a debit to accounts receivable and a credit to sales. The debit to accounts receivable increases the asset of the company, while the credit to sales increases equity. When the customer pays the amount owed to the company, the company records the transaction as a debit to cash and a credit to accounts receivable. Accounts receivable also decreases when a customer returns products and when uncollectible accounts are written off. The journal entries for sales returns and allowances, along with sales discounts, have been covered in earlier accounting courses. Bad debt, the reason why accounts need to be written off, is discussed next.

Accounting for Bad Debt

There is an upside and a downside to selling goods and services to customers on credit. The upside is that selling on credit encourages people to buy. For the most part, people pay their bills when they are due. The downside is that there will inevitably be customers who will either delay paying their bills or will never pay. The latter is referred to as **bad debt.**

Bad debt is considered an operating expense, and must be recorded in a way that is consistent with ASPE or IFRS principles. Because expense recognition states that expenses must be recorded during the same period in which the related revenue is generated, bad debt expense must be recorded during the same period in which credit sales are generated. Accurately determining the amount of bad debt in the same period as credit sales can be challenging because it is sometimes difficult to know if a customer is just late with the payment or is unable to pay. Assumptions must be made in this regard because the records must reflect the company's current financial position as accurately as possible. The methods used for estimating the amount of bad debt will be explored later in this chapter.

To record bad debt in a way that satisfies expense recognition, accountants have created an account called **allowance for doubtful accounts (AFDA)**. It is located directly beneath accounts receivable on the Accounting Map, and is a contra account. A contra account is linked directly to another account and is used to decrease the account balance. In this case, the AFDA contra account is linked directly to accounts receivable. The AFDA account has a normal credit balance, unlike accounts receivable which has a normal debit balance. The use of the AFDA account in recording bad debt is referred to as the allowance method of accounting for bad debts.

The allowance method estimates an amount that will be bad debt and records it in the books. Recording bad debt will decrease the equity of the company by recognizing an expense on the income statement, and will decrease assets by using the AFDA account. Bad debt is recorded in the same period in which revenue is generated in order to adhere to expense recognition.

For example, assume that you own Columbo Company and that at the end of 2016 your customers owe a total of $100,000. After analyzing the existing data and the current economy, it has been determined that $5,000 of the accounts receivable may not be collectable. However, since there is still a chance that you will collect, you will not remove them from the accounts receivable list. Note that the amount estimated to be uncollectable is not based on one specific customer but is an overall estimate for the entire accounts receivable.

The accounts receivable account of $100,000 does not change. It remains as a debit on the balance sheet. Instead, the AFDA contra account is credited with $5,000, resulting in a net realizable value of $95,000. The **net realizable value** of accounts receivable is defined as the amount of cash that the accounts receivable are likely to turn into, or in other words, the accounts receivable balance net of the AFDA. For the debit side of this transaction, bad debt expense is increased by $5,000 and this amount is reported as an expense for the period in the income statement. The journal entry at the end of 2016 for this transaction is shown in Figure 2.3.

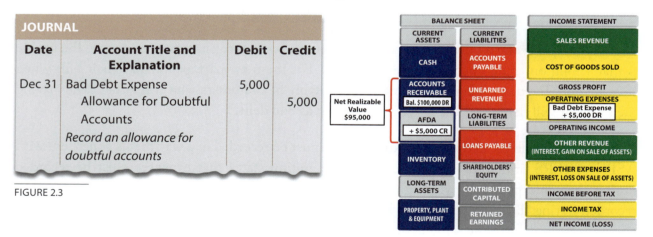

FIGURE 2.3

The net realizable value of accounts receivable is $95,000 and this figure would be presented on the balance sheet. The presentation of this part of the balance sheet for Columbo Company is shown in Figure 2.4.

Columbo Company
Partial Balance Sheet
As at December 31, 2016

Current Assets		
Cash		$12,500
Accounts Receivable	$100,000	
Less: Allowance for Doubtful Accounts	(5,000)	
Net Accounts Receivable		95,000
Inventory		210,000
Prepaid Insurance		12,000
Total Current Assets		$329,500

FIGURE 2.4

The AFDA contra account allows a company to account for the possibility that some of the accounts receivable generated in the current period will not be collected. The debit to bad debt expense supports expense recognition since this amount will be deducted as an expense in the period during which the sale was recorded. Note that the company's equity decreases as a result of recognizing the bad debt expense.

According to ASPE and IFRS, any amount of receivables that are deemed uncollectible, thus credited to the AFDA, must be justified with backup documentation. In other words, a company must have a good reason to believe that some amounts will not be paid in order to justify the adjustments made to the assets and expenses. Such measures are warranted because estimates such as AFDA are easy targets for manipulation by management.

After companies anticipate bad debt by setting up the AFDA contra account, several scenarios can exist.

1. A customer is unable or unwilling to pay the debt and the amount is considered uncollectible.
2. After an account is written off as uncollectible, the customer informs you that he or she will pay the amount.
3. The customer is unable to pay the debt when it is due, but will be able to pay it in the future.

We will examine each scenario as a continuation of the estimation of bad debt from Figure 2.3.

Scenario 1: On February 16, 2017, a customer who owes you $250, informs you that he is unable or unwilling to pay his account.

The amount is now considered uncollectible and needs to be written off.

Since the allowance method was used, the bad debt expense was previously entered to match prior period revenue, and the AFDA account has been established. Now, the AFDA account will be debited and the accounts receivable account credited to remove the amount from the company's records. The entry shown in Figure 2.5 will have no impact on the company's equity, since this was already accounted for by the original debit to bad debt expense in 2016.

Usually, a company will attempt to contact and collect from a customer for many months. After a period of time, the company may realize the customer just will not pay or cannot be contacted. Figure 2.5 is the journal entry to write off that account.

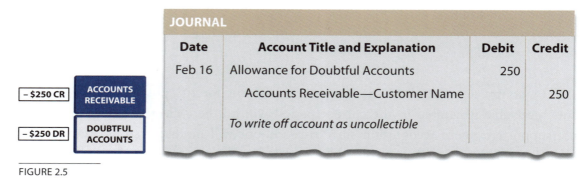

FIGURE 2.5

Scenario 2: The customer in scenario 1 has improved his cash flow and is now willing to pay his account (which was previously written off as uncollectible). He pays the amount on June 25, 2017.

Two journal entries must be made in this scenario. The first journal entry is to reinstate the customer's account balance (by reversing the entry in Figure 2.5). The second journal entry records the amount being paid. These journal entries are shown in Figures 2.6 and 2.7 respectively.

1. Reinstate the customer's account balance.

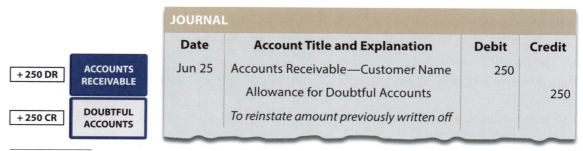

FIGURE 2.6

2. Record receipt of payment on account.

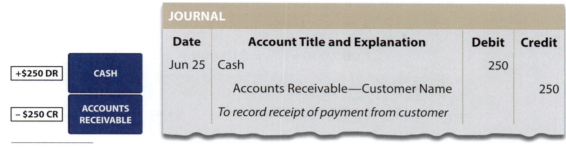

	JOURNAL			
Date	**Account Title and Explanation**	**Debit**	**Credit**
Jun 25	Cash	250	
	Accounts Receivable—Customer Name		250
	To record receipt of payment from customer		

+$250 DR — CASH

− $250 CR — ACCOUNTS RECEIVABLE

FIGURE 2.7

Scenario 3: The customer is unable to pay the debt by the due date, but will be able to pay in the future.

Even customers with a good credit record sometimes take time to settle their bills. After many months of attempting to collect from a customer, a company would face the decision of writing off the account as uncollectable. If the amount is written off, the transaction in scenario 1 would be made. When the customer finally does pay, the two transactions in scenario 2 would be made.

However, if it is relatively certain that the customer will pay eventually, the company can decide to take no action, except to periodically issue a reminder to the customer. The original amount in accounts receivable will remain on the books and will be credited when the account is finally paid. Another alternative is to convert the accounts receivable into a notes receivable, which will be covered later in this chapter.

Approaches to Estimate Bad Debt

Managing accounts receivable includes assessing how much of it will end up as bad debt. This has an impact on how a company reflects its financial position on a timely basis, and also has implications for meeting ASPE or IFRS requirements. In other words, businesses should always have good reasons for their treatment of bad debt and should maintain the necessary documentation to justify it.

We will examine two approaches for estimating bad debt: the income statement approach and the balance sheet approach.

The Income Statement Approach

The income statement approach, or the percentage of sales method, is so called because credit sales from the income statement are used as a basis to predict future bad debt. More specifically, the current year's bad debt expense is calculated by multiplying credit sales by a percentage. Different companies use different percentages based on their own collection history and credit policy.

For example, if the collection history of a company suggests that 1% of credit sales will result in bad debt, that rate is used to estimate the portion of each period's sales that will not be collectible.

Total credit sales for Columbo Company in 2016 amounted to $1,000,000, of which $200,000 is currently owing by customers. On the basis of historical sales, 1% of $1,000,000 is expected to be uncollectible. Therefore, the bad debt expense for the period is shown in Figure 2.8.

$1,000,000 x 1% = $10,000

JOURNAL			
Date	**Account Title and Explanation**	**Debit**	**Credit**
Dec 31	Bad Debt Expense	10,000	
	Allowance for Doubtful Accounts		10,000
	To record bad debt expense based on percentage of credit sale		

FIGURE 2.8

As previously discussed, the accounts receivable account, or control account, maintains the same debit amount, which in this case is $200,000. The amount calculated above will be added to the current balance in the AFDA account. Assuming that the AFDA starts with a zero balance, it will now have a $10,000 credit balance. This leaves a net accounts receivable balance of $190,000. The AFDA credit balance of $10,000 represents a decrease in the company's assets. The income statement includes a debit balance of $10,000 for bad debt expense. This is shown in Figure 2.9.

This approach is called the income statement approach because the name is taken from the way the bad debt expense is calculated. Nevertheless, adjustments must be made to both the income statement and the balance sheet accounts when accounting for the bad debt expense.

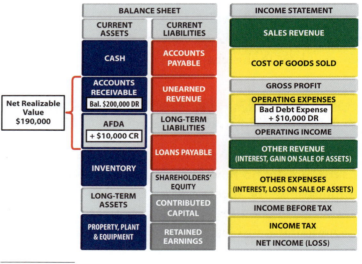

FIGURE 2.9

The Balance Sheet Approach

Under the balance sheet approach, a company can calculate allowance for bad debt using either the percentage of total accounts receivable method or the aging method. The percentage of total accounts receivable method, as the name implies, uses a percentage of receivables to estimate bad debt. The percentage is applied to the ending accounts receivable balance. For example, if the accounts receivable balance at the end of the period is $200,000, and the company estimates based on its experience that 4% of total accounts receivable will become uncollectible, the allowance for bad debt in this period would be $8,000 ($200,000 x 0.04). Therefore, the AFDA account must be adjusted to have a credit balance of $8,000. We will show entries to adjust the AFDA balance later in this section.

Under the aging method, percentages are applied to groupings based on the age of outstanding accounts receivable amounts. We will use an example to illustrate this procedure.

The chart in Figure 2.10 contains three groups of customers and their outstanding balances on December 31, 2016.

1.   Those who have not paid within 30 days.

2.   Those who have not paid for 31 to 60 days.

3.   Those who have not paid for more than 60 days.

Aging Category	Bad Debt % (probability of being uncollectible)	Balance of Accounts Receivable
30 days	2%	$80,000
31–60 days	3%	90,000
more than 60 days	5%	30,000
Total		$200,000

The above percentages are based on historical performance.

FIGURE 2.10

A percentage is applied to each aging category. A 2% rate is applied to the first group, 3% to the second group and 5% to the third group. These percentages are the probability, or likelihood, that these amounts will be uncollectible. The longer that a customer takes to pay, the less likely he or she will pay; that is the reason why the highest rate is used for the third group.

The Balance of Accounts Receivable column of the chart in Figure 2.11 shows the amount that each group still owes the company. The percentages are applied to these amounts to calculate the expected total bad debt per customer group. These amounts are then added to give us the total amount of estimated bad debt.

Aging Category	Bad Debt % (probability of being uncollectible)	Balance of Accounts Receivable	Estimated Bad Debt*
30 days	2%	$80,000	$1,600
31–60 days	3%	90,000	2,700
more than 60 days	5%	30,000	1,500
Total		$200,000	$5,800

* Balance x Bad Debt %

FIGURE 2.11

In this example, $5,800 of the gross accounts receivable balance of $200,000 is estimated to be uncollectible. The $5,800 of estimated bad debt will become the ending balance of AFDA for the period regardless of AFDA's existing balance. Regardless of whether the percentage of total accounts receivable method or the aging method is used, the calculated uncollectible accounts receivable amount is what the AFDA's ending credit balance will be. Under the balance sheet approach, the adjustments required could be grouped into three different scenarios based on AFDA having a credit, zero or debit balance. These scenarios are presented through the following examples.

Scenario 1: AFDA has a credit balance of $3,000.

If there is already a credit balance in the AFDA account, it needs to be subtracted from the $5,800 total to give us the bad debt expense for the period. A credit balance indicates the company has overestimated bad debt expense in the past. In this example, the AFDA account had a credit balance of $3,000. Subtracting that from the calculated amount of $5,800 leaves us with an adjustment in the AFDA account of $2,800. In effect, this "tops up" the AFDA account, because we are adjusting it to reflect the total amount of bad debt expected. Figure 2.12 shows the journal entry for this transaction and the accounting map shows the impact of scenario 1 on the balance sheet and income statement.

Scenario 2: AFDA has a balance of zero.

If AFDA has a zero balance, then the amount calculated as uncollectible becomes the amount of the adjustments. The amount of the credit to the AFDA account would be $5,800. Figure 2.12 shows the journal entry for this transaction.

Scenario 3: AFDA has a debit balance of $1,000.

If there is already a debit balance in the AFDA account, it is added to the $5,800 total to give us the bad debt expense for the period. A debit balance indicates the company has underestimated bad debt expense in the past. In this example, the AFDA account had a debit balance of $1,000. Adding that to the calculated amount of $5,800 leaves us with an adjustment in the AFDA account of $6,800. Figure 2.12 shows the journal entry for this transaction.

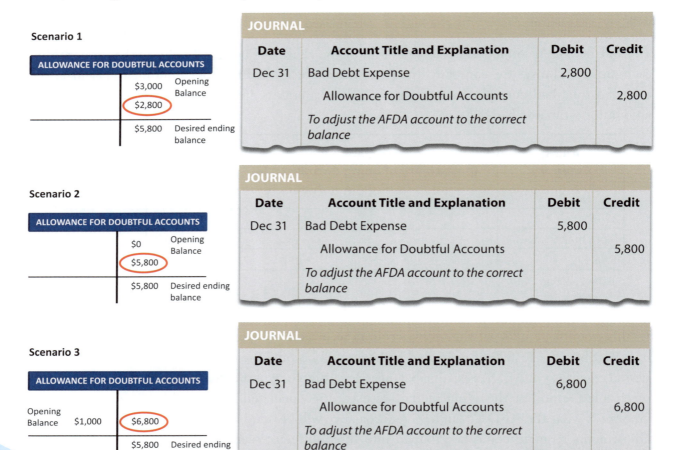

Scenario 1

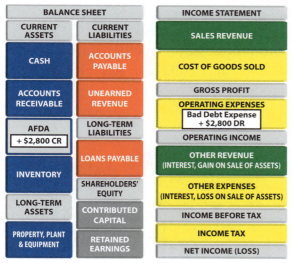

FIGURE 2.12

Note that the net adjustment of accounts receivable adheres to conservatism, which requires assets to be valued at the lower amount of possible alternatives and, as a result, reflects a reduced income for the period. This approach allows the business to make decisions based on figures that don't overstate assets, net income or the financial position of the company.

Rather than using only the income statement approach or only the balance sheet approach, a company can also use a mix of procedures. The mix of procedures involves the initial use of the income statement approach and later adjusting AFDA using the balance sheet approach. Specifically, in the initial stage, bad debt is calculated as a percentage of sales while ignoring the existing AFDA balance. At the end of the period, accounts receivable is reviewed to check the appropriateness of the AFDA balance, and adjustments to the AFDA balance are made as required.

Managing Accounts Receivable Information Using Reports

Much of our analysis of accounts receivable has involved accounting for receivables in the company's books. This is important because these records give management accurate information with which to make good business decisions. This also allows companies to adhere to external reporting standards and principles.

Another important aspect of accounts receivable is managing or controlling them. It is important for a business to know not only the amount of its accounts receivable but also which policies and procedures will lead to the collection of the maximum possible amount.

Having too many customers owing the company too much money on overdue bills restricts cash flow and working capital. Among other things, it limits the ability of the company to meet its commitments, such as accounts payable and loans.

A CLOSER LOOK

A number of strategies will ensure that a company manages and controls its accounts receivable. These include

- Commitment to efficiency. Management commits to ensuring that accounts receivable are handled efficiently.

- Measuring results. After using ratios and reports to manage information, it is essential to determine whether these measures are working.

- Cutting-edge technology. Having the company's technology up-to-date to provide accurate and useful information about accounts receivable will assist in informed decision-making.

Since accounts receivable plays such a prominent role in the financial well-being of a company, it is important that information about this asset is efficiently organized.

Computer software is available to collect, organize and process information in different ways. Reports can be produced to give management insight into financial affairs in ways that raw data cannot.

The Accounts Receivable Subledger

The list in Figure 2.13 is a customer-by-customer list of outstanding amounts owing to a company; these amounts represent the total in the accounts receivable control account.

Accounts Receivable listing as at July 31					
	Current	31–60 days	61–90 days	91 days +	Total
Archer Limited	1,300	900	1,500		3,700
Beta Company	1,200	1,800	1,300	150	4,450
Cooper Limited	1,800	150			1,950
Dunwoody Company	200	500	200		900
Harry's Supplies	4,000	3,000	1,600	1,200	9,800
Lino Inc.	400	600	100		1,100
Total	**8,900**	**6,950**	**4,700**	**1,350**	**21,900**
	40.64%	31.74%	21.46%	6.16%	

FIGURE 2.13

Presenting the data in this form facilitates the analysis of accounts receivable by customer. It also highlights the figures that stand out from the others. In this case, the areas of note have been marked in yellow, red and green in the revised chart in Figure 2.14.

Accounts Receivable listing as at July 31					
	Current	31–60 days	61–90 days	91 days +	Total
Archer Limited	1,300	900	1,500		3,700
Beta Company	1,200	1,800	1,300	150	4,450
Cooper Limited	1,800	150			1,950
Dunwoody Company	200	500	200		900
Harry's Supplies	4,000	3,000	1,600	1,200	9,800
Lino Inc.	400	600	100		1,100
Total	**8,900**	**6,950**	**4,700**	**1,350**	**21,900**
	40.64%	31.74%	21.46%	6.16%	

FIGURE 2.14

As the yellow and red areas show, two customers have bills outstanding more than 90 days.

The yellow area shows an amount of $150 from Beta Company that has not been paid for more than 90 days. However, this is a relatively small amount, especially in comparison with Beta's total amount owing. It could be the result of an invoice discrepancy or some other minor issues. Although Beta is one of only two customers with balances owing for more than 90 days, management may not be too concerned about this balance. There should still be controls in place to follow up with the customer either to correct or adjust the amount.

The other customer with a balance exceeding 90 days, Harry's Supplies, is certainly a cause for concern. The amount marked in red, $1,200, represents a significant portion of the outstanding balance. Furthermore, the amount might be even more problematic, given that the same customer was given $4,000 credit in the current month. This account is not being well managed, and management should follow up with the company and reconsider the credit policies that allowed this situation to develop.

The green area of this chart is notable because, unlike all the other customers on the list, Cooper Limited does not have an outstanding balance for the 61–90 day period. Furthermore, it has only $150 outstanding for the 31–60 day period. Therefore the $1,800 credit given to Cooper in the current period appears to be justified: this customer has paid bills promptly, and providing more credit for this customer would make good business sense.

Alternative Presentation Formats

The preceding examples represent just a few ways in which accounts receivable information can be organized and presented. Computer software allows for multiple methods of analysis. Management should tailor computer programs to meet the specific needs and objectives of the company with regard to information about accounts receivable, bad debt internal controls and all other related issues.

The reports that can be generated involving accounts receivable include

- Current active customers
- Past customers not active for the last 12 months
- Customer activities listing value of sales per month
- Customer activities listing value of sales per product
- Categorization of customers according to sales representative or geographic location
- Overdue accounts

Measuring the Effectiveness of Collections Using Ratios

Another approach to measuring the effectiveness of the company's collection efforts is through the use of financial ratios. We examine two types of ratios: days sales outstanding and accounts receivable turnover.

Days Sales Outstanding

One way of organizing accounts receivable information is to use days sales outstanding (DSO). **Days sales outstanding** tracks how long customers take to pay their bills. This is done by using two basic figures from the financial records: average net accounts receivable and net credit sales for the past 12 months. Recall that the net accounts receivable is equal to the gross accounts receivable less allowance for doubtful accounts, and the net credit sales is equal to the total of credit sales less sales discount, returns and allowances. The formula is shown below.

$$\text{Days Sales Outstanding} = \frac{\text{Average Net Accounts Receivable}}{\text{Net Credit Sales}} \times 365$$

As shown in the formula, the average net accounts receivable figure is divided by the net credit sales of the past 12 months. The result is then multiplied by 365 (days in the year). The result provides the company with the average number of days that customers take to pay their bills. The following two examples illustrate the use and function of this particular ratio.

Company 1

Assume that the total average net accounts receivable amount for Company 1 is $200,000, and the total net credit sales amount for the past year was $1,200,000. Our DSO ratio is calculated as shown below.

$$\text{Days Sales Outstanding} = (\$200,000 \div \$1,200,000) \times 365$$
$$= 61 \text{ days}$$

In other words, it takes an average of 61 days to collect amounts outstanding.

Company 2

Assume that the total average net accounts receivable amount for Company 2 is $135,000, and the total net credit sales for the past year was $1,650,000. Our DSO ratio is calculated as shown below.

$$(\$135,000 \div \$1,650,000) \times 365 = 30 \text{ days}$$

On the basis of these calculations, Company 2 is collecting its accounts receivable from customers twice as fast as Company 1. Because of the importance of cash in operating a business, it is in the company's best interest to collect outstanding accounts receivable as quickly as possible. By quickly turning sales into cash, a company has the opportunity to effectively use the cash for reinvestment and to produce more revenue. One of the most important factors that affect DSO is the company's credit terms.

If both companies allow customers 30 days to pay for their purchase on account, Company 2 is doing well in terms of collection whereas Company 1 is doing poorly.

Accounts Receivable Turnover Ratio

The **accounts receivable turnover** (ART) ratio measures how often during the year a company will collect its entire accounts receivable amount. The formula is shown below.

$$\text{Accounts Receivable Turnover} = \frac{\text{Net Credit Sales}}{\text{Average Net Accounts Receivable}}$$

Company 1

In the example above, Company 1 had an average net accounts receivable of $200,000 and net credit sales of $1,200,000. The accounts receivable turnover is calculated as shown below.

$$\text{ART} = \$1,200,000 \div \$200,000 = 6 \text{ times}$$

The turnover of six times per year is in line with the days outstanding ratio. Since it takes the company approximately 61 days to collect accounts receivable, they only collect the entire amount of accounts receivable six times in the year.

Company 2

In the example above, Company 2 had an average net accounts receivable of $135,000 and net credit sales of $1,650,000. The accounts receivable turnover is calculated as shown below.

$$\text{ART} = \$1,650,000 \div \$135,000 = 12.2 \text{ times}$$

The turnover of 12 times per year is in line with the days outstanding ratio. Since it takes the company approximately 30 days to collect accounts receivable, they only collect the entire amount of accounts receivable 12 times in the year, or every month.

Accounts Receivable Controls

Now that we have examined various ways of organizing, presenting and managing accounts receivable information, the information can be used to implement sound control policies. There is no value in collecting all that data unless it is used to better manage a company's accounts receivable.

This is the purpose of accounts receivable internal controls—to help a company get the most out of one of its largest and most crucial assets. We will look specifically at how a credit policy can serve as a control mechanism to ensure that the accounts receivable asset is managed, protected and maximized in value.

Credit Policies

One of the first issues a company should consider when establishing a credit policy is whether to adopt a lenient or restrictive approach to providing credit. Two factors can influence the decision: the company's own financial position and its market position relative to the competition.

If a company is financially constrained, it probably cannot risk extending credit to customers. Similarly, low sales volumes for custom-made products leave a company with less room to extend generous credit terms. A company with little or no competition does not need to increase market share, and has no incentive to adopt lenient credit policies.

WORTH REPEATING

Two factors are taken into consideration when deciding on how stringent or lenient the company's credit policy should be:

- The company's own financial situation. The stronger it is, the better it can afford to make sales on credit.
- The company's competitive situation. The more competition a company has, the greater the pressure to extend credit in order to increase sales.

Decisions involving credit terms can have a significant impact on sales volume. The more lenient a company's credit policy, the more likely it is to generate additional sales. It provides potential customers with the incentive to buy goods without having to pay for them immediately. Therefore, a more competitive market environment, homogeneous products and high sales volumes provide a company with greater incentive to extend more lenient credit terms to customers.

Credit Approval

Providing payment terms to customers involves making unsecured loans to the customers so that they can buy the company's product or service. Instead of automatically offering these terms, a company can implement various measures to better understand their customers and follow up when necessary. This is the essence of credit approval. It can involve having the customer complete a credit application and update the information regularly. The company can also request a customer's financial statements to ensure that it is in a position to pay its bills.

Credit Information

Of course, customers may not always be completely open about their financial health or ability to pay their bills. Companies therefore get independent credit information about customers from credit reporting agencies, financial institutions and even from other vendors.

Credit agency reports can be very useful in getting up-to-date information on current and potential customers. They can provide payment history, claims against the customer, banking information, existing credit granted, a record of recent inquiries as well as any credit ratings.

Terms of Sale

Setting the terms of sale is another credit control a company can apply. A certain period, such as 30 days, can be used and enforced with all customers.

Credit Collection

Finally, deciding on the methods of collecting from customers is yet another control in credit policy. The invoice is always the first tool of collection. If a customer is overdue with payment, the company can send a copy of the invoice as a reminder. If that does not prove successful, other measures such as letters, phone calls and even personal visits can be used to put pressure on the customer. If all else fails, a collection agency can be hired to enforce payment, especially when the account is long overdue.

Other controls for accounts receivable that may be implemented are

- Keeping individual records for each customer.
- Following up on large accounts that are overdue.
- Writing off a bad debt when it has been determined that all reasonable measures have been exhausted to collect the debt.
- Ensuring that the original write-off is reversed when payments are received for a previously written-off account.

A CLOSER LOOK

An important objective for any successful business is to maximize its control and management of accounts receivable. To that end, a company can establish a checklist of items to monitor how well it is doing in meeting this objective. Such a checklist may include the following items.

- Is the staff fully trained to handle accounts receivable issues?

- Is all sensitive accounts receivable information adequately secured?

- Are invoices being processed accurately?

- Are customers informed quickly enough of credit decisions made by the company?

- Are third-party collection agencies being properly monitored?

IN THE REAL WORLD

Companies have various means at their disposal to convert their accounts receivable into cash. One that has become more frequent in recent years is known as factoring, which can help a company's cash flow and working capital in the short term.

Factoring involves selling accounts receivable assets at a discount price to a third party, the factor. The factor is then responsible for collecting payment from the debtor.

At one time, a factor was brought in as a last resort—only after all previous attempts at collecting failed, including the use of a collection agency.

However, factoring has become quite commonplace, with tens of billions of dollars being factored each year.

Today, as it becomes increasingly difficult for businesses to secure loans, factoring is turning into a viable option for raising funds. The cost to the seller involves receiving a discounted price for the total value of accounts receivable. In essence, this amounts to decreasing the value of the company assets. However, it receives cash for its accounts receivable, and the discount price may be worth more than the amount the company could hope to collect from its customers on its own.

Setting Firm Credit Terms

Perhaps most important, a company should try to assess whether its collection period is stringent enough. Accounts receivable should not be extended more than 10 or 15 days beyond the credit terms. Industry standards differ, so assessing what the competition is doing, then setting a benchmark to meet or surpass those expectations, may be a wise business strategy. Setting a high standard and routinely enforcing it might improve the collection of accounts.

The Promissory Note and Notes Receivable

There is another way to look at accounts receivable. In a sense, the transaction is much like a loan. Since the customers do not initially pay for the goods or services they receive from the company, the selling company is in effect lending customers the money to pay for them until the loan is due. However, this loan usually does not come with interest within the credit period.

A **promissory note**, or **note receivable** makes an account receivable resemble a formal loan by adding precise terms of repayment to which the customer adds her signature.

For example, if a customer is overdue on her account, the company may request that the customer sign a promissory note, which would formalize the arrangements involved in the repayment of the debt, similar to how a formal loan specifies its terms of repayment. Both a loan and a promissory note can set terms that include naming the parties to the document, the amount to be paid, when the amounts are due, as well as the interest charges related to the payments.

A promissory note, or note receivable, is used to formalize an accounts receivable item and also to extend unusual credit terms to a specific customer. For example, an agreement may involve lengthening the terms of repayment to more than one year. In addition, the note can be used to extend credit to a customer with no formal credit history. The stronger legal claim associated with a note provides greater protection for the selling company when dealing with uncertain or riskier customer accounts. Provided that the seller is confident the customer will eventually pay the note, there should be no objection to issuing the note.

PROMISSORY NOTE

_____ , 201__

At any time after the above date, the undersigned promises to pay the lender the sum of $_____ with _____ % interest until _____ 201__.
The makers, endorsers, and guarantors hereof waive presentment, demand of payment, notice of nonpayment, protest, notice of protest, and all exemptions.

_____
NAME OF LENDER

_____
LENDER'S SIGNATURE

_____
NAME OF BORROWER

_____
BORROWER'S SIGNATURE

For example, on April 1, 2016, Kay Fernandez Alonso has $1,000 of outstanding accounts receivable with Columbo Company. Columbo's year-end is October 31. Kay cannot pay the amount immediately, but is willing to sign a note. The interest is 6% per annum, to be collected when the note is due. Kay promises to pay on April 1, 2017. The entry to record the conversion of the accounts receivable to a note receivable on April 1, 2016 is shown in Figure 2.15.

WORTH REPEATING

The formula to calculate interest is

Interest = Principal x Interest x Time

Interest rates are given as an annual rate, so if the amount of time is less than one year, you must adjust the interest for the partial year. For example, interest for seven months would require $7/12$ as the fraction for Time in the formula.

JOURNAL			
Date	Account Title and Explanation	Debit	Credit
Apr 1	Notes Receivable	1,000	
	Accounts Receivable		1,000
	Converted accounts receivable to a note receivable		

ACCOUNTS RECEIVABLE

– $1,000 CR

NOTES RECEIVABLE

+ $1,000 DR

FIGURE 2.15

On October 31, when Columbo Company prepares its financial statements, it will need to accrue the interest earned from Kay. The interest is 6% of $1,000 that has been earned from April 1 to October 31, 2016. Notice from Figure 2.16 that the interest earned is classified as "Other Revenue" rather than sales revenue.

JOURNAL			
Date	Account Title and Explanation	Debit	Credit
Oct 31	Interest Receivable	35	
	Interest Revenue		35
	To record accrued interest revenue $1,000 \times 6\% \times 7/12$		

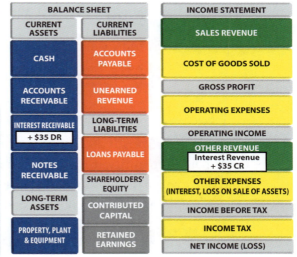

FIGURE 2.16

When Kay pays the amount due on April 1, 2017, the entry in Figure 2.17 is recorded on the statements of Columbo Company.

BALANCE SHEET		INCOME STATEMENT
CURRENT ASSETS	**CURRENT LIABILITIES**	SALES REVENUE
CASH + $1,060 DR	**ACCOUNTS PAYABLE**	COST OF GOODS SOLD
ACCOUNTS RECEIVABLE	**UNEARNED REVENUE**	GROSS PROFIT
INTEREST RECEIVABLE - $35 CR	**LONG-TERM LIABILITIES**	OPERATING EXPENSES
		OPERATING INCOME
NOTES RECEIVABLE - $1,000 CR	**LOANS PAYABLE**	OTHER REVENUE Interest Revenue + $25 CR
LONG-TERM ASSETS	**SHAREHOLDERS' EQUITY**	OTHER EXPENSES (INTEREST, LOSS ON SALE OF ASSETS)
	CONTRIBUTED CAPITAL	INCOME BEFORE TAX
PROPERTY, PLANT & EQUIPMENT	**RETAINED EARNINGS**	INCOME TAX
		NET INCOME (LOSS)

The explanation for this transaction is as follows.

- Kay paid $1,060 (debit to cash).
- An amount of $25 was recorded as interest revenue earned from November 1, 2016 to April 1, 2017 by crediting interest revenue.
- The interest receivable of $35 which was recorded on October 31, 2016 was eliminated by crediting the account.
- The note receivable of $1,000 was eliminated by crediting the notes receivable account.

JOURNAL

Date	Account Title and Explanation	Debit	Credit
Apr 1	Cash	1,060	
	Interest Receivable		35
	Interest Revenue		25
	Notes Receivable		1,000
	Record the receipt of note principal & interest ($1,000 x 6% x $^5/_{12}$)		

FIGURE 2.17

It is possible that on April 1, 2017, Kay may not pay the amount owing to Columbo Company. If a note is not paid at maturity, it is considered a **dishonoured note**. Since the notes receivable is no longer valid due to expiry, Columbo Company cannot keep it as a notes receivable in its books. Thus, it will convert the note back to accounts receivable with the transaction shown in Figure 2.18.

JOURNAL

Date	Account Title and Explanation	Debit	Credit
Apr 1	Accounts Receivable—Kay	1,060	
	Interest Receivable		35
	Interest Revenue		25
	Notes Receivable		1,000
	To record a dishonoured note		

FIGURE 2.18

The amount recorded in accounts receivable for Kay is the total amount owing, including interest. Columbo Company will continue to attempt to collect from Kay, just as they would any other customer. If at some point a decision is made to stop trying to collect, Columbo will write off the account in the manner described earlier in the chapter.

An Ethical Approach to Managing Accounts Receivable

The company and its accounting department are responsible for managing accounts receivable accurately and ethically. This includes properly recording credit sales and receipt of cash, as well as properly estimating bad debt. Accounts receivable is an important asset on the balance sheet and management and accounting for this asset is open to manipulation.

Various ethical principles and standards have been established to prevent or detect manipulation of accounts receivable. The following case study illustrates unethical behaviour, which violates the full disclosure principle.

Charles owns a manufacturing business, which has been growing steadily. His bank wants to examine his financial statements before approving his loan to finance his increasing need for additional capital. His records show a total of $250,000 in accounts receivable, and he has earned net income of $80,000 for the current year. Charles is also aware that there is an amount of $50,000 that is likely to be uncollectible; however, he knows that if he allows for the bad debt in his statements, he may not be successful in securing the loan. Charles justifies his non-disclosure by committing himself to allowing for the bad debt the following year because there is a slight chance that he may still get paid.

What Charles did was unethical. He deliberately overstated the value of his assets to try to secure the loan. He believed that the debt was not going to be paid, but he represented it otherwise to distort the current value of the accounts receivable.

Charles consciously violated the full disclosure principle by withholding information relevant to the valuing of these assets.

Consider another example of unethical behaviour. This time we will examine the importance of maintaining the integrity of the accounts receivable information that a company collects and manages. Failure to do so can put into doubt the accuracy of the company's books, and the ethics of the people in charge.

Sophie has been hired by the controller, Rick, to manage the company's accounts receivable. Upon assuming the job, Sophie soon notices that the company's accounts receivable have been poorly managed. The computer system was old and the invoices were not detailed enough, thus leading to customers questioning their invoices. Furthermore, the company would increase prices on the date of shipment instead of using the prices on the date the order was placed. Customers would complain and did not want to pay invoices showing prices they had not agreed to.

Sophie brought her concerns to Rick, who told her to keep quiet about her concerns and to do the best she could. Rick was afraid that he would be held accountable if the extent of the problems were made known to upper management, so he tried to hide the problems as much as he could. Sophie did not know what to do about the unethical accounting practices. If she remained silent, the integrity of the company's accounts receivable would be in serious jeopardy.

An accountant is responsible for maintaining the integrity of the information in the books. Rick should have dealt with these problems as soon as he became aware of them. Instead, when these problems were identified, he tried to hide them and absolve himself of any responsibility. The company's customers were being treated unfairly, the integrity of the financial information of the company was compromised and the tactics used in response to the problems were ethically unacceptable. Furthermore, Rick imposed an unacceptable dilemma on his employee, Sophie, requiring her to choose between her job and the proper management of the company's assets.

Unless Rick accepts responsibility for the problems and corrects them, he puts both himself and his company in a vulnerable position both financially and ethically.

A CLOSER LOOK

An important feature of the income statement approach is that the calculation produces an amount by which the bad debt expense needs to be recorded regardless of what the existing balance of AFDA is. On the other hand, the balance sheet approach's calculation produces an amount which would be the ending balance of AFDA and not necessarily the amount of adjustment required.

Under the income statement approach, after the amount based on a percentage of credit sales is calculated, the amount is then debited to bad debt expense and credited to AFDA. The idea behind basing the expense on sales is to appropriately match the bad debt expense with the credit sales of the period. The total amount of the allowance is essentially ignored. If the percentage of credit sales used realistically reflects the actual amount of bad debt experienced, the allowance account will reflect a reasonable balance.

If the actual bad debt experienced is materially lower than the estimate (based on a percentage of sales), the allowance for doubtful accounts may build to an unrealistically large amount. This would occur because the increase in AFDA based on the estimate of bad debt is not consistent with a corresponding reduction resulting from actual bad debt write-offs.

If you observe that the allowance account is becoming unusually large, you could forego recording additional bad debt expenses (and the corresponding credit to the allowance account), until debits (i.e. actual bad debt write-offs) reduce the allowance account to a reasonable balance once again. What is a reasonable balance? As with many items in accounting, the answer is based on professional judgment.

 Access **ameengage.com** for integrated resources including tutorials, practice exercises, the digital textbook and more.

In Summary

Explain the importance of accounts receivable

➪ Accounts receivable often represent a significant percentage of a company's assets.

➪ Allowing the existence of accounts receivable, i.e. allowing customers to buy on credit, is instrumental in increasing sales in a modern economy.

➪ While most companies find day-to-day administration of accounts receivable burdensome, effective and efficient management of accounts receivable can help improve cash flows and customer satisfaction.

Account for bad debt using the allowance method

➪ Since a portion of debt from credit sales may be uncollectible, the expense recognition principle of accounting requires bad debt expense to be estimated and accounted for in the same period that sales are recorded. The allowance method satisfies expense recognition through the use of an allowance for doubtful accounts (AFDA), which is a contra account attached to the accounts receivable account. The allowance method conforms to both ASPE and IFRS rules.

Estimate bad debt using income statement and balance sheet approaches

➪ The income statement approach estimates bad debt based on credit sales of the year.

➪ The balance sheet approach estimates bad debt based the balance of accounts receivable or on the aging of accounts receivable at year end.

Utilize reports, including the accounts receivable subledger, to manage accounts receivable information

➪ The accounts receivable subledger shows accounts receivable balance by customer and by the length of time the debt has been outstanding. Detailed examination of the accounts receivable subledger can help the company highlight important areas that require management focus or changes in credit policies.

➪ Using computer software, a company can generate various accounts receivable related reports that are tailored to management's needs.

Calculate financial ratios pertaining to accounts receivable

➪ The effectiveness of accounts receivable collections can be gauged with the use of two ratios: days sales outstanding (DSO) and accounts receivable turnover (ART).

Apply controls relating to accounts receivable

➪ Credit controls and policies are necessary to manage and protect the accounts receivable asset.

➪ Examples of controls relating to accounts receivable include setting competitive yet firm credit terms and getting independent credit information about customers before approving their credit.

Record promissory notes and notes receivable

➥ Accounts receivable can be converted into promissory notes, or notes receivable, which are legally binding documents. The conversion from accounts receivable to notes receivable is recorded in the journal with a debit to notes receivable and a credit to accounts receivable.

➥ The company that issued the notes receivable must record accrued interest revenue at the end of an accounting period.

Apply ethics relating to accounts receivable and notes receivable

➥ Management must ensure that accounts receivable is properly managed and any estimates for bad debt are recorded as accurately as possible.

Review Exercise 1

ABC Company uses the allowance method to account for bad debt. During 2016, the company had $350,000 in sales of which 80% were on account and 20% were cash sales.

During the year the company received $250,000 from customers as payment on their accounts. In June, it also wrote off $1,500 for a customer who notified them it was filing for bankruptcy and would not be able to pay. However, some time after the account was written off, the same customer notified ABC Company that it had received money from a wealthy relative and would be able to pay the account early in the new year. The company expects that $5,000 of the accounts receivable balance at the end of the year may be uncollectible.

Required

a) Using the general journal and December 31 as the date for all transactions, record the sales, collections for customers on account, write-off of accounts and bad debt expense for 2016. You may omit explanations for each entry.

Assume accounts receivable had a debit balance of $35,000 and that the AFDA had a credit balance of $2,500 at the beginning of the year (January 1, 2016).

b) Show how the above transactions would be posted in the related T-accounts

c) Show how accounts receivable would be reported on the December 31, 2016 balance sheet after the above entries had been posted.

d) Assume that instead of using the balance sheet approach, the company uses the income statement approach and expects that 1% of credit sales may be uncollectible. Record the journal entry to estimate bad debt on December 31. Assume that the AFDA had a credit balance of $2,500 at the beginning of the year.

Note: do not consider cost of goods sold in the above transactions.

See Appendix I for solutions.

a) Show how the above transactions would be recorded in the journal.

Date	Account Title and Explanation	Debit	Credit

b) Show how the above transactions would be posted in the related T-accounts

Cash	Accounts Receivable	Sales Revenue

	Allowance for Doubtful Accounts	Bad Debt Expense

c) Show how accounts receivable would be reported on the December 31, 2016 balance sheet after the above entries had been posted

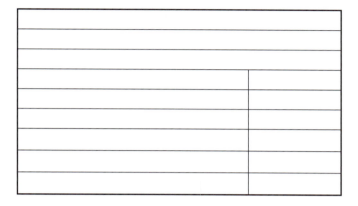

d) Record the journal entry for bad debt using the income statement approach.

Date	Account Title and Explanation	Debit	Credit

Review Exercise 2

You are the accountant for Booe Company. Record the following transactions assuming the company has an August 31 year end.

1. Sale to Guy Tygart on account—1,000 gadgets @ $5 on June 30, 2016.
2. Guy Tygart cannot pay on July 31, but signed a note with an annual 6% interest rate, to be collected on December 31, 2016.
3. Guy Tygart pays the amount due on December 31.
4. Assume instead that Guy dishonoured the note on December 31.

Do not record cost of goods sold for the transactions above.

Assume that $5,000 had been credited to the allowance account for the year.

See Appendix I for solutions.

Date	Account Title and Explanation	Debit	Credit

Chapter 3
LONG-TERM ASSETS

AMEENGAGE™ Access **ameengage.com** for integrated resources including tutorials, practice exercises, the digital textbook and more.

LEARNING OUTCOMES

❶ Identify the characteristics of long-term assets

❷ Record the acquisition and changes in the value of property, plant and equipment

❸ Apply the three methods of depreciation of property, plant and equipment

❹ Account for the gain or loss on the disposal of asset and changes in depreciation estimates

❺ Account for natural resources

❻ Define and account for intangible assets and describe the different types of intangible assets

❼ Calculate and interpret asset turnover and return on asset ratios

❽ Describe controls related to long-term assets

❾ Describe ethical approach related to long-term assets

Long-Term Assets

Current assets are defined as those owned for the short term. On the other hand, long-term assets are those that are owned and will be used by the company as part of normal operations for the long term. Specifically, long-term assets must possess the following three characteristics.

1. They provide the infrastructure necessary for operating the business.

2. They are expected to be used on an ongoing basis. Typically, an "ongoing basis" means longer than one accounting period or one year.

3. They are not intended to be sold to customers.

Long-term assets are also commonly referred to as long-lived assets, non-current assets, fixed assets or capital assets.

Long-term assets can be either tangible or intangible by nature. Tangible assets have physical substance, which can be perceived with our senses, especially by touch. Intangible assets have no physical substance and can only be perceived by the mind or imagination.

FIGURE 3.1

Subsequently, the long-term assets section of the Accounting Map is divided into separate parts containing tangible and intangible assets. As shown in Figure 3.1, "Property, Plant and Equipment" pertains to a company's long-term assets that are of a tangible nature, such as buildings, machinery, vehicles, computer equipment and software. The intangible part is labelled "Intangible Assets" and includes items such as patents and trademarks. Goodwill is also intangible by nature, but it has distinctive characteristics deserving of its own section. Each group of assets will be covered in this chapter. Long-term investments, while considered a part of long-term assets, are covered in a separate chapter.

A company must have long-term tangible assets to get physical tasks accomplished. Examples include machines that package bottles, trucks that deliver products and computers that scan and calculate inventory data. Long-term tangible assets often form the physical backbone of a company. Without them, a business will not have the property, buildings and machinery it needs to deliver goods and services to its customers. This is particularly true for manufacturers or companies involved in the transportation industry whose long-term assets are often the largest assets on the balance sheet.

For example, Figure 3.2 shows an excerpt of Amtrak's balance sheet for the years ended September 30, 2013 and September 30, 2012.

National Railroad Passenger Corporation and Subsidiaries (Amtrak) Consolidated Balance Sheet For the Year Ended September 30 (In Thousands of Dollars, Except Share Data)		
ASSETS	**2013**	**2012**
Current Assets		
Cash and Cash Equivalents	$282,280	$210,820
Restricted Cash	6,813	8,130
Accounts Receivable, net of allowances of $3,076 and $7,236 at September 30, 2013 and 2012, respectively	202,702	210,634
Materials and Supplies—net	258,133	234,896
Prepaid Expenses	16,223	13,712
Other Current Assets	14,972	24,114
Total Current Assets	**$781,123**	**$702,306**
Property and Equipment		
Locomotives	$1,531,045	$1,487,227
Passenger Cars and Other Rolling Stock	2,922,180	2,859,918
Right-of-Way and Other Properties	11,321,458	10,729,363
Construction in Progress	1,126,936	1,020,317
Leasehold Improvements	498,153	496,353
Property and Equipment, Gross	17,399,772	16,593,178
Less: Accumulated Depreciation and Amortization	(6,455,403)	(5,970,354)
Total Property and Equipment, net	**$10,944,369**	**$10,622,824**
Other Assets, Deposits and Deferred Charges		
Notes Receivable on Sale-Leasebacks	$53,755	$51,850
Deferred Charges, Deposits and Other	149,906	213,266
Total Other Assets, Deposits and Deferred Charges	**203,661**	**265,116**
Total Assets	**$11,929,153**	**$11,590,246**

FIGURE 3.2

For both fiscal years 2013 and 2012, the company's largest assets were its property, plant and equipment. These are important investments for the business and need to be properly managed to achieve long-term success. Because long-term assets tend to be worth large amounts of money and constitute major items on a company's balance sheet, it is tremendously important for accountants to properly classify, record and monitor the value of long-term assets. This chapter will discuss in detail how accountants perform these tasks.

The Acquisition and Changes in Value of Long-Term Assets

The initial purchase of property, plant and equipment requires a journal entry to record the value of the asset purchased. Following the cost principle, an asset must be recorded at its actual cost. The first step in accounting for the acquisition of property, plant and equipment is to determine the cost of the acquired item.

When a company purchases physical items such as land, buildings and equipment, the company usually pays not only for the purchase price of such items, but also for other costs associated with acquiring the assets. For example, when a company buys land with the intention of building a factory, it may have to pay for land drainage before the factory can be built. When a company buys a vehicle, it must pay for the vehicle's insurance and license before the vehicle can be legally driven. Some of these expenditures have to be included in the cost of the asset and reported on the balance sheet, while others must be expensed and reported on the income statement. Accountants must pay attention to the nature of the expenditures related to asset acquisition to properly classify which costs should be included

ASPE vs IFRS

ASPE allows the cost model only. Under ASPE, the acquisition of long-term assets must always be recorded at cost.

However, under IFRS, companies may choose to record acquisition of long-term assets using either the cost model or the revaluation model. Under the revaluation model, assets are revalued periodically to reflect their fair market value.

WORTH REPEATING

Buying assets as well as selling assets at book value has no impact on the value of owner's equity.

in the asset cost and which costs should be expensed. Specifically, two categories of expenditures have to be included in the cost of the asset in addition to its purchase price.

1. The costs necessary for getting the asset ready for use

2. Asset retirement obligations

The costs necessary for getting the asset ready for use represent the costs that are directly related to having the asset set up at its intended location and in a ready-for-use condition. Examples of such expenditures include legal fees for closing a building purchase, the costs of clearing land for its intended use and the costs of machine delivery, handling, installation, assembly and testing. These expenditures benefit the company not only in the current period, but also in future periods as long as the long-term asset is still being used.

Asset retirement obligations represent estimated costs of removing the purchased asset and restoring the site once the asset is retired. This usually applies to land that is being disrupted or destroyed, such as for mining. The company must usually restore the land by returning it to its original state (e.g. filling in mining pits). Estimation and accounting of asset retirement obligations can be complicated, and will be discussed in a more advanced accounting textbook. For examples in this textbook, assume that none of the company's long-term assets have an asset-retirement obligation.

Since the costs in both categories are directly related to the asset itself, they are not treated as expenses but as part of the cost of the asset. This cost is then recorded on the company's balance sheet. Other costs that are not directly attributable to getting the asset ready for use, such as the costs of advertising products that a recently acquired machine will be producing, are expensed rather than capitalized. Recurring costs that benefit the company only in the current period (without providing long-term benefits, such as the costs of a vehicle's license and insurance) are also expensed.

The value of a long-term asset also dictates whether its purchase should be capitalized or expensed. The materiality principle allows the company to expense low-cost, long-term assets that are below the company's materiality threshold. In other words, an item can be considered an expense in the income statement instead of a long-term asset on the balance sheet if it has no material value relative to the size of the business.

Recording the Acquisition of Property, Plant and Equipment

The asset's purchase price, the costs necessary for getting the asset ready for use and the asset retirement obligations are combined into a single amount representing the cost of the asset. The amount is then debited to the appropriate asset account.

For example, the Sunshine Juice Company has purchased a new bottling machine for its orange juice line on February 1, 2016. It was purchased at a price of $120,000 and shipped at a cost of $5,000, with installation costs of $2,000. Assuming one invoice for all these costs, Figure 3.3 shows the journal entry for the acquisition of this long-term asset.

JOURNAL			
Date	**Account Title and Explanation**	**Debit**	**Credit**
Feb 1	Machine	127,000	
	Accounts Payable		127,000
	Record the purchase of a machine for $120,000 plus $2,000 for installation and $5,000 for shipping		

FIGURE 3.3

When totalled, the costs amount to $127,000. This is debited to an account that is part of property, plant and equipment and credited to accounts payable, since the company was invoiced and owes this amount to the bottling machine manufacturer. Of course, once the bill is paid, accounts payable will be debited and cash will be credited.

Although some prepared financial statements may show a single property, plant and equipment line item, there are actually separate accounts for each long-term asset within that category.

Lump Sum Purchases of Property, Plant and Equipment

Companies sometimes purchase property, plant and equipment in bundles, or what is known as a "basket of assets." Instead of buying property, plant and equipment individually from different vendors, a company may get a good price for a basket of assets by buying them from the same vendor in one transaction, called a **lump sum purchase** or a **basket purchase**.

The challenge with this type of transaction is that by paying a lower price for the assets, the buyer acquires them for less than their appraised value. In this case, the lump sum paid for all the assets is divided and allocated to each item according to percentages based on the appraised values or fair values. For example, on August 1, 2016 the Huge Bargain Store purchased land, a building and a parking lot for the purpose of opening a new store. It bought all these assets in a bundle for the lump sum payment of $800,000. However, each asset has its own appraised value, as listed in Figure 3.4.

Item	Appraised Value
Land	600,000
Building	300,000
Parking Lot	100,000
Total	1,000,000

FIGURE 3.4

The total of all the appraised values is $1,000,000, which is $200,000 more than the purchase price. The first step is to take each item's appraised value and divide it by the total appraised value. This produces a percentage that should be allocated to each asset and is shown in Figure 3.5.

Land	600,000 ÷ 1,000,000	60%
Building	300,000 ÷ 1,000,000	30%
Parking Lot	100,000 ÷ 1,000,000	10%

FIGURE 3.5

These percentages are now allocated to the amount actually paid, which was $800,000. For example, land made up 60% of the total appraised value, so it makes up 60% of the price paid, which is $480,000. This is shown in Figure 3.6.

Land	800,000 × 60%	480,000
Building	800,000 × 30%	240,000
Parking Lot	800,000 × 10%	80,000
Total		800,000

FIGURE 3.6

Figure 3.7 shows the journal entry after calculating the actual value applied to the assets. Each asset is debited by the value calculated and cash is credited by the purchase price of $800,000.

JOURNAL			
Date	**Account Title and Explanation**	**Debit**	**Credit**
Aug 1	Land	480,000	
	Building	240,000	
	Parking Lot	80,000	
	Cash		800,000
	Record the purchase of land, building and parking lot		

FIGURE 3.7

Changes in Property, Plant and Equipment

Property, plant and equipment can change in value as a result of two factors: depreciation, which will be examined shortly, and changes made to the asset itself. One challenge with property, plant and equipment is determining whether an item should be classified as a long-term asset or simply recorded as an expense in the current year. This challenge is even more difficult when there is a change to the asset. If the change improves the service potential of the asset, it is considered "betterment." If the change involves repair or routine maintenance that does not improve the service potential of the asset, it is considered "repair." The classification affects how the change is recorded. Expenditures classified as betterment are capitalized as an asset, while those classified as repair are considered an expense.

The betterment versus repair classification is important every time money is spent on property, plant and equipment. To assess whether the expenditure is considered an asset or an expense ask four questions.

1. Does the expenditure extend the life of the asset?
2. Does the expenditure improve the productivity of the asset or improve the quality of the asset's output?
3. Does the expenditure reduce the company's operating costs?
4. Is the expenditure a material amount?

We will examine each question separately through examples.

1. Does the expenditure extend the life of the asset?

Assume that a company has a large stamping press that runs on an electric motor. The maintenance department has been buying and using replacement parts to keep the motor in operation. The head of the maintenance department tells the owner that these replacement parts are becoming harder to find and the motor has only one year of operation left. The maintenance manager recommends that the company buy a new motor for the stamping press, which would extend the life of the machine by about 10 years.

If the maintenance department continues buying new parts for the motor, no material changes or upgrades are made to the stamping press; the motor's life span is not extended. These expenditures are considered repair and therefore classified as expenses in the income statement. However, if the company buys a new motor, a material improvement or betterment will be made to the stamping press. Its life span will significantly increase, as will its total cost as a long-term asset on the balance sheet.

2. Does the expenditure improve the productivity of the asset or improve the quality of the asset's output?

Assume that a company originally bought a machine without the optional lighting system that would allow the machine to be operated at night. Management later decided to have a night production shift, and needed to install the lighting system at a substantial cost. This installation significantly increased the machine's productivity, since it could make more products within the work week. The lighting system, along with all additional costs associated with its delivery and installation, should be considered a betterment, and added to the original cost of the machine.

3. Does the expenditure reduce the company's operating costs?

Many pieces of equipment require routine maintenance by paid staff or outsourced help. A company's internet server is an example of equipment that requires routine maintenance. Technicians periodically check the server to ensure that everything is running smoothly. However, technology is available to enable the server itself to perform many routine checks. If the company were to purchase such technology, it would reduce some of the expense of having personnel perform the maintenance, thereby reducing operating costs of the company. The new technology would be classified as a capital expenditure and added to the cost of the server on the company's balance sheet.

4. Is the expenditure a material amount?

As mentioned earlier, the amount of expenditure should be capitalized (added to the cost of the asset) if the money was spent for one of the purposes described in items 1 to 3 above. However, accountants need to consider whether the expenditure is a material amount. Companies often have accounting policies that determine what dollar amount is considered to be material. If the amount is material, the cost is capitalized. If the amount is immaterial, the cost is expensed.

For example, a company that owns a $50 million long-term asset may decide that any asset-related cost below $600 is automatically expensed. Therefore, when a $100 betterment is made to the asset, the cost will be considered immaterial and expensed even though it achieves one of the three purposes above. It is management's responsibility to decide what amount is considered material for the company.

The Concept of Depreciation

In any discussion of expenses arising from assets, expense recognition must be considered. Expenses associated with assets need to be matched with associated revenues. Property, plant and equipment are typically used for long periods of time and the asset's cost must be allocated over its life span. This allocation is called **depreciation**. We will examine various aspects of depreciation and how long-term assets on the balance sheet are affected.

ASPE vs IFRS

Under ASPE, the periodic allocation of property, plant and equipment cost is called "amortization", although the term "depreciation" is also allowed.

IFRS uses only the term "depreciation" for the same concept.

Residual Value

Before discussing specific methods of depreciation, we should first examine what an asset's residual value is and how it affects depreciation calculations. Depreciation is the process by which accountants allocate the cost of an asset over time. At the end of its useful life, the asset might still be worth something. The estimated value of the asset at the end of its useful life is called **residual value**, because the asset is considered to have some value, despite no longer being useful to the company.

For example, a company may no longer be using a delivery truck that has been on the road for six years. A buyer might see some residual value in the truck, buy it and sell its spare parts or the scrap metal it contains. People might want an item for a number of purposes, which is the reason why a long-term asset might carry a residual value even after it is unable to do what it was designed for.

The total amount depreciated for a long-term asset is affected by the residual value that is expected to remain at the end of the asset's useful life. An asset's residual value is not depreciated. In other words, if a company purchases an item of property, plant and equipment for $5,000, and determines that its residual value will eventually be $1,000, the amount depreciated over the useful life of the asset is $4,000. Even though the asset can no longer be used for business after its useful life expires, the company may be able to get some money for it and this price should be subtracted from the depreciation calculations made by the company.

Actual Salvage Value

The actual **salvage value** of an asset, defined as the proceeds from selling the scrap at the end of the asset's life less its disposal cost, may turn out to be different from its originally estimated residual value. One of the realities confronting accountants is that depreciation is a theoretical concept. The market value of a long-term asset may not decrease at the same rate as its depreciation schedule. The decrease in the market value of an item of property, plant and equipment over time depends on the supply and demand mechanism of the market, which has nothing to do with how much the item has been depreciated in the books. In other words, depreciation involves an accountant's best estimate, which requires justified calculations of a long-term asset's value over its useful life with the company. Depreciation does not dictate an asset's market value.

For example, a long-term asset might be purchased at an initial cost of $100,000. The accountant will examine the asset, study its potential worth over time, and make an educated guess at what someone might be willing to pay to salvage it. This is not an easy task. At the end of the asset's life, if the actual salvage value is different from the accountant's original estimate, a gain (or loss) on asset disposal will be recorded.

Assume that the accountant estimates a residual value of $10,000. Ten years later, the item is salvaged for $6,000. Since the residual value was higher than the selling price the accountant records a loss of $4,000. The overestimation is not an issue as long as the accountant was justified in making the initial estimate and adjusts for a loss once the asset is salvaged. Similarly, if the asset is sold for more than its estimated residual value, the difference is recorded as a gain.

Three Methods of Depreciation

As time goes by and an asset is used, its value on the market will decline. The asset's book value should also decline as its cost is spread out over its useful life. Since no one knows what an asset will be worth until it is actually sold, an accountant must estimate how much a long-term asset should be depreciated while being used by the company.

In addition to estimating the depreciation amount, an accountant must also decide which of the three depreciation methods to use. The accountant should try to choose the depreciation method that best reflects the pattern in which the asset will be used by the company in practice. Additionally, once this method is chosen, adherence to the consistency principle requires that the same method be used for the entire time the company uses the asset (unless special conditions are met).

The simplest method of depreciating a long-term asset is to take its total cost, deduct any residual value it is expected to have and divide the balance by the amount of years the asset is expected to be useful. This would produce the same depreciation amount year after year and is called the **straight-line depreciation** method. Its primary appeal is that it is simple. Its weakness is that it may not reflect a realistic decline in the value of the asset. That is why other methods of depreciation have been developed.

We will now examine three methods of depreciation related to long-term assets. The three methods are listed in Figure 3.8.

The Straight-Line Method	Uses simple average
The Declining-Balance Method	Try to reflect a more realistic decline in asset value
The Units-of-Production Method	

FIGURE 3.8

The Straight-Line Method

The straight-line depreciation method takes the entire cost of the long-term asset, less any estimated residual value, and divides it by the number of years of its estimated useful life. This produces an average depreciation expense, which is applied each year until the asset is sold or reaches the end of its useful life.

In the example below, the straight-line method is applied to an asset that is expected to have a residual value once its useful life is over. Remember, only the value related to an asset's useful life is depreciated. This means that the residual value is subtracted from the initial cost before the depreciation method is applied.

$$\text{Amount Depreciated} = \text{Total Cost of Asset} - \text{Residual Value}$$

Smith Tools buys a machine for $5,000. The machine is expected to have a useful life of five years and its residual value is estimated to be $1,000. The amount to be depreciated is as follows.

$$\text{Amount Depreciated} = \$5,000 - \$1,000 = \$4,000$$

Under the straight-line method, the average is calculated by dividing the amount to be depreciated (cost − residual value) by the number of years of the asset's useful life.

$$\text{Yearly Depreciation} = \frac{\text{Amount Depreciated}}{\text{Years of Useful Life}} = \frac{\$4,000}{5}$$

$$= \$800 \text{ depreciation per year}$$

If the machine was purchased on January 1, 2016, the annual depreciation would be applied to the machine as shown in Figure 3.9.

Year	Cost of Machine	Depreciation Expense	Accumulated Depreciation	Net Book Value
2016	5,000	800	800	4,200
2017	5,000	800	1,600	3,400
2018	5,000	800	2,400	2,600
2019	5,000	800	3,200	1,800
2020	5,000	800	4,000	1,000

FIGURE 3.9

Depreciation of $800 is accumulated each year until the end of the asset's useful life. At that time, all that is left of the asset's book value is its residual value. In this case, the amount is $1,000, the final net book value at the bottom right-hand corner of the table.

Continuing with the Smith Tools example, assume that the asset will have no residual value at the end of its useful life. This means that the total amount to be depreciated will be $5,000, which was the original cost of the asset. The annual depreciation amounts would be recorded as shown in Figure 3.10.

Year	Depreciation Expense
2016	1,000
2017	1,000
2018	1,000
2019	1,000
2020	1,000

As is common in accounting, the calculations are only part of the process. The next step is to record the results of those calculations in the financial statements.

FIGURE 3.10

Accountants want to see the original value of the asset on the balance sheet, but also want to see the net book value change over time. Contra accounts allow both the asset's original value and the net book value to be reflected on the balance sheet. Remember, a contra-asset account is linked to another asset account to reduce the value of the asset. The contra account for a long-term asset is called **accumulated depreciation**. It reflects the decrease in value of the long-term asset over time. The original cost of the long-term asset account remains constant. The net book value of the asset equals its original cost less its accumulated depreciation.

Figure 3.11 shows the corresponding journal entry for recording $1,000 of depreciation expense of a long-term asset on December 31, 2016.

JOURNAL			
Date	**Account Title and Explanation**	**Debit**	**Credit**
Dec 31	Depreciation Expense	1,000	
	Accumulated Depreciation—Machine		1,000
	Record the depreciation of long-term asset for the first year		

FIGURE 3.11

Figure 3.11 shows the accounts related to long-term assets at the end of 2016. The initial purchase of the asset from January 1 is shown as a debit balance in property, plant and equipment. The entry for depreciation on December 31 is recorded as a credit to accumulated depreciation. This reduces the net book value of the long-term asset to $4,000. Equity decreases with the depreciation expense that is recorded on the income statement.

Each year depreciation is recorded, the amount of accumulated depreciation increases and the net book value of the long-term asset decreases. This is illustrated in Figure 3.12. Notice that as accumulated depreciation increases by $1,000 each year, the net book value decreases by $1,000.

Year	Cost of Long-Term Asset	Depreciation Expense	Accumulated Depreciation	Net Book Value
2016	5,000	1,000	1,000	4,000
2017	5,000	1,000	2,000	3,000
2018	5,000	1,000	3,000	2,000
2019	5,000	1,000	4,000	1,000
2020	5,000	1,000	5,000	0

FIGURE 3.12

The Declining and Double-Declining-Balance Method

One drawback to the straight-line method is that it may not accurately reflect how the cost of the asset should be allocated, thus showing an inaccurate net book value for the asset. This is because the net book value of long-term assets does not always decrease by the same amount each year. Alternative depreciation methods have been developed by the accounting profession. One of them is the **declining-balance method.**

The most common real-life example of asset depreciation is the car. Usually, the largest decrease in net book value of a car occurs the moment it is driven off the dealership's lot. In other words, the greatest depreciation in value occurs during the early years of the car's useful life and that is one reason why the declining balance method is used. This concept applies to many long-term assets.

While the straight-line method simply applies an average depreciation rate, the declining-balance method applies an annual percentage for the calculation of depreciation against the net book value of the asset. As a result, a higher level of depreciation is recorded in the early years of the asset's useful life.

Consider the purchase of equipment worth $10,000 that has a useful life of five years with no residual value.

The percentage for the declining-balance method is calculated below.

$$\text{Annual Depreciation} = \frac{100\%}{\text{Years of Useful Life (5)}} = 20\%$$

The 20% calculated is applied to the net book value of the asset to calculate depreciation for the year. If the useful life of an asset is 10 years, then the base depreciation rate applied is 10% (100% ÷ 10). If the useful life is 20 years, the depreciation rate applied each year is 5% (100% ÷ 20).

The depreciation rate can be multiplied based on the accountant's estimation of how fast the asset's value will depreciate. One of the most commonly used depreciation rates doubles the declining-balance rate of depreciation. This method is called the **double-declining-balance method**, by which twice the depreciation rate is used each year. With the same percentages already calculated, a double-declining depreciation rate of 40% (20% × 2) would be used when the useful life of an asset is five years. When the useful life is 10 years, a double-declining depreciation rate of 20% would be used (10% × 2). For a useful life of 20 years, an annual rate of 10% would be used (5% × 2).

The formula for calculating the double-declining balance rate is

Double-Declining Rate = Yearly Depreciation Rate Using Declining Balance Method × 2

Using a double-declining rate amounts to exaggerating the declining effect by the order of two. This ensures that much of the depreciation occurs during the early years of an asset's life span.

The declining method applies the depreciation rate to the net book value of the asset. Since the net book value of the asset decreases every year, it does not apply the same amount of depreciation every year. Instead, it applies the same depreciation percentage rate to the net book value every year.

In the example of the $10,000 piece of equipment with a useful life of five years, assume the company uses the double-declining-balance method. The depreciation for the first year will be

$10,000 x 40% = $4,000

The net book value for the beginning of the second year would be

$10,000 − $4,000 = $6,000

The double-declining depreciation rate of 40% is applied to this new balance to determine the depreciation amount for the second year.

$$\$6,000 \times 40\% = \$2,400$$

The same double-declining rate is applied to a decreasing net book value on an annual basis. This means that over the years, the depreciation amounts are reduced substantially, which generally reflects the way long-term assets decline in value.

The rest of the depreciation amounts in the example are shown in Figure 3.13.

Year	Beginning of Year Book Value	@ 40% Double-Declining Depreciation Rate	Remaining Book Value
1	$10,000	minus $4,000 equals	$6,000
2	$6,000	$2,400	$3,600
3	$3,600	$1,440	$2,160
4	$2,160	$864	$1,296
5	$1,296	$518.40	$777.60

FIGURE 3.13

Applying a percentage rate to a balance every year means there will always be a remaining balance when the double-declining method is used. In this example, the remaining book value at the end of five years is $777.60 because there was no residual value. However, if the asset has a residual value when the declining-balance (or double-declining-balance) method is used, the asset should not be depreciated below the residual value. For example, if the residual value is $1,000 for the example shown above, Figure 3.14 shows the depreciation amounts. Notice that in the last year, depreciation can only be $296 to drop the net book value to the residual amount of $1,000.

Year	Beginning of Year Book Value	@ 40% Double Declining Depreciation Rate	Remaining Book Value
1	$10,000	$4,000	$6,000
2	$6,000	$2,400	$3,600
3	$3,600	$1,440	$2,160
4	$2,160	$864	$1,296
5	$1,296	$296	$1,000

FIGURE 3.14

The Units-of-Production Method

The **units-of-production method** involves a different procedure for depreciating property, plant and equipment. The level of asset usage is the basis for calculating depreciation. The methods studied so far use a predetermined formula that is not based on usage. The first step in the units-of-production method is to choose a unit for measuring the usage of the long-term asset. If the asset is a vehicle, the unit can be the number of kilometres driven. If the asset is a machine, the unit can be the number of hours operated. These measures are known as units-of-production, hence the name of this method.

Once the type of unit is chosen, the next step is to estimate the number of units used for the entire life of the asset. The total cost of the asset is divided by this number to arrive at a cost per unit. This cost per unit is applied to the number of units produced in a year to determine that year's depreciation amount. The same procedure is followed each year until the end of the asset's estimated useful life.

Here is an example to illustrate how the units-of-production method can be applied in depreciation of property, plant and equipment.

Deliveries Are Us bought a truck for $110,000 for deliveries. The truck has an estimated residual value of $10,000. The company wants all its trucks to be in top condition, so it retires them after 200,000 kilometres of usage. The calculation for the per unit amount is shown below.

$$\text{Cost per Unit Amount} = \frac{\text{Cost} - \text{Residual Value}}{\text{Total Units of Production}} = \frac{\$110,000 - \$10,000}{200,000 \text{ km}} = \$0.50 \text{ per unit}$$

If the truck is driven 30,000 kilometres for the first year, the depreciation for that year is calculated as shown below.

$$\text{Depreciation} = \text{Units of Production Used for Year} \times \$0.50 = 30,000 \text{ km} \times \$0.50 = \$15,000$$

The amount of depreciation for a year is entirely dependent on its usage. For example, if in the second year the truck was driven for 25,000 kilometres, the depreciation for that year would be

$$25,000 \text{ km} \times \$0.50 = \$12,500$$

If in the third year, the truck was driven for 35,000 kilometres, the year's depreciation would be

$$35,000 \text{ km} \times \$0.50 = \$17,500$$

This depreciation procedure would be applied annually until the truck had been driven for 200,000 kilometres, the initial estimation for the life of the truck. Once the usage exceeds the estimated units of production, no additional depreciation expense should be allocated to the units produced.

Which Depreciation Method Should Be Used?

As is common in accounting, no single method of calculating a balance sheet item is necessarily better or preferable than another. The challenge for the accountant is to choose a method that best reflects the nature of the asset involved. Perhaps most important, the accountant must continue to use the initial method chosen. This is the consistency principle so that manipulation of financial figures after the fact is prevented.

However, the consistency principle does not prevent an accountant from using different methods of depreciation for different types of company assets—so long as the same method is used for the life of the particular asset. For example, a company might use the straight-line method to depreciate an advertising sign, but use the declining-balance method to depreciate a company-owned vehicle, since the value of cars and trucks decreases most during their early years.

Depreciation For Partial Years

Our examination of depreciation has been based on the assumption that property, plant and equipment are purchased on the first day of a year and sold on the last day of another year. Of course, business executives do not allow depreciation methods to dictate when assets are bought and sold. Various tactics can be employed to accommodate the realities of the calendar year when depreciating a company's long-term assets. Once a long-term asset has been purchased, the accountant must choose a depreciation schedule that accommodates the timing of asset ownership. She may decide to depreciate the asset for the full month of purchase, depreciate monthly thereafter until the asset is sold and not depreciate for the month of sale.

A number of possible combinations are available to the accountant to depreciate during the year of purchase or sale, or month of purchase or sale. These combinations provide the accountant with the flexibility to develop a depreciation schedule that best reflects the business reality of the company.

Examine the situation that arises from the purchase of a $120,000 packaging machine by the Jones Cookie Factory on March 27, 2008. The company determines that the packager will have a useful life of 10 years, after which it will not be salvageable; thus no residual value needs to be estimated. The machine will be depreciated by $12,000 annually and $1,000 monthly. The machine is eventually sold on October 1, 2015 at a price of $32,000. The fiscal year-end for the Jones Cookie Factory is November 30.

The company decides to use the following depreciation rules: no depreciation in the month of purchase and monthly depreciation thereafter, including the month of sale.

Figure 3.15 displays the annual depreciation calculated after the application of the chosen schedule. For fiscal years 2009 to 2014, each year includes 12 full months and will have $12,000 of annual depreciation at $1,000 per month. That is the easy part. The challenge is dealing with the partial years of 2008 (year of purchase) and 2015 (year of sale).

In fiscal year 2008, the month of purchase was March. The chosen schedule dictates that there is no depreciation in that month, as illustrated in Figure 3.16. That leaves eight months of depreciation in the fiscal year, or $8,000.

	Months	Depreciation
2008	8	8,000
2009	12	12,000
2010	12	12,000
2011	12	12,000
2012	12	12,000
2013	12	12,000
2014	12	12,000
2015	11	11,000
	Total	91,000

FIGURE 3.15

FIGURE 3.16

In fiscal year 2015, the month of sale was October. The chosen schedule dictates that even though the sale occurred on the first day of the month, depreciation for the entire month is calculated, as shown in Figure 3.17. This means that there will be 11 months of depreciation for the fiscal year amounting to a total of $11,000.

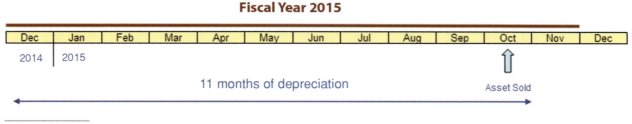

FIGURE 3.17

As Figure 3.18 shows, the total amount depreciated for the packaging machine is $91,000. Subtracting this amount from the original purchase price of $120,000 produces a net book value of $29,000. If the machine was sold for $32,000, it would generate a gain of $3,000 on the sale. A different depreciation method would likely result in a different amount for the gain, or even a loss on the sale. For example, another common practice of the partial depreciation would be a full depreciation in the year of acquisition and no deprecation in the year of sale. If the company chooses to use this method, the gain or loss on the sale will likely change. Although depreciation is an estimate, the accountant should try to make the estimate as accurate as possible.

Packaging Machine

$91,000 Depreciated

$32,000 Sale Price − $29,000 Book Value = $3,000 Gain

FIGURE 3.18

Disposal of Assets and Revision of Depreciation

When a long-term asset is disposed of, a gain or loss is usually generated from disposal of the asset. The accountant must remove from the books all the accumulated depreciation for the asset in question, since the company no longer owns the item. For example, a company has equipment (long-term asset) that costs $5,000, with a useful life of five years and a residual value of $1,000. The asset is eventually sold after five years on December 31, 2016 for $1,000. The journal entry needed to record the transaction at sale is shown in Figure 3.19.

JOURNAL			
Date	**Account Title and Explanation**	**Debit**	**Credit**
Dec 31	Cash	1,000	
	Accumulated Depreciation - Equipment	4,000	
	Equipment		5,000
	To record the sale of used asset for $1,000		

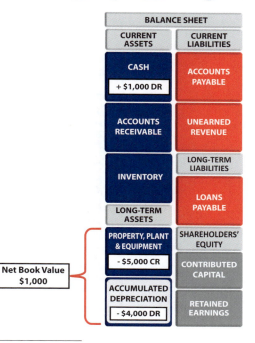

FIGURE 3.19

The amount of $1,000 is received for the asset and debited to cash. An amount of $4,000 is debited to the accumulated depreciation account, which initially had a credit balance of $4,000 due to adjusting entries made over the years. This amount is now cleared. Lastly, $5,000 is credited to the property, plant and equipment account to clear the value of the asset since the company no longer owns it.

Now assume that the equipment was sold for $500, half the estimated residual value. Since only $500 was received for the asset, this amount is debited to cash and the $500 loss is recorded as an other expense in the income statement. The $4,000 in accumulated depreciation is still debited to that account, and the initial cost of $5,000 is still credited to the property, plant and equipment asset account. The transaction is shown in Figure 3.20.

JOURNAL			
Date	**Account Title and Explanation**	**Debit**	**Credit**
Dec 31	Cash	500	
	Accumulated Depreciation—Equipment	4,000	
	Loss on Disposal of Asset	500	
	Equipment		5,000
	To record the sale of used asset for $500		

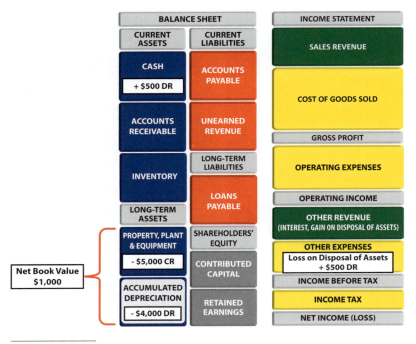

FIGURE 3.20

If the equipment was sold for $1,500, then a $500 gain is recorded since the equipment sold for more than the net book value. This is shown in Figure 3.21.

JOURNAL			
Date	**Account Title and Explanation**	**Debit**	**Credit**
Dec 31	Cash	1,500	
	Accumulated Depreciation—Equipment	4,000	
	Gain on Disposal of Asset		500
	Equipment		5,000
	To record the sale of used asset for $1,500		

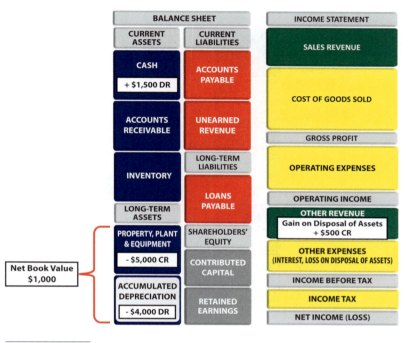

FIGURE 3.21

The $500 gain on disposal of asset will appear as part of other revenue in the income statement.

Instead of trying to sell the long-term asset, a company may decide to donate it to charity. The transaction would involve a loss for the company and would be recorded as a donation expense. Assume the company donated the equipment from the previous example to a local charity.

JOURNAL			
Date	**Account Title and Explanation**	**Debit**	**Credit**
Dec 31	Accumulated Depreciation—Equipment	4,000	
	Donation Expense	1,000	
	Equipment		5,000
	To record the donation of used asset		

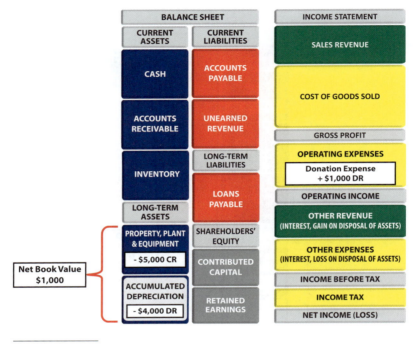

FIGURE 3.22

Rather than selling or donating the old asset that the company no longer wants, it may trade the old asset with its supplier for a newer one. Often, the company has to pay cash in addition to giving up the old asset. To record the exchange transaction, the old asset and its accumulated depreciation are removed from the company's books by crediting the original cost of the old asset and debiting the associated accumulated depreciation balance. Cash is credited for the amount paid. The new asset is debited at the fair value of the old asset plus the cash paid. The difference between the fair value of the old asset and its net book value is then recorded as gain or loss on disposal of the old asset.

To illustrate the accounting of long-term assets exchange, consider the following example. Suppose the company traded its old truck for a new one at a truck dealership on June 1, 2016. The company's old truck and an additional $95,000 cash were exchanged for a brand new truck. The old truck originally cost $100,000. The old truck had a fair value of $20,000, and an accumulated depreciation of $70,000 on the day of the trade. The following journal entry in Figure 3.23 is made to record the truck exchange.

JOURNAL			
Date	**Account Title and Explanation**	**Debit**	**Credit**
Jun 1	Truck (new)	115,000	
	Accumulated Depreciation—Truck (old)	70,000	
	Loss on Disposal of Asset	10,000	
	Truck (old)		100,000
	Cash		95,000
	To trade old truck for a new truck		

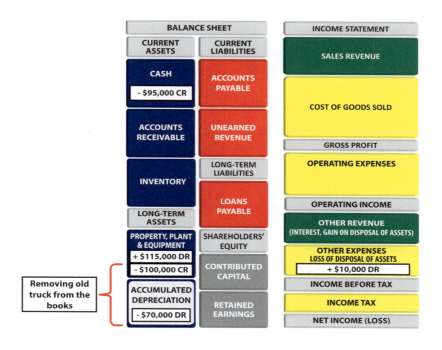

FIGURE 3.23

To remove the old truck from the company's books, the old truck's original book value of $100,000 is credited and its accumulated depreciation of $70,000 is debited. Because $95,000 is paid, cash is credited at $95,000. The new truck is valued at $115,000, which is equal to the fair value of the old truck ($20,000) plus cash paid ($95,000). Because the fair value of the old truck ($20,000) is less than its net book value $30,000 ($100,000 − $70,000) on the day of the exchange, loss on disposal of asset is recorded at $10,000.

As explained earlier, a long-term asset can be disposed of in many ways that do not involve selling the item. For the purpose of this textbook, we have discussed only the routine methods of disposal and provided a solid foundation for understanding the accounting concept in general. Here is one final change to the initial example in this section. Instead of five years, the life of the equipment ends up being four years, and the asset is sold for $500.

When the useful life was five years, $4,000 of total depreciation had to be spread out over those five years, using the straight-line method. This amounted to $800 of depreciation per year. If the actual life of the asset ends up being four years, then only four years' worth of depreciation was accumulated, for a total of $3,200 ($800 × 4). The remaining book value, or amount yet to be depreciated, is $1,800. Since the asset was sold for $500, this results in a loss of $1,300.

In summary, $500 is debited to cash; $3,200 in accumulated depreciation is taken off the books by debiting that amount; $1,300 is debited as a loss in the income statement; and the original cost of the asset ($5,000) is removed from the books by crediting that amount to the account. The journal entry for this is shown in Figure 3.24.

JOURNAL			
Date	**Account Title and Explanation**	**Debit**	**Credit**
Dec 31	Cash	500	
	Accumulated Depreciation - Equipment	3,200	
	Loss on Disposal of Asset	1,300	
	Equipment		5,000
	To record the sale of used asset for $500		

FIGURE 3.24

If the company wants to retire this equipment at the end of the fourth year but cannot find a buyer for the equipment, the transaction still needs to be recorded even though the company does not gain any proceeds from the asset retirement. When the equipment is retired, the accumulated depreciation of $3,200 and the original cost of $5,000 would be removed from the books, while the loss on disposal of asset would now increase to $1,800. In fact, even if there is no gain or loss on disposal of asset, the journal entry still needs to be made whenever a long-term asset is retired. The retirement of an asset that has been fully depreciated without any salvage value would simply involve debiting accumulated depreciation and crediting the asset account at the original cost of the asset. This would completely remove the asset and its accumulated depreciation from the company's books.

One final note: going back to our original example, if the company uses the asset for longer than the estimated useful life of five years, the remaining book value would be $1,000, which is the estimated residual value. In this case, no adjustments would be made and the company would continue to use the asset without further depreciation.

Revising Depreciation

Our examination of depreciation in this chapter has included numerous references to estimates. We have also looked at examples in which the residual value or the asset's useful life, or both, were incorrectly estimated. Let us take a closer look at these scenarios with a more comprehensive example.

Brian's Bricks bought a new brick molding machine for its factory at a cost of $300,000. It was expected to have a useful life of 10 years and a salvage value of $20,000.

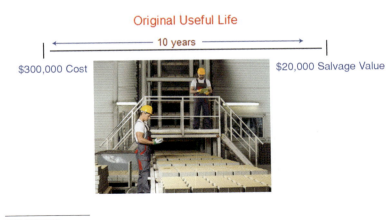

FIGURE 3.25

After five years of use, the molding machine is not deteriorating as quickly as expected. After consulting with the machine's manufacturer, management determines that the useful life of this asset could be extended to 15 years, and the salvage value increased to $40,000 as illustrated in Figure 3.26.

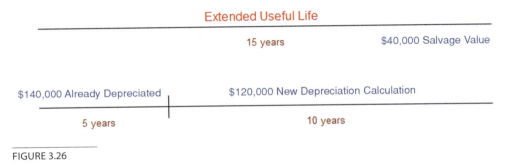

FIGURE 3.26

Using the straight-line method, the company's accountants had recorded depreciation of [($300,000 − 20,000) ÷ 10] × 5 = $140,000, which produced a net book value of $300,000 − 140,000 = $160,000.

Brian's Bricks then started a new depreciation schedule, assuming the straight-line method again, in which the amount to be depreciated for the rest of the asset's new useful life would be $160,000 − $40,000 (new salvage value) = $120,000. This amount is divided by the number of years left in the new useful life (15 years − 5 years already recorded = 10 years), to produce an annual depreciation amount of $12,000.

Note that the company should not change the depreciation already accumulated during the first five years of using the molding machine. An accountant should only make or change depreciation estimates for the future. Any changes that are made need to be justified with the appropriate documentation. In this case, that documentation would include consultation with the asset's manufacturer.

Depreciation also needs to be revised when the value of the asset decreases due to impairment. **Impairment** occurs when the asset's recoverable amount drops to a point that is below its net book value. An asset's **recoverable amount** is equal to the asset's market price less costs of disposal, or its future value, whichever is higher. Future value represents future revenue that the asset will generate for the company. Both external factors (such as changes in technology that reduce the older-technology asset's market price) and internal factors (such as physical damage to the asset) may provide indicators of impairment. When there is an indicator that a long-term asset may be impaired, the company must conduct impairment tests to find out whether the asset's recoverable amount is in fact lower than its net book value. When any long-term asset, either tangible or intangible, becomes impaired, the book value of the asset must be written down in the balance sheet to match the asset's recoverable amount. Impairment loss will then be recorded as an expense on the company's income statement. The calculations of future depreciation must also be revised based on the reduced asset's value due to impairment.

To further illustrate the accounting of impairment, assume that on December 31 a company realizes that the value of its factory machinery has been impaired due to physical damage. The machinery's recoverable amount is determined to be $60,000 while the machinery's original cost was $130,000. Up to this date, the accumulated depreciation is recorded as $40,000. The company should record an impairment loss of $30,000 as calculated below.

$$\text{Net Book Value} = \$130,000 - \$40,000 = \$90,000$$

$$\text{Impairment Loss} = \text{Net Book Value} - \text{Recoverable Amount} = \$90,000 - \$60,000 = \$30,000$$

The recoverable amount of $60,000 is less than the net book value of $90,000 by $30,000. Figure 3.27 shows that the $30,000 impairment should be recorded by debiting the impairment loss account and by crediting the accumulated depreciation account. As indicated in the Accounting Map, on the income statement the loss increases the operating expenses; on the balance sheet, it decreases the net book value of the machinery by increasing the accumulated depreciation account.

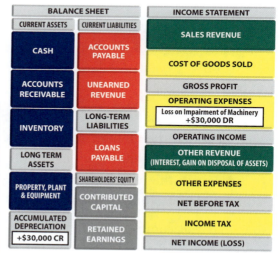

JOURNAL			
Date	Account Title and Explanation	Debit	Credit
Dec 31	Loss on Impairment of Machinery	30,000	
	Accumulated Depreciation—Machinery		30,000
	To record impairment loss		

FIGURE 3.27

ASPE vs IFRS

Under ASPE, a company must conduct impairment tests whenever the company becomes aware of an impairment indication. An impairment loss that has been previously recorded can never be reversed.

Under IFRS, a company must conduct impairment tests on goodwill and intangible assets with indefinite lives every year, even if there is no indication of impairment. However, for intangible assets with finite lives and property, plant and equipment, IFRS requires the company to actively look for impairment indicators every year, and only conduct impairment tests if indicators exist. IFRS allows reversal of previously recorded impairments for all tangible and intangible assets, except goodwill.

Natural Resources

Natural resources have a physical nature, but are different from the nature of property, plant and equipment. In fact, some companies place natural resources in a separate asset category on the balance sheet. For our present purpose, we will examine these types of assets in our broader discussion of long-term assets and how we account for natural resources in the company's books.

First, natural resources come at a cost. This includes any expenditure made in acquiring the asset such as preparing resources for extraction. It also includes any expenditure for restoring the land upon completion of use. The total cost is recorded in the appropriate asset account on the balance sheet.

Second, the value of natural resources decreases over time as more natural resources are extracted from the ground. This is called **depletion** and needs to be accounted for in the books just as depreciation is with property, plant and equipment.

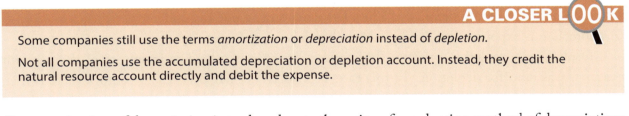

A CLOSER LOOK

Some companies still use the terms *amortization* or *depreciation* instead of *depletion*.

Not all companies use the accumulated depreciation or depletion account. Instead, they credit the natural resource account directly and debit the expense.

Our examination of depreciation introduced us to the units-of-production method of depreciation; the method that involves actual usage of an asset. It is therefore most appropriate for use in calculating the depletion natural resources, where actual units, such as cubic metres, barrels or tonnes, can be used in the calculation.

The example of the Standing Tall Timber Company will be used to illustrate how the units-of-production method is applied to a natural resource asset. The company has bought land to be harvested for timber, at a total cost of $10 million. It estimates that once all the land is harvested, the land will be worth $2 million. This is the asset's residual value. Furthermore, the company estimates that the total timber to be harvested will amount to $80 million Multiple of the Foot, Board Measure (MFBM). Equivalent to one thousand board feet, MFBM is a commonly used unit in North America to measure lumber.

$$\frac{\text{Total Cost} - \text{Residual Value}}{\text{Total Units}} = \frac{\$10,000,000 - \$2,000,000}{80,000,000 \text{ MFBM}} = \$0.10 \text{ per MFBM}$$

If two million MFBM were harvested in the first year, the depletion for the year would be

$$2,000,000 \times \$0.10 = \$200,000$$

JOURNAL			
Date	Account Title and Explanation	Debit	Credit
Dec 31	Inventory	200,000	
	Accumulated Depletion—Timber		200,000
	To record depletion for the year for Standing Tall Timber		

BALANCE SHEET

CURRENT ASSETS	CURRENT LIABILITIES
CASH	ACCOUNTS PAYABLE
ACCOUNTS RECEIVABLE	UNEARNED REVENUE
	LONG-TERM LIABILITIES
INVENTORY + $200,000 DR	LOANS PAYABLE
LONG-TERM ASSETS	
PROPERTY, PLANT & EQUIPMENT	SHAREHOLDERS' EQUITY
	CONTRIBUTED CAPITAL
ACCUMULATED DEPRECIATION + $200,000 CR	RETAINED EARNINGS

FIGURE 3.28

The three figures above (total cost, residual value and total units) are used to calculate a per-unit depletion cost that is applied for every unit of timber depleted within a year.

In this example, $200,000 of timber is depleted in the first year. The journal entry to record the timber depletion and the Accounting Map are illustrated in Figure 3.28. To record this amount, $200,000 is credited to the accumulated depreciation account, and $200,000 is debited as inventory on the balance sheet. Note that unlike depreciation for property, plant and equipment, the $200,000 depletion is not debited to depreciation expense. This is because timber inventory is generated as a result of the depletion process. The harvested timber is valued as inventory at the per-unit rate that was used for depletion. In this case, it is $0.10 per MFBM. The inventory value is then transferred to cost of goods sold in the income statement when the inventory is sold. The timber that is yet to be harvested remains a separate asset on the balance sheet and is valued at cost less any depletion.

Since we have learned the calculation and journal entries underlying natural resource transactions, we can look at how the information is presented by a Canadian mining company in the real world. Potash Corporation of Saskatchewan Inc. (PotashCorp) is our example. Headquartered in Canada, PotashCorp is the world's largest fertilizer company. The company produces all three nutrients that are important ingredients for fertilizer by mining potash and phosphate from the ground and capturing nitrogen from the air. Fertilizer production requires a lot of investments in terms of property, plant and equipment. Figure 3.29 represents the components of PotashCorp's property, plant and equipment.

	Land and Improvements	Buildings and Improvements	Machinery and Equipment	Mine Development Costs	Assets Under Construction	Total
Carrying Amount—December 31, 2013	$525	$3,557	$6,459	$530	$1,162	$12,233
Additions	–	–	19	55	1,043	1,117
Changes in Investment Tax Credits	–	–	(4)	–	4	–
Disposals	–	(1)	(2)	–	–	(3)
Transfers	46	135	742	93	(1,016)	–
Change in Asset Retirement Costs	–	–	–	25	–	25
Depreciation	(25)	(76)	(475)	(122)	–	(698)
Carrying Amount—December 31, 2014	$546	$3,615	$6,739	$581	$1,193	$12,674
Balance as at December 31, 2014 Comprised of						
Cost	$697	$4,099	$10,660	$ 1,301	$1,193	$17,950
Accumulated Depreciation	(151)	(484)	(3,921)	(720)	–	(5,276)
Carrying Amount	$546	$3,615	$6,739	$581	$1,193	$12,674

FIGURE 3.29

Figure 3.29 shows the balances included in Note 13 in the Notes to the Financial Statements section of PotashCorp's 2014 annual report. It provides the details of PotashCorp's property, plant and equipment, which show balances of $12,674 and $12,233 in 2014 and 2013 balance sheets respectively. Remember, all costs involved in preparing resources for extraction are capitalized. For PotashCorp, these costs include items such as expenses in constructing equipment used in mining natural resources. Construction may take more than a year to complete. At the end of the year, the costs associated with constructing assets that have not been finished are capitalized as "assets under construction." Once asset construction is complete and the asset is ready for use, the balance will then be transferred from the assets under construction account to the appropriate account. For example, if the company is constructing equipment, the balance will be transferred from assets under construction to machinery and equipment once the equipment is ready for use. This is why the assets under construction are not depreciated, while all other four components of property, plant and equipment are. Depreciation does not start until the asset under construction is complete and ready for its intended use. Once this happens, the asset must be depreciated or depleted as discussed earlier.

ASPE vs IFRS

Under IFRS, every company (regardless of whether it is in the natural resources industry or not) must show the reconciliation of the beginning and the ending balances for each class of property, plant and equipment. Figure 3.28 illustrates an example of how to present the reconciliation required under IFRS.

Under ASPE, such reconciliation is not required.

Intangible Assets and Goodwill

The previous discussion of long-term assets covered tangible assets, which are physical in nature and can be touched or sensed. In contrast, **intangible assets** are conceptual in nature. They are identifiable assets that have no physical form and largely constitute intellectual property, such as patents and trademarks. An asset is considered to be identifiable if it

1. is separable, meaning it is capable of being separated from the company and sold; or
2. emerges from contractual or legal rights, regardless of whether it is separable or transferable from the company.

An asset that is not identifiable does not count as an intangible asset. Goodwill, for example, is not identifiable, since it does not fit any of the above two criteria. Therefore, it is accounted for differently and reported separately from other intangible assets. We will discuss other intangible assets first, and save goodwill until the end of this section.

Different intangible assets differ in their lengths of useful life. Some intangible assets are likely to benefit the company only for a finite number of years, while others have a potential to bring future benefits for the company indefinitely. Just as property, plant and equipment need to be depreciated, intangible assets with finite useful lives need to go through a similar process. However, the process of allocating the cost of intangible assets over their useful lives is usually called *amortization* instead of depreciation. In addition to amortization, the value of intangible assets (including both those with finite useful lives and those with infinite useful lives) may also decrease due to impairment, which is similar to the impairment of property, plant and equipment discussed earlier.

Intangible Assets with Finite Useful Lives

Patents, copyrights and research and development costs are the most obvious examples of intangible assets that have limited useful lives.

Patents

Individuals and companies invent and develop innovative products, usually at enormous cost of both money and time. Inventors need to protect their intellectual property and this is achieved through patenting.

A **patent** grants the patentee the exclusive right, for a set period of time, to prevent others from making, using, selling or distributing the patented invention without permission. In most international jurisdictions, including Canada, a patent term lasts for 20 years, but the duration can differ according to the type of patent. This gives the inventor or inventing company the right to enjoy the rewards of creating a new and successful product.

A patent can be purchased from another party or filed by the company. If the company purchases the patent from another party, the cost of the patent is equal to the purchase price plus any legal costs involved. If the company files its own patent, the application process typically requires the use of patent lawyers (as does the defense and management of a patent). All legal and associated costs in acquiring and defending a patent are capitalized in the long-term assets section of the balance sheet. The value of the assets is then amortized for the amount of time left in the patent's legal term or its estimated useful life, whichever is shorter.

This example illustrates how to record journal entries for patent acquisition and amortization. Assume Henry's Lights purchases a patent from Crazy Larry Light Bulb for $28,000 on January 1, 2016. The patent has seven years remaining in its term and is expected to bring in revenues to the company for the whole seven years. The entries to record the purchase on January 1, 2016, as well as one year's amortization for the year ending December 31, 2016 would be recorded as shown in Figure 3.30.

JOURNAL			
Date	**Account Title and Explanation**	**Debit**	**Credit**
Jan 1	Patents	28,000	
	Cash		28,000
	To record purchase of patent with seven years remaining		
Dec 31	Amortization Expense—Patents	4,000	
	Accumulated Amortization—Patents		4,000
	To record amortization expense for one year		

FIGURE 3.30

The $4,000 annual amortization amount is calculated using the straight-line method. The straight-line method divides the amortizable amount ($28,000 less salvage value of zero) by the number of years remaining (7 years). This method is usually used for amortizing patents and other intangible assets.

Copyright

Copyright is similar to a patent in that it gives exclusive rights of ownership to a person or group that has created something. The difference with copyright, is that it applies to artistic work, such as music and literature, and can exist even if the work has not been registered. For example, it is automatically assumed that an article or photo posted on the Internet is protected by copyright. A person cannot simply assume that he has unlimited rights to use or copy a work from the Internet. Registration with the Canadian Intellectual Property Office, however, puts a copyright holder in a stronger position if litigation arises over the copyright. In Canada, the laws regarding copyrights are governed by the Copyright Act which states that, generally, the life of a copyright lasts throughout the life of the author plus 50 years from the end of the calendar year of his or her death. This means that estimates of a copyright's legal life depend on when the work was first created and how long the author lived. The copyright's useful life, however, is usually shorter than its legal life in practice.

Overall, copyright is treated in much the same way as a patent. The costs may include the purchase price in obtaining the copyright from someone else, legal fees paid to register and defend the copyright, and any other fees involved in its acquisition and defense. The cost of the copyright is amortized over the number of years of its legal term, or its estimated useful life, whichever is shorter.

Research and Development Costs

Research and development (R&D) costs are expenditures incurred during the pre-operating period to develop new products or processes that will bring financial benefits to the company in the future. Theoretically, the portion of the R&D costs that result in successful products or processes should be considered long-term assets and recorded in the balance sheet, while the portion of R&D costs that do not result in successful products or processes should be considered expenses and recorded in the income statement. In practice, accounting for R&D costs is complex because it is usually difficult to know in the same accounting period whether money spent on R&D will be fruitful. To deal with this complexity, accountants separate R&D costs into research costs and development costs, and treat them differently.

Research costs include the expenditures from undertaking original investigation to gain new knowledge and understanding. Examples of research activities include the search for raw material alternatives and the design of potential new products. In this preliminary phase, it is still unclear whether the search for raw material alternatives or the new product design will actually be successful. Therefore, all research costs are expensed.

Development costs include the expenditures from applying research findings and knowledge to plan or design how to produce new products or significantly improve processes. Examples of development activities include designing prototypes and testing new raw materials. Development is a more advanced phase than the research phase, and has a much higher probability of generating future benefits for the company. As a result, the company may capitalize the development costs if they meet all of the following criteria.

1. The new products or processes being developed are technically feasible.
2. The company intends to complete the project.
3. The company has an ability to use the new processes or sell the new products.
4. A market exists for the new products, or the processes are useful for generating future economic benefits.
5. The company has adequate resources to complete the project.
6. The company can reliably measure the expenditure attributable to the project.

If the development costs meet all of the criteria, the company can choose whether to capitalize or expense them. If the development costs do not meet all of the criteria, they must be expensed. If the company cannot distinguish development costs from research costs, the expenditures must also be expensed.

Intangible Assets with Indefinite Useful Lives

Some intangible assets do not have an expiry date, and will keep generating economic benefits for the company as long as the company still owns them. Some examples of these assets include trademarks, trade names, franchises and licenses.

Trademark and Trade Name

A **trademark** is similar to a patent and copyright except that it grants ownership rights for a recognizable symbol or logo. A **trade name** grants exclusive rights to a name under which a company or product trades for commercial purposes, even though its legal or technical name might differ. Some corporations have numerous trademarks and trade names that they protect on a continuing basis. For example, McDonald's is not only a trade name that the company protects but it serves as an umbrella brand for numerous other trademarks, such as the Golden Arches, the Extra Value Meal and Hamburger University.

Any internal costs incurred for developing and maintaining a trademark or trade name, such as those involved with advertising, are considered indistinguishable from other costs of developing the company's business, and are expensed during the year they are incurred. However, just as with patents and copyrights, legal fees for registering the name or logo are capitalized. Alternatively, trademarks and trade names can be purchased from someone else. Because these can be separately measured, they are capitalized as an intangible asset on the balance sheet.

Franchises and Licenses

A **franchise** is a contract that allows the franchisee to operate a branch using the franchisor's brand name and business model. For example, one can buy a franchise to run a KFC branch, Mac's convenience store, or Petro-Canada gas station. The franchisee receives operating support from the franchisor such as marketing and training, while the franchisor maintains some control of how the franchisee operates the branch.

A **license** is a contract that permits the licensee to use the licensor's product or brand name under specified terms and conditions. For example, one can buy a license from Marvel to sell T-shirts with Iron Man printed on them. A license usually does not come with an ongoing formal support from the licensor, and the licensor usually does not have much control over how the licensee operates the business.

The franchisee or licensee usually has to pay initial franchise fees or license fees when acquiring the franchise or license. These initial fees are capitalized as long-term assets on the balance sheet. Normally, there is no expiry date on the franchise or license, meaning the franchisee or licensee can keep operating the branch or selling the product under the contract as long as annual payments called royalties are made. Because there is no expiry date on the franchise or license, if the franchisee or the licensee plans to operate the franchise or sell the licensed product indefinitely, the initial fees are not amortized. Royalties that are paid annually are expensed.

Goodwill

Goodwill arises when a company purchases another company at a cost that is greater than the market value of that company's net assets. The excess of the cost of the company over the total of the market value of its assets, less its total liabilities, is recorded as goodwill.

Goodwill can be attributed to factors such as a recognizable brand name, experienced management, a skilled workforce or a unique product. Unlike other assets, items representing goodwill do not come with an easily determinable market price to be amortized over time. Nevertheless, businesses are willing to pay for goodwill, and it increases equity on the balance sheet. We will use an example to explain how goodwill works and how accountants should record such items in the company's books.

Vicky's Entrepreneurial Enterprises decides to buy the net assets Jack's Sweets, a relatively new but established candy maker on June 1, 2016. The purchase price is $1 million. At the time of purchase, Jack's Sweets has assets with a market value of $1.5 million and liabilities totalling $700,000, giving the purchased company a net asset value of $800,000.

The extra $200,000 in the company's purchase price constitutes goodwill. Vicky is willing to pay for the brand name, because Jack's Sweets is known for great tasting candies. Jack's Sweets' memorable commercials featured a fictional "Uncle Jack" handing out treats to beloved customers. Vicky considers $200,000 for this brand to be a bargain and is willing to pay this amount for goodwill. However, she also expects a good return on her investment for the premium paid for the business.

To record the purchase of Jack's Sweets, Vicky's accountant adds the value of the assets and liabilities to Vicky's balance sheet. This results in a debit to assets of $1,500,000 and a credit to liabilities of $700,000. The cash payment amount of $1,000,000 is recorded as a credit to cash. The premium paid is recorded as goodwill and increases that asset account by $200,000. Figure 3.31 shows this transaction.

JOURNAL			
Date	Account Title and Explanation	Debit	Credit
Jun 1	Assets	1,500,000	
	Goodwill	200,000	
	Liabilities		700,000
	Cash		1,000,000
	Purchase net assets of Jack's Sweets, including goodwill		

Note: we use the title "Assets" and "Liabilities" in this journal for demonstration purpose. In reality, each asset and liability would be recorded in its specific account.

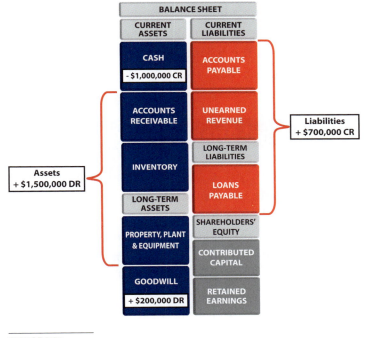

FIGURE 3.31

Unlike most other long-term assets, items categorized as goodwill do not have their value amortized over time. However, this does not mean that the value of goodwill cannot decrease. Events may occur that impair the value of goodwill.

For example, assume that Company A bought Company B because the latter was producing a unique product that the rest of the market could not match. Company A paid a premium of $150,000 over the net asset value of Company B, so this premium is goodwill. However, since the purchase, advances in technology allowed a competitor to create a new product to compete with the one produced by Company B. The new product is still undergoing development and testing, but will almost certainly enter the market within a decade.

The value of goodwill associated with the innovative quality of Company B's product will be seriously reduced. But it will not be negated altogether, since it is estimated that the product will still be competitive, even after the introduction of a competing product.

A decrease in the value of goodwill for the current year is estimated at $50,000. The journal entry to record this is shown in Figure 3.32. The impairment of goodwill is recorded as an expense on the income statement, which reduces the equity of the company.

JOURNAL			
Date	Account Title and Explanation	Debit	Credit
Dec 31	Loss on Impairment of Goodwill	50,000	
	Goodwill		50,000
	Loss on impairment of goodwill		

FIGURE 3.32

The value of goodwill should never be adjusted upward above cost. This violates the accounting principle of conservatism, which was previously covered. Internally generated goodwill also cannot be recognized or recorded in the balance sheet because the value of goodwill cannot be objectively separated from the value of the company's other assets.

Presentation and Financial Analysis of Long-Term Assets

The details of PotashCorp's property, plant and equipment was examined in Figure 3.28. We will return to PotashCorp to see how the company's long-term assets and their depreciation and amortization are presented on its financial statements. Figure 3.33 shows the assets portion of PotashCorp's balance sheet (called "Consolidated Statements of Financial Position"), its income statement (called "Consolidated Statements of Income") and a portion of Note 4 that describes PotashCorp's nature of expenses, including depreciation and amortization.

As illustrated in PotashCorp's balance sheet, long-term assets (or non-current assets) are below current assets in the assets section. Tangible assets (property, plant and equipment) are separate from intangible assets. Notice that PotashCorp presented its long-term assets on the balance sheet at their net book value. The $12,674 balance of PotashCorp's property, plant and equipment on the company's 2014 balance sheet is the net book value, less accumulated depreciation. A company must always present the costs and accumulated depreciation or amortization of its long-term assets either in the notes or on the balance sheet itself. PotashCorp included this detail in the notes.

Because PotashCorp's income statement is by function rather than by nature, depreciation and amortization are not presented directly on the company's income statement. Instead, as the company stated in Note 4, "depreciation and amortization" are included in both cost of goods sold and selling and administrative expenses. It is common for mining companies to charge depreciation and amortization of long-term assets that are deemed necessary for mining operations to the cost of goods sold. Depreciation and amortization of other long-term assets that are used for administrative purposes are charged to selling and administrative expenses.

Consolidated Statements of Financial Position

As at December 31

in millions of Canadian dollars

The Consolidated statements of financial position show assets, liabilities and equity.

Notes		2014	2013
	Assets		
	Currents Assets		
	Cash and Cash Equivalents	$215	$628
Note 11	Receivables	1,029	752
Note 12	Inventories	646	728
	Prepaid Expenses and Other Current Assets	48	81
		1,938	2,189
	Non-current assets		
Note 13	Property, Plant and Equipment	12,674	12,233
Note 14	Investments in Equity-Accounted Investees	1,211	1,276
Note 14	Available for-sale Investments	1,527	1,722
Note 15	Other Assets	232	401
Note 16	Intangible Assets	142	137
	Total Assets	$17,724	$17,958

Consolidated Statements of Income

For the years ended December 31

in millions of US dollars except as otherwise noted

The Consolidated statements of income provide a summary of the earnings for the year.

Notes		2014	2013	2012
Note 3	**Sales**	$7,115	$7,305	7,927
Note 4	Frieght Transportation and Distribution	(609)	(507)	(494)
Note 4	Cost of Goods Sold	(3,859)	(3,943)	(4,023)
	Gross Margin	2,647	2,790	3,410
Note 4	Selling and Sdministrative Expenses	(245)	(231)	(219)
Note 5	Provincial Mining and Other Taxes	(257)	(194)	(180)
	Share of Earnings of Equity-Accounted Investees	102	195	278
	Dividend Income	117	92	144
Note 14	Impairment of Available-for-Sale Investment	(38)	—	(341)
Note 6	Other Income (Expenses)	22	(36)	(73)
	Operating Income	2,348	2,616	3,019
Note 7	Finance Costs	(184)	(144)	(114)
	Income Before Income Taxes	2,164	2,472	2,905
Note 8	Income Taxes	(628)	(687)	(826)
	Net Income	$1,536	$1,785	$2,079

NOTE 4 Nature of Expenses

Accounting Policies

Cost of goods sold is costs primarily incurred at, and charged to, an active producing facility and primary components include: labor, employee benefits, services, raw materials (including inbound freight adn purchasing and receiving costs), operating supplies, energy costs, on-site warehouse costs, royalties, property and miscellaneous taxes, and depreciation and amortization.

The primary components of selling and administrative expenses are compensation, other employee benefits, supplies, communications, travel, professional services and depreciation and amortization.

FIGURE 3.33

The values of the assets on the balance sheet provide an idea of the amount invested in the company to run its operations. However, these values alone do not indicate whether these assets are being used effectively and efficiently. We will examine two ratios that can provide insight on how well assets are being used.

Asset Turnover

A turnover ratio measures how rapidly an asset's status changes and becomes productive. Recall that inventory turnover measures how quickly an asset converts from inventory to becoming a sale. **Asset turnover** measures how quickly a company converts its total assets, including long-term assets, into revenue.

To calculate asset turnover, we need net sales from the income statement and the average total assets, which is produced by taking the average of beginning and ending total assets.

$$\text{Average Total Assets} = (\text{Beginning of Year Total Assets} + \text{End of Year Total Assets}) \div 2$$

$$\text{Asset Turnover} = \frac{\text{Net Sales}}{\text{Average Total Assets}}$$

Return on Assets

A company's return on assets is similar to asset turnover except that its focus is on net income instead of revenue. Return on assets measures the relationship between net income and assets. In other words, is the company making enough profit from investment in its total assets? Since the two ratios involve similar analyses, they also involve similar calculations.

$$\text{Return on Assets} = \frac{\text{Net Income}}{\text{Average Total Assets}}$$

Note that the ratios have the same denominator: Average Total Assets. It is the numerators that differ. One uses revenue, the other uses net income. Another difference is that turnover is expressed as a decimal number, while return is expressed as a percentage.

Using the Ratios

Apply these two ratios by using the financial information made available by Amtrak and Union Pacific, two U.S. companies in the railway transportation industry. Using the formulas already outlined, the ratios are calculated in Figure 3.34.

Selected Financial Information (in millions)			
Year 2013		Amtrak	Union Pacific
A	Net Sales	2,991	21,963
B	Total Assets—Beginning of Year	11,590	47,153
C	Total Assets—End of year	11,929	49,731
D = (B+C)÷2	Average Total Assets	11,760	48,442
E = A÷D	Asset Turnover	0.25	0.45
F	Net Income	-1,276	4,388
G = F÷D	Return on Assets	-10.85%	9.06%

FIGURE 3.34

For Amtrak and Union Pacific, both net sales and net income were divided by average total assets to produce the two financial ratios.

With regard to asset turnover, Amtrak has a figure of 0.25 and Union Pacific has a figure of 0.45. This means that Union Pacific generated more revenue dollars per investment in assets than Amtrak.

With regard to return on assets, Amtrak has a rate of -10.85% and Union Pacific's rate is 9.06%. This means that Union Pacific generated significantly more net income per investment in assets than Amtrak.

All financial ratios represent a simple snapshot of company performance. They tend to focus on one aspect of a business and provide different kinds of information about how well a company is doing. In this case, Union Pacific appears to be using its investment in assets to generate revenue and net income more effectively than Amtrak.

Controls Related To Long-Term Assets

Tangible assets are purchased by a company, used to earn an income and eventually disposed of. In the meantime, the value of a long-term asset depreciates over the period of its estimated useful life. Accounting procedures are used to control and safeguard all tangible assets while the company possesses them. Different companies and industries depend on long-term assets to varying degrees. For instance, auto manufacturers General Motors and Ford rely heavily on long-term assets such as machines, robots and factories. It is sometimes possible for people to steal large assets of a company. Security measures such as physical barriers and security personnel can protect large items from theft.

Insurance is a more useful measure to protect large long-term assets. Insurance can protect not only in the event of theft, but also in the event of catastrophic situations such as extreme weather or unforeseen breakdowns. It is important for management to make sure that the best possible insurance policies are in place and are updated or adjusted when needed. Some companies may even want to consider some self-insurance options to help protect their long-term assets from catastrophic risk.

Big or small, expensive or inexpensive, all types of tangible assets should be tracked properly and relevant transactions recorded accurately in the company's books. Experienced accountants should perform these control procedures. Each long-term asset should be tagged in some way, perhaps by bar code and scanner. The tags should be read, compared with accounting records and vice versa. Physical audits should be performed on a regular basis to ensure that all assets on the books are on the premises, still in use and accounted for.

For all company assets, paperwork and records should be completed correctly and handled securely. The first priority is to record the correct amount of cost for the long-term asset. As always, any costs related to the acquisition of the asset must be included in the total cost. These can include freight, installation and even invoicing costs related to the asset.

As emphasized throughout our discussion of asset controls, policies, plans and procedures need to be in place, and regulations and laws followed. For example, a large company may have a policy of classifying items as long-term assets only if they cost more than $1,000. A smaller company may institute a lower threshold for its policy. These policies need to be clearly communicated to the staff responsible for their implementation. Adherence to all related policies, plans, procedures and regulations should be monitored, with audits when necessary.

Economic and efficient use of tangible assets involves purchasing assets at the best possible price. It also means that internal controls should include a bidding process for suppliers, which helps to ensure the best possible price. Financial ratios, discussed earlier in this chapter, can be used on a regular basis to monitor the efficient use of a company's long-term assets. If the ratios indicate an inefficient use of these assets, measures can be taken to either dispose of or make better use of them. If sales are sluggish, this may mean that long-term assets are not being used to their full capacity. A business may also find that too much money has been invested in its long-term assets. Leasing them could free up some capital. As always, company goals and objectives related to long-term assets should be stated, implemented, reviewed and changed when necessary.

Controls related to intangible assets are not very different from those relating to tangible assets. As always, qualified staff should be available to ensure that transactions are recorded and classified properly in the company's books and all payments are properly documented. Costs should be objectively verified and any supporting documentation should be properly maintained. The procedures involved are similar for both tangible and intangible assets.

However, with intangible assets, the only physical evidence of their existence often comes in the form of contracts, accompanying invoices and supporting cost documentation. That is why it is so important to physically protect such documents. They can be placed in a vault on the premises or a safe deposit box in a bank. These documents can be referenced when changes are made or when the company's books need updating.

IN THE REAL WORLD

Although businesses should make certain that all their assets are insured and that potential liabilities are also covered, this does not always mean that an insurance company need be involved. Businesses can self-insure to cover various risks. Companies that self-insure are sometimes regarded as being uninsured. In other words, "self-insurance" can be seen as an attempt to avoid paying for insurance. Indeed, this can be true, since some companies fail to adequately self-insure.

Proper self-insurance involves a company setting aside enough capital reserves to cover itself in case of a catastrophic event. If something happens to a company's long-term assets, these capital reserves can be used to cover the loss. The advantage of self-insurance is that a company will avoid paying premiums that are often very high.

The disadvantage of self-insurance is that a company needs to tie up a certain amount of its capital to cover a disaster, and even that is sometimes insufficient. To minimize this disadvantage, alternative self-insurance strategies can be undertaken. For example, a business can still buy some insurance, but add self-insurance. Alternatively, businesses can form collaborative self-insurance groups, whereby a group of companies contributes to a pool of funds that can be used if one or more of them suffer a catastrophic event.

As with most aspects of today's business environment, various innovative solutions can be found to resolve inadequacies in the market. Self-insurance is an example of one of those innovations.

Beyond initial registration or purchase, ongoing valuation of intangible assets needs to take place. For example, market conditions may affect the value of goodwill, or competing trademarks may diminish the value of a brand name. Furthermore, companies that own patents, copyright and trademarks should be on the lookout for entities that are using such intellectual property without permission. Any such use diminishes the value of the protected asset. All proper legal avenues should be pursued, including legal action or the threat of legal action, when improper use of protected intellectual assets has taken place.

An Ethical Approach To Long-Term Assets

Accounting for a firm's long-term assets can be manipulated to produce fraudulent figures. Decisions regarding classifying long-term assets, depreciating them and calculating residual values can have a significant impact on a company's financial statements. It is important for accountants to understand the ethical principles that help prevent abuse.

When accountants are faced with a decision, they should ask if it should be done because it is an accurate reflection of the business or for some other reason. Other reasons could be to hide one's own incompetence, seek financial gain, succumb to pressure from management or meet public expectation of company performance.

A good accountant should always raise a red flag when the answer to the question is anything other than, "This is being done because it is an accurate reflection of the financial condition of the business."

Figures for long-term assets can be manipulated to present a financial picture that does not accurately reflect the financial state of the company. One of the first decisions that an accountant must make is whether it is in fact a long-term asset. An attempt to falsely classify the item as an expense reduces the company's net income. Conversely, an attempt to classify an expense as a long-term asset does not reduce the company's equity. Any result that does not reflect the true nature of the asset is an ethical breach and should always be avoided.

Estimating the useful life of a long-term asset is also open to manipulation. Intentionally shortening an asset's life span can unduly increase the annual depreciation charges recorded in the company's books. Intentionally increasing a long-term asset's residual value decreases the amount to be depreciated and the depreciation charges. An accountant has an ethical obligation to detect and avoid these abuses at all times.

Ethical considerations of intangible assets relate mostly to their correct reporting in financial statements. This includes determining the appropriate cost, calculating the correct amortization and impairment and accurately reporting all amounts in the statements of operation and financial position.

Companies should always set up internal controls to ensure that ongoing transactions involving intangible assets are expensed or capitalized properly. Review procedures should be in place to ensure that annual amortization is verified and properly reported. Any review procedure should be the joint responsibility of both management and company auditors. Executives and accountants must take responsibility for the company's books; not doing so can lead to serious consequences.

IN THE REAL WORLD

The year 2001 saw the beginning of numerous corporate and accounting scandals, amounting to breaching ethical standards. Authorities began investigating some of America's largest corporations regarding, among other things, accounting fraud. The corporations investigated included three telecommunications companies: Global Crossing, Qwest and WorldCom.

Some of these investigations found a distortion of gains and expenses as a result of misclassifying long-term assets. These errors may have been a result of incompetence. Alternatively, they may have been a deliberate attempt to mislead the public. Either way, accounting standard violations were found in numerous instances. For example, both Global Crossing and Qwest engaged in billions of dollars of what are known as swaps. These companies purchased telecom capacity from customers who then bought it back from the companies. These were falsely treated as long-term assets rather than as current operating expenses. The result was that both companies recorded the revenue upfront, then expensed the amount over a period of time. This violates, among other things, expense recognition.

In addition, WorldCom classified billions of dollars of current operating expenses as long-term assets. This was done over a period of 15 months. The auditing firm Arthur Andersen failed to raise any red flags over the practice.

AMEENGAGE™ *Access **ameengage.com** for integrated resources including tutorials, practice exercises, the digital textbook and more.*

In Summary

Identify the characteristics of long-term assets

- ➪ Long-term assets provide the infrastructure necessary for operating the business.
- ➪ They are expected to be used on an ongoing basis, typically longer than one year.
- ➪ They are not intended to be sold to customers.

Record the acquisition and changes in the value of property, plant and equipment

- ➪ Cost of property, plant and equipment includes purchase price, expenditures necessary to get the asset ready for operation and asset retirement obligations. The whole cost is debited to the appropriate long-term asset account.
- ➪ In the case of lump sum purchase, the amount paid for all the assets is divided and allocated to each item according to percentages based on the appraised values or fair values.
- ➪ Changes made to property, plant and equipment subsequent to their acquisition must be classified as either "betterment" or "repair." Betterment is capitalized. Repair is expensed.
- ➪ Property, plant and equipment (except land) decrease in value (depreciate) over time. Depreciation is the process of allocating the cost of the asset over its useful life.

Apply the three methods of depreciation of property, plant and equipment

- ➪ The straight-line method of depreciation uses simple average, resulting in the same amount of depreciation every year.
- ➪ The declining and double-declining-balance method applies a depreciation rate to the remaining balance of the book value of the asset.
- ➪ The units-of-production method utilizes the level of asset usage as the basis for calculating depreciation.
- ➪ An accountant should choose the depreciation method that best reflects the nature of the asset involved.

Account for the gain or loss on the disposal of asset and changes in depreciation estimates

- ➪ The disposal of an asset will usually involve either a gain or a loss relative to the item's book value. Gains and losses appear on the income statements.
- ➪ Revisions can be made to a depreciation schedule. However, proper justification should always be used and prior depreciation deductions should never be changed.

Account for natural resources

- ➪ The natural resources that a company owns—such as minerals, oil or timber—are physical in nature, and are capitalized under long-term assets section on the balance sheet. Some companies categorize them separately from other non-current assets.
- ➪ The value of natural resources gets depleted over time, using the units-of-production method.

Define and account for intangible assets and describe the different types of intangible assets

↪ Intangible assets are defined as identifiable assets that have no physical form. An asset is considered to be identifiable if it either is separable from the company or emerges from contractual or legal rights.

↪ The decrease in intangible asset's value due to amortization and impairment is recorded as an expense or a loss in income statement. While impairment loss may be recorded directly against the asset account, amortization must be recorded in an accumulated amortization account.

↪ A patent gives the inventor the exclusive right to use a product. The cost of the patent is for legal fees or the purchase of rights from someone else. This cost is amortized over the remaining term of the patent, or its expected useful life, whichever is shorter.

↪ Copyright gives exclusive rights of a creation to its creator. Copyright is granted automatically to works produced and published.

↪ Research and development (R&D) costs are expenditures incurred during the pre-operating period. Research costs are always expensed. Development costs can either be expensed or capitalized.

↪ A trademark gives exclusive rights to logos and other company symbols. A trade name provides exclusive rights to names of companies and products.

↪ A franchise is a contract that allows the franchisee to operate a branch using the franchisor's brand name and business model. A license is a contract that permits the licensee to use the licensor's product or brand name under the specified terms and conditions. The initial franchise fees or license fees are capitalized.

Calculate and interpret asset turnover and return on asset ratios

↪ Asset turnover measures the revenue a company generates relative to its investment in total assets.

↪ Return on assets measures the net income a company generates relative to total assets.

Describe controls related to long-term assets

↪ Controls to protect a company's long-term assets can include accurate recording and tracking procedures or proper insurance in case of catastrophic events. Qualified accounting personnel should always supervise the policies and measures that a company implements.

Describe ethical approach related to long-term assets

↪ Net income figures and net asset values can be distorted by manipulating decisions regarding the classification of long-term assets, the estimation of residual value and useful life and other aspects of depreciation. Unethical manipulations must always be avoided.

Review Exercise 1

Nelson Rugasa is an entrepreneur who has just started a consulting business. On December 31, 2016, Nelson purchased a laptop computer for $3,000 and office equipment for $10,000.

Required

a) Record the purchase of long-term assets, assuming Nelson paid with cash.

Research Component (to be done outside of class time)

b) Research the useful life of long-term assets, and suggest the useful life for the computer and office equipment.

c) Research the way in which the value of long-term assets decline, and suggest the depreciation method(s) that should be used for the computer and office equipment.

d) Based on your research on useful life, and the ways in which the value of long-term assets decline, prepare a table showing the cost, depreciation, accumulated depreciation, and net book value of the computer, and office equipment for the first three years.

e) Explain how you calculate the profit or loss on disposal of a long-term asset.

See Appendix I for solutions.

a)

Date	Account Title and Explanation	Debit	Credit

b)

_____

_____

_____

_____

_____

_____

c)

_____

_____

_____

_____

_____

_____

_____

d)

Year	Cost	Depreciation	Accumulated Depreciation	Net Book Value

Year	Cost	Depreciation	Accumulated Depreciation	Net Book Value

e) _____

_____

_____

_____

_____

_____

_____

_____

_____

_____

_____

_____

_____

_____

_____

_____

_____

_____

_____

_____

_____

_____

_____

Review Exercise 2

Rulison Company had the following transactions during 2016.

Jan 1   Paid $250,000 to purchase Regnier Ltd. Regnier had $500,000 in assets and $300,000 in liabilities.

Jan 1   Purchased patents from Saundra Arneson for $50,000. The remaining life of the patents is four years.

Jan 1   Purchased a trademark, which will be applied to the patented product for $20,000. Management believes that the trademark's remaining useful life will be double that of the patent's, and the trademark will have the residual value of $100.

Jan 30   Purchased mineral rights for $100,000. The company needs to extract a mineral that goes into the patented product. Rulison Company expects to extract 500,000 kg of mineral before the rights expire.

Jun 30   The senior executives that came from Regnier Ltd. resigned en masse. The directors felt that the loss of the senior executives seriously affected the company's goodwill. They felt that the decrease in the value of goodwill was estimated to be $25,000.

Rulison Company prepares its financial statements with a year-end of December 31. Amortization policy states that one half year's amortization is taken in both the year of purchase and year of sale. Depletion is based on units extracted. The company extracted 10,000 kg of mineral from the beginning of February to the end of December. Assume all purchases are made with cash and that the straight-line method of depreciation is used for the patent and trademark.

Prepare the journal entries to record the above transactions. Also prepare the year-end adjusting entries associated with the long-term assets.

See Appendix I for solutions

Date	Account Titles and Explanation	Debit	Credit

Notes

Chapter 4
CURRENT LIABILITIES

AMEENGAGE™ Access **ameengage.com** *for integrated resources including tutorials, practice exercises, the digital textbook and more.*

LEARNING OUTCOMES

❶ Define and differentiate between determinable and non-determinable liabilities

❷ Record accounts payable

❸ Record payroll liabilities

❹ Record transactions with sales tax

❺ Record unearned revenue

❻ Record short-term notes payable

❼ Record transactions related to the current portion of non-current liabilities

❽ Record estimated liabilities

❾ Apply controls relating to current liabilities

Current Liabilities

BALANCE SHEET	
CURRENT ASSETS	**CURRENT LIABILITIES**
CASH	BANK OVERDRAFT & OPERATING LINE OF CREDIT
SHORT-TERM INVESTMENTS	ACCOUNTS PAYABLE & ACCRUED LIABILITIES
ACCOUNTS RECEIVABLE	
DOUBTFUL ACCOUNTS	UNEARNED REVENUE
INVENTORY	LOANS PAYABLE (CURRENT)
PREPAID EXPENSES	NON-CURRENT LIABILITIES

FIGURE 4.1

This chapter deals with **current liabilities**, which are obligations expected to be paid within one year of the balance sheet date or the company's normal operating cycle. Obligations due beyond one year are classified as **non-current liabilities**, which will be covered in Chapter 8.

The balance sheet presentation of current liabilities is comparable to the balance sheet presentation of current assets. The main difference in the way they are listed on the balance sheet is that the order of liabilities is dictated by the timing of settlement whereas assets are placed in the order of their liquidity. Figure 4.1 illustrates this difference. Bank overdraft and line of credit are listed first among the current liabilities, followed by accounts payable, which is a common type of trade payable. Accrued liabilities include such liabilities as payroll liabilities, sales taxes payable to the government and interest payable on notes and loans. Unearned revenue and the current portion of long-term loans are also listed as current liabilities.

A company's liabilities can be divided into two categories: known liabilities and unknown liabilities. These categories are sometimes referred to as *determinable liabilities* and *non-determinable liabilities*, respectively.

Determinable liabilities have a precise value. In other words, the businesses that have determinable liabilities know exactly who they owe, how much they owe and when they are supposed to pay. Amounts owed to suppliers (trade payables), employees (payroll liabilities) and the government (e.g. sales taxes) are determinable liabilities. All determinable liabilities should leave an easily recognizable and traceable paper trail, and may include documents such as invoices and contracts. The exact amounts due, and when they are due, should be clearly identified.

A company's unknown or **non-determinable liabilities** include estimated liabilities. They are non-determinable because the exact amount owing or when it is supposed to be paid is unknown on the date of financial statement issuance. This is similar to a topic we studied on the assets side of the balance sheet, where the exact amount of bad debt for the year was unknown on the date of financial statement issuance.

We will first discuss each important type of determinable liability, starting with bank overdraft and operating line of credit. Non-determinable liabilities, as well as controls and ethics related to current liabilities, will be examined at the end of the chapter.

Bank Overdraft and Operating Line of Credit

A company faced with short-term financial needs can borrow from a financial institution through a bank overdraft or a line of credit. **Bank overdraft** refers to the financial institution's extension of credit to cover the portion of cash withdrawal that is more than the account balance. The financial institution will automatically deposit amounts into the company's cash account if it goes into a negative balance up to a pre-specified amount. The negative balance could be due to issues with cash flow or simply timing differences between deposits and withdrawals.

Alternatively, many businesses have an operating line of credit with their financial institution. An **operating line of credit** refers to the maximum loan balance that a business may draw upon at any time without having to visit or request approval from the bank. The business negotiates a predetermined maximum balance that it is allowed to owe as well as the interest rate charged on the outstanding balance of this account.

If the company's cash account has a negative balance as of the balance sheet date, the bank overdraft is reported as a current liability. Likewise, if the company owes a financial institution on its line of credit as of the balance sheet date, the line of credit is reported as a current liability. Both bank overdraft and line of credit are reported ahead of accounts payable and any other determinable liabilities on the balance sheet.

Accounts Payable

Accounts payable is a known liability. A company purchases goods or services from a vendor and that vendor issues the company an invoice, which must be paid by a certain date. The terms of the liability are easily recognized and recorded by the company.

In previous chapters, we pointed out that selling an item on account means debiting accounts receivable and crediting sales. With accounts payable there is a mirror transaction: an asset or expense account is debited and the accounts payable account is credited.

Figure 4.2 shows an example of a purchase on credit. A company bought a repair service on credit from Plumbers Inc. for $1,000 on September 30, 2016.

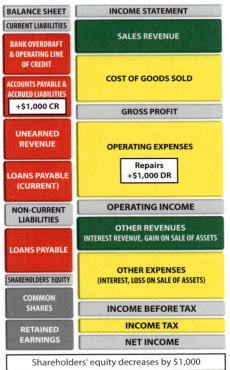

JOURNAL

Date	Account Title and Explanation	Debit	Credit
Sep 30	Repairs Expense	1,000	
	Accounts Payable		1,000
	Record invoice #1425 owing to Plumbers Inc.		

FIGURE 4.2

The amount of money owed by customers is controlled by using an accounts receivable subledger (subsidiary ledger). The same principle applies when maintaining control of the amount of money owed to suppliers. This is controlled by using the accounts payable subledger.

For accounts payable, the control account in the general ledger includes the total amount of credit balances in the individual subledger accounts.

Figure 4.3 shows an example of a purchases journal used to record transactions on a daily basis.

	Purchase Journal		Repairs & Maintenance	Legal	Office Supplies	Inventory Purchases	Accounts Payable
Date	Vendor/Account Name	Vendor Invoice No.	Debit	Debit	Debit	Debit	Credit
Jan 2	Antonio's Electrical	5125	82.65				82.65
Jan 2	Vander Berkel Distributors	2089				1,707.60	1,707.60
Jan 3	Wong Imports Limited	2360				1,498.80	1,498.80
Jan 8	Yonge Office Supplies	5890			76.14		76.14
Jan 9	Designer's Choice	1925				1,137.00	1,137.00
Jan 15	Designer's Choice	1966				1,862.40	1,862.40
Jan 16	Rawlston Equipment Suppliers	6091			25.89		25.89
Jan 18	Sanders Multi-Media Ltd.	26				1,915.20	1,915.20
Jan 21	Yonge Office Supplies Limited	6198			91.26		91.26
Jan 22	Western Plumbers	121	536.23				536.23
Jan 30	Becker & Partner—Lawyers	7001		468.46			468.46
	Totals		**618.88**	**468.46**	**193.29**	**8,121.00**	**9,401.63**

The total of $9,401.63 will be recorded in the accounts payable control account in the general ledger.

FIGURE 4.3

Expense and inventory debits are recorded when amounts are payable for invoices received from vendors, as shown in Figure 4.4. The corresponding credits are recorded in the accounts payable control account.

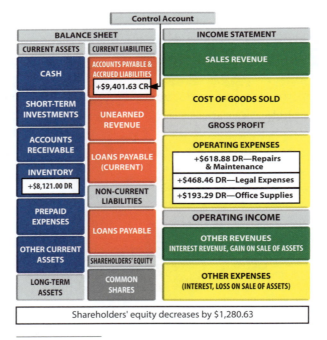

FIGURE 4.4

From Figure 4.3 and Figure 4.4, note that the total amount of $9,401.63 owing is recorded in the accounts payable control account. The subledger contains various levels of detail pertaining to the purchase of products or services. Examples are listed in Figure 4.5.

	Antonio's Electrical	Invoice	Current	60 days	90 days	90 days +	Total
Dec 20	Service performed on transformer	5035		426.22			
Jan 2	Replaced light fitting	5125	82.65				
	Total		82.65	426.22	0	0	508.87

	Vander Berkel Distributors	Invoice	Current	60 days	90 days	90 days +	Total
Dec 14	Purchased product	2010		5,312.23			
Jan 2	Purchased product	2089	1,707.60				
	Total		1,707.60	5,312.23	0	0	7,019.83

FIGURE 4.5

The circled amounts are totalled for each supplier and eventually represented as one credit increase in the accounts payable account in the general ledger.

Alternatively, if an automated system is used, all transactions are entered automatically into the general ledger and the details are used to generate reports on accounts payable.

WORTH REPEATING

It should be noted that equity decreases when the expense actually occurs—even though cash has yet to exchange hands. This concept adheres to the expense recognition principle.

The Accounts Payable Subledger Report

One of the reports that could be generated from the information in a computerized system is the **accounts payable subledger report**, which presents specific information related to vendors and amounts owing to them.

Keeping accounts payable subledgers is important for forward-looking businesses for a number of reasons. The subledgers

- help monitor the amounts owing to specific suppliers and their corresponding due dates
- provide the company with information regarding when to pay its bills, which allows for important planning relating to cash flow—for example, if a company has surplus cash, early payments of bills may lead to discounts

- enable company accountants and managers to look up specific information related to suppliers and purchases made from them
- allow for trend analysis to help in negotiating volume discounts with the suppliers
- provide decision makers with information that allows for better planning and implementation of goals

Payroll as an Accrued Liability

An **accrued liability** is a result of an expense that is recognized for a current period, but is not paid until the next period. Even though cash payment is not made at the time the expense is incurred, the payment is mostly predictable and will occur on an established schedule. This is why accrued liabilities, similar to accounts payable, are normally categorized as known liabilities.

Payroll provides an excellent example of accrued liabilities because payroll journal entries are often recorded in one period, but amounts are not paid until the next period. We will use an example involving payroll for a full-time employee named Glen Booth to demonstrate how to account for accrued liabilities. Assume Glen Booth earns a salary of $54,000 per year and is paid on a monthly basis. This means his monthly gross pay is $4,500. Figure 4.6 shows a breakdown of the calculation for his monthly net pay.

Gross Pay		$4,500.00
Deductions		
CPP	$208.31	
EI	84.60	
Income taxes	802.90	
Total deduction		1,095.81
Net pay		$3,404.19

FIGURE 4.6

Gross pay is the amount an employee earns. Deductions such as the Canada Pension Plan (CPP), Employment Insurance (EI) and income tax are required by law to be withheld by the employer and sent to the tax authorities. Net pay is the actual amount received by the employee after all deductions have been taken from the gross pay.

From the chart in Figure 4.6, the journal entry in Figure 4.7 is recorded. We will use T-accounts to account for all transactions related to the payroll.

JOURNAL			
Date	Account Title and Explanation	Debit	Credit
Jan 31	Salaries Expense	4,500.00	
	CPP Payable		208.31
	EI Payable		84.60
	Income Tax Payable		802.90
	Salaries Payable		3,404.19
	To record employee payroll		

− CPP PAYABLE +	− EI PAYABLE +
208.31	84.60

− INCOME TAXES PAYABLE +	− SALARIES PAYABLE +
802.90	3,404.19

FIGURE 4.7

The transaction shows the salaries expense broken down into various liability amounts. All the deductions are recorded in liability accounts until it is time to send these amounts to the tax authority in Canada, which is the Canada Revenue Agency (CRA). In a perfect world with no liabilities, all the amounts withheld from the employee's paycheque would immediately be paid, with cash, to the CRA. In reality, there is usually a difference in timing from withholding the deductions to actually sending them to the CRA. Businesses act as an intermediary, taking the money from the employee and sending it to the CRA at a later date. The business effectively has a debt (liability) for a short period of time until it sends the money where it is supposed to go.

The net pay may be recorded as a liability (salaries payable) if the actual cash payment will happen a few days later. If, however, the employee is paid immediately, cash is credited for the net pay amount instead of salaries payable.

The second portion of a payroll journal entry is to record the employer's portion of the deductions. In this example, the employer will

- match the employees' CPP deduction of $208.31
- pay 1.4 times the amount of the employees' EI deduction of $118.44

The journal entry to record the employer contributions on January 31, 2016 is shown in Figure 4.8.

JOURNAL			
Date	Account Title and Explanation	Debit	Credit
Jan 31	Employee Benefits Expense	326.75	
	CPP Payable		208.31
	EI Payable		118.44
	To record employer payroll expenses		

− CPP PAYABLE +	
208.31	Employee deduction
208.31	Employer contribution
416.62	

− EI PAYABLE +	
84.60	Employee deduction
118.44	Employer contribution
203.04	

FIGURE 4.8

The employer portions of CPP and EI are added to the existing liability accounts. These liability accounts already have the employee portions recorded in them from Figure 4.7. A single expense account called employee benefits expense is used to record the extra employer expenses.

At this point, payroll for the employee is complete. The employer must now pay the payroll liabilities that have been created.

Paying the Payroll Liabilities

Amounts deducted from payroll are owed to the government. After recording the journal entries for the employee payroll and the employer contributions, the employer has a number of liability accounts that must be paid.

First, the employer must actually pay the employee. Initially the net pay was recorded in salaries payable because the actual pay is going to be paid on a different day. To pay the employee, cash and liability are decreased, as shown in Figure 4.9. Remember, if the employee was paid on the same day as the payroll entry, cash would have been credited in Figure 4.7 instead of salaries payable and this entry on February 1 would not be needed.

JOURNAL			
Date	Account Title and Explanation	Debit	Credit
Feb 1	Salaries Payable	3,404.19	
	Cash		3,404.19
	To pay employee		

- SALARIES PAYABLE +

Feb 1 3,404.19	3,404.19 Jan 31

FIGURE 4.9

Next, CPP, EI and income tax amounts must be sent to the CRA. This is called a payroll remittance. This remittance includes the employee and employer portion of CPP, the employee and employer portion of EI and the income tax.

We will assume the remittance must be made by February 15, 2016. The journal entry to make the payment is shown in Figure 4.10. All the liability accounts are debited by the amount of their balances to clear them, and the total cash amount is sent to the CRA.

JOURNAL			
Date	**Account Title and Explanation**	**Debit**	**Credit**
Feb 15	CPP Payable	416.62	
	EI Payable	203.04	
	Income Taxes Payable	802.90	
	Cash		1,422.56
	To remit deductions to the CRA		

−	**CPP PAYABLE**	+	
Remittance	416.62	208.31	Employee deduction
		208.31	Employer contribution
		416.62	

−	**EI PAYABLE**	+	
Remittance	203.04	84.60	Employee deduction
		118.44	Employer contribution
		203.04	

−	**INCOME TAXES PAYABLE**	+	
Remittance	802.90	802.90	

FIGURE 4.10

Another area in which accrued liabilities commonly occur is sales tax, discussed in the next section.

Sales Tax

Sales tax is a tax applied by the government to goods or services that are sold. Sales taxes can be applied by both the federal and provincial government. They are calculated as a percentage of a sale, and the percentages can vary from province to province. Some provinces have a provincial sales tax (PST) that is applied by the provincial government. The federal government applies a federal sales tax called the goods and services tax (GST). Some provinces have partnered with the federal government and combined both the provincial and federal sales tax into a harmonized sales tax (HST). Figure 4.11 shows examples of provinces and the sales taxes they charge.

Ontario
HST

Manitoba
GST + PST

Alberta
GST

FIGURE 4.11

Although sales tax must be paid to the government, it would be impractical, if not impossible, for individual customers to send the sales tax owed to the government every time they bought something. Imagine buying a coffee and having to send the government a few cents in sales tax.

Instead, businesses act as tax collectors for the government by collecting the sales tax from their customers and sending it to the government. Businesses must be careful and accurate in collecting sales taxes from customers. These taxes collected are not money that the business can spend; the money does not belong to the business, it belongs to the government.

For example, if a business receives $1,500 from a customer, which includes $150 in sales tax, the business must make sure it does not spend the $150 in taxes collected. This money must eventually be sent to the government, as illustrated in Figure 4.12.

FIGURE 4.12

The due date for a business to send the collected sales tax to the government can vary. Companies that have a very small amount of sales may be required to send in the sales tax once a year. As the amount of sales increases and the amount of sales tax collected increases, the business may be required to submit the money on a quarterly or monthly basis. Failure to send this money, or sending the money late, results in interest and penalties being charged to the business by the government.

Provincial Sales Tax

Provincial sales tax (PST) is paid by the final consumer of a product. A retailer buying inventory for resale from a supplier does not pay the PST because the retailer is not the final consumer of the inventory. But when the retailer sells the inventory to customers, the customers pays the PST.

The retailer is responsible for collecting the PST from the customer and eventually sending (remitting) the amount collected to the provincial government. The amount collected is recorded in a current liability account until it is remitted.

As an example, assume Hardware Store sells inventory to a customer for $1,000 cash on June 15, 2016. The provincial sales tax rate is 6%. The transaction is shown in Figure 4.13. For this example, ignore the cost of goods sold.

Each sale gradually increases the amount in the PST payable account until it is time for the company to send it to the provincial government. Assume the payment is made on August 31, 2016 and the account only has a $60 credit balance. Figure 4.14 shows the transaction.

The PST payable account essentially acts as a clearing account. It accumulates the PST collected over a period of time, and then is cleared to $0 when a payment is sent to the provincial government.

The retailer must pay PST on purchases that will not be resold to customers. In this case, the retailer is considered to be the final consumer of the product and must pay the PST. In cases like this, the PST is calculated and added to the cost of the asset or expense that is being purchased.

BALANCE SHEET		INCOME STATEMENT

CURRENT ASSETS	CURRENT LIABILITIES	SALES REVENUE
CASH +$1,060 DR	ACCOUNTS PAYABLE & ACCRUED LIABILITIES	+$1,000 CR
		COST OF GOODS SOLD
SHORT-TERM INVESTMENTS	SALES TAX PAYABLE +$60 CR	
		GROSS PROFIT
ACCOUNTS RECEIVABLE	SALES TAX RECOVERABLE	OPERATING EXPENSES
INVENTORY	NON-CURRENT LIABILITIES	OPERATING INCOME

JOURNAL

Date	Account Title and Explanation	Debit	Credit
Jun 15	Cash	1,060	
	PST Payable		60
	Sales Revenue		1,000
	Sold inventory		

FIGURE 4.13

JOURNAL

Date	Account Title and Explanation	Debit	Credit
Aug 31	PST Payable	60	
	Cash		60
	Remit PST to government		

FIGURE 4.14

BALANCE SHEET	
CURRENT ASSETS	CURRENT LIABILITIES
CASH -$60 CR	ACCOUNTS PAYABLE & ACCRUED LIABILITIES
SHORT-TERM INVESTMENTS	SALES TAX PAYABLE -$60 DR
ACCOUNTS RECEIVABLE	SALES TAX RECOVERABLE
INVENTORY	NON-CURRENT LIABILITIES

Goods and Services Tax

The **goods and services tax (GST)** is a sales tax imposed by the federal government on most transactions between businesses and between businesses and consumers. The GST rate is currently 5% of the sales amount. Similar to the provincial sales tax, the business that is selling a product or service must collect the GST on the sale and record it in a liability account.

Where the GST differs from the provincial sales tax is that it is considered a recoverable sales tax. This means that a business is able to reduce the amount of GST that must be paid to the government by the amount of GST the business spends. The amount of GST that the business spends is usually recorded in a contra liability account called **GST Recoverable**. The following transactions illustrate how these accounts are used.

Suppose Hardware Store purchases inventory for resale on June 1. As discussed, it does not have to pay PST on the purchase, but does have to pay GST. The GST is recorded in the contra liability account to eventually reduce the amount owing to the government. The transaction is shown in Figure 4.15.

JOURNAL			
Date	**Account Title and Explanation**	**Debit**	**Credit**
Jun 1	Inventory	600	
	GST Recoverable	30	
	Cash		630
	Purchased inventory		

BALANCE SHEET

CURRENT ASSETS	CURRENT LIABILITIES
CASH -$630 CR	ACCOUNTS PAYABLE & ACCRUED LIABILITIES
SHORT-TERM INVESTMENTS	SALES TAX PAYABLE
ACCOUNTS RECEIVABLE	SALES TAX RECOVERABLE +$30 DR
INVENTORY +$600 DR	NON-CURRENT LIABILITIES

FIGURE 4.15

Now, Hardware Store makes a sale to a customer for $1,000 cash. This was shown in Figure 4.13, but now we will include the GST as part of the sale.

As we focus on the GST in Figure 4.16, Hardware Store owes the government $50 from the sale. However, it can reduce the amount owing by the $30 it spent earlier during the month. To make the payment to the federal government on June 30, the transaction shown in Figure 4.17 must be made.

The cash payment is for the difference between the two accounts ($20). Both GST accounts act as clearing accounts. They accumulate the GST collected and GST paid over a period of time, and then the accounts are cleared to $0 when a payment is made to the federal government.

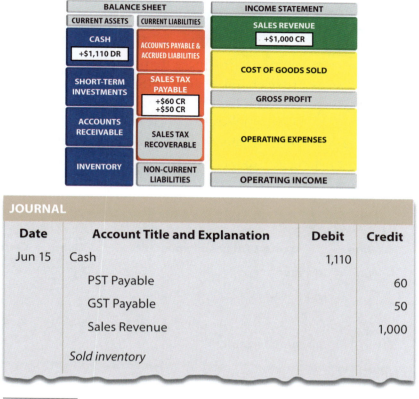

JOURNAL			
Date	Account Title and Explanation	Debit	Credit
Jun 15	Cash	1,110	
	PST Payable		60
	GST Payable		50
	Sales Revenue		1,000
	Sold inventory		

FIGURE 4.16

In the end, the customer pays the entire amount of GST, but the amount sent to the government is sent by different companies. In the example, the customer paid $50 GST to Hardware Store. Hardware Store sent $20 to the government and its supplier of inventory sent the other $30.

JOURNAL			
Date	Account Title and Explanation	Debit	Credit
Jun 30	GST Payable	50	
	GST Recoverable		30
	Cash		20
	Remit GST to government		

FIGURE 4.17

Harmonized Sales Tax

The **harmonized sales tax (HST)** is a sales tax that combines the provincial and federal taxes into one sales tax amount. Provinces that have the HST will not charge separate PST or GST amounts. Instead they charge a single HST amount.

Harmonized sales tax is applied to almost all of the same transactions that GST is applied to, and is sent to the federal government. HST is also a recoverable sales tax, like GST. Using Hardware Store and assuming an HST rate of 13%, a purchase is recorded as shown in Figure 4.18.

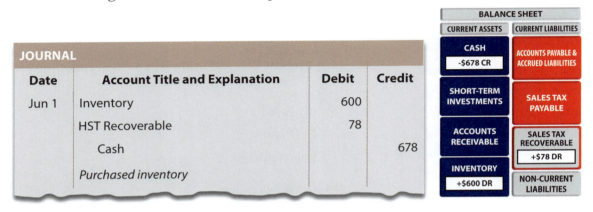

FIGURE 4.18

The cash sale for $1,000 is shown in Figure 4.19.

The payment to the federal government is similar to the way the GST is paid. Both the HST recoverable account and the HST payable account are cleared when the payment is made. The journal entry for HST payment transaction is shown in Figure 4.20.

The cash payment is for the difference between the two accounts ($52). Both HST accounts act as clearing accounts. They accumulate the HST collected and HST

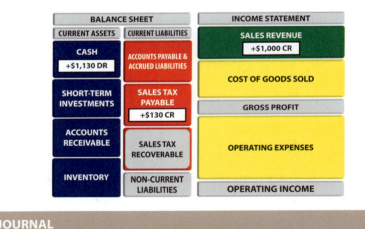

JOURNAL			
Date	Account Title and Explanation	Debit	Credit
Jun 15	Cash	1,130	
	HST Payable		130
	Sales Revenue		1,000
	Sold inventory		

FIGURE 4.19

paid over a period of time, and then they are cleared to $0 when a payment is made to the federal government.

JOURNAL			
Date	**Account Title and Explanation**	**Debit**	**Credit**
Jun 30	HST Payable	130	
	HST Recoverable		78
	Cash		52
	Remit HST to government		

BALANCE SHEET

CURRENT ASSETS	CURRENT LIABILITIES
CASH -$52 CR	**ACCOUNTS PAYABLE & ACCRUED LIABILITIES**
SHORT-TERM INVESTMENTS	**SALES TAX PAYABLE** (balance) $130 -$130 DR
ACCOUNTS RECEIVABLE	**SALES TAX RECOVERABLE** (balance) $78 -$78 CR
INVENTORY	**NON-CURRENT LIABILITIES**

FIGURE 4.20

In the end, the customer pays the entire amount of HST, but the amount sent to the government is sent by different companies. In the example, the customer paid $130 HST to Hardware Store. In turn, Hardware Store sent $52 to the government and its supplier of inventory sent the other $78.

A CLOSER LOOK

Some companies may choose to include sales tax in the selling price of their goods or services. To determine the amount of selling price before tax, you would simply divide the tax-inclusive selling price by 100% plus the applicable percentage of tax. For example, assume the selling price of an item is $113, and it already includes HST of 13%. To determine the selling price before sales tax on this item, you would simply divide $113 by 1.13, resulting in the $100 selling price before taxes. In other words, the sales tax is equal to $13 ($113 − $100).

Sales Tax Remittances

When making remittances, or payments, to the government, some businesses use government forms and make the payment by cheque. Others use an online form and electronically transfer the funds.

The sales tax forms have various numbered lines, which must be filled out. Instructions are available on the form or online regarding which information must be entered in each line and how to calculate the amount of HST owing.

The purpose of the HST remittance form is to have companies report the total HST they collected and the total HST they paid out during the period. If the total HST collected is greater than the total HST paid out, the difference is a balance owing to the government. If HST collected is less than HST paid out, the difference is a refund for the company that the government will pay out. The company's total sales before tax is also listed on the form for informative purposes and to reconcile the amount of HST collected.

Returning to Hardware Store we will determine the company's HST balance owing or refund. From Figure 4.19, the HST collected is $130. From Figure 4.18, the HST paid is $78. The difference, also known as net tax, is $52 ($130 − $78). There are various adjustments that might be made after this point that may change the balance owing or refund. In this case, assuming there are no adjustments, the $52 is a balance owing and a cheque or electronic payment must be sent to the government.

Unearned Revenue

The accrual basis of accounting applies to both expenses and revenue, as illustrated in Figure 4.21. As you have learned, expenses are recognized during the period in which they are incurred, and not when they are actually paid. The same applies to unearned revenue. For example, a publishing company might receive payment in advance for a one-year subscription to its magazine. The money is paid, but the magazine has not yet been supplied to the customer. Until the product exchanges hands, the amount paid in advance cannot be recognized as revenue. The payment is therefore considered unearned revenue, which is a liability.

Businesses sometimes misunderstand how accruals work. This can lead to mistakes and bad decisions. For example, management may be tempted to treat unearned revenue as though it is already earned. Using the example of a magazine subscription again, what would happen if a customer later decided to cancel the subscription and the magazine publisher had considered the money as earned? Until the product has been delivered, no transaction has been finalized with the customer. The money should be paid back to the customer.

Accrued Expense

Expense Incurred	Expense Paid
Month 1	Month 2

Accrual recognizes expense in month incurred

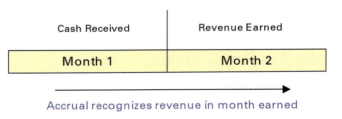

Unearned Revenue

Cash Received	Revenue Earned
Month 1	Month 2

Accrual recognizes revenue in month earned

This diagram illustrates how the accrual concept works for both expenses (e.g., salaries) and revenues (e.g., magazine subscriptions).

FIGURE 4.21

With a non-refundable subscription, the same principle would apply. It is still the obligation of the company to deliver goods or services that have been paid for and to treat the money as unearned until completion of the transaction.

If a customer voluntarily cancels his or her rights to the goods or services and notifies the company to that effect, the revenue will be treated as earned and classified as such on the books. An example of this might be a subscriber moving overseas and informing the publisher that delivery of the magazine is no longer necessary. If the subscription is non-refundable, the customer would have no right to demand repayment. Of course, if the subscription were refundable, the publisher would have to reverse the initial transaction and refund the subscriber. This is another example of why the publisher should treat the cash received as a liability instead of earned revenue.

Here is an example to illustrate the concept of accruals and revenue. Tracking Time is the publisher of a magazine with a fiscal year-end of December 31. In December, Tracking Time receives $120,000 from subscribers to cover the delivery of magazines for one year starting on January 1. The delivery will be made on a monthly basis.

The transaction is recorded in the company's books as shown in Figure 4.22.

FIGURE 4.22

The money is received and debited in the cash account in December. However, the money is yet to be earned, so the amount is credited to the unearned revenue account. Since revenue is not yet earned, there is no change in the company's equity.

On January 1, the magazine is delivered to customers for that month. This means that Tracking Time's obligation to the customer has been met for the month and the corresponding revenue is now earned. One month of subscriptions equals one-twelfth of the whole year subscription; therefore, the amount of $10,000 is recognized as revenue for the month of January, as shown in Figure 4.23.

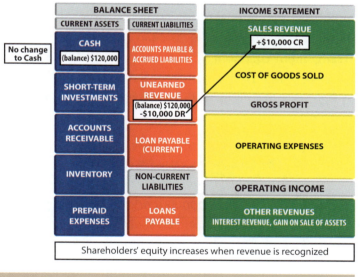

FIGURE 4.23

Unearned revenue originally had a credit balance of $120,000. Of that amount, $10,000 is now debited to the unearned revenue account and credited to the revenue account in the income statement. Although cash remains the same, the recognition of the unearned revenue means that equity has increased by $10,000. The obligation that Tracking Time now has to its customers is reduced to $110,000 from the original total of $120,000.

Another type of unearned liability gaining popularity in recent years, possibly due to the increase in online sales, is for gift cards or gift certificates. Similar to the Tracking Time example above, when a business sells a gift card or certificate, it debits cash account and credits an unearned revenue account.

Short-Term Notes Payable

With regard to accounts receivable, companies sometimes want greater assurance that a customer will pay its bill. Instead of issuing an invoice and creating an account receivable, a company might make a more formal arrangement in the form of a note receivable.

In the same way that a company can have a customer agree to the terms of a note receivable, a supplier can have a company agree to the terms of a **note payable**. These notes are legally binding documents that obligate the borrower to certain terms, much like a loan.

Such documents outline the amount owed, when it is due and the interest payable. They are signed by the parties involved and constitute a more formal arrangement than a basic account payable. If the due date is one year or less, the note is reported as a current liability on the balance sheet, as highlighted in Figure 4.24. Figure 4.25 is an example of a note payable.

FIGURE 4.24

Note Payable For Value Received, the undersigned promises to pay to the order of:

Trimore Distributors the sum of:

***** $5,000 and 00/100 Dollars ********************($5,000.00)

with annual interest of 5% on any unpaid balance. This note shall mature and be payable, along with accrued interest on:

July 31, 2016

February 1, 2016	_Oren Vance_	_Ahmed Karat_
Issue Date	Borrower's Signature	Witness Signature

FIGURE 4.25

In the note payable presented above, Oren Vance borrowed $5,000 from Trimore Distributors on February 1, 2016. The interest rate is 5% and both principal and interest are payable in six months. The journal entry used to record the note payable is shown in Figure 4.26.

JOURNAL			
Date	**Account Title and Explanation**	**Debit**	**Credit**
Feb 1	Cash	5,000	
	Notes Payable		5,000
	Record a 6-month, 5% note payable		

FIGURE 4.26

Accrued Interest and Notes Payable

Using the above example, let us assume the borrower has a June 30 year-end date. The matching principle dictates that we must report expenses in the period in which they helped to earn revenue; since no payment has been made or interest expense recognized, we must accrue the interest owing on the note to June 30. The journal entry in Figure 4.27 would be required.

JOURNAL			
Date	**Account Title and Explanation**	**Debit**	**Credit**
Jun 30	Interest Expense	104	
	Interest Payable		104
	Record interest on a 6-month, 5% note payable ($5,000 x 5% x $\frac{5}{12}$ = $104.17)		

FIGURE 4.27

In addition to the note payable for $5,000, the company would report interest payable of $104 on its June 30 year-end balance sheet within the Accounts Payable and Accrued Liabilities section.

On July 31, both principal and interest will be paid to Trimore Distributors. The entry to record repayment of the note, plus interest, is presented in Figure 4.28.

JOURNAL			
Date	**Account Title and Explanation**	**Debit**	**Credit**
Jul 31	Interest Payable	104	
	Interest Expense	21	
	Notes Payable	5,000	
	Cash		5,125
	Record interest and payment for a 6-month, 5% note payable ($5,000 × 5% × $\frac{1}{12}$ = $21, $5,000 + $5,000 × 5% × $\frac{6}{12}$ = $5,125)		

FIGURE 4.28

Note that the interest payable account is debited to remove the accrual recorded in the previous period and interest expense is debited with $21, which represents the interest expense for the month of July. In total, six months worth of interest has been recorded: five months in the previous period and one month in the current period.

Current Portion of Non-Current Liabilities

When the term of a note payable (loan payable) is longer than one year, the liability should be classified as a non-current liability called *loans payable*. If a portion of the loan will be paid within the next 12 months, that portion is considered current. Although the entire portion will be contained within the non-current loans payable account, the current portion must be reported separately when the balance sheet is prepared.

For example, a company manufactures a wide range of products for consumers. It wants to purchase a new processing machine to keep up with growing demand for its product. The company has insufficient cash reserves on hand to finance the purchase. Management decides to obtain a loan from a bank to finance an important capital investment.

On January 2, 2016, the company negotiates a loan from the bank of $50,000 with a term of five years, bearing an annual interest rate of 5%. Of that debt, $10,000 plus interest is payable every December 31. Figure 4.29 shows how the bank loan is recorded in the company's books.

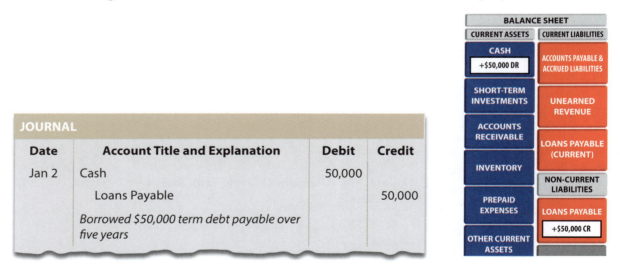

FIGURE 4.29

On December 31, the first installment plus interest was paid. The transaction is recorded as shown in Figure 4.30.

JOURNAL			
Date	**Account Title and Explanation**	**Debit**	**Credit**
Dec 31	Loans Payable	10,000	
	Interest Expense	2,500	
	Cash		12,500
	Record payment for first loan installment plus interest		

FIGURE 4.30

After the first payment, the balance of the loan decreases to $40,000, $10,000 of which is still considered current. When the balance sheet is prepared at the year-end, $10,000 will show as part of current liabilities and $30,000 will show as part of non-current liabilities.

Estimated and Contingent Liabilities

We have already discussed various forms of known liabilities, also referred to as determinable liabilities, which are debts taken on by the company for which the terms are readily known. However, some company liabilities exist for which the exact terms are not precisely known and cannot be determined until future events occur. These unknown liabilities are also referred to as non-determinable liabilities, and can be divided further into estimated liabilities and contingent liabilities.

Estimated Liabilities

Estimated liabilities are financial obligations that a company cannot exactly quantify. Examples include product warranties and customer loyalty programs. A company needs to adhere to the expense recognition principle when it makes an estimate of the amount of the upcoming liability.

Product Warranties

Just as a company needs to estimate how much bad debt it will have in the upcoming period, when a company sells products with warranties it needs to estimate how much warranty liability it will have. Warranties are one way a company guarantees that its product will be free of defects for a certain period of time, and any defects during that period will be the responsibility of the company. By estimating the warranty liability, the company can expense this liability in the period in which related revenues are generated. Any errors in estimation can be adjusted once the actual figures are known.

There are two approaches to accounting for product warranties: the revenue approach and the expense approach. This textbook will focus only on the expense approach, which involves using an estimate of the expected cost the company will incur due to warranty claims. The revenue approach will be addressed at the intermediate accounting level.

For example, Star Machines is a manufacturer of industrial labelling machines. It offers customers a warranty of three years on the purchase of each machine. If a machine breaks down during this warranty period, Star Machines is obliged to repair it, provide necessary parts and, if necessary, replace the machine.

On the basis of an analysis of historical company trends, the company's accountant determines that an average of $100 per machine is paid out in warranty obligations. The company has sold 50 of these labelling machines during the 2016 fiscal year; therefore, the journal entry in Figure 4.31 is made to recognize the warranty expense for 2016.

The $5,000 is expensed for this period in the income statement since these estimates cover expected warranties for the year. The estimated warranty liability of $5,000 is credited in the corresponding liability account.

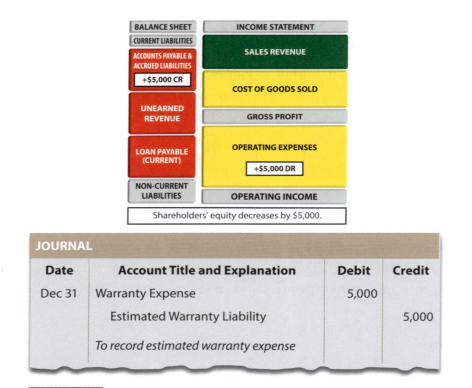

FIGURE 4.31

During the next year, Star Machines receives some warranty claims and has actual expenditure in meeting those claims. Let us assume that Star Machines uses $500 in parts from its own inventory, and maintenance staff report $1,500 worth of billable hours related to warranty claims. Figure 4.32 illustrates how Star's accountant records these transactions.

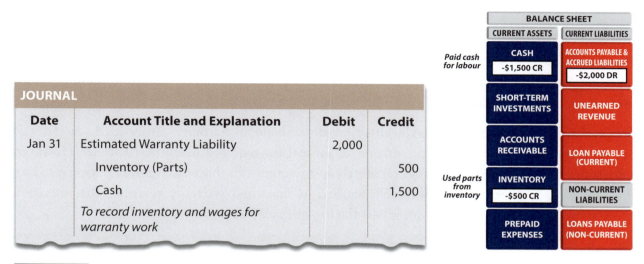

FIGURE 4.32

The estimated warranty liability account is debited with $2,000, leaving a balance of $3,000 to satisfy warranty claims over the remaining two-year period. On the credit side, $500 worth of inventory is taken off the books, and $1,500 is recorded as a decrease in the bank account.

There is no change to the income statement since the estimated warranty was expensed in the year the machine was sold. The company will calculate and record a debit to warranty expense and a credit to estimated warranty liability accounts on the basis of the number of machines sold that year.

Assuming that this amount does not change for the remainder of the warranty period (i.e. no one else makes any warranty claims), Star Machines will have to reverse the original estimate with the actual claims made. Figure 4.33 shows how that process is transacted.

The remaining $3,000 in the estimated warranty liability account is removed with a debit. In the income statement, $3,000 in expenses is removed from the books with a credit (decrease) of that amount. The company is reversing the original expense for the amount that remains in the estimated warranty liability account.

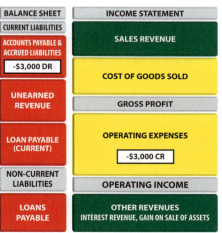

FIGURE 4.33

Of course, no company wants to find itself in a position of significantly erring in estimating certain liabilities as this would result in large adjustment entries after the fact.

Accountants should provide an accurate snapshot of company finances. Large errors in estimating liabilities will distort that snapshot.

To avoid such difficulties, a company should always closely monitor its estimated liability accounts. If estimates are continually and significantly wrong, then reviews should be conducted and changes made to historical and other analyses that are producing these errors. For example, if liabilities keep increasing, it would indicate that a manufacturing problem exists.

The example above demonstrated a situation of embedded warranty. Embedded warranty is provided with a product or service with no additional fee required from the customer. However, sometimes companies sell warranties separately to customers. In those cases, revenue generated on the sale of these warranties is initially recorded as unearned warranty revenue. The unearned warranty revenue is recognized throughout the life of the warranty contract.

Let us assume that Star Machines sold $60,000 worth of three-year warranties as a separate product to its customers on June 1, 2016. Figure 4.34 illustrates how the transaction is recorded in the company's books.

JOURNAL			
Date	Account Title and Explanation	Debit	Credit
Jun 1	Cash	60,000	
	Unearned Warranty Revenue		60,000
	Record the sale of three-year warranties		

FIGURE 4.34

The receipt of $60,000 is recorded as a debit to cash and as a credit to unearned warranty revenue. Since this is a three-year warranty, $20,000 will be recognized at the end of each year. At the end of the first year, the company recorded the appropriate adjustment (see Figure 4.35).

The $20,000 is recorded as a debit to the unearned warranty revenue and as a credit to the warranty revenue account. The rest of the revenue will be earned as the warranty periods elapse. At present, the unearned warranty revenue account has a $40,000 balance

JOURNAL			
Date	Account Title and Explanation	Debit	Credit
May 31	Unearned Warranty Revenue	20,000	
	Warranty Revenue		20,000
	Recognize one year unearned warranty revenue as earned		

FIGURE 4.35

because there are two more years left in the warranty period. Note that only the unearned revenue in the next twelve months is counted as current liabilities.

Customer Loyalty Programs

Customer loyalty programs have gained popularity in recent years as companies look for creative ways to retain or attract customers. Such programs result in the need for the business to record an estimated liability for the amount the customers will receive in the future if they use up their accumulated rewards. The rewards are often in the form of points, store currencies or travel miles. Reward redemption by a customer represents a reduction in future sales. Therefore, when rewards are issued to a customer, a sales discounts account is normally debited instead of an expense account, and a redemption rewards liability account is credited. The dollar amount of redemption rewards liability recognized would be estimated based on past redemption history.

For example, assume that Zen Gen is a teahouse chain that offers a customer loyalty program whereby customers are rewarded one loyalty point for every dollar of tea and other refreshments purchased. One hundred loyalty points can be redeemed for a one-dollar discount toward future purchase. In June 2016, Zen Gen sold $150,000 worth of refreshments. Historically, an average of 70% of the points issued is redeemed. Following past experience, Zen Gen's accountant would recognize redemption rewards liability of $1,050 ($150,000 × 70% × $0.01). Figure 4.36 shows the journal entry to record Zen Gen's customer loyalty points issued in June 2016.

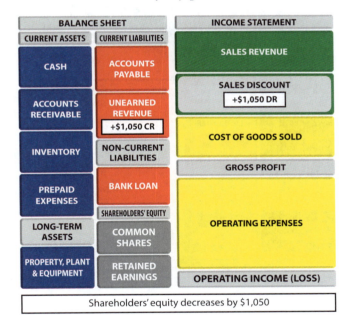

JOURNAL			
Date	Account Title and Explanation	Debit	Credit
Jun 30	Sales Discount—Loyalty Programs	1,050	
	Redemption Rewards Liability		1,050
	Record customer loyalty point issuance		

FIGURE 4.36

As a result of this transaction, net sales (and thus equity) decrease, and liabilities increase. Similar to the sales returns and allowances account, the sales discount account is a contra account linked to the sales revenue account. Both sales discounts and sales returns and allowances are deducted from sales revenue to reveal the net sales amount on an income statement.

Redemption rewards liability is a current liability. Specifically, the redemption rewards liability account is considered unearned revenue because issuing loyalty points based on a current transaction's sales dollar amount is similar to Zen Gen accepting money from a customer in advance in exchange for a potential future discount. Once loyalty points are redeemed, Zen Gen's obligation or liability is nullified, and its unearned revenue becomes earned.

Zen Gen's sales transaction in July will be used to illustrate an example of loyalty point redemption journal entry. Assume that the total value of sales in July was $180,000, of which $179,250 was received in cash, and $750 was redeemed in points. Figure 4.37 shows the journal entry to record the sales through cash and loyalty point redemption in July. For simplicity, the cost of refreshments is ignored.

BALANCE SHEET		INCOME STATEMENT
CURRENT ASSETS	CURRENT LIABILITIES	SALES REVENUE +$180,000 CR
CASH +$179,250 DR	ACCOUNTS PAYABLE	SALES DISCOUNT
ACCOUNTS RECEIVABLE	UNEARNED REVENUE -$750 DR	COST OF GOODS SOLD
INVENTORY	NON-CURRENT LIABILITIES	GROSS PROFIT
PREPAID EXPENSES	BANK LOAN	OPERATING EXPENSES
LONG-TERM ASSETS	SHAREHOLDERS' EQUITY COMMON SHARES	
PROPERTY, PLANT & EQUIPMENT	RETAINED EARNINGS	OPERATING INCOME (LOSS)

Shareholders' equity increases by $180,000

JOURNAL			
Date	Account Title and Explanation	Debit	Credit
Jul 31	Redemption Rewards Liability	750	
	Cash	179,250	
	Sales Revenue		180,000
	Record July sales through cash and loyalty point redemption		

FIGURE 4.37

From Figure 4.37, you can see that even though Zen Gen sold $180,000 worth of refreshments in July, the company received only $179,250 in cash due to the sales discount through loyalty points. Because sales discount was recorded at the time of loyalty point issuance in June, the difference between sales amount and cash receipt of $750 in July is recorded as a reduction in redemption rewards liability. The redemption rewards liability account should be reviewed regularly and adjusted as needed to make sure that the balance always reflects the company's best estimate based on past redemption rates.

Contingent Liabilities

Unlike estimated liabilities, a company's **contingent liabilities** involve a financial obligation that will occur only if a certain event takes place. As a result, not only are contingent liabilities estimated, but they are also dependent upon another event taking place.

According to the accounting rules, a company will only establish a contingent liability if payment is likely and the amount of liability can be reasonably estimated. Since it is difficult to determine what is and what is not possible, and how much of a contingency should be estimated, these items usually involve discretion and judgment by the accountants on behalf of the company.

Perhaps the most common reason to establish a contingent liability is to anticipate a costly lawsuit. If such a lawsuit does happen, it could seriously affect a company's bottom line. It would be prudent to include a note in the company's financial statements outlining any contingencies that may lead to a liability.

In summary, Figure 4.38 shows an example of how both determinable and non-determinable liabilities would appear in the current liabilities section for a business' balance sheet.

ASPE vs IFRS

The financial obligation that will occur if a certain event takes place is referred to as a "contingent liability" in ASPE and a "provision" in IFRS. A provision usually refer to cash or assets set aside to meet future liabilities.

Both ASPE and IFRS require the contingent liability to be recognized as an actual liability when the company determines that the payment is probable. However, IFRS defines the word *probably* as "more likely than not," whereas ASPE defines it as "likely."

Red Carpet Inc.
Partial Balance Sheet
December 31, 2016

Current Liabilities	
Operating Line of Credit	$12,500
Accounts Payable & Accrued Liabilities	15,760
Unearned Revenue	2,500
Notes Payable	10,000
Current Portion of Non-current Liabilities	3,460
Estimated Warranty Liabilities	3,457
Contingent Liabilities (Note 4)	28,500
Total Current Liabilities	**$76,177**

FIGURE 4.38

Controls Relating to Current Liabilities

One of the first, basic controls over a company's liabilities involves a simple principle: keep track of company bills and budget well enough to pay them on time. The inability to pay suppliers could cause serious inventory shortages. Even more importantly, not paying suppliers risks a company's reputation and ability to do business with others.

Controls should be implemented to ensure that the right bills are paid at the right time. To that end, all relevant documents should be gathered, such as purchase orders, receipts and original invoices, to ensure the legitimacy of the invoices.

After an invoice is paid, it should be marked as such and kept on file for verification purposes. A company would never want to pay the wrong bills or pay the same bills more than once. Controls related to invoices should prevent this from happening.

Accounting controls also involve ensuring that a company's resources are used efficiently and economically. This includes paying bills on time and making use of any payment discounts that are available. Automated systems can alert the appropriate personnel when payments should be made. Manual systems can make use of "tickler files," which allow placement of time-sensitive documents in labelled folders that are quickly and easily accessible.

The amount of current liabilities in a company can play a part in applying for a bank loan. Too many current liabilities compared to current assets may prevent the company from securing a loan. The comparison of current assets to current liabilities is called the *current ratio* and is an indicator of how liquid the company is. A higher current ratio indicates better liquidity.

WORTH REPEATING

The formula for the current ratio is

$$\frac{\text{Current Assets}}{\text{Current Liabilities}}$$

If a company has a current ratio of 1.5, this means they have $1.50 in current assets for every $1 in current liabilities.

If the company is showing poor liquidity, this might lead management to either hide current liabilities by not recording them or reclassify them as non-current liabilities. Both actions would be unethical and could lead to fines if found out.

IN THE REAL WORLD

One of the oldest yet still successful scams in business is sending a phony invoice to a company. Honest businesses often get fooled by this practice and end up wasting their money in the process.

In fairness, many of these invoices look real. They often use names similar to businesses dealt with on a regular basis, such as an Internet service provider or a club offering membership. Furthermore, the people who pay these bills are often not the people responsible for making the purchases.

There are various ways in which such fraud can be detected. Collecting all necessary internal documentation is one approach. Relying on a copy of an invoice without a purchase order is a mistake. Another approach is to simply call the number provided on the invoice to see if it is a legitimate business.

Businesses have enough of a challenge to meet financial obligations they actually owe. So ensuring that phony invoices are detected and dealt with appropriately not only makes good business sense but also helps prevent one of the oldest and most embarrassing scams around.

 Access **ameengage.com** *for integrated resources including tutorials, practice exercises, the digital textbook and more.*

In Summary

Define and differentiate between determinable and non-determinable liabilities
- ⇨ The listing order of liabilities on the balance sheet is dictated by the timing of the amount owed.
- ⇨ A company's known liabilities, or determinable liabilities, are financial obligations with fixed terms that can be traced using documentation (e.g. accounts payable).
- ⇨ Non-determinable liabilities include estimated liabilities for amounts that are not known as of the balance sheet date.

Record accounts payable
- ⇨ An accounts payable is the flip side of an accounts receivable. Instead of sending a customer a bill, an accounts payable involves receiving an invoice for goods or services received.

Record payroll liabilities
- ⇨ An accrued liability is how expenses are reconciled with the expense recognition principle. Even though an expense such as an employee's salary may not be paid until the next period, the expense itself must be recognized in the current period with an accrual.

Record transactions with sales tax
- ⇨ Sales taxes are charged on sales. The amount collected by the business must be sent to the government.

Record unearned revenue
- ⇨ Unearned revenue relates to the way revenues are reconciled with the revenue recognition principle. Even though an amount may have been paid by customers, the revenue itself can only be recognized in a later period when goods or services are delivered.

Record short–term notes payable
- ⇨ Notes payable are the flip side of a promissory note from a customer. They represent a more formal contract between a company and a supplier after a sale has been made, as opposed to a standard bill or invoice.

Record transactions related to the current portion of non-current liabilities
- ⇨ If a liability will be paid out over several years, the amount to be paid in the next year is separated on the balance sheet and called the current portion of long-term liabilities.

Record estimated liabilities
- ⇨ Estimated liabilities, such as product warranties, represent financial obligations whose specific amount will not be known until some future time. Contingent liabilities represent a financial obligation that will need to be met only if a certain event occurs. The possibility of a lawsuit might necessitate the establishment of a contingent liability.

Apply controls relating to current liabilities

➭ Controls related to current liabilities should include proper tracking and monitoring of invoices and all related documentation. This ensures that the correct bills are paid on time, which is a crucial part of maintaining the company's finances.

➭ A company should not attempt to understate current liabilities by not recording them or reclassifying them as non-current.

Review Exercise

Elnora Yearby Limited buys and resells machines. During the year, the following transactions took place.

Jan 15   Bought a machine for resale for $105,000 plus 13% HST. The amount is payable in 30 days. The company uses a perpetual inventory system.

Jan 30   Sold the machine for $214,000 plus 13% HST cash including a five-year warranty. Based on past experience, the accountant determines that an amount of $20,000 will probably be paid out in warranty obligations.

Jan 30   Paid the HST amount owing to the federal government.

Feb 15   Paid for the machine purchased on Jan 15.

Mar 27   Elnora Yearby must repair the machine under warranty. The company uses $200 in parts from its own inventory.

Record the journal entries for the above transactions.

See Appendix I for solutions

JOURNAL

Date	Account Title and Explanation	Debit	Credit

Chapter 5
PARTNERSHIPS

LEARNING OUTCOMES

❶ Describe the characteristics, advantages and disadvantages of a partnership

❷ Describe different types of partnerships

❸ Record the formation of a partnership

❹ Record the division of income or loss

❺ Record partners' drawings

❻ Prepare financial statements for a partnership

❼ Account for the addition or withdrawal of a partner

❽ Record the liquidation of a partnership

AMEENGAGE™ Access **ameengage.com** *for integrated resources including tutorials, practice exercises, the digital textbook and more.*

The Partnership Form of Business

In your previous accounting studies, you learned about the three primary options for structuring the ownership of a business.

1. In a proprietorship, only one person owns the business and keeps all the profits, which are taxed at the personal level. The owner is personally responsible for all the liabilities of the business. This means that if creditors are looking for payment, they will pursue the owner's personal assets.

2. A **partnership** is an association of two or more people who jointly own a business, its assets and liabilities, and share in its gains or losses; profits are taxed personally. Some partners may be brought in for their technical expertise and others for their ability to raise capital. There are many similarities in accounting for partnerships and proprietorships.

3. In a corporation, there can be a large number of owners known as shareholders, many of whom may not participate in the running of the business. A corporation has many rights and duties because it is a legal entity distinct from its owners. All profits are taxed at the corporate level when they are earned and at the personal level when dividends are distributed to shareholders. Corporations can raise funds from the general public by issuing shares. The shareholders (owners) of a corporation are not personally responsible for the company's debt.

While the examples in other chapters of this textbook focus primarily on proprietorships and corporations, this chapter examines the characteristics of partnerships in detail. We will explore business partnerships and demonstrate the effect of transactions and financial reporting on the asset, liability and partners' equity accounts and how various accounting principles are applied.

Figure 5.1 shows a simple comparison of the equity component of a proprietor's balance sheet to that of a partnership. In a sole proprietorship, owner's capital records the total equity of the business. The total investment by the owner, plus any profit or loss is reported in this one account. In a partnership, each partner has their own separate capital account. Details on each partner's investment and share of profit or loss is recorded separately.

FIGURE 5.1

Many professional businesses are structured as partnerships, such as consulting firms, law firms and accounting firms. Regardless of which industries they operate in, all partnerships have certain characteristics in common that govern the duties, rights and responsibilities of all partners. Certain advantages and disadvantages are associated with conducting a business as a partnership. The characteristics, advantages and disadvantages of partnership will be discussed in detail.

Characteristics

Legal Entity

As with a proprietorship, a partnership can sue or be sued. Although a partnership is considered a legal entity, for some purposes it is not considered legally separate from its owners. While the partnership itself does not pay taxes, it must still file a report on the profits of the partnership, as well as each partner's share of profits. Each partner is then required to report their share of profits (or losses) on their individual tax return, and (as with a proprietorship) they must pay taxes at their own personal tax rate regardless of whether the profits were actually withdrawn from the partnership.

Division of Profit and Losses

Even though a legal partnership agreement is not required for a partnership, it is generally advisable for partners to draw up a legal partnership agreement that specifies the division of partnership profits and losses. These terms can be changed by agreement of the partners by having a new legal partnership agreement drawn up. A new partnership agreement cancels and replaces the previous agreement. The division of profits and losses are discussed later in this chapter.

Right to Own Property

A partnership can own assets in its name, such as property, land and equipment. In fact, partners will often bring existing individual assets into the partnership for use by the business. The partnership's assets are jointly owned by all partners. This means that if a partner brings an existing individual asset into the partnership, the asset becomes the partnership's, and it is not legally returnable to the partner who contributed it. If the partnership dissolves, the asset would be sold along with other partnership assets and the proceeds (or losses) divided according to the terms of the original partnership agreement. The treatment of partnership assets will be discussed in more detail. Also, just as in a proprietorship, the accounting records for all partnership assets, liabilities and business activities are kept separately from the partners' personal accounting records.

Advantages

Instead of one person owning and operating a business as with a proprietorship, a partnership involves two or more people combining resources, both human and financial. This provides two advantages. First, the combination of human resources means that the business should benefit from the skills and experience of each partner. To illustrate, assume two lawyers, Helen White and Greg Harris decide to form the partnership White & Harris, Attorneys at Law. Helen specializes in family law and Greg specializes in criminal law. Together they are able to service twice as many clients in two different areas of law. Second, due to their combined financial resources, they are more likely than a proprietorship to be able to provide sufficient cash flow to the business without having to rely on external financing.

Another advantage of the partnership form of business is the relative ease of formation. As with a proprietorship, a partnership is relatively easy to set up. Some small partnerships of two or more individuals may be based on just a verbal agreement or a handshake. On the other hand, many professional partnerships, such as those of legal and accounting firms, may have hundreds of partners located in offices all over the world. Regardless of the number of partners, it is always wise to have a legal agreement setting out the rights and obligations of all partners. A legal agreement formalizes the arrangement for sharing profits and losses and for other eventualities such as the addition or withdrawal of a partner, or the dissolution of the partnership. In the absence of a written agreement, individuals could find themselves liable for the actions of their partners whether or not they were involved in decisions made by one partner on behalf of the partnership. Partnership agreements are discussed in more depth later in the chapter.

Disadvantages

Perhaps the most serious disadvantage of the partnership form of business is that each partner is responsible for the liabilities of the business; this is referred to as having unlimited liability. For instance, consider our legal partnership, White & Harris, Attorneys at Law. Assume that Helen White has no personal assets other than what she invested in the partnership. Greg Harris, on the other hand, owns his own home, a rental property, a cottage, a sailboat and several valuable paintings. The business suffered losses for several years and was then sued for $1.5 million by a dissatisfied client. As the partnership has very little remaining cash or assets, the partners were personally liable for the $1.5 million liability. Since Ms. White had no assets, Mr. Harris, because of unlimited liability, was required to pay the debt on behalf of the partnership.

As with a proprietorship, one of the disadvantages of a partnership is its limited life. In the event of the death of one of the partners, bankruptcy or the addition or withdrawal of a partner, the existing partnership ends (although not necessarily the business). A new partnership can be formed based on the new circumstance, and with the agreement of all partners, the business continues.

Another disadvantage is **mutual agency**, which means that each partner can authorize contracts and transactions on behalf of the partnership provided the activity is within the scope of the partnership's business. This is a disadvantage because it places the other partners at risk if the authorizing partner does not act in the best interests of the partnership.

Figure 5.2 summarizes the characteristics of partnerships and compares them with the characteristics of proprietorships. You will notice similarities between the two forms of business ownership, as well as some differences. Despite the differences in some characteristics, the accounting treatment for both forms of ownership are virtually the same.

Partnerships and Proprietorships—A Summary of Characteristics

Characteristics	Proprietorship	Partnership
# of owners	One	Two or more
Control	Owner has complete control	Decisions are shared among partners, with possibility of disagreement and conflict
Raising capital	Small—since only one person is raising money	Larger—since more than one person is responsible for raising money
Profits	Proprietor receives 100% of profits	Partners share profits in proportion to terms of the partnership agreement
Formation	Relatively simple to set up	Simple to set up, but details require close attention
Liability	Proprietor is responsible for all debts and/or legal obligations	Partners are responsible jointly and individually for actions of other partners
Skills	Reliance on the skills of the proprietor alone	Partners offer different skills in various areas of the business
Dissolution	Relatively simple to dissolve	May be dissolved upon death or withdrawal of a partner; partnership has limited life
Taxation	Profits are taxed whether or not cash is withdrawn from the business	Partners share profits and are taxed whether or not cash is withdrawn

FIGURE 5.2

To overcome the most serious disadvantage of the partnership form of business, which is unlimited liability, different types of partnerships have been introduced to limit liability. These are known as limited partnerships, and limited liability partnerships. In addition to the general form of partnership, these two special types of partnership are discussed in detail in the following section.

Types of Partnerships

General Partnership

A **general partnership** means that all partners share the responsibility for the liabilities of the business—that is, they have unlimited liability.

Limited Partnership

Businesses sometimes find themselves in the position of being legally obligated to pay other parties a considerable amount of money. These obligations can take the form of debt owed to creditors or financial sums awarded to other parties in a lawsuit. In other words, a business is liable to others for its actions. Proprietorships and partnerships generally extend unlimited liability to all the owners of the business. Unlimited liability in a partnership can be particularly damaging because if one partner is unable to meet liability obligations that are related to the partnership, the other partners are obliged to pay. This could mean having to sell off personal assets such as houses, cars and cottages. Limited partnerships resolve the potential problem of unlimited liability by creating two categories of partners within the business: the **general partner** and the **limited partner**.

Unlimited liability is assigned to a general partner, who is legally authorized to manage the day-to-day operations of the business and to make decisions on behalf of the business.

Limited liability is assigned to a limited partner, who is responsible only for providing the capital to finance the business. This partner should not be involved in day-to-day operations and is therefore not considered liable for decisions made by the business that can lead to a liability. As a result, limited partners are liable only for the amount they have invested in the business.

Limited Liability Partnership

Another business legal entity—the **limited liability partnership** or **LLP**—has been developed in some jurisdictions to deal with liability. Unlike a limited partnership, the limited partners usually participate in managing the business. LLPs are primarily used in professional partnerships to protect one partner from another partner's negligence. For example, if a lawyer is sued for negligence, other lawyers in the firm are not automatically considered liable; however, as with limited partnerships, partners usually cannot escape liability entirely. In the case of LLPs, this means that all partners are still liable for any unpaid debts to creditors. Although the details of an LLP will vary from province to province, generally an LLP can protect partners from some forms of liability, but not all.

Formation of a Partnership

In the formation stage of a partnership, all partners should collectively draw up a legal partnership agreement as a written contract. A partnership agreement will lessen the chance of legal and ethical conflict between the partners, and specify the purpose of the business as well as the relationships between the partners. In the absence of a partnership agreement, individuals could find themselves liable for the actions of their partners. Also, without an agreement, all partnership profits and losses must be shared equally, which may not be what the partners intended.

A partnership agreement should normally include

- the date of inception of the partnership
- the legal name and address of the business
- the purpose of the business
- names and addresses of all partners
- contribution of each partner
- the duties, rights and responsibilities of the partners
- the terms for sharing profits and losses
- procedures for addition or withdrawal of a partner
- terms of withdrawal of assets from the business
- provisions for the death of a partner
- the terms for liquidation of the partnership

Partnership agreements can be as varied as the businesses themselves, but any contract should include clear provisions for a full range of eventualities.

Once the partnership agreement has been drawn up, the next step is to record the initial journal entries to set up the asset, liability and equity accounts. The partners may have assets (other than cash) and liabilities that they would like to bring into the business. An independent market evaluation, or appraisal, of the items is required. Assume that on January 1, 2017, Lee Wang and Kim Chow decide to form the partnership Wang & Chow. Figure 5.3 is a summary of the amounts contributed by each partner.

Lee Wang		Kim Chow	
Cash	$8,000	Cash	$10,000
Accounts receivable	10,000	Building	170,000
Allowance for doubtful accounts	890	Bank loan	100,000
Equipment	18,000		
Accumulated depreciation	2,000		
Accounts payable	1,800		
Notes payable	6,000		

FIGURE 5.3

An independent appraiser determined that the allowance for doubtful accounts should be $1,200 and the market value of the equipment is $11,000. All other assets are recorded at the values presented.

The journal entries to set up assets, liabilities and equity accounts based on Wang's and Chow's initial investments are shown in Figure 5.4.

JOURNAL			
Date	**Account Title and Explanation**	**Debit**	**Credit**
Jan 1	Cash	8,000	
	Accounts Receivable	10,000	
	Equipment	11,000	
	Allowance for Doubtful Accounts		1,200
	Accounts Payable		1,800
	Notes Payable		6,000
	Capital—Wang		20,000
	To record Wang's investment in the partnership		
Jan 1	Cash	10,000	
	Building	170,000	
	Bank Loan		100,000
	Capital—Chow		80,000
	To record Chow's investment in the partnership		

FIGURE 5.4

The amount of accumulated depreciation is not set up in the books of the partnership because the market value of the equipment, $11,000, represents the cost of the asset in the new business. A method of depreciation, useful life and residual value will all need to be determined to calculate depreciation for current and future years. Each owner's opening capital is calculated by deducting the total amount of liabilities from the total amount of assets.

Lee Wang, Capital = $8,000 + $10,000 + $11,000 − $1,200 − $1,800 − $6,000 = $20,000

Kim Chow, Capital = $10,000 + $170,000 − $100,000 = $80,000

Division of Income or Loss

A key difference between a partnership, a proprietorship and a corporation is the way in which profits are distributed. In a proprietorship, the proprietor simply receives all the profits. In a corporation, profits are distributed in the form of dividend payments (profits paid out to shareholders). If all the assets are sold and all debts paid, the remaining cash would be distributed among the shareholders in proportion to the number of shares owned. For example, a shareholder with 10 times more shares than another shareholder would receive 10 times more of the remaining cash.

In a partnership, profits are distributed differently than they are in a proprietorship or a corporation. Since partners are involved, profits must be shared, but not always on an equal basis. A partnership agreement sets out the terms of ownership, including how profits are to be divided. In the absence of a partnership agreement, all profits and losses are shared equally among the partners. A partnership's equity account on the balance sheet is referred to as the capital account. Figure 5.5 shows an example how partnership equity would change over a period of time.

	J. Witner	R. Pierce	Total
Capital Balance (beginning)	25,000	50,000	75,000
Add: Additional Contribution	0	0	0
Share of Partnership Net Income for the Period	50,000	100,000	150,000
Subtotal	75,000	150,000	225,000
Less: Drawings	40,000	80,000	120,000
Capital Balance (ending)	35,000	70,000	105,000

FIGURE 5.5

The partnership's capital account is broken down by partner. In this case, J.Witner had a beginning capital balance of $25,000 and R.Pierce had a beginning capital balance of $50,000. During the year, they did not contribute additional capital to the business. At the end of the year, J.Witner's share of net income is $50,000 and $40,000 was withdrawn. R.Pierce's share of net income is $100,000 and $80,000 was withdrawn. The closing capital account balance is the net worth of the partnership.

One of the primary purposes of a partnership agreement is to stipulate how earnings are to be divided. Each partner's share of profits and losses is determined by the partnership's profit and loss ratio. In Figure 5.5, it is assumed that the partner's share of net income is calculated according to the capital contribution of each partner.

J.Witner's share of net income of $50,000 = ($25,000 ÷ $75,000) × $150,000

R.Pierce's share of net income of $100,000 = ($50,000 ÷ $75,000) × $150,000

Profit and loss ratios can take many forms, such as

- by dividing equally amongst all partners
- according to an agreed-upon ratio, such as 2:1, or 60% to 40%
- according to the capital contribution of each partner
- according to agreed-upon salary and interest allocations, plus a share of the remainder

Each of these methods will be examined separately.

Dividing Profits Equally

The simplest method of dividing profits is on an equal basis. For example, assume L. Wang and K. Chow earned $46,000 in net income for the year. The net income is credited in the income summary account after the revenue and expense accounts have been closed. For the partners to share the profits equally, a debit is then made to the income summary account for the entire amount, while credits of $23,000 ($46,000 ÷ 2) each are made to the capital accounts of the two partners, as shown in the journal entry in Figure 5.6.

JOURNAL				
Date	**Account Title and Explanation**		**Debit**	**Credit**
Dec 31	Income Summary		46,000	
	Capital—Wang			23,000
	Capital—Chow			23,000
	To adjust partners' capital accounts for their share of net income			

FIGURE 5.6

WORTH REPEATING

Closing the books for a company transfers the values in the revenue and expense accounts to the income summary account, leaving the revenue and expense accounts with a zero balance. The income summary account is then closed to the capital account. If the company had a net income for the year, the income summary account will be debited and the capital account will be credited, leaving the income summary account with a zero balance.

Dividing Profits According to an Agreed-Upon Ratio

The allocation of business profits can be done according to an agreed-upon ratio. For example, if L. Wang receives 60% of the profits and K. Chow receives 40%, the split is recorded in the books as shown in Figure 5.7. As a result of the $46,000 net income, L. Wang's capital balance increases by $27,600 ($46,000 × 60%), and K. Chow's capital balance increases by $18,400 ($46,000 × 40%).

JOURNAL			
Date	Account Title and Explanation	Debit	Credit
Dec 31	Income Summary	46,000	
	Capital—Wang		27,600
	Capital—Chow		18,400
	To adjust partners' capital accounts for their share of net income		

FIGURE 5.7

Dividing Profits According to the Capital Contribution of Each Partner

Another method of allocating the profits among partners is to base it on the amount that each partner invested in the business. For example, if L. Wang contributes $20,000 (one-fifth or 20%) of the capital and K. Chow contributes $80,000 (four-fifths or 80%), they are entitled to their proportion of the profits, as shown in Figure 5.8. As a result of the $46,000 net income, L. Wang's capital balance increases by $9,200 ($46,000 × 20%), and K. Chow's capital balance increases by $36,800 ($46,000 × 80%).

JOURNAL			
Date	Account Title and Explanation	Debit	Credit
Dec 31	Income Summary	46,000	
	Capital—Wang		9,200
	Capital—Chow		36,800
	To adjust partners' capital accounts for their share of net income		

FIGURE 5.8

Dividing Profits According to Agreed-Upon Salary and Interest Allocations, Plus a Share of the Remainder

Profits can also be divided by using a fixed salary allocation, interest allocation, or both for each partner, and then dividing the remaining profits equally. For example, if the partnership agreement stipulates that L. Wang's salary is $18,000, K. Chow's salary is $20,000, and interest allowance is 5% of each partner's capital balance at the beginning of the year then those are the first amounts to be deducted from the net income of the business and distributed to the partners. These amounts are shown in orange in Figure 5.9.

	Total	L. Wang	K. Chow
Net Income	$46,000		
Salary to Wang	−18,000	$18,000	
Salary to Chow	−20,000		$20,000
Interest allowance to Wang (20,000 × 5%)	−1,000	1,000	
Interest allowance to Chow (80,000 × 5%)	−4,000		4,000
Remainder	3,000		
Share of profit to Wang (3,000 × 50%)	−1,500	1,500	
Share of profit to Chow (3,000 × 50%)	−1,500		1,500
Transferred to partners' capital accounts		$20,500	$25,500

FIGURE 5.9

The $3,000 remaining after the salaries are distributed is divided equally among the partners. These amounts are shown in green on the chart.

If the distributed amounts are added up for each partner, the totals come to $20,500 ($18,000 + $1,000 + $1,500) for L. Wang and $25,500 ($20,000 + $4,000 + $1,500) for K. Chow, as shown in red on the chart. These allocations are recorded to each partner capital account as shown in Figure 5.10.

JOURNAL			
Date	**Account Title and Explanation**	**Debit**	**Credit**
Dec 31	Income Summary	46,000	
	Capital—Wang		20,500
	Capital—Chow		25,500
	To adjust partners' capital accounts for their share of net income		

FIGURE 5.10

The number of ways that profits can be divided between partners is unlimited. For example, interest can first be allocated (out of net income) at a fixed rate on each partner's capital account. The remaining amount of net income could then be divided according to a predetermined ratio or salary. The method chosen should meet the needs and interests of the partners involved and be clearly stated in the partnership agreement. The salary and interest allocations are not expenses and are not to be deducted from the partnership's revenues in determining net income for the period.

It is important to note that the method of distributing the earnings is just allocation, not actual payments and not actual expenses. Even the salary and interest amounts are allocations. The allocation is to assign to each partner's capital account their share of the earnings. If they wish to take money from the business, it is considered a drawing, which will be discussed in the next section.

If the partners have agreed to allocate salary and interest, then salary and interest are allocated regardless of whether or not the net income can cover all the salary and interest amounts. Suppose the net income in Figure 5.9 was only $40,000. In this case the remainder would have been a negative $3,000, indicating an over allocation of salary and interest. The over allocation would be covered by subtracting $1,500 from each partner, reducing the total allocation of income to their capital accounts.

Partner Drawings

The amount reported as partner's drawings does not represent the amount that has been earned by the partner during the period, but the amount that has been withdrawn from the partner's equity. During the year, partners may withdraw cash or other assets from the business for personal use. Assume that on November 5, 2017, L. Wang and K. Chow withdrew from the partnership $8,000 and $15,000, respectively. The journal entries to record the withdrawals and related year-end closing entries for the Wang & Chow partnership are as shown in Figure 5.11.

JOURNAL			
Date	Account Title and Explanation	Debit	Credit
Nov 5	Drawings—Wang	8,000	
	Drawings—Chow	15,000	
	Cash		23,000
	To record partners' drawings during the year		

JOURNAL			
Date	Account Title and Explanation	Debit	Credit
Dec 31	Capital—Wang	8,000	
	Capital—Chow	15,000	
	Drawings—Wang		8,000
	Drawing—Chow		15,000
	To close the partners' drawings account		

FIGURE 5.11

Partnership Financial Statements

There are three basic financial statements that are prepared by partnerships: the income statement, statement of partners' equity and the balance sheet. Partnership financial statements are quite similar to those of proprietorships. The main difference is that a partnership is an association of two or more people, and so there is a bit more involved in accounting for equity and the division of profits and losses of the partners.

For instance, Figure 5.12, shows an income statement for Wang & Chow, the partnership discussed earlier regarding formation of a partnership. We have assumed all the balances in the statement simply for demonstration purposes.

Wang & Chow Income Statement For the Year Ended December 31, 2017		
Revenue		
Service Revenue		$60,000
Expenses		
Depreciation	$1,000	
Bank Charges	230	
Insurance	425	
Professional Fees	945	
Property Taxes	1,300	
Repairs and Maintenance	100	
Salaries	10,000	
Total Expenses		14,000
Net Income		$46,000

FIGURE 5.12

Notice that the partnership income statement is almost identical to a proprietorship income statement. Partners' share of the income is divided according to the terms in the partnership agreement. Any detailed calculations for the distribution of profit (or losses) is usually included as a separate schedule in notes to the income statement.

Partnerships must also prepare a **statement of partners' equity**, which is a statement explaining the changes to the balance of each partner's capital account from the beginning to the end of the year. Changes are normally in the form of drawings from the business, investments added to the business and each partner's share of profit or loss.

Now look at a statement of partners' equity for Wang & Chow. Using the beginning partners' capital balances information from the journal entry in Figure 5.4, a statement can be prepared for

Wang & Chow for the year ended December 31, 2017 (Figure 5.13). For simplicity, assume that the date of inception of the partnership was January 1, 2017, that Lee Wang added an investment of $4,500 during the year, that the two partners share profits and losses equally and that Lee Wang and Kim Chow withdrew $8,000 and $15,000 from the business in 2017, respectively. Net income is taken from the partnership's income statement in Figure 5.12.

Wang & Chow Statement of Partners' Equity For the Year Ended December 31, 2017			
	Lee Wang	Kim Chow	Total
Partners' Capital, January 1	$20,000	$80,000	$100,000
Add: Investments	4,500	0	4,500
Net Income	23,000	23,000	46,000
	47,500	103,000	150,500
Less: Drawings	8,000	15,000	23,000
Partners' Capital, December 31	$39,500	$88,000	$127,500

FIGURE 5.13

The information for the statement of partners' equity is taken from the partnership income statement, the partners' capital accounts and the partners' drawings accounts.

A partnership balance sheet is very similar to that of a proprietorship. The main difference is that, for a partnership, the balance sheet shows the balance of each partner's capital account in a section called partners' capital. Using the ending partners' capital balances information from the statement of partners' equity in Figure 5.13, a balance sheet can be prepared for Wang & Chow for December 31, 2017 as shown in Figure 5.14.

Wang & Chow Balance Sheet As at December 31, 2017			
Assets		**Liabilities and Partners' Capital**	
Cash	$32,500	**Liabilities**	
Accounts Receivable	16,750	Accounts Payable	$1,000
Equipment	11,000	Notes Payable	4,000
Accumulated Depreciation—Equipment	(1,500)	Bank Loan	48,000
Building	170,000	**Total Liabilities**	53,000
Accumulated Depreciation—Building	(8,750)	**Partners' Capital**	
		Capital—Wang	39,500
		Capital—Chow	127,500
Total Assets	$220,000	**Total Liabilities and Partners' Capital**	$220,000

FIGURE 5.14

Addition and Withdrawal of a Partner

The legal basis for any partnership is the partnership agreement. Once a partner leaves, or another is added, a new partnership agreement should be prepared and signed by all parties. However, this does not mean that the business needs to open a new set of books. Instead, adjustments can be made to the current set of books to reflect any change in partner status.

Addition of a Partner

An existing partnership may want to add a new partner if they require additional capital or another skilled person. The new partner will either invest assets in the partnership (similar to Figure 5.4), or can purchase part of an existing partner's equity. To help illustrate the transactions to add or remove a partner from a partnership, we will examine a sample partnership with three existing partners, A, B and C.

In Figure 5.15, the first row shows the existing capital balances of the three partners before the addition of Partner D.

	Partner A	Partner B	Partner C	Partner D	Total
Balance before admitting new partner (includes all earnings to date)	120,000	150,000	50,000		320,000
Admission of new partner				100,000	100,000
Balance after admitting new partner	120,000	150,000	50,000	100,000	420,000

FIGURE 5.15

Partner D is the new addition; therefore, his opening balance is zero. The total of all the opening balances is $320,000. On January 1, 2016, Partner D contributes $100,000 to the partnership, which creates a new balance of $420,000.

Figure 5.16 shows how the admission of the new partner is recorded in journal format.

JOURNAL			
Date	**Account Title and Explanation**	**Debit**	**Credit**
Jan 1	Cash	100,000	
	Capital—Partner D		100,000
	To record admission of new partner		

FIGURE 5.16

The receipt of $100,000 represents a debit in the company's cash account, and a corresponding credit of $100,000 is added to Partner D's capital account.

Another way a partner can be added is if they purchase part of the equity of one or more existing partners. In this scenario, part of the capital of one or more partners is transferred to the new partner. In Figure 5.17, $100,000 of the capital of Partner A is transferred to Partner D.

	Partner A	Partner B	Partner C	Partner D	Total
Balance before admitting new partner (includes all earnings to date)	120,000	150,000	50,000		320,000
Admission of new partner	−100,000			100,000	0
Balance after admitting new partner	20,000	150,000	50,000	100,000	320,000

FIGURE 5.17

In the second row, $100,000 is deducted from Partner A's balance, and added to Partner D's balance. The journal entry would be as shown in Figure 5.18.

JOURNAL			
Date	Account Title and Explanation	Debit	Credit
Jan 1	Capital—Partner A	100,000	
	Capital—Partner D		100,000
	To record admission of new partner		

FIGURE 5.18

Note that the above transaction did not involve cash. In cases like this, any cash that changes hands between Partner A and Partner D is done outside of the partnership's books. In fact, the amount of cash paid by Partner D could be more or less than $100,000, however from the partnership's books perspective, that is irrelevant. Only the transfer of capital is what is recorded.

The partnership's total net assets after the transfer remain at $320,000, instead of the $420,000 shown in Figure 5.15. Instead of adding new cash to the partnership, Partner D purchased most of Partner A's capital (equity). Partner A would receive the cash personally from Partner D.

Withdrawal of a Partner

At times, a partner may wish to leave the partnership, or the others may wish a partner to leave. When a partner leaves, their capital account is closed and they receive a cash payout. The cash payout can either be a private transaction between partners, or the partnership itself can pay the leaving partner. Figure 5.19 illustrates a private cash transaction between partners. Partners A and B each use their personal cash to pay Partner C for a portion of Partner C's capital.

	Partner A	Partner B	Partner C	Total
Balance before withdrawal of Partner C	120,000	150,000	50,000	320,000
Withdrawal of Partner C	25,000	25,000	−50,000	0
Balance after withdrawal of Partner C	145,000	175,000	0	320,000

FIGURE 5.19

After the withdrawal of Partner C, the total partnership capital of the business remained the same. It is important to understand that the cash payment to Partner C is not recorded using the cash account because Partner C's shares were paid by Partners A and B personally, and not from the business. Assuming Partner A and B will each receive an equal share of Partner C's capital, the capital of Partner A and B will each increase by $25,000 and the capital of Partner C will decrease by $50,000.

Figure 5.20 shows how the withdrawal of Partner C is recorded in journal format.

JOURNAL			
Date	**Account Title and Explanation**	**Debit**	**Credit**
Jan 1	Capital—Partner C	50,000	
	Capital—Partner A		25,000
	Capital—Partner B		25,000
	To record withdrawal of Partner C		

FIGURE 5.20

If the withdrawal of Partner C was paid from partnership assets, this will reduce both net assets and total partnership capital, as shown in Figure 5.21.

	Partner A	Partner B	Partner C	Total
Balance before withdrawal of Partner C	120,000	150,000	50,000	320,000
Withdrawal of Partner C			−50,000	−50,000
Balance after withdrawal of Partner C	120,000	150,000	0	270,000

FIGURE 5.21

Figure 5.22 shows how the withdrawal of Partner C is recorded in journal format.

JOURNAL			
Date	**Account Title and Explanation**	**Debit**	**Credit**
Jan 1	Capital—Partner C	50,000	
	Cash		50,000
	To record withdrawal of Partner C		

FIGURE 5.22

When Market Value Differs from Book Value

The discussion so far has assumed that the cash received from a new partner or paid to a leaving partner is the same as the value shown in the capital account. However, sometimes the cash amount is different from the capital amount. When new partnership agreements are negotiated, the partners usually come to an understanding of what the business is really worth, relative to its stated book value. This understanding then forms the foundation of how much new partners must pay to receive a percentage or share of ownership in the business.

Let us build upon two examples that were already looked at in this chapter. The opening balance originally looked as shown in Figure 5.23.

	Partner A	Partner B	Partner C	Partner D	Total
Balance before admitting new partner (includes all earnings to date)	120,000	150,000	50,000		320,000

FIGURE 5.23

In the first example, assume that Partner D (the new partner) is willing to pay a premium for a share of the business. He would be willing to do this because the business could have a value that is not reflected in the capital account, such as an increase in the value of the good name of the business (goodwill), or a higher market value for assets such as land or copyright.

After negotiating the new partnership agreement, Partner D agrees to contribute $200,000 on January 1, 2016 to receive a $130,000 share of the business' book value, which amounts to a quarter of the business. Figure 5.24 and Figure 5.25 show how that transaction would be recorded.

	Partner A	Partner B	Partner C	Partner D	Total
Balance before admitting new partner (includes all earnings to date)	120,000	150,000	50,000		320,000
Admission of new partner	23,334	23,333	23,333	130,000	200,000
Balance after admitting new partner	143,334	173,333	73,333	130,000	520,000

FIGURE 5.24

The addition of Partner D's $200,000 contribution raises the total level of net assets from $320,000 to $520,000. One quarter of the new total of $520,000 amounts to $130,000, which is Partner D's new share. The remaining balance of Partner D's $200,000 investment, amounting to $70,000, is divided equally among the other three partners, as shown in Figure 5.25. The premium paid is sometimes called a bonus, which is allocated to the existing partners. We assume the bonus is divided equally among the original partners in this example, but the bonus would be divided however the partnership agreement states.

JOURNAL			
Date	**Account Title and Explanation**	**Debit**	**Credit**
Jan 1	Cash	200,000	
	Capital—Partner A		23,334
	Capital—Partner B		23,333
	Capital—Partner C		23,333
	Capital—Partner D		130,000
	To record admission of new partner		

FIGURE 5.25

In our second example, assume that Partner D is a partner who adds value to the business. Perhaps Partner D has a client list that would increase the value of the business once the new partnership is formed. Figure 5.26 shows what happens when Partner D pays $100,000 on January 1, 2016 to receive a quarter share of the business, for a value of $105,000.

	Partner A	Partner B	Partner C	Partner D	Total
Balance before admitting new partner (includes all earnings to date)	120,000	150,000	50,000		320,000
Admission of new partner	−1,666	−1,667	−1,667	105,000	100,000
Balance after admitting new partner	118,334	148,333	48,333	105,000	420,000

FIGURE 5.26

The $100,000 contribution made by Partner D creates total net assets of $420,000. One quarter of the new total of $420,000 is $105,000, which is Partner D's share. Since Partner D only paid $100,000 for this share, the $5,000 difference is a bonus to the new partner which is paid for by the capital of the original partners. This means that approximately $1,667 is deducted from the account balances of partners A, B and C, as shown in Figure 5.27.

JOURNAL			
Date	**Account Title and Explanation**	**Debit**	**Credit**
Jan 1	Cash	100,000	
	Capital—Partner A	1,666	
	Capital—Partner B	1,667	
	Capital—Partner C	1,667	
	Capital—Partner D		105,000
	To record admission of new partner		

FIGURE 5.27

The withdrawal of a partner can also be accomplished when the cash given to a leaving partner is not equal to the capital in their account. Suppose Partner C really wanted to leave the business. This could be due to unresolved conflict with the other partners, unexpected life changes or any other reason. The desire to leave immediately may lead Partner C to accept a lesser amount of cash than what their capital account says they should receive.

Suppose Partner C decides to leave and accepts $40,000 cash. In this scenario, both of the remaining partners receive a bonus based on the amount of Partner C's capital that was not paid out. This bonus to the remaining partners is split evenly. The impact on capital is shown in Figure 5.28.

	Partner A	Partner B	Partner C	Partner D
Balance before withdrawal of Partner C	120,000	150,000	50,000	320,000
Withdrawal of Partner C	5,000	5,000	−50,000	−40,000
Balance after withdrawal of Partner C	125,000	155,000	0	280,000

FIGURE 5.28

Equity and net assets decrease by the $40,000 cash received by the departing partner. The journal entry to record this transaction is shown in Figure 5.29.

JOURNAL			
Date	Account Title and Explanation	Debit	Credit
Jan 1	Capital—Partner C	50,000	
	Cash		40,000
	Capital—Partner A		5,000
	Capital—Partner B		5,000
	To record the withdrawal of a partner		

FIGURE 5.29

Alternatively, a partner may be leaving because the remaining partners want him out of the business. In this case, the incentive to Partner C to leave is cash payment in excess of the stated value of Partner C's capital.

Suppose Partner C is willing to leave if he receives $58,000 cash. In this scenario, both remaining partners give a bonus to the leaving partner. This bonus to the leaving partner is split evenly between the remaining partners. The impact on capital is shown in Figure 5.30.

	Partner A	Partner B	Partner C	Partner D
Balance before withdrawal of Partner C	120,000	150,000	50,000	320,000
Withdrawal of Partner C	−4,000	−4,000	−50,000	−58,000
Balance after withdrawal of Partner C	116,000	146,000	0	262,000

FIGURE 5.30

Equity and net assets decrease by the $58,000 cash received by the departing partner. The journal entry to record this transaction is shown in Figure 5.31.

JOURNAL				
Date	Account Title and Explanation		Debit	Credit
Jan 1	Capital—Partner C		50,000	
	Capital—Partner A		4,000	
	Capital—Partner B		4,000	
	Cash			58,000
	To record the withdrawal of a partner			

FIGURE 5.31

Liquidation of a Partnership

A partnership has a limited life. If the partnership changes due to the addition or withdrawal of a partner, the existing partnership ends. Similarly, if the partners decide to end or sell the business, or if the partnership dissolves due to bankruptcy or other factors, a process known as a **partnership liquidation** takes place. Liquidation means that the partnership as a business entity will legally cease to exist. The liquidation process involves selling off any partnership assets, paying off liabilities, and distributing any remaining proceeds to the partners according to their individual profit and loss ratios.

As with the end of any business, the accounting cycle must first be completed in order to determine a starting point for the liquidation process. By now you are likely quite knowledgeable about the entire accounting cycle, from journalizing and posting transactions to preparing a trial balance, to preparing the financial statements, closing entries and the post-closing trial balance. Once these tasks are complete, the liquidation process can begin. This involves

1. Selling off partnership assets for cash, and realizing a gain or loss
2. Allocating any gain or loss to the partners according to their individual profit and loss ratios
3. Paying partnership liabilities (in cash) to creditors
4. Distributing remaining proceeds to partners according to their partnership agreement

Note that step 4 entails distributing remaining proceeds to partners according to their capital account balances. In many cases, all partners will have credit balances in their capital accounts, meaning that they have no capital deficiency. However, there are also many cases in which one or more partners has a debit balance in their capital account, and this is known as a **capital deficiency**. Both situations will be examined, starting with the most straightforward situation, where there is no capital deficiency.

Liquidation with No Capital Deficiency

First consider a partnership liquidation based on the simplified balance sheet for ABC Partnership, in which there is no capital deficiency.

In Figure 5.32, the balance sheet of ABC Partnership is shown after liquidation. Since the only remaining asset consists of $100,000 in cash, this is distributed to the partners in proportion to their equity in the business. The transaction would appear as shown in Figure 5.32.

ABC Partnership Balance Sheet As at December 31, 2016			
Assets		**Liabilities and Partners' Capital**	
Cash	$100,000	**Partners' Capital**	
		Capital—Partner A	35,000
		Capital—Partner B	40,000
		Capital—Partner C	25,000
Total Assets	$100,000	**Total Liabilities and Partners' Capital**	$100,000

JOURNAL			
Date	**Account Title and Explanation**	**Debit**	**Credit**
Dec 31	Capital—Partner A	35,000	
	Capital—Partner B	40,000	
	Capital—Partner C	25,000	
	Cash		100,000
	To record cash distribution among partners		

FIGURE 5.32

This was a relatively simple example. The amounts of cash received by the partners were equal to their share of equity. This example also assumes that assets were sold at their book value, which rarely happens. Suppose before liquidation, ABC Partnership had assets valued at $700,000 and liabilities valued at $600,000, as shown in the balance sheet in Figure 5.33. Thus, net assets are equal to $100,000. If the business' net assets are sold for $70,000, representing a loss of $30,000, the journal entry in Figure 5.33 would be made.

ABC Partnership			
Balance Sheet			
As at December 31, 2016			
Assets		**Liabilities and Partners' Capital**	
Cash	$100,000	**Liabilities**	
Accounts Receivable	200,000	Loan Payable	$200,000
Equipment	700,000	Accounts Payable	400,000
Less: Accumulated Depreciation	(300,000)	**Total Liabilities**	$600,000
		Partners' Capital	
		Capital—Partner A	35,000
		Capital—Partner B	40,000
		Capital—Partner C	25,000
		Total Partners' Capital	$100,000
Total Assets	$700,000	**Total Liabilities and Partners' Capital**	$700,000

JOURNAL			
Date	**Account Title and Explanation**	**Debit**	**Credit**
Dec 31	Cash	570,000	
	Accumulated Depreciation	300,000	
	Loss on Sale of Assets	30,000	
	Accounts Receivable		200,000
	Equipment		700,000
	Sold asset for a loss		
Dec 31	Loan Payable	200,000	
	Accounts Payable	400,000	
	Cash		600,000
	Paid all liabilities		

FIGURE 5.33

The net result is that cash decreases to $70,000 and all assets and liabilities are removed from the balance sheet. The loss of $30,000 is recorded as an additional expense.

This loss is then allocated to the partners according to the same formula that would be used when distributing earnings, or whatever terms were agreed upon in the partnership agreement. For the purpose of this example, assume that the earnings (or losses) are distributed equally, as shown in Figure 5.34.

JOURNAL			
Date	**Account Title and Explanation**	**Debit**	**Credit**
Dec 31	Capital—Partner A	10,000	
	Capital—Partner B	10,000	
	Capital—Partner C	10,000	
	Loss on Sale of Net Assets		30,000
	To allocate loss on sale of net assets		

FIGURE 5.34

The cash is then distributed to the partners based on the closing balance of their equity, as shown in Figure 5.35.

JOURNAL			
Date	**Account Title and Explanation**	**Debit**	**Credit**
Dec 31	Capital—Partner A	25,000	
	Capital—Partner B	30,000	
	Capital—Partner C	15,000	
	Cash		70,000
	To record cash distribution among partners		

FIGURE 5.35

This example involved allocating a loss on sale of assets. Any gain would be allocated in the same manner—equally, unless otherwise provided for—and the cash would be divided according to each partner's final balance of equity in the business.

To summarize, liquidation of a partnership primarily involves the following chronological steps.

1. Selling off partnership assets for cash, and realizing a gain or loss
2. Allocating any gain or loss to the partners according to their profit and loss ratios
3. Paying partnership liabilities (in cash) to creditors
4. Distributing remaining proceeds to partners equally (per their partnership agreement)

The effects on the partners' capital account balances using the figures from the most recent example, in which the net assets were sold at a loss, are summarized in Figure 5.36.

	Assets			=	Liabilities + Partners' Capital				
	Cash	Accounts Receivable	Equip- ment (Net)	Loan Payable	Accounts Payable	Capital— Partner A	Capital— Partner B	Capital— Partner C
Before liquidation	$100,000	$200,000	$400,000	$200,000	$400,000	$35,000	$40,000	$25,000
Sell assets and realize loss	570,000	–200,000	–400,000			–10,000	–10,000	–10,000
Pay partnership liabilities	670,000 –600,000	0	0	200,000 –200,000	400,000 –400,000	25,000	30,000	15,000
Distribute remaining proceeds to partners	70,000 –70,000	0	0	0	0	25,000 –25,000	30,000 –30,000	15,000 –15,000
Final balances	$ 0	$ 0	$ 0	$ 0	$ 0	$ 0	$ 0	$ 0

FIGURE 5.36

Liquidation with a Capital Deficiency

Often, one or more partners have a debit balance in their capital account, which is known as a capital deficiency. Capital deficiencies occur for many reasons, including normal business losses, cash withdrawals that exceed a partner's capital account balance, or a negative balance that arises during the process of liquidation. Look at the previous example, but under different circumstances. Refer to the balance sheet for ABC Partnership in Figure 5.33.

Suppose that before liquidation, ABC Partnership has assets valued at $700,000 and liabilities valued at $600,000. Thus, the net assets are

JOURNAL			
Date	Account Title and Explanation	Debit	Credit
Dec 31	Cash	517,500	
	Accumulated Depreciation	300,000	
	Loss on Sale of Assets	82,500	
	Accounts Receivable		200,000
	Equipment		700,000
	Sold asset for a loss		
Dec 31	Loan Payable	200,000	
	Accounts Payable	400,000	
	Cash		600,000
	Paid all liabilities		

FIGURE 5.37

equal to $100,000. This time, the assets can only be sold for $517,500, generating a loss of $82,500. Figure 5.37 shows the journal entry.

Once these journal entries are posted, there is a $17,500 cash balance remaining. Figure 5.38 shows the effects on the partners' capital accounts as a result of the liquidation process. Since Partner A ($7,500) and Partner B ($12,500) have credit balances in their capital accounts, they each receive cash in accordance with their capital balances. Partner C, however, has a debit balance in his capital account of $2,500 (that is, a negative balance). This represents a capital deficiency, meaning that Partner C owes the partnership $2,500. There are two possible scenarios to consider: one in which Partner C has sufficient personal cash to pay the $2,500 deficit to the partnership, and one in which Partner C does not have enough cash to pay what he owes.

	Assets			=	Liabilities	+	Partners' Capital		
	Cash	Accounts Receivable	Equipment (Net)	Loan Payable	Accounts Payable	Capital— Partner A	Capital— Partner B	Capital— Partner C
Before liquidation	$100,000	$200,000	$400,000	$200,000	$400,000	$35,000	$40,000	$25,000
Sell assets and realize loss	517,500	–200,000	–400,000			–27,500	–27,500	–27,500
Pay partnership liabilities	617,500 –600,000	0	0	200,000 –200,000	400,000 –400,000	7,500	12,500	–2,500
Balance after selling assets and paying off liabilities	$17,500	$0	$0	$0	$0	$7,500	$12,500	–$2,500

FIGURE 5.38

If Partner C has sufficient personal cash to pay the $2,500 deficit to the partnership, the following journal entry would be made to record his payment as shown in Figure 5.39. This payment would bring Partner C's capital account balance to zero, thereby fulfilling his obligation to the partnership and completing the liquidation process. The accompanying table in Figure 5.39 also shows the effects on the accounts as a result of the payment of capital deficit by Partner C.

JOURNAL			
Date	Account Title and Explanation	Debit	Credit
Dec 31	Cash	2,500	
	Capital—Partner C		2,500
	To record the payment of capital deficit by Partner C		

	Assets			=	Liabilities	+	Partners' Capital		
	Cash	Accounts Receivable	Equip-ment (Net)	Loan Payable	Accounts Payable	Capital— Partner A	Capital— Partner B	Capital— Partner C
Balance after selling assets and paying off liabilities	$17,500	$0	$0	$0	$0	$7,500	$12,500	–$2,500
Payment of capital deficit	+2,500							+2,500
Balance after deficit payment	20,000					7,500	12,500	0
Distribute remaining proceeds to partners	–20,000					–7,500	–12,500	
Final balances	$ 0	$ 0	$ 0	$ 0	$ 0	$ 0	$ 0	$ 0

FIGURE 5.39

What if Partner C does not have enough cash to pay the $2,500 he owes to the partnership? The partnership characteristic of unlimited liability means that if one partner is unable to meet obligations related to the partnership, the other partners are obliged to pay. Partner A and Partner B must absorb the loss according to their agreement—in this case, equally. Partner A and Partner B would each need to decrease their own capital by $1,250 to cover the $2,500 capital deficiency, bringing Partner C's capital account balance to zero. The journal entry for this transaction and its impacts on accounts are shown in Figure 5.40.

JOURNAL			
Date	Account Title and Explanation	Debit	Credit
Dec 31	Capital—Partner A	1,250	
	Capital—Partner B	1,250	
	Capital—Partner C		2,500
	To record the payment of Partner C's capital deficit by Partner A and Partner B		

	Assets			=	Liabilities	+	Partners' Capital		
	Cash	Accounts Receivable	Equip- ment (Net)	Loan Payable	Accounts Payable	Capital— Partner A	Capital— Partner B	Capital— Partner C
Balance after selling assets and paying off liabilities	$17,500	$0	$0	$0	$0	$7,500	$12,500	–$2,500
Write off of capitals						–1,250	–1,250	+2,500
Balance after write off of capitals	17,500					6,250	11,250	0
Distribute remaining proceeds to partners	–17,500					–6,250	–11,250	
Final balances	$0	$0	$0	$0	$0	$0	$0	$0

FIGURE 5.40

The partners would now be able to close the partnership accounts and complete the liquidation process. Beyond this, Partners A and B may decide to pursue Partner C legally to get back the money they lost, although if Partner C cannot pay the partnership the amount owed, it is unlikely he would be able to pay Partners A and B.

IN THE REAL WORLD

Some of the world's most famous ventures and corporations started out as partnerships.

Richard and Maurice McDonald were brothers from New Hampshire who moved to California in the late 1920s to seek their fortune. They eventually fine-tuned their hot dog stand and barbecue restaurant to limit the number of items on the menu, eliminated utensils and plates, and made the kitchen more efficient. After selling 21 franchises by the mid-1950s, Ray Kroc came along and purchased all the rights to the business for $2.7 million. There are now approximately 31,000 McDonald's restaurants around the globe with sales of over $22 billion a year.

Bill Hewlett and David Packard graduated with engineering degrees from California's Stanford University in 1934. A few years later, they started working together on a technical sound device; Disney Studios bought eight of these devices. Their partnership was formalized in 1939 and they went on to innovate in the fields of technology and management style. Today, Hewlett-Packard generates more than $100 billion in sales from computer-related equipment. The name of the company was decided on a coin toss. You can guess who won.

 Access **ameengage.com** for integrated resources including tutorials, practice exercises, the digital textbook and more.

In Summary

Describe the characteristics, advantages and disadvantages of a partnership

↪ A partnership is an association of two or more people who jointly own a business, for which earnings are taxed at a personal level only.

↪ A partnership is a legal entity, however partners generally have unlimited liability.

↪ Partnership advantages include raising more capital and having more expertise, since more people are involved in creating the business. Partnerships can also be easy to create.

↪ Disadvantages can include unlimited liability and mutual agency

Describe different types of partnerships

↪ A general partnership means that all partners have unlimited liability.

↪ A limited partnership divides a company's partners into two categories: general partners and limited partners. Unlimited liability extends to general partners because they are involved in the day-to-day decision making of the business. Limited partners, on the other hand, are only liable for the amount of capital they invest in the business. This is known as limited liability.

↪ A limited liability partnership or LLP is a legal ownership structure, used in some jurisdictions, that usually protects professionals from a partner's negligence. If one of the partners is sued, the others are not necessarily liable. However, all the partners are liable for any debts owed to regular day-to-day creditors.

Record the formation of a partnership

↪ Even though a partnership agreement in the form of a legal written contract is not required to form a partnership, having a partnership agreement will lessen the chance of legal and ethical conflict between partners and specify the purpose of the business and the relationships between the partners.

↪ Assets that partners bring into the business are recorded at their fair market values. Each owner's opening capital is calculated by deducting the total amount of liabilities from the total amount of assets that each owner brings into the business.

Record the division of income or loss

↪ A partnership's earnings can be divided in a number of different ways; these are usually outlined in the partnership agreement. Four common methods of dividing earnings are the following: equally; based on a ratio; based on the capital contribution of each partner; and drawing salaries and intereset before dividing the rest.

↪ To record the division of income, the income summary account is debited and the partners' capital accounts are credited. To record the division of loss, the partners' capital accounts are debited and the income summary account is credited.

Record partners' drawings

- ✪ When a partner withdraws cash from the business for personal use, the partners' drawings account is debited and cash is credited.

- ✪ The partners' drawings account is closed at the end of each accounting period by debiting the partners' capital account and crediting the partners' drawings account.

Prepare financial statements for a partnership

- ✪ There are three basic financial statements that are prepared by partnerships: the income statement, statement of partners' equity, and the balance sheet. Partnership financial statements are quite similar to those of proprietorships, except that they include capital accounts for each partner.

Account for the addition or withdrawal of a partner

- ✪ A new partner can simply add in a new portion of partner's equity, or purchase some or all of another partner's share.

- ✪ When a partner withdraws from a partnership, the capital of the withdrawn partner can be bought out using either the existing partners' personal assets or the partnership's assets. If the personal assets of the existing partners are used, a credit or an increase in the existing partners' capital is recorded in the partnership's journal. If the partnership's assets are used, a credit or a decrease in the partnership's assets is recorded.

- ✪ If the amount of capital allocated to a new partner is different than the cash invested, a bonus is either allocated to the existing partners or the new partner.

- ✪ If the amount of cash paid to a departing partner is different than their capital account, a bonus is either allocated to the existing partners or the leaving partner.

Record the liquidation of a partnership

- ✪ The partnership agreement should stipulate how the liquidation should be done. If assets are sold above or below book value, the corresponding gains or losses are shared among the partners. The remaining cash can be distributed according to each partner's proportion of equity in the business.

Review Exercise

On January 1, 2016, Zelma Rapoza, Serena Dennen and Sharron Throop have decided to set up a spa and operate it as a partnership. They will each contribute $10,000 to buy equipment and help pay for lease expenses. Zelma is also contributing $25,000 of her own equipment.

They agree to pay themselves a yearly salary of $5,000 each. Since Zelma contributed the equipment, she expects $3,000 "rent" per year on the equipment for ten years. Each partner is to earn 5% on their investment (cash contribution). The net income for the year was $25,000. The profit remaining after salaries, rent and interest is to be distributed at ratio of their cash contribution.

Required

a) Prepare a schedule showing the changes in capital during 2016.

b) Prepare journal entries for the following transactions.

Jan 1	Record the initial cash contribution.
Jan 1	Record the equipment contribution.
Dec 31	Record the division of partnership income. Assume that revenues and expenses have already been closed to the income summary account.
Jan 2, 2017	Sharron retires from the partnership. To buy Sharron's shares, Zelma and Serena contribute $10,000 and $7,333 of their personal assets respectively. Prepare a journal entry to record Sharron's withdrawal from the partnership.

See Appendix I for solutions.

a)

_____

_____

_____

_____

_____

_____

_____

_____

_____

_____

b)

Date	Account Title and Explanation	Debit	Credit

Chapter 6

CORPORATIONS: CONTRIBUTED CAPITAL AND DIVIDENDS

AMEENGAGE™ *Access **ameengage.com** for integrated resources including tutorials, practice exercises, the digital textbook and more.*

LEARNING OUTCOMES

❶ Describe the characteristics of corporate organizations

❷ Describe differences between public and private corporations

❸ Explain shareholders' equity

❹ Record the issuance of shares

❺ Record the payment of cash dividends

❻ Record stock splits and stock dividends

❼ Record income tax expense

❽ Record the closing entries for a corporation

❾ Calculate retained earnings

❿ Explain the importance of ethics for corporate reporting

Appendix

⓫ Record the reacquisition of shares

The Corporate Form of Organization

So far we have demonstrated accounting practices related to proprietorships and partnerships. These two types of business are usually operated and managed by their owners. In proprietorships and partnerships, the owners provide their own funding for the business. They can fund the business with their personal assets or by taking out a loan, thereby incurring a debt. Whether the owners use their own assets or they borrow money, they are personally liable for all debts of the business. A proprietorship or a partnership exists as long as the owners are alive and decide to continue its operation.

There is also a different type of business, known as a corporation. A **corporation** is a legal entity that is separate from its owners. In a corporation, the owners are known as **shareholders**, because they hold shares of equity in the corporation. Corporations are chartered (or incorporated) under federal or provincial law, and there are legal restrictions on how they are set up and how they must be governed. Figure 6.1 shows how proprietorships and partnerships differ from corporations in terms of equity.

All corporations have certain characteristics in common that govern their duties, rights and responsibilities and we will look at those in more detail.

SOLE PROPRIETORSHIP	PARTNERSHIP	CORPORATION
OWNER'S EQUITY	PARTNERS' EQUITY	SHAREHOLDERS' EQUITY
OWNER'S CAPITAL	CAPITAL—PARTNER A	COMMON SHARES
	CAPITAL—PARTNER B	RETAINED EARNINGS

FIGURE 6.1

Separate Legal Existence

A corporation is a separate legal entity that has the rights and responsibilities of a person. This means that the corporation is legally separate from its owners, known as shareholders. A corporation can enter into its own contracts, and it can buy and sell property. It is responsible for its own actions and for its own debts. It has the right to sue, and it can also be sued. The shareholders cannot be held personally liable for the debts of the corporation.

Limited Liability of Shareholders

Because a corporation is legally separate from its owners, the shareholders are not responsible for any actions or debts of the business. Shareholders are only liable for the amount that they have invested in the company, giving them what is called **limited liability**.

Formal Organizational Structure

At the heart of a corporation is the separation of ownership and management. In a large corporation, the company's shareholders do not necessarily run the business. In some cases, the owners of a corporation may have very little to do with managing the business. As owners of the business, shareholders are responsible for electing a board of directors who will manage the business on their behalf. The board of directors is responsible for deciding on the corporation's operational policies. The board also appoints the external auditors and an executive management team. The executive management team acts as the company's legal agents and is usually headed by a chief executive officer (CEO).

Unlimited Life

A corporation is considered a *going concern,* which means that it remains an entity regardless of the comings and goings of shareholders.

Ability to Raise Capital

When a corporation needs to raise capital for day-to-day operations or to invest in property and equipment, it can issue units of its equity, known as **shares**, or stock. Those who own shares in a corporation's equity are known as shareholders. Shares are an attractive investment for shareholders because they not only offer limited liability but also have the potential to increase in value. They also offer liquidity, which is the ability to buy and sell them.

Income Tax Treatment

As a separate legal entity, a corporation must file a tax return and pay federal and provincial income tax on its earnings. Shareholders do not pay income tax on the earnings of the corporation. However, they are required to pay personal income tax on any income that they receive in the form of dividends. A **dividend** is a distribution of the corporation's earnings (net income) to shareholders based on the shares that they own. You will learn more about dividends later in this chapter.

Because a corporation pays income tax on its earnings and shareholders pay personal income tax on their dividends, this is referred to as **double taxation**. This does not necessarily mean that the government will receive $2 in income tax instead of $1. It simply means that tax is paid twice (at different rates) on earnings. The corporation earns income, pays corporate income tax, and from the remaining income after tax, it pays dividends to shareholders. Shareholders then pay personal income tax on the dividends. In Canada, there are various tax credits such as the federal dividend tax credit to help reduce the amount of tax paid by shareholders.

Government Requirements

A corporation is owned by its shareholders, and it is responsible to them for its financial results. Corporations are required to meet strict federal and provincial government regulations. When a corporation is formed, it must file government documents known as articles of incorporation. The **articles of incorporation** (or corporate charter) contain the operational details of the corporation, including its name, purpose and general objectives.

Corporations must also meet certain requirements for issuing shares and distributing income to shareholders. They must regularly report on their financial results and operations and conduct formal shareholder meetings. Although the corporate structure has many advantages, it also has legal obligations that require lawyers to be hired, forms to be completed and documents to be prepared and filed.

Figure 6.2 compares the characteristics of a sole proprietorship, a partnership and a corporation.

Characteristics of Business Organizations			
	Sole Proprietorship	**Partnership**	**Corporation**
Owners	One individual	Two or more individuals	One or more shareholders
Owner liability	Unlimited	Unlimited	Limited
Life of business	Limited	Limited	Unlimited
Taxation of earnings	• Taxed at the individual's personal tax rate • Paid by owner	• Taxed at each partner's personal tax rate • Paid by partners	• Taxed at corporate tax rate • Paid by corporation
Example	Indra's Bookkeeping Services	PricewaterhouseCoopers	Telus Corp.

FIGURE 6.2

The corporate form of organization allows businesses to do things on a larger scale and in a formally structured way. It also has certain duties, rights and responsibilities that can be viewed as advantages and disadvantages, as shown in Figure 6.3.

Advantages	Disadvantages
• Separate legal existence • Limited liability of shareholders • Formal organizational structure • Unlimited life • Ability to raise capital	• Strict government requirements • Double taxation of corporation and shareholders

FIGURE 6.3

WORTH REPEATING

There are three main forms of organizations, each with a different ownership structure.

1. A sole proprietorship is a business owned and generally operated by one owner.
2. A partnership is a non-corporate entity owned by two or more partners.
3. A corporation is a business that is a legal entity separate from its owners, known as shareholders.

Corporations can be classified by their purposes into for-profit corporations and not-for-profit corporations. **For-profit corporations** are formed for the purpose of generating profits for their shareholders. Examples of for-profit corporations include McDonald's, Bombardier and Facebook. **Not-for-profit corporations** are formed for such purposes as advancing social and environmental causes rather than generating financial returns for their shareholders. Examples of not-for-profit organizations include World Wide Fund for Nature, Toronto Symphony Orchestra and Breast Cancer Society of Canada. The accounting practices of for-profit corporations are different from those of not-for-profit corporations. This textbook focuses on the accounting practices of for-profit corporations, which can be further classified into public and private corporations, as will be discussed next.

Public vs. Private Corporations

The corporate form of organization has a formal organizational structure with separate legal existence. As a separate legal entity, a corporation has the right to be formed as either a public or private corporation. A **public corporation** is one that trades its shares on a stock exchange, such as the Toronto Stock Exchange (TSX) or the Montreal Stock Exchange (MSE). Trading simply means buying or selling shares. That is, its shares are available to be traded publicly from one member of the general public (the current shareholder) to another (the purchaser). A public corporation is also commonly referred to as a publicly accountable enterprise.

A **private corporation** is one that does not offer its shares to the public. The company's shares are instead owned and exchanged privately. For example, a private corporation may have a single owner who wishes never to sell the shares publicly. Or a private corporation may be a company with several owners who belong to the same family, who have no intention of selling shares on a stock exchange. A private corporation is also commonly known as a closed corporation or a privately held corporation.

IN THE REAL WORLD

A Canadian-controlled private corporation (CCPC) is a private corporation that is entitled to certain tax rates and deductions if it meets specific guidelines. Not all private corporations that operate in Canada are classified as CCPCs.

A private enterprise might choose to become a CCPC for the corporate tax advantages. A discussion of the specific tax benefits are outside the scope of this course. Some of these tax advantages include additional time to pay some types of taxes, higher investment tax credits, and potential capital gains exemptions.

Below are some of the requirements for a company to qualify as a registered CCPC in Canada.

- The company's shares are not traded on any stock exchange.
- The corporation is a resident in Canada.
- The corporation is not directly or indirectly controlled by a non-resident shareholder.

The financial reporting requirements for private companies are different from those of public companies. The reporting standards for public corporations are generally more strict and detailed than those for private companies since more external users depend on the financial statements of public corporations. We will explore these differences.

Public and Private Corporations: IFRS vs. ASPE

As of January 1, 2011, Canada adopted International Financial Reporting Standards (IFRS) as the accounting standards guideline for publicly traded corporations. Therefore, all public corporations in Canada must now be IFRS-compliant.

On the other hand, private corporations in Canada have a choice of following IFRS or Accounting Standards for Private Enterprises (ASPE), as shown in Figure 6.4. A private corporation usually has only a few shareholders, most of whom may be closely related and involved in the day-to-day operation of the business. A private corporation does not sell its shares to the general public. For this reason, its few shareholders may not see the need for the more stringent reporting standards required under IFRS. The one exception is if a private corporation has issued publicly-held bonds, in which case IFRS must be used. The standards under ASPE are continually evolving: for instance, some substantial changes were made effective in 2014, and other changes take effect in 2016 and beyond.

Reporting Options for Private Corporations

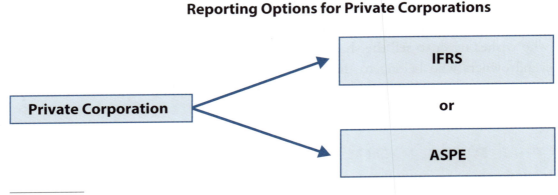

FIGURE 6.4

A private corporation may choose to use ASPE rather than incur the high costs of retraining staff and converting to IFRS. ASPE requires fewer disclosures in financial reporting than IFRS. IFRS can be much more technically complex.

On the other hand, a private corporation may choose to switch from ASPE to IFRS if its owners are considering making it a public corporation. In order to issue shares to the public, the corporation must comply with IFRS. A private corporation may also choose to switch to IFRS if it has international operations or wants the ability to compare its own financial statements to international competitors. Whichever standard the company decides to follow, it is required to include this information in its financial statements so that users are informed.

In the next chapter, financial statements will be shown in accordance with IFRS guidelines in addition to ASPE guidelines. But first, some of the specific accounting requirements of corporations will be discussed in more detail.

Accounting for Shareholders' Equity

In a proprietorship, owner's equity is a simple figure that represents the net worth of the business. In a partnership, equity is divided into separate capital accounts for each partner's stake in the business. With a corporation, things become more complex. As the ownership structure gets more complicated, so does the recording and reporting of equity on the company's balance sheet. In the simplest terms, equity represents the owners' claims on the assets of the business.

In a corporation, the shareholders actually own the company and so owners' equity is called **shareholders' equity**. Shareholders' equity is comprised of two components: contributed capital and retained earnings.

Contributed capital is generally comprised of two sub-categories called share capital and contributed surplus. **Share capital** refers to capital raised from the sale of shares and **contributed surplus** contains other types of additions to shareholders' contributions. In the real world, the use of the term contributed capital is often omitted and the term share capital is used instead.

Retained earnings are the earnings that are kept and accumulated by the company after dividends have been paid to the shareholders. In other words, the earnings not paid out to shareholders are retained in the business. Share capital and retained earnings are reported as two separate items in the shareholders' equity section of the financial statements.

A corporation's charter (or articles of incorporation) specifies the number of shares it will issue, the types of shares to be issued and the rights of the shareholders for each type of share. A corporation can offer for sale an unlimited number of shares, or it can specify a particular number of shares. If the company later decides it needs to issue more shares, additional authorization is required. The maximum number of shares that can legally be issued is known as the company's **authorized shares**.

When authorized shares are sold to shareholders, they become **issued shares**. Once shares have been issued, they can be sold or transferred to other investors without involving the corporation. This is known as trading on the secondary market. **Outstanding shares** are those shares that have already been authorized and issued and are held by shareholders. Outstanding shares can be traded on the secondary market by those who own them.

In the secondary market, shares are sold at a price known as their **market value**. The market value is determined by the amount that investors are willing to pay for them. This means that the shares may be sold at a higher or lower price than what the original holder paid for them.

When we examine the balance sheet of a corporation, the shares figure shows the total amount of money received by the corporation when it initially sold the shares to shareholders. This value is the book value of the shares and has no bearing on the market value of the shares. If the company is doing well, the market value will likely be higher than the book value. If the company is not doing well, the market value will likely be lower than the book value.

Later in this chapter, you will learn how to calculate retained earnings. You will also see how retained earnings are presented in the shareholders' equity section of a corporation's balance sheet.

The Classes of Shares: Common and Preferred

All public corporations must issue common shares. Some corporations also offer another class of shares known as preferred shares. **Common shares** are a type of equity that gives shareholders ownership in the corporation, along with voting rights to elect a board of directors and the potential to receive a share of the company's earnings in the form of dividends. Investors buy common shares with the expectation that the corporation will remain or become profitable, although the payment of dividends is not guaranteed.

A corporation may also issue preferred shares, a type of share with features that are not available with common shares. **Preferred shares** receive preference because dividends must first be paid on them before any dividends are paid on common shares. This preference, however, does not guarantee that dividends will be paid. Preferred shares usually indicate the amount of dividends that each share will receive. In the event of a company liquidation, preferred shareholders also have priority over common shareholders over the assets of the liquidating company. However, preferred shareholders have no voting rights to influence the direction of the company. In this sense, it is only common shareholders that maintain this specific right of company ownership, and it is an important one.

Some preferred shares have a **cumulative** feature allowing them the right to be paid the current year's dividends and to accumulate any unpaid dividends from previous years. With cumulative preferred shares, if no dividend is declared by the board of directors, or if a dividend payment is otherwise missed, the dividends owing will accumulate and must be paid before any dividends are paid to the common shareholders. With cumulative preferred shares, any unpaid dividends from prior periods are known as **dividends in arrears**. Preferred shares that do not have the right to receive any accumulated unpaid dividends are known as **non-cumulative** shares.

Figure 6.5 summarizes the most important features of common and preferred shares.

Features of Common Shares	Features of Preferred Shares
• Represent ownership in the corporation • Owners elect the board of directors • Owners vote on corporate policy • Owners rank after bondholders and preferred shareholders in the event of a liquidation • Owners have a right to receive dividends only if declared by the board of directors	• Owners have a higher claim on assets and earnings than do common shareholders • Owners generally get paid a regular dividend, especially before any dividends are paid to common shareholders • Cumulative preferred shares have the right to accumulate unpaid dividends from previous years

FIGURE 6.5

Par Value Shares and No-Par Value Shares

In some countries, both common and preferred shares can be sold at par value or no-par value. **Par value shares** are shares that are issued with an assigned value. **No-par value shares** are shares issued with no assigned value. When no-par value shares are issued, the equity account is credited for the entire proceeds of the sale. In some jurisdiction, only no-par value shares are allowed to be issued. For this chapter, we will assume all shares are no-par value shares.

Issuing Shares

One of the advantages of the corporate form of ownership is the ability of public corporations to raise cash by selling shares to the public. However, shares can also be issued in non-monetary exchanges for long-term assets or services.

We will look at three different ways a corporation can issue shares and how the transactions are recorded in the company's accounting records.

Issuing Shares in Exchange for Cash

The most common reason for issuing shares is to raise needed financial capital. Suppose that on February 8, 2016, a corporation issues 1,000 common shares at $10 per share, to raise a total of $10,000 cash.

Figure 6.6 shows how the transaction would be recorded in the journal, and how it would affect the balance sheet accounts.

JOURNAL			
Date	**Account Title and Explanation**	**Debit**	**Credit**
Feb 8	Cash	10,000	
	Common Shares		10,000
	To record issue of 1,000 common shares for cash		

FIGURE 6.6

The receipt of $10,000 is recorded as a debit to the cash account, and the corresponding credit is made to the common shares account and reported in the share capital section of the balance sheet.

However, not every type of share issuance is as straightforward as this exchange for cash. It is also possible to make non-monetary exchanges of shares for goods and services.

Issuing Shares in Exchange for Assets or Services

If a corporation has limited cash, it may offer shares to a supplier in exchange for assets such as land, property or equipment. Since shares offer liquidity, which is the ability to trade the shares at their market value, and there is potential for the market value to increase, some suppliers may be willing to exchange an asset for shares.

In a non-monetary exchange, the parties to the transaction still need to determine the value of assets that are being exchanged. Most importantly, the corporation will need to know the dollar amount at which the transaction will be recorded. Accountants and other professionals determine this amount using the concept of **fair value**, which is the amount that the asset could be sold for in the open market. Depending on the accounting standards used, the share issuance transaction can be recorded at either the fair value of the goods and services or the fair value of the shares being exchanged.

Public corporations, which must report under IFRS, must use the fair value of the goods or services received to record the transaction. If this value is difficult to determine, then the fair value of the shares exchanged should be used. For example, if a corporation wants to issue shares to purchase used equipment, but the fair value of the equipment cannot be determined, then the fair value of the shares traded on the stock market will be used as the value of the equipment.

Figure 6.7 shows how the transaction would be recorded if, on February 25, 2016, the corporation issues 20,000 common shares at their current market value (the fair value) of $40 each in exchange for the equipment. The corporation cannot readily determine the fair value of the equipment.

JOURNAL			
Date	Account Title and Explanation	Debit	Credit
Feb 25	Equipment	800,000	
	Common Shares		800,000
	To record issue of 20,000 common shares for equipment		

FIGURE 6.7

In a private corporation reporting under ASPE, the transaction can also be valued at whichever value is more easily determined: the fair value of the goods and services, or the fair value of the shares being issued. This is slightly complicated by the fact that a private corporation's shares are not normally traded on the open market, so it is difficult to determine their fair value. Often a professional appraisal must be done to establish a fair value for the goods or services, and that is the value that will be used to record the transaction.

For example, Figure 6.8 shows how the transaction would be recorded if, on March 18, 2016, a private corporation issues 1,000 common shares in exchange for land that is valued (appraised) at $1,000,000.

JOURNAL			
Date	Account Title and Explanation	Debit	Credit
Mar 18	Land	1,000,000	
	Common Shares		1,000,000
	To record issue of 1,000 common shares for land valued at $1,000,000		

FIGURE 6.8

The purchase increases the long-term asset account land with a debit. The corresponding $1,000,000 credit is recorded in the common shares account, and reported in the share capital section of the balance sheet.

The concept and determination of fair value can also be used if a corporation wants to issue shares in exchange for professional services it has received.

Suppose that a new corporation required the services of an accountant. The accounting services performed come to a total of $10,000. For a new corporation, the $10,000 expenditure might be considered costly and hard on its cash flow. On March 21, 2016, the company offers to issue to the accountant 1,000 common shares at their current market value of $10 each, to equal the fair value of $10,000. The accountant accepts the offer of shares in exchange for her accounting services. Figure 6.9 shows how the transaction is recorded on the company's books. On the income statement, the $10,000 is included as a debit to an operating expense account, and the corresponding credit is made to the common shares account and reported in the share capital section of the balance sheet. Given the nature of such a transaction, the cash account remains untouched.

JOURNAL

Date	Account Title and Explanation	Debit	Credit
Mar 21	Accounting Fees Expense	10,000	
	Common Shares		10,000
	To record issue of 1,000 common shares in exchange for accounting services		

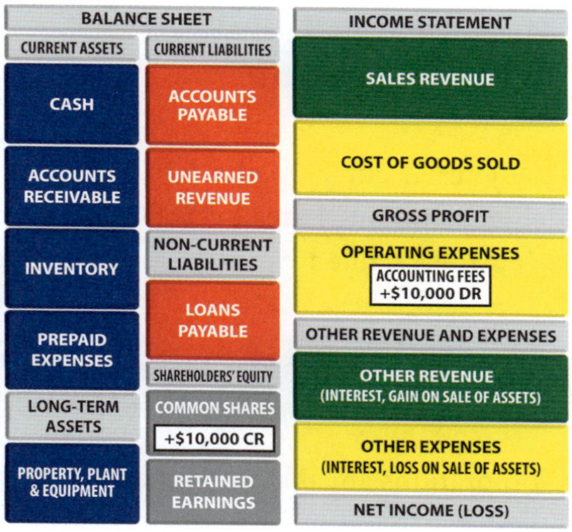

FIGURE 6.9

Accounting for Share Issue Costs

Earlier we established that all corporations have certain duties, rights and responsibilities. Along with the advantage of being able to raise large amounts of financial capital, public corporations are also responsible for the costs associated with raising that capital.

When a corporation issues shares to the public, there are certain costs associated with the share issue such as registration fees, legal and accounting fees, regulatory fees and printing of share certificates and other required documentation. These costs are not considered regular operating costs, but are referred to as **share issue costs**. The share issue costs can be accounted for using either the offset method or the retained earnings method. If the offset method is used, then the share issue costs are recorded as a debit to the appropriate share account (common or preferred). If the retained earnings method is used, then the share issue costs are debited directly to retained earnings.

For example, suppose that on February 10, 2016, a company issues 1,000 common shares in exchange for $10,000 cash, and incurs a total of $600 in share issue costs. Figure 6.10 shows the entry that would be made for this transaction.

JOURNAL			
Date	Account Titles and Explanation	Debit	Credit
Feb 10	Cash	9,400	
	Common Shares	600	
	Common Shares		10,000
	To record issue of 1,000 common shares for cash, with $600 in share issue costs		

JOURNAL			
Date	Account Titles and Explanation	Debit	Credit
Feb 10	Cash	9,400	
	Retained Earnings	600	
	Common Shares		10,000
	To record issue of 1,000 common shares for cash, with $600 in share issue costs		

FIGURE 6.10

The journal entry on the left hand side shows the transaction using the offset method, which debits common shares by $600. The journal entry on the right hand side shows the transaction using the retained earnings method, which debits retained earnings by $600.

Accounting for Cash Dividends

Corporations are able to raise capital by offering several attractive investment options to potential investors. Investors are not only attracted by the potential for increased market value of their shares, but also by an opportunity to receive a portion of the company's profits in the form of dividends. Corporations commonly issue two types of dividends: cash dividends and stock (or share) dividends. We will discuss cash dividends first, and stock dividends in a later section.

A corporation's share price is not entirely within the corporation's control as it fluctuates with changes in the economy, investor confidence and investment analysts' recommendations. The frequency and level of dividend payments, however, are within the corporation's control because the board of directors can set the terms of dividend payments. Dividends are often paid once a year, if the directors decide to pay them.

There are three important dates related to the accounting treatment of dividends

- The **date of declaration** is the date on which the board of directors announces (declares) that dividends will be paid to shareholders.
- The **date of record** is the date on which the corporation lists all those who currently hold shares and are therefore eligible to receive dividend payments.
- The **date of payment** is the date on which the company actually makes the dividend payment to eligible shareholders.

To illustrate the relationship between these three dates, suppose Zuti Corporation's board of directors declared a cash dividend on its common shares on March 31, 2016, and the dividend is to be paid on June 30, 2016. The board announces that all shareholders who hold common shares as of April 30, 2016 will be eligible to receive the dividend. We would express this as: on March 31, 2016, Zuti Corporation declared a cash dividend to be distributed on June 30, 2016 to all shareholders of record as of April 30, 2016.

Next we will examine Zuti Corporation's accounting responsibilities related to each of these dates.

A CLOSER LOOK

Before cash dividends can be paid, three important conditions must be met.

1. The board of directors must declare that a dividend will be paid.

2. The corporation must have enough cash to cover its ongoing operations and other obligations.

3. The corporation must have enough legal capital; that is, it must maintain enough assets to fulfill its obligations to creditors, and ensure that any dividend payments would not result in a deficit to retained earnings.

On the Date of Declaration

Suppose that Zuti Corporation's board of directors declares on March 31, 2016 that a dividend payment of $1 per share will be paid to shareholders of all 10,000 outstanding common shares.

Although the dividends are not paid right away, the company must record the obligation to pay them on the date that the dividends are declared. The accounting entry for a dividend declaration can be done in one of two ways: using a cash dividends account, or using the retained earnings account.

Using the Cash Dividends Account

When the dividend is declared, a debit is made to a temporary account known as the cash dividends account, and a credit is made to the dividends payable account. The cash dividends account reduces the equity of the corporation and behaves like owner drawings in a proprietorship. It is used to accumulate all of the dividends declared for the period. Note that in the accounting records and financial statements, dividends must be divided between common shares and preferred shares. This example will only deal with common shares.

Figure 6.11 shows the related accounting entry for Zuti Corporation. In this example, a debit of $10,000 is made to cash dividends. The cash dividends account behaves like owner's drawings. The debit to the cash dividends account will eventually decrease the balance of retained earnings on the balance sheet at the end of the period. The credit appears on the balance sheet as an increase of $10,000 to the dividends payable account, which is considered a current liability. In other words, the dividend payment is accrued until the payment is finally made.

JOURNAL			
Date	Account Title and Explanation	Debit	Credit
Mar 31	Cash Dividends—Common	10,000	
	Dividends Payable		10,000
	To record declaration of cash dividend on 10,000 common shares at $1 per share		

FIGURE 6.11

Using the Retained Earnings Account

Some companies choose an alternative method to record dividends on the date of declaration. Dividends eventually decrease the balance of retained earnings at the end of the period. This occurs when the cash dividends account is closed to retained earnings at the end of the period. You will learn more about closing entries later in this chapter. To save time and simplify their accounting entries, some companies choose to forego using the cash dividends account, and immediately debit the retained earnings account for the amount of the dividends. The related accounting entry is shown in Figure 6.12. This method has the same effect on the balance sheet as the method that uses the cash dividends account.

JOURNAL			
Date	Account Title and Explanation	Debit	Credit
Mar 31	Retained Earnings	10,000	
	Dividends Payable		10,000
	To record declaration of cash dividend on 10,000 common shares at $1 per share		

FIGURE 6.12

BALANCE SHEET

CURRENT ASSETS	CURRENT LIABILITIES
CASH	ACCOUNTS PAYABLE
ACCOUNTS RECEIVABLE	DIVIDENDS PAYABLE +$10,000 CR
INVENTORY	NON-CURRENT LIABILITIES
PREPAID EXPENSES	LOANS PAYABLE
	SHAREHOLDERS' EQUITY
LONG-TERM ASSETS	CONTRIBUTION CAPITAL
PROPERTY, PLANT & EQUIPMENT	RETAINED EARNINGS -$10,000 DR

Whichever method is used, this transaction does not involve the income statement. This is because dividend payments are not an operating expense, but a distribution of the corporation's earnings to its shareholders.

On the Date of Record

The date of record is the date on which the corporation determines who the existing shareholders are and how many shares each shareholder owns. The company must determine who its shareholders are on the date of record so that it knows who is eligible for the declared dividend payment.

No accounting entry is made for the date of record, but the corporation does keep detailed records of all shareholders. The person responsible for this is the corporate secretary, who is in charge of all official company documentation. Among other duties, the corporate secretary maintains the company's share register, which is much like a subledger. Some large corporations use the services of a transfer agent to record changes in ownership of shares as a result of trading on the stock market.

On the Date of Payment

On the payment date, dividend payments are made to the shareholders by cheque or by electronic transfer to their investment account at a financial institution. Using our previous example, assume that on June 30, 2016, Zuti Corporation pays the dividends that were declared on March 31, 2016. Figure 6.13 shows the related accounting entry for this transaction.

JOURNAL			
Date	**Account Title and Explanation**	**Debit**	**Credit**
Jun 30	Dividends Payable	10,000	
	Cash		10,000
	To record payment of cash dividend declared on March 31, 2016		

FIGURE 6.13

The debit to dividends payable decreases the current liability on the balance sheet. The credit to cash decreases the current assets on the balance sheet. Note that this accounting entry will be the same no matter which method was used to record the dividend declaration: the cash dividends method or the retained earnings method. This is because both methods originally set up the liability as a credit to dividends payable.

The preceding examples show the accounting entries for cash dividends on common shares. This was done to keep the examples easy to follow. However, the accounting entries would be done in a similar manner if cash dividends were only paid out to preferred shareholders.

Dividends in Arrears

Cumulative preferred shares entitle shareholders to receive any unpaid dividends from prior periods—that is, **dividends in arrears**. Conversely, preferred shares without this cumulative feature are known as non-cumulative shares. Non-cumulative preferred shares do not accumulate unpaid dividends, and so they are treated in the accounting records much the same way as common shares. The discussion that follows will demonstrate the accounting treatment for all three types of shares: non-cumulative preferred shares, cumulative preferred shares and common shares.

Suppose that on December 31, 2015, Yarind Corporation had on its balance sheet the following share capital.

- 10,000, $2 cumulative preferred shares with the book value of $60,000
- 25,000, $2 non-cumulative preferred shares with the book value of $100,000
- 100,000 common shares with the book value of $200,000

Note that for the two types of preferred shares, the $2 refers to the annual dividend per share that shareholders are entitled to receive when dividends are declared.

Figure 6.14 shows how the share capital would appear in the shareholders' equity section of the company's balance sheet on December 31, 2015.

Yarind Corporation Shareholders' Equity (partial Balance Sheet) December 31, 2015	
Share Capital	
Preferred shares, $2 cumulative, 15,000 shares authorized, 10,000 shares issued and outstanding	$60,000
Preferred shares, $2 non-cumulative, 30,000 shares authorized, 25,000 shares issued and outstanding	100,000
Common shares, unlimited shares authorized, 100,000 shares issued and outstanding	200,000
Total Share Capital	$360,000
Retained Earnings	500,000
Total Shareholders' Equity	$860,000

FIGURE 6.14

In reality, the financial statements presentation can be done in a single column or in multiple columns. In this example, a single column format is shown. In the review exercise of this chapter, you can find an example of a two-column presentation format.

Suppose that during the year 2016, the company's board of directors neither declared nor paid any dividends. Then, on December 15, 2017, the board of directors declares $100,000 in dividends, payable on February 10, 2018 to the shareholders of record on December 31, 2017. No other dividends have been declared to date. To summarize this information

For the year ended December 31, 2016, dividends declared: $0
For the year ended December 31, 2017, dividends declared: $100,000

When dividends on cumulative preferred shares remain unpaid from prior periods, the corporation must keep track of the amount that is still owing to the cumulative preferred shareholders. This means the corporation owes the cumulative preferred shareholders a total of $40,000 as shown below.

Dividends in arrears on cumulative preferred shares from 2016 ($2 × 10,000) $20,000
Dividends on cumulative preferred shares for 2017 ($2 × 10,000)   20,000
Total cumulative preferred dividends $40,000

For 2017, the corporation also owes the non-cumulative preferred shareholders an amount equal to the dividends of 2017 only for a total of $50,000 ($2 × 25,000).

After the preferred shareholders have been paid, the remainder of the dividends will be paid to the common shareholders, as follows.

Dividends declared (December 15, 2017) $100,000
Payable on cumulative preferred shares (2016 and 2017) $40,000
Payable on non-cumulative preferred shares (2017)   50,000
Total preferred dividends payable   90,000
Remainder of dividends—payable to common shareholders $10,000

The journal entry to record the declaration of dividends on December 15, 2017, and the effect on the balance sheet, is shown in Figure 6.15. This accounting entry shows the cash dividends method of accounting for the dividend declaration, but Yarind Corporation could alternatively use the retained earnings method.

JOURNAL			
Date	**Account Title and Explanation**	**Debit**	**Credit**
Dec 15	Cash Dividends—Preferred, cumulative	40,000	
	Cash Dividends—Preferred, non-cumulative	50,000	
	Cash Dividends—Common	10,000	
	Dividends payable		100,000
	To record declaration of cash dividends on common and preferred shares		

FIGURE 6.15

The journal entry to record the subsequent payment of the dividends on February 10, 2018, and the effect on the balance sheet, is shown in Figure 6.16.

JOURNAL			
Date	**Account Title and Explanation**	**Debit**	**Credit**
Feb 10	Dividends payable	100,000	
	Cash		100,000
	To record payment of cash dividends declared		

FIGURE 6.16

As before, the payment reduces the dividend liability and cash balances.

Stock Splits and Stock Dividends

Among the advantages of the corporate form of organization is the right of a corporation to manage and reorganize its equity structure. For various reasons, a corporation's board of directors may decide to retain cash and, rather than declare a cash dividend, offer shareholders a different type of payment. This payment might be in the form of either a stock split or a stock dividend.

A **stock split** is an action that increases the number of a corporation's outstanding shares, which in turn decreases the individual price of each share traded on the stock market. For example, if a corporation declares a two-for-one stock split, it calls in all outstanding shares of existing shareholders, and exchanges each share for two shares. The shareholder now owns two shares for every one share they previously held in the company; however, the value of each share is reduced by half. Stock splits can be done with any other ratio that the corporation decides on, such as three-for-one or four-for-one. Consider this example of a stock split.

Suppose that as of December 31, 2016, Standard Corporation has 10,000 common shares outstanding, and the shares are currently traded at $40 each on the stock market. The book value of the common shares on the balance sheet is $200,000. On January 15, 2017, the company's board of directors declares a two-for-one stock split. The stock split results in twice as many shares (10,000 shares × 2 = 20,000 shares), but at the same overall book value of $200,000. Each shareholder now owns two shares for every one that they originally held, but the market will respond by dropping the market value from $40 per share to $20 per share. Figure 6.17 shows the effect on Standard Corporation's shareholders' equity if it declares a stock split. As shown below, a stock split increases the number of common shares issued with no impact on the total shareholders' equity. The overall result is that there is no change in each shareholder's percentage ownership and the total values of both share capital and shareholders' equity remain the same after the stock split.

Standard Corporation Shareholders' Equity (Partial Balance Sheet) December 31, 2016 (Before Stock Split)	
Share Capital	
Common shares, unlimited shares authorized, 10,000 shares issued and outstanding	$200,000
Retained Earnings	500,000
Total Shareholders' Equity	$700,000

Standard Corporation Shareholders' Equity (Partial Balance Sheet) January 15, 2017 (After Stock Split)	
Share Capital	
Common shares, unlimited shares authorized, 20,000 shares issued and outstanding	$200,000
Retained Earnings	500,000
Total Shareholders' Equity	$700,000

FIGURE 6.17

One of the main reasons for splitting shares is to increase their liquidity. If a share price is too high on the stock market, some investors may feel the shares are too expensive or unaffordable. A lower share price makes the shares attractive to more investors, which can potentially benefit all the investors. Because the total book value of the shares outstanding is not affected, no journal entry is needed to account for a stock split. A memorandum (note) is usually recorded to indicate the increased number of shares outstanding.

A CLOSER LOOK

A corporation can also do a stock split on preferred shares in addition to common shares. The increasing or decreasing of the amounts of preferred shares is handled the same as common shares. The difference is how the dividends for preferred shares are handled. Suppose a corporation is going to issue a two-for-one preferred stock split, and there are 20,000 preferred shares which currently pay $4 dividends. After the stock split, there will be 40,000 preferred shares which will pay $2 dividends. The preferred stock split will have to be mentioned in the notes.

Conversely, if a company wants to decrease its number of outstanding shares, it may decide to do a **reverse stock split**. In a two-for-one reverse stock split, each current shareholder would receive one share for every two shares they held in the company; however, the market value of each share would double. Figure 6.18 shows the effect on Standard Corporation's shareholders' equity if it declares a reverse stock split. A reverse stock split reduces the number of common shares issued from 10,000 to 5,000 with no impact on the total shareholders' equity. The market will respond by increasing the market price from $40 per share to $80 per share. As with a regular stock split, there is zero overall effect on shareholders' equity and no change in each shareholder's percentage ownership. Reverse stock splits may be done when a company's share price is becoming too low to be listed on a particular stock exchange.

Standard Corporation Shareholders' Equity (Partial Balance Sheet) December 31, 2016 (Before a Reverse Stock Split)	
Share Capital	
Common shares, unlimited shares authorized, 10,000 shares issued and outstanding	$200,000
Retained Earnings	500,000
Total Shareholders' Equity	$700,000

Standard Corporation Shareholders' Equity (Partial Balance Sheet) January 15, 2017 (After Stock Split)	
Share Capital	
Common shares, unlimited shares authorized, 5,000 shares issued and outstanding	$200,000
Retained Earnings	500,000
Total Shareholders' Equity	$700,000

FIGURE 6.18

A **stock dividend** may be issued in lieu of a cash dividend for several reasons. First, a company may wish to retain its cash in order to expand the business, which will eventually increase the value for shareholders. Another reason is to keep the share price affordable for new investors; the company can increase the number of outstanding shares to reduce the market price per share. A stock dividend can also satisfy investors with a dividend, even though cash will not be paid.

To demonstrate a stock dividend, return to Standard Corporation. Figure 6.19 shows the shareholders' equity section of the company's balance sheet before the stock dividend is declared. On December 31, 2016, Standard Corporation has 10,000 outstanding common shares. The current market price is $40 per share.

Standard Corporation Shareholders' Equity (partial Balance Sheet) December 31, 2016 (Before a Stock Dividend)	
Share Capital	
Common shares, unlimited shares authorized, 10,000 shares issued and outstanding	$200,000
Retained Earnings	500,000
Total Shareholders' Equity	$700,000

FIGURE 6.19

On January 15, 2017, the company's board of directors decides to declare a 20% stock dividend on all 10,000 outstanding shares. The dividend is to be distributed on February 20, 2017 to all shareholders of record as of January 31, 2017. Public corporations, which must report under IFRS, must use the market value of the shares to record the stock dividend on the date of declaration. To calculation of the value of the shares in this stock dividend assuming the market price on the date of declaration is $40 per share is shown below.

Total number of outstanding common shares = 10,000

20% stock dividend on 10,000 shares = 10,000 × 0.20 = 2,000 shares

2,000 shares at a current market price of $40 per share = 2,000 × $40 = $80,000

The total value of shares to be issued in the form of stock dividends is $80,000. Figure 6.20 shows the journal entry to record the declaration of the stock dividend and the effect on the shareholders' equity section of the balance sheet. A debit is made to the account called stock dividends, which is similar in purpose to the cash dividends account used when a cash dividend is declared. The stock dividends account, like any dividend, will reduce retained earnings. Alternatively, we could directly debit retained earnings.

JOURNAL			
Date	**Account Title and Explanation**	**Debit**	**Credit**
Jan 15	Stock Dividends	80,000	
	Stock Dividends Distributable		80,000
	To record declaration of 20% stock dividends on common shares		

FIGURE 6.20

Stock dividends distributable is an equity account, not a liability, but it is used in a similar way that the dividends payable account is used for cash dividends. It keeps track of the amount that will be distributed to the shareholders. The end result of a stock dividend is a rearrangement of the components of shareholders equity—that is, some of the value of retained earnings is shifted to the common shares account. Stock dividends are never considered a liability, because the company does not actually owe shareholders a stock dividend.

Figure 6.21 shows the journal entry to record the distribution of the stock dividend on February 20, 2017, and the effect on the shareholders' equity section of the balance sheet.

JOURNAL			
Date	**Account Title and Explanation**	**Debit**	**Credit**
Feb 20	Stock Dividends Distributable	80,000	
	Common Shares		80,000
	To record distribution of 20% stock dividends on common shares		

ACCOUNTS RECEIVABLE	NON-CURRENT LIABILITIES
INVENTORY	LOANS PAYABLE
	SHAREHOLDERS' EQUITY
PREPAID EXPENSES	COMMON SHARES +$80,000 CR
LONG-TERM ASSETS	STOCK DIVIDENDS DISTRIBUTABLE -$80,000 DR
PROPERTY, PLANT & EQUIPMENT	RETAINED EARNINGS

FIGURE 6.21

This distribution of the stock dividend completes the transfer of part of retained earnings to the value of common shares. Figure 6.22 shows the shareholders' equity section of the balance sheet for Standard Corporation before the stock dividend was declared and after the stock dividend was distributed. Notice that total shareholders' equity has not changed, just the values of retained earnings, common shares and the number of common shares issued and outstanding.

Standard Corporation Shareholders' Equity (Partial Balance Sheet) January 15, 2017 (Before Stock Dividend)		Standard Corporation Shareholders' Equity (Partial Balance Sheet) February 20, 2017 (After Stock Dividend)	
Share Capital		**Share Capital**	
Common shares, unlimited shares authorized, 10,000 shares issued and outstanding	$200,000	Common shares, unlimited shares authorized, 12,000 shares issued and outstanding	$280,000
Retained Earnings	500,000	Retained Earnings	420,000
Total Shareholders' Equity	$700,000	**Total Shareholders' Equity**	$700,000

FIGURE 6.22

All of the above transactions illustrate how public corporations account for issuing shares and recording dividends. For private corporations, issuing shares would be recorded in the same manner. However, the recording and payment of dividends is usually less formal for private corporations because the shares are not publicly traded and the list of shareholders is usually quite short. Figure 6.23 below shows the impact of cash dividends, stock dividends and stock splits.

	Common Shares		Retained Earnings	Shareholders' Equity	Assets
	Value	**Quantity**			
Cash Dividend	No Change	No Change	Decrease	Decrease	Decrease
Stock Dividend	Increase	Increase	Decrease	No Change	No Change
Stock Split	No Change	Increase	No Change	No Change	No Change

FIGURE 6.23

The Canada Business Corporations Act requires the value assigned to stock dividends be at the market price on the declaration date. This is called the fair value method. Other countries may use other methods such as the stated value method or the memo method. These two alternative valuation methods are beyond the scope of this textbook.

Income Tax Expense for Corporations

Unlike a proprietorship or partnership, a corporation is considered a separate legal entity from its owners. A corporation must therefore file and pay taxes on its net income; this amount that the corporation is obligated to pay is known as **income tax**. Federal income tax laws, including the income tax rates, are determined by the Government of Canada and published in the Income Tax Act.

Income tax expense is recorded in a corporation's accounting records on an accrual basis. For accounting purposes, the company applies the prescribed percentage from the Income Tax Act to its net income for its fiscal period. This amount is then recorded as its income tax expense, and its income tax payable. Consider this example.

Suppose that for the fiscal year ended December 31, 2016, Star Company reported a net income before tax of $266,000. Assume the company is subject to income tax at a rate of 30% on its net income for the period. Based on the net income according to its accounting records, Star Company would record an income tax expense of $266,000 × 30% = $79,800 for the year ended December 31, 2016. Figure 6.24 shows the recorded transaction, and the effects on the balance sheet and income statement.

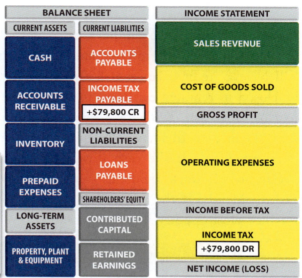

JOURNAL			
Date	Account Title and Explanation	Debit	Credit
Dec 31	Income Tax Expense	79,800	
	Income Tax Payable		79,800
	To record income tax expense at the year end		

FIGURE 6.24

Note that the transaction is recorded with an increase to an expense and an increase to a liability. The liability will eventually be paid to the government.

We used the term "net income according to accounting records" because there is a difference between IFRS and the Income Tax Act when it comes to calculating taxable income. This can lead to different amounts of tax being calculated based on which income figures are used. A discussion of the difference is beyond the scope of this textbook, so we will simply use net income as calculated by the corporation for our tax calculations.

Closing Entries for Corporations

At the end of a period, a business must close revenue and expense accounts to equity. A corporation is no different. At the end of the period, a corporation's revenue and expense accounts are closed to a temporary account called income summary. The income summary and any cash or stock dividends are then closed to retained earnings.

Figure 6.25 shows the sample closing entries for a small company using its income summary account. After closing revenue and expenses to income summary, the income summary account will have a credit balance of $50,000, indicating a net income for the year. That amount will be closed to retained earnings, increasing the equity of the corporation. An entry is also made to close the cash dividends account at the end of the period. For this example, assume that $10,000 in cash dividends on common shares were declared during 2016. This closing entry is required only if the cash dividends method was used to record dividends on the date of declaration. If stock dividends were declared, they would also be closed in the same manner as cash dividends. If the retained earnings account was debited on the date of declaration, then this last closing entry is not required.

JOURNAL			
Date	**Account Titles and Explanation**	**Debit**	**Credit**
Dec 31	Sales Revenue	200,000	
	Income Summary		200,000
	To close revenue account		
Dec 31	Income Summary	150,000	
	Cost of Goods Sold		80,000
	Salaries Expense		35,000
	Rent Expense		25,000
	Income Tax Expense		10,000
	To close expense accounts		
Dec 31	Income Summary	50,000	
	Retained Earnings		50,000
	To close net income to retained earnings		
Dec 31	Retained Earnings	10,000	
	Cash Dividends—Common		10,000
	To close cash dividends account		

FIGURE 6.25

Calculating Retained Earnings

Share capital and retained earnings are reported separately in the shareholders' equity section of the financial statements. Share capital is what has been invested by shareholders or the owners of a corporation when they purchase shares. Now examine how to calculate retained earnings, and look at how retained earnings are presented in the shareholders' equity section of a company's balance sheet.

To properly create the shareholders equity portion of a corporation's balance sheet, several values must be calculated. The quantity of shares that have been sold (issued) through the stock market must be shown for all classes of shares (common and preferred). Also, the total value that the shares were sold for must be shown. This is considered the book value of the shares, and the value does not change as market prices for the shares increase or decrease.

To calculate retained earnings, suppose Mamae Company started 2016 with a balance of $100,000 in its retained earnings account. During the year, the company earned a net income of $40,000. It also paid cash dividends to shareholders in the amount of $10,000, and stock dividends at a value of $5,000 (both dividends were paid on common shares). The balance of the retained earnings account on December 31, 2016 would be calculated as shown in Figure 6.26.

Calculation of Retained Earnings For Year Ended December 31, 2016		
Retained Earnings, January 1, 2016		$100,000
Add: Net Income for year		40,000
Less: Cash Dividends—Common	$10,000	
Stock Dividends	5,000	15,000
Retained Earnings, December 31, 2016		$125,000

FIGURE 6.26

Figure 6.27 shows how the December 31 balance of retained earnings fits into the shareholders' equity section of the balance sheet for Mamae Company as at December 31, 2016.

Mamae Company Shareholders' Equity As at December 31, 2016	
Share Capital	
Preferred shares, $2, 10,000 shares authorized, 3,000 shares issued and outstanding	$12,000
Common shares, unlimited shares authorized, 50,000 shares issued and outstanding	5,000,000
Total Share Capital	5,012,000
Retained Earnings	125,000
Total Shareholders' Equity	$5,137,000

FIGURE 6.27

For private corporations following ASPE, a calculation of retained earnings must be included in a formal statement of retained earnings. Under ASPE, a company is not required to disclose in the statement the number of authorized shares, only their rights and privileges. You will learn how to prepare a statement of retained earnings in the next chapter.

For all public corporations, and for private corporations that follow IFRS, a calculation of retained earnings must be included in a formal statement of changes in shareholders' equity, along with additional information that you will learn about when we discuss financial statements in the next chapter.

Ethics

It is very important that information provided to the shareholders of a corporation is accurate and that any unethical actions taken by individuals running the corporation are handled properly and not covered up.

In 2009, the Ontario Securities Commission charged four employees from Research in Motion (RIM) $77 million for backdating stock options. The Ontario Securities Commission ensures laws regarding stocks are properly followed by corporations.

A stock option is the right of an employee to purchase company shares at a set purchase price. The purchase price is usually the market price on the day stock options are granted to the employees. No matter what happens to the stock price after that date, the price remains fixed for the employees. By backdating the stock option, executives of RIM were able to set the price at a low purchase price, purchase shares at that lower price and then immediately sell at a higher price to make a profit.

Although the individuals were not accused of fraud, what they did was negligent and unethical. These individuals were required to pay back the profits they made due to the backdating, plus penalties. Securities commissions and auditors help provide confidence that financial statements are reporting on the corporation properly, and if something unethical is being done, it will be caught.

 Access **ameengage.com** for integrated resources including tutorials, practice exercises, the digital textbook and more.

 In Summary

Describe the characteristics of corporate organizations

⇨ A corporation is a legal entity that is separate from its owners known as shareholders.

⇨ Some characteristics of corporations are: limited liability of shareholders, formal organizational structure, unlimited life and the ability to raise capital.

Describe differences between public and private corporations

⇨ Public corporations sell a portion of their shares to the public through stock markets. Private corporations do not sell their shares to the public.

⇨ Public corporations must be IFRS-compliant. Private corporations have a choice of following IFRS or Accounting Standards for Private Enterprises (ASPE).

Explain shareholders' equity

⇨ Shareholders' equity is made up of two components: contributed capital and retained earnings.

⇨ Contributed capital generally consists of two sub-categories, called share capital and contributed surplus.

⇨ There are two types of share capital: common shares and preferred shares.

⇨ Common shares constitute ownership in the company, but do not come with guaranteed dividend payments.

⇨ Preferred shares do not come with voting rights, but do come with regular dividend payments and a higher claim to company assets than common shares.

⇨ Retained earnings are the earnings that are kept and accumulated by the company after dividends have been paid to the shareholders.

Record the issuance of shares

⇨ A company can issue shares in exchange for cash, assets owned or services rendered.

⇨ Par value shares are shares that are issued with a stated (par) value. In Canada, shares can be issued with no stated value and are therefore called no-par value shares.

⇨ Share issue costs are certain costs associated with the share issue. Share issue costs are recorded as a reduction to either retained earnings or common (or preferred) shares.

Explain the importance of ethics for corporate reporting

⇨ Auditors will review corporate statements to ensure they are reported properly and ethically.

Record the payment of cash dividends

- ➪ There are three important dates related to the accounting treatment of dividends. The date of declaration, the date of record and the date of payment.

- ➪ The accounting entry for a dividend declaration can be made in one of two ways: using a cash dividends account, or using the retained earnings account.

Record stock splits and stock dividends

- ➪ A stock split is a corporate action that increases the number of a corporation's outstanding shares, which in turn decreases the individual price of each share.

- ➪ If a company wants to decrease its number of outstanding shares, it may decide to do a reverse stock split.

- ➪ A stock dividend may be issued in lieu of a cash dividend if a company wants to retain its cash in order to expand the business, or to keep the share price affordable for new investors.

Record income tax expense

- ➪ A corporation must file and pay taxes on its net income; this amount that the corporation is obligated to pay is known as income tax.

- ➪ Income tax expense is recorded in a corporation's accounting records on an accrual basis.

- ➪ Taxable income represents the company's net income as defined by the Income Tax Act.

Record the closing entries for a corporation

- ➪ A corporation's revenue and expense accounts are closed at the end of the period either using the Income Summary account or directly to the retained earnings account.

Calculate retained earnings

- ➪ Retained earnings represent the amount of equity that the company has earned and kept in the business and not distributed to shareholders.

- ➪ Share capital and retained earnings are reported separately in the shareholders' equity section of the financial statements.

- ➪ Shareholders' equity is made up of two main components: contributed capital and retained earnings.

Explain the importance of ethics for corporate reporting

- ➪ Auditors will review corporate statements to ensure they are reported properly and ethically.

Review Exercise

Marcel Campos and Fidel Feisthamel have operated their company as a partnership for several years. Over the years the company has grown, and the partners believe it is appropriate to incorporate their company as Camphamel Inc., a publicly traded company, and raise more capital to expand.

Accordingly, Marcel and Fidel engaged a qualified bookkeeper to provide accounting services for their new corporation. The corporate charter authorized the company to issue an unlimited number of common shares and 200,000, $3 non-cumulative preferred shares worth $100 each. On March 3, 2016, the partners transferred assets worth $2,000,000 and liabilities worth $1,250,000 to the company in exchange for 20,000 no-par value common shares.

Then, Marcel and Fidel sought investment capital from investors. On April 15, 2016, a group of investors agreed to buy an additional 20,000 common shares for $1,000,000 cash.

Instead of paying the accountant $100,000 of fees in cash, Marcel and Fidel gave the accountant 10,000, $3 non-cumulative preferred shares on April 30, 2016. The corporation cannot readily determine the fair value of the preferred shares.

To inject more capital into the business, on November 10, 2016, the company issued 5,000 more common shares at their current market value of $50 each in exchange for equipment.

On November 15, 2016, the company declared a 5% stock dividend on all the common shares outstanding. The market value of each common share was $60 on this date. Stock dividend was later distributed to shareholders on December 2, 2016.

At the directors' meeting on December 15, 2016, Marcel, Fidel, and a director appointed by the shareholders decided to pay cash dividends of $180,000 to preferred and common shareholders of record on January 30, 2017. For the year ended December 31, 2016, the newly incorporated company made a net income of $900,000. The dividend is to be paid on February 28, 2017. During the period January 1–February 28, 2017, the company produced a net income of $30,000.

Required

a) Record the required journal entries for 2016 and 2017.

b) Prepare a calculation showing the change in retained earnings during the year 2016.

c) Prepare the shareholders' equity section of the balance sheet as at December 31, 2016.

See Appendix I for solutions.

a) Journal Entries

Date	Account Title and Explanation	Debit	Credit

Date	Account Title and Explanation	Debit	Credit

b) Calculation of Retained Earnings

c) Shareholders' Equity for 2016

Appendix 6A: Reacquisition of Common Shares

In addition to issuing shares, a corporation can also buy back its own shares from shareholders. The reacquisition of shares may take place for a number of different reasons. For example, a corporation may purchase its shares to reduce the number of shares outstanding, hence increasing earnings per share. A company may also purchase its own shares with the intention of increasing its shares' market price by attracting interest in the stock with a larger trading volume in the stock market. When they have enough cash on hand, some corporations may also reacquire shares to give back cash to shareholders or to remove a specific group of shareholders. Regardless of the reason for reacquisition, in most provinces of Canada, the reacquired shares must be retired and cancelled. This means that those reacquired shares are brought back to the pool of authorized shares that remain unissued. However, in the US and some Canadian provinces, those shares are allowed to be held as **treasury shares** to be reissued instead of being retired or cancelled. Treasury shares have no rights until they are reissued. They can be held by the corporation for an indefinite period of time and can be either reissued or retired later on.

In this Appendix, we will explore accounting treatments for the reacquisition of common shares that are cancelled by a corporation.

Average Cost of Shares

When a business retires or disposes of a long-term asset such as equipment, it removes the cost of that asset from the balance sheet. The same is true for retiring common shares. A corporation should remove from its books the cost of reacquired shares. However, since it would be nearly impossible to find out the exact cost of each share, an average cost per share is used instead. The **average cost per share** is calculated by dividing the book value of the common shares account by the number of common shares issued and outstanding at the transaction date. Usually shares would be reacquired at a price that is different than their average cost, as demonstrated in the following sections.

Reacquiring Shares: Less than the Average Cost

If a corporation repurchases its shares for less than the average cost, a gain is made. However, since corporations are not allowed to record gains or losses from transactions with their shareholders, nothing can be recorded on the income statement. This gain is treated as an addition to shareholders' equity. More specifically, this gain is recorded as part of the contributed capital as a contributed surplus. Recall that contributed capital contains *share capital* and *contributed surplus* as shown in Figure 6A.1. Share capital is the capital raised from the sale of shares. Contributed surplus contains other types of additions to shareholders' contributions.

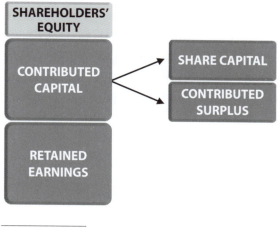

FIGURE 6A.1

Since most of the corporation's transactions do not involve the contributed surplus account, we generally referred to the contributed capital as share capital throughout the textbook, except for this Appendix. We will illustrate how a contributed surplus is affected when shares are reacquired for less than their average cost.

Assume that Pokadot Corporation paid $15,000 to reacquire 5,000 of its own common shares on October 2, 2016. Prior to the share reacquisition, Pokadot had 100,000 outstanding common shares. Its balance sheet before recording the share reacquisition transaction shows a balance of $400,000 for the common shares. Thus, Pokadot's average cost per share is $4 ($400,000 ÷ 100,000 outstanding shares). Because the price of $3 ($15,000 ÷ 5,000 shares) that Pokadot paid for each share is lower than its average cost per share of $4, the difference is treated as an addition to shareholders' equity through the contributed surplus account. The journal entry to record the reacquisition of Pokadot's shares for less than its average cost per share and its impact on the balance sheet are shown in Figure 6A.2.

| JOURNAL | | | |
Date	Account Title and Explanation	Debit	Credit
Oct 2	Common Shares	20,000	
	Contributed Surplus		5,000
	Cash		15,000
	To record reacquiring and retiring of shares		

BALANCE SHEET

CURRENT ASSETS	CURRENT LIABILITIES
CASH -$15,000 CR	ACCOUNTS PAYABLE
ACCOUNTS RECEIVABLE	UNEARNED REVENUE
INVENTORY	NON-CURRENT LIABILITIES
PREPAID EXPENSES	LOANS PAYABLE
LONG-TERM ASSETS	SHAREHOLDERS' EQUITY
	COMMON SHARES -$20,000 DR
PROPERTY, PLANT & EQUIPMENT	CONTRIBUTED SURPLUS + $5,000 CR
	RETAINED EARNINGS

FIGURE 6A.2

The amounts paid to buy back the shares is credited to cash. The 5,000 reacquired common shares are removed from the company's books by debiting the common shares account using the shares' average cost ($5,000 shares × $4 per share = $20,000). To balance the transaction, the difference of $5,000 ($20,000 – $15,000) is recorded as a credit to the contributed surplus.

Pokadot now has 95,000 common shares outstanding (100,000 shares – 5,000 shares) with the remaining common shares balance of $380,000 ($400,000 – $20,000) after the share reacquisition. The average cost per share remains the same ($380,000 ÷ 95,000 outstanding shares = $4 per share). Assuming that contributed surplus has a beginning balance of zero, the contributed surplus of $5,000 would be presented under contributed capital in the shareholders' equity section of the balance sheet.

Reacquiring Shares: More than the Average Cost

If a corporation repurchases its shares for more than the average cost, a loss is made. This loss would be treated as a reduction in shareholders' equity. This loss is recorded by debiting the contributed surplus account, but only if the contributed surplus account has an existing credit (or positive) balance. The contributed surplus account cannot have a debit (or negative) balance. Therefore, if the size of the loss is larger than the existing balance of the contributed surplus account, or if the contributed surplus account has a zero balance, the part of the loss that cannot be absorbed by the contributed surplus would be deducted against the retained earnings account, which can have a debit (or negative) balance. We will illustrate how to account for this loss when the contributed surplus account has a positive balance, and when the contributed surplus account balance is zero.

Assume that after Pokadot Corporation reacquired a portion of its shares on October 2, 2016, it did so again one month later. On November 2, 2016, Pokadot paid $60,000 to repurchase 10,000 shares. There is no other change in the common shares between October 2 and November 2, so the average amount per share is still $4. Because the amount that Pokadot paid on November 2 of $6 ($60,000 ÷ 10,000 shares) per share is higher than Pokadot's average cost per share of $4, Pokadot incurred a total loss of $20,000 [($6 per share – $4 per share) × 10,000 shares]. To completely deplete the contributed surplus account, $5,000 of the total loss of $20,000 would be deducted against the account. The remaining $15,000 loss would then be deducted against retained earnings, as shown in the journal entry in Figure 6A.3.

JOURNAL			
Date	Account Title and Explanation	Debit	Credit
Nov 2	Common Shares	40,000	
	Contributed Surplus	5,000	
	Retained Earnings	15,000	
	Cash		60,000
	To record reacquiring and retiring of shares		

FIGURE 6A.3

Pokadot now has 85,000 common shares outstanding (95,000 shares – 10,000 shares) with the remaining common shares balance of $340,000 ($380,000 – $40,000) after the share reacquisition on November 2, 2016. The average cost per share remains the same ($340,000 ÷ 85,000 outstanding shares = $4 per share). Because the contributed surplus has been completely depleted, the account now has a zero balance.

If the company reacquires its shares for more than the average cost when the contributed surplus account has no balance, the loss is recorded directly to retained earnings. Assume that Pokadot reacquired an additional 1,000 shares on January 17, 2017 with $4,500 cash. There is no other change in the common shares between November 2, 2016 and January 17, 2017, so the average cost per share is still $4. Because the amount that Pokadot paid on January 17 of $4.50 ($4,500 ÷ 1,000 shares) per share is higher than Pokadot's average cost per share of $4, Pokadot incurred a total loss of $500 [($4.50 per share – $4 per share) × 1,000 shares]. The whole $500 loss is recorded as a debit to retained earnings because there is a zero balance in the contributed surplus account as shown in the journal entry in Figure 6A.4.

JOURNAL			
Date	Account Title and Explanation	Debit	Credit
Jan 17	Common Shares	4,000	
	Retained Earnings	500	
	Cash		4,500
	To record reacquiring and retiring of shares		

BALANCE SHEET

CURRENT ASSETS	CURRENT LIABILITIES
CASH - $4,500 CR	ACCOUNTS PAYABLE
ACCOUNTS RECEIVABLE	UNEARNED REVENUE
INVENTORY	NON-CURRENT LIABILITIES
PREPAID EXPENSES	LOANS PAYABLE
	SHAREHOLDERS' EQUITY
LONG-TERM ASSETS	COMMON SHARES - $4,000 DR
PROPERTY, PLANT & EQUIPMENT	CONTRIBUTED SURPLUS
	RETAINED EARNINGS - $500 DR

FIGURE 6A.4

The loss from share reacquisition that is recorded as a debit to retained earnings is never reversed even if the company subsequently reacquires a portion of its shares at less than the average cost. In other words, whenever shares are reacquired at less than the average cost, the difference is always recorded as a credit to the contributed surplus account.

 Access **ameengage.com** *for integrated resources including tutorials, practice exercises, the digital textbook and more.*

In Summary

Record the reacquisition of shares

↪ The reacquisition of shares means that a corporation buys back its own shares from shareholders. In most provinces of Canada, the reacquired shares must be retired and cancelled.

↪ A corporation reacquires its shares for a number of different reasons including reducing the number of shares outstanding, increasing share market price or giving back cash to shareholders.

↪ The average cost per share is calculated by dividing the book value of the common shares account by the number of common shares issued and outstanding at the transaction date.

↪ The accounts affected by share reacquisition depend on whether the repurchase price is more or less than the average cost per share. When shares are reacquired at less than the average cost, the difference is recorded as a credit to the contributed surplus account. When shares are reacquired for more than the average cost, the difference is first deducted against the contributed surplus account. Once the contributed surplus account is depleted, the remaining difference is debited to the retained earnings account.

—————— **Review Exercise** ——————

Raktor Inc.'s balance sheet on December 31, 2016 reported that Raktor had 200,000 outstanding common shares with a book value of $1,000,000, and that Raktor had a contributed surplus account balance of zero. On March 10, 2017, Raktor paid $70,000 to repurchase 15,000 common shares. On June 15, 2017, Raktor repurchased an additional 15,000 common shares, but paid $90,000 this time. There had been no other changes in the number or value of the company's common shares.

See Appendix I for solutions.

Required

a) Record the share reacquisition journal entry on March 10, 2017.

Date	Account Title and Explanation	Debit	Credit

b) What is the average cost of shares after the share reacquisition on March 10, 2017?

_____

_____

c) Record the share reacquisition journal entry on June 15, 2017.

Date	Account Title and Explanation	Debit	Credit

Notes

Chapter 7
CORPORATIONS: THE FINANCIAL STATEMENTS

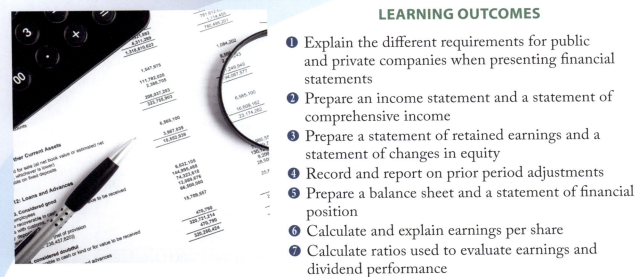

LEARNING OUTCOMES

❶ Explain the different requirements for public and private companies when presenting financial statements

❷ Prepare an income statement and a statement of comprehensive income

❸ Prepare a statement of retained earnings and a statement of changes in equity

❹ Record and report on prior period adjustments

❺ Prepare a balance sheet and a statement of financial position

❻ Calculate and explain earnings per share

❼ Calculate ratios used to evaluate earnings and dividend performance

AMEENGAGE *Access **ameengage.com** for integrated resources including tutorials, practice exercises, the digital textbook and more.*

Preparation of Financial Statements

In the news, you may come across articles about large companies such as Google or Microsoft releasing their quarterly or annual reports. These companies are presenting their financial performance for the last period. Most stock exchanges require public companies to prepare financial statements every three months in addition to the annual report.

You have already learned how to prepare financial statements for a proprietorship and partnership. The logic behind preparing statements for a corporation is the same, although these statements are generally more complex than those of a proprietorship. Corporations have access to more sources of financing, so the debt and equity sections of the balance sheet may appear to be quite different. Additionally, a corporation may offer more diverse products and services, which can make the income statement more complex.

One reason for the complexity is because a corporation's financial statements serve a much wider audience group. While a sole proprietorship may have a few financial statement users, a corporation can have hundreds or thousands of financial statement users. Corporation ownership is determined by shares, so all shareholders are users of the financial statements. Also, a public corporation has potential shareholders, or investors, who may purchase the corporation's shares. These investors are also users of the financial information. A corporation's statement users want different financial information for different purposes, so the corporation is subject to more complex disclosure requirements.

This chapter illustrates how a corporation's financial statements can be prepared to satisfy disclosure requirements. Financial disclosure requirements for a Canadian corporation can be found in Accounting Standards for Private Enterprises (ASPE) and International Financial Reporting Standards (IFRS). Public corporations must prepare financial statements according to IFRS, while private corporations can prepare statements according to IFRS or ASPE. To illustrate the financial statements of a corporation, Figure 7.1 shows the adjusted trial balance of a fictitious company, Darma Corporation. Two statements will be prepared in this chapter. The first will assume Darma Corporation is private and follows ASPE; the second will assume the company is public and follows IFRS.

Darma Corporation Adjusted Trial Balance December 31, 2016		
Account Titles	**Debit**	**Credit**
Cash	$87,650	
Short-Term Investments	287,580	
Accounts Receivable	685,725	
Inventory	1,652,840	
Prepaid Expenses	16,840	
Property, Plant and Equipment (net)	3,206,740	
Goodwill	777,185	
Accrued Liabilities		$145,845
Accounts Payable		426,890
Current Portion of Non-Current Debt		43,870
Non-Current Debt		568,750
Deferred Tax Liability		24,800
Common Shares		3,900,000
Retained Earnings		1,340,000
Cash Dividends	400,000	
Sales Revenue		2,505,750
Sales Discounts	1,200	
Sales Returns and Allowances	3,800	
Gain on Sale of Assets		4,500
Gain on Foreign Currency Translation		5,200
Gain on Value of Investments		8,700
Operating Income from Discontinued Operations		125,000
Gain on Sale of Assets from Discontinued Operations		45,000
Cost of Goods Sold	1,100,000	
Interest Expense	21,000	
Salaries Expense	275,000	
Depreciation Expense	44,000	
Administrative Expenses	300,000	
Income Tax Expense—Continuing Operations	233,745	
Income Tax Expense—Discontinued Operations	51,000	
Total	$9,144,305	$9,144,305

FIGURE 7.1

Income Statement and Statement of Comprehensive Income

Recall from previous chapters that the purpose of a proprietorship's income statement is to display the company's profitability during a specific period. The income statement shows the amount of revenue, from which expenses are deducted to provide the net income figure for the period. This section will first show the components of the income statement under ASPE, and later show the components of the statement of comprehensive income under IFRS.

ASPE

The sample income statement for Darma Corporation under ASPE is shown in Figure 7.2. ASPE requires companies to separate continuing operations from discontinued operations in their income statement presentation. Therefore, Darma Corporation's income statement is divided into two major components: the continuing operations component and the discontinued operations component.

Darma Corporation Income Statement For the Year Ended December 31, 2016		
Sales Revenue		$2,505,750
Less: Sales Discounts	$1,200	
Sales Returns and Allowances	3,800	5,000
Net Sales		2,500,750
Cost of Goods Sold		1,100,000
Gross Profit		1,400,750
Operating Expenses		
Salaries Expense	275,000	
Depreciation Expense	44,000	
Administrative Expenses	300,000	619,000
Income from Operations		781,750
Other Income (Expenses)		
Gain on Sale of Assets	4,500	
Gain on Foreign Currency Translation	5,200	
Gain on Value of Investments	8,700	
Interest Expense	(21,000)	(2,600)
Income before Taxes and Discontinued Operations		779,150
Income Tax Expense		233,745
Income before Discontinued Operations		545,405
Discontinued Operations		
Operating Income from Discontinued Operations	125,000	
Gain on Sale of Assets from Discontinued Operations	45,000	
Income Tax Expense	(51,000)	119,000
Net Income		**$664,405**

Continuing Operations (left bracket covering upper section)

Discontinued Operations (left bracket covering lower section)

FIGURE 7.2

Continuing Operations

Income before discontinued operations shows the results of the company's operations that are ongoing. It is the component of the income that is from the **continuing operations** only. A large corporation may have several different lines of business that serve different types of customers or provide different goods and services. Each of these different operations is known as a **business segment**. Occasionally, a company may sell or discontinue a business segment. The requirement under ASPE is to report separately the results of discontinued operations, as will be discussed later. The income before discontinued operations represents the results of only business segments that have not been sold or discontinued.

The income before discontinued operations can be calculated in multiple steps. The first step is to calculate income from operations as follows.

Net Sales of $2,500,750 – Cost of Goods Sold of $1,100,000 = Gross Profit of $1,400,750

Gross Profit of $1,400,750 – Total Operating Expenses of $619,000 = Income from Operations of $781,750

After figuring out the income from operations, other income (or expenses) is then added (or subtracted) to provide income before income tax and discontinued operations. **Other income (expenses)** includes items that are not part of the company's regular day-to-day operations. For example, any gain or loss on the sale of property, plant and equipment would be listed as other income or expenses. In Darma's case, there are three gains and one loss from the other income (expenses) category. Other income (expenses) is added to (subtracted from) the income from operations to calculate income before income tax and discontinued operations, as shown below.

Income from Operations of $781,750 + Other Income of $18,400 ($4,500 + $5,200 + $8,700) – Other Expenses of $21,000 = Income before Taxes and Discontinued Operations of $779,150

Taxes are calculated on the income before taxes and discontinued operations. Similar to how income from continuing operations is reported separately from the income from discontinued operations, continuing operations' taxes must be reported separately from discontinued operations' taxes. Income taxes should be shown following the related business segments. Corporate income tax calculation in the real world can be quite complex and is beyond the scope of this textbook. In this textbook, income tax presentation will be illustrated using straightforward tax calculation by multiplying a tax percentage by an income figure. Assume Darma must pay income tax at 30%. Darma's income tax expense based on its income before taxes and discontinued operations is equal to $233,745 ($779,150 × 30%). This income tax expense is deducted from the income before taxes and discontinued operations to determine the income before discontinued operations, as shown below.

Income before Taxes and Discontinued Operations of $779,150 – Income Tax Expense of $233,745 = Income before Discontinued Operations of $545,405

Discontinued Operations

A **discontinued operation** is a business segment that is no longer part of the company's regular operating activities. During the year, Darma discontinued a segment of its business operations. This segment generated an operating income of $125,000 before its disposal and a $45,000 gain on the sale of the assets. Darma must pay 30% tax on the income and gain. Discontinued operations' income tax expense of $51,000, equivalent to 30% of $170,000 ($125,000 + $45,000), is presented separately from the income tax expense related to continuing operations. The after-tax income from continuing operations and the after-tax income from discontinued operations leave Darma with a total net income of $664,405. The calculation of income from discontinued operations and net income is illustrated below.

Operating Income (Loss) from Discontinued Operations of $125,000 + Gain (Loss) on Sale of Assets from Discontinued Operations of $45,000 – Income Tax Expense (Benefit) of $51,000 = Income from Discontinued Operations of $119,000

The income from discontinued operations and the net income are calculated as follows.

Income before Discontinued Operations of $545,405 + Income from Discontinued Operations of $119,000 = Net Income of $664,405

If the discontinued segment showed a loss from its operations or from the sale of assets, Darma would recognize a savings of income tax. For example, suppose Darma has an operating loss from the discontinued operations and the assets were sold at a loss for a total of $100,000. Darma would save 30% (or $30,000) of that in income tax, so the net loss would be $70,000.

Another scenario is that Darma may have an operating income from the discontinued segment but incur a loss in the sale of assets. Suppose Darma has an operating income of $100,000 from the discontinued segment but the assets were sold at a loss of $30,000. Darma would need to pay income tax expense of $30,000 ($100,000 × 30%) but would also have an income tax benefit of $9,000 ($30,000 × 30%). The net effect is paying tax of $21,000 ($30,000 – $9,000) for this discontinued segment.

It is important to report the income from continuing operations and from discontinued operations separately because investors and creditors rely on this accounting information to make decisions. Reporting separately allows the users of financial information to identify what is not relevant to the company's ongoing performance. This especially helps users predict future results,

weak
No discussion as to WHY the focus is on continuing operations!

OK

such as how much profit the company will make in the following year and how competitive the company will be after eliminating a segment. Both ASPE and IFRS require companies to report discontinued operations separately from continuing operations.

IFRS

If Darma Corporation was a public corporation, it would prepare a **statement of comprehensive income** under IFRS guidelines. Some of the IFRS requirements on how to present the statement of comprehensive income are similar to ASPE's requirements on how to present the income statement. For example, both must separate continuing operations income from discontinued operations. However, the comprehensive income statement under IFRS is more complex because of three additional requirements.

1. comprehensive income
2. presentation of expenses by function or by nature
3. presentation of earnings per share

Each of these additional requirements is discussed below.

Comprehensive Income

Comprehensive income is the total of net income plus other comprehensive income (or loss). **Other comprehensive income** (**OCI**) is a category of income resulting from transactions that are beyond company owners' or management's control, such as a change in market value of investments. Other comprehensive income can arise from adjustments in fair value of investments, pension, or property, plant and equipment, and also differences arising from foreign currency translation transactions. IFRS does not allow these items to be reported as a part of net income, but they do affect the equity accounts. Other comprehensive income is presented on the statement showing classification of expenses by function in Figure 7.3. (We will examine what "by function" means a little later.) As shown in Figure 7.3, a section called Other Comprehensive Income appears below net income. Other comprehensive income (or loss) is added to net income to arrive at total comprehensive income. The details of the items in other comprehensive income are beyond the scope of this textbook.

Darma Corporation		
Statement of Comprehensive Income (by Function)		
For the Year Ended December 31, 2016		
Continuing Operations		
Sales Revenue, Net		$2,500,750
Cost of Goods Sold		1,100,000
Gross Profit		1,400,750
Gain on Sale of Assets		4,500
Distribution Expense	$309,500	
Administrative Expense	309,500	
Interest Expense	21,000	640,000
Net Income before Tax		765,250
Income Tax Expense		229,575
Income from Continuing Operations		535,675
Discontinued Operations		
Income from Discontinued Operations, Net of $51,000		
of Income Tax Expense		119,000
Net Income		654,675
Other Comprehensive Income, Net of Income Tax		
Foreign Currency Translation Difference	3,640	
Net Change in Fair Value of Investments	6,090	9,730
Total Comprehensive Income		$664,405
Earnings Per Share		
Basic and Diluted		$3.27

FIGURE 7.3

IFRS requires that other comprehensive income (or loss) be reported either

1. in its own section on the statement of comprehensive income; or
2. in a separate statement that accompanies the traditional income statement.

This textbook will present other comprehensive income in its own section on the statement of comprehensive income. IFRS requires that each item listed under other comprehensive income be reported net of income tax. If the company chooses to report the total comprehensive income as one line item, the number shown must be net of income tax. This is why the sample statement in Figure 7.3 includes the heading "Other Comprehensive Income, Net of Income Tax." Reporting of other comprehensive income net of income tax explains why Darma's statements of comprehensive income under IFRS in Figures 7.3 and 7.4 show income tax expense from continuing operations of $229,575. This number is $4,170 lower than the income tax expense from continuing operations of $233,745 in Darma's adjusted trial balance in Figure 7.1 and income statement under ASPE in Figure 7.2. This is because Darma's other comprehensive income is reported net of $4,170 income tax. Darma's statement of comprehensive income under IFRS does not show the $4,170 portion of income tax that is related to other comprehensive income.

Presentation of Expenses by Function or by Nature

IFRS requires that expenses be analyzed and presented on the statement of comprehensive income (or loss) by function or by nature. A corporation is allowed to choose the more suitable of the two methods for its statement presentation, based on which format is considered most reliable and relevant to its users. IFRS also allows the expenses to be listed in any order within each classification.

Classifying expenses **by function** means that expenses are presented on the statement according to the various functions of the entity. Expenses are allocated to their functions, such as selling expenses and administrative expenses. One advantage to disclosing expenses by function is that users can more easily see how gross profit and operating income are calculated. When a company uses the by function presentation for its income statement, it must still disclose the individual expenses by nature in notes to the statement. Figure 7.3 demonstrates how Darma Corporation would present its statement of comprehensive income with expenses analyzed by function.

Classifying expenses **by nature** means that expenses are presented on the statement according to their natural classification, such as salary expense, employee benefits, advertising expense, depreciation, and such. Expenses analyzed by nature are *not* allocated to the different functions of the business. Figure 7.4 demonstrates how Darma Corporation would present its statement of comprehensive income with expenses analyzed by nature.

Darma Corporation Statement of Comprehensive Income (by Nature) For the Year Ended December 31, 2016		
Continuing Operations		
Revenue		
Sales Revenue, Net	$2,500,750	
Gain on Sale of Assets	4,500	$2,505,250
Expenses		
Cost of Goods Sold	1,100,000	
Salaries Expense	275,000	
Depreciation Expense	44,000	
Administrative Expense	300,000	
Interest Expense	21,000	1,740,000
Net Income before Tax		765,250
Income Tax Expense		229,575
Income from Continuing Operations		535,675
Discontinued Operations		
Income from Discontinued Operations, Net of $51,000 of Income Tax Expense		119,000
Net Income		654,675
Other Comprehensive Income, Net of Income Tax		
Foreign Currency Translation Difference	3,640	
Net Change in Fair Value of Investments	6,090	9,730
Total Comprehensive Income		$664,405
Earnings Per Share		
Basic and Diluted		$3.27

(Handwritten note: "No depn in COGS!" with a bracket pointing to Cost of Goods Sold, Salaries Expense, Depreciation Expense, Administrative Expense, Interest Expense)

FIGURE 7.4

Presentation of Earnings Per Share

While the presentation of earnings per share is not required under ASPE, it is required on the statement of comprehensive income under IFRS. The earnings per share figure for Darma Corporation is presented at the bottom of the statement in both Figure 7.3 and Figure 7.4. Earnings per share and its calculation will be discussed in more detail later in this chapter.

Summary of Differences between ASPE's Income Statement and IFRS' Statement of Comprehensive Income

The recognition and measurement of items on an income statement are intended to be much less complex under ASPE than IFRS. This is why ASPE does not require the recognition of other comprehensive income items and there is no requirement to prepare income statements with expenses detailed by function or nature. ASPE does mandate minimum disclosures on the face of the financial statements to ensure that the information provided to lenders is useful. The main differences between ASPE's income statement and IFRS' statement of comprehensive income are summarized in Figure 7.5.

Topic of Interest	IFRS	ASPE
Statement name	"Statement of Comprehensive Income" or "Statement of Income and Comprehensive Income"	"Income Statement" or "Statement of Income"
Presentation of expenses	Expenses should be classified by either their nature or their function.	There is no specific rule on how to present the expenses as long as items that are required to be presented are adhered to.
Other comprehensive income/comprehensive income	Items must be classified as either comprehensive income or net income. Other comprehensive income must be presented either in a stand-alone statement or as a separate section within the statement of comprehensive income.	All profit and loss items are included in net income without being separated into other comprehensive income.
Earnings per share (EPS)	Basic and diluted EPS must be presented in the statement.	Not mentioned

FIGURE 7.5

The net income figure from the income statement or the statement of comprehensive income is added to the beginning retained earnings balance in the statement of retained earnings (under ASPE) or the statement of changes in equity (under IFRS), as explained in the next section.

Statement of Retained Earnings and Statement of Changes in Equity

Similar to how sole proprietorships report the changes to owner's equity on the statement of owner's equity, all corporations, whether private or public, are required to report on the changes to retained earnings during the accounting period. Net income from the income statement is added to, and dividends are subtracted from, the beginning balance of retained earnings to determine the ending balance of retained earnings. For private corporations following ASPE, this is reported in a statement of retained earnings. ASPE also requires that changes in other shareholders' equity accounts be presented in the notes to the financial statements. For public corporations, IFRS requires that changes to all equity accounts (not just to the retained earnings account) be shown on a statement of changes in equity. You will learn more about the requirements under IFRS later in this chapter. For now, we will discuss the requirements under ASPE.

ASPE

Under ASPE, the retained earnings account is the only equity account for which a private corporation must report changes in a separate statement, called the **statement of retained earnings.** Retained earnings are the earnings that are kept and accumulated by the company after dividends have been paid to the shareholders. Note that the income statement must be prepared before the statement of retained earnings because the net income (or loss) from the income statement must be added to (or subtracted from) the retained earnings at the beginning of the period. Retained earnings will increase if the company reported a net income and decrease if the company reported a net loss or paid out dividends.

Assume Darma had an opening balance of retained earnings of $1,340,000 and paid $400,000 in cash dividends. As shown in Figure 7.6, the statement of retained earnings is prepared in a similar way to the statement of owner's equity in a proprietorship. The net income is taken from the income statement already prepared.

Darma Corporation	
Statement of Retained Earnings	
For the Year Ended December 31, 2016	
Retained Earnings, January 1, 2016	$1,340,000
Add: Net Income for the Period	664,405
	2,004,405
Less: Cash Dividends	(400,000)
Retained Earnings, December 31, 2016	$1,604,405

FIGURE 7.6

IFRS

For public corporations, IFRS requires that all changes to the equity accounts be shown on a **statement of changes in equity**. This statement must include changes in retained earnings, the changes in share capital and any other items that affected equity during the period. Figure 7.7 shows the statement of changes in equity for Darma Corporation for the year ended December 31, 2016. For this example, assume that Darma is a public corporation that follows IFRS.

The statement of changes in equity has a column for each item that makes up shareholders' equity. Net income from the statement of comprehensive income is added to retained earnings, and dividends are subtracted from retained earnings. Any issuance of common shares and preferred shares are added to share capital and preferred shares, respectively. In reality, public companies usually have other comprehensive income (OCI). The OCI from the statement of comprehensive income is added to the beginning balance of **accumulated OCI** to determine the ending OCI balance. In this case, assume that the accumulated other comprehensive income account has a zero beginning balance, and that Darma issued common shares worth $1.3 million in 2016.

A total column combines all values and shows how equity changed from the beginning of the period to the end.

Darma Corporation Statement of Changes in Equity For the Year Ended December 31, 2016				
	Common Shares	Retained Earnings	Accumulated Other Comprehensive Income	Total Equity
Beginning Balance, January 1, 2016	$2,600,000	$1,340,000	$0	$3,940,000
Comprehensive Income				
Net Income		654,675		654,675
Increase in OCI			9,730	9,730
Dividends to Shareholders				
Common		(400,000)		(400,000)
Issue of Equity				
Common Shares	1,300,000			1,300,000
Ending Balance	$3,900,000	$1,594,675	$9,730	$5,504,405

FIGURE 7.7

Summary of Differences between ASPE's Statement of Retained Earnings and IFRS' Statement of Changes in Equity

The main differences between ASPE's statement of retained earnings and IFRS' statement of changes in equity are summarized in Figure 7.8.

Topic of Interest	IFRS	ASPE
Statement name	Statement of Changes in Equity	Statement of Retained Earnings
Content	Changes in all equity accounts are presented on the face of the statement.	Only changes in retained earnings are presented on the face of the statement. Changes in other shareholders' equity accounts are presented in the notes to the financial statements.

FIGURE 7.8

The statement of retained earnings in Figure 7.6 and the statement of changes in equity in Figure 7.7 are prepared based on the assumption that no adjustment needs to be made to the beginning retained earnings balance. Sometimes, this balance needs to be adjusted due to accounting changes and prior period adjustments, which will be discussed next.

Accounting Changes and Prior Period Adjustments

Sometimes errors are discovered in the accounting records. A correcting entry can be made, but it must be journalized and posted before the closing entries at the end of that period. That way, the information will be included in the period to which it belongs. For example, if a company's accounting clerk discovers an error in a journal entry that was made on June 15, 2016 and corrects it on June 22, 2016, the financial statements for June will be accurate.

But what happens when an error is found after the period has been closed? The error must be corrected so that the information is included in the period to which it belongs, and it remains comparable from one period to the next. A correcting entry that is made to a previous period is known as a **prior period adjustment**. Prior period adjustments are particularly important because they can affect net income (or loss) of the prior period, and therefore affect the beginning retained earnings balance for the current period.

Accounting errors are just one of three types of accounting changes that can affect a prior period's financial information. The three types of accounting changes are as follows.

- correction of prior period errors
- change in accounting policy
- change in accounting estimate

The mechanics of how the prior period adjustments are made and how they are presented on the statement of retained earnings will be discussed.

Correction of Prior Period Errors

Correction of prior period errors are actions taken to correct errors made in previous financial statements by the business. Suppose the $25,000 purchase of equipment was mistakenly recorded as maintenance expense. The original entry was made in 2015 but is not discovered until 2016. Because the error overstated the repairs and maintenance expenses, income for 2015 was understated by $25,000. Simply transferring $25,000 from maintenance expense to equipment is not appropriate because maintenance expense would be understated for 2016. The transfer would also not address the fact that retained earnings should be increased when this error is corrected.

The solution is to increase the balance of the equipment account by $25,000 so that the asset is properly recorded. The balance in retained earnings should also increase; however, we must also take into account income taxes that are now owed on the extra amount of income. If Darma pays 30% income tax, it will owe $7,500 in taxes based on the increase of $25,000 in income. The final result is shown in Figure 7.9. Notice that this entry only affects balance sheet accounts and does not affect the income statement.

→ this ignores depn expense on the $25,000 capital item !!!

JOURNAL			
Date	**Account Title and Explanation**	**Debit**	**Credit**
Jan 31	Equipment	25,000	
	Retained Earnings		17,500
	Income Tax Payable (25,000 × 30%)		7,500
	To record correction for error in June 15, 2015 journal entry, expensed to Repairs and Maintenance		

FIGURE 7.9

The error caused net income for 2015 to be understated by $17,500 ($25,000 less the income tax at a rate of 30%). By crediting retained earnings for the net effect of the error, this account was corrected to reflect the income that would have been recorded. Income taxes payable are also corrected to reflect the actual amount owing on the income earned.

When a company has a prior period error, adjustments to retained earnings must be included in the statement of retained earnings if the company uses ASPE, or the statement of changes in equity if the company uses IFRS. The adjustments are on the statement of retained earnings under ASPE and on the statement of changes in equity under IFRS in a similar manner. Specifically, the adjustment to retained earnings is listed before any other items are added or subtracted. The statement of retained earnings and the statement of changes in equity with the prior period adjustment are shown in Figure 7.10 and Figure 7.11 respectively.

Darma Corporation Statement of Retained Earnings For the Year Ended December 31, 2016	
Retained Earnings, January 1, 2016	$1,340,000
Add: Prior Year Adjustment	17,500
Add: Net Income for the Period	664,405
	2,021,905
Less: Cash Dividends	(400,000)
Retained Earnings, December 31, 2016	$1,621,905

FIGURE 7.10

Darma Corporation Statement of Changes in Equity For the Year Ended December 31, 2016				
	Common Shares	**Retained Earnings**	**Accumulated Other Comprehensive Income**	**Total Equity**
Beginning Balance, January 1, 2016	$2,600,000	$1,340,000	$0	$3,940,000
Adjustment to correct error from 2015		17,500		17,500
Restated Balance	2,600,000	1,357,500	0	3,957,500
Comprehensive Income				
Net Income		654,675		654,675
Increase in OCI			9,730	9,730
Dividends to Shareholders				
Common		(400,000)		(400,000)
Issue of Equity				
Common Shares	1,300,000			1,300,000
Ending Balance	$3,900,000	$1,612,175	$9,730	$5,521,905

FIGURE 7.11

Change in Accounting Policy

Suppose that in fiscal year 2016, Darma Corporation changes its method of depreciation from the straight-line to the double-declining balance method. The decision to change its depreciation method represents a **change in accounting policy**. Under IFRS, this can be undertaken by a company only if the change is either required by IFRS or when the change will result in more reliable and relevant information for users of its financial statements. Under ASPE, a company does not need to meet the reliability/relevance test to change an accounting policy.

If Darma always reports comparative numbers (statements for two or more years) on its financial statements, then this change in depreciation policy means the 2015 and 2016 values for depreciation expense and net income are not comparable. When there is a change in accounting policy, accounting standards require a restatement of previously reported information. The new accounting policy must be retroactively applied to the prior period's accounting information, which is presented in comparison with current period's information, as if the new accounting policy had always been used. The approach of changing accounting information on financial statements of prior period is also known as the **retroactive approach**. Darma has to restate the 2015 comparative amounts in the 2016 financial statements. In addition, the beginning balances of 2015 and 2016 retained earnings have to be adjusted for the cumulative effect of using the double-declining balance method over the straight-line method. The adjustment would reflect a larger depreciation expense (lower net income) for prior periods up until 2015, assuming the asset is relatively new, thus depreciation expense under the double-declining balance method is higher than the depreciation expense under the straight-line method up until 2015. Similar to the correction of prior period errors, the cumulative effect of the change in accounting policy would be added to (or subtracted from) the beginning retained earnings balance in the statement of retained earnings.

Change in Accounting Estimate

Often, items that are recorded in a company's accounting records and reported on its financial statements are based on estimates. For example, the useful life of an asset is usually estimated to calculate its depreciation over time. But what if the useful life of an asset turns out to be significantly longer (or shorter) than originally estimated? This is not an error, but represents a **change in accounting estimate**. In such a case, no prior period adjustment is necessary. This type of change would simply be handled by using the new estimate to calculate depreciation for the current and future periods also known as **prospective approach**.

Figure 7.12 summarizes the accounting treatment of three types of accounting changes previously discussed. The three types of accounting changes are presented similarly in ASPE and IFRS.

Accounting Changes	Accounting Treatment
Correction of Prior Period Errors	Retrospective approach with restatement, including the presentation of prior period error corrections as an addition to (or deduction from) the beginning retained earnings balance in the statement of retained earnings
Accounting Policy Changes	Retrospective approach with restatement as if the new policy had always been used
Accounting Estimate Changes	Prospective approach affecting only current and future periods

FIGURE 7.12

Balance Sheet and Statement of Financial Position

The statement of retained earnings (or the statement of changes in equity) links the income statement and the balance sheet together. The net income figure from the income statement is used in the statement of retained earnings to calculate the ending balance of retained earnings. The ending balance of retained earnings from the statement of retained earnings is then presented under the shareholders' equity section on the balance sheet. The balance sheet under ASPE is illustrated next, followed by the statement of financial position under IFRS.

ASPE

A classified balance sheet prepared under ASPE looks very similar to a sole proprietorship's balance sheet. Assets and liabilities are often listed on the basis of liquidity from most liquid to least liquid (i.e., the current items are usually listed first). ASPE allows a company the flexibility to call this statement either a balance sheet or a statement of financial position. The normal presentation of a balance sheet includes an asset section with the following classification of assets.

- Current Assets
- Long-Term Investments
- Property, Plant and Equipment
- Intangible Assets
- Goodwill

The liabilities section will include both current and long-term liabilities.

The shareholders' equity section will include

- Share Capital (i.e., common and preferred shares)
- Contributed Surplus
- Retained Earnings

Figure 7.13 shows the classified balance sheet for Darma Corporation if it were a private corporation following ASPE.

Darma Corporation Balance Sheet As at December 31, 2016		
Assets		
Current Assets		
Cash	$87,650	
Short-Term Investments	287,580	
Accounts Receivable	685,725	
Inventory	1,652,840	
Prepaid Expenses	16,840	
Total Current Assets		$2,730,635
Long-Term Assets		
Property, Plant and Equipment (net)	3,206,740	
Goodwill	777,185	3,983,925
Total Assets		$6,714,560
Liabilities		
Current Liabilities		
Accrued Liabilities	$145,845	
Accounts Payable	426,890	
Current Portion of Non-Current Debt	43,870	
Total Current Liabilities		$616,605
Long-Term Liabilities		
Non-Current Debt		568,750
Deferred Tax Liability		24,800
Total Liabilities		1,210,155
Shareholders' Equity		
Common Shares		
200,000 shares issued and outstanding	3,900,000	
Retained Earnings	1,604,405	
Total Shareholders' Equity		5,504,405
Total Liabilities and Shareholders' Equity		$6,714,560

FIGURE 7.13

The balance sheet shows the common practice of presenting the individual items under each classification ordered by liquidity (most liquid to least liquid). Many companies choose to reverse the order of the individual items from least liquid to most liquid. There is currently no specific requirement for the order of these sections according to ASPE.

— why ?
explain this !

IFRS

Under IFRS, the balance sheet is often called the statement of financial position although IFRS allows a company to call this statement either one. Assets and liabilities are still classified as current and long-term. However, the term *non-current* is used instead of *long-term.* Similar to ASPE, there is currently no specific requirement for the order of these sections. However, the typical order of presentation is a little different from the balance sheet under ASPE.

- non-current items are usually listed before current items
- equity is usually listed before liabilities

in Europe.
Canada ???

Figure 7.14 shows the statement of financial position for Darma Corporation under IFRS guidelines. Under IFRS, financial statements must show the number of shares authorized and the number of shares issued. ASPE does not require disclosure of the number of shares authorized likely because private corporations are not traded on the stock market and this information is not as relevant for users.

Darma Corporation **Statement of Financial Position** **As at December 31, 2016**		
Assets		
Non-Current Assets		
Property, Plant and Equipment (net)	$3,206,740	
Goodwill	777,185	$3,983,725
Current Assets		
Prepaid Expenses	16,840	
Inventory	1,652,840	
Accounts Receivable	685,725	
Short-Term Investments	287,580	
Cash	87,650	
Total Current Assets		2,730,635
Total Assets		$6,714,560
Shareholders' Equity		
Common Shares,		
unlimited shares authorized,		
200,000 shares issued and outstanding	$3,900,000	
Retained Earnings	1,594,675	
Accumulated Other Comprehensive Income	9,730	
Total Shareholders' Equity		5,504,405
Liabilities		
Non-Current Liabilities		
Non-Current Debt	568,750	
Deferred Tax Liabilities	24,800	593,550
Current Liabilities		
Accrued Liabilities	145,845	
Accounts Payable	426,890	
Current Portion of Non-Current Debt	43,870	
Total Current Liabilities		616,605
Total Liabilities		1,210,155
Total Liabilities and Shareholders' Equity		$6,714,560

FIGURE 7.14

Summary of Differences between ASPE's Balance Sheet and IFRS' Statement of Financial Position

The main differences between ASPE's and IFRS' balance sheets or statements of financial position are summarized in Figure 7.15.

Topic of Interest	IFRS	ASPE
Statement name	Both names of "Balance Sheet" and "Statement of Financial Position" are acceptable, although "Statement of Financial Position" is more often used.	Both names of "Balance Sheet" and "Statement of Financial Position" are acceptable, although "Balance Sheet" is more often used.
Listing order	Listing order is not specified, but companies adopting IFRS tend to list items from least liquid to most liquid. Shareholders' equity is usually presented before liabilities.	Listing order is not specified, but companies adopting ASPE tend to list items from most liquid to least liquid. Liabilities are usually presented before shareholders' equity.
Shareholders' equity section	Retained earnings and accumulated other comprehensive income are reported separately.	Because companies that use ASPE do not report other comprehensive income, the accumulated other comprehensive income account does not exist on the balance sheet.

FIGURE 7.15

Earnings Per Share (EPS)

The previous chapter discussed corporations raising capital by offering shares of their equity to the public. For investors, or shareholders, there are two monetary reasons to buy shares in a company. One reason is the potential of making a profit from an increase in the share price (what is known as a *capital gain*). The other reason to buy shares is the anticipation of regular payments of cash dividends. All public corporations must issue common shares. Many public corporations also issue preferred shares.

WORTH REPEATING

Shares are an attractive investment for shareholders because they offer limited liability and have the potential to increase in value. They also offer liquidity, which is the ability to sell or transfer shares at their market value. The market value of shares is determined by the amount that investors are willing to pay for them at that particular point in time. This means that the shares may be sold at a higher or lower price than the current holder paid for them.

Every corporation issues common shares. Common shares are a type of equity that gives shareholders ownership in the corporation, along with voting rights to elect a board of directors, and the potential to receive a share of the company's equity in the form of dividends. Investors buy common shares with the expectation that the corporation will remain or become profitable, although the payment of dividends is not guaranteed. Some corporations also offer another class of shares known as preferred shares.

When potential investors are deciding which company's shares to buy, they first want to know something about the company's profitability. One key indicator of a company's profitability is a value known as earnings per share, which a public company must present on its statement of comprehensive income under IFRS. **Earnings per share** (**EPS**) is a ratio that indicates the profit earned by each common share. EPS enables shareholders to evaluate the potential return on their investment. We will look at the formula for calculating earnings per share.

First, recall the discussion about dividends from the previous chapter. When a company issues both preferred and common shares, dividends must be paid to preferred shareholders first. The remainder of profits available for dividends is declared to the common shareholders. Because EPS is only calculated on common shares, the current year's preferred dividends is subtracted from profits to calculate earnings per share. The number that results from deducting preferred dividends from net income is the numerator in calculating EPS. The denominator is the weighted average number of common shares outstanding. The **weighted average number of shares** outstanding is determined by taking the number of shares outstanding multiplied by the fraction of the year during which those shares were outstanding. This ensures that the number of shares outstanding is matched to the amount of income that was earned on them. The formula for calculating earnings per share is presented below.

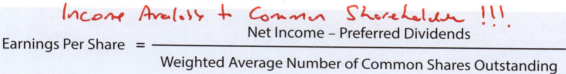

Income Analysis + Common Shareholders !!!

$$\text{Earnings Per Share} = \frac{\text{Net Income} - \text{Preferred Dividends}}{\text{Weighted Average Number of Common Shares Outstanding}}$$

All calculations in this chapter will be based on the example of Darma Corporation. From Figure 7.3 or 7.4, Darma's 2016 net income (profits) of $654,675 is used. Note that other comprehensive income is not included in this calculation. Assume that Darma has 200,000 common shares outstanding on December 31, 2016, and no preferred shares outstanding. For now assume that there were no changes to the number of shares outstanding for 2016; that is, all 200,000 common shares were outstanding for the entire year. Darma's earnings per share (EPS) would be calculated as follows.

$$\text{Earnings Per Share} = \frac{(\$654{,}675 - \$0)}{200{,}000}$$

$$= \frac{\$654{,}675}{200{,}000}$$

$$= \$3.27$$

For the year ended December 31, 2016, Darma Corporation had earnings per share (EPS) of $3.27. The company is making $3.27 profit for every common share outstanding. The general interpretation is that the larger the EPS, the more profitable the company. Figure 7.3 and Figure 7.4 show how the earnings per share figure is presented on Darma's statement of comprehensive income for 2016.

A CLOSER LOOK

When examining corporate financial statements, it is common to see two earnings per share figures: basic earnings per share and fully diluted earnings per share. **Basic earnings per share** is based on actual shares that have been issued to shareholders, and it is shown in this textbook. **Fully diluted earnings per share** is based on actual and potential shares that have or could be issued. Potential shares can arise from a few places:

- Management compensation: Some corporations give senior management options to purchase shares of the company at a reduced price.

- Convertible bonds: Corporations can sell bonds that are convertible into shares in the company.

- Convertible preferred shares: Corporations may issue preferred shares with the "convertible" feature, which allows preferred shareholders to convert their preferred shares into common shares.

The fully diluted EPS is calculated as if all existing management options, convertible bonds and convertible preferred shares were converted into common shares. This will cause the fully diluted EPS to be a smaller figure than the basic EPS. The concept of fully diluted EPS is covered in more advanced accounting courses.

When earnings per share was calculated in Figure 7.3 or 7.4, it was assumed that there was no change in the number of outstanding common shares for the entire year. That is, Darma had 200,000 common shares outstanding on January 1, 2016 and 200,000 common shares outstanding on December 31, 2016. What if Darma issued an additional 10,000 common shares on July 1, 2016; that is, 10,000 additional shares were outstanding for six months, from July 1 to December 31? This is where the calculation of weighted average number of shares comes into play. Figure 7.16 summarizes the numbers needed to calculate EPS.

Date 2016	Actual Number of Shares	Fraction of Year	Weighted Average Number of Shares
Jan 1	200,000	x 12 months/12 months	200,000
Jul 1	10,000	x 6 months/12 months	5,000
	210,000		205,000

FIGURE 7.16

In addition, assume that Darma Corporation has preferred shares and declared preferred dividends of $50,000 for 2016. The calculation of earnings per share for 2016 would now look like this.

$$\text{Earnings Per Share} = \frac{\text{Net Income} - \text{Preferred Dividends}}{\text{Weighted Average Number of Common Shares Outstanding}}$$

$$\text{Earnings Per Share} = \frac{(\$654,675 - \$50,000)}{205,000}$$

$$= \frac{\$604,675}{205,000}$$

$$= \$2.95$$

For the year ended December 31, 2016, Darma Corporation had earnings per share (EPS) of $2.95. Under these changed conditions, the company is making $2.95 profit for every common share outstanding.

Under IFRS, public corporations must disclose earnings per share (EPS) on their statement of comprehensive income, or the income statement if it is presented separately. EPS must also be explained in notes to the financial statements. Private companies that report under ASPE are not required to report their earnings per share.

Calculation of Financial Ratios

Earnings per share (EPS) is a financial ratio that is used to evaluate a company's profitability. In addition to EPS, there are several other ratios of interest to potential investors, shareholders and other users of financial information: book value per common share, the dividend payout ratio and the price-earnings (P/E) ratio. These three ratios and how they are used to evaluate a company's earnings and dividend performance is discussed in this section.

Book Value per Common Share

Like earnings per share (EPS), book value per common share is considered a profitability ratio. It enables shareholders to evaluate the potential return on their investment. **Book value per common share**, often called *book value per share*, is a value that indicates what a common share would be worth to common shareholders if the company were to be liquidated (dissolved).

nonsense!

A company's shares can be valued at either their market value or their book value. Market value represents the price at which shares are publicly traded on the stock market. Book value represents the theoretical value of a share based on a shareholder's claim to the company's assets.

Theoretically, a share's market value should mirror its book value. What the company is worth according to its financial statements should be reflected in the price at which its shares are trading. However, shares are often bought and sold for a very different price than what is reflected on the company's financial statements; the book value does not usually match the market value.

Book value per common share is calculated using the following formula.

$$\text{Book Value per Common Share} = \frac{\text{Shareholders' Equity} - \text{Preferred Equity}}{\text{Number of Common Shares Outstanding}}$$

From Figure 7.14, the shareholders' equity section of Darma's December 31, 2016 statement of financial position is used. On Darma's balance sheet, the value of shareholders' equity is $5,504,405 and Darma does not have any preferred shares. The number of common shares outstanding is 200,000. Darma's book value per common share would be calculated as follows.

$$\text{Book Value per Common Share} = \frac{\$5,504,405}{200,000}$$

$$= \$27.52$$

Therefore, as of December 31, 2016, Darma Corporation's book value per common share is $27.52. This figure would be of interest to investors and others who want to evaluate a share's value against its market price; that is, as a comparison against what a share in the company is currently selling for.

way too vague... no value added

Note that book value per share can be calculated per common share and per preferred share. This textbook shows the calculation for book value per common share.

Dividend Payout Ratio

For investors, there are two monetary reasons to buy shares in a company. One is the potential of profit from an increase in the share price. The other is the anticipation of regular payments of cash dividends. The **dividend payout ratio** shows potential investors what percentage of company earnings is paid out to shareholders in dividends. This enables investors to evaluate which company, or companies, they want to invest in. A stable dividend payout ratio indicates

helps

that a company's board of directors has a consistent record of paying out dividends. For this reason, the dividend payout ratio is considered a good market analysis tool.

The dividend payout ratio is calculated using the following formula.

$$\text{Dividend Payout Ratio} = \frac{\text{Dividends Paid for the Year}}{\text{Net Income}}$$

Darma's statement of changes in equity in Figure 7.7 shows that the company paid $400,000 in dividends to shareholders during 2016. This is the numerator. The denominator is the 2016 net income figure, $654,675, from Darma's statement of comprehensive income in Figure 7.3 or 7.4. Darma's dividend payout ratio would be calculated as follows.

$$\text{Dividend Payout Ratio} = \frac{\$400,000}{\$654,675}$$

$$= 61\%$$

The company is paying out 61% of its earnings in the form of dividends, and the rest of net income, which is 39%, is being kept in the business in the form of retained earnings.

Price-Earnings Ratio

Another good indicator of company performance is the **price-earnings (P/E) ratio**, which divides the market price per common share by earnings per share. The price-earnings ratio is considered a good market analysis tool that provides the investor with an indicator of future growth, as well as risk, of the company's earnings. It is often used by investors and investment advisors as an indicator to buy, sell or hold on to shares.

assuming it is representative of the future !

The price-earnings ratio is calculated using the following formula.

$$\text{Price-Earnings Ratio} = \frac{\text{Market Price per Share}}{\text{Earnings Per Share}}$$

Earlier it was calculated that Darma had 2016 earnings per common share of $3.27. Assume that, on December 31, 2016, Darma's common shares were selling at $24 per share. Darma's price-earnings ratio would be calculated as follows.

$$\text{Price-Earnings Ratio} = \frac{\$24.00}{\$3.27}$$

$$= 7.3$$

This price-earnings (P/E) ratio indicates that, as of December 31, 2016, Darma's common shares were selling at 7.3 times their earnings. If it is assumed that Darma always reports comparative numbers (statements for two or more years) on its financial statements, then its price-earnings ratio can be compared from one period to the next. Investors generally look at a high P/E ratio as an indicator of earnings growth in the future. It can be useful to compare a company's ratio from one period to another, to compare it to the ratios of other companies within the same industry or to ratios in the market in general.

It is important to note that no one particular financial ratio tells the whole story about a company's performance. Investors and other users of financial information must evaluate a combination of factors when deciding whether and when to invest in a company.

In Summary

Explain the different requirements for public and private companies when presenting financial statements

↪ Public companies must use IFRS. Private companies may choose to use either ASPE or IFRS. ASPE and IFRS have different financial statement presentation requirements.

↪ In terms of the frequency of reporting, both ASPE and IFRS require companies to issue their financial statements at least annually. However, public companies are usually required by stock exchanges to prepare financial statements every three months in addition to the final annual report.

Prepare an income statement and a statement of comprehensive income

↪ The statement displaying a company's profitability is called an income statement under ASPE and a statement of comprehensive income under IFRS.

↪ Both ASPE and IFRS require companies to present income (or loss) and taxes from continuing operations separately from those from discontinued operations.

↪ A statement of comprehensive income under IFRS differs from an income statement under ASPE based on differentiation between comprehensive income and net income, presentation of expenses by function or by nature and presentation of earnings per share required by IFRS.

Prepare a statement of retained earnings and a statement of changes in equity

↪ In both the statement of retained earnings under ASPE and the statement of changes in equity under IFRS, net income from the income statement is added to, and dividends are subtracted from, the beginning balance of retained earnings to derive at the ending balance of retained earnings.

↪ In a statement of retained earnings under ASPE, only changes in retained earnings are presented on the face of the statement. Changes in other shareholders' equity accounts are presented in the notes to the financial statements.

↪ In a statement of changes in equity under IFRS, changes in all equity accounts are presented on the face of the statement.

Record and report on prior period adjustments

↪ Three types of accounting changes include a correction of prior period errors, a change in accounting policy and a change in accounting estimate.

↪ Only two types of accounting changes, namely a correction of prior period errors and a change in accounting policy, require retrospective approach of adjustments. No prior period adjustment is necessary for a change in accounting estimate, which affects only current and future periods.

⮡ If prior period adjustments are needed, adjustments to retained earnings must be listed before any other items are added or subtracted on the statement of retained earnings under ASPE or on the statement of changes in equity under IFRS.

Prepare a balance sheet and a statement of financial position

⮡ A statement that lists a company's assets, liabilities and shareholders' equity is often called a balance sheet under ASPE and a statement of financial position under IFRS, although both names are acceptable under both accounting standards.

⮡ Both ASPE and IFRS currently do not specify how items should be listed on a balance sheet or a statement of financial position. Companies that use ASPE tend to list assets and liabilities on the basis of liquidity from most liquid to least liquid, while companies that use IFRS tend to list items in the reverse order.

⮡ A statement of financial position prepared under IFRS presents accumulated other comprehensive income separately from retained earnings. The accumulated other comprehensive income account does not exist under ASPE.

Calculate and explain earnings per share

⮡ Earnings per share (EPS) can be calculated by dividing the net income available for common shareholders by weighted average number of common shares outstanding.

⮡ EPS measures dollars of profit for every common share outstanding. The larger the EPS, the more profitable the company.

Calculate ratios used to evaluate earnings and dividend performance

⮡ Book value per common share is calculated by dividing equity net of preferred shares by number of common shares outstanding. It is a value that indicates what a common share would be worth to common shareholders if the company were to be liquidated (dissolved).

⮡ Dividend payout ratio is calculated by dividing dividends paid for the year by net income after tax. It shows what percentage of company earnings is paid out to shareholders in dividends.

⮡ Price to earnings (P/E) ratio is calculated by dividing market price per share by earnings per share. It compares a company's current share price to its EPS.

Review Exercise

The following information was taken from the accounting records of Shah Company at December 31, 2016. Assume the tax rate is 35%. Also assume that Shah's preferred shares are not convertible, and that Shah does not have any outstanding securities that can be converted into common shares.

FINANCIAL STATEMENT ITEMS	Amount
Prior-year error—debit to Retained Earnings	$7,500
Income tax expense on operating income from discontinued operations	12,250
Total dividends	25,000
Common shares, unlimited shares authorized, 40,000 shares issued and outstanding	155,000
Sales revenue	710,000
Interest expense	30,000
Operating income, discontinued operations	35,000
Loss due to lawsuit	11,000
Sales Discounts	15,000
Income tax savings on sale of discontinued operations (sold at a loss)	14,000
General expenses	62,000
Income tax expense on continuing operations	74,200
Preferred shares, non-cumulative, $5.00, 10,000 shares authorized, 1,000 shares issued	50,000
Retained Earnings, January 1, 2016 (prior to adjustment)	110,000
Loss on sale of discontinued operations	40,000
Cost of goods sold	380,000

Required

a) Prepare a statement of comprehensive income for the year ended December 31, 2016.
b) Prepare a statement of change in equity for Shah Company for the year ended December 31, 2016.
c) Prepare a partial statement of financial position that shows only the shareholders' equity portion as at December 31, 2016.
d) Calculate the EPS ratio.

Review Exercise — Answer

a) Prepare a statement of comprehensive income.

b) Prepare a statement of changes in equity.

c) Prepare a partial statement of financial position that shows only the shareholders' equity portion.

d) Calculate the EPS ratio.

_____

_____

_____

_____

_____

_____

_____

_____

Notes

Chapter 8
NON-CURRENT LIABILITIES

LEARNING OUTCOMES

❶ State the characteristics and different types of bonds

❷ Apply the concept of present value

❸ Record bonds issued at par

❹ Record bonds issued at a discount or a premium

❺ Record the retirement of bonds

❻ Record instalment notes payable

❼ Describe how non-current liabilities are presented on the balance sheet

❽ Apply controls and ethics related to non-current liabilities

AMEENGAGE™ *Access **ameengage.com** for integrated resources including tutorials, practice exercises, the digital textbook and more.*

Non-Current Liabilities: An Introduction

The liabilities side of the balance sheet contains two main sections: current liabilities (discussed in Chapter 4) and non-current liabilities. The focus of this chapter is non-current liabilities, which are obligations due beyond one year (12 months) of the balance sheet date. A non-current liability is also known as a long-term liability. Some common types of non-current liabilities of business organizations are bonds payable, term loans and financing leases.

The most common form of non-current financing used by a company is a loan. Term loans were partly covered in the current liabilities section because the portion of the loan due within one fiscal period is presented as a current liability on the balance sheet.

An alternative to borrowing money from a bank is to borrow money from private investors. This is done by issuing bonds, which can be sold to raise cash for the business. Bonds will be discussed in detail in this chapter.

FIGURE 8.1

Characteristics and Types of Bonds

Companies cannot always secure sufficient financing from a bank or selling shares. Instead, a large company may choose to borrow money by offering investors a type of non-current debt known as a bond. A bond represents a promise to pay a specified amount to the investor on a specific date, known as the bond's maturity date.

The company that issues the bond is called the **bond issuer**. The investor who purchases the bond is known as the **bondholder**. Like a company's shares, bonds are sold to investors on the stock (or securities) exchange. Bonds are typically sold in small denominations, in multiples of $1,000. Bond investors are often large organizations such as pension funds but can also include smaller institutions or individuals. The primary difference between a bond and a loan is that there is a market in which bonds are actively traded. A loan is usually a private agreement between two parties that is non-tradeable.

There are several types of bonds.

- **Term bonds** mature on a specific date, whereas serial bonds are a set of bonds that mature at different intervals.

- **Debenture bonds**, often just referred to as "debentures," are unsecured bonds that are backed only by the bondholder's faith in the company's good reputation.

- **Redeemable** (or callable) **bonds** have a callable feature whereby the company has the right to buy back the bonds before maturity at a set or "call" price.

- **Mortgage bonds**, or secured bonds, can be issued when companies put up specific assets as collateral in the event that it defaults on interest or principal repayments.

- **Convertible bonds** give bondholders the option of converting or exchanging the bonds for a specific number of the company's shares.

- **Registered bonds** list the bondholders as registered owners who receive regular interest payments on the interest payment dates.

- **Coupon bonds** contain detachable coupons that state the amount and due date of the interest payment. These coupons can be removed and cashed by the holder separately.

Bond Issuance

Similar to a company's shares, a bond issue must first be authorized by the corporation's board of directors. To authorize a bond issue, the board of directors must determine the following.

- the total number of bonds to authorize and issue
- the **face value** of the bonds, which is the amount to be paid to the investor upon maturity date; the face value is also sometimes referred to as the bond's par value
- the contractual interest rate, which is the annual percentage rate of interest the investor receives on the face value of each bond; the contractual rate is also sometimes referred to as the bond's coupon rate
- the **maturity date,** which is the date on which the final payment is due to the investor

All of these details are stated in a bond certificate, a document that is issued as an official record to investors when they purchase their bonds.

A bond is an interest-bearing investment vehicle whereby money is received from investors in exchange for interest payments. Interest payments are determined by the bond's contractual interest rate (or coupon rate), which is written on the bond. The contractual interest rate is an annual rate. For example, if an investor buys a $100,000 bond with a 10% interest rate, the investor will earn $10,000 every year ($100,000 × 10%). However, most bonds pay out interest semi-annually (twice a year). To calculate this the annual interest is simply divided by two. So the semi-annual interest for the above bond would be $5,000 ($10,000 ÷ 2).

Companies that issue bonds want to pay the lowest interest possible, but must remain competitive with other investment opportunities or potential buyers will invest elsewhere. That is why companies generally issue bonds at the going or **market interest rate,** the interest rate that investors can demand in return for lending their money. For example, if the market rate is 10%, the company is likely to issue the bond with a 10% interest rate; this is known as issuing a bond at par (face value). But, since it takes time to arrange the printing and distribution of bonds, rates of existing bonds can differ significantly from current market rates. When investors consider purchasing bonds, they want to know how much they must invest at today's market interest rate to get the equivalent of the bonds' coupon rate. The amount the investor will pay today is known as the bonds' present value, and it involves a concept known as the time value of money, which is discussed next.

The Concept of Present Value

In this discussion of accounting methods, round figures have been used, to demonstrate various procedures. It has also been assumed that the value of money remains constant; one dollar in a person's hand at one moment is equal in value to a dollar in that person's hand at a later time. In fact, the value of money changes over time. This is what interest rates are all about.

Money itself has a price. If it is lent, it gets repaid with interest. A deposit in a bank account is essentially a loan to a bank, with interest. Of course, a loan from a bank also comes with a price tag (in the form of interest).

The world of finance often refers to this phenomenon as the **time value of money**. It is important for accountants to be familiar with this because it is a basic principle of economics and finance. Furthermore, it affects the amounts in transactions that an accountant records over time. If a company keeps money in a bank, its value will change even if nothing is done to it.

In the context of the current discussion of bonds payable, the time value of money matters because it will help determine the price the bonds will sell for when the market rate of interest differs from the stated rate. Here is a simple example to show how a company can pay both the principal and interest over time. This involves making calculations concerning the value of money at some future point in time.

Suppose Samuel has one dollar and invests it for one year at an interest rate of 10%. At the end of the year, Samuel has made 10 cents in interest and has a total of $1.10.

At the start of the second year, Samuel starts with $1.10. The interest for the year amounts to 11 cents ($1.10 × 10%) for a year-end balance of $1.21.

There is a pattern developing. The more money that is left in an interest-bearing account, the more the interest grows each year. In the first year, interest was 10 cents. In the second year, it was 11 cents. Figure 8.2 shows the interest that would accumulate in the account over a period of 10 years.

The amount of interest earned in Year 10 is over 23 cents, more than double the amount of interest earned in Year 1.

Year	Opening Balance	Interest at 10%	Closing Balance
1	1.0000	0.1000	1.1000
2	1.1000	0.1100	1.2100
3	1.2100	0.1210	1.3310
4	1.3310	0.1331	1.4641
5	1.4641	0.1464	1.6105
6	1.6105	0.1611	1.7716
7	1.7716	0.1772	1.9487
8	1.9487	0.1949	2.1436
9	2.1436	0.2144	2.3579
10	2.3579	0.2358	2.5937

FIGURE 8.2

This phenomenon is referred to as **compound interest**, which is the piling on effect that applying the same interest rate has on an account over a period of time. With each passing period, the interest rate is applied to interest on top of the principal.

The amount in the bottom right-hand corner of the chart ($2.59) is the value of the money in the account after Year 10, also referred to as the **future value**.

Following this basic logic, the future value of the money after Year 2 is $1.21. After Year 5, it is $1.61, and so on.

Calculating the value of money can work in reverse, too. An accountant can try to calculate what amount needs to be invested today to produce a certain amount in the future. This is known as the **present value**.

Figure 8.3 shows the present values of $1.00 over 10 years, given an interest rate of 10%. The factors are calculated using a formula that is beyond the scope of this book. However, these factors can be found in many mathematical textbooks, and are commonly included as tables in professional accounting exams. Most business calculators include functions which use the factors, as do common spreadsheet programs.

The chart provides answers for the following question: What amount needs to be invested now to create $1 in x number of years, with x representing Years 1 to 10 and assuming an interest rate of 10%?

	10%
Year	Factor
1	0.9091
2	0.8264
3	0.7513
4	0.6830
5	0.6209
6	0.5645
7	0.5132
8	0.4665
9	0.4241
10	0.3855

Excerpt from Present Value table.

FIGURE 8.3

An investor requiring $1.00 after one year would have to invest about 91 cents (as indicated on the first line of the chart). If the investor wanted $1 after 10 years, 39 cents would have to be invested now (as shown on the last line of the chart). The difference between the amounts is a testament to the power of compound interest. Waiting nine years to get the same payoff means initially investing less than half the money. The greater the interest rate, and the longer this interest rate is applied, the more compound interest is earned.

It should be noted that Figure 8.3 applies only to an interest rate calculation of 10%. Separate charts need to be used when other interest rates are involved in calculating present and future values.

Time Value of Money and Bonds Payable

When bonds are sold at their par or face value, both the present value of the principal and future interest payments can be calculated. In the previous calculations, interest was stated at an annual rate and paid once per year. Interest on bonds is normally paid semi-annually. Therefore, when applying present value concepts, the number of periods is doubled and the interest rate is divided by two.

A $100,000 bond issued with 10% interest payable semi-annually over the next five years is used for the following calculations.

$$\text{Future Value } (FV) = \$100,000$$
$$\text{Semi-Annual Interest Rate } (i) = 10\% \times \tfrac{1}{2} = 5\%$$

$$\text{Semi-Annual Interest Payments } (PMT) = \$100,000 \times 5\% = \$5,000$$
$$\text{Number of Periods } (n) = 5 \times 2 = 10$$

The present value of the $100,000 principal repayment is

$$\$100,000 \times 0.6139 = \$61,390$$

The interest payments are different from the principal repayment in that they represent an **annuity** because they are periodic and recurring fixed payments. One of two methods can be used to calculate the present value of the interest payment annuity.

1. The present value of each interest payment can be calulated individually. For example, the first interest payment of $5,000 in six months is multiplied by the period 1 factor to determine the present value of that particular payment. To this amount, add the second $5,000 payment in 12 months and multiply it by the period 2 factor. After this, add the third $5,000 payment in 18 months and multiply it by the period 3 factor. This goes on for all ten interest payments, which can get tedious and is prone to

Present Value	5%
Periods	Factor
1	0.9524
2	0.9070
3	0.8638
4	0.8227
5	0.7835
6	0.7462
7	0.7107
8	0.6768
9	0.6446
10	0.6139

Excerpt from Present Value of Annuity table.

FIGURE 8.4

error. For a five-year bond this calculation would be repeated 10 times (once for each interest payment) to determine the present value of all the interest payments.

2. Since annuities are a common occurrence in the financial industry, tables containing factors for annuities have been developed (see Figure 8.5). Using this table, the present value of *all* interest payments can be made in just one calculation.

Calculate the present value of the future interest payments.

Present Value of $5,000 payments (annuity) made over 10 periods
= $5,000 x 7.7217
= $38,608.50 (round to $38,610)

Present Value of Annuity	5%
Periods	Factor
1	0.9524
2	1.8594
3	2.7232
4	3.5460
5	4.3295
6	5.0757
7	5.7864
8	6.4632
9	7.1078
10	7.7217

FIGURE 8.5

Summary

Present value of principal	= $61,390
Present value of interest payments	= $38,610
Total proceeds	$100,000

Note: The present value of the interest payments is rounded to $38,610 for illustrative purposes.

A spreadsheet or financial calculator with the present value function would not require rounding. This text uses the tables at the end of the chapter for illustration and exercise purposes. Figures may be slightly different if a spreadsheet or financial calculator are used.

It is important to note that the present value of the principal and interest payments equal the face value of the bond ($100,000). This occurred because we have discounted the 5% bond using the 5% interest rate. This shows that the face value of the bond is equal to the present value of the payments when the market rate is equal to the interest rate of the bond.

A CLOSER LOOK

Present value *(PV)* and future value *(FV)* can also be calculated using either a business or financial calculator, or a spreadsheet program. These tools use the same factors as you find in charts or tables, but they allow you to eliminate steps in calculations. Rather than separately calculating the PV or FV of the bond's face value and then its interest, these tools enable you to find the total value using one calculation. All you need to know is the input values: the bond's face value, the market rate of interest per period *(i)*, the number of periods *(n)*, and the interest payment *(PMT)*. You may find that you get slightly different answers using the tables than you do using a digital tool; this is simply due to rounding factors used in the PV and FV tables. Different calculators may vary in their method of operation, but they are based on the same concepts and use the same inputs. Check the user manual or help file for your calculator or spreadsheet.

Issuing Bonds at Par

Business Time Inc., a publisher of investment-related books, magazines and newspapers, wants to raise money for long-term financing by issuing bonds. On December 31, 2016, the company issues 1,000, 10-year bonds at par, at a price of $100 each with 5% annual interest. Figure 8.6 shows how the transaction is recorded by the company's accountant.

JOURNAL			
Date	**Account Title and Explanation**	**Debit**	**Credit**
Dec 31	Cash	100,000	
	Bonds Payable		100,000
	Issue of $100,000 worth of bonds at par (due in 2026)		

FIGURE 8.6

The total amount of $100,000 is debited in the cash account. A corresponding liability shows a credit increase of $100,000 in the bonds payable account. Since the principal for the bonds is due in 10 years, the liability is classified as non-current and placed in that section of the balance sheet.

Issuing the bond for a 10-year term means that a company will have to make interest payments to its bondholders every year for 10 years. Most bonds call for semi-annual (twice per year) interest payments. For simplicity, interest is paid annually in this illustration.

A $5,000 credit represents a decrease in cash, while a $5,000 debit represents an increase in interest expense. This is illustrated in Figure 8.7.

JOURNAL			
Date	**Account Title and Explanation**	**Debit**	**Credit**
Dec 31	Interest Expense	5,000	
	Cash		5,000
	Pay interest on bonds ($100,000 × 5%)		

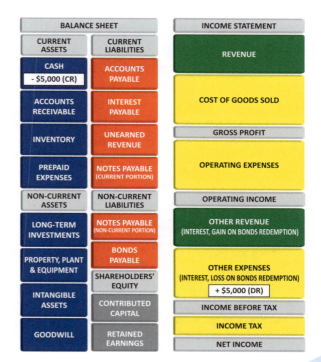

FIGURE 8.7

During the 10-year term that Business Time Inc. is making interest payments to its bondholders, the year-end may occur before the payment is made. A portion of the payment may be due, but the interest is actually paid in the following period.

The company is therefore required to expense the interest during the period in which it was incurred; this is regarded as an accrual and represents a decrease in the company's equity for the period. According to the matching principle, this keeps the company's books in good standing until the payment is made in the following period.

Assume for a moment that the company's year-end is October 31, but the bond anniversary date is December 31. On October 31, when the company prepares its financial statements, it will accrue only 10/12 of the annual interest, as shown in Figure 8.8.

JOURNAL			
Date	Account Title and Explanation	Debit	Credit
Oct 31	Interest Expense	4,167	
	Interest Payable		4,167
	Interest on bonds: $100,000 x 5% x 10/12		

FIGURE 8.8

As with the other interest payments on the bond, $4,167 is expensed as a debit (increase) to bond interest on October 31. However, unlike the previous transaction, interest payable (accrued liabilities) is credited instead of cash.

Continuing the above example, when interest is paid on December 31, the payment is recorded as shown in Figure 8.9.

JOURNAL			
Date	Account Title and Explanation	Debit	Credit
Dec 31	Interest Expense	833	
	Interest Payable	4,167	
	Cash		5,000
	Interest paid: $100,000 x 5%		

FIGURE 8.9

This transaction pays $5,000 to the bondholder. The $4,167 interest accrued at year-end is cleared with the payment. Interest expense of $833 is recorded for the two months between the year end and the interest payment date.

There is another principle involved in making annual interest payments on bonds: on the first day of every year, the company knows that interest payments will be due before the end of the year. Therefore, that year's interest payable gets classified as a current liability.

On the other hand, the original principal (which will be paid back at the end of the 10-year term of the bond) is classified as a non-current liability by the company. This is like a 10-year term loan where you only pay the interest.

We have demonstrated how a bond issue is treated at par. However, the period from the time that a business decides to issue the bonds to the time they are printed for distribution can be several months. In the meantime, the market rate is likely to have changed. This means that the interest rate on the bond may end up being higher—or lower—than that of the market. This will affect the demand for the company's bonds. The price of the bond must, therefore, be adjusted accordingly.

A bond's face value is printed on the face of the bond. The face value is the same as the principal. The principal amount gets paid back to the bondholder, regardless of any changes in market price. In other words, *regardless of the price paid for the bond*, the business needs to pay the full face value of the bond to the bondholder when the bond matures.

However, the market value and the face value of a bond are not always the same. There are two scenarios to consider when such situations occur.

Scenario 1: Market value is less than face value. The bond will be sold at a discount.

Scenario 2: Market value is more than face value. The bond will be sold at a premium.

Issuing Bonds at a Discount

When the bonds were sold at par (or face value), the resulting transaction was relatively simple. From the previous section, the company received a lump sum of $100,000 and established a bonds payable for that same amount.

Things change when market interest rates rise above the interest rate attached to the bond. When that happens, investors can receive higher interest payments from other bonds and market investments.

To deter investors from those other investments and to attract them to the issuer's bonds, the company should offer the bonds at a more attractive price—at a discount. The **discount** is the difference between the price paid and the par value.

But what should that discount price be? The company sets a discount price which compensates the investor for the money lost with the bond's lower interest rate. Here is a demonstration of how this is done.

Assume on January 1, 2016, Energy Bite Inc. issued bonds with a maturity value of $100,000 when the market rate of interest was 12%. The bonds have an annual coupon interest rate of 10% and mature in five years. Interest on the bonds is payable semi-annually on July 1 and January 1 of each year. The company's year-end is September 30. The principal is $100,000, which means that the semi-annual interest payment is $5,000 ($10,000 × ½). Payment of the full amount of principal, or face value of the bond, returns a yield of 5% (10% × ½) semi-annually.

However, since the market rate is 12%, receiving an interest payment of 10% is not high enough to attract investors. In that case, the company must essentially lower the price of the bond to below face value so that the buyer can get an effective interest rate of 12%. It is important to understand that the buyer still expects to get $100,000 for the bond when it matures plus the $5,000 interest every period regardless of what was initially paid. Using the same present value concepts as shown above, here is how the price of the bond is determined.

> Note: Use Table 8-1 and Table 8-2 at the end of the chapter for factors used in the following calculations.

Future Value *(FV)* = $100,000
Semi-Annual Payment *(PMT)* = 5% x $100,000 = $5,000
Semi-Annual Interest Rate *(i)* = 10% x ½ = 5%
Number of Periods *(n)* = 5 x 2 = 10

Present Value of the Principal *(PV)* = $100,000 x 0.5584 = $55,840
(Semi-Annual Market Interest Rate *(i)* of 6%, 10 periods *(n)*)

Present Value of Future Interest Payments *(PV)* = $5,000 x 7.3601 = $36,801
(6% Semi-Annual Interest *(i)*, 10 periods *(n)*)

Total price bondholders are willing to pay for their investment = $55,840 + $36,801 = $92,641

Remember to always use the market interest rate to determine the present value factor because that is what investors use to determine what they should pay for the bonds. However, the bond coupon rate should be used to determine the interest payment as that is the rate attached to the bond. The price investors are willing to pay is lower than the par value because the market rate is 12%, meaning the investors can easily get a return higher than 10% elsewhere in the market. Therefore, the price they are willing to pay will be lower.

The difference between the price paid and the par value is known as the discount. Accounting for the bond discount requires the use of a contra account. As you learned in your previous accounting studies, a contra account is linked to another account and records decreases in the value of that account. This is done so that the original value of the related account remains unchanged. For example, a contra account is used when accounting for the depreciation of an asset such as property, plant and equipment (PPE).

Figure 8.10 shows how the receipt of $92,641 for the issue of Energy Bite Inc. bonds (at discount) is recorded by the company using the contra account Discount on Bonds.

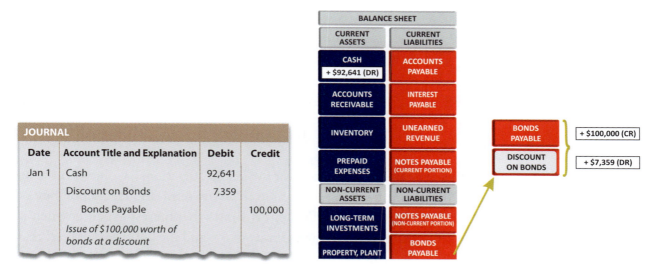

FIGURE 8.10

So although Energy Bite has issued a $100,000 bond, and this amount must be paid when the bond matures, they only received $92,641 from the bondholder.

The bond discount is amortized using the **effective interest method**. This method uses the market interest rate at the date the bonds are issued as the basis to calculate the interest expense. The effective interest rate is applied to the amortized cost of the bonds payable and reflects the actual cost of borrowing.

Because of the discount, issuing bonds below the market rate make it more costly for the company to borrow money. At the maturity date, the company will need to repay the face value of $100,000, rather than the issue price of $92,641; the discount itself ($7,359) is an additional cost of borrowing. Over the life of the bonds, the total cost of borrowing (interest and discount) must be allocated to the interest expense account. This process is called **amortizing the discount** and increases the amount of interest expense reported in each period.

Semi-Annual Interest Period	A Interest Payment ($100,000 × 5%)	B Interest Expense (D × 6%)	C Discount Amortization (B − A)	D Bond Amortized Cost (D + C)
0				$92,641
1	$5,000	$5,558	$558	93,199
2	5,000	5,592	592	93,791
3	5,000	5,627	627	94,418
4	5,000	5,665	665	95,083
5	5,000	5,705	705	95,788
6	5,000	5,747	747	96,535
7	5,000	5,792	792	97,327
8	5,000	5,840	840	98,167
9	5,000	5,890	890	99,057
10	5,000	5,943	943	$100,000
	$50,000	$57,359	$7,359	

FIGURE 8.11

Figure 8.11 shows the amortization table of the bond over five years (10 periods). Column A shows the interest payment of $5,000 which is fixed in each period since the semi-annual coupon rate of 5% and the face value of $100,000 stay the same. Column B shows the interest expense which is calculated by multiplying the semi-annual interest market rate of 6% and the bond's amortized cost at the end of the previous period. The values in this column increase over time since although the market rate is fixed, the bond's amortized cost increases over time. Column C shows the amount of discount amortized over the periods by calculating the difference between the interest expense and the interest payment. The values in this column increase as well since the interest expense increases. Column D shows the bonds amortized cost. Note that this continues to increase by the amount of discounts amortized each period until it reaches the face value of $100,000.

On July 1, 2016, the first payment of interest would be recorded as shown in Figure 8.12. Going back to the table in Figure 8.11, in period 1, the interest expense is debited for $5,558 (column B). The discount on bonds is also amortized

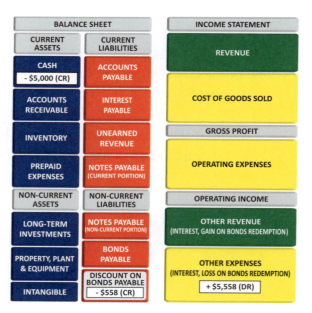

JOURNAL			
Date	Account Title and Explanation	Debit	Credit
July 1	Interest Expense	5,558	
	Discount on Bonds		558
	Cash		5,000
	Record interest and the amortization of the discount for the current year		

FIGURE 8.12

and credited for $558 (column C). The cash is credited for the payment of interest of $5,000 (column A).

On July 1 and January 1 in each of the next five years, the bond issuer will pay $5,000 interest on the bond in cash to the bondholder. The amortization of the discount is just an adjustment and calculated as a difference between the interest payment and the interest expense. After each period, the value of the discount on the bonds will decrease and the book value (or carrying value) of the bond will increase. By the end of the five years, the discount will be reduced to zero and the book value of the bond will be the face value, $100,000.

Since the year-end is September 30, 2016, Energy Bite needs to accrue interest expense before the second payment date on January 1, 2017. Figure 8.13 shows that at each year-end for the next five years, the interest expense is accrued and the discount is amortized for three months, from July 1 to September 30. The interest expense and the amortized discounts for period 2 (six months) can be found in the table from Figure 8.11. These numbers must be adjusted to reflect only three months instead of six months. As shown in Figure 8.13, the interest expense is debited for $2,796 ($5,592 × ³⁄₆), discount is amortized (credited) for $296 ($592 × ³⁄₆) and interest payable is credited for 2,500 ($2,796 − $296).

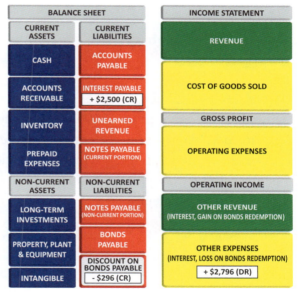

JOURNAL			
Date	Account Title and Explanation	Debit	Credit
Sep 30	Interest Expense	2,796	
	Discount on Bonds		296
	Interest Payable		2,500
	Accrued interest expense and amortized discount at year-end		

FIGURE 8.13

As shown in Figure 8.14, on January 1, 2017, the cash payment is made for $5,000. Interest payable is debited for $2,500 and interest expense is also debited for the remaining balance of period 2 which is $2,796 ($5,592 − $2,796). The rest of the discount of period 2 is also amortized and credited for $296 ($592 − $296).

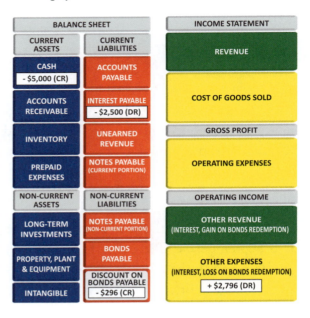

JOURNAL			
Date	**Account Title and Explanation**	**Debit**	**Credit**
Jan 1	Interest Payable	2,500	
	Interest Expense	2,796	
	Discount on Bonds		296
	Cash		5,000
	Payment of interest and amortized discount		

FIGURE 8.14

At the end of the five-year term, as shown in Figure 8.15, cash is credited in the amount of $100,000, and the same amount is debited to bonds payable as a non-current debt, thereby clearing the liability. It is assumed that all interest payments are made and recorded prior to this journal entry. Any outstanding interest payments will be included with this final payment.

JOURNAL			
Date	**Account Title and Explanation**	**Debit**	**Credit**
Jan 1, 2021	Bonds Payable	100,000	
	Cash		100,000
	Repay $100,000 to bondholder		

FIGURE 8.15

Issuing Bonds at a Premium

We have already discussed why companies issue bonds at a discount. The higher market interest rate makes the bond's interest rate less competitive, so the selling price is reduced to make up the difference with potential investors.

Of course, there is a flip side to that scenario. By the time a company's bond issue reaches the market, the market interest rate may decline. This means that the bond's interest rate would be higher than that of the market, and produce a higher rate of return for an investor than what the market is currently offering. This creates a greater demand for the company's bond, which means the company can now sell the bond at a premium (at a price that is higher than its face value).

IN THE REAL WORLD

Although companies are required to use effective-interest method under IFRS, ASPE allows private companies to choose either the effective-interest method or other methods such as the straight-line method. Under ASPE, the straight-line method can only be used if the results are not significantly different from the effective-interest method.

In the real world, private companies would mostly choose the effective-interest method. This is because the calculation for the straight-line method does not accurately reflect the change in value of an item over time. This is true with regard to the value of assets, and is also true with regard to the value of bonds issued at a discount or premium.

A company that issues bonds at a premium takes the same steps in recording the transaction as it would with a discount, except in reverse. Let us review those steps with an example using Energy Bite Inc. again.

On January 1, 2016, Energy Bite Inc. issued bonds with a maturity value of $100,000. The bonds have an annual coupon interest rate of 10% and mature in five years. Interest on the bonds is payable semi-annually on July 1 and January 1 of each year. The company's year-end is September 30. A market rate of 10% means that the bonds could be issued at par. A market rate of 12% means that the bonds were issued at discount. What happens when the market rate is 8%?

> Note: Use Table 8-1 and Table 8-2 at the end of the chapter for factors used in the following calculations.

Future Value *(FV)* = $100,000

Semi-Annual Payment *(PMT)* = 5% x $100,000 = $5,000

Semi-Annual Interest Rate *(i)* = 8% x ½ = 4%

Number of Periods *(n)* = 5 x 2 = 10

Present Value of the Principal *(PV)* = $100,000 x 0.6756 = $67,560
(Semi-Annual Market Interest Rate (i) of 4%, 10 periods *(n)*)

Present Value of Future Interest Payments = $5,000 x 8.1109 = $40,555
(4% Semi-Annual Interest (i), 10 Periods *(n)*)

Total price bondholders are willing to pay   = $67,560 + $40,555 = $108,115
for their investment

The price investors are willing to pay is higher than the par value because the market rate is 8%, meaning it is difficult for investors to get a return as high as 10% elsewhere in the market. Therefore, the price they are willing to pay will be higher.

Figure 8.16 shows how this bond issue is recorded on the company's books.

JOURNAL

Date	Account Title and Explanation	Debit	Credit
Jan 1	Cash	108,115	
	Premium on Bonds		8,115
	Bonds Payable		100,000
	Issue of $100,000 worth of bonds at a premium		

FIGURE 8.16

As always, proceeds from the sale are deposited and recorded as a debit to the cash account. On the other side of the balance sheet, the principal amount of the bond ($100,000) is credited to bonds payable (a non-current liability) account. Finally, the premium on the bond of $8,115 is recorded as a credit in an account called premium on bonds. Premium on bonds appears directly below the bonds payable account on the balance sheet. So far, there is no change to equity; therefore the income statement is not impacted.

Unlike the discount on a bond, which is recorded in a contra liability account, the premium is recorded in a separate liability account. Since it is credited, it represents an amount owing. If a discount is considered an expense, why should a premium not be regarded as revenue? A discount is an increase to an expense (DR) while the premium simply offsets the bond account and decreases the expense (CR).

Similar to a discount on a bond issue, a premium must be amortized as periodic interest payments are made. In other words, the premium liability of $8,115 should be amortized over the term of the bond using the effective-interest method. Figure 8.17 shows the amortization table of the bond over five years. Column A shows the interest payment of $5,000 which will be fixed in five years (10 periods) since the semi-annual coupon rate of 5% and the face value of $100,000 would stay the same. Column B shows the interest expense which is calculated by multiplying the semi-annual interest market rate of 4% and the bond's amortized cost from the end of the previous period. The values in this column decrease over time since although the market rate is fixed, the bond's amortized cost decreases over time. Column C shows the amount of premium amortized over the periods by calculating a difference between the interest expense and the interest payment. The values in this column increase since the interest expense decreases while the interest payment remains constant. Column D shows the bond's amortized cost. Note that the bond's amortized cost continues to decrease by the amount of premium amortized each period until it reaches the face value of $100,000.

Semi-Annual Interest Period	A Interest Payment ($100,000 × 5%)	B Interest Expense (D × 4%)	C Premium Amortization (A − B)	D Bond Amortized Cost (D − C)
0				$108,115
1	$5,000	$4,325	$675	107,440
2	5,000	4,298	702	106,738
3	5,000	4,270	730	106,008
4	5,000	4,240	760	105,248
5	5,000	4,210	790	104,458
6	5,000	4,178	822	103,636
7	5,000	4,145	855	102,781
8	5,000	4,111	889	101,892
9	5,000	4,076	924	100,968
10	5,000	4,032*	968	$100,000
	$50,000	$41,885	$8,115	

* $7 difference due to rounding. The final interest expense is adjusted due to rounding to ensure the final bond amortized cost is equal to $100,000.

FIGURE 8.17

Figure 8.18 shows how that transaction would be recorded for the first year if the effective-interest rate method is used.

On July 1, 2016, the first payment date, the $5,000 (column A) interest payment is recorded and is represented by a credit to cash. The expense to the company is only $4,325 (column B) and the rest of the debit is taken care of by the $675 (column C) first period's amortization of the premium calculated using the effective-interest rate method.

JOURNAL

Date	Account Title and Explanation	Debit	Credit
July 1	Interest Expense	4,325	
	Premium on Bonds	675	
	Cash		5,000
	Payment of interest and amortization of premium		

FIGURE 8.18

On July 1 and January 1 in each of the next five years, the bond issuer will pay $5,000 interest on the bond in cash to the bondholder. The amortization of the premium is just an adjustment and calculated as a difference between the interest payment and the interest expense.

When financial statements are prepared, the premium on bonds is added to the face value of the bonds. The balance sheet would look like Figure 8.19 at the end of the first period, after the amortization of the premium.

Bonds Payable	$100,000
Add: Unamortized Premium	7,440
Book Value	$107,440

FIGURE 8.19

Since the year-end is September 30, 2016, Energy Bite needs to accrue interest expense before the second payment date on January 1, 2017. Figure 8.20 shows that at each year-end for the next five years, the interest expense is accrued and the premium is amortized for three months, from July 1 to September 30. The interest expense and the amortized premium for period 2 (six months) can be found in the table from Figure 8.17. These numbers must be adjusted to reflect only three months instead of six months. As shown in Figure 8.20, the interest expense is debited for $2,149 ($4,298 × ³⁄₆), premium is amortized (debited) for $351 ($702 × ³⁄₆) and interest payable is credited for 2,500 ($2,149 + $351).

JOURNAL

Date	Account Title and Explanation	Debit	Credit
Sep 30	Interest Expense	2,149	
	Premium on Bonds	351	
	Interest Payable		2,500
	Accrued interest expense and amortized premium at year end		

FIGURE 8.20

As shown in Figure 8.21, on January 1, 2017, the cash payment is made for $5,000. Interest payable is debited for $2,500 and interest expense is also debited for the remaining balance of period 2 which is $2,149 ($4,298 − $2,149). The rest of the premium of period 2 should also be amortized and debited for $351 ($702 − $351).

JOURNAL

Date	Account Title and Explanation	Debit	Credit
Jan 1	Interest Payable	2,500	
	Interest Expense	2,149	
	Premium on Bonds	351	
	Cash		5,000
	Payment of interest and amortized discount		

FIGURE 8.21

Because of the premium, issuing bonds above the market rate makes it less costly for the company to borrow money. At the maturity date, the company will need to repay the face value of $100,000, rather than the issue price of $108,115. In other words, the premium itself ($8,115) is reducing the cost of borrowing. Over the life of the bonds, the total cost of borrowing (interest payment less premium) must be allocated to the interest expense account. This process of allocating the premium is called **amortizing the premium**. This process decreases the amount of interest expense reported in each period.

Similar to Figure 8.15 from the discount discussion, on the maturity date, cash is credited in the amount of $100,000, and the same amount is debited to bonds payable to remove the debt from the books.

A CLOSER LOOK

Recording the bond premium or discount using a separate premium on bonds or discount on bonds account is called the gross method. Alternatively, a bond issuer can account for bond premiums or discounts using the net method by recording them directly in the bonds payable account. This method eliminates the use of separate accounts to track premiums or discounts. To illustrate the differences between the two methods, the transactions below compare how issuing bonds at a discount is recorded under the net method and the gross method.

Net Method			
Jan 1	Cash	92,641	
	Bonds Payable		92,641

Gross Method			
Jan 1	Cash	92,641	
	Discount on Bonds	7,359	
	Bonds Payable		100,000

The transactions below compare how the interest payment and discount amortization are recorded under the net and gross methods.

Net Method			
July 1	Interest Expense	5,558	
	Bonds Payable		558
	Cash		5,000

Gross Method			
July 1	Interest Expense	5,558	
	Discount on Bonds		558
	Cash		5,000

If the bonds had been issued at a premium, the differences between the two methods of accounting would still be similar. The premium amount would have been included in the bonds payable account on the date of bond issuance, making the balance of bonds payable higher than the par value. When the premium is amortized, instead of debiting the premium on bonds account, the issuing company would debit the bonds payable account, thus lowering the bonds payable account balance.

Retiring Bonds

Regardless of the price at which a bond was issued, whether at par, discount or premium, the underlying terms of the bond remain the same. That means that an interest payment is made regularly according to the rate on the bond. It also means that the principal amount is paid back in full. The original investor essentially loans the issuing company the principal amount.

When the bond matures, that principal amount is paid back to the current owner of the bond. This transaction is also referred to as redeeming the bond, or buying it back.

Using our example of Energy Bite Inc., Figure 8.22 shows how the final bond redemption is recorded. Cash is credited in the amount of $100,000. The original bonds payable, created five years earlier at the time of bond issue, is finally taken off the books with a $100,000 debit to that account. This transaction of bonds redemption is identical to what is shown earlier in Figure 8.15 under the assumption that the bonds were issued at a discount.

JOURNAL			
Date	**Account Title and Explanation**	**Debit**	**Credit**
Jan 1	Bonds Payable	100,000	
	Cash		100,000
	Redemption of $100,000 worth of bonds at par		

FIGURE 8.22

BALANCE SHEET

CURRENT ASSETS	CURRENT LIABILITIES
CASH - $100,000 (CR)	ACCOUNTS PAYABLE
ACCOUNTS RECEIVABLE	INTEREST PAYABLE
INVENTORY	UNEARNED REVENUE
PREPAID EXPENSES	NOTES PAYABLE (CURRENT PORTION)
NON-CURRENT ASSETS	NON-CURRENT LIABILITIES
LONG-TERM INVESTMENTS	NOTES PAYABLE (NON-CURRENT PORTION)
PROPERTY, PLANT & EQUIPMENT	BONDS PAYABLE - $100,000 (DR)
INTANGIBLE ASSETS	SHAREHOLDERS' EQUITY
	CONTRIBUTED CAPITAL
GOODWILL	RETAINED EARNINGS

This transaction takes care of the redemption of the bond. However, a company sometimes issues what are known as **callable bonds**. These give the issuing company the option to buy back the bonds before the stated maturity date. The issuer might want to do this to take advantage of lower market interest rates, which would allow for the issuance of new bonds to match those lower rates. The company could now make lower annual interest payments on its bonds.

In addition to redeeming the bonds to remove them from the books, any premium or discount must be addressed. If the bond is removed from the books, any remaining premium or discount must also be removed.

Consider our earlier example of Energy Bite Inc. bonds which were issued at a discount. If the company was to exercise a call option on the bonds at the end of Year 4 (which includes eight periods of paid interest) then according to the amortization table in Figure 8.11, the unamortized discount would amount to the following.

$$\$7,359 - \$5,526 = \$1,833$$
or
$$\$890 + \$943 = \$1,833$$

The book value of the bond on this date is $98,167 ($100,000 – $1,833), however it is likely that the amount of cash paid to redeem this bond early will be different from the book value. If the amount of cash paid is greater than the book value, a loss must be recognized. If the amount of cash paid is less than the book value, a gain must be recognized.

If Energy Bite paid $99,000 to redeem the bonds early, they would record a loss of $833, as shown in Figure 8.23.

JOURNAL			
Date	**Account Title and Explanation**	**Debit**	**Credit**
Jan 1	Bonds payable	100,000	
	Loss on Bond Redemption	833	
	Discount on Bonds		1,833
	Cash		99,000
	Redemption of $100,000 worth of bonds		

FIGURE 8.23

The debit to bond payable and the credit to discounts on bonds are to remove both items from the books of the company. The loss is reported on the income statement under Other Revenue and Expenses. If the cash paid is less than the bond's book value, a gain would be recorded and also reported on the income statement.

If we use the bonds which were issued at a premium, then the same type of transaction would take place, except that a debit would be recorded to the premium on bonds to close the account. Any gain or loss on the redemption would be recorded in the same manner illustrated.

Notes Payable

In Chapter 4 you learned about short-term notes payable, which represent a current liability that is due within 12 months of the date of issue. Short-term notes payable are shown as current liabilities on the balance sheet at the end of the period. A **note payable** is a legally binding document that represents money owed to the bank, an individual, corporation or other lender. Short-term notes are usually paid in full at their maturity date.

A **non-current notes payable**, on the other hand, represents a long-term liability that is due beyond 12 months of the date of issue. Non-current notes payable are repayable in periodic payments, such as monthly, quarterly or semi-annually. These periodic payments on the notes are usually referred to as **instalments**.

Notes payable are similar to bonds payable in some respects. Like bonds, notes represent a promise to pay a specified amount (the face value) on a specific date, known as the maturity date. Also, both bonds and notes require interest payments. However, whereas bonds have a stated contractual interest rate (or coupon rate), notes can have two types of interest rates. The first, a **fixed interest rate**, is a rate that remains constant for the entire term of the note. The second type of rate is a **variable interest rate**, also referred to as a "floating" rate because it fluctuates according to market interest rates.

When the periodic payments, or instalments, are paid on notes payable, the amount consists of both a payment toward the note's principal (its face value), and interest on the unpaid balance of the note. The amount of the instalment payment is normally paid in one of two ways: as fixed principal plus interest, or as blended principal plus interest. We will look at both of these payment types next.

Fixed Principal Payments

One of two ways to calculate the instalment payments on notes payable is as fixed principal plus interest. As an example, suppose that Trigraph Inc. issues a $300,000 five-year, 5% note payable on January 1, 2016. The journal entry to record the issue of the note payable is shown in Figure 8.24.

JOURNAL			
Date	**Account Title and Explanation**	**Debit**	**Credit**
Jan 1	Cash	300,000	
	Notes Payable		300,000
	Issue five-year, 5% note payable		

FIGURE 8.24

According to the terms of the note, the note is repayable in 60 monthly instalments (5 years × 12 months/year = 60 instalment payments), plus interest on the outstanding principal, due on the first day of each month. The payments will consist of an equal monthly reduction of the principal of $5,000 ($300,000 × 1/60), and the monthly interest expense of 5% on the outstanding principal. You learned in the earlier section on bonds about the effective-interest rate method to calculate interest expense. The effective-interest rate method is also used to calculate the interest expense on notes payable.

For Trigraph's note payable, the first monthly instalment payment on February 1 is calculated as follows.

Principal:	$300,000 ÷ 60 monthly payments = $5,000
Interest (5%):	($300,000 × 5% × 1/12) = $1,250
Cash Payment:	$5,000 + $1,250 = $6,250

Figure 8.25 shows an instalment payment schedule for Trigraph Inc.'s note payable for the first four payment periods.

Date	A Cash Payment (B + C)	B Interest Expense (D × 5% × $\frac{1}{12}$)	C Reduction of Principal ($300,000 ÷ 60)	D Principal Balance (D – C)
Jan 1				$300,000
Feb 1	$6,250	$1,250	$5,000	$295,000
Mar 1	$6,229	$1,229	$5,000	$290,000
Apr 1	$6,208	$1,208	$5,000	$285,000

FIGURE 8.25

As shown in Figure 8.25, column A represents the total cash payment which includes both interest expense (column B) and the monthly principal payment (column C). This approach is called a fixed principal payment since a monthly reduction of the principal ($5,000) is fixed for each interest period. As the payments are made, the principal balance (column D) is reduced; therefore, the interest expense on the remaining principal decreases resulting in decreasing monthly cash payments.

As Figure 8.25 shows, the principal balance after the February 1 payment is as follows.

$$\$300,000 - \$5,000 = \$295,000$$

The journal entry to record the first instalment payment on the note payable is shown in Figure 8.26. Interest expense and notes payable are both debited for $1,250 and $5,000 respectively. Cash is also credited for $6,250. As shown in the Accounting Map, the interest expense for the period is shown on the income statement under Other Expenses. On the balance sheet, the principal amount of $5,000 reduces the current portion of the notes payable

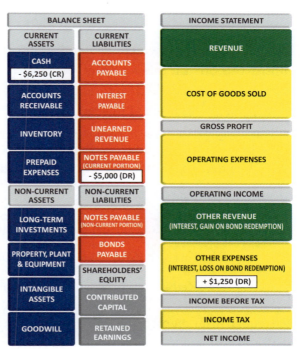

JOURNAL			
Date	Account Title and Explanation	Debit	Credit
Feb 1	Interest Expense	1,250	
	Notes Payable	5,000	
	Cash		6,250
	Record monthly payment of principal and interest on note payable		

FIGURE 8.26

due within the next 12 months. The presentation of current and non-current portions will be further explained later in this chapter.

A similar journal entry is made monthly for the remainder of the term of the note, but it will be based on the interest expense on the outstanding principal balance as of that particular period. As seen already in Figure 8.25, the interest expense will decrease with each period as the principal balance decreases.

Blended Payments

Another way to calculate the instalment payments on notes payable is as blended principal plus interest. Let us look at an example of this method, once again using Trigraph Inc. Suppose that Trigraph issues a $300,000 five-year, 5% note payable on January 1, 2016. The journal entry to record the issue of the note payable is the same as before, and is shown again in Figure 8.27.

JOURNAL			
Date	**Account Title and Explanation**	**Debit**	**Credit**
Jan 1	Cash	300,000	
	Notes Payable		300,000
	Issue five-year, 5% note payable due 2021		

FIGURE 8.27

According to the terms of the note, the note is repayable in 60 monthly instalments. However, unlike the fixed principal payment method (where the payment consists separately of an equal monthly reduction of the principal, and the monthly interest expense on the outstanding principal), the blended payments will *include* the interest on the outstanding principal. This type of payment is often used for mortgages, car loans, student loan payments, and so on.

With the blended payment method, the instalments are made in equal monthly payments that consist of both the reduction of the principal and the monthly interest expense of 5% on the outstanding principal. Therefore, the interest expense will decrease with each period as with the fixed principal method. However, the portion of the payment that is applied to the principal will increase with each period. Let us look at how this happens.

With blended payments, the first monthly instalment on February 1 is calculated as follows.

Principal:	$300,000
Payment Terms:	60 equal instalment payments of $5,661
Interest (5%):	($300,000 × 5% × 1/12) = $1,250
Reduction of Principal:	$5,661 − $1,250 = $4,411

The equal instalment payments are calculated using PV factors or a calculator. The calculation of the instalment payment is beyond the scope of this course, so we will provide the payment amount. The key is determining how much of the instalment payment is interest and how much is principal. Figure 8.28 shows an instalment payment schedule for Trigraph Inc.'s note payable for the first four payment periods.

Date	A Cash Payment	B Interest Expense (D × 5% × $\frac{1}{12}$)	C Reduction of Principal (A – B)	D Principal Balance (D – C)
Jan 1				$300,000
Feb 1	$5,661	$1,250	$4,411	$295,589
Mar 1	$5,661	$1,232	$4,429	$291,160
Apr 1	$5,661	$1,213	$4,448	$286,712

FIGURE 8.28

As shown in Figure 8.28, column A represents the total cash payment which is fixed on each interest period and equals $5,661. The interest expense (column B) is calculated by multiplying the interest rate by the outstanding principal. The principal reduction (column C) is equal to the difference between the fixed cash payment and the interest expense. As the payments are made, the principal balance (column D) decreases.

As Figure 8.26 shows, the principal balance after the February 1 payment is as follows.

$$\$300,000 - \$4,411 = \$295,589$$

The journal entry to record the first instalment payment on the note payable is shown in Figure 8.29. Interest expense and notes payable are both debited for $1,250 and $4,411 respectively. Cash is also credited for $5,661. As shown in the Accounting Map, the interest expense for the period is shown on the income statement under Other Expenses. On the balance sheet, the principal amount of $4,411 reduces the current portion of the notes payable.

JOURNAL			
Date	Account Title and Explanation	Debit	Credit
Feb 1	Interest Expense	1,250	
	Notes Payable	4,411	
	Cash		5,661
	Record monthly payment of principal and interest on note payable		

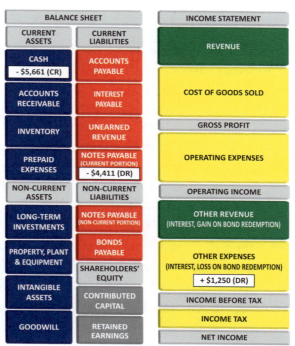

FIGURE 8.29

A similar journal entry is made monthly for the remainder of the term of the note, but it will be based on the decreasing interest expense as the portion of the payment that is applied to the principal increases with each period.

The blended method ensures the cash payments made are always equal. As more payments are made, the amount going toward reducing the principal increases while the amount of interest decreases. The fixed method ensures that the reduction of the principal is consistent from payment to payment, however the amounts of cash paid each period decreases as the amount of interest decreases.

Current vs. Non-Current Notes Payable

By now you are quite familiar with the difference between current and non-current (or long-term) liabilities—that is, current liabilities are those payable within 12 months of the balance sheet date, while non-current liabilities are those payable beyond 12 months. Using this concept, the amount of a note payable must be reported on the balance sheet in its respective categories: the amount of principal to be reduced over the next 12 months from the balance sheet date is reported as "Current portion of Note Payable," the balance of the principal to be reduced beyond the 12-month period is reported as "Non-current portion of Note Payable." You will see just how this financial statement presentation is accomplished in the next section.

Financial Statement Presentation of Non-Current Liabilities

In the normal presentation of a balance sheet, assets and liabilities are classified as current and non-current. This level of detail is required by users of the financial statements so that they can fully understand and assess a company's financial position and its ability to pay its debts.

We have just discussed the concept of separately reporting current and non-current portions of notes payable on the balance sheet. This same practice applies to bonds payable, which was covered earlier in this chapter. Let us look at an example of financial statement presentation for both types of non-current liabilities, starting with notes payable.

Notes Payable on the Financial Statements

The example of the notes payable of Trigraph Inc. under the fixed principal payments method will be used to illustrate the balance sheet presentation. Fast-forward to the end of the first 12 months after the note was issued, to the balance sheet date of December 31, 2016. First, determine the current and non-current portions of the note as of December 31. Based on the instalment payment schedule in Figure 8.25, the schedule for 2016 would appear as in Figure 8.30. (Note that the January 1, 2017 payment is shown, because up until that payment is made, it also represents the December 31, 2016 balance.)

Date	A Cash Payment (B + C)	B Interest Expense (D × 5% × ¹⁄₁₂)	C Reduction of Principal ($300,000 ÷ 60)	D Principal Balance (D − C)
Jan 1, 2016				$300,000
Feb 1	$6,250	$1,250	$5,000	$295,000
Mar 1	$6,229	$1,229	$5,000	$290,000
Apr 1	$6,208	$1,208	$5,000	$285,000
May 1	$6,188	$1,188	$5,000	$280,000
Jun 1	$6,167	$1,167	$5,000	$275,000
Jul 1	$6,146	$1,146	$5,000	$270,000
Aug 1	$6,125	$1,125	$5,000	$265,000
Sep 1	$6,104	$1,104	$5,000	$260,000
Oct 1	$6,083	$1,083	$5,000	$255,000
Nov 1	$6,063	$1,063	$5,000	$250,000
Dec 1	$6,042	$1,042	$5,000	$245,000
Jan 1, 2017	$6,021	$1,021	$5,000	$240,000

$5,000 × 12 = $60,000

FIGURE 8.30

As Figure 8.30 shows in Column C, the reduction of principal is $5,000 per month, or $60,000 per year. So, as of December 31, 2016, the current portion of the note payable, the amount to be paid over the next 12 months, will again be $60,000 ($5,000 × 12 months). As of December 31, 2016, the non-current portion of the note payable, the amount to be paid beyond the next 12 months, is as follows.

Non-current portion of note payable = Principal Balance (Dec. 31, 2016) − Reduction of Principal over next 12 months

= $240,000 − $60,000

= $180,000

Figure 8.31 presents the partial balance sheet for Trigraph Inc., focusing on the liabilities section of the statement. Note that all other amounts in the partial balance sheet are assumed for our illustration purposes.

Trigraph Inc.
Balance Sheet (partial)
As at December 31, 2016

Current Liabilities		
Accounts Payable	$70,000	
Interest Payable	10,000	
Current Portion of Notes Payable	60,000	
Total Current Liabilities		140,000
Non-Current Liabilities		
Notes Payable, 5%, due 2021	180,000	
Total Non-Current Liabilities		180,000
Total Liabilities		$320,000

FIGURE 8.31

Bonds Payable on the Financial Statements

Bonds payable affect the balance sheet accounts in different ways, depending on whether the bonds are issued at par, at a discount or at a premium. Generally, the presentation of bonds payable on the balance sheet can be summarized as follows.

- Bonds issued at par—The balance sheet reports the non-current liability (as of the end of the period) equal to the bonds' face value, until the bonds' maturity.

- Bonds issued at a discount—The balance sheet reports the non-current liability (as of the end of the period) equal to the bonds' carrying value (its book value), until the bond's maturity. For bonds issued at a discount, the carrying value is the bonds' face value minus the total unamortized discount. Each year, the bond's carrying value will increase until the amount reported on the balance sheet equals the bond's face value.

- Bonds issued at a premium—The balance sheet reports the non-current liability (as of the end of the period) equal to the bonds' carrying value (its book value), until the bond's maturity. For bonds issued at a premium, the carrying value is the bond's face value plus the total unamortized premium. Each year, the bond's carrying value will decrease until the amount reported on the balance sheet equals the bond's face value.

To illustrate the balance sheet presentation, we will use an example of bonds issued at a discount. Return to the earlier example in which Energy Bite issued $100,000 five-year, 10% interest bonds on January 1, 2016. At the then-current market interest rate of 12% with semi-annual interest payments, the bonds were issued at a discount for $92,641; this is the carrying value of the bonds on their issue date. Referring to the amortization table in Figure 8.11, at the end of the first fiscal year of September 30 (semi-annual interest period 2), the unamortized discount on the bond payable would be $6,505 ($7,359 − $558 − $296). Notice that since the year-end is September 30, only three months of period 2 should be accounted for when it comes to calculating the year-end adjustments ($592 × $^{1}/_{2}$ = $296) We know that the face value of the bonds is $100,000. Energy Bite's partial balance sheet for September 30, 2016 is shown in Figure 8.32.

Energy Bite Inc. Balance Sheet (partial) As at September 30, 2016		
Non-Current Liabilities		
Bond Payable, 10%, due January 1, 2021	$100,000	
Less: Discount on Bond Payable	6,505	
Total Non-Current Liabilities		$93,495

FIGURE 8.32

Note that as of September 30, 2016, the bonds' carrying value is now $93,495, which represents its amortized cost.

If Energy Bite were to issue the same bonds on January 1, 2016, at a then-current market interest rate of 8% with semi-annual interest payments, the bonds would be issued at a premium for $108,115; this would be the carrying value of the bonds on their issue date. Referring to the amortization table in Figure 8.17, at the end of the first fiscal year (semi-annual interest period 2), the unamortized premium on the bond payable would be $7,089 ($8,115 − $675 − $351). Since the year-end is September 30, only three months of period 2 should be accounted for when calculating the year-end adjustments ($702 × 1/2 = $351) We know that the face value of the bonds is $100,000. Energy Bite's partial balance sheet for September 30, 2016 is shown in Figure 8.33.

	Energy Bite Inc. Balance Sheet (partial) As at September 30, 2016	
Non-Current Liabilities		
Bond Payable, 10%, Due January 1, 2021	$100,000	
Add: Premium on Bond Payable	7,089	
Total Non-Current Liabilities		$107,089

FIGURE 8.33

Interest expense, and the amortization of bond discount and premium, affect the income statement accounts in different ways, depending on whether the bonds are issued at par, at a discount or at a premium. Generally, the presentation of interest expense from the bonds payable on the income statement can be summarized as follows.

- Bonds issued at par—The income statement reports interest expense for the period equal to the bond's contractual interest rate.

- Bonds issued at a discount—The income statement reports interest expense for the period equal to the bond's contractual interest rate plus the amortized portion of the discount.

- Bonds issued at a premium—The income statement reports interest expense for the period equal to the bond's contractual interest rate minus the amortized portion of the premium.

As the Accounting Maps showed in the section on bonds payable, the income statement includes interest expense for the period under Other Expenses.

At the beginning of this section, you learned that users of the financial statements require this level of detail. Creditors and investors require complete and accurate financial information so that they can make informed business decisions. This is why accounting standards require full disclosure of all current and non-current debt.

Controls and Ethics Related to Non-Current Liabilities

Non-current liabilities play a key role in helping a company finance its business. At the same time, lenders and investors are also interested in ensuring that they will receive their money back by the payment dates. That is why a company needs to monitor the level of debt and its accompanying interest expense. Taking too much debt could jeopardize a company's ability to maintain a good credit rating and may consequently limit future borrowing. For the same reasons, banks and other creditors use various measurement tools to confirm whether or not a company can handle its obligations.

In general, different financial measurements can be applied to control a company's ability to pay off its non-current debt. For example, analysts could take a look at the amount of a company's total assets financed by creditors or the amount of interest obligations in compared to its earnings. The financial ratios used for non-current liabilities will be discussed in detail in the last chapter.

A company must comply with all relevant policies, plans, procedures, laws and regulations. With regard to loans, this means that all documents pertaining to the loan should be reviewed by legal counsel. Strong controls surrounding the negotiation of non-current liabilities should result in obtaining the best possible interest rates. A lower interest rate will increase cash flow which can then be used for other activities of the business. In addition, robust cash controls ensure that interest and principal payments are made on time. Other controls include verifying that interest and principal payments have been received by lenders.

We will now examine ethical violations related to non-current liabilities.

Companies assume non-current liabilities, such as term loans and bond issues, to finance large items and projects that often take years to complete. The sheer magnitude of these transactions makes them vulnerable to abuse.

IN THE REAL WORLD

In the fall of 2008, the world was hit by the worst financial crisis since the Depression. Global financial institutions had too much money invested in bad credit, especially sub-prime mortgages. The economy started to slow down when these bad debts went unpaid and the credit market crashed as a result.

In the aftermath of the crash, leading financial minds looked for solutions to problems that had gone unsolved for years. Although many experts looked for ways to better regulate the markets, some analysts started pointing fingers at the accounting profession.

Specifically, a long-running criticism of accounting standards is that they do not require an appropriate level of disclosure. A perfect example of this is off-balance-sheet financing—the practice of keeping some forms of long-term financing off the company books.

Another example of poor disclosure is reporting pension fund assets and liabilities only in footnote form. Recent standards are now forcing companies to disclose a net amount on the balance sheet itself.

Critics of the accounting profession believe that it is only through fair and open reporting that companies can gain the trust of investment markets in general. How can companies expect people to trust them with money if they are not fully open about what is reported in the financial statements?

Open and fair accounting practices can help bring back some stability and trust in world markets at a time when it is most needed.

Management is often closely involved when large sums of money are dealt with. Since at this level there can be fewer internal controls, those in place must be thorough and complete. Reviews by top-level executives and audits should be performed internally and externally.

Individuals can be tempted to siphon off or redirect money when dealing with large amounts of money. Staying alert and attentive to these risks is one of the primary responsibilities of those who own and run the company.

Additionally, it is necessary to be vigilant with transactions conducted with financial institutions, where unauthorized commissions may exist. Some part of the loan money might end up in the hands of individuals who work out a side deal for themselves. That is why it is always important for companies to keep track of all the money.

The final type of fraud discussed here is off-balance sheet financing. Some businesses engage in accounting practices that keep some large financing schemes off the books. This allows a business to keep its debt to equity and leverage ratios low, which might artificially inflate share prices by overstating a company's equity position. Examples include joint ventures, research and development partnerships and operating leases.

A **lease** is a contract between the owner of an asset and another party who uses the asset for a given period of time. One form is an **operating lease,** such as a car rental, where the ownership is not transferred to another party over the term of the agreement.

Operating leases were once a common example of off-balance sheet financing. Instead of owning the asset, a company could lease it and expense any rental fees. Accounting rules have been changed so that some leases, depending on their terms, are treated as a form of financing. This forces the company to record an asset and the accompanying liability on its balance sheet. This increases its debt-to-equity ratio and gives users of its financial statements a more accurate picture of the company's financial position.

 *Access **ameengage.com** for integrated resources including tutorials, practice exercises, the digital textbook and more.*

In Summary

State the characteristics and different types of bonds

⇨ The company that issues the bond is called the bond issuer. The investor who purchases the bond is the bondholder.

⇨ The investor provides principal loan to the issuing company. In return, the company makes interest payments to the investor, in addition to eventually repaying the principal.

⇨ There are several types of bonds, such as term bonds, debenture bonds, redeemable bonds, mortgage bonds, convertible bonds, registered bonds and coupon bonds.

Apply the concept of present value

⇨ The time value of money involves the concept that interest is earned on top of interest year after year. This is called compound interest.

⇨ Future value determines the value of an investment in the future if an amount is invested today. Present value determines the amount invested today to produce a certain amount in the future.

Record bonds issued at par

⇨ When the bond interest rate equals the market interest rate, the company can sell the bond at par.

Record bonds issued at a discount or a premium

⇨ When the bond interest rate is lower than the market interest rate, the company sells the bond at a discount.

⇨ When the bond interest rate is higher than the market interest rate, the company can sell the bond at a premium.

⇨ Both the discount and premium attached to the bond price should be amortized over the term of the bond until maturity.

Record the retirement of bonds

⇨ When the bond reaches maturity, it is time for the issuing company to repay the principal to whoever holds the bond at the time. This is also called redemption.

⇨ The issuing company may have the option to redeem a bond early. Such securities are referred to as callable bonds.

Record instalment notes payable

⇨ A company usually has three basic options when it comes to long-term financing: bank loans, bond issues and notes payable.

⇨ Non-current notes payable are repayable in periodic payments, such as monthly, quarterly or semi-annually.

⇨ A non-current note payable represents a long-term liability that is due beyond 12 months of the date of issue.

Describe how non-current liabilities are presented on the balance sheet

⇨ Non-current liabilities must be split into a current portion (amount owed in the next 12 months) and non-current portion (amount owed beyond 12 months). These amounts are reported on the balance sheet in the current liabilities and non-current liabilities sections respectively.

Apply controls and ethics related to non-current liabilities

⇨ Controls related to non-current liabilities should ensure that all documents are in order and that cash flow planning accommodates future payments for loans and bonds.

⇨ Ethics related to non-current liabilities should ensure the integrity of large amounts of cash that upper management has the responsibility of handling. Unauthorized commissions are always a risk when dealing with financial institutions. Off-balance-sheet financing is also a practice that can skew the way in which company finances are reported to the public.

Table 8-1
Present Value of $1

Periods	1%	2%	3%	4%	5%	6%
1	0.9901	0.9804	0.9709	0.9615	0.9524	0.9434
2	0.9803	0.9612	0.9426	0.9246	0.9070	0.8900
3	0.9706	0.9423	0.9151	0.8890	0.8638	0.8396
4	0.9610	0.9238	0.8885	0.8548	0.8227	0.7921
5	0.9515	0.9057	0.8626	0.8219	0.7835	0.7473
6	0.9420	0.8880	0.8375	0.7903	0.7462	0.7050
7	0.9327	0.8706	0.8131	0.7599	0.7107	0.6651
8	0.9235	0.8535	0.7894	0.7307	0.6768	0.6274
9	0.9143	0.8368	0.7664	0.7026	0.6446	0.5919
10	0.9053	0.8203	0.7441	0.6756	0.6139	0.5584
11	0.8963	0.8043	0.7224	0.6496	0.5847	0.5268
12	0.8874	0.7885	0.7014	0.6246	0.5568	0.4970
13	0.8787	0.7730	0.6810	0.6006	0.5303	0.4688
14	0.8700	0.7579	0.6611	0.5775	0.5051	0.4423
15	0.8613	0.7430	0.6419	0.5553	0.4810	0.4173

Table 8-2
Present Value of Annuity $1

Periods	1%	2%	3%	4%	5%	6%
1	0.9901	0.9804	0.9709	0.9615	0.9524	0.9434
2	1.9704	1.9416	1.9135	1.8861	1.8594	1.8334
3	2.9410	2.8839	2.8286	2.7751	2.7232	2.6730
4	3.9020	3.8077	3.7171	3.6299	3.5460	3.4651
5	4.8534	4.7135	4.5797	4.4518	4.3295	4.2124
6	5.7955	5.6014	5.4172	5.2421	5.0757	4.9173
7	6.7282	6.4720	6.2303	6.0021	5.7864	5.5824
8	7.6517	7.3255	7.0197	6.7327	6.4632	6.2098
9	8.5660	8.1622	7.7861	7.4353	7.1078	6.8017
10	9.4713	8.9826	8.5302	8.1109	7.7217	7.3601
11	10.3676	9.7868	9.2526	8.7605	8.3064	7.8869
12	11.2551	10.5753	9.9540	9.3851	8.8633	8.3838
13	12.1337	11.3484	10.6350	9.9856	9.3936	8.8527
14	13.0037	12.1062	11.2961	10.5631	9.8986	9.2950
15	13.8651	12.8493	11.9379	11.1184	10.3797	9.7122

Review Exercise 1

Hohl Company is planning to expand its facilities by constructing a new building and installing new machines. To complete this project, the company has decided to issue $2,000,000 worth of 20-year 4% callable bonds, with interest paid every six months.

On April 1, 2016 the company completed all the necessary paperwork, and is now ready to issue the bonds. Fortunately, just as Hohl Company was issuing its bonds, the current market rate dropped to 3.5%. Their financial advisor recommended issuing the bonds at a premium of $142,968.

On March 31 of 2021, interest rates dropped to 2%. At this point, the company issues $2,200,000 of 10-year 2% bonds at par to redeem all outstanding 4% bonds. The company paid $2,110,000 to redeem the 4% bonds.

Required

a) Prepare the bond premium amortization table from period 1 to period 10 (covers 2016 to 2021).
b) Record the journal entry for the issuance of bonds on April 1, 2016.
c) Record the payment of interest on September 30, 2016.
d) Record any required journal entries as of the company year-end, February 28, 2017. Note that the company pays interest semi-annually.
e) Record journal entries for retirement of the 4% bonds and issue of new 2% bonds.
f) Record the first interest payment on the 2% bonds.

See Appendix I for answers.

a)

Semi-Annual Interest Period	A Interest Payment	B Interest Expense	C Premium Amortization	D Bond Amortized Cost

b) to f)

Date	Account Title and Explanation	Debit	Credit

Review Exercise 2

On April 1, 2016, Hohl Company issued a two-year notes payable of $200,000 for purchasing equipment from one of the company's suppliers. The interest rate is 4% and payments are made semi-annually. Assume all other conditions remain unchanged and the company's year-end is February 28.

See Appendix I for answers.

Required

a) Using the table below, calculate cash payment, interest expense, reduction of principal and principal balance on each payment date, using the fixed principal payment method.

Date	A Cash Payment	B Interest Expense	C Reduction of Principal	D Principal Balance

b) Using the table below, calculate cash payment, interest expense, reduction of principal and principal balance on each payment date, with an equal instalment payment of $52,525 using the blended payment method.

Date	A Cash Payment	B Interest Expense	C Reduction of Principal	D Principal Balance

c) Record journal entries of issuing day, first payment day, first year-end and second payment day, using the blended payment method from part b).

Date	Account Titles and Explanations	Debit	Credit

Notes

Chapter 9
INVESTMENTS

LEARNING OUTCOMES

❶ Describe and classify different types of investments

❷ Prepare journal entries for non-strategic debt and equity investments

❸ Prepare journal entries for strategic equity investments

❹ Describe how the different types of investments are presented in the financial statements

AMEENGAGE *Access **ameengage.com** for integrated resources including tutorials, practice exercises, the digital textbook and more.*

Investments: An Introduction and Classification

Because cash is the lifeblood of a business, cash management means ensuring not only that the business has enough cash to cover its operations and debt obligations, but also that the business is able to maximize returns on its excess cash. When a company has more cash on hand than it immediately needs for general operations and debt payment, the company can invest the surplus to generate investment income rather than leaving it in a bank account and receiving a much lower return. This chapter covers how to account for and report on these investments.

The Accounting Map in Figure 9.1 shows how investments appear on the balance sheet. Balance sheet presentation of an investment depends on whether the investment is considered short- or long-term. A **short-term investment** is intended to be held for less than a year and is reported in the current assets section of the balance sheet. A **long-term investment** is intended to be held for longer than a year, and is reported in the non-current (or long-term) assets section of the balance sheet.

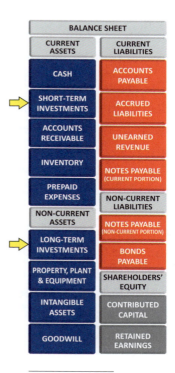

FIGURE 9.1

Investments usually take the form of either debt or equity: a business can try to generate investment return by either lending money to someone else (debt) or by buying a stake in the ownership of another organization (equity). Investing excess cash by lending money to someone else for interest income is commonly known as investment in **debt instruments** (or **debt securities**). Examples of debt instruments include money market funds, term deposits, treasury bills and bonds. Investing excess cash by buying a stake in the ownership of another organization is also known as investment in **equity instruments** (or **equity securities**), which include preferred and common shares of another company. The company that purchases and owns the debt or equity issued by another company is known as the **investor**. The company that issues (sells) the debt or equity to another company is the **investee**. This chapter focuses on investment mostly from the point of view of the investor.

Debt and equity instruments that can be bought and sold on the securities market are generally very liquid. The market value of debt and equity securities may fluctuate over time based on factors such as the investee's financial performance, fluctuations in market interest rate and the global economy.

On the investor's books, an investment is classified based on the investor's intent. Investors may invest having either of the following intentions.

1. An investor may simply try to generate investment income without intending to establish a long-term relationship with, influence or control the investee. Such an investment is classified as a **non-strategic investment**.

2. Alternatively, an investor may intend to establish a long-term relationship with, influence or control the investee. Such an investment is classified as a **strategic investment**.

The classification, intents and types of investments are summarized in Figure 9.2. Notice that debt instruments are always considered a non-strategic investment. This is because purchasing debt instruments does not give the investor ownership rights in the investee. Investors with ownership rights through investee's shares (particularly common shares) can vote on important matters such as electing the investee's board of directors, and thus have an opportunity to establish and maintain a meaningful long-term relationship with, influence or control the investee.

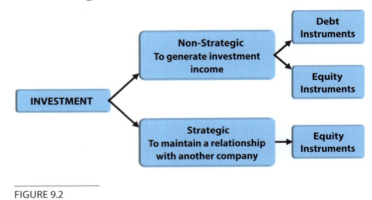

FIGURE 9.2

Let us explain the concept of intention in more detail. A company will have a plan when it comes to investing. They may want to invest their money for a few months, or may plan on getting long-term returns or having a long-term relationship with the investee. The plan of the company highlights their intention. It is important to note that the intention at the time the investment is purchased may not always be the actual outcome. For example, a company may plan to invest for long-term, but an unexpected event happens which causes them to sell their investment early to get the cash. In accounting, the intention at the purchase date determines how the investment is initially classified.

Classification of debt and equity securities are important because different types of securities are subject to different accounting treatments under both ASPE and IFRS. Specifically, how a security is classified determines how it should be valued and presented on the financial statements. We will discuss how to account for non-strategic investment first, followed by strategic investment.

> ## WORTH REPEATING
>
> Debt involves lending money to someone else in return for interest. Debt generally has a fixed maturity.
>
> Equity involves investing in another organization in the form of ownership, with the expectation that its value will increase over time while profits are shared in the form of dividends. Unlike debt, equity does not have a maturity.

Non-Strategic (Trading) Investments in Debt and Equity

A company may invest in another corporation for several reasons. It may purchase securities to earn interest on long-term debt, or to earn dividends on share equities. Alternatively, it may trade securities on a short-term basis to quickly make a gain from selling them at a higher price than what they were purchased for. When debt or equity securities are purchased with the intention of selling them in the short term at a gain, they are known as **trading investments**, or trading securities. Because the investor that owns trading investments does not intend to establish any form of long-term relationship with the investee, trading investments are considered non-strategic investments.

Non-strategic investments are classified as either debt investments or equity investments. This section will first look at non-strategic debt investments and then discuss non-strategic equity investments.

Non-Strategic Debt Investments

A debt instrument (or security) is classified and reported according to its maturity and its purpose. A debt instrument that will mature within 12 months is considered a **short-term debt instrument**. A short-term debt instrument is usually a highly liquid, low-risk **money market instrument** such as a treasury bill, term deposit or a money market fund.

A debt instrument that will take more than 12 months to mature is considered a **long-term debt instrument**. A common example of a long-term debt instrument is bonds, which provide a steady source of interest income.

Non-strategic debt investments, both short- and long-term, are valued using one of two methods.

1. the amortized cost method

2. the fair value through profit and loss method

The amortized cost method is most often used in the valuation of debt investments. The fair value through profit and loss method is used for debt investment valuation only if the company adopts IFRS, and if the debt instruments are invested for trading purposes. Figure 9.3 shows the required valuation methods under ASPE and IFRS, and balance sheet presentation for debt investments based on their maturity and the investor's intent.

ASPE vs IFRS

Under ASPE, all debt instruments are valued at amortized cost.

Under IFRS, only debt instruments that are invested for interest revenue purposes are valued at amortized cost. Those invested for trading purposes are valued at fair value.

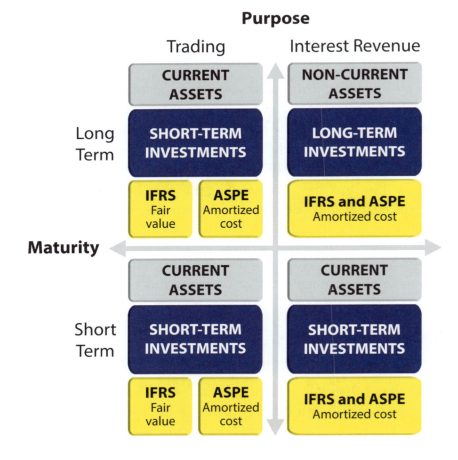

FIGURE 9.3

There are several important events during the lifetime of a debt investment that must be accounted for. These concepts will all be familiar from the discussion of bonds in Chapter 8. These important events are

- Acquisition, at the purchase price of the instrument

- Recording interest revenue, recognized as it accrues

- Amortization of discount or premium, using the effective-interest method

- Sale or disposition at maturity, including the receipt of cash, the removal of amortized cost from the books, and recording any gain or loss on early redemption

We will first examine the accounting entries required for each of these events under the amortized cost method, starting with an example of a short-term debt instrument, a treasury bill.

The Amortized Cost Method

Short-Term Debt Instrument

Let us first use the amortized cost method when accounting for a short-term debt instrument. The Government of Canada Treasury bill (T-bill) will be used in the example. T-bills are short-term debt instruments issued and backed by the federal government. The maturity date of T-bills are between one month to one year. T-bills are zero-coupon bonds. In other words, investors buy T-bills at a price that is less than their face value, and receive the amount equal to the face value back on the maturity date.

Acquisition. On November 1, 2016, Maynard Company (the investor) purchases a $10,000, Government of Canada 120-day Treasury bill (T-bill) for $9,838. The investment will mature on February 28, 2017. It is trading at a market interest rate of 5% annually. Maynard's year-end is December 31. Note that the purchase price of $9,838 is equal to the present value of $10,000 that will be received in 120 days using the annual market interest rate of 5%. The acquisition is recorded at the purchase price, as shown in Figure 9.4.

JOURNAL			
Date	**Account Title and Explanation**	**Debit**	**Credit**
Nov 1	Short-Term Investment—Treasury Bill	9,838	
	Cash		9,838
	To record purchase of Canada 120-day treasury bill at 5%		

FIGURE 9.4

Maynard has purchased a $10,000 bond for only $9,838, which is a discount of $162. The investee will have to pay back the full $10,000 at maturity, meaning Maynard will have earned a 5% return ($162) on their investment. Maynard will report this short-term debt investment in the current assets section of their balance sheet.

Recording interest revenue and amortization of the discount (or premium). Interest revenue on the debt investment is recognized as it accrues. As well, the discount should be amortized over the term of the T-bill (120 days) using the effective-interest method (discussed in Chapter 8). Maynard Company must accrue the interest revenue for the months of November and December so that it can be included in Maynard's year-end financial statements. Note that with the short term of the T-bill (120 days), interest is received at maturity; therefore, the amortization of the discount will be the same amount as the interest earned. Interest revenue is calculated by multiplying the carrying value of the investment ($9,838) by the market interest rate (5%), resulting in interest revenue of $82 ($9,838 × 5% × $^{61}/_{365}$). The journal entry for December 31 would be recorded as in Figure 9.5.

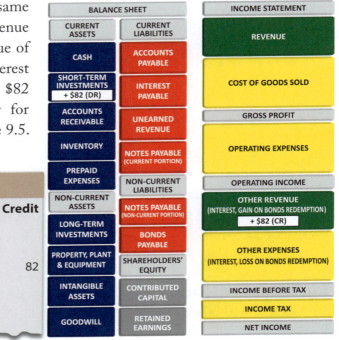

JOURNAL			
Date	Account Title and Explanation	Debit	Credit
Dec 31	Short-Term Investment—Treasury Bill	82	
	Interest Revenue		82
	To accrue interest revenue and amortize discount on Canada 120-day treasury bill at 5%		

FIGURE 9.5

The T-bill will be reported as a current asset on Maynard Company's December 31 balance sheet at its amortized cost of $9,920 ($9,838 + $82). The interest revenue of $82 will be reported as other revenue on Maynard's income statement.

Disposition at Maturity. When the Treasury bill matures on February 28, 2017, Maynard will need to record the following in its journals.

1. the interest revenue for January and February

2. the amortization of the discount for January and February

3. the receipt of cash

4. the removal of the amortized cost from the books

If the Treasury bill had been sold before its maturity date, Maynard would also need to record any gain or loss on early redemption.

First, the interest revenue for January and February is $80, which is the difference between the face value of the T-bill ($10,000) and the amortized cost ($9,920). As with the journal entry in Figure 9.5, the interest revenue and discount amortization are recorded together, as in Figure 9.6.

JOURNAL			
Date	Account Title and Explanation	Debit	Credit
Feb 28	Short-Term Investment—Treasury Bill	80	
	Interest Revenue		80
	To accrue interest revenue and amortize discount on Canada 120-day treasury bill at 5%		

FIGURE 9.6

Next, the company records the receipt of cash for the face value of the Treasury bill, which is $10,000 ($9,920 + $80). The journal entry is shown in Figure 9.7.

BALANCE SHEET	
CURRENT ASSETS	CURRENT LIABILITIES
CASH + $10,000 (DR)	ACCOUNTS PAYABLE
SHORT-TERM INVESTMENTS - $10,000 (CR)	INTEREST PAYABLE
ACCOUNTS RECEIVABLE	UNEARNED REVENUE
INVENTORY	NOTES PAYABLE (CURRENT PORTION)
PREPAID EXPENSES	NON-CURRENT LIABILITIES
NON-CURRENT ASSETS	NOTES PAYABLE (NON-CURRENT PORTION)
LONG-TERM INVESTMENTS	BONDS PAYABLE
PROPERTY, PLANT & EQUIPMENT	SHAREHOLDERS' EQUITY
INTANGIBLE ASSETS	CONTRIBUTED CAPITAL
GOODWILL	RETAINED EARNINGS

JOURNAL			
Date	Account Title and Explanation	Debit	Credit
Feb 28	Cash	10,000	
	Short-Term Investment—Treasury Bill		10,000
	To record the receipt of cash for matured Canada 120-day treasury bill		

FIGURE 9.7

Long-Term Debt Instrument

Next we will use the amortized cost method to account for a long-term debt instrument, a bond.

Chapter 8 discussed recording and reporting bonds payable as a long-term liability from the perspective of the issuer (or investee). From the perspective of the bondholder (the investor), a bond is considered a long-term asset and appears on the balance sheet just before property, plant and equipment. Let us look at how a bond would be accounted for in the investor's accounting records.

Acquisition. As with a short-term debt instrument, the acquisition of a long-term investment such as a bond is recorded at its purchase price. Recall that a bond can be sold at a premium or a discount. We can use the example of Energy Bite Inc. from Chapter 8 to illustrate this concept once again—only we will look at the investment from the investor's viewpoint.

On January 1, 2016, Energy Bite Inc. (the investee, or issuer) issued five-year $100,000 bonds paying 10% interest annually, when the market rate was 8%. The bonds pay interest semi-annually. Maynard Company (the *investor*) purchases all of these bonds for a market price of $108,115. This means that Maynard has purchased the bonds at a premium of $8,115 ($108,115 – $100,000). Maynard records the acquisition of the bonds at their purchase price, as in Figure 9.8. The bonds are reported as non-current assets on Maynard's balance sheet. To keep things simple, Maynard has a December 31 year-end.

JOURNAL			
Date	Account Title and Explanation	Debit	Credit
Jan 1	Long-Term Investment—Energy Bite Inc. Bonds	108,115	
	Cash		108,115
	To record purchase of Energy Bite Inc. bonds		

FIGURE 9.8

The section in Chapter 8 on issuing bonds at a premium shows that this is also the amount of cash that Energy Bite Inc. recorded when it sold the bonds.

Recording interest revenue and amortization of the premium (or discount). Using the amortized cost method, any premium (or discount) is amortized to interest revenue over the term of the bonds (in this case, five years). Since we are dealing with a premium, interest revenue will be reduced by the amount of amortization. If this were a discount, interest revenue would be increased by the amortization amount. Once again, we use the effective-interest rate method. For this example, refer to Figure 8.17, the amortization table for the bond over five years.

On the first interest payment date, July 1, 2017, Maynard Company records the interest received, $5,000 ($100,000 × 10% × 6/12), as a debit to Cash. The interest revenue is calculated as the amortized cost of the bonds ($108,115, since none of the bonds' cost has yet been amortized) multiplied by the market rate of interest (8%). This is recorded as a credit to interest revenue of $4,325 ($108,115 × 8% × 6/12). The amortization of the premium is the difference between the interest received and the interest revenue, or $675 ($5,000 − $4,325). Figure 9.9 shows the associated journal entries.

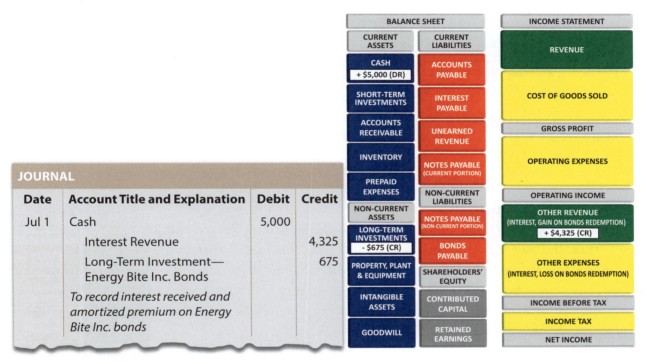

FIGURE 9.9

The section in Chapter 8 on issuing bonds at a premium shows that $4,325 is also the amount of interest expense that Energy Bite Inc. recorded for the first interest period, and $675 is the amount of premium that was amortized for that same period. Notice that the amortized premium is directly recorded to the bonds investment account. Chapter 8 discussed how to use the discount and premium accounts to record bonds discount and premium. That is usually done by the issuing company. On the investors' books, it is common to record this amount directly to the investment account.

The investor's transactions for bonds are a flip side of the investee's transactions that you learned in the last chapter. If Energy Bite Inc. had used the net method (i.e. recording bond premium as a part of the bonds payable account) rather than the gross method (i.e. recording bond premium using a separate premium on bonds account), its transactions would exactly mirror Maynard's transactions. For example, the following transactions would be recorded by Energy Bite and Maynard when Maynard purchased the bonds from Energy Bite.

Investee: Energy Bite Inc.		
Dec 31	Cash	108,115	
	Bonds Payable		108,115

Investor: Maynard		
Dec 31	Long-Term Investment— Energy Bite Inc. Bonds	108,115	
	Cash		108,115

The following transactions would be recorded on July 1, when Energy Bite paid interest to Maynard.

Investee: Energy Bite Inc.		
Jul 1	Interest Expense	4,325	
	Bonds Payable	675	
	Cash		5,000

Investor: Maynard		
Jul 1	Cash	5,000	
	Interest Revenue		4,325
	Long-Term Investment— Energy Bite Inc. Bonds		675

Disposition at maturity. If Maynard Company holds the bonds until maturity, the carrying value (amortized cost) of the long-term investment will equal the face value of the bonds, $100,000. This means that the premium (or discount, if we were dealing with discounted bonds) has been fully amortized. Maynard will record the receipt of cash at maturity, and the removal of the fully amortized cost of the bonds from the company's books, as in Figure 9.10.

JOURNAL			
Date	**Account Title and Explanation**	**Debit**	**Credit**
Jan 1	Cash	100,000	
	Long-Term Investment—Energy Bite Inc. Bonds		100,000
	To record cash received on maturity of Energy Bite Inc. bonds		

FIGURE 9.10

Next, let us see what would happen if the bonds were sold before their maturity date.

Sale before maturity. Chapter 8 explained early redemption of bonds and why the issuer may want to buy back the bonds before maturity. Conversely, an investor may want to redeem their bonds early if they need the cash immediately, or if they find that interest rates are now higher and they could earn a better return by reinvesting their cash. When bonds are redeemed before their maturity date, the process involves one additional step—to record any gain or loss arising from the early redemption.

The first step is to recognize any unrecorded interest as well as any unrecorded amortization of the premium or discount. Once this has been done, the investor can record the receipt of cash, remove the fully amortized cost of the bonds from the company's books and recognize any gain or loss. If the bonds are redeemed between interest payment dates, any interest earned for that partial period must also be recorded. For this next example, refer to Figure 8.17, the amortization table for the bond over five years.

For example, if Maynard Company decides to redeem the Energy Bite bonds for $98,000 on January 1, 2020 (at the end of semi-annual interest period 8), rather than waiting until their maturity in 2021, the unamortized premium amounts to

$$\$8,115 - \$6,223 = \$1,892$$

In this case, assume that the interest was received up to and including the end of interest period 8, and that the appropriate journal entry was made at that time.

Referring to Figure 8.17, at the end of semi-annual interest period 8 the bonds' unamortized cost is $101,892. Since Maynard is selling the bonds for $98,000 cash, this represents a loss on the sale of

$$\$101,892 - \$98,000 = \$3,892$$

Maynard's journal entry for the early redemption is shown in Figure 9.11.

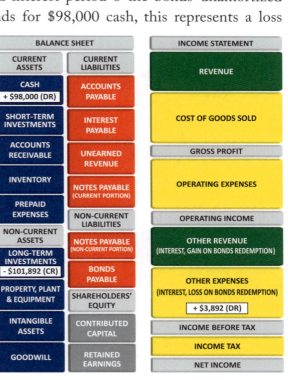

JOURNAL			
Date	Account Title and Explanation	Debit	Credit
Jan 1	Cash	98,000	
	Loss on Sale of Energy Bite Inc. Bonds	3,892	
	Long-Term Investment— Energy Bite Inc. Bonds		101,892
	To record cash received on early redemption of Energy Bite Inc. bonds		

FIGURE 9.11

The loss on sale of the bonds is reported on Maynard's income statement as other expenses. Note that if Maynard had redeemed the bonds for greater than their amortized cost, this would have represented a gain on the sale of the bonds, and the gain would have been reported on the income statement as other revenues.

The presentation of long-term debt instruments on the investing company's balance sheet depends on the purpose of the instruments to the investing company. The investing company may invest in debt instruments either for interest revenue purpose or for trading purposes. If the investing company purchases long-term debt instruments with the purpose of holding on to them to gain interest revenue, the long-term debt instruments will be presented in the long-term assets section of the lending company's balance sheet. On the other hand, if the investing company purchases long-term debt instruments for short-term trading purposes, hoping to simply sell them higher than their purchase prices, the instruments must be presented in the current assets portion of the investing company's balance sheet.

The Fair Value through Profit and Loss Method

Recall that debt instruments such as bonds are a form of debt that can be readily bought and sold on a bond market, making them good trading investments. When debt and equity instruments are purchased for the primary purpose of trading, they are reported at their fair value. **Fair value** is the amount that an asset can be sold for in the public market. Recording an investment by the fair value through profit and loss method enables investors to evaluate the issuer's financial solvency and predict their future cash flows.

There are several important events during the lifetime of a debt investment that must be accounted for. When using the fair value through net income method, the important events are

- Acquisition, at the fair value of the instrument

- Recording interest revenue, recognized as it accrues

- Fair value adjustments, to record changes in carrying value due to changes in fair value

We have already examined the accounting entries required for the first two events under the amortized cost method. When using the fair value through net income method, an additional entry must be made.

On October 1, 2016, Maynard Company pays $9,500 for Energy Bite Inc. 10% interest bonds with a par value of $10,000. Assume that the bonds pay interest semi-annually on April 1 and October 1. The bonds will mature in 2021. Maynard Company (the investor) intends to trade the bonds within six to eight months, therefore making them (from the investor's perspective) short-term investments rather than long-term. Maynard records the acquisition of the bonds as in Figure 9.12.

JOURNAL			
Date	**Account Title and Explanation**	**Debit**	**Credit**
Oct 1	Short-Term Investment—Energy Bite Inc. Bonds	9,500	
	Cash		9,500
	To record purchase of Energy Bite Inc. bonds held as a short-term investment		

FIGURE 9.12

Assuming Maynard has a year-end of December 31, the entry in Figure 9.13 is made to accrue the interest receivable on the Energy Bite Inc. bonds.

JOURNAL			
Date	**Account Title and Explanation**	**Debit**	**Credit**
Dec 31	Interest Receivable	250	
	Interest Revenue		250
	To record interest revenue on Energy Bite Inc. bonds held as short-term investment ($10,000 × 10% × 3/12)		

FIGURE 9.13

Now, assume that during the period October 1 to December 31, the market interest rate decreases. Energy Bite's bonds, which pay a higher interest rate and are a more desirable investment, have increased in fair value. (Conversely, if the market interest rate increased, the fair value of Energy Bite's bonds would decrease.) If Energy Bite's bonds are now trading in the market at $10,500, the entry in Figure 9.14 is needed to record what is known as a **fair value adjustment**.

JOURNAL			
Date	**Account Title and Explanation**	**Debit**	**Credit**
Dec 31	Short-Term Investment—Energy Bite Inc. Bonds	1,000	
	Gain on Fair Value Adjustment of Trading Investment		1,000
	To record fair value adjustment to Energy Bite Inc. bonds held as short-term investment		

FIGURE 9.14

Any gain (or loss) must be recorded on Maynard's income statement as other revenues (or other expenses, for a loss). The bonds are reported as current assets on Maynard's balance sheet at their fair value of $10,500. This becomes the new carrying value of the bonds.

Non-Strategic Equity Investments

When debt and equity instruments are purchased for the primary purpose of trading they are reported at their fair value, which is usually their market price. When accounting for trading equity investments at fair value, the important events that require journal entries are

- Acquisition, at the fair value of the instrument on the date of purchase

- Recording dividend revenue, recognized when the investor becomes entitled to the dividend

- Fair value adjustments, to record changes in carrying value due to changes in fair value

- Sale of the investment, including the receipt of cash, the removal of the investment from the books and recording any gain or loss on the sale

Chapter 6 explained that shares represent part ownership of a company. Equity instruments are classified based on their purpose to the investor. A company may invest in equity instruments for a trading purpose. An investment in equity instruments is considered to have a trading or non-strategic purpose if the company purchases common or preferred shares of another company to earn dividend income and/or to sell the shares for a gain. Equity instruments that are held for trading purposes at the end of an accounting period are reported in the current assets section of the balance sheet.

ASPE vs IFRS

Under ASPE, trading investments in equity are valued at fair value. However, trading investments in debt are valued at amortized cost.

Under IFRS, trading investments in both debt and equity are valued at fair value.

We can look at an example to illustrate the key events in accounting for equity instruments that are purchased for trading. Assume that Maynard Company purchases 100 common shares in Dempton Corporation on January 1, 2016 at $400 per share.

Acquisition. Because the equity instrument is purchased for the purpose of trading, Maynard records it at its fair value as shown in Figure 9.15.

JOURNAL			
Date	Account Title and Explanation	Debit	Credit
Jan 1	Short-Term Investment—Dempton Corporation Common Shares	40,000	
	Cash		40,000
	To record purchase of 100 Dempton Corporation common shares ($400 × 100)		

FIGURE 9.15

As an investment made for the purpose of trading and selling it for a profit, it is reported on the balance sheet as a current asset.

Recording dividend revenue. If Dempton Corporation pays a $2 per share cash dividend on March 31, 2016, Maynard Company records the dividend revenue as in Figure 9.16.

JOURNAL			
Date	Account Title and Explanation	Debit	Credit
Mar 31	Cash	200	
	Dividend Revenue		200
	To record receipt of cash dividend on Dempton Corporation common shares (100 × $2)		

FIGURE 9.16

The dividend revenue is reported on Maynard's income statement under other revenues.

Fair value adjustments. By Maynard's year-end, December 31, 2016, Dempton Corporation's common shares are trading on the market at $425, an increase of $25 ($425 − $400) per share over their initial purchase price. This results in a gain, and requires a fair value adjustment as shown in Figure 9.17.

JOURNAL			
Date	Account Title and Explanation	Debit	Credit
Dec 31	Short-Term Investment—Dempton Corporation Common Shares	2,500	
	Gain on Fair Value Adjustment of Trading Investment		2,500
	To record fair value adjustment to Dempton Corporation common shares (100 x $25)		

FIGURE 9.17

The shares are reported on Maynard's December 31, 2016 balance sheet at their new fair value of $42,500 ($40,000 + $2,500). This becomes the new carrying value of the investment. The gain on fair value adjustment is reported on Maynard's income statement under other revenues.

Sale of the investment. When Maynard Company sells its common shares, a gain or loss must be recognized for the difference between the proceeds of the sale and the carrying value of the investment. In this case, let us assume that on January 31, 2017, Maynard sells all 100 shares of Dempton common stock for a total price of $43,000 (100 × $430). With a carrying value of $42,500, this represents a gain of $500 ($43,000 − $42,500), and is recorded as in Figure 9.18.

JOURNAL			
Date	Account Title and Explanation	Debit	Credit
Jan 31	Cash	43,000	
	Short-Term Investment— Dempton Corporation Common Shares		42,500
	Gain on Sale of Dempton Corporation Common Shares		500
	To record sale of Dempton Corporation common shares		

FIGURE 9.18

Maynard reports this gain on its income statement under other revenues.

Strategic Investments In Equity

A company may choose to invest in another corporation for strategic reasons. First, the investor may want to build a long-term relationship with a key customer or vendor by investing in it. The company may want to venture into a new industry by investing in another company in that industry. Alternatively, the company may invest strategically in common stock of another company in the same industry because it wants to expand its market base, tap into new technologies used by another company or to eliminate competition.

Another reason that an investor might purchase equity instruments is to hold enough equity in another corporation so that it can control how that business operates. In other cases, the investor may wish to hold an amount of equity that gives it partial influence over the investee company's financing and investing decisions. Regardless of the reasons for investing, equity instruments that are held for strategic purposes are always considered long-term investments. The amount of influence that the investor has depends on the percentage of common shares it owns of the other company (the investee). Also, the method of accounting required for strategic investments in equity depends on how much influence the investor has over the investee. Next, we will take a closer look at the levels of influence and how they are determined.

Significantly Influenced Investments

When anyone purchases common shares in a company, they become part-owner of that company. For many shareholders, the level of ownership is minimal because they own such a small percentage of the total number of shares outstanding. For instance, if you own 10 shares out of the 1,000,000 common shares outstanding, your votes will do little to elect a board of governors or influence the operation of the company you have invested in. Accordingly, you would have an insignificant influence on the investee corporation. This applies to any shareholder who owns less than 20% of the common shares outstanding.

On the other hand, a significant influence is assumed to exist if one shareholder owns between 20% and 50% of the common shares outstanding. This gives the investor the right to participate in decisions over the investee's operating and financial policies. At this level of influence, the investor has a non-controlling interest in the investee company and is sometimes referred to as an associate. We will use this term in a later section of this chapter.

If one shareholder or investor owns more than 50% of the common shares outstanding, that investor holds a **controlling interest**, which means that they have control over how the investee company operates. At this level of share ownership, the investor has the right to direct the operating and financial activities of the investee. Note that in the real world, an investor's level of influence can often be affected by other circumstances, such as "hostile takeovers," or legal circumstances. However, such issues are beyond the scope of this textbook.

Figure 9.19 illustrates the levels of influence that investors can have, and the associated reporting requirements.

Number of Common Shares Owned by Investor	Investor's Level of Influence on Investee	Method of Accounting and Reporting Required
Less than 20%	Insignificant	Fair value method
20% to 50%	Significant ("non-controlling interest")	Equity or cost method
More than 50%	Control ("controlling interest")	Consolidation method

FIGURE 9.19

We will examine the fair value method and equity methods used by IFRS, and the cost method used by ASPE. Consolidation is a topic covered in more advanced accounting courses. First, recall the financial reporting concept of comprehensive income. The concept is briefly explained in the Worth Repeating segment on the next page.

Fair Value Method

The previous section of this chapter discussed the fair value method of accounting for non-strategic (trading) investments. For strategic (equity) investments, an investor who owns less than 20% of another company's common shares is required to use the fair value method of reporting. When accounting for strategic investments at fair value, the important events that require journal entries are

- Acquisition, at the fair value of the equity on the date of purchase

- Recording dividend revenue, recognized when the investor becomes entitled to the dividend

- Fair value adjustments, to record a gain or loss due to changes in fair value

We can look at an example to illustrate the key events in accounting for the purchase of strategic equity instruments. Assume that Maynard Company purchases 1,000 common shares in Dempton Corporation on January 1, 2016 at $400 per share. The 1,000 common shares represent less than 20% of Dempton's total outstanding common shares, which means that Maynard does not have significant influence over Dempton. Recall that equity instruments that are held for strategic purposes are always considered long-term investments. Note in particular that Maynard Company follows IFRS, and so reports any fair value adjustments on its statement of comprehensive income under other comprehensive income.

Acquisition. Because the equity instrument is purchased for strategic purposes, Maynard records it at its fair value as shown in Figure 9.20.

JOURNAL			
Date	**Account Title and Explanation**	**Debit**	**Credit**
Jan 1	Long-Term Investment—Dempton Corporation Common Shares	400,000	
	Cash		400,000
	To record purchase of 1,000 Dempton Corporation common shares ($400 × 1,000)		

FIGURE 9.20

As an investment made for strategic (i.e. long-term) purposes, it is reported on Maynard's balance sheet as a non-current asset.

Recording dividend revenue. If Dempton Corporation pays a $2 per share cash dividend on March 31, 2016, Maynard Company records the dividend revenue as in Figure 9.21.

JOURNAL			
Date	Account Title and Explanation	Debit	Credit
Mar 31	Cash	2,000	
	Dividend Revenue		2,000
	To record receipt of cash dividend on Dempton Corporation common shares (1,000 × $2)		

FIGURE 9.21

The dividend revenue is reported on Maynard's statement of comprehensive income under other comprehensive income.

Fair value adjustments. By Maynard's year-end, December 31, 2016, Dempton Corporation's common shares are trading on the market at $425, an increase of $25 ($425 − $400) per share over their initial purchase price. This results in a gain, and requires a fair value adjustment as shown in Figure 9.22.

JOURNAL			
Date	Account Title and Explanation	Debit	Credit
Dec 31	Long-Term Investment—Dempton Corporation Common Shares	25,000	
	Other Comprehensive Income—Gain on Fair Value Adjustment		25,000
	To record fair value adjustment to Dempton Corporation common shares (1,000 × $25)		

FIGURE 9.22

There is one additional consideration when reporting the gain on fair value adjustment on Maynard's statement of comprehensive income. As discussed in Chapter 7, IFRS requires that each item listed under other comprehensive income be reported net of income tax. If Maynard Company has a 30% tax rate, this gain will only increase other comprehensive income by $17,500 ($25,000 − [$25,000 × 30%]). The gain on fair value adjustment is reported on Maynard's statement of comprehensive income in its own section called "Other Comprehensive Income, net of income tax."

Equity Method

The **equity method** is used to record and report strategic equity investments when the investor owns 20% to 50% of the investee's outstanding common shares. Recall from an earlier section of this chapter that an investor at this level referred to as an associate.

When accounting for strategic investments under the equity method, the important events that require journal entries are

- Acquisition, at cost (the purchase price) of the instrument on the date of purchase

- Recording investment revenue, the share of associate's profit or loss, as an adjustment to the investor's equity account

- Recording dividend received, recognized when the investor becomes entitled to the dividend

We will once again use the example of Maynard Corporation, but this time we will apply the equity method for recording and reporting the investment. For this purchase, there are some transaction costs (i.e. brokerage fees) for purchasing the shares, but assume that these costs are included in the $400 price per share. The main point is that under the equity method any transaction costs must be included to record the purchase "at cost."

Assume that Maynard Company purchases 1,000 common shares in Dempton Corporation on January 1, 2016 at $400 per share. The 1,000 common shares represent 25% of Dempton's total outstanding common shares, which means that Maynard has a significant influence over Dempton.

Acquisition. When the shares are initially purchased, they are recorded at cost in a non-current, asset account. In this case, the account is called "Investment in Associate." It is listed on the balance sheet along with any other long-term investments. The entry to record the acquisition is shown in Figure 9.23.

JOURNAL			
Date	**Account Title and Explanation**	**Debit**	**Credit**
Jan 1	Investment in Associate—Dempton Corporation	400,000	
	Cash		400,000
	To record purchase of 1,000 Dempton Corporation common shares		

FIGURE 9.23

Recording Investment Revenue and Dividend Received. Assume that for the year ended December 31, 2016, Dempton Corporation has a profit of $200,000. It also declares and pays a $20,000 cash dividend. Recall that Maynard Company owns a 25% stake in Dempton's total outstanding common shares. Maynard must first calculate its share of Dempton's profit, which is $50,000 ($200,000 × 25%). Then, Maynard calculates the cash dividend it received, which is $5,000 ($20,000 × 25%). The cash dividend of $5,000 is a reduction of its investment since Dempton Corporation's net assets are reduced as a result of the dividends paid. Maynard records the investment revenue and dividend received as in Figure 9.24.

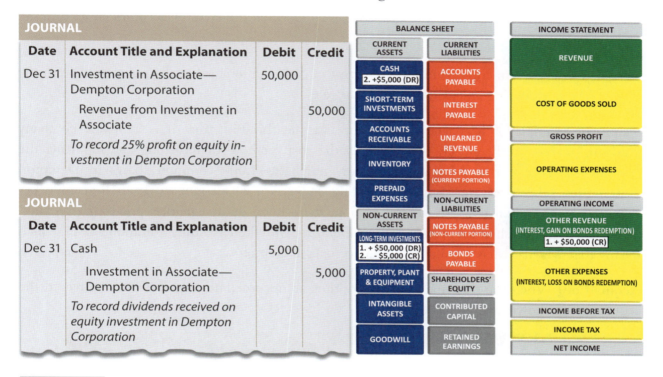

FIGURE 9.24

As a result of these transactions, Maynard Company's equity investment in Dempton Corporation as of December 31, 2016 is as follows.

Investment in Dempton Corporation = Initial Investment + Revenue from Investment − Cash Dividend Received

= $400,000 + $50,000 − $5,000

= $445,000

Cost Method

Companies reporting under ASPE can choose to use the cost method to report on strategic investments when the investor has a significant influence. This method can be used when there is no quoted market price. When accounting for strategic investments under the cost method, the important events that require journal entries are as follows.

- Acquisition, at cost of the instrument on the date of purchase

- Recording dividend revenue, recognized as income when the investor becomes entitled to the dividend

- Sale of the investment, including the receipt of cash, the removal of the investment from the books and recording any gain or loss on the sale

Using the example of Maynard Corporation, assume this time that it is a private company reporting under ASPE and chooses to apply the cost method for recording and reporting the investment. Assume that Maynard Company purchases 1,000 common shares in Dempton Corporation (also a private company reporting under ASPE) on January 1, 2016 at $400 per share. Since Dempton is a private corporation, there is no quoted market price for its shares. The 1,000 common shares represent 25% of Dempton's total outstanding common shares, which means that Maynard has significant influence over Dempton's.

Acquisition. When the shares are purchased, they are recorded at cost. The entry to record the acquisition is shown in Figure 9.25.

JOURNAL			
Date	**Account Title and Explanation**	**Debit**	**Credit**
Jan 1	Long-Term Investment—Dempton Corporation Common Shares	400,000	
	Cash		400,000
	To record purchase of 1,000 Dempton Corporation common shares ($400 × 1,000)		

FIGURE 9.25

Maynard reports this investment as a non-current asset on its balance sheet.

Recording dividend revenue. If Dempton Corporation pays a $2 per share cash dividend on March 31, 2016, Maynard Company records the dividend revenue as in Figure 9.26.

JOURNAL			
Date	**Account Title and Explanation**	**Debit**	**Credit**
Mar 31	Cash	2,000	
	Dividend Revenue		2,000
	To record receipt of cash dividend on Dempton Corporation common shares (1,000 × $2)		

FIGURE 9.26

The dividend revenue is reported on Maynard's income statement under other revenues.

Recording sale of shares. When Maynard Company sells its common shares, it must record the following: the receipt of cash, the removal of the investment from the books and any gain or loss on the sale. Assume that on January 31, 2017, Maynard sells all 1,000 shares of Dempton at $425 per share, for a total price of $425,000 (1,000 × $425). The shares originally cost $400,000, so this represents a gain of $25,000 ($425,000 − $400,000), and is recorded as in Figure 9.27.

JOURNAL			
Date	**Account Title and Explanation**	**Debit**	**Credit**
Jan 31	Cash	425,000	
	Long-Term Investment—Dempton Corporation Common Shares		400,000
	Gain on Sale of Dempton Corporation Common Shares		25,000
	To record sale of Dempton Corporation common shares ($425,000 − $400,000 = $25,000)		

FIGURE 9.27

The gain on sale of the shares is reported on Maynard's income statement under other revenues.

Presentation Of Investments On The Financial Statements

Financial disclosure requirements for a Canadian corporation are found in ASPE or IFRS. Public corporations are required to prepare financial statements according to IFRS, while private corporations have the option to prepare statements according to IFRS or ASPE. The examples in this chapter have been based on corporations that report under IFRS. Although the names of the financial statements have been used interchangeably; for example, either income statement or statement of comprehensive income, they generally have the same purpose (although the IFRS statement of comprehensive income has some additional components).

The Balance Sheet

Debt or equity instruments are reported on the investor's balance sheet according to their purpose (strategic or non-strategic) and expected time to maturity.

Investments Classified as Current Assets

Non-strategic investments, those debt or equity instruments that are purchased with the intention of selling them in the short term at a gain, are always classified as current assets on the investor's balance sheet. They are reported on the balance sheet at their amortized cost.

Long-term debt instruments, such as bonds, are investments that will take more than 12 months to mature; however, they are considered short-term (trading) investments if the investor's actual intent is to sell them in the near future to make a gain. These are reported on the balance sheet at fair value. According to IFRS, these investments must be separately reported from those reported at their amortized cost.

Figure 9.28 is one example of how these two classifications of short-term, or trading, investments would be presented on Maynard Company's (partial) balance sheet.

Maynard Company Inc. Balance Sheet (partial) December 31, 2016	
Current Assets	
Cash and Cash Equivalents	$70,000
Treasury Bills—at Amortized Cost	9,920
Trading Investments—at Fair Value	400,000

FIGURE 9.28

Investments Classified as Non-Current Assets

When long-term debt instruments such as bonds are purchased for interest revenue purpose, they are classified on the balance sheet according to their time to maturity; any investments that are due to mature within 12 months are classified as current assets, while any investments maturing beyond 12 months are classified as non-current assets. When equity instruments are purchased for strategic purposes, they are reported as non-current assets on the investor's balance sheet.

Accounting standards require separate disclosure for long-term investments according to their valuation and reporting methods; that is, whether they are valued at fair value, the equity method or the cost or amortized cost method.

The Income Statement (and Statement of Comprehensive Income)

Other comprehensive income can arise from changes in the value of assets such as long-term investments. Such increases or decreases in the value of assets will appear on the statement as gains or losses on the investment. A gain is an increase in the value of the asset; a loss is a decrease in the value of the asset.

Figure 9.29 is one example of how these two classifications of short-term, or trading, investments would be presented on Maynard Company's (partial) income statement.

Maynard Company Inc. Income Statement (partial) For Year Ended December 31, 2016	
Income from Operations	$765,000
Other Revenues	
Earnings from Equity Investment	27,000

FIGURE 9.29

There are various types of income that an investor can earn on investments. To summarize, the sources of income (or loss) on investments include the following.

- interest earned
- dividends received
- gain or loss on sale of investments
- fair value adjustments
- income on equity in a strategic investment

It is important to properly classify debt and equity investments according to their purpose and their time to maturity. This determines their different accounting treatments under ASPE and IFRS. If you return to Figure 9.3, you will have a new understanding of the valuation and reporting of debt investments.

 Access **ameengage.com** for integrated resources including tutorials, practice exercises, the digital textbook and more.

In Summary

Describe and classify different types of investments

⇨ Investments can be made by purchasing debt in the form of debt instruments (or debt securities) such as money market funds, term deposits, treasury bills and bonds. Investments can also be made by purchasing equity instruments (or equity securities) such as preferred and common shares of another company.

⇨ Investors can purchase debt and equity instruments to generate investment income (a non-strategic investment) or to establish a long-term relationship with another company (a strategic investment).

⇨ Under ASPE, all debt instruments are valued at amortized cost. Under IFRS, only debt instruments that are invested for interest revenue purposes are valued at amortized cost. Those invested for trading purposes are valued at fair value.

Prepare journal entries for non-strategic debt and equity investments

⇨ Debt or equity securities purchased with the intention of selling them in the short term at a gain are known as trading investments, or trading securities.

⇨ Non-strategic investments are classified as either debt investments or equity investments.

⇨ A debt instrument that will mature within 12 months is considered a short-term debt instrument.

⇨ Non-strategic debt investments are recorded using one of two methods: the amortized cost method; or the fair value through net income method.

Prepare journal entries for strategic equity investments

⇨ Equity instruments held for strategic purposes are always considered long-term investments.

⇨ A shareholder owning less than 20% of an investee's common shares outstanding has an insignificant influence on the investee corporation. A significant influence exists if one shareholder owns between 20% and 50% of the common shares outstanding. An investor owning more than 50% of the common shares outstanding holds a controlling interest.

Describe how the different types of investments are presented in the financial statements

⇨ Non-strategic investments are always classified as current assets on the investor's balance sheet.

➪ Long-term debt instruments, such as bonds, are investments that will take more than 12 months to mature; however, they are considered short-term (trading) investments if the investor's actual intent is to sell them in the near future to make a gain.

➪ When long-term debt instruments such as bonds are purchased as strategic investments, they are classified on the balance sheet according to their time to maturity: any investments that are due to mature within 12 months are classified as current assets, while any investments maturing beyond 12 months are classified as non-current assets.

➪ Other comprehensive income can arise from changes in the value of assets such as long-term investments. Such increases or decreases in the value of assets will appear on the statement as gains or losses on the investment.

Review Exercise

Benita Sikorsky is the controller for Travel Time Inc., a medium-sized enterprise that has a July 31 year-end. From time to time, her company has "surplus" cash on hand that it uses to make short-term investments. All of the investments are intended to be sold in less than one year. The types of investments vary from period to period, depending on which investments produce the highest return for the company.

During the past year, the company completed the following transactions.

Jan 1   Lent $50,000 to another company at an annual rate of 4% and due in 6 months.

Apr 1   Purchased 1,000 Drake Company bonds priced at $100 each with interest payable semi-annually on July 1 and December 31 at an annual rate of 6%. Also paid for any accrued interest owing.

May 10   Purchased 1,000 shares of Coretex Company at $50 per share.

Jul 1   Received interest payment for six months on the Drake Company bonds.

Jul 1   Received full proceeds from the loan of Jan 1, including interest.

Jul 10   Received the quarterly dividend of $100 on the Coretex Company shares.

Jul 31   Year-end adjustment: Recorded the interest accrued on the Drake bonds.

Oct 1   Sold 100 Coretex shares for proceeds of $47 per share.

Dec 15   Sold 900 Coretex shares for proceeds of $52 per shares.

Dec 31   Received the second interest payment on the Drake Company bonds then immediately sold the bonds for $102,500.

Record journal entries for each of the above transactions.

See Appendix I for solutions.

Date	Account Title and Explanation	Debit	Credit

Date	Account Title and Explanation	Debit	Credit

Chapter 10
THE STATEMENT OF CASH FLOWS

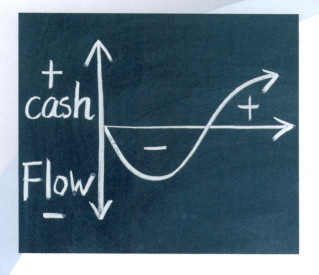

LEARNING OUTCOMES

❶ Classify operating, investing and financing activities

❷ Prepare a cash flow statement using the indirect method

❸ Calculate book value and cash received for selling long-term assets

❹ Explain the concept of free cash flow and its importance for potential investors

❺ Discuss ethics and control issues related to cash flow

Appendix

❻ Prepare a cash flow statement using the direct method

AMEENGAGE™ *Access **ameengage.com** for integrated resources including tutorials, practice exercises, the digital textbook and more.*

The Importance of Cash Flow

Most of our discussion of accounting procedures and principles so far has focused on two types of financial statements: the balance sheet and the income statement. Indeed, these financial statements have become synonymous with the accounting profession. When people think about business finance, they usually think about balance sheets and income statements.

However, analyzing the income statement and balance sheet does not provide all the information needed by users. This is because balance sheets and income statements are prepared on an accrual basis. Revenue and expense recognition dictate that revenues and expenses be recorded for the period in which they are earned or incurred. However, these types of transactions do not always involve an actual exchange of cash. Conversely, other transactions such as borrowing or repaying loans affect cash but do not affect net income.

Why is cash so important? Without cash, a company cannot pay its bills. Without cash, a company cannot purchase and pay for new inventory or other assets required to run the business. Thus, determining how cash is generated and spent is an important way to determine how well the company is performing.

To some extent, recording accruals masks the sources and uses of cash in a business. Thus, both ASPE and IFRS require the preparation of a statement to track the sources and uses of cash in a business. ASPE calls this the **cash flow statement** and IFRS calls it the **statement of cash flows**. Both terms will be used throughout this chapter. For the most part, both accounting standards require the statements to be prepared in the same manner, although IFRS does allow some options on where certain items are reported.

These statements ignore accruals and just focus on cash. Users can use this information to make decisions such as whether a company can pay its debts as they mature, or pay for expenses in its day-to-day operations or whether the company must borrow cash to make large asset purchases.

Three Ways of Generating Cash Flow

A business generates and consumes cash in one of the following three ways.

- **operating activities**
- **investing activities**
- **financing activities**

In fact, all cash flow statements are structured in this manner.

Cash Flow from Operating Activities

This component of the cash flow statement tracks the movement of cash within a business on the basis of day-to-day activities. All items in this section are directly related to items on the income statement (revenue and expenses) and the current assets and current liabilities on the balance sheet. This includes transactions involving customers, suppliers, inventory, and so on. It is the most important section of the cash flow statement because the future of a business largely depends on the activities reported in this section.

Cash Flow from Investing Activities

This component of the cash flow statement tracks the movement of cash in a business on the basis of the purchases and sales of long-term assets. This section shows how the business is investing cash back into itself. For example, if a truck was sold during the year, cash flow would have increased. Alternatively, if the business purchased land, cash flow would have decreased, since the business had to use cash to invest in the land.

Cash Flow from Financing Activities

This component of the cash flow statement tracks cash received from investors and lenders to help run, or finance, the business and cash paid back to the investors (dividends) and lenders (principal repayment). Financing generally deals with non-current liabilities such as receiving bank loans, and equity financing such as selling shares. Bank loan payments and dividend payments to shareholders are also reported here.

Figure 10.1 summarizes the events that are recorded in each of the three sections of the cash flow statement.

Operating Activities	Cash sales and collecting cash from customers
	Cash received from short-term investments
	Cash received from interest revenue and dividends from investment
	Payments made to suppliers for current assets or expenses
	Paying employee salaries
	Paying interest of loan
	Paying other operating expenses
Investing Activities	Buying or selling long-term assets
Financing Activities	Issuing or reacquiring shares
	Issuing short-term loan payable
	Receiving long-term debt
	Paying dividends to shareholders
	Payments made to reduce principal of long-term debt
	Payments made to reduce principal of note payable

FIGURE 10.1

ASPE vs IFRS

Although both standards require the creation of the cash flow statements, IFRS does allow for some options on how a few items are reported. Under ASPE, interest or dividends received from a short- or long-term investment are reported as operating activities. IFRS, however, allows the option to report as either operating or investing activities.

Under ASPE, interest paid on loans is an operating activity. Dividends paid to shareholders are a financing activity. IFRS, however, allows the option to report either as operating or financing activities. Of course for IFRS statements to be consistent, once a decision is made about where to report interest and dividends, it must always be reported in that manner.

Preparing a Statement of Cash Flows

Two methods are used to prepare a statement of cash flows.

The **indirect method** analyzes cash flow from operating activities indirectly by starting with accrual-based net income, adding or subtracting certain items from the income statement and changes in current assets and current liabilities on the balance sheet. Investing activities and financing activities are determined by analyzing the long-term assets, non-current liabilities and the equity portions of the balance sheet.

Like the indirect method, the **direct method** breaks down the three ways of generating and using cash into operating, investing and financing activities. However, unlike the indirect method, the direct method calculates cash flow from operating activities by directly analyzing cash received from sales and collections and directly analyzing cash spent on expenses. Although both IFRS and ASPE suggest that all cash flow statements should be prepared using the direct method, they also allow the indirect method to be used. The indirect method is most commonly used since it is generally easier to prepare. This chapter will focus on the indirect method, while the Appendix will focus on the direct method.

IN THE REAL WORLD

Academic studies have shown that if two versions of the cash flow statement are shown (i.e. direct and indirect method), investors can make better decisions. By disclosing both the direct and indirect method, a company would be improving its accounting transparency. Furthermore, through statistical studies, it has been shown that the indirect method is more useful than the direct method. However, a reason for this discrepancy was not revealed by the studies. Furthermore, the direct method is usually more easily understood by users than the indirect method.

Before preparing the statement of cash flows, the balance sheet and income statement must be prepared and examined. The statement of cash flows presents the change in cash over a period of time and is presented with a date format covering a specified time period similar to the income statement.

Examine the Balance Sheet and the Income Statement

The first document we need is a comparative balance sheet for two periods that shows both periods' cash balances. Consider Soho Supplies, a manufacturer of office supplies with a year-end of December 31. Soho's financial statements will be used for cash flow analysis in this chapter. We will use this specific balance sheet for Soho Supplies for the remainder of the chapter, and keep referring to it as we move along.

The last column of the balance sheet in Figure 10.2 shows the difference between 2015 and 2016 amounts. This difference is used when preparing the cash flow statement. The first line of the balance sheet shows that the cash account decreased by $46,207 from $396,142 in 2015 to $349,935 in 2016.

Soho Supplies			
Balance Sheet			
As at December 31			
Assets	**2016**	**2015**	**Change**
Current Assets			
Cash	$349,935	$396,142	($46,207)
Accounts Receivable	1,286,138	1,065,812	220,326
Inventory	1,683,560	840,091	843,469
Prepaid Insurance	48,612	42,625	5,987
Total Current Assets	3,368,245	2,344,670	1,023,575
Property, Plant and Equipment[1]			
Land	0	50,000	(50,000)
Equipment	322,518	120,000	202,518
Less: Accumulated Depreciation	(79,262)	(36,000)	(43,262)
Total Assets	$3,611,501	$2,478,670	$1,132,831
Liabilities			
Current Liabilities			
Accounts Payable	$783,602	$475,645	$307,957
Salaries Payable	25,000	50,000	(25,000)
Interest Payable	15,650	23,500	(7,850)
Income Tax Payable	280,117	250,000	30,117
Current Portion of Bank Loan	380,000	240,000	140,000
Notes Payable	170,000	200,000	(30,000)
Total Current Liabilities	1,654,369	1,239,145	415,224
Non-Current Portion of Bank Loan	420,000	356,000	64,000
Total Liabilities	2,074,369	1,595,145	479,224
Shareholders' Equity			
Common Shares	15,000	5,000	10,000
Retained Earnings[2]	1,522,132	878,525	643,607
Total Shareholders' Equity	1,537,132	883,525	653,607
Total Liabilities and Equity	$3,611,501	$2,478,670	$1,132,831

Additional Information

[1] Property, Plant and Equipment:
   a) During 2016, land, which cost $50,000, was sold for $60,000, resulting in a $10,000 gain on sale. The gain is reported on the Income Statement in the Other Revenue (Expense) section.
   b) During 2016, Soho made purchases of equipment for $202,518.

[2] Retained Earnings:
   Soho declared and paid $10,000 in dividends in 2016.

FIGURE 10.2

Soho's income statement is shown in Figure 10.3.

Soho Supplies
Income Statement
For the Year Ended December 31, 2016

Sales		$8,685,025
Cost of Goods Sold		5,998,612
Gross Profit		2,686,413
Operating Expenses		
Salaries		1,416,135
Other Operating Expenses		235,417
Depreciation Expense		43,262
Insurance Expense		16,000
Total Operating Expenses		1,710,814
Operating Income		975,599
Other Revenue (Expenses)		
Interest Expense	($51,875)	
Gain on Sale of Land	10,000	(41,875)
Operating Income before Tax		933,724
Income Tax Expense		280,117
Net Income		$653,607

FIGURE 10.3

The company's net income is $653,607 for 2016. This income statement will be used for the remainder of the chapter, so keep it handy as we assemble our cash flow statement for 2016.

An obvious question after noticing a decrease of $46,207 in the cash account and a net income of $653,607 is: What happened to all the cash? This can be answered by the cash flow statement, which ignores accruals and reflects only transactions involving cash. To help illustrate how cash changed using the indirect method, we will start with the opening cash balance in 2016 (or the ending cash balance in 2015) which is $396,142. The opening cash balance is presented at the top in Figure 10.4, which shows the first portion of cash flow from operating activities within the cash flow statement. As shown in the figure, net income, depreciation and gain on sale of land are added to and subtracted from the cash opening balance. We'll explain these steps and the rationale behind them next.

Soho Supplies
Cash Flow Statement (Partial)
For the Year Ended December 31, 2016

	Amount	Updated Cash Balance
Opening Cash Balance		$396,142
Cash Flow from Operating Activities		
Net income	$653,607	1,049,749
Add: Depreciation Expense	43,262	1,093,011
Less: Gain on Sale of Land	(10,000)	1,083,011

The Updated Cash Balance column is used to calculate the updated cash balance to help you understand the process.

You will not see this theoretical column illustrated in a proper cash flow statement. It is a learning tool only.

FIGURE 10.4

Cash Flow from Operating Activities

Remember that cash flow from operating activities under the indirect method starts with net income and then adds or subtracts certain items from the income statement and changes on the balance sheet. In the current example, the company's net income for 2016 is $653,607.

Net income is added to (or net loss is deducted from) the opening cash account balance. As shown in Figure 10.4, net income of $653,607 is added to the opening cash balance of $396,142, bringing the updated cash balance to $1,049,749. This figure means that if all revenues and expenses shown in the income statement were received and paid in cash, Soho Supplies' cash balance after adding all cash receipts from revenues and deducting all cash payments for expenses would have been $1,049,749. However, in reality, not all revenues and expenses involve cash due to the accrual basis of accounting required under ASPE and IFRS. Since the focus is on cash flow instead of accruals, only the money that actually changes hands during a period needs to be accounted for. Therefore, in the cash flow from operations section, we begin with net income and initially add or subtract non-cash items from the income statement.

Depreciation

Depreciation is a non-cash expense and thus must be added to the net income balance to convert the accrual-based net income to cash-based net income. Since depreciation simply decreases the book value of an asset without any change to cash, depreciation deductions must be excluded from any equations involving cash flow. To illustrate this point, a journal entry for depreciation would entail a debit to depreciation expense, and a credit to accumulated depreciation for the particular asset—neither the debit nor the credit involves cash. Therefore, Soho Supplies' depreciation expense of $43,262 from the income statement in Figure 10.3 is added to the net income on the cash flow statement, as shown in Figure 10.4.

Gain on Sale of Land

In 2016, Soho Supplies' land with a book value of $50,000 was sold for $60,000. This means that the company made a profit (or gain) of $10,000, which appears in the other revenue (expenses) section of Soho Supplies' income statement. When long-term assets are sold for more than their book value, a gain is recorded. If the sale price is less than the book value, a loss is recorded. The gain (or loss) on sale of non-current assets is reported separately from sales (or operating expenses) because it is not part of day-to-day operations.

Soho Supplies' net income of $653,607 includes the $10,000 gain on sale of land. However, because the gain is not part of day-to-day operating activities, it must be removed from the cash flow from operating activities section of the cash flow statement. This is why the $10,000 gain on sale of land is deducted from net income in the cash flow from operating activities section. Although the gain will be removed from the cash flows from operating activities section, the $60,000 proceeds from the sale of land will be reported in the cash flow from investing activities section, which will be explained later. *Therefore, the $10,000 gain is deducted from net income in the cash flow from operations section to avoid double counting.* If, instead, Soho incurred a *loss* from the sale of land, the amount would be added back to net income in the cash flow from operations section.

In summary, the first step to prepare the cash flow statement is to add net income to the opening cash balance. Then, depreciation is added back since it is a non-cash item. The gain on the sale of land is deducted since this is not an operating activity. This concludes the first part of the cash flow statement shown in Figure 10.4.

Changes in Current Assets and Current Liabilities

The next step is to add or subtract changes in items related to operating activities that do not flow through the income statement. These items include all the current assets and current liabilities on the balance sheet.

As the value of various current assets and liabilities change from one period to another, cash flow is affected. Figures 10.5 to 10.8 illustrate this principle.

FIGURE 10.5

If accounts receivable decreases, it means that cash has been collected, resulting in an increase to cash (as shown in Figure 10.5).

If inventory increases, it means that cash has been used (or will be used) to pay for it, resulting in a decrease in cash (as shown in Figure 10.6).

If accounts payable decreases, it means that cash has been used to pay it off, resulting in a decrease in cash (as shown in Figure 10.7).

If prepaid expenses increase, it means that cash has been used to pay for them, resulting in a decrease in cash (as shown in Figure 10.8).

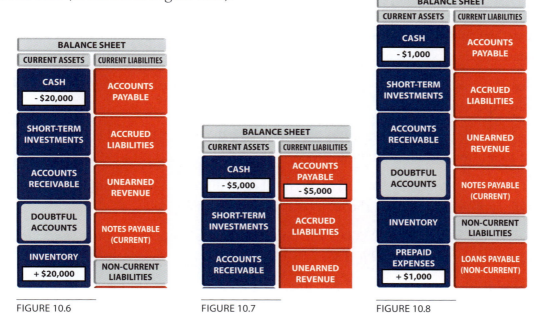

FIGURE 10.6   FIGURE 10.7   FIGURE 10.8

Figure 10.9 shows the rest of the cash flow from operating activities with all the changes in current assets and current liabilities. A discussion of these items follows after the figure.

	Amount	Updated Cash Balance
Soho Supplies		
Cash Flow Statement (Partial)		
For the Year Ended December 31, 2016		
Opening Cash Balance		$396,142
Cash Flow from Operating Activities		
Net income	$653,607	1,049,749
Add: Depreciation Expense	43,262	1,093,011
Less: Gain on Sale of Land	(10,000)	1,083,011
Changes in Current Assets and Current Liabilities		
Increase in Accounts Receivable	(220,326)	862,685
Increase in Prepaid Expenses	(5,987)	856,698
Increase in Inventory	(843,469)	13,229
Increase in Accounts Payable	307,957	321,186
Decrease in Salaries Payable	(25,000)	296,186
Decrease in Interest Payable	(7,850)	288,336
Increase in Income Taxes Payable	30,117	$318,453
Change in Cash due to Operating Activities	($77,689)	

FIGURE 10.9

The first listed current asset in the comparative balance sheet (after cash) is accounts receivable. As indicated in the balance sheet, this account increased by $220,326 from 2015 to 2016. Remember that since accounts receivable increased, it will decrease cash because it is yet to be collected. We therefore deduct this amount from the cash balance of $1,083,011. As indicated in Figure 10.9, the updated cash balance is $862,685.

Prepaid expenses increased by $5,987, resulting in a decreased cash balance of $856,698 because the prepaid expenses must have been paid with cash.

Inventory increased by $843,469, decreasing the cash balance to $13,229 because cash must have been used to pay for the additional inventory.

Accounts payable increased by $307,957. This resulted in more cash in the bank since Soho deferred paying their suppliers, increasing the cash balance to $321,186.

Salaries payable decreased by $25,000. This means Soho paid out more cash owing for salaries, decreasing the cash balance to $296,186.

Interest payable also decreased by $7,850, meaning Soho used cash to pay for the interest owed. The cash balance decreased to $288,336.

Lastly, income taxes payable increased by $30,117. This means Soho has deferred payment of income taxes and therefore has more cash. This increases the cash balance to $318,453.

The updated cash balance has gone from the beginning balance of $396,142 to $318,453, a drop of $77,689. This indicates that cash decreased by $77,689 due to operating activities.

Under the indirect method of preparing cash flow statements, Figure 10.10 outlines the impact on the cash flow statement an increase or decrease to current assets or current liabilities will have.

Impact on Cash Flow Statement:
Change in Current Assets and Current Liabilities

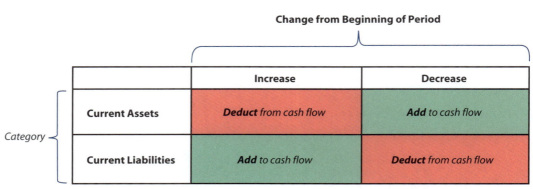

FIGURE 10.10

Cash Flow from Investing Activities

Changes in the value of long-term assets (i.e. property, plant and equipment) affect cash flow. However, measuring the affect is not as straightforward as observing the change in the property, plant and equipment balance from one year to the next.

This section of the cash flow statement deals with the way cash flow changes through the investment in or sale of long-term assets. In the current example with Soho Supplies, the information required to complete the cash flow from investing activities section is provided in the Additional Information portion below Soho's balance sheet (Figure 10.2).

The proceeds from the sale of the land in the amount of $60,000 is added to the updated cash balance since the transaction represents a cash inflow. The proceeds include the $10,000 gain, which was previously deducted from the operating activities section of the cash flow statement. The $202,518 purchase of equipment is deducted from the updated cash balance because it represents a cash outflow. In Figure 10.11, the cash flow from the investing activities section is added to the illustrative cash flow statement.

Soho Supplies
Cash Flow Statement (Partial)
For the Year Ended December 31, 2016

	Amount	Updated Cash Balance
Opening Cash Balance		$396,142
Cash Flow from Operating Activities		
Net income	$653,607	1,049,749
Add: Depreciation Expense	43,262	1,093,011
Less: Gain on Sale of Land	(10,000)	1,083,011
Changes in Current Assets and Current Liabilities:		
Increase in Accounts Receivable	(220,326)	862,685
Increase in Prepaid Expenses	(5,987)	856,698
Increase in Inventory	(843,469)	13,229
Increase in Accounts Payable	307,957	321,186
Decrease in Salaries Payable	(25,000)	296,186
Decrease in Interest Payable	(7,850)	288,336
Increase in Income Taxes Payable	30,117	318,453
Change in Cash due to Operating Activities	77,689	
Cash Flow from Investing Activities		
Sale of Land	60,000	378,453
Purchase of Equipment	(202,518)	$175,935
Change in Cash due to Investing Activities	($142,518)	

FIGURE 10.11

This is Soho's change in cash due to investing activities and constitutes the entire cash flow from investing activities section of the cash flow statement.

Cash Flow from Financing Activities

Cash flow from financing activities is the last section of the cash flow statement that needs to be prepared. As loans or equity increase or decrease, cash flow is affected. Note that this does not only refer to non-current loans, but also any current liabilities that have an interest component to them, such as notes payable.

If loans or common shares increase, cash has been received, resulting in an increase in cash. If loans or common shares decrease, this leads to a decrease in cash.

Remember that this section accounts for cash resulting from any financing activities during the year. It includes borrowing money or receiving cash as a result of a share issue. This section also includes any payments involved with financing, such as dividend payments or loan repayments. While repayments of loan principal amounts are an outflow in this section, the interest expense related to this loan has already been accounted for in the operating activities section as part of net income.

First, all aspects pertaining to financing must be checked on the balance sheet. The three parts that are affected are notes payable, bank loans and shares.

Look at notes payable in the current liabilities section of the balance sheet. This is relatively simple since there is only one account here. The decrease in notes payable of $30,000 implies that cash also decreased by $30,000 from 2015 to 2016. Notes payable could be classified as either non-current (long-term) or short-term depending on its due date. In Soho's case, it is due in less than one year; therefore, it appears as part of the current liability section. Regardless of whether it is short-term or non-current, notes payable would be part of the financing activities section of the cash flow statement.

Now look at bank loans. An extra step is involved because bank loans are divided into two areas on the balance sheet: current and non-current. We must extract from the balance sheet the changes from period to period that occurred for both combined.

As shown in Figure 10.12 (the liabilities portion of the balance sheet), the current portion of the bank loan increased by $140,000 from 2015 to 2016. The non-current portion of the bank loan increased by $64,000. Therefore, the total increase in the bank loan balance is $204,000 ($140,000 + $64,000). This amount is an increase to cash since Soho received additional money as a loan. Therefore, it represents a cash inflow.

Liabilities	2016	2015	Change	
Accounts Payable	$783,602	$475,645	$307,957	
Salaries Payable	25,000	50,000	(25,000)	
Interest Payable	15,650	23,500	(7,850)	
Income Tax Payable	280,117	250,000	30,117	
Current Portion of Bank Loan	380,000	240,000	140,000	
Notes Payable	170,000	200,000	(30,000)	❶ Sum=$204,000
Total Current Liabilities	$1,654,369	$1,239,145	$415,224	
Non-Current Portion of Bank Loan	420,000	356,000	64,000	
Total Liabilities	$2,074,369	$1,595,145	$479,224	

FIGURE 10.12

Dividends are considered next. In the Additional Information section under Soho's balance sheet (Figure 10.2), it is mentioned that Soho declared and paid $10,000 in dividends during 2016. This represents a decrease to cash because it is a cash outflow.

Although there is a note regarding the amount of dividends paid, the amount of dividends paid can be calculated by examining the financial statements.

DECREASE (DR)		INCREASE (CR)
−	RETAINED EARNINGS	+
Dividends	$10,000	$878,525 Opening Balance
		$653,607 2016 Net Income
		$1,522,132 Closing Balance

FIGURE 10.13

Previous chapters explained that the retained earnings account will increase if there is a net income for the year and decrease if there is a net loss for the year. Additionally, dividends are paid out of the retained earnings account, decreasing its value. The balance sheet in Figure 10.13 shows that the retained earnings account increased by $643,607 in 2016, however the income statement shows that net income was $653,607. Therefore, the difference of $10,000 must be the dividends paid. This will represent a decrease in cash flow in the financing section of the cash flow statement.

Lastly, the balance of common shares increased by $10,000 from 2015 to 2016. This means that new shares were issued for $10,000 in cash. Therefore, the cash balance increased by $10,000.

Changes in cash due to financing activities account for an increase to the cash account of $174,000 (−$30,000 + $204,000 − $10,000 + $10,000). The cash flow from financing section is added on in Figure 10.14.

	Amount	Updated Cash Balance
Soho Supplies		
Cash Flow Statement (Partial)		
For the Year Ended December 31, 2016		
Opening Cash Balance		$396,142
Cash Flow from Operating Activities		
Net income	$653,607	1,049,749
Add: Depreciation Expense	43,262	1,093,011
Less: Gain on Sale of Land	(10,000)	1,083,011
Changes in Current Assets and Current Liabilities		
Increase in Accounts Receivable	(220,326)	862,685
Increase in Prepaid Expenses	(5,987)	856,698
Increase in Inventory	(843,469)	13,229
Increase in Accounts Payable	307,957	321,186
Decrease in Salaries Payable	(25,000)	296,186
Decrease in Interest Payable	(7,850)	288,336
Increase in Income Taxes Payable	30,117	318,453
Change in Cash due to Operating Activities	**(77,689)**	
Cash Flow from Investing Activities		
Sale of Land	60,000	378,453
Purchase of Equipment	(202,518)	175,935
Change in Cash due to Investing Activities	**(142,518)**	
Cash Flow from Financing Activities		
Payment towards Notes Payable	(30,000)	145,935
Proceeds from Bank Loan	204,000 ❶	349,935
Payment of Cash Dividend	(10,000)	339,935
Issuance of Common Shares	$10,000	$349,935
Change in Cash due to Financing Activities	**$174,000**	

*Note that the $204,000 proceeds from the bank loan is from the calculation in Figure 10.12.

FIGURE 10.14

Summary of the Indirect Method

Three sections of the cash flow statement have been completed: cash flow from operating activities, investing activities and financing activities. They can now be put all together to form one complete cash flow statement in proper format for 2016 as shown in Figure 10.15.

Soho Supplies
Cash Flow Statement
For the Year Ended December 31, 2016

Cash Flow from Operating Activities

Net Income	$653,607	
Depreciation	43,262	
Gain on Sale of Land	(10,000)	
Changes in Current Assets and Current Liabilities		
Increase in Accounts Receivable	(220,326)	
Increase in Prepaid Insurance	(5,987)	
Increase in Inventory	(843,469)	
Increase in Accounts Payable	307,957	
Decrease in Salaries Payable	(25,000)	
Decrease in Interest Payable	(7,850)	
Increase in Income Tax Payable	30,117	
Change in Cash due to Operating Activities		($77,689)
Cash Flow from Investing Activities		
Sale of Land	60,000	
Purchase of Equipment	(202,518)	
Change in Cash due to Investing Activities		(142,518)
Cash Flow from Financing Activities		
Payment towards Notes Payable	(30,000)	
Proceeds from Bank Loan	204,000	
Payment of Cash Dividends	(10,000)	
Proceeds from Issuance of Common Shares	$10,000	
Change in Cash due to Financing Activities		174,000
Net Increase (Decrease) in Cash		($46,207)
Cash at the Beginning of the Year		396,142
Cash at the End of the Year		$349,935

FIGURE 10.15

Analysis of the Cash Flow Statement

Once the cash flow statement is completed, an analysis should be performed to see if there are any concerns. The first item to note is that cash decreased during the year even though there was a net income. Part of that decrease was due to an outflow of cash from operating activities of $77,689. This can be a problem for the company, since it indicates that day-to-day operations are not generating a cash inflow. In other words, the company is not being self-sufficient with its operations.

The two major contributors to this cash outflow from operations were an increase in accounts receivable and an increase in inventory. Both can indicate trouble for the company. An increase in accounts receivable can result from an increase in sales on account instead of cash, or from customers taking longer to pay their bills. Either situation means the company is not receiving cash on a timely basis. The large increase in inventory can indicate that the company is buying too much inventory, which eventually has to be paid with cash. Alternatively, it could mean that inventory is not turning into cost of goods sold, which would mean that the quantity of sales has decreased.

The company purchased some new equipment during the year and also sold some land. Both can be considered normal, assuming the equipment is needed and the plan was to sell the land. However, considering the cash flow problems from operations, the question may be asked whether the sale of land was simply to raise some cash to pay for operating expenses. Financing operations by selling long-term assets is not a sustainable practice.

The financing activities section of the cash flow statement is the only one showing a cash inflow. This is primarily due to a large bank loan. The bank loan may have been borrowed to pay for the equipment. Overall, there are concerns due to the negative cash flow from operations and the apparent financing of operating activities by selling assets and taking loans.

Selling Long-Term Assets

In the example of Soho Supplies, land was sold and reported in the investing activities section of the cash flow statement. Since land does not depreciate, the decrease in the value of land was equal to the book value of the land. A gain is reported if the amount received is greater than the book value of the land, and a loss is reported if the amount is less than the book value of the land.

When selling equipment or any other long-term asset that depreciates in value, determining the book value of the item is an important step in calculating cash flow. Figure 10.16 presents the assets section of the balance sheet for Soho Supplies. For demonstration purposes, information regarding the long-term assets section has been changed. It is now different from Figure 10.2.

Soho Supplies Balance Sheet (Partial) As at December 31			
Assets	**2016**	**2015**	**Change**
Current Assets			
Cash	$349,935	$396,142	($46,207)
Accounts Receivable	1,286,138	1,065,812	220,326
Inventory	1,683,560	840,091	843,469
Prepaid Insurance	48,612	42,625	5,987
Total Current Assets	$3,368,245	$2,344,670	$1,023,575
Long-Term Investments[1]	400,000	500,000	(100,000)
Equipment[2]	420,000	170,000	250,000
Less: Accumulated Depreciation	(61,262)	(36,000)	(25,262)
Total Assets	$4,126,983	$2,978,670	$1,130,313

Additional Information:
[1] During 2016, Soho did not purchase any long-term investments.
[2] During 2016, Soho made purchases of equipment for $375,000.

FIGURE 10.16

The additional information below the partial balance sheet in Figure 10.16 indicates that there were no purchases of long-term investments, so the decrease in that account is due only to the sale of investments. However, the actual cash received does not necessarily match the decrease in value. Also, Soho purchased equipment worth $375,000; however, the value of that account only increased by $250,000. This would indicate that some equipment was sold. The income statement in Figure 10.17 will provide more information on these accounts.

Soho Supplies
Income Statement
For the Year Ended December 31, 2016

Sales	$8,685,025
Cost of Goods Sold	5,998,612
Gross Profit	2,686,413
Operating Expenses	
Salaries Expense	1,416,135
Other Operating Expenses	235,417
Depreciation Expense	43,262
Insurance Expense	16,000
Total Operating Expenses	1,710,814
Operating Income	975,599
Other Revenue (Expense)	
Loss on Sale of Investments	($5,000)
Gain on Sale of Equipment	16,000 11,000
Operating Income before Tax	986,599
Income Tax Expense	280,117
Net Income	$706,482

FIGURE 10.17

Property, Plant and Equipment with Depreciation

The cash involved for both sale of long-term investments and the sale and purchase of equipment is reported in the investing activities section. In this example, the income statement indicates that some equipment has been sold for a gain. To determine how much cash was actually received, the book value of the asset must be determined. This is done by examining the changes in the balance sheet accounts. Figure 10.18 helps illustrate this.

FIGURE 10.18

The balance sheet shows that equipment increased by $250,000; however, the additional information indicates that $375,000 was purchased during the year. The $125,000 difference represents the original cost of the equipment that was sold in 2016. Also from the balance sheet, accumulated depreciation increased by $25,262; however, depreciation expense on the income statement was $43,262. This means that $18,000 was removed from accumulated depreciation when the equipment was sold.

The difference between the cost of the equipment and the associated accumulated depreciation indicates the equipment had a book value of $107,000 when it was sold. The income statement tells us that the equipment was sold at a gain of $16,000, which means the total amount of cash received must have been $123,000 ($107,000 + $16,000). If there had been a loss instead of a gain on the sale of the equipment, the cash received would have been calculated by deducting the loss from the book value of the equipment. The proceeds from the sale of equipment represents an increase in cash flow in the investing activities section of the cash flow statement.

Long-Term Investments

Long-term investments held at cost were also sold during the year, as shown by the account's decrease on the balance sheet in Figure 10.16.

FIGURE 10.19

However, the $100,000 decrease represents the cost of the investment, not necessarily the amount of cash received. The income statement indicates there was a loss of $5,000 when the investment was sold. Thus, the amount of cash received, as shown in Figure 10.19, was $95,000 ($100,000 – $5,000), representing an increase in cash flow in the investing activities section of the cash flow statement. Note that a gain on the sale would be added to the cost of the investment for calculating the amount of cash received on the sale.

In this example for long-term investments, it was assumed that there were no additional purchases in the year. If there were any purchases of long-term investments during the year, the amount would be added to the debit side of the investment account and then the amount (cost) of investment sold would be calculated. The calculation is similar to the example shown in the equipment account from Figure 10.18.

Based on the information given in Figures 10.16 and 10.17, the investing activities section of the cash flow statement would be reported as in Figure 10.20.

Soho Supplies Statement of Cash Flows (Partial) For the Year Ended December 31, 2016		
Cash Flow from Investing Activities		
Sale of Equipment	$123,000	
Sale of Investments	95,000	
Purchase of Equipment	(375,000)	
Change in Cash due to Investing Activities		($157,000)

FIGURE 10.20

Additional Items for the Cash Flow Statement

We already discussed some of the non-cash items such as depreciation and a gain or loss on the sale of assets under the operating activities section of the cash flow statement. As for the investing and financing activities, there could also be some non-cash transactions. For instance, the company may issue some shares to pay off a note payable or they may buy assets in exchange for shares. Note that although these non-cash transactions are not shown on the cash flow statement, accounting standards require their disclosure in the notes to the financial statements.

Additionally, an income statement may report discontinued operations in addition to regular operations. When it comes to the cash flow statement, the cash flows related to discontinued items should be presented separately based on the appropriate operating, investing or financing activities.

Free Cash Flow

Throughout this course, it is continually emphasized that the fundamental objective of accounting is to provide financial information that readers can use to make appropriate decisions. A group of readers—the external users—is made up of those outside the organization, primarily existing of potential investors, creditors and lenders. These external users want to ensure that their investment is protected, and so they require information on the company's economic resources and any claims on those resources. Some of the information most crucial to their decisions can be found on the cash flow statement, in a concept known as *free cash flow*.

Free cash flow is the amount of cash remaining after a business has covered its operating activities and capital expenditures (investing in long-term assets). This remaining cash is available for uses such as reducing debt, buying back shares or paying dividends. Free cash flow relies partly on the company's cash from operating activities, which in turn is based on the company's net income. However, the investing activities section of the cash flow statement does not separate capital expenditures into those that are *investments* in productive assets versus those that involve *maintenance* of productive assets. Since it can be difficult to determine exactly which items in the investing section are only related to actual investment in the business (rather than maintenance), companies quite often just use net cash from investing activities in the calculation of free cash flow.

Free cash flow is calculated by deducting the net cash flow of investing activities from the net cash flow of operating activities. If cash flow from investing activities is negative, it means that cash has been spent on assets. This number must be subtracted from the cash flow from operating activities. If cash flow from investing activities is positive, it means that cash was received from selling assets. This number must be added to the cash flow from operating activities.

Free Cash Flow = Net Cash Flow from Operating Activities – Net Cash Flow from Investing Activities

The information from Soho's cash flow statement in Figure 10.15 can be used to calculate free cash flow. Soho Supplies' cash flow statement for the year ended December 31, 2016 reported a decrease in cash due to operations of $77,689, and a decrease in cash due to investments of $142,518. Using the equation above, Soho's free cash flow can be calculated as follows.

Free Cash Flow = – $77,689 – $142,518

= – $220,207

The negative free cash flow is an unfavourable indicator of Soho's financial health. Investors often use free cash flow as a measure of a business' cash-generating ability and, in theory, should be looking for a positive or increasing cash flow. The cash flow statement provides additional insight into Soho's activities during the year.

External users of the financial statements must be aware of the many factors that affect a company's reported cash flow, and that different companies may interpret accounting guidelines differently. As well, companies can influence their cash flow in various ways, and external users need to be particularly well informed before making any decisions.

Ethics and Controls

The accounting scandals that began in 2001 with Enron served as a warning to much of the financial community that income statements and balance sheets can be manipulated to present a false financial picture of a business. As a result, an increasing number of people started using the cash flow statement as a more revealing snapshot of a company's financial well-being.

Indeed, the motivation behind relying more on cash flow statements to analyze company performance is understandable. Cash flow statements are supposed to show where the money is coming from and where it is going. However, no financial statement is immune from flaws, and this is certainly also the case with cash flow statements.

The following three situations should be viewed with caution when analyzing the cash flow statement of a business.

- **Some companies may stretch out their payables.** One way of artificially enhancing a company's cash position from operations is to deliberately delay paying bills. In fact, some companies will even go so far as to institute such a policy and label it as a form of good cash flow decision making. Of course, the company has not improved its underlying cash flow, but has simply manipulated it.

- **Some companies may finance their payables.** Some companies try to manipulate their cash flow statements by having a third party pay their payables for them, although regulators have tried to crack down on this practice. This means that the company itself shows no payments in its cash flow and, instead, pays a fee to the third party at a later date. Picking and choosing the periods in which this is done artificially manipulates the cash flow statement.

- **Some companies may shorten their collection on receivables.** While not necessarily a bad decision to collect faster from customers, this can have implications if it is done just to improve perceived cash flow. If collections that would normally happen in the next fiscal year are collected immediately to improve the cash flow this fiscal year, then the next fiscal year may show poor cash flow. This type of action merely delays reporting a poor cash flow.

 *Access **ameengage.com** for integrated resources including tutorials, practice exercises, the digital textbook and more.*

In Summary

Classify operating, investing and financing activities

⮞ Balance sheets and income statements are prepared on an accrual basis, which involves recording transactions that do not necessarily involve any exchange of money. Cash flow statements differ in that they reveal both the sources and uses of cash within a business.

⮞ The cash flow statement contains three sections: cash flow from operating activities, cash flow from investing activities and cash flow from financing activities.

⮞ The cash flow from operating activities tracks the movement of cash related to day-to-day activities of the business.

⮞ The cash flow from investing activities tracks the movement of cash on the basis of the purchases and sales of long-term assets.

⮞ The cash flow from financing activities tracks the movement of cash related to the way a company receives money for financing purposes and pays it back.

Prepare a cash flow statement using the indirect method

⮞ The indirect method of preparing cash flow statements starts with accrual-based net income from the income statement and adjusts it by adding or subtracting non-cash items and changes in current assets and current liabilities to reveal net cash flow from operating activities.

⮞ The indirect method tends to be more commonly used in preparing cash flow statements, since the direct method takes a more burdensome approach to tracking cash receipts and payments.

Calculate book value and cash received for selling long-term assets

⮞ When selling long-term assets, the accumulated depreciation must also be cleared out. Accumulated depreciation, along with assets' book value and gain (or loss) on disposal must be taken into account in calculating cash proceeds from the disposal.

Explain the concept of free cash flow and its importance for potential investors

⮞ Free cash flow is the amount of cash remaining after a business has covered its operating activities and capital expenditures.

⮞ Investors often use free cash flow as a measure of a business' cash-generating ability and its overall financial health.

Discuss ethics and control issues related to cash flow

⮞ Three situations should be viewed with caution when analyzing the cash flow statement of a business: some companies may stretch out their payables; some companies may finance their payables; and some companies may shorten their collections.

Review Exercise

Shown below is the balance sheet, income statement and notes for Dellray Inc.

Dellray Inc.
Balance Sheet
As at December 31

	2016	2015
Assets		
Current Assets		
Cash	$1,085,700	$27,000
Accounts Receivable	370,000	400,000
Inventory	290,000	250,000
Prepaid Expenses	29,000	21,000
Total Current Assets	1,774,700	698,000
Long-Term Investments[1]	560,000	600,000
Equipment[2]	1,300,000	1,100,000
Less: Accumulated Depreciation	(206,000)	(156,000)
Total Long-Term Assets	1,654,000	1,544,000
Total Assets	$3,428,700	$2,242,000
Liabilities		
Current Liabilities		
Accounts Payable	$461,000	$342,000
Current Portion of Bank Loan	75,000	65,000
Notes Payable	96,000	90,000
Total Current Liabilities	632,000	497,000
Non-Current Portion of Bank Loan	275,000	215,000
Total Liabilities	907,000	712,000
Shareholders' Equity		
Common Shares	400,000	320,000
Retained Earnings	2,121,700	1,210,000
Total Shareholders' Equity	2,521,700	1,530,000
Total Liabilities and Equity	$3,428,700	$2,242,000

Additional Information

[1] During 2016, Dellray Inc. did not purchase any long-term investments.

[2] During 2016, Dellray Inc. made purchases of equipment for $400,000.

Dellray Inc.
Income Statement
For the Year Ended December 31, 2016

Sales	$5,600,000
Cost of Goods Sold	2,968,000
Gross Profit	2,632,000
Operating Expenses	
Depreciation Expense	80,000
Insurance Expense	8,000
Salaries Expense	766,000
Other Operating Expenses	367,300
Total Operating Expenses	1,221,300
Operating Income	1,410,700
Other Revenue and Expenses	
Gain on Sale of Investments	8,000
Loss on Sale of Factory Equipment	(10,000)
Net Income before Tax	1,408,700
Income Tax Expense	422,000
Net Income	$986,700

See Appendix I for solutions.

Required

a) Prepare the cash flow statement for 2016 using the indirect method.

_____

_____

_____

_____

_____

_____

_____

_____

_____

_____

_____

_____

_____

_____

_____

b) Calculate and analyze Dellray's free cash flow for 2016.

_____

_____

_____

_____

_____

_____

_____

_____

_____

_____

Appendix 10A: The Direct Method

Earlier in this chapter, a cash flow statement was assembled using the indirect method. The term "indirect" refers to tracking the changes to cash without direct reference to cash receipts or payments. The indirect method analyzes cash flow by starting with accrual-based net income and making related adjustments for changes on the balance sheet and income statement.

The direct method is the other way to prepare the cash flow statement. Like the indirect method, the direct method breaks down the three ways of generating and using cash into operating activities, investing activities and financing activities. The difference is that the direct method prepares the operating activities section so that each income statement item is reported on a cash-basis. Each income statement item is adjusted to remove any accruals and just report cash. The investing and financing activities sections are prepared the same way as with the indirect method.

To illustrate the direct method, we will use the same Soho Supplies balance sheet and income statement that were used for the indirect method. The balance sheet is shown in Figure 10A.1 and the income statement is shown in Figure 10A.2.

Soho Supplies
Balance Sheet
As at December 31

Assets	2016	2015	Change
Current Assets			
Cash	$349,935	$396,142	($46,207)
Accounts Receivable	1,286,138	1,065,812	220,326
Inventory	1,683,560	840,091	843,469
Prepaid Insurance	48,612	42,625	5,987
Total Current Assets	$3,368,245	$2,344,670	$1,023,575
Property, Plant and Equipment[1]			
Land	0	50,000	(50,000)
Equipment	322,518	120,000	202,518
Less: Accumulated Depreciation	(79,262)	(36,000)	(43,262)
Total Assets	$3,611,501	$2,478,670	$1,132,831
Liabilities			
Current Liabilities			
Accounts Payable	$783,602	$475,645	$307,957
Salaries Payable	25,000	50,000	(25,000)
Interest Payable	15,650	23,500	(7,850)
Income Tax Payable	280,117	250,000	30,117
Current Portion of Bank Loan	380,000	240,000	140,000
Notes Payable	170,000	200,000	(30,000)
Total Current Liabilities	$1,654,369	$1,239,145	$415,224
Non-Current Portion of Bank Loan	420,000	356,000	64,000
Total Liabilities	$ 2,074,369	$ 1,595,145	$ 479,224
Shareholders' Equity			
Common Shares	15,000	5,000	10,000
Retained Earnings[2]	1,522,132	878,525	643,607
Total Shareholders' Equity	$ 1,537,132	$ 883,525	$ 653,607
Total Liabilities and Equity	$ 3,611,501	$ 2,478,670	$ 1,132,831

Additional Information

[1]   Property, Plant and Equipment:
   a)   During 2016, land, which cost $50,000, was sold for $60,000 resulting in a $10,000 gain on sale. The gain is reported on the Income Statement in the Other Revenue (Expense) section.
   b)   During 2016, Soho made purchases of equipment for $202,518.

[2]   Retained Earnings:
   Soho declared and paid $10,000 in dividends in 2016.

FIGURE 10A.1

Soho Supplies
Income Statement
For the Year Ended December 31, 2016

Sales	$8,685,025
Cost of Goods Sold	5,998,612
Gross Profit	2,686,413
Operating Expenses	
Salaries Expense	1,416,135
Other Operating Expenses	235,417
Depreciation Expense	43,262
Insurance Expense	16,000
Total Operating Expenses	1,710,814
Operating Income	975,599
Other Revenue (Expenses)	
Interest Expense	($51,875)
Gain on Sale of Land	10,000 (41,875)
Operating Income before Tax	933,724
Income Tax Expense	280,117
Net Income	$653,607

FIGURE 10A.2

For the operating activities section, the focus is on operating items that affect cash. Thus, depreciation will be ignored, since depreciation is a transaction that does not affect cash. Also, the gain on the sale of land will be ignored, since the sale of land is an investing activity. All other items on the income statement will be examined and recorded on the cash flow statement.

Cash Receipts

The first item on the cash flow statement prepared using the direct method is cash receipts. For simplicity, let us assume that Soho Supplies' only source of cash receipts is from sales to its customers. Also assume that all sales are credit sales. For the purpose of cash flow statement preparation, the credit sales balance has to be converted to the actual amount of cash collected from customers during 2016. The amount of sales revenue from Soho's income statement and the beginning and ending accounts receivable balances from Soho's balance sheet can be used to calculate the amount of cash collection from customers, as shown below.

An analysis of the T-account in Figure 10A.3 will help visualize the calculation.

FIGURE 10A.3

Credit sales (from income statement)	$8,685,025
Less: ending accounts receivable balance for 2016 (not yet collected in cash)	1,286,138
Add: opening accounts receivable balance for 2016 (collected during 2016)	($1,065,812)
Cash collected from sales on credit during 2016	$8,464,699

We now know that $8,464,699 cash was collected from sales during 2016.

Cash Payments

Next, Soho's cash payments are calculated by analyzing the changes to each of the expenses listed on the income statement and their related balance sheet accounts.

Cash Payments for Inventory

There are two steps involved in calculating the cash payments for inventory purchased.

First, the amount of merchandise purchased during the year must be calculated. From the balance sheet, we know the beginning and ending balances of inventory. The income statement tells us the amount of cost of goods sold. Based on the cost of goods sold and inventory balances, the amount of purchases can be calculated by solving the missing number in the inventory T-account, as shown in Figure 10A.4.

FIGURE 10A.4

Without using the T-account, the calculation for the amount of purchases is

Cost of goods sold for 2016 (from income statement)	$5,998,612
Add: increase in inventory for 2016 ($1,683,560 − $840,091)	843,469
Inventory purchased on credit during 2016	$6,842,081

Now that the amount of inventory purchased during the year is known, this figure can be used to determine the cash payments for inventory.

A few assumptions have to be made about how inventory is purchased and paid for. One assumption is that inventory is purchased on credit and paid for at a later date. Another assumption is that accounts payable is only used for suppliers of inventory. With two assumptions in place, the inventory purchases for 2016 can be added to accounts payable to determine how much cash was paid for inventory.

This is shown in the T-account in Figure 10A.5.

DECREASE (DR)		INCREASE (CR)
−	**ACCOUNTS PAYABLE**	**+**
Payments to Suppliers 6,534,124	475,645 Opening Balance	
	6,842,081 Purchases 2016	
	$783,602 Closing Balance	

FIGURE 10A.5

The calculation without the T-account for the cash payments for inventory is

Balance of accounts payable, Jan 1, 2016 (from balance sheet)	$475,645
Add: merchandise purchased on credit during 2016	6,842,081
Less: balance of accounts payable, Dec 31, 2016 (from balance sheet)	783,602
Cash payments for merchandise	$6,534,124

Cash Payments to Employees

To analyze Soho's cash payment to employees for salaries expense for the year, start with the expense on the income statement. Next, adjust this amount by the change in salaries payable during the year. Because salaries are normally paid within a short time period of when they are accrued (usually weeks or a month), we can assume that all salaries payable at January 1, 2016 were fully paid during the year.

The analysis of the salaries payable T-account in Figure 10A.6 shows the calculation.

DECREASE (DR)　　　　　　　　　　　　　INCREASE (CR)

-	SALARIES PAYABLE	+

Payments to employees in 2016 (1,441,135)	50,000 Opening Balance
	1,416,135 Expense for 2016
	$25,000 Closing Balance

FIGURE 10A.6

Salaries expense for 2016 (from income statement)	$1,416,135
Add: change in salaries payable for 2016 ($50,000 – $25,000)	25,000
Cash payments to employees for salaries during 2016	$1,441,135

Cash Payments for Other Operating Expenses

The next expense on the income statement is other operating expenses. None of the remaining current assets or current liabilities is related to this item on the income statement. For example, prepaid insurance is related to insurance expense and interest payable is related to interest expense.

Thus, there are no adjustments to the amount of cash for other operating expenses and the amount shown on the income statement ($235,417) will be the amount reported as cash payments on the cash flow statement.

Cash Payments for Insurance

Cash paid for insurance will be based on the insurance expense reported on the income statement and adjusted by the change in prepaid insurance on the balance sheet. Recall that insurance premiums that are paid in advance are recorded in the prepaid insurance account until the amount has been used. Since the prepaid insurance account increased, we can assume that more cash was paid for prepaid insurance over the year. This will be added to the amount of the insurance expense.

The analysis of the prepaid insurance T-account in Figure 10A.7 shows the calculation.

INCREASE (DR)　　　　　　　　　　　　　DECREASE (CR)

+	PREPAID INSURANCE	-

Opening Balance 42,625	16,000 Insurance expense 2016
Paid during 2016 (21,987)	
Closing Balance $48,612	

FIGURE 10A.7

Insurance expense incurred during 2016 (from income statement)	$ 16,000
Add: Change in prepaid insurance for 2016 ($48,612 – $42,625)	5,987
Cash payments for insurance during 2016	$ 21,987

Cash Payments for Interest

Interest expense is the next cash item on the income statement. The amount reported as an expense will be adjusted by the change in interest payable. The decrease in interest payable indicates that more cash was paid to cover interest owed during the year. This decrease will be added to the interest expense.

The analysis of the interest payable T-account in Figure 10A.8 shows the calculation.

DECREASE (DR)	INCREASE (CR)
- INTEREST PAYABLE	+
Payment during 2016 59,725	23,500 Opening Balance
	51,875 Interest expense 2016
	$15,650 Closing Balance

FIGURE 10A.8

Interest expense incurred during 2016 (from income statement)	$51,875
Add: change in interest payable for 2016 ($23,500 – $15,650)	7,850
Cash payments for interest during 2016	$59,725

Cash Payments for Income Taxes

The last cash expense is income taxes. The balance sheet account, income tax payable, is used to adjust the expense to determine the actual cash amount paid. Since income tax payable increased over the year, it indicates that the company was able to defer paying income taxes. This saves cash, thus reducing the amount of cash paid for income tax during 2016 to $250,000.

The analysis of the income tax payable T-account in Figure 10A.9 shows the calculation.

DECREASE (DR)	INCREASE (CR)
- INCOME TAX PAYABLE	+
Payment during 2016 250,000	250,000 Opening Balance
	280,117 Income tax expenses for 2016
	$280,117 Closing Balance

FIGURE 10A.9

Income tax expense for 2016 (from income statement)	$280,117
Less: Change in Income Tax Payable for 2016 ($250,000 – $280,117)	(30,117)
Cash payments for income tax during 2016	$250,000

Now that all the cash related income statement items are complete, the operating activities section of the cash flow statement can be prepared, as shown in Figure 10A.10. The section is divided into the cash receipts and the cash payments, which matches with the adjusted sales and adjusted expenses from the income statement.

Soho Supplies
Cash Flow Statement
For the Year Ended December 31, 2016

Cash Flow from Operating Activities		
Cash Receipts		
Cash Received from Customers		$8,464,699
Cash Payments		
Payments for Inventory	$6,534,124	
Payments to Employees	1,441,135	
Payments for other Operating Expenses	235,417	
Payments for Insurance	21,987	
Payments for Interest	59,725	
Payments for Income Taxes	250,000	
Total Cash Payments		8,542,388
Change in Cash due to Operating Activities		($77,689)

FIGURE 10A.10

You will notice that the decrease in cash from operating activities of $77,689 matches the cash flow statement prepared under the direct method in Figure 10.15.

The investing and financing activities of the cash flow statement under the direct method are analyzed and prepared in the same manner as for the indirect method. These two sections are explained in Chapter 10. The completed cash flow statement prepared using the direct method is shown in Figure 10A.11.

Soho Supplies
Cash Flow Statement
For the Year Ended December 31, 2016

Cash Flow from Operating Activities

Cash Receipts

Cash Received from Customers		$8,464,699

Cash payments

Payments for Inventory	$6,534,124	
Payments to Employees	1,441,135	
Payments for other Operating Expenses	235,417	
Payments made for Insurance	21,987	
Payments for Interest	59,725	
Payments made for Income taxes	250,000	
Total Cash Payments		$8,542,388
Cash Flows from Operating Activities		($77,689)

Cash Flow from Investing Activities

Sale of Land	60,000	
Purchase of Equipment	(202,518)	
Change in Cash due to Investing Activities		(142,518)

Cash Flow from Financing Activities

Payments towards Notes Payable	(30,000)	
Proceeds from Bank Loan	204,000	
Payment of Cash Dividends	(10,000)	
Proceeds from Issuance of Common Shares	$10,000	
Change in Cash due to Financing Activities		174,000
Net Increase (Decrease) in Cash		($46,207)
Cash at the Beginning of the Year		396,142
Cash at the End of the Year		$349,935

FIGURE 10A.11

  Access **ameengage.com** for integrated resources including tutorials, practice exercises, the digital textbook and more.

In Summary

Prepare a cash flow statement using the direct method

↪ The direct method applies only to the operating activities section of the cash flow statement.

↪ Under the direct method, all cash items on the income statement are reported separately on the cash flow statement, after being adjusted by changes in related accounts from the balance sheet.

Review Exercise

Shown below is the balance sheet, income statement and notes for Harmony Inc. Prepare the cash flow statement for 2016 using the direct method.

Harmony Inc. Balance Sheet As at December 31		
	2016	**2015**
Assets		
Current Assets		
Cash	$1,085,700	$27,000
Accounts Receivable	370,000	400,000
Inventory	290,000	250,000
Prepaid Insurance	29,000	21,000
Total Current Assets	1,774,700	698,000
Long-Term Investments[1]	560,000	600,000
Equipment[2]	1,300,000	1,100,000
Less: Accumulated Depreciation	(206,000)	(156,000)
Total Long-Term Assets	1,654,000	1,544,000
Total Assets	$3,428,700	$2,242,000
Liabilities		
Current Liabilities		
Accounts Payable[3]	$461,000	$342,000
Current Portion of Bank Loan	75,000	65,000
Notes Payable	96,000	90,000
Total Current Liabilities	632,000	497,000
Non-Current Portion of Bank Loan	275,000	215,000
Total Liabilities	907,000	712,000
Shareholders' Equity		
Common Shares	400,000	320,000
Retained Earnings	2,121,700	1,210,000
Total Shareholders' Equity	2,521,700	1,530,000
Total Liabilities And Equity	$3,428,700	$2,242,000

Additional Information

[1]During 2016, Harmony Inc. did not purchase any long-term investments.

[2]During 2016, Harmony Inc. made purchases of equipment for $400,000.

[3]Assume accounts payable is only used for suppliers of inventory.

Harmony Inc.
Income Statement
For the Year Ended December 31, 2016

Sales	$5,600,000
Cost of Goods Sold	2,968,000
Gross Profit	2,632,000
Operating Expenses	
Depreciation Expense	80,000
Insurance Expense	8,000
Salaries Expense	766,000
Other Operating Expenses	367,300
Total Operating Expenses	1,221,300
Operating Income	1,410,700
Other Revenue and Expenses	
Gain on Sale of Investments	8,000
Loss on Sale of Factory Equipment	(10,000)
Net Income before Tax	1,408,700
Income Tax Expense	422,000
Net Income	$986,700

See Appendix I for solutions.

Calculations for the Operating Activities—Direct Method

_____

_____

_____

_____

_____

_____

_____

_____

_____

_____

_____

_____

_____

_____

_____

_____

_____

_____

_____

_____

_____

_____

_____

_____

_____

_____

_____

_____

Notes

Chapter 11
FINANCIAL STATEMENT ANALYSIS

LEARNING OUTCOMES

❶ Explain the importance of analyzing financial statements

❷ Conduct horizontal and vertical analysis of financial statements

❸ Calculate and apply liquidity ratios

❹ Calculate and apply profitability ratios

❺ Calculate and apply operation management and leverage ratios

❻ Calculate and apply capital market ratios

❼ Identify the limitations of financial statement analysis

AMEENGAGE Access **ameengage.com** for integrated resources including tutorials, practice exercises, the digital textbook and more.

The Importance of Financial Statement Analysis

In this textbook, you have learned how to prepare the financial statements for partnerships and corporations. These statements provide the basic set of information about a company and are used in decision-making processes internally and externally. This chapter will show how these financial statements can be used to help users make decisions.

Financial statements are useful for both internal and external users. Internal users such as managers and executives analyze financial information to correct negative results and take advantage of positive results. External users, such as investors and suppliers, analyze financial information to determine whether to invest money or extend credit terms.

There are different ways to analyze a company's financial statements. One way is to perform a horizontal or vertical analysis of the financial statements. Another way is to calculate ratios based on the numbers from a company's financial statements. Some ratios have been presented before in the previous chapters. Each of those ratios represents a piece of the puzzle. Each piece of the puzzle or each ratio has its own merits, but it alone does not provide users with the complete picture of a company's financial health. This chapter illustrates how to compute important ratios and how to analyze them to better understand the complex nature of a corporation's financial status. We will begin our discussion with horizontal and vertical analysis of the statements.

Horizontal and Vertical Analysis

We will inspect the balance sheet of Star Hotel, a fictitious Canadian hotel corporation. Suppose this company is planning to renovate to offer more rooms and services. It has contacted the bank to secure a bank loan, but the bank must determine whether the company is profitable and will be able to afford the loan and interest payments. The bank has asked for Star Hotel's financial statements for the last three years. Star Hotel's comparative balance sheet is presented in Figure 11.1. A **comparative balance sheet** is simply a balance sheet that shows the balances for multiple years for easy comparison. For readability, a single column is used for each year.

Star Hotel Comparative Balance Sheet As at December 31, 2014–2016			
	2016	**2015**	**2014**
Assets			
Current Assets			
Cash	$8,000	$20,000	$32,000
Accounts Receivable	100,000	70,000	40,000
Food Inventory	40,000	28,000	16,000
Prepaid Expenses	12,000	12,000	12,000
Total Current Assets	160,000	130,000	100,000
Property, Plant and Equipment			
Building, Net	390,000	400,000	410,000
Equipment, Net	50,000	55,000	60,000
Total Long-Term Assets	440,000	455,000	470,000
Total Assets	$600,000	$585,000	$570,000
Liabilities			
Current Liabilities			
Accounts Payable	$50,000	$60,000	$80,000
Unearned Revenue	30,000	25,000	20,000
Total Current Liabilities	80,000	85,000	100,000
Total Liabilities	80,000	85,000	100,000
Shareholders' Equity			
Share Capital			
Common Shares—10,000 outstanding	100,000	100,000	100,000
Preferred Shares—5,000 outstanding	20,000	10,000	10,000
Retained Earnings	400,000	390,000	360,000
Total Shareholders' Equity	520,000	500,000	470,000
Total Liabilities and Shareholders' Equity	$600,000	$585,000	$570,000

FIGURE 11.1

The comparative balance sheet is a tool used to perform **horizontal analysis** because it compares information from one accounting period to another, usually from year to year. This means that you can compare similar line items to see how that item has changed from year to year.

Using the comparative balance sheet, the bank can easily see the increases and decreases in assets and liabilities, and estimate the future trends of the financial information. Specifically, we can quickly see that total assets have increased while total liabilities have decreased, which is a good sign. However, the company's cash balance is dwindling while accounts receivable significantly increased, indicating that there may be some cash or collection issues. To make its decision, the bank needs more in-depth information.

Figure 11.2 summarizes some key financial information for Star Hotel's previous three years. Just examining dollar amounts may not reveal trends in the company. Instead we can present the values as percentages. This will show the value of the item compared to a base year. A **base year** is usually the earliest year shown and will be the basis for comparison.

To calculate the percentages, we will use the following formula.

$$\text{Percentage of Base-Year} = \frac{\text{New Account Balance}}{\text{Base-Year Account Balance}}$$

In this example, 2014 will be the base-year. For each line, the 2014 value is the denominator in the calculation. So for cash, we will always divide by $32,000. For 2014, $32,000 divided by $32,000 is 100%. For 2016, the calculation would look like this.

$$\frac{\$8,000}{\$32,000} = 0.25 \text{ or } 25\%$$

A way to describe this trend is that cash in 2016 is at 25% of the balance in 2014. Repeat this calculation for each separate line item across the years.

Star Hotel Key Figures As at December 31, 2014–2016			
	2016	**2015**	**2014**
Cash	$8,000	$20,000	$32,000
Total Current Assets	160,000	130,000	100,000
Property, Plant and Equipment	440,000	455,000	470,000
Total Assets	600,000	585,000	570,000
Total Current Liabilities	80,000	85,000	100,000
Total Shareholders' Equity	520,000	500,000	470,000

Star Hotel Percentage of 2014 Base-Year As at December 31, 2014–2016			
	2016	2015	2014
Cash	25%	63%	100%
Total Current Assets	160%	130%	100%
Property, Plant and Equipment	94%	97%	100%
Total Assets	105%	103%	100%
Total Current Liabilities	80%	85%	100%
Total Shareholders' Equity	111%	106%	100%

FIGURE 11.2

Using this method, the bank can see trends emerging in the data. Despite cash significantly decreasing over time, total current assets have been steadily increasing. Liabilities have been reduced while shareholders' equity has been increasing since 2014. There are no major concerns with these observations.

Alternatively, there is another calculation method which describes percentage changes between years for line items. The method simply subtracts an old figure from a new figure, and then it divides the result by the old figure of the same line item. The formula is as follows.

$$\text{Percentage Change since Base-Year} = \frac{\text{New Account Balance} - \text{Base-Year Account Balance}}{\text{Base-Year Account Balance}}$$

Figure 11.3 summarizes some key financial information for Star Hotel's previous three years. As before, 2014 is selected as the base-year. For cash, we will always subtract $32,000 from the year we are examining and divide the result by $32,000. For example, the balance of cash in 2016 was $8,000.

$$\frac{\$8,000 - \$32,000}{\$32,000} = -0.75 \; or - 75\%$$

A way to describe this trend is that the cash balance decreased by 75% between 2014 and 2016. This could be the reason why Star Hotel needs a loan, because the company does not have enough cash to pay for renovations.

Star Hotel Key Figures As at December 31, 2014–2016			
	2016	2015	2014
Cash	$8,000	$20,000	$32,000
Total Current Assets	160,000	130,000	100,000
Property, Plant and Equipment	440,000	455,000	470,000
Total Assets	600,000	585,000	570,000
Total Current Liabilities	80,000	85,000	100,000
Total Shareholders' Equity	520,000	500,000	470,000

Star Hotel Percentage Changed with 2014 Base-Year As at December 31, 2014–2016	2016	2015	2014
Cash	–75%	–38%	0%
Total Current Assets	60%	30%	0%
Property, Plant and Equipment	–6%	–5%	0%
Total Assets	5%	3%	0%
Total Current Liabilities	–20%	–15%	0%
Total Shareholders' Equity	11%	6%	0%

FIGURE 11.3

One item to note in Figure 11.3 is the 0% changes for 2014. There is no percent change from the base-year figure, because they are the same dollar amounts (i.e. $32,000 – $32,000 = $0. Next, $0 ÷ $32,000 = $0).

Instead of comparing the dollars to a base-year, the bank could use one of the line items as a base figure. Usually, the **base figure** is a total dollar amount such as total assets. Figure 11.4 shows the percentage of line items by using total assets as the base. This is called **vertical analysis** because each separate line item is being compared to the base-figure within the specific year.

Star Hotel Key Percentages As at December 31, 2014–2016	2016	2015	2014
Cash	1%	3%	6%
Total Current Assets	27%	22%	18%
Property, Plant and Equipment	73%	78%	82%
Total Assets	100%*	100%	100%
Total Current Liabilities	13%	15%	18%
Total Shareholders' Equity	87%	85%	82%

*$600,000 ÷ $600,000 = 100%

FIGURE 11.4

To calculate the percentages, we will use the following formula.

$$\text{Percentage of Base-Figure} = \frac{\text{Line Item Account Balance}}{\text{Base-Figure Account Balance}}$$

To start, a base-figure must be selected. In 2016, Star Hotel had a total asset balance of $600,000. Next, divide all line items in the 2016 balance sheet by the base-figure selected. For cash, divide the balance of $8,000 by the total assets. The result is 0.01 or 1%.

$$\frac{\$8,000}{\$600,000} = 0.01 \ or \ 1\%$$

This type of analysis reveals that cash currently only represents 1% of total assets. Star Hotel should consider holding more cash in case of unexpected events. Fortunately, current assets represent 27% of total assets and have grown to more than double that of current liabilities. Using this information, the bank decides that Star Hotel is in an overall healthy financial position.

The next step is to use the same tools to analyze the company's income statement. Horizontal analysis is done in much the same way on the income statement as it is on the balance sheet. Star Hotel's comparative income statement is shown in Figure 11.5 for the past three years.

Star Hotel Comparative Income Statement For the Year Ended December 31, 2014–2016			
	2016	**2015**	**2014**
Revenue			
Service Revenue	$270,000	$200,000	$180,000
Food Sales Revenue	80,000	50,000	40,000
Total Revenue	350,000	250,000	220,000
Cost of Goods Sold	50,000	30,000	25,000
Gross Profit	300,000	220,000	195,000
Operating Expenses			
Advertising Expense	33,000	15,000	5,000
Depreciation Expense	15,000	15,000	15,000
Insurance Expense	12,000	12,000	12,000
Salaries Expense	200,000	150,000	140,000
Supplies Expense	20,000	18,000	15,500
Total Expenses	280,000	210,000	187,500
Net Income	$20,000	$10,000	$7,500

FIGURE 11.5

The comparative income statement allows the bank to quickly see which revenue and expenses have increased or decreased and whether net income is rising or falling. Star Hotel has seen a large increase in revenue, perhaps attributable to an increased advertising budget. The company's net income has doubled since 2015 which is a good sign of profitability. However, if the bank grants a loan, Star Hotel will be required to incur an interest expense, which would reduce the profitability of the company. The bank decides to look at other trends in the company.

Figure 11.6 lists the key figures from the income statement for the previous three years as dollars, percentage of, as well as percentage changed from the base-year of 2014.

Star Hotel Key Figures For the Year Ended December 31, 2014–2016			
	2016	2015	2014
Total Revenue	$350,000	$250,000	$220,000
Cost of Goods Sold	50,000	30,000	25,000
Gross Profit	300,000	220,000	195,000
Total Expenses	280,000	210,000	187,500
Net Income	20,000	10,000	7,500

Star Hotel Percentage of 2014 Base-Year For the Year Ended December 31, 2014–2016			
	2016	2015	2014
Total Revenue	160%	114%	100%
Cost of Goods Sold	200%	120%	100%
Gross Profit	154%	113%	100%
Total Expenses	150%	112%	100%
Net Income	267%	133%	100%

Star Hotel Percentage Changed with 2014 Base-Year For the Year Ended December 31, 2014–2016			
	2016	2015	2014
Total Revenue	60%	14%	0%
Cost of Goods Sold	100%	20%	0%
Gross Profit	54%	13%	0%
Total Expenses	50%	12%	0%
Net Income	167%	33%	0%

FIGURE 11.6

Star Hotel's sales have been increasing at a faster rate than its expenses, resulting in higher net income. After seeing these trends, the bank decides that the company is likely to continue operating profitably into the future.

Finally, the bank can also use vertical analysis on Star Hotel's income statement by converting everything to a percentage of total revenue for each year, as shown in Figure 11.7.

Star Hotel Percentage of Base-Figure Total Revenue For the Year Ended December 31, 2014–2016			
	2016	**2015**	**2014**
Total Revenue	100%	100%	100%
Cost of Goods Sold	14%	12%	11%
Gross Profit	86%	88%	89%
Total Expenses	80%	84%	85%
Net Income	6%	4%	3%

FIGURE 11.7

This analysis reveals that gross profit has remained quite steady, but operating expenses have been gradually falling in relation to total revenue. This indicates that sales have risen without causing much of an increase to operating expenses, allowing for more net income per dollar of sales.

Considering all of the conclusions, the bank approves the loan to Star Hotel because it has been growing steadily over the past three years and is in a healthy enough financial position to expand operations without much risk.

The Star Hotel example used horizontal and vertical analysis tools to make a decision. While these tools are helpful in providing insight regarding a company's financial position, there are limitations to what they can actually show. The tools do not consider errors in the figures. Also, the trends may not continue because businesses change and evolve constantly. Fortunately, there are many other analysis tools available to users. These will be discussed next.

Liquidity Analysis

For the next type of analysis, we will use the financial statements of Second Cup Coffee Co. (Second Cup), a Canadian corporation that sells specialty coffee and baked goods. The comparative balance sheet is shown in Figure 11.8. The comparative balance sheet is not only an important tool in conducting horizontal and vertical analysis, but it also allows users to easily calculate various financial ratios for the company to even better understand its finances.

We will dissect sections of the balance sheet to perform our initial analysis. The analysis will involve the calculation of ratios. Ratios measure different aspects of a company's financial situation, and they are divided into four categories based on what they measure: liquidity, profitability, operations management and leverage. For a public company, we can also measure corporate performance. For all ratios, we can compare to a similar company in the same industry, or to industry averages to determine whether the company is performing relatively well or poorly. During our discussion of Second Cup, we will compare from one year to the next, to Starbucks' ratios (in Appendix III) and to sample industry averages. Second Cup's and Starbucks' financial statements in this chapter and in Appendix III are publicly available information, which was obtained from the respective companies' websites. The industry averages in this chapter are not based on real industry information and are presented here for illustrative purposes only.

Second Cup Coffee Co. Statement of Financial Position As at December 27, 2014 and December 28, 2013 (expressed in thousands of Canadian dollars)		
	2014	**2013**
Assets		
Current Assets		
Cash	$10,918	$6,501
Accounts Receivable	4,026	4,368
Notes and Leases Receivable	81	220
Inventory	221	123
Prepaid Expenses	485	190
Income Tax Recoverable	699	-
Total Current Assets	16,430	11,402
Non-Current Assets		
Notes and Leases Receivable	302	701
Property and Equipment	4,380	3,507
Intangible Assets	32,337	61,730
Total Assets	$53,449	$77,340
Liabilities		
Current Liabilities		
Accounts Payable	$6,011	$4,586
Provisions	1,937	847
Other Liabilities	512	717
Income Tax Payable	-	138
Gift Card Liability	3,727	3,895
Deposits From Franchises	378	878
Current Portion of Long-Term Debt	11,119	-
Total Current Liabilities	23,684	11,061
Non-Current Liabilities		
Provisions	1,133	1,380
Other Liabilities	368	428
Long-Term Debt	-	11,089
Deferred Income Taxes	3,270	7,418
Total Liabilities	28,455	31,376
Shareholders' Equity		
Share Capital—Common Shares	8,652	1,000
Contributed Surplus	61,651	61,557
Retained Earnings (Deficit)	(45,309)	(16,593)
Total Shareholders' Equity	24,994	45,964
Total Liabilities and Shareholders' Equity	$53,449	$77,340

FIGURE 11.8

Liquidity refers to the ability of a company to repay its debt obligations as they become due. The more liquid a company is, the easier it is to cover obligations such as accounts payable and loan payments. There are several ways to measure liquidity.

Working Capital

Working capital is a measure of liquidity that assesses the adequacy of a company's current assets to cover its current liabilities. It can be quickly calculated and easily understood. The formula for working capital is shown below.

$$\text{Working Capital} = \text{Current Assets} - \text{Current Liabilities}$$

Working capital is a dollar figure, not a ratio, so it is difficult to say how much working capital is enough. A positive working capital indicates that the company has enough liquid assets to pay off its upcoming debts. The working capital of Second Cup is calculated in Figure 11.9 for 2013 and 2014.

	2014	2013
Current Assets	$16,430	$11,402
Current Liabilities	$23,684	$11,061
Working Capital	**($7,254)**	**$341**
Industry Average	**$62**	**$325**

FIGURE 11.9

The working capital has gone from positive to negative which is an indication of poor liquidity. The company may have to sell a long-term asset or raise cash through other means to pay off its current liabilities. When compared to the industry, other companies on average have also shown a decrease in working capital. However, Second Cup has experienced a much larger decrease in working capital. Appendix III shows that Starbucks performed better than Second Cup in this area because Starbucks had a positive working capital in both 2013 and 2014. Contrary to Second Cup and the industry average, Starbucks' working capital is significantly higher in 2014 than in 2013.

Current Ratio

The **current ratio** is a useful ratio for determining the company's ability to repay its upcoming debts and obligations. The current ratio is calculated as shown below.

$$\text{Current Ratio} = \frac{\text{Current Assets}}{\text{Current Liabilities}}$$

The current ratio assesses business liquidity by determining the extent to which current assets can cover current liabilities. This means establishing the business' ability to pay off its debt due within one year. No business wants to find itself in a position of having to sell long-term assets to pay current bills. A current ratio of 1.0 indicates that the business has just enough current assets to pay for its current liabilities.

Depending on the industry, the higher the current ratio, the more assurance that the business has enough of a cushion that it can afford to have some cash tied up in current assets, such as inventory and accounts receivable. However, a very high current ratio could indicate poor management of current assets. For example, if the current ratio of a business is 5.0, it has $5.00 in current assets for every dollar that it owes in the next 12 months. This indicates that the business may have too much cash. Money in a bank account earning 0.1% interest is not an efficient use of assets, especially if the business can earn a better rate of return elsewhere. Cash should either be invested in new long-term assets or perhaps invested in the short term until a better use for the cash can be established.

The chart in Figure 11.10 calculates the current ratio using the numbers provided in Second Cup's financial statements.

	2014	2013
Current Assets	$16,430	$11,402
Current Liabilities	$23,684	$11,061
Current Ratio	0.69	1.03
Industry Average	0.88	0.97

FIGURE 11.10

In this case, the ratio indicates an unhealthy situation. Not only is the ratio well below 1 in the most recent year, but it has decreased from one year to the next. Second Cup may run into cash flow problems within the next year. The industry has also experienced a decrease in current ratio, although not as great a decrease as Second Cup. In 2013, Starbucks' current ratio was 1.02, which is about the same as Second Cup's 2013 current ratio of 1.03. However, in 2014, Starbucks' current ratio of 1.37 is significantly higher than both Second Cup's and the industry average, suggesting that Starbucks was in a much healthier situation in terms of liquidity than Second Cup and other companies in the same industry on average.

Quick Ratio

Another ratio that is relevant to the analysis of a business' liquidity is the **quick ratio** (also known as the acid test). The ratio measures the adequacy of highly liquid assets (including cash, short-term investments and accounts receivable) to cover current liabilities. The formula for the quick ratio is shown below.

$$\text{Quick Ratio} = \frac{\text{Cash} + \text{Short-Term Investments} + \text{Accounts Receivable}}{\text{Current Liabilities}}$$

The quick ratio is much like the current ratio; the only difference is that the quick ratio excludes some current assets which cannot be quickly converted to cash (such as inventory and prepaid expenses). Short-term investments occur when a company has excess cash and wishes to invest it. This cash can be invested in debt and equity instruments such as bonds and shares of other companies. The accounting for short-term investments has been covered in an earlier chapter.

In essence, the quick ratio assesses the ability of the business to meet its most immediate debt obligations without relying on the liquidation of inventory (which may take some time to sell). A quick ratio of 1 indicates that the business has just enough liquid assets to pay for its current liabilities. Anything below 1 might mean the business has too much of its money tied up in inventory or other less liquid assets and may be unable to pay its short-term bills.

Quick ratios have been calculated in Figure 11.11 using the numbers from Second Cup's balance sheet. Note that Second Cup does not have any short-term investments.

	2014	2013
Cash + Short-Term Investments + Accounts Receivable	$14,944	$10,869
Current Liabilities	$23,684	$11,061
Quick Ratio	0.63	0.98
Industry Average	0.86	0.94

FIGURE 11.11

In 2013, Second Cup had a better short-term liquidity than Starbucks since Second Cup's quick ratio of 0.98 was higher than Starbucks' quick ratio of 0.71. However, Starbucks' quick ratio improved in 2014 to be 0.81, while Second Cup's quick ratio dropped to 0.63. This means that Second Cup has gone from a nearly adequate short-term liquidity position to a dangerous one.

Second Cup's liquidity situation could have worsened if the company had invested even more money in inventory or fixed assets. To address any potential problems here, and since the balance sheet provides only a snapshot of business finances, further analyses should be performed over the next few months on the specific assets and liabilities of the business. A review should be performed to address the situation and rectify any problems found. This is to ensure that bills can be paid on time.

Profitability Analysis

Profitability refers to the ability of a company to generate profits. The greater the profitability, the more valuable the company is to shareholders. A consistently unprofitable company is likely to go bankrupt. There are several ratios available to help analyze the profitability of a company. They are calculated using figures from the income statement as well as the balance sheet. The income statement for Second Cup is shown in Figure 11.12.

Second Cup Coffee Co. Statement of Comprehensive Income For the Periods Ended December 27, 2014 and December 28, 2013 (expressed in thousands of Canadian dollars, except for per share amounts)		
	2014	**2013**
Revenue		
Royalties	$12,350	$14,117
Sale of Goods	9,287	5,506
Services and Other Revenue	6,535	7,565
Total Revenue	28,172	27,188
Cost of Services	7,679	4,054
Gross Profit	20,493	23,134
Operating Expenses		
Salaries, Benefits, and Incentives	6,496	6,866
Coffee Central Overheads	6,700	5,647
Depreciation Expense	933	749
Amortization Expense	339	502
Lease Expense	2,692	1,775
Loss (Gain) on Disposal of Equipment	34	(197)
Total Expenses	17,194	15,342
Operating Income	3,299	7,792
Other Revenue and Expenses		
Restructuring Charges	2,166	883
Provisions for Cafe Closures	1,630	479
Impairment Charges	29,708	13,552
Loss on Acquisition of Cafes	692	-
Interest and Financing Expense	478	516
Loss Before Income Taxes	(31,375)	(7,638)
Income Tax Recovery	4,343	269
Net Loss	($27,032)	($7,369)
Basic and Diluted Loss Per Share	($2.66)	($0.74)

FIGURE 11.12

Figure 11.12 shows Second Cup's comparative income statement, allowing users to easily compare the financial results of the company over two years. We can instantly see, for example, that Second Cup has not generated a profit for the past two years. We can also see that revenue has remained somewhat level while expenses have significantly increased overall, resulting in a higher net loss for 2014. In contrast, Starbucks' comparative income statement in Appendix III reveals that Starbucks was profitable. In addition to these observations, several more ratios can be calculated to assess profitability.

Gross Profit Margin

The gross profit margin is used to demonstrate the impact of cost of goods sold on the income statement. In other words, the gross profit margin subtracts cost of goods sold from sales revenue, the result of which is divided by sales revenue. The formula is shown below.

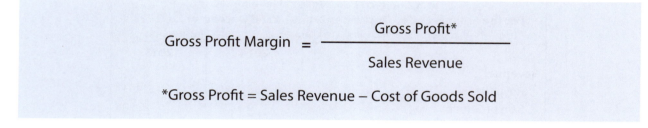

$$\text{Gross Profit Margin} = \frac{\text{Gross Profit*}}{\text{Sales Revenue}}$$

$$\text{*Gross Profit} = \text{Sales Revenue} - \text{Cost of Goods Sold}$$

Gross profit margin reveals the percentage of revenue left after the costs that are directly involved in producing the goods or services (for manufacturers) or in buying the goods for resale (for retailers) are deducted. That is, the amount of profit remaining after deducting the cost of goods sold. The remaining profit is used to pay for operating and other expenses. Figure 11.13 calculates the gross profit margin using figures from Second Cup's income statement for 2013 and 2014.

	2014	2013
Gross Profit	$20,493	$23,134
Total Revenue	$28,172	$27,188
Gross Profit Margin	73%	85%
Industry Average	71%	82%

FIGURE 11.13

A higher gross profit margin means that the company has an easier time covering its expenses and is more likely to be profitable. However, gross profit margins should be compared to an industry average to determine whether they are healthy or not. A decline in the gross profit margin, such as with Second Cup, indicates that the company is either not generating enough revenue, has experienced an increase in inventory costs or both.

The industry has also experienced a decrease in gross profit margin. This could indicate that industry wide there is an increase in the cost of coffee and other items being sold. It could also indicate that prices are driven down by an increase in competition as a whole. Notice that Second Cup does have a better margin than the industry average. Perhaps it is able to find better deals when purchasing inventory or is able to charge a higher price than the industry average due to its branding. In comparison, Starbucks had a lower gross profit margin than both Second Cup and the industry average, as its gross profit margin was lower than 60% for both 2013 and 2014.

Net Profit Margin

The **net profit margin** assesses a company's profitability after all expenses have been deducted. This is the amount of net profit or loss per dollar of revenue. The formula is shown below.

$$\text{Net Profit Margin} = \frac{\text{Net Income}}{\text{Sales Revenue}}$$

As with the gross profit margin, a higher net profit margin is generally considered a better sign than a lower one, although it should always be compared to an industry average and previous results. Figure 11.14 calculates the net profit margins for Second Cup for both 2013 and 2014.

	2014	2013
Net Income (Loss)	($27,032)	($7,369)
Total Revenue	$28,172	$27,188
Net Profit Margin	**−96%**	**−27%**
Industry Average	**5%**	**4%**

FIGURE 11.14

Although total revenue has increased since 2013, net income has remained negative and significantly worsened. This is a bad sign for the shareholders because their investments have not earned a return in more than two years. To perform a complete analysis of net profit margins, comparisons should be made on a monthly and yearly basis to historical company performance, industry averages and direct competitors. Only then will these net income figures be placed in context so that conclusions can be drawn.

The industry and Starbucks are showing positive net profit margins for both years. This is of concern to Second Cup, since it has posted negative profit margins for the past two years.

Earnings Before Interest and Taxes (EBIT)

To get a clearer look at profitability, it is useful to examine line items other than just gross profit or net income. Some costs on an income statement are not directly under the control of management. These costs are interest and taxes and are added to net income. This amount is called **earnings before interest and taxes**, or EBIT. Starbucks was also able to generate a positive EBIT in 2014 despite its negative EBIT in 2013.

Adding these costs to net income essentially levels the playing field when analyzing the performance of one business compared to another. Taxes are not the result of day-to-day managerial decision-making and interest rates are determined by the bank. These types of costs can vary from jurisdiction to jurisdiction or from one business to another. Thus, EBIT properly reflects the performance of the business based on what the business can control. The calculation of EBIT for Second Cup is shown in Figure 11.15. Since income tax is recovered and is not an expense in this example, income tax recovery is subtracted from the loss.

	2014	2013
Net Income (Loss)	($27,032)	($7,369)
Income Tax Recovery	$4,343	$269
Interest and Financing Expense	$478	$516
EBIT	**($30,897)**	**($7,122)**
Industry Average	**$5,342**	**$4,986**

FIGURE 11.15

Generally, the greater the dollar value of EBIT the better the company is performing. However, as we observed with net income, EBIT is negative despite an increase in total revenue since 2013. This indicates that controllable expenses within the company have grown in the past year. The growth of controllable expenses is greater than the growth in sales. This is also of concern since the industry is able to generate a positive EBIT. Starbucks was also able to generate a positive EBIT in 2014 despite its negative EBIT in 2013.

EBIT Percentage to Sales

Another way to analyze EBIT is to compare it to sales. **EBIT percentage to sales** indicates how efficient the company is at controlling expenses in relation to revenue. The formula is shown below.

$$\text{EBIT Percentage to Sales} = \frac{\text{EBIT}}{\text{Sales Revenue}}$$

It is possible for a company to show an increase in EBIT from one year to the next yet have a lower EBIT percentage to sales. If the EBIT percentage to sales decreases over time, this indicates the company is becoming less efficient. If the EBIT percentage to sales increases over time, then the company is becoming more efficient at controlling its expenses.

As we look at Second Cup, we know its EBIT is negative, so its EBIT percentage to sales will also be negative. The calculations for both years is shown in Figure 11.16.

	2014	2013
EBIT	($30,897)	($7,122)
Total Revenue	$28,172	$23,134
EBIT Percentage to Sales	**−110%**	**−31%**
Industry Average	**16%**	**14%**

FIGURE 11.16

The EBIT percentage to sales shows a large decrease from one year to the next. This likely means that the business has become less efficient during the period, and further analysis needs to be done to find out which expenses are contributing to the decline. On the income statement, there are significant increases in restructuring charges, provisions for cafe closures and impairment charges. These may indicate the company has made significant changes to its organization during the recent year to bring improvements in coming years. It could also mean that the company is losing ground to competitors. An examination of the notes that accompany the financial statements would provide more insight.

If the company successfully makes improvements to its organization, it should be able to return to the industry average of a positive EBIT percentage to sales. Starbucks' EBIT percentage to sales was negative in 2013, but it was able to return to a positive EBIT percentage to sales of 19% in 2014.

Return on Equity (ROE)

Return on equity (ROE) is a measure of what the owners are getting out of their investment in the company. It is often the most important ratio for investors because it has a large impact on the value of an investment. This ratio requires information from both the balance sheet and income statement to be calculated. The formula is shown below.

$$\text{Return on Equity} = \frac{\text{Net Income}}{\text{Average Shareholders' Equity}}$$

The return on equity formula assumes that there is no preferred share equity included in shareholders' equity. If preferred equity exists, the formula would be as follows:

Return on Equity = (Net Income − Preferred Dividends) ÷ Average Common Shareholders' Equity

Notice that the calculation requires average shareholders' equity. Whenever a ratio is calculated that uses some information from the balance and some from the income statement, the balance sheet information is always averaged. This is because the balance sheet represents a snapshot in time while the income statement represents an entire accounting period. By averaging the balance sheet accounts, we are simulating a figure that covers the same period of time as the income statement. This makes the ratio more comparable and reliable.

Although not shown in Figure 11.8, we need to know the balance of shareholders' equity at December 29, 2012 to calculate the average shareholders' equity for 2013. Assume that the balance on this date was $56,700. (All numbers presented for Second Cup in this chapter are in thousands.) Then, the calculations of ROE for Second Cup in 2013 and 2014 are shown in Figure 11.17.

	2014	2013
Net Income (Loss)	($27,032)	($7,369)
Average Shareholders' Equity[1]	$35,479	$51,332
Return on Equity	−76%	−14%
Industry Average	13%	16%

(1) Average Shareholders' Equity for 2013: ($56,700 + $45,964) ÷ 2 = $51,332
Average Shareholders' Equity for 2014: ($45,964 + $24,994) ÷ 2 = $35,479

FIGURE 11.17

A high ROE is desirable because it means that investors made a good decision to invest in the company. Shareholders like to see a return that is as good as or better than they could have received by investing elsewhere. A negative ROE indicates that shareholders actually lost money on their investments over the year. It deters investors from investing more money because of the risk of losing it. Second Cup's return on equity has gone from bad to worse recently while other companies in the same industry have been able to generate a positive return for their shareholders. In comparison, Starbucks significantly improved from a lower-than-industry-average ROE of 0.2% in 2013 to a higher-than-industry-average ROE of 42% in 2014. Based on its high ROE in 2014, Starbucks would provide a more attractive investment than Second Cup.

IN THE REAL WORLD

 One of the most important assessments business owners can make is to know if they are getting a decent return on their investment. How is this done and how do they know if they are getting their money's worth out of the business?

Any determination of return on investment revolves around shareholders' equity. In other words, how much cash would the owners have left if they sold all the assets of the business and paid off all their debt? Given that this is a hypothetical question, and that the owners do not have to sell everything to assess the return on investment, there are other ways of assessing the value of the investment in the business.

For example, the owners could ask themselves another practical question: Should we keep our money in the business, or put it elsewhere? Safe investments such as fixed deposit accounts come with relatively lower returns on investment. Investing in a friend's new business comes with a potentially much larger return on investment—but also with greater risk.

In fact, a general rule of thumb can be applied to assessing return on investment associated with certain levels of risk. Generally speaking, investments in publicly traded companies come with the expectation of a return ranging from 15%–25%. Alternatively, the rate of return associated with private companies is expected to be much higher. In fact, it is not unusual to expect a rate of return of 100% or more for an investment in a small private company.

As with most things in life, everything comes at a price. With return on investment, the price can be a matter of risk. If owners want a better return, they must have a greater tolerance for risk.

Return on Assets (ROA)

Return on assets (ROA) essentially provides an assessment of what the company does with what it has; it measures every dollar earned against each dollar's worth of assets. A business invests in assets for the purpose of generating sales and making a profit. ROA is a measure of how effective the investment in assets is. Although assessing ROA depends on the type of business being analyzed, a higher ROA number is generally considered better than a lower one. A higher ratio means that the business is earning more money on its investment in assets.

$$\text{Return on Assets} = \frac{\text{Net Income}}{\text{Average Total Assets}}$$

Now calculate ROA for Second Cup. The net income (loss) comes from the income statement. The total asset figures are found on the balance sheet. Assume that the balance of total assets at the year-end in 2012 was $96,500. The calculation is shown in Figure 11.18.

	2014	2013
Net Income (Loss)	($27,032)	($7,369)
Average Total Assets[1]	$65,395	$86,920
Return on Assets	**−41%**	**−8%**
Industry Average	**12%**	**11%**

(1)   Average Total Assets for 2013: ($77,340 + $96,500) ÷ 2 = $86,920
      Average Total Assets for 2014: ($53,449 + $77,340) ÷ 2 = $65,395

FIGURE 11.18

As expected, since the company has losses in both years, the return on assets is negative. There was a significant drop in the ROA in 2014. What the ROA means is that in 2013, Second Cup lost $0.08 for every $1 invested in assets. In 2014, this loss increased to $0.41 for every $1 invested in assets. Various factors might explain the the bigger loss per $1 invested in assets in 2014 including selling long-term assets (which would result in a smaller denominator in the ROA formula), or an increase in costs of goods sold or other expenses. Ultimately, if resources are properly allocated and assets are efficiently used, ROA should increase. The industry and Starbucks are showing a positive return on their investments in assets.

As a general rule, a business in an industry with a low ROA usually indicates the business is capital-intensive or asset-heavy. This means that the business is investing a considerable amount in assets relative to profits. Industries that tend to display low ROA figures include manufacturers and large transportation companies such as railroads. Alternatively, a business in an industry with a high ROA is less capital-intensive or asset-heavy. Examples include professional practices, software companies and retailers.

Asset Turnover

Another way to assess how well business assets are being utilized is to test how much revenue is generated for every dollar of assets. This is calculated by dividing revenue by average total assets.

$$\text{Asset Turnover} = \frac{\text{Sales Revenue}}{\text{Average Total Assets}}$$

Asset turnover measures the ability of a company to generate sales revenue from asset investments—the higher the number, the better. Figure 11.19 shows the asset turnover for Second Cup.

	2014	2013
Total Revenue	$28,172	$27,188
Average Total Assets[(1)]	$65,395	$86,920
Asset Turnover	**0.43 times**	**0.31 times**
Industry Average	**0.39 times**	**0.34 times**

(1) Average Total Assets for 2013: ($77,340 + $96,500) ÷ 2 = $86,920
Average Total Assets for 2014: ($53,449 + $77,340) ÷ 2 = $65,395

FIGURE 11.19

In 2014, the business generated $0.43 of revenue for every dollar tied up in assets. This is an increase from the previous year. This indicates the business has become more efficient at generating revenue with its assets. Since we know the amount of assets decreased between the two years, it means the business is "selling more with less."

When compared to the industry, Second Cup performed better than the industry in 2014. It is generating more revenue for every dollar invested in assets. However, when compared to Starbucks, Second Cup performed a lot worse in both years. Starbucks was able to generate $1.51 and $1.48 of revenue for every dollar tied up in assets in 2013 and 2014, respectively. Starbucks' asset turnover figures for both 2013 and 2014 more than doubled those of Second Cup's and the industry's.

The DuPont Framework

Return on equity is one of the most important profitability ratios frequently reviewed by investors. In this chapter, we learned that the ratio is calculated using the following equation

$$\text{ROE} = \frac{\text{Net Income}}{\text{Average Shareholders' Equity}}$$

Return on equity measures the amount of return earned in comparison to the resources the owners provide. In general, the higher the ROE, the more efficient a company is in using its owners' resources.

Suppose that you are examining the return on equity ratio for a company in two consecutive years. If the ratio remains the same from the first to second year, it may be easy to conclude that the company performed equally well in both years. However, the manner in which the company generated the ROE can be drastically different and would be of interest to shareholders.

Looking back to the concepts taught in this course, shareholders' equity is equal to assets minus liabilities (denominator of ROE). Based on the ROE equation, this indicates that an increase in

ROE can be caused by an increase in net income, a decrease in assets, or an increase in liabilities. If a company's ROE increases or decreases, examining ROE in its simplest form does not provide information on what caused ROE to change.

The **DuPont Framework** resolves this problem by breaking the ROE equation into three components to provide more information on where the changes in ROE are coming from. The ROE equation can be expanded and rearranged to formulate the DuPont formula as shown below.

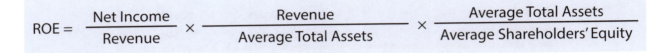

$$ROE = \frac{\text{Net Income}}{\text{Revenue}} \times \frac{\text{Revenue}}{\text{Average Total Assets}} \times \frac{\text{Average Total Assets}}{\text{Average Shareholders' Equity}}$$

The formulation of this equation from ROE is mainly mathematical and easy to understand. It starts with the basic ROE equation.

$$ROE = \frac{\text{Net Income}}{\text{Average Shareholders' Equity}}$$

Then apply two common multipliers (revenue and average total assets) to both numerator and denominator.

Apply the first common multiplier.

$$ROE = \frac{\text{Net Income}}{\text{Average Shareholders' Equity}} \times \frac{\text{Revenue}}{\text{Revenue}}$$

$$= \frac{\text{Net Income}}{\text{Revenue}} \times \frac{\text{Revenue}}{\text{Average Shareholders' Equity}}$$

Apply the second common multiplier.

$$ROE = \frac{\text{Net Income}}{\text{Revenue}} \times \frac{\text{Revenue}}{\text{Average Shareholders' Equity}} \times \frac{\text{Average Total Assets}}{\text{Average Total Assets}}$$

Finally, the equation can be rearranged to formulate the DuPont framework.

$$ROE = \frac{\text{Net Income}}{\text{Revenue}} \times \frac{\text{Revenue}}{\text{Average Total Assets}} \times \frac{\text{Average Total Assets}}{\text{Average Shareholders' Equity}}$$

The DuPont framework provides important insight to ROE by connecting the following three measurements.

1. Net Profit Margin (Net Income ÷ Revenue): This measures operating efficiency
2. Asset Turnover Ratio (Revenue ÷ Average Total Assets): This measures asset usage efficiency
3. Total assets as a percentage of shareholders' equity (Average Total Assets ÷ Average Shareholders' Equity): This measures how much a company relies on the use of equity vs. debt. In financial accounting, this ratio is called an equity multiplier.

Substituting the above three measurements, ROE can be represented as:

$$\text{ROE} = \text{Net Profit Margin} \times \text{Asset Turnover Ratio} \times \text{Equity Multiplier}$$

Based on this DuPont framework, an increase in ROE can be caused by an increase in one of the three components or a combination of all components. Recall that an increase in net profit margin and total assets turnover is generally a positive sign for a company. However, an increase in equity multiplier could mean that a company is using more debt (i.e. hence lower shareholders' equity) to finance its business. While this could represent an efficient use of debt to generate returns, it also makes the business riskier.

Return to the Second Cup financial statements. Recall that ROE decreased from –14% in 2013 to –76% in 2014. Using the values calculated earlier in the chapter, we can calculate the components of ROE for the two years as follows:

	2014	2013
Net Profit Margin	–96%	–27%
Asset Turnover	0.43	0.31
Equity Multiplier	1.84	1.69

FIGURE 11.20

The net profit margins and asset turnover ratios were taken from Figure 11.14 and Figure 11.19 respectively. The equity multiplier was calculated using average total assets (from Figure 11.19) divided by average shareholders' equity (from Figure 11.17).

For Second Cup, ROE in 2014 dropped of 62 percentage points from 2013. This is primarily caused by the large decrease in the net profit margin (a drop of 69 percentage points). Asset turnover improved, which lessened the impact of the poor profit margin on ROE. The increase in the equity multiplier also lessened the impact of the poor profit margin. The decline in net profit margin suggests that the company was not able to properly control expenses in 2014. The increase in the equity multiplier suggests that the company was relying more on debt and less on equity (as a percentage) in 2014 to finance its assets. Starbucks' situation was the opposite. In 2014, Starbucks' ROE increased significantly from 0.2% to 42% due primarily to the large increase in the net profit margin (from 0.1% in 2013 to 13% in 2014).

The DuPont framework demonstrates that examining ROE as a single number is not enough to make sound business decisions. Even if a company's ROE stays the same from year to year, applying the DuPont framework can provide useful insights. If a company's net profit margin and total assets turnover have increased from year 1 to year 2 but the equity multiplier has decreased, this is generally a good indicator although the overall ROE may remain the same. On the other hand, if the company's net profit margin and total assets turnover have decreased from year 1 to year 2 but equity multiplier has increased significantly, this most likely is not a favourable sign.

Operations Management and Leverage Analysis

Operations management refers to the ability of a company to manage its assets such as inventory and accounts receivable. Accounts receivable may be a large source of cash for a company, but it is not worth anything if it cannot be collected. As well, inventory is converted into cash by selling it, but it must be managed properly to ensure that it can be sold in a timely manner. To determine whether inventory is being managed properly, there are two ratios that can be calculated.

Inventory Turnover Ratio

Management is often concerned with the company's ability to sell, or "turn over," inventory. In industries that deal with food and beverage sales, it is especially important because of the short product life of the inventory. Throwing away expired products is just like throwing away cash. The inventory turnover ratio is calculated as shown below.

$$\text{Inventory Turnover Ratio} = \frac{\text{Cost of Goods Sold}}{\text{Average Inventory}}$$

The **inventory turnover ratio** represents the number of times that the company sold its entire inventory. The industry the company is in determines the desirable value for this ratio. For example, hardware stores may only turn over inventory once or twice per year because the goods do not expire or become obsolete very quickly. The fashion industry may turn over inventory four times per year because fashion trends tend to change quickly and with the seasons. Second Cup's inventory turnover ratio is calculated in Figure 11.21. Assume that the inventory balance at December 29, 2012 was $137,000.

	2014	2013
Cost of Gods Sold	$7,679	$4,054
Average Inventory[(1)]	$172	$130
Inventory Turnover	**44.6**	**31.2**
Industry Average	**25.8**	**23.1**

(1)   Average Inventory for 2013: ($123 + $137) ÷ 2 = $130
       Average Inventory for 2014: ($221 + $123) ÷ 2 = $172

FIGURE 11.21

Second Cup's high inventory turnover ratio indicates that it has very little wastage, which is important in the food and beverage industry. This is a sign of good inventory management. Also, Second Cup has a much better inventory turnover than the industry and Starbucks, meaning it is managing its inventory better than competitors. To get a better understanding of what this ratio means, we can also calculate the inventory days on hand.

Inventory Days on Hand

This ratio states the same thing as the inventory turnover ratio but in a different way. **Inventory days on hand** is equal to the average number of days that it took to turn over inventory during the year. Some users prefer to use this ratio because they are familiar with working in units such as days and months. The formula is shown below.

$$\text{Inventory Days on Hand} = \frac{\text{Average Inventory}}{\text{Cost of Goods Sold}} \times 365$$

This ratio converts the number of times inventory is turned over into the average number of days it took to turn over inventory. For example, a company that sells its entire inventory twice a year would have an inventory turnover ratio of 2 and an inventory days on hand of 182.5 days. The ratio is calculated for Second Cup in Figure 11.22.

	2014	2013
Average Inventory	$172	$130
Cost of Goods Sold	$7,679	$4,054
Days in a year	× 365	× 365
Inventory Days on Hand	8.2	11.7
Industry Average	14.1	15.8

FIGURE 11.22

The lower the result, the faster inventory is sold on average. This means that on average it took just over a week for Second Cup to sell the inventory on hand in 2014 , compared to about two months for Starbucks. Second Cup likely purchased new inventory once a week to keep its products fresh. This is a sign of good inventory management.

The other aspect of operating management is the ability to collect on its bills. Sales have to result in cash. If customers are buying a product or service on credit, they have to pay within a reasonable amount of time to ensure proper cash flow and good financial health for the business. To determine whether accounts receivable is being managed properly, there are two ratios that can be calculated.

Days-Sales-Outstanding (DSO)

Days-Sales-Outstanding (DSO) measures the average number of days that a company takes to collect its receivables. The formula for DSO is as follows.

$$\text{Days-Sales-Outstanding} = \frac{\text{Average Accounts Receivable}}{\text{Net Credit Sales}} \times 365$$

Second Cup's accounts receivable primarily comprise of royalty fees owed from franchisees. From an external point of view, we do not know what portion of the total revenue of Second Cup is cash versus credit. For our discussion, we will assume that all Second Cup branches are owned by franchisees and thus all revenue is credit. The DSO provides an indication of how many days it takes for customers to pay their bills. This number is important because late payments can cost a business lost interest from cash deposits in a bank, or additional administration costs required to collect payments from customers.

The calculation of DSO for Second Cup is shown in Figure 11.23. Assume that the accounts receivable balance at the year-end in 2012 was $4,263.

	2014	2013
Average Accounts Receivable[1]	$4,197	$4,316
Net Credit Sales (Total Revenue)	$28,172	$27,188
Number of Days in the year	× 365	× 365
Days-Sales-Outstanding	**54 days**	**58 days**
Industry Average	**55 days**	**57 days**

(1)   Average Accounts Receivable for 2013: ($4,368 + $4,263) ÷ 2 = $4,316
      Average Accounts Receivable for 2014: ($4,026 + $4,368) ÷ 2 = $4,197

FIGURE 11.23

As you can see, the business is improving its ability to collect from customers. The DSO decreased from 58 days in 2013, to below 54 days in 2014. This is also in line with the industry values and lower than Starbucks' DSO (over 60 days for both 2013 and 2014). Second Cup is performing as well as the industry and better than Starbucks in collecting from customers. If the DSO increased, it might be an indication of disputes with customers, a slowdown in sales resulting in slower payments to the company, or problems in the billing and credit function of the company. None of these items would be considered favourably by owners, investors or analysts.

However, there are some cautionary notes to keep in mind related to the DSO. First, the revenue figure used in the ratio should exclude all cash sales, since only sales on account (credit sales) are of concern, relative to collecting customer payments. Second, outliers in sales data such as sales to a major customer, who was given a different credit policy from other customers, should be kept out of the total revenue figure used to calculate DSO, because they can skew the ratio. While data such as Starbucks' and Second Cup's credit sales as a percentage of total sales and credit policies to franchisees are not available on the public financial statements, Second Cup's and Starbucks' management should track and analyze their credit sales and receivables data internally to be able to manage its DSO.

Accounts Receivable Turnover (ART)

The **accounts receivable turnover ratio (ART)** is similar to DSO. It involves dividing a company's net credit sales by the average amount of accounts receivable.

$$\text{Accounts Receivable Turnover} = \frac{\text{Net Credit Sales}}{\text{Average Accounts Receivable}}$$

The calculation for Second Cup is shown in Figure 11.24.

	2014	2013
Net Credit Sales (Total Revenue)	$28,172	$27,188
Average Accounts Receivable	$4,197	$4,316
Accounts Receivable Turnover	**6.7 times**	**6.3 times**
Industry Average	**6.6 times**	**6.4 times**

FIGURE 11.24

A higher ratio indicates a greater ability to convert accounts receivable into cash. If a business turns over its receivables 12 times per year, it would mean that it is collecting the average balance of receivables every month. In Second Cup's case, an accounts receivable turnover of slightly over six times per year means that it collected receivables almost every two months on average in 2013 and 2014. By the same token, Starbucks' accounts receivable turnover of almost six means that it takes slightly longer than two months on average to collect its receivables.

Leverage Analysis

There are two ways to finance a business: debt and equity. Debts are the liabilities of the business, such as bank loans and accounts payable. Equity is generated by selling shares and generating profits. **Leverage** relates to the amount of debt and risk the company has. Companies often take on debt to finance the purchase of large assets. They then use these assets to expand operations and generate sales. However, there is usually a high cost of debt in the form of interest expense, which is where the risk comes in. A company must be able to increase profits by more than the interest expense to benefit the shareholders. One measure of leverage is the debt-to-equity ratio.

Debt-to-Equity Ratio (D/E)

The **debt-to-equity ratio (D/E)** is used to assess the balance of debt and equity in a business. The debt-to-equity ratio is calculated as shown below.

$$\text{Debt-to-Equity Ratio} = \frac{\text{Total Liabilities}}{\text{Total Shareholders' Equity}}$$

It is not healthy for a business to borrow too much relative to what it is worth. This is because there is a cost of debt in the form of interest. The industry a business is in usually influences how much should be borrowed. For example, capital-intensive industries such as auto manufacturers have higher

WORTH REPEATING

Acquiring loans or paying back loan principals has no effect on equity. However, paying interest on a loan has a negative effect on equity.

debt-to-equity ratios than software developers. Second Cup's debt-to-equity ratios for the years 2013 and 2014 are calculated in Figure 11.25. The industry averages are also shown for comparison purposes.

	2014	2013
Total Liabilities	$28,455	$31,376
Shareholders' Equity	$24,994	$45,964
Debt-to-Equity Ratio	1.14	0.68
Industry Average	2.08	2.24

FIGURE 11.25

As you can see, the debt-to-equity ratio increased from 2013 to 2014 and has risen above 1. This is not a good sign, especially considering the significant decrease in shareholders' equity. It implies that Second Cup has suffered a loss and was unable to pay off much debt during the year. While Second Cup's debt-to-equity ratios in both 2013 and 2014 are lower than the industry average, its debt-to-equity ratio is higher than that of Starbucks' (1.04 in 2014).

There are a few ways a business can improve the debt-to-equity ratio. First, making more profit might do the trick (although it is easier said than done), since it directly results in an increase to shareholders' equity. Second, the business might consider issuing more shares in exchange for cash.

Interest Coverage Ratio

There is a cost to borrowing money. We can use the **interest coverage ratio** to determine whether the company is able to cover the interest charged on its debt. This ratio divides EBIT by interest expense. This ratio measures the extent to which earnings before interest and taxes cover the interest payments that are to be made by the business. The formula is shown below.

$$\text{Interest Coverage Ratio} = \frac{\text{EBIT}}{\text{Interest Expense}}$$

For example, an interest coverage ratio of only 1 time would mean that the business has just enough earnings (before interest and tax expenses are deducted) to cover the amount of interest paid during the year.

For Second Cup, the calculation of the interest coverage ratio is shown in Figure 11.26. Again, because the company has a negative EBIT, we know it is not making enough to cover interest expense. The EBIT value was calculated in Figure 11.15.

	2014	2013
EBIT	($30,897)	($7,122)
Interest and Financing Expense	$478	$516
Interest Coverage Ratio	**−65 times**	**−14 times**
Industry Average	**6 times**	**5 times**

FIGURE 11.26

Although the actual amount of interest to be paid in 2014 has decreased from the previous year, the significantly lower EBIT means the company is in even worse shape when it comes to being able to cover the interest it owes. This would be a key ratio that a lender would be interested in when making a decision to lend money to a company. A poor interest coverage ratio such as shown by Second Cup may mean the company will have difficulty securing loans in the future. While Starbucks also had a negative interest coverage ratio in 2013, its performance later improved significantly in this area. In 2014, Starbucks' interest coverage ratio increased to 48 times, which means that Starbucks earned more than enough in 2014 to cover its interest expense.

Debt-to-Assets Ratio

The **debt-to-assets** ratio shows how much debt a company has as a percentage of assets.

$$\text{Debt-to-Assets Ratio} \ = \ \frac{\text{Total Liabilities}}{\text{Total Assets}}$$

The calculation for Second Cup is shown in Figure 11.27.

	2014	2013
Total Liabilities	$28,455	$31,376
Total Assets	$53,449	$77,340
Debt-to-Assets Ratio	53%	41%
Industry Average	42%	40%

FIGURE 11.27

As the debt-to-assets ratio increases, this indicates that more debt is being used to finance the business relative to its assets. This increases the risk the company takes on. Debt accrues interest and interest must be paid. Failure to pay interest or debt can lead to bankruptcy in worst-case scenarios.

Different industries have different tolerances for the amount of debt the business should incur. In 2013, Second Cup had an acceptable debt-to-assets ratio; however, the ratio for 2014 is significantly higher than the industry average and slightly higher than that of Starbucks'.

Capital Market Performance Analysis

In addition to calculating financial ratios for internal measurements, some ratios are used by investors to determine whether a public corporation's shares are a desirable purchase. The ratios that measure the stock performance of a public corporation were covered in a previous chapter and are briefly reviewed here.

Shares that are publicly traded on the stock markets can experience price changes daily, hourly or even by the minute. The changes in market value affect investors as they buy and sell shares, but the corporation does not record any of these changes in its books.

Second Cup does not have any preferred shares; however, its financial statement notes show that it had 9,903,045 common shares outstanding at the year-end of 2013. Toward the end of 2014, the company issued an additional 2,927,900 common shares and ended 2014 with 12,830,945 common shares outstanding.

Book Value per Common Share

Book value per common share represents the theoretical value of a common share based on a shareholder's claim to the company assets. This assumes that all assets would be sold for their book value and all liabilities would be paid off. However, book value will not necessarily match the market value of the shares.

The calculation of book value per share is shown below.

$$\text{Book Value per Share} = \frac{\text{Shareholders' Equity} - \text{Preferred Equity}}{\text{Number of Common Shares Outstanding}}$$

Note that preferred equity would include preferred dividends if there are any preferred dividends outstanding. The formula calculates the amount of money that a holder of each common share would receive if all the company's assets were immediately liquidated.

For Second Cup, the book value per share at the end of 2014 is calculated below.

$$\text{Book Value per Share} = \frac{\$24,994,000}{12,830,945}$$

$$= \$1.95$$

This means that Second Cup common shareholders could expect to receive about $1.95 per share if the company decided to liquidate its assets and pay all its debts. In comparison, Starbucks common shareholders could expect to receive about $7 per share if the company liquidates.

Dividend Payout Ratio

Since dividends, or at least the potential for dividends, must form part of an analysis of a company, the investing community developed a ratio to assess just how much in dividends a corporation is paying out to shareholders. This is called the **dividend payout ratio** and calculates dividends paid as a percentage of net income. The basic formula is as follows.

$$\text{Dividend Payout Ratio} = \frac{\text{Dividends Paid in a Year}}{\text{Net Income}}$$

Second Cup paid $1,684 in dividends in 2014. The calculation of the dividend payout ratio is shown below.

$$\text{Dividend Payout Ratio} = \frac{\$1,684}{\$(27,032)}$$

$$= -6.2\%$$

Second Cup paid dividends in 2014, even though the company generated a net loss. This may have been done to keep investors confident even though Second Cup suffered a loss as it restructured the organization. A negative payout ratio should serve a warning to investors and shareholders, since it may mean the company had to raise additional cash just to pay the dividends. Starbucks performed better than Second Cup in this area, having positive payout ratios for both 2013 and 2014.

Earnings per Share (EPS)

Earnings per share (EPS) is a key corporate measure for investors. This measures how much profit is earned for each outstanding share. The formula for earnings per share is shown below.

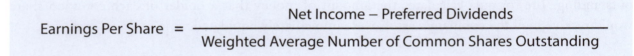

$$\text{Earnings Per Share} = \frac{\text{Net Income} - \text{Preferred Dividends}}{\text{Weighted Average Number of Common Shares Outstanding}}$$

Second Cup's financial statements present the weighted average number of common shares for 2014 as 10,151,716. We will use this number in our calculation.

$$\text{Earnings Per Share} = \frac{-\$27,032,000}{10,151,716}$$

$$= -\$2.66$$

Second Cup had a loss per share of $2.66, as shown on its statement of comprehensive income. Starbucks had a positive earnings per share of $2.75 in 2014, making it more attractive for investors compared to Second Cup.

We learned in a previous chapter how to calculate the weighted average number of common shares; however, companies may use slightly different variations in their calculation. Thus, since Second Cup provided its weighted number of common shares, we used that in our calculation. If we had to calculate the weighted number based on the information given, we might end up with a slightly different weighted average and a different EPS.

Price-Earnings Ratio

Another ratio commonly used by stockholders to evaluate their investment in a corporation is the **price-earnings ratio (P/E ratio),** which provides the investor with a measurement of share price to actual earnings of the corporation. It is used as an indicator of company growth and risk. It can be used as an indicator to buy, sell or hold shares. The formula is shown below.

$$P/E \text{ Ratio} = \frac{\text{Market Price per Share}}{\text{Earnings Per Share}}$$

Second Cup had a year end of December 27, 2014. On that date, the market value of its shares was $3.05 per share. Thus, the price-earnings ratio for Second Cup is calculated below.

$$\text{Price-Earnings Ratio} = \frac{\$3.05}{-\$2.66}$$

$$= -1.15$$

Because of the loss in 2014, the price-earnings ratio is negative. In the investment community, a negative P/E ratio is not informative and is usually reported as not applicable. Investors should be aware, however, that this company is currently losing money per share.

When a company has a positive P/E ratio, the ratio indicates the shares are selling for a multiple of its earnings. For example, Starbucks' P/E ratio of 27.11 in 2014 indicates a company's shares on the market are selling 27.11 times its EPS. The P/E ratio can be used when comparing shares between companies, although the comparison should be done with companies in the same industry. This will allow for a more even and fair comparison.

We have just examined many different ratios. Examining only one ratio will not provide a complete picture of the financial status of a company. Many values are needed to form a proper picture. Figure 11.28 summarizes the formulas used to determine different valuations and indicates whether a higher or lower value is desirable for each ratio.

Ratio	Formula	Ideal Value
Working Capital	Current Assets – Current Liabilities	Higher
Current Ratio	$\dfrac{\text{Current Assets}}{\text{Current Liabilities}}$	Higher
Quick Ratio	$\dfrac{\text{Cash + Short-Term Investments + Accounts Receivable}}{\text{Current Liabilities}}$	Higher
Gross Profit Margin	$\dfrac{\text{Gross Profit}}{\text{Sales Revenue}}$	Higher
Net Profit Margin	$\dfrac{\text{Net Income}}{\text{Sales Revenue}}$	Higher
EBIT	Net Income + Interest + Tax	Higher

Ratio	Formula	Ideal Value
EBIT Percentage to Sales	$\dfrac{EBIT}{Sales\ Revenue}$	Higher
Return on Equity	$\dfrac{Net\ Income}{Average\ Shareholders'\ Equity}$	Higher
Return on Assets	$\dfrac{Net\ Income}{Average\ Total\ Assets}$	Higher
Asset Turnover	$\dfrac{Sales\ Revenue}{Average\ Total\ Assets}$	Higher
Inventory Turnover Ratio	$\dfrac{Cost\ of\ Goods\ Sold}{Average\ Inventory}$	Higher
Inventory Days on Hand	$\dfrac{Average\ Inventory}{Cost\ of\ Goods\ Sold} \times 365$	Lower
Days-Sales-Outstanding	$\dfrac{Average\ Accounts\ Receivable}{Net\ Credit\ Sales} \times 365$	Lower
Accounts Receivable Turnover Ratio	$\dfrac{Net\ Credit\ Sales}{Average\ Accounts\ Receivable}$	Higher
Debt-to-Equity Ratio	$\dfrac{Total\ Liabilities}{Total\ Shareholder's\ Equity}$	Lower
Interest Coverage Ratio	$\dfrac{EBIT}{Interest\ Expense}$	Higher
Debt-to-Assets Ratio	$\dfrac{Total\ Liabilities}{Total\ Assets}$	Lower
Book Value per Share	$\dfrac{Shareholders'\ Equity - Preferred\ Equity}{Number\ of\ Common\ Shares\ Outstanding}$	Higher
Dividend Payout Ratio	$\dfrac{Dividends\ Paid\ in\ a\ Year}{Net\ Income}$	Higher
Earnings Per Share	$\dfrac{Net\ Income - Preferred\ Dividends}{Weighted\ Average\ Number\ of\ Common\ Shares\ Outstanding}$	Higher
Price-Earnings Ratio	$\dfrac{Market\ Price\ per\ Share}{Earnings\ per\ Share}$	Higher

FIGURE 11.28

Keep in mind that an extremely high value on a ratio where higher is better, or an extremely low value on a ratio where a lower value is better may not always be a good outcome. For example, if inventory days on hand is too low, it could indicate a situation where the company is always running out of products. Too high a quick ratio may indicate the company is not re-investing cash into the business to improve operations.

Limitations of Financial Analysis

Although financial analysis of a company's statements can be beneficial, there are several instances where the comparison will not be entirely accurate, or the information provided may not be useful.

For example, when comparing results between companies, different accounting policies can alter the values and make a comparison more difficult. Different accounting policies could include how inventory is valued (FIFO, weighted average or specific identification), and how property, plant and equipment is depreciated (straight-line, declining balance or unit of production). Also, a private corporation following ASPE may find it difficult to compare with competitors that are public companies and follow IFRS.

To work around this challenge, some may adjust the stated values in the financial statements for comparison purposes. The statements are not re-issued; this is simply an internal process for ratio comparison. By changing the account values based on similar accounting policies, a more accurate comparison can be made.

A second limitation arises from how IFRS presents certain information. Comprehensive income is not usually included in profitability or other ratios. In most cases, using net income instead of comprehensive income will not cause any significant change in the ratios presented. For example, a change in profitability ratio from 6.3% to 6.6% due to including comprehensive income will not affect decision makers. However, if comprehensive income makes up a large portion of the income reported by a company, it may wish to include comprehensive income in the ratio calculations so the relevant information is available to users.

Lastly, the economy and other external factors can affect how ratios are interpreted. For example, if a company is affected by a recession and reports a net loss for the year, comparing the current year to previous years really does not provide much useful information. A net loss can also cause other ratios to lose their meaning. Second Cup, for example, had a negative price earnings ratio and a negative dividend payout ratio, both of which do not mean much.

When a company experiences a loss, in which case some ratios and analysis are not productive, it may be more beneficial to examine what caused the loss. If the loss is due to an economic downturn, is the company able to survive the loss and is it positioned to bounce back once the economy recovers? If the loss is due to selling off a portion of the company and restructuring, does the company have a sound plan in place to maximize remaining resources to begin generating a profit again?

In Summary

Explain the importance of analyzing financial statements

⇨ There are different ways to analyze a company's financial statements, such as horizontal analysis, vertical analysis and financial ratio analysis. These analyses are tools that both external and internal financial statement users can utilize in making their decisions.

⇨ Internal users, such as managers and executives, analyze financial information to correct negative results and take advantage of positive results.

⇨ External users, such as investors and suppliers, analyze financial information to determine whether to invest money or extend credit terms.

Conduct horizontal and vertical analysis of financial statements

⇨ The comparative balance sheet is used to perform horizontal analysis because it compares information from one accounting period to another.

⇨ One way of conducting horizontal analysis is by calculating succeeding year's balance sheet items as a percentage of the base-year's number.

⇨ Another way of conducting horizontal analysis is by calculating the percentage change from a base-year to show percentage increase or decrease of each balance sheet item over time.

⇨ Vertical analysis is conducted by converting each separate line item in a financial statement into percentage of the base-figure within the specific year.

Calculate and apply liquidity ratios

⇨ A company's liquidity can be assessed using working capital, current ratio, and quick ratio.

⇨ Working capital is calculated by deducting current liabilities from current assets. A positive working capital indicates that the company has enough liquid assets to pay off its upcoming debts.

⇨ The current ratio is calculated by dividing current assets by current liabilities. It assesses business liquidity by determining the extent to which current assets can cover current debts.

⇨ The quick ratio is calculated the same way as the current ratio, except that the quick ratio includes only the assets that can be quickly converted to cash in the numerator (cash, short-term investments and accounts receivable). It assesses the ability of the business to meet its short-term debt obligations without relying on the liquidation of inventory.

Calculate and apply profitability ratios

⇨ A company's profitability can be assessed using gross profit margin, net profit margin, EBIT percentage to sales, return on equity (ROE) and return on assets (ROA).

⇨ Gross profit margin is calculated by dividing gross profit by sales revenue. It reveals the percentage of revenue left after cost of goods sold is deducted.

⇨ Net profit margin is calculated by dividing net income by sales revenue. It assesses a company's profitability after all expenses have been deducted.

⇨ EBIT percentage to sales is calculated by dividing EBIT by sales revenue. It assesses how efficient the company is at controlling expenses in relation to revenue.

⇨ Return on equity (ROE) is calculated by dividing net income by average shareholders' equity. It is a measure of what the shareholders are getting out of their investment in the company.

⇨ Return on assets (ROA) is calculated by dividing net income by average total assets. It measures every dollar earned against each dollar's worth of assets.

Calculate and apply operations management and leverage ratios

⇨ A company's operations management can be assessed using inventory turnover, inventory days on hand, accounts receivable turnover and days-sales-outstanding.

⇨ A company's leverage can be assessed using debt-to-equity ratio, interest coverage ratio and debt-to-assets ratio.

Calculate and apply capital market ratios

⇨ Public corporations can be analyzed to determine if they are desirable as investments.

⇨ Company performance can be assessed using book value per share, dividend payout ratio, earnings per share and the price-earnings ratio.

Identify the limitations of financial statement analysis

⇨ Ratio analysis may not present an accurate picture if the companies being compared use different accounting policies or if one follows ASPE while another follows IFRS.

⇨ Under IFRS, comprehensive income is usually not included in ratio analysis. Comprehensive income may need to be included if the amount is significant.

⇨ Economic situation, or losses, can cause some ratios to lose their meaning. A closer look at the cause of a loss may be beneficial in addition to ratio analysis.

Review Exercise

Use the financial statements for Basil's Bakery to perform a horizontal and vertical analysis and calculate the following financial ratios and figures for 2016.

- Working Capital
- Current Ratio
- Quick Ratio
- Gross Profit Margin
- Net Profit Margin
- EBIT
- EBIT Percentage to Sales
- Return on Equity
- Return on Assets
- Asset Turnover
- Inventory Turnover Ratio
- Inventory Days on Hand
- Days-Sales-Outstanding
- Accounts Receivable Turnover
- Debt-to-Equity Ratio
- Interest Coverage Ratio
- Debt-to-Assets Ratio

After calculating the ratios, comment on the result for each ratio. In your explanation, ensure you state whether or not the result is good along with the reasoning behind that determination.

Basil's Bakery
Balance Sheet
As at December 31, 2016 and 2015

	2016	2015
Assets		
Current Assets		
Cash	$1,605	$987
Accounts Receivable	1,175	573
Inventory	396	256
Other Current Assets	301	103
Total Current Assets	3,477	1,919
Property, Plant and Equipment	2,034	1,170
Total Assets	$5,511	$3,089
Liabilities and Equity		
Liabilities		
Current Liabilities	$1,474	$547
Non-Current Liabilities	104	58
Total Liabilities	1,578	605
Shareholders' Equity	3,933	2,484
Total Liabilities and Equity	$5,511	$3,089

*Note: The numbers in this financial statement are expressed in thousands of Canadian dollars.

Basil's Bakery
Income Statement
For the Year Ended December 31, 2016

Sales Revenue	$6,009
Cost of Goods Sold	2,928
Gross Profit	3,081
Operating Expenses	
Depreciation	108
Interest	518
Other Operating Expenses	723
Total Operating Expenses	1,349
Income from Operations	1,732
Investment Income	79
Operating Income before Tax	1,811
Income Tax	516
Net Income	$1,295

*Note: The numbers in this financial statement are expressed in thousands of Canadian dollars.

Assume all sales are credit sales.

In addition to the financial statements above, the following data is known. The bakery industry average for gross profit margin is 49.47% for 2016, and the industry average for net profit margin is 20.36% of the same time period.

In 2015, Basil's Bakery had a gross profit margin of 52.13% and a net profit margin of 21.95%.

See Appendix I for solutions.

Basil's Bakery Percentage Change and Vertical Analysis As at December 31, 2016				
	2016	2015	% Change	% of Base-Figure 2016
Cash	$1,605	$987		
Accounts Receivable	1,175	573		
Inventory	396	256		
Other Current Assets	301	103		
Total Current Assets	3,477	1,919		
Property, Plant and Equipment	2,034	1,170		
Total Assets	$5,511	$3,089		
Current Liabilities	$1,474	$547		
Non-Current Liabilities	104	58		
Total Liabilities	1,578	605		
Shareholders' Equity	3,933	2,484		
Total Liabilities and Equity	$5,511	$3,089		

_____

_____

_____

_____

_____

_____

_____

_____

_____

Financial Ratio or Figure	Calculation	Result
Working Capital		
Current Ratio		
Quick Ratio		
Gross Profit Margin		
Net Profit Margin		
EBIT		
EBIT Percentage to Sales		
Return on Equity		
Return on Assets		
Asset Turnover		
Inventory Turnover Ratio		
Inventory Days on Hand		
Days-Sales-Outstanding		
Accounts Receivable Turnover		
Debt-to-Equity Ratio		
Interest Coverage Ratio		
Debt-to-Assets Ratio		

_____

_____

_____

_____

_____

_____

Notes

Appendix I

REVIEW EXERCISE SOLUTIONS

Chapter 1 Review Exercise 1—Solutions

	Relevant components of the conceptual framework	Violation? (Y/N)	Explanation
a)	Relevance, completeness and comparability (faithful representation)	Y	Closure and environmental liabilities and expenses are important aspects of mining operations and thus are most likely relevant for financial statement users' decisions. Failure to disclose the information about them violates completeness and comparability characteristics because financial statement users would not have complete information to compare Golden Opportunity Mining's performance with other companies' performance. The understandability characteristic does not mean that the company is allowed to omit relevant information because it may lead to confusion by some users. It means that the company must provide all relevant information and try to explain it in a way that is understandable to financial statement users with a reasonable knowledge of accounting.
b)	Revenue recognition, relevance	Y	Recognizing revenue before the risks and reward of ownership are transferred to the customer is a violation of revenue recognition criteria. Even though the transaction amount of $3,000 is usually considered immaterial for the company, in this case it is material to determine the manager's bonus. Therefore, it is inappropriate and unethical for the manager to recognize revenue too early for his own benefit.
c)	Cost constraint	N	The company did not violate any principles by not listing all suppliers and the amounts due to each of them because doing so is not required by IFRS or ASPE. In addition, the company is under cost constraint because the benefits are lower than the costs of reporting such information.
d)	Expense recognition	Y	According to expense recognition principle, expenses must be recorded in the same period in which they were used to generate revenue. Because wages of temporary workers were incurred to generate revenue in 2016, wages expenses should be recorded in 2016, not 2017.
e)	Going concern	Y	Because the owner intends to close the restaurant soon, financial statements should not be prepared based on a going concern assumption. In other words, the company's balance sheet must show the value for which assets could be sold, not the value of assets based on historical cost net of accumulated depreciation. The owner's intention to close the restaurant must also be disclosed in the notes to the financial statements.

Chapter 1 Review Exercise 2—Solutions

Year	Costs Incurred	Percentage of Completion	Revenue Recognized	Gross Profit
2016	$150 million	20%	$175.0 million	$25.0 million
2017	225 million	30%	262.5 million	37.5 million
2018	300 million	40%	350.0 million	50.0 million
2019	75 million	10%	87.5 million	12.5 million
Total	$750 million	100%	$875.0 million	$125.0 million

Chapter 2 Review Exercise 1—Solutions

a)

JOURNAL			
Date	**Account Title and Explanation**	**Debit**	**Credit**
Dec 31	Cash	70,000	
	Accounts Receivable	280,000	
	Sales Revenue		350,000
	To record sales for the year		
Dec 31	Cash	250,000	
	Accounts Receivable		250,000
	To record collection of accounts for the year		
Dec 31	Allowance for Doubtful Accounts	1,500	
	Accounts Receivable		1,500
	To write-off uncollectible account		
Dec 31	Accounts Receivable	1,500	
	Allowance for Doubtful Accounts		1,500
	To reverse write-off of account		
Dec 31	Bad Debt Expense	2,500	
	Allowance for Doubtful Accounts		2,500
	To estimate bad debt for the year		

b)

Cash	
$70,000	
250,000	
$320,000	

Accounts Receivable	
Beg. Bal.: $35,000	$250,000
280,000	1,500
1,500	
$65,000	

Sales Revenue	
	$350,000

Allowance for Doubtful Accounts	
$1,500	Beg. Bal.: $2,500
	1,500
	2,500
	$5,000

Bad Debt Expense	
$2,500	

c)

Partial Balance Sheet	
Accounts Receivable	$65,000
Less: Allowance for Doubtful Accounts	5,000
Net Accounts Receivable	$60,000

d)

JOURNAL			
Date	Account Title	Debit	Credit
Dec 31	Bad Debt Expense	2,800	
	Allowance for Doubtful Accounts		2,800
	To estimate bad debt for the year		

If the company uses the income statement approach, it does not take the AFDA beginning balance into account when it records the journal entry to estimate bad debt. Simply calculate 1% of credit sales (350,000 x 0.8 = 280,000), which is equal to $2,800, and use this number in the journal entry.

Chapter 2 Review Exercise 2—Solutions

JOURNAL			
Date	**Account Title and Explanation**	**Debit**	**Credit**
Jun 30	Accounts Receivable—Tygart	5,000	
	Sales Revenue		5,000
	To record sale on credit		
Jul 31	Notes Receivable	5,000	
	Accounts Receivable—Tygart		5,000
	Converted accounts receivable to a note receivable		
Aug 31	Interest Receivable	25	
	Interest Revenue		25
	To record accrued interest revenue $5,000 x 6% × 1/12		
Dec 31	Cash	5,125	
	Interest Receivable		25
	Interest Revenue		100
	Notes Receivable		5,000
	Receipt of note principal and interest		
Dec 31	Accounts Receivable—Tygart	5,125	
	Interest Receivable		25
	Interest Revenue		100
	Notes Receivable		5,000
	To record a dishonoured note		

Chapter 3 Review Exercise 1—Solutions

a)

JOURNAL			
Date	Account Title and Explanation	Debit	Credit
Dec 31	Computer	3,000	
	Office Equipment	10,000	
	Cash		13,000
	Purchase of computer and office equipment for cash		

b) A reasonable life for a computer would be three years, and for equipment would be 5–10 years. Students will arrive at various numbers based on their research.

c) Because computers are upgraded quickly, a declining balance method would be appropriate with large amounts of depreciation early on. For office equipment, straight-line depreciation would be reasonable.

d)

Year	Cost	Depreciation	Accumulated Depreciation	Net Book Value
2017	3,000.00	1,000.00	1,000.00	2,000.00
2018	2,000.00	666.67	1,666.67	1,333.33
2019	1,333.33	444.44	2,111.11	888.89

Year	Cost	Depreciation	Accumulated Depreciation	Net Book Value
2017	10,000	2,000	2,000	8,000
2018	10,000	2,000	4,000	6,000
2019	10,000	2,000	6,000	4,000
2020	10,000	2,000	8,000	2,000
2021	10,000	2,000	10,000	0

e) The profit or loss on disposal of a long-term asset is the difference between the amount received, and the net book value of the asset at the time of disposal.

Chapter 3 Review Exercise 2—Solutions

JOURNAL			
Date	**Account Title and Explanation**	**Debit**	**Credit**
Jan 1	Assets	500,000	
	Goodwill	50,000	
	Liabilities		300,000
	Cash		250,000
	Purchase of assets and liabilities of		
	Regnier company		
Jan 1	Patents	50,000	
	Cash		50,000
	Purchase of patents for cash		
Jan 1	Trademarks	20,000	
	Cash		20,000
	Purchase of trademarks for cash		
Jan 30	Mineral Rights	100,000	
	Cash		100,000
	Purchase of mineral rights for cash		
Jun 30	Loss Due to Impairment of Goodwill	25,000	
	Goodwill		25,000
	To record impairment of goodwill		
Dec 31	Amortization Expense—Patents	6,250	
	Accumulated Amortization—Patents		6,250
	Amortization for the period $(50,000 \div 4) \times$		
	½ year		
Dec 31	Amortization Expense—Trademarks	1,244	
	Accumulated Amortization—Trademarks		1,244
	Amortization for the period $((20,000 - 100) \div$		
	$8) \times$ ½ year		
Dec 31	Inventory	2,000	
	Accumulated Depletion—Mineral Rights		2,000
	Depletion for the period $10,000 \times (100,000 \div$		
	500,000)		

Chapter 4 Review Exercise—Solutions

JOURNAL			
Date	**Account Title and Explanation**	**Debit**	**Credit**
Jan 15	Inventory	105,000	
	HST Recoverable	13,650	
	Accounts Payable		118,650
	Bought machine for resale		
Jan 30	Cash	241,820	
	HST Payable		27,820
	Sales Revenue		214,000
	Sold machine for cash		
Jan 30	Cost of Goods Sold	105,000	
	Inventory		105,000
	Record COGS for above sale		
Jan 30	Warranty Expense	20,000	
	Estimated Warranty Liability		20,000
	Accrued for estimated warranty costs		
Jan 30	HST Payable	27,820	
	HST Recoverable		13,650
	Cash		14,170
	Paid HST to the government		
Feb 15	Accounts Payable	118,650	
	Cash		118,650
	Paid for machine bought on account on Jan 15		
Mar 27	Estimated Warranty Liability	200	
	Inventory		200
	To record inventory for warranty work		

Chapter 5 Review Exercise—Solutions

a)

	Total	Zelma	Serena	Sharron
Cash Contribution	$30,000	$10,000	$10,000	$10,000
Contribution of Equipment	25,000	25,000		
Partner Contributions	$55,000	$35,000	$10,000	$10,000
Net Income	$25,000			
Salaries	−15,000	5,000	5,000	5,000
Equipment Rental	−3,000	3,000		
Interest	−1,500	500	500	500
Division of Income	5,500	1,834	1,833	1,833
Addition to Partners' Capital		$10,334	$7,333	$7,333
Capital Balance, December 31, 2016	$80,000	$45,334	$17,333	$17,333

b)

JOURNAL			
Date	**Account Title and Explanation**	**Debit**	**Credit**
Jan 1, 2016	Cash	30,000	
	Capital—Rapoza		10,000
	Capital—Dennen		10,000
	Capital—Throop		10,000
	To record set up of partnership		
Jan 1, 2016	Equipment	25,000	
	Capital—Rapoza		25,000
	To record contribution of equipment		
Dec 31, 2016	Income Summary	25,000	
	Capital—Rapoza		10,334
	Capital—Dennen		7,333
	Capital—Throop		7,333
	To adjust partners' capital accounts for		
	their share of net income		
Jan 2, 2017	Capital—Throop	17,333	
	Capital—Rapoza		10,000
	Capital—Dennen		7,333
	To record Throop's withdrawal from		
	partnership		

Chapter 6 Review Exercise - Solutions

a) Journal Entries

JOURNAL			
Date	**Account Title and Explanation**	**Debit**	**Credit**
Mar 3, 2016	Assets	2,000,000	
	Liabilities		1,250,000
	Common Shares		750,000
	Issued 20,000 common shares for net assets of partnership		
Apr 15, 2016	Cash	1,000,000	
	Common Shares		1,000,000
	Issued 20,000 common shares for cash		
Apr 30, 2016	Accounting Fee Expense	100,000	
	Preferred Shares		100,000
	Issued preferred shares in exchange for accounting services		
Nov 10, 2016	Equipment	250,000	
	Common Shares		250,000
	Issued common shares in exchange for equipment		
Nov 15, 2016	Stock Dividends	135,000	
	Stock Dividends Distributable		135,000
	Recorded declaration of stock dividends on common shares		
	(5% x 45,000 outstanding common shares= 2,250)		
	(2,250 X $60 = $135,000)		
Dec 2, 2016	Stock Dividends Distributable	135,000	
	Common Shares		135,000
	Recorded distribution of stock dividends		
Dec 15, 2016	Cash Dividends-Preferred	30,000	
	Cash Dividends-Common	150,000	
	Dividends Payable		180,000
	Declared dividend on common and preferred shares in 2016		
Dec 31, 2016	Income Summary	900,000	
	Retained Earnings		900,000
	Closed income summary account		

JOURNAL			
Date	**Account Title and Explanation**	**Debit**	**Credit**
Dec 31, 2016	Retained Earnings	315,000	
	Cash Dividends-Preferred		30,000
	Cash Dividends-Common		150,000
	Stock Dividends		135,000
	Closed dividend accounts		
Jan 30, 2017	No journal entry required on date of record		
Feb 28, 2017	Dividends Payable	180,000	
	Cash		180,000
	Recorded payment of dividends declared		

b) Calculation of Retained Earnings

Calculation of Retained Earnings		
December 31, 2016		
Retained Earnings, January 1, 2016		$0
Add: Net Income		900,000
Less: Cash Dividends-Preferred	30,000	
Cash Dividends-Common	150,000	
Stock Dividends	135,000	315,000
Retained Earnings, December 31, 2016		$585,000

c) Shareholders' Equity for 2016

CamphamelInc.		
Shareholders' Equity (Partial Balance Sheet)		
December 31, 2016		
Share Capital		
Preferred shares, $3, 200,000 authorized, 10,000 shares outstanding	$100,000	
Common shares,unlimited authorized, 47,250 shares outstanding	2,135,000	
Total Share Capital		$2,235,000
Retained Earnings		585,000
Total Shareholders'Equity		$2,820,000

Chapter 6 Appendix Review Exercise—Solutions

a)

JOURNAL			Page	
Date	**Account Title and Explanation**	**Debit**	**Credit**
Mar 10	Common Shares	75,000	
	Contributed Surplus		5,000
	Cash		70,000
	To record reacquiring and retiring of shares		
	[($1,000,000 ÷ 200,000) × 15,000]		

b)   Average cost of shares remains unchanged at $5. [($1,000,000-$75,000) ÷ 185,000 shares]

c)

JOURNAL			Page	
Date	**Account Title and Explanation**	**Debit**	**Credit**
Jun 15	Common Shares	75,000	
	Contributed Surplus	5,000	
	Retained Earnings	10,000	
	Cash		90,000
	To record reacquiring and retiring of shares		
	(15,000 shares x $5 per share)		

Chapter 7 Review Exercise—Solutions

a)

Shah Company		
Statement of Comprehensive Income		
For the Year Ended December 31, 2016		
Continuing Operations		
Sales Revenue		$710,000
Less: Sales Discounts		(15,000)
Net Sales		695,000
Cost of Goods Sold		(380,000)
Gross Profit		315,000
Less: Operating Expenses		
General Expenses		62,000
Operating Income		253,000
Less: Other Expenses		
Interest Expenses	$30,000	
Loss Due to Lawsuit	11,000	
Income Tax Expense	74,200	115,200
Income from Continuing Operations		137,800
Discontinued Operations		
Operating Income	35,000	
Less: Income Tax	(12,250)	22,750
Loss on Sale of Discontinued Operations	(40,000)	
Less: Income Tax Saving	14,000	(26,000)
Net Income		$134,550
Earnings Per Share		
Basic and Diluted		$3.24

b)

Shah Company Statement of Changes in Equity For the Year Ended December 31, 2016				
	Common Shares	Preferred Shares	Retained Earnings	Total Equity
Beginning Balance, January 1, 2016	$155,000	$50,000	$110,000	$315,000
Adjustment to Correct Error from 2015			(7,500)	(7,500)
Restated Balance	155,000	50,000	102,500	307,500
Comprehensive Income				
Net Income			134,550	134,550
Dividends to Shareholders				
Preferred and Common			(25,000)	(25,000)
Ending Balance	$155,000	$50,000	$212,050	$417,050

c)

Shah Company Statement of Financial Position (partial) As at December 31, 2016	
Shareholders' Equity	
Preferred shares, non-cumulative, $5,	
10,000 shares authorized, 1,000 shares issued	$50,000
Common Shares, unlimited shares authorized,	
40,000 shares issued and outstanding	155,000
Retained Earnings	212,050
Total Shareholders' Equity	$417,050

d)

$$EPS = \frac{\text{Net Income} - \text{Preferred Dividends}}{\text{Weighted Average Number of Common Shares Outstanding}}$$

Since Preferred Dividends = $5.00 × 1000 = $5,000 and assuming the same number of shares has been outstanding throughout the year

EPS = (134,550 − 5,000) ÷ 40,000 = $3.24

Chapter 8 Review Exercise 1—Solutions

Premium bond price = $2,000,000 + $142,968 = $2,142,968

a)

Semi-Annual Interest Period	A Interest Payment ($2,000,000 × 2%)	B Interest Expense (D × 1.75%)	C Premium Amortization (A – B)	D Bond Amortized Cost (D – C)
0				$2,142,968
1	$40,000	$37,502	$2,498	2,140,470
2	40,000	37,458	2,542	2,137,928
3	40,000	37,414	2,586	2,135,342
4	40,000	37,368	2,632	2,132,710
5	40,000	37,322	2,678	2,130,032
6	40,000	37,276	2,724	2,127,308
7	40,000	37,228	2,772	2,124,536
8	40,000	37,179	2,821	2,121,715
9	40,000	37,130	2,870	2,118,845
10	40,000	37,080	2,920	2,115,925

b) to f)

JOURNAL			
Date	**Account Title and Explanation**	**Debit**	**Credit**
Apr 1, 2016	Cash	2,142,968	
	Premium on Bonds		142,968
	Bonds Payable		2,000,000
	Issue of $2 million worth of bonds at a		
	premium, due in 20 years		
Sep 30, 2016	Interest Expense	37,502	
	Premium on Bonds	2,498	
	Cash		40,000
	Payment of interest and amortization of		
	premium		
Feb 28, 2017	Interest Expense	31,215	
	Premium on Bonds	2,118	
	Interest Payable		33,333
	To accrued interest at year-end		
	$2,000,000 × 4% × 5⁄12		
	$2,542 × 5 ÷ 6		
Mar 31, 2021	Cash	2,200,000	
	Bonds Payable		2,200,000
	Issuance of new bonds		
Mar 31, 2021	Bonds Payable	2,000,000	
	Premium on Bonds	115,925	
	Gain on Bond Redemption		5,925
	Cash		2,110,000
	Redemption of bonds		
Sep 30, 2021	Interest Expense	22,000	
	Cash		22,000
	To record interest		
	$2,200,000 × 2% × 5⁄12		

Chapter 8 Review Exercise 2 - Solutions

a)

Date	A Cash Payment (B + C)	B Interest Expense (D × 4% × 6/12)	C Reduction of Principal (D × 6/24)	D Principal Balance (C – D)
Apr 1, 2016				$200,000
Oct 1, 2016	$54,000	$4,000	$50,000	150,000
Apr 1, 2017	53,000	3,000	50,000	100,000
Oct 1, 2017	52,000	2,000	50,000	50,000
Apr 1, 2018	51,000	1,000	50,000	0

b)

Date	A Cash Payment	B Interest Expense (D × 4% × 6/12)	C Reduction of Principal (A – B)	D Principal Balance (C – D)
Apr 1, 2016				$200,000
Oct 1, 2016	$52,525	$4,000	$48,525	151,475
Apr 1, 2017	52,525	3,030	49,495	101,980
Oct 1, 2017	52,525	2,040	50,485	51,495
Apr 1, 2018	52,525	1,030	51,495	0

c)

JOURNAL			
Date	**Account Titles and Explanations**	**Debit**	**Credit**
Apr 1, 2016	Cash	200,000	
	Notes Payable		200,000
	Issue of note payable of $200,000, at 4%		
	annual interest rate, paid semi-annually		
Oct 1, 2016	Interest Expense	4,000	
	Notes Payable	48,525	
	Cash		52,525
	Instalment payment of principal and interest		
	$200,000 x 4% x $^6/_{12}$		
	$52,525 − $4,000		
Feb 28, 2017	Interest Expense	2,525	
	Interest Payable		2,525
	To recognize accrued interest at year-end		
	$3,030 x $^5/_6$		
Apr 1, 2017	Interest Expense	505	
	Interest Payable	2,525	
	Notes Payable	49,495	
	Cash		52,525
	To record payments of interest and principal		
	$3,030 − $2,525		

Chapter 9 Review Exercise - Solutions

JOURNAL			
Date	**Account Title and Explanation**	**Debit**	**Credit**
Jan 1	Short-Term Investments—Trading	50,000	
	Cash		50,000
	Six-month, 4% loan to another company		
Apr 1	Short-Term Investments—Trading	100,000	
	Interest Receivable	1,500	
	Cash		101,500
	Purchased 1,000 bonds at $100 each plus accrued interest		
	(100,000 × .06 × $^3/_{12}$)		
May 10	Short-Term Investments-Trading	50,000	
	Cash		50,000
	Purchased 1,000 shares of Coretex Company		
	at $50 per share		
Jul 1	Cash	3,000	
	Interest Receivable		1,500
	Interest Revenue		1,500
	Received 6 months interest on bonds (100,000 × .06 × $^6/_{12}$)		
Jul 1	Cash	51,000	
	Short-Term Investments-Trading		50,000
	Interest Revenue		1,000
	Received proceeds from loan plus interest (50,000 × $^6/_{12}$ × 4%)		
Jul 10	Cash	100	
	Dividend Revenue		100
	Received quarterly dividend on Coretex shares		
Jul 31	Interest Receivable	500	
	Interest Revenue		500
	Accrued interest on bonds at year end (100,000 × .06 × $^1/_{12}$)		
Oct 1	Cash	4,700	
	Loss on Sale of Investment	300	
	Short-Term Investments—Trading		5,000
	Sale of Coretex shares at a loss		
	$(47–50) × 100		

JOURNAL			
Date	**Account Title and Explanation**	**Debit**	**Credit**
Dec 15	Cash	46,800	
	Gain on Sale of Investment		1,800
	Short-Term Investments—Trading		45,000
	Sale of Coretex shares at a gain		
	$(52–50) × 900		
Dec 31	Cash	3,000	
	Interest Revenue		2,500
	Interest Receivable		500
	Received six months interest on bonds (100,000 × .06 × 5/12)		
Dec 31	Cash	102,500	
	Short-Term Investments—Trading		100,000
	Gain on Sale of Investment		2,500
	Sale of Drake bonds at a gain		

Chapter 10 Review Exercise - Solutions

a)

Dellray Inc. Statement of Cash Flows For the Year Ended December 31, 2016		
Cash Flow from Operating Activities		
Net Income	$986,700	
Add: Depreciation	80,000	
Add: Loss on Sale of Equipment	10,000	
Deduct: Gain on Sale of Investments	(8,000)	
Changes in Current Assets and Current Liabilities		
Decrease in Accounts Receivable	30,000	
Increase in Inventory	(40,000)	
Increase in Prepaid Expenses	(8,000)	
Increase in Accounts Payable	119,000	
Change in Cash due to Operating Activities		$1,169,700
Cash Flow from Investing Activities		
Sale of Equipment	160,000	
Sale of Investments	48,000	
Purchase of Equipment	(400,000)	
Change in Cash due to Investing Activities		(192,000)
Cash Flow from Financing Activities		
Payment towards Notes Payable	6,000	
Proceeds from Bank Loan	70,000	
Payment of Cash Dividend	(75,000)	
Issuance of Common Shares	80,000	
Change in Cash due to Financing Activities		81,000
Net Increase (Decrease) in Cash		1,058,700
Cash at the Beginning of the Year		27,000
Cash at the End of the Year		$1,085,700

| Cost of equipment sold | $= \$1,100,000 + \$400,000 - \$1,300,000$ |
| | $= \$200,000$ |

| Depreciation of equipment sold | $= \$156,000 + \$80,000 - \$206,000$ |
| | $= \$30,000$ |

Book value	$= \$200,000 - \$30,000$
	$= \$170,000 - \$10,000$ loss
	$= \$160,000$ cash received on sale of equipment

Cost of investment	$= \$600,000 - \$560,000$
	$= \$40,000 + \$8,000$
	$= \$48,000$ cash received on sale of investments

| Dividends paid | $= \$1,210,000 + \$986,700 - \$2,121,700$ |
| | $= \$75,000$ cash paid for dividends |

| Increase from bank loan | $= (\$75,000 + \$275,000) - (\$65,000 + \$215,000)$ |
| | $= \$70,000$ proceeds from bank loan |

b)

Free Cash Flow = Net Cash Flow from Operating Activities – Net Cash Flow from Investing Activities

$= \$1,169,700 - \$192,000$

$= \$977,700$

Dellray has a positive free cash flow, which means that the company generated more than enough cash from operations to cover its capital expenditures in 2016. It has $977,700 remaining cash that it could have used to reduce debt, buy back shares or pay dividends. In addition, Dellray's free cash flow is more than enough to cover its total current liabilities, which is equal to $632,000 at the end of 2016. Analysis of Dellray's free cash flow together with the income statement and balance sheet reveals favorable conditions for Dellray because the company is profitable and would not have a liquidity crisis even if it has to repay all of its current liabilities right away.

Chapter 10 Appendix Review Exercise - Solutions

Harmony Inc.
Statement of Cash Flows
For the Year Ended December 31, 2016

Cash Flow from Operating Activities		
Cash Receipts		
Cash Received from Customers		$5,630,000
Cash Payments		
Payments for Inventory	$ 2,889,000	
Payments for Insurance	16,000	
Payments to Employees	766,000	
Payments for Other Operating Expenses	367,300	
Payments for Income Taxes	422,000	
Total Cash Payments		4,460,300
Change in Cash due to Operating Activities		1,169,700
Cash Flow from Investing Activities		
Sale of Equipment	160,000	
Sale of Investments	48,000	
Purchase of Equipment	(400,000)	
Change in Cash due to Investing Activities		(192,000)
Cash Flow from Financing Activities		
Payment toward Notes Payable	6,000	
Proceeds from Bank Loan	70,000	
Payment of Cash Dividend	(75,000)	
Issuance of Common Shares	80,000	
Change in Cash due to Financing Activities		81,000
Net Increase (Decrease) in Cash		1,058,700
Cash at the Beginning of the Year		27,000
Cash at the End of the Year		$1,085,700

*Note that the investing and financing sections are calculated the same way under both direct and indirect methods.

Calculations for the Operating Activities—Direct Method

Cash Received from Customers	
Sales of 2016	$5,600,000
Add: Increase of Account Payable Changes ($400,000 – $370,000)	30,000
Cash Received from Customers	$5,630,000
Payments for Inventory	
Cost of goods sold for 2016 (from income statement)	$2,968,000
Add: Increase in Inventory for 2016	40,000
Inventory purchased on credit during 2016	$3,008,000
Balance of Accounts Payable, Jan 1, 2016 (from balance sheet)	$342,000
Add: Merchandise purchased on credit during 2016	3,008,000
Less: Balance of Accounts Payable, Dec 31, 2016 (from balance sheet)	461,000
Cash payments for merchandise	$2,889,000
Payments for Insurance	
Insurance expense for 2016 (from income statement)	$8,000
Add: Change in prepaid insurance for 2016	8,000
Cash payments for insurance during 2016	$16,000
Payments to Employees	
Salaries expense for 2016 (from income statement)	$766,000
Add: Change in salaries payable for 2016	0
Cash payments to employees for salaries during 2016	$766,000
Payments for other operating expenses = Other Operating Expenses	$367,300
Payments made for Income taxes	
Income tax expense for 2016 (from income statement)	$422,000
Less: Change in Income Tax Payable for 2016	0
Cash payments for income tax during 2016	$422,000

Cost of equipment sold
$$= \$1,100,000 + \$400,000 - \$1,300,000$$
$$= \$200,000$$

Depreciation of equipment sold
$$= \$156,000 + \$80,000 - \$206,000$$
$$= \$30,000$$

Book value on sale of equipment
$$= \$200,000 - \$30,000$$
$$= \$170,000 - \$10,000 \text{ loss}$$
$$= \$160,000 \text{ cash received}$$

Cost of investment on sale of investments
$$= \$600,000 - \$560,000$$
$$= \$40,000 + \$8,000$$
$$= \$48,000 \text{ cash received}$$

Dividends paid
$$= \$1,210,000 + \$986,700 - \$2,121,700$$
$$= \$75,000 \text{ cash paid for dividends}$$

Increase from bank loan
$$= (\$75,000 + \$275,000) - (\$65,000 + \$215,000)$$
$$= \$75,000 \text{ proceed from bank loan}$$

Chapter 11 Review Exercise - Solutions

	Basil's Bakery Percentage Change and Vertical Analysis As at December 31, 2016			
	2016	**2015**	**% Change**	**% of Base- Figure 2016**
Cash	$1,605	$987	62.61%	29.12%
Accounts Receivable	1,175	573	105.06%	21.15%
Inventory	396	256	54.69%	7.13%
Other Current Assets	301	103	192.23%	5.42%
Total Current Assets	3,477	1,919	81.19%	63.09%
Property, Plant and Equipment	2,034	1,170	73.85%	36.61%
Total Assets	$5,511	$3,089	78.41%	100.00%
Current Liabilities	$1,474	$547	169.47%	26.53%
Non-Current Liabilities	104	58	79.31%	1.87%
Total Liabilities	1,578	605	160.83%	28.40%
Shareholders' Equity	3,933	2,484	58.33%	71.36%
Total Liabilities and Equity	$5,511	$3,089	78.41%	100.00%

Basil's Bakery has grown considerably in 2016 compared to 2015, as witnessed by the positive percentage changes in all categories. While shareholders' equity increased 58.33% from 2015, total liabilities increased even more at 160.83%. This larger percentage increase in liabilities is not necessarily a bad thing, considering that the total liabilities balance is still much lower than shareholders' equity balance. As shown in the vertical analysis, total liabilities are only 28.40% of total assets, compared to shareholders' equity, which is 71.36% of total assets. Additionally, liquidity does not appear to be a problem, considering that Basil's Bakery has far more current assets (63.09% of total assets) than current liabilities (26.53% of total assets). Therefore, the company is in a good position to take advantage of higher leverage provided it can cover the interest expense that comes with more debt. Another important thing to note from the annual percentage change is the 105.06% increase in accounts receivable, which is higher than the percentage increases of cash and inventory. This means that Basil's Bakery has been growing its business partly by increasing credit sales. The company may need to put more focus on management and control of accounts receivable, as the company's success will increasingly depend on its ability to collect its accounts receivable.

Financial Ratio or Figure	Calculation	Result
Working Capital	$3,477 − $1,474	$2,003
Current Ratio	$\dfrac{\$3,477}{\$1,474}$	2.36
Quick Ratio	$\dfrac{\$1,605 + \$1,175}{\$1,474}$	1.89
Gross Profit Margin	$\dfrac{\$3,081}{\$6,009}$	0.5127 or 51.27%
Net Profit Margin	$\dfrac{\$1,295}{\$6,009}$	0.2155 or 21.55%
EBIT	$1,295 + $516 + $518	$2,329
EBIT Percentage to Sales	$\dfrac{\$2,329}{\$6,009}$	0.3876 or 38.76%
Return on Equity	$1,295 ÷ $\dfrac{(\$3,933 + \$2,484)}{2}$	0.4036 or 40.36%
Return on Assets	$1,295 ÷ $\dfrac{(\$5,511 + \$3,089)}{2}$	0.3012 or 30.12%
Asset Turnover	$\dfrac{\$6,009}{(\$5,511 + \$3,089) ÷ 2}$	1.40 times
Inventory Turnover Ratio	$2,928 ÷ $\dfrac{(\$396 + \$256)}{2}$	8.98
Inventory Days on Hand	$\dfrac{(\$396 + \$256) ÷ 2}{\$2,928} × 365$	40.64 days
Days-Sales-Outstanding	$\dfrac{(\$1,175 + \$573) ÷ 2}{\$6,009} × 365$	53.09 days
Accounts Receivable Turnover	$6,009 ÷ $\dfrac{(\$1,175 + \$573)}{2}$	6.88
Debt-to-Equity Ratio	$\dfrac{\$1,578}{\$3,933}$	0.4012 or 40.12%
Interest Coverage Ratio	$\dfrac{\$2,329}{\$518}$	4.50 times
Debt-to-Assets Ratio	$\dfrac{\$1,578}{\$5,511}$	0.2863 or 28.63%

Basil's Bakery has a positive **working capital** of $2,003 which indicates that the company has enough liquid assets to pay off its upcoming short-term debts.

The company has a **current ratio** of 2.36 which indicates that the business has double and a bit of current assets to pay for its current liabilities. It could be argued that the bakery has enough of a cushion that it could afford to have more cash tied up in current assets, such as inventory and accounts receivable. It could also invest a small portion to earn more investment income.

The bakery has a **quick ratio** of 1.89 which indicates that the business can meet its most immediate debt obligations without relying on the liquidation of inventory. In terms of liquidity as a whole, Basil's Bakery is highly liquid based on the above three financial ratios and figures, indicating a strong financial position in meeting short-term debt obligations.

Basil's Bakery has a **gross profit margin** of 51.27%, which means that after deducting cost of goods sold from sales revenue, the company still has a little more than half of sales revenue left to cover other expenses. Compared to 2015, the gross profit margin declined, indicating that the company is either generating less revenue, has experienced an increase in inventory costs or both. This should be a point of concern, indicating a downward trend. Comparing 2016's gross profit margin to the industry average of 49.47% shows that the bakery is doing better than the average company in the same industry. It must work to ensure that it remains above this amount by setting appropriate prices and properly managing inventory costs.

The business has a **net profit margin** of 21.55% which means that the company is earning 21 cents of net income for every one dollar of revenue earned. Compared to 2015, the net profit margin declined, indicating that the company's costs have increased. This should be a point of concern, indicating a downward trend. Comparing 2016's net profit margin to the industry average of 20.36% shows that the bakery is doing better than the average company in the same industry. It must work to ensure that it remains above this amount by managing costs and expenses.

The company has a positive **EBIT** of $2,329. This shows the dollar amount the company earned taking into account only controllable expenses.

When we apply EBIT as a percentage to sales, we see Basil's Bakery kept more than 38% of its sales revenue before controllable expenses. Interest and taxes dropped the EBIT percentage to sales down to the 21.55% net profit margin. The EBIT percentage to sales can be compared to prior years or other bakeries to see how well this company is performing.

Basil's Bakery has a positive 40.36% **return on equity (ROE)**. A positive return on equity is favourable for investors. As always, shareholders can compare the company's ROE with other companies' ROE to see whether the return from investing in Basil's Bakery provides at least as high of a return as they could have received if they had invested elsewhere. In terms of profitability, the company is doing well.

Basil's Bakery had a **return on assets** of about 30%. This means the company made a profit of $0.30 for every dollar invested in assets in the business. This appears to be a good return, but can be compared to other bakeries for a more thorough assessment.

The **asset turnover** is 1.4 times. This means the bakery generates $1.40 of revenue for every one dollar of assets. This is a good indicator that the company is using its assets efficiently.

Basil's Bakery has an **inventory turnover ratio** of 8.98 which represents the number of times that the company sold its entire inventory within the year. Bakeries should have a higher turnover ratio because some of the input products they use can expire, such as milk and eggs. Once items are baked, they have a short shelf life as efficiently.

The company has an **inventory days on hand ratio** of 40.64 days. This indicates that the inventory is sold rather slowly. This paired with the inventory turnover ratio, shows that the bakery could be selling inventory faster. This is a point of concern. In terms of operations management, inventory must be addressed immediately. Inventory should be turning over more quickly to ensure that the bakery is not throwing out expired products. A turnaround in operations management could mean more success in profitability and liquidity.

The **accounts receivable turnover** and the **days-sales-outstanding** ratio indicate the company collects its accounts receivable every 53 days, or turns over it accounts receivable almost seven times a year. This is not a very healthy ratio. Long collection periods can mean that the company's credit policy is too lenient, or that there are billing disputes, resulting in a delay in receivables collection from customers. It can lead to cash flow problems if cash is not being received in a timely manner.

The bakery has a **debt-to-equity ratio** of 40.12% indicating that the total debt is significantly lower than equity. Having relatively low debt compared to equity is considered low risk because the company has a low cost of debt in the form of interest. Therefore, the company's leverage appears to be at an acceptable level.

The **interest coverage ratio** appears healthy. Basil's Bakery has enough EBIT to cover its interest obligations 4.5 times. The bakery currently has a debt-to-equity ratio of 40%, but if the amount of debt were to increase, the bakery should still be able to cover the interest on the debt. This should be monitored to ensure the interest coverage does not get too low.

The **debt-to-assets ratio** is sitting at a little more than 28%. This may be a relatively low value for debt-to-assets, which would indicate the company is not relying too heavily on debt to finance its assets. A comparison with other bakeries would place this in perspective.

Notes

Appendix II

PRESENT VALUE FACTORS

Present Value Factors for a Single Value

Interest Rate

Period	1%	2%	3%	4%	5%	6%	7%	8%	9%	10%	11%	12%	13%	14%	15%	16%	17%	18%	19%	20%
1	0.9901	0.9804	0.9709	0.9615	0.9524	0.9434	0.9346	0.9259	0.9174	0.9091	0.9009	0.8929	0.8850	0.8772	0.8696	0.8621	0.8547	0.8475	0.8403	0.8333
2	0.9803	0.9612	0.9426	0.9246	0.9070	0.8900	0.8734	0.8573	0.8417	0.8264	0.8116	0.7972	0.7831	0.7695	0.7561	0.7432	0.7305	0.7182	0.7062	0.6944
3	0.9706	0.9423	0.9151	0.8890	0.8638	0.8396	0.8163	0.7938	0.7722	0.7513	0.7312	0.7118	0.6931	0.6750	0.6575	0.6407	0.6244	0.6086	0.5934	0.5787
4	0.9610	0.9238	0.8885	0.8548	0.8227	0.7921	0.7629	0.7350	0.7084	0.6830	0.6587	0.6355	0.6133	0.5921	0.5718	0.5523	0.5337	0.5158	0.4987	0.4823
5	0.9515	0.9057	0.8626	0.8219	0.7835	0.7473	0.7130	0.6806	0.6499	0.6209	0.5935	0.5674	0.5428	0.5194	0.4972	0.4761	0.4561	0.4371	0.4190	0.4019
6	0.9420	0.8880	0.8375	0.7903	0.7462	0.7050	0.6663	0.6302	0.5963	0.5645	0.5346	0.5066	0.4803	0.4556	0.4323	0.4104	0.3898	0.3704	0.3521	0.3349
7	0.9327	0.8706	0.8131	0.7599	0.7107	0.6651	0.6227	0.5835	0.5470	0.5132	0.4817	0.4523	0.4251	0.3996	0.3759	0.3538	0.3332	0.3139	0.2959	0.2791
8	0.9235	0.8535	0.7894	0.7307	0.6768	0.6274	0.5820	0.5403	0.5019	0.4665	0.4339	0.4039	0.3762	0.3506	0.3269	0.3050	0.2848	0.2660	0.2487	0.2326
9	0.9143	0.8368	0.7664	0.7026	0.6446	0.5919	0.5439	0.5002	0.4604	0.4241	0.3909	0.3606	0.3329	0.3075	0.2843	0.2630	0.2434	0.2255	0.2090	0.1938
10	0.9053	0.8203	0.7441	0.6756	0.6139	0.5584	0.5083	0.4632	0.4224	0.3855	0.3522	0.3220	0.2946	0.2697	0.2472	0.2267	0.2080	0.1911	0.1756	0.1615
11	0.8963	0.8043	0.7224	0.6496	0.5847	0.5268	0.4751	0.4289	0.3875	0.3505	0.3173	0.2875	0.2607	0.2366	0.2149	0.1954	0.1778	0.1619	0.1476	0.1346
12	0.8874	0.7885	0.7014	0.6246	0.5568	0.4970	0.4440	0.3971	0.3555	0.3186	0.2858	0.2567	0.2307	0.2076	0.1869	0.1685	0.1520	0.1372	0.1240	0.1122
13	0.8787	0.7730	0.6810	0.6006	0.5303	0.4688	0.4150	0.3677	0.3262	0.2897	0.2575	0.2292	0.2042	0.1821	0.1625	0.1452	0.1299	0.1163	0.1042	0.0935
14	0.8700	0.7579	0.6611	0.5775	0.5051	0.4423	0.3878	0.3405	0.2992	0.2633	0.2320	0.2046	0.1807	0.1597	0.1413	0.1252	0.1110	0.0985	0.0876	0.0779
15	0.8613	0.7430	0.6419	0.5553	0.4810	0.4173	0.3624	0.3152	0.2745	0.2394	0.2090	0.1827	0.1599	0.1401	0.1229	0.1079	0.0949	0.0835	0.0736	0.0649
16	0.8528	0.7284	0.6232	0.5339	0.4581	0.3936	0.3387	0.2919	0.2519	0.2176	0.1883	0.1631	0.1415	0.1229	0.1069	0.0930	0.0811	0.0708	0.0618	0.0541
17	0.8444	0.7142	0.6050	0.5134	0.4363	0.3714	0.3166	0.2703	0.2311	0.1978	0.1696	0.1456	0.1252	0.1078	0.0929	0.0802	0.0693	0.0600	0.0520	0.0451
18	0.8360	0.7002	0.5874	0.4936	0.4155	0.3503	0.2959	0.2502	0.2120	0.1799	0.1528	0.1300	0.1108	0.0946	0.0808	0.0691	0.0592	0.0508	0.0437	0.0376
19	0.8277	0.6864	0.5703	0.4746	0.3957	0.3305	0.2765	0.2317	0.1945	0.1635	0.1377	0.1161	0.0981	0.0829	0.0703	0.0596	0.0506	0.0431	0.0367	0.0313
20	0.8195	0.6730	0.5537	0.4564	0.3769	0.3118	0.2584	0.2145	0.1784	0.1486	0.1240	0.1037	0.0868	0.0728	0.0611	0.0514	0.0433	0.0365	0.0308	0.0261
21	0.8114	0.6598	0.5375	0.4388	0.3589	0.2942	0.2415	0.1987	0.1637	0.1351	0.1117	0.0926	0.0768	0.0638	0.0531	0.0443	0.0370	0.0309	0.0259	0.0217
22	0.8034	0.6468	0.5219	0.4220	0.3418	0.2775	0.2257	0.1839	0.1502	0.1228	0.1007	0.0826	0.0680	0.0560	0.0462	0.0382	0.0316	0.0262	0.0218	0.0181
23	0.7954	0.6342	0.5067	0.4057	0.3256	0.2618	0.2109	0.1703	0.1378	0.1117	0.0907	0.0738	0.0601	0.0491	0.0402	0.0329	0.0270	0.0222	0.0183	0.0151
24	0.7876	0.6217	0.4919	0.3901	0.3101	0.2470	0.1971	0.1577	0.1264	0.1015	0.0817	0.0659	0.0532	0.0431	0.0349	0.0284	0.0231	0.0188	0.0154	0.0126
25	0.7798	0.6095	0.4776	0.3751	0.2953	0.2330	0.1842	0.1460	0.1160	0.0923	0.0736	0.0588	0.0471	0.0378	0.0304	0.0245	0.0197	0.0160	0.0129	0.0105
30	0.7419	0.5521	0.4120	0.3083	0.2314	0.1741	0.1314	0.0994	0.0754	0.0573	0.0437	0.0334	0.0256	0.0196	0.0151	0.0116	0.0090	0.0070	0.0054	0.0042
40	0.6717	0.4529	0.3066	0.2083	0.1420	0.0972	0.0668	0.0460	0.0318	0.0221	0.0154	0.0107	0.0075	0.0053	0.0037	0.0026	0.0019	0.0013	0.0010	0.0007
50	0.6080	0.3715	0.2281	0.1407	0.0872	0.0543	0.0339	0.0213	0.0134	0.0085	0.0054	0.0035	0.0022	0.0014	0.0009	0.0006	0.0004	0.0003	0.0002	0.0001

Present Value Factors for an Annuity

Period	1%	2%	3%	4%	5%	6%	7%	8%	9%	10%	11%	12%	13%	14%	15%	16%	17%	18%	19%	20%
1	0.9901	0.9804	0.9709	0.9615	0.9524	0.9434	0.9346	0.9259	0.9174	0.9091	0.9009	0.8929	0.8850	0.8772	0.8696	0.8621	0.8547	0.8475	0.8403	0.8333
2	1.9704	1.9416	1.9135	1.8861	1.8594	1.8334	1.8080	1.7833	1.7591	1.7355	1.7125	1.6901	1.6681	1.6467	1.6257	1.6052	1.5852	1.5656	1.5465	1.5278
3	2.9410	2.8839	2.8286	2.7751	2.7232	2.6730	2.6243	2.5771	2.5313	2.4869	2.4437	2.4018	2.3612	2.3216	2.2832	2.2459	2.2096	2.1743	2.1399	2.1065
4	3.9020	3.8077	3.7171	3.6299	3.5460	3.4651	3.3872	3.3121	3.2397	3.1699	3.1024	3.0373	2.9745	2.9137	2.8550	2.7982	2.7432	2.6901	2.6386	2.5887
5	4.8534	4.7135	4.5797	4.4518	4.3295	4.2124	4.1002	3.9927	3.8897	3.7908	3.6959	3.6048	3.5172	3.4331	3.3522	3.2743	3.1993	3.1272	3.0576	2.9906
6	5.7955	5.6014	5.4172	5.2421	5.0757	4.9173	4.7665	4.6229	4.4859	4.3553	4.2305	4.1114	3.9975	3.8887	3.7845	3.6847	3.5892	3.4976	3.4098	3.3255
7	6.7282	6.4720	6.2303	6.0021	5.7864	5.5824	5.3893	5.2064	5.0330	4.8684	4.7122	4.5638	4.4226	4.2883	4.1604	4.0386	3.9224	3.8115	3.7057	3.6046
8	7.6517	7.3255	7.0197	6.7327	6.4632	6.2098	5.9713	5.7466	5.5348	5.3349	5.1461	4.9676	4.7988	4.6389	4.4873	4.3436	4.2072	4.0776	3.9544	3.8372
9	8.5660	8.1622	7.7861	7.4353	7.1078	6.8017	6.5152	6.2469	5.9952	5.7590	5.5370	5.3282	5.1317	4.9464	4.7716	4.6065	4.4506	4.3030	4.1633	4.0310
10	9.4713	8.9826	8.5302	8.1109	7.7217	7.3601	7.0236	6.7101	6.4177	6.1446	5.8892	5.6502	5.4262	5.2161	5.0188	4.8332	4.6586	4.4941	4.3389	4.1925
11	10.3676	9.7868	9.2526	8.7605	8.3064	7.8869	7.4987	7.1390	6.8052	6.4951	6.2065	5.9377	5.6869	5.4527	5.2337	5.0286	4.8364	4.6560	4.4865	4.3271
12	11.2551	10.5753	9.9540	9.3851	8.8633	8.3838	7.9427	7.5361	7.1607	6.8137	6.4924	6.1944	5.9176	5.6603	5.4206	5.1971	4.9884	4.7932	4.6105	4.4392
13	12.1337	11.3484	10.6350	9.9856	9.3936	8.8527	8.3577	7.9038	7.4869	7.1034	6.7499	6.4235	6.1218	5.8424	5.5831	5.3423	5.1183	4.9095	4.7147	4.5327
14	13.0037	12.1062	11.2961	10.5631	9.8986	9.2950	8.7455	8.2442	7.7862	7.3667	6.9819	6.6282	6.3025	6.0021	5.7245	5.4675	5.2293	5.0081	4.8023	4.6106
15	13.8651	12.8493	11.9379	11.1184	10.3797	9.7122	9.1079	8.5595	8.0607	7.6061	7.1909	6.8109	6.4624	6.1422	5.8474	5.5755	5.3242	5.0916	4.8759	4.6755
16	14.7179	13.5777	12.5611	11.6523	10.8378	10.1059	9.4466	8.8514	8.3126	7.8237	7.3792	6.9740	6.6039	6.2651	5.9542	5.6685	5.4053	5.1624	4.9377	4.7296
17	15.5623	14.2919	13.1661	12.1657	11.2741	10.4773	9.7632	9.1216	8.5436	8.0216	7.5488	7.1196	6.7291	6.3729	6.0472	5.7487	5.4746	5.2223	4.9897	4.7746
18	16.3983	14.9920	13.7535	12.6593	11.6896	10.8276	10.0591	9.3719	8.7556	8.2014	7.7016	7.2497	6.8399	6.4674	6.1280	5.8178	5.5339	5.2732	5.0333	4.8122
19	17.2260	15.6785	14.3238	13.1339	12.0853	11.1581	10.3356	9.6036	8.9501	8.3649	7.8393	7.3658	6.9380	6.5504	6.1982	5.8775	5.5845	5.3162	5.0700	4.8435
20	18.0456	16.3514	14.8775	13.5903	12.4622	11.4699	10.5940	9.8181	9.1285	8.5136	7.9633	7.4694	7.0248	6.6231	6.2593	5.9288	5.6278	5.3527	5.1009	4.8696
21	18.8570	17.0112	15.4150	14.0292	12.8212	11.7641	10.8355	10.0168	9.2922	8.6487	8.0751	7.5620	7.1016	6.6870	6.3125	5.9731	5.6648	5.3837	5.1268	4.8913
22	19.6604	17.6580	15.9369	14.4511	13.1630	12.0416	11.0612	10.2007	9.4424	8.7715	8.1757	7.6446	7.1695	6.7429	6.3587	6.0113	5.6964	5.4099	5.1486	4.9094
23	20.4558	18.2922	16.4436	14.8568	13.4886	12.3034	11.2722	10.3711	9.5802	8.8832	8.2664	7.7184	7.2297	6.7921	6.3988	6.0442	5.7234	5.4321	5.1668	4.9245
24	21.2434	18.9139	16.9355	15.2470	13.7986	12.5504	11.4693	10.5288	9.7066	8.9847	8.3481	7.7843	7.2829	6.8351	6.4338	6.0726	5.7465	5.4509	5.1822	4.9371
25	22.0232	19.5235	17.4131	15.6221	14.0939	12.7834	11.6536	10.6748	9.8226	9.0770	8.4217	7.8431	7.3300	6.8729	6.4641	6.0971	5.7662	5.4669	5.1951	4.9476
30	25.8077	22.3965	19.6004	17.2920	15.3725	13.7648	12.4090	11.2578	10.2737	9.4269	8.6938	8.0552	7.4957	7.0027	6.5660	6.1772	5.8294	5.5168	5.2347	4.9789
40	32.8347	27.3555	23.1148	19.7928	17.1591	15.0463	13.3317	11.9246	10.7574	9.7791	8.9511	8.2438	7.6344	7.1050	6.6418	6.2335	5.8713	5.5482	5.2582	4.9966
50	39.1961	31.4236	25.7298	21.4822	18.2559	15.7619	13.8007	12.2335	10.9617	9.9148	9.0417	8.3045	7.6752	7.1327	6.6605	6.2463	5.8801	5.5541	5.2623	4.9995

Appendix III

STARBUCKS' FINANCIAL STATEMENTS AND RATIO ANALYSIS

CONSOLIDATED STATEMENTS OF EARNINGS

(in millions, except per share data)

Fiscal Year Ended	Sep 28, 2014	Sep 29, 2013	Sep 30, 2012
Net revenues:			
Company-operated stores	$ 12,977.9	$ 11,793.2	$ 10,534.5
Licensed stores	1,588.6	1,360.5	1,210.3
CPG, foodservice and other	1,881.3	1,713.1	1,532.0
Total net revenues	16,447.8	14,866.8	13,276.8
Cost of sales including occupancy costs	6,858.8	6,382.3	5,813.3
Store operating expenses	4,638.2	4,286.1	3,918.1
Other operating expenses	457.3	431.8	407.2
Depreciation and amortization expenses	709.6	621.4	550.3
General and administrative expenses	991.3	937.9	801.2
Litigation charge/(credit)	(20.2)	2,784.1	—
Total operating expenses	13,635.0	15,443.6	11,490.1
Income from equity investees	268.3	251.4	210.7
Operating income/(loss)	3,081.1	(325.4)	1,997.4
Interest income and other, net	142.7	123.6	94.4
Interest expense	(64.1)	(28.1)	(32.7)
Earnings/(loss) before income taxes	3,159.7	(229.9)	2,059.1
Income tax expense/(benefit)	1,092.0	(238.7)	674.4
Net earnings including noncontrolling interests	2,067.7	8.8	1,384.7
Net earnings/(loss) attributable to noncontrolling interests	(0.4)	0.5	0.9
Net earnings attributable to Starbucks	$ 2,068.1	$ 8.3	$ 1,383.8
Earnings per share — basic	$ 2.75	$ 0.01	$ 1.83
Earnings per share — diluted	$ 2.71	$ 0.01	$ 1.79
Weighted average shares outstanding:			
Basic	753.1	749.3	754.4
Diluted	763.1	762.3	773.0

CONSOLIDATED STATEMENTS OF COMPREHENSIVE INCOME

(in millions)

	Sep 28, 2014	Sep 29, 2013	Sep 30, 2012
Net earnings including noncontrolling interests	$ 2,067.7	$ 8.8	$1,384.7
Other comprehensive income/(loss), net of tax:			
Unrealized holding gains/(losses) on available-for-sale securities	1.6	(0.6)	0.7
Tax (expense)/benefit	(0.6)	0.2	(0.3)
Unrealized gains/(losses) on cash flow hedging instruments	24.1	47.1	(42.2)
Tax (expense)/benefit	(7.8)	(24.6)	4.3
Unrealized gains/(losses) on net investment hedging instruments	25.5	32.8	1.0
Tax (expense)/benefit	(9.4)	(12.1)	(0.4)
Reclassification adjustment for net (gains)/losses realized in net earnings for cash flow hedges and available-for-sale securities	(1.5)	46.3	14.8
Tax expense/(benefit)	3.8	(3.5)	(4.3)
Translation adjustment	(75.8)	(41.6)	6.1
Tax (expense)/benefit	(1.6)	0.3	(3.3)
Other comprehensive income/(loss)	(41.7)	44.3	(23.6)
Comprehensive income including non-controlling interests	2,026.0	53.1	1,361.1
Comprehensive income/(loss) attributable to non-controlling interests	(0.4)	0.5	0.9
Comprehensive income attributable to Starbucks	$ 2,026.4	$ 52.6	$ 1,360.2

CONSOLIDATED BALANCE SHEETS

(in millions, except per share data)

	Sep 28, 2014	Sep 29, 2013
ASSETS		
Current assets:		
Cash and cash equivalents	**$ 1,708.4**	$ 2,575.7
Short-term investments	**135.4**	658.1
Accounts receivable, net	**631.0**	561.4
Inventories	**1,090.9**	1,111.2
Prepaid expenses and other current assets	**285.6**	287.7
Deferred income taxes, net	**317.4**	277.3
Total current assets	**4,168.7**	5,471.4
Long-term investments	**318.4**	58.3
Equity and cost investments	**514.9**	496.5
Property, plant and equipment, net	**3,519.0**	3,200.5
Deferred income taxes, net	**903.3**	967.0
Other assets	**198.9**	185.3
Other intangible assets	**273.5**	274.8
Goodwill	**856.2**	862.9
TOTAL ASSETS	**$ 10,752.9**	$ 11,516.7
LIABILITIES AND EQUITY		
Current liabilities:		
Accounts payable	**$ 533.7**	$ 491.7
Accrued litigation charge	**—**	2,784.1
Accrued liabilities	**1,514.4**	1,269.3
Insurance reserves	**196.1**	178.5
Deferred revenue	**794.5**	653.7
Total current liabilities	**3,038.7**	5,377.3
Long-term debt	**2,048.3**	1,299.4
Other long-term liabilities	**392.2**	357.7
Total liabilities	**5,479.2**	7,034.4
Shareholders' equity:		
Common stock ($0.001 par value) — authorized, 1,200.0 shares; issued and outstanding, 749.5 and 753.2 shares, respectively	**0.7**	0.8
Additional paid-in capital	**39.4**	282.1
Retained earnings	**5,206.6**	4,130.3
Accumulated other comprehensive income	**25.3**	67.0
Total shareholders' equity	**5,272.0**	4,480.2
Noncontrolling interest	**1.7**	2.1
Total equity	**5,273.7**	4,482.3
TOTAL LIABILITIES AND EQUITY	**$ 10,752.9**	$ 11,516.7

CONSOLIDATED STATEMENTS OF CASH FLOWS

(in millions)

Fiscal Year Ended	Sep 28, 2014	Sep 29, 2013	Sep 30, 2012
Operating Activities			
Net earnings including noncontrolling interests	$ 2,067.7	$ 8.8	$ 1,384.7
Adjustments to reconcile net earnings to net cash provided by operating activities:			
Depreciation and amortization	748.4	655.6	580.6
Litigation charge	—	2,784.1	—
Deferred income taxes, net	10.2	(1,045.9)	61.1
Income earned from equity method investees	(182.7)	(171.8)	(136.0)
Distributions received from equity method investees	139.2	115.6	86.7
Gain resulting from sale of equity in joint ventures and certain retail operations	(70.2)	(80.1)	—
Stock-based compensation	183.2	142.3	153.6
Excess tax benefit on share-based awards	(114.4)	(258.1)	(169.8)
Other	36.2	23.0	23.6
Cash (used)/provided by changes in operating assets and liabilities:			
Accounts receivable	(79.7)	(68.3)	(90.3)
Inventories	14.3	152.5	(273.3)
Accounts payable	60.4	88.7	(105.2)
Accrued litigation charge	(2,763.9)	—	—
Income taxes payable, net	309.8	298.4	201.6
Accrued liabilities and insurance reserves	103.9	47.3	(8.1)
Deferred revenue	140.8	139.9	60.8
Prepaid expenses, other current assets and other assets	4.6	76.3	(19.7)
Net cash provided by operating activities	607.8	2,908.3	1,750.3
INVESTING ACTIVITIES:			
Purchase of investments	(1,652.5)	(785.9)	(1,748.6)
Sales of investments	1,454.8	60.2	—
Maturities and calls of investments	456.1	980.0	1,796.4
Acquisitions, net of cash acquired	—	(610.4)	(129.1)
Additions to property, plant and equipment	(1,160.9)	(1,151.2)	(856.2)
Proceeds from sale of equity in joint ventures and certain retail operations	103.9	108.0	—
Other	(19.1)	(11.9)	(36.5)
Net cash used by investing activities	(817.7)	(1,411.2)	(974.0)
FINANCING ACTIVITIES:			
Proceeds from issuance of long-term debt	748.5	749.7	—
Principal payments on long-term debt	—	(35.2)	—
Payments on short-term borrowings	—	—	(30.8)
Proceeds from issuance of common stock	139.7	247.2	236.6
Excess tax benefit on share-based awards	114.4	258.1	169.8
Repurchase of common stock	(758.6)	(588.1)	(549.1)
Cash dividends paid	(783.1)	(628.9)	(513.0)
Minimum tax withholdings on share-based awards	(77.3)	(121.4)	(58.5)
Other	(6.9)	10.4	(0.5)
Net cash used by financing activities	(623.3)	(108.2)	(745.5)
Effect of exchange rate changes on cash and cash equivalents	(34.1)	(1.8)	9.7
Net (decrease)/increase in cash and cash equivalents	(867.3)	1,387.1	40.5
CASH AND CASH EQUIVALENTS:			
Beginning of period	2,575.7	1,188.6	1,148.1
End of period	$ 1,708.4	$ 2,575.7	$ 1,188.6
SUPPLEMENTAL DISCLOSURE OF CASH FLOW INFORMATION:			
Cash paid during the period for:			
Interest, net of capitalized interest	$ 56.2	$ 34.4	$ 34.4
Income taxes, net of refunds	$ 766.3	$ 539.1	$ 416.9

CONSOLIDATED STATEMENTS OF EQUITY

(in millions)

	Common Stock		Additional Paid-in Capital	Retained Earnings	Accumulated Other Comprehensive Income/(Loss)	Shareholders' Equity	Non-controlling Interest	Total
	Shares	Amount						
Balance, October 2, 2011	$744.8	$0.7	$40.5	$4,297.4	$46.3	$4,384.9	$2.4	$4,387.3
Net earnings	—	—	—	1,383.8	—	1,383.8	0.9	1,384.7
Other comprehensive income/(loss)					(23.6)	(23.6)	—	(23.6)
Stock-based compensation expense	—	—	155.2	—	—	155.2	—	155.2
Exercise of stock options/vesting of RSUs, including tax benefit of $167.3	16.5	—	326.1	—	—	326.1	—	326.1
Sale of common stock, including tax benefit of $0.2	0.3	—	19.5	—	—	19.5	—	19.5
Repurchase of common stock	(12.3)	—	(501.9)	(91.3)	—	(593.2)	—	(593.2)
Cash dividends declared, $0.72 per share	—	—	—	(543.7)	—	(543.7)	—	(543.7)
Noncontrolling interest resulting from acquisition	—	—	—	—	—	—	2.2	2.2
Balance, September 30, 2012	749.3	$0.7	$39.4	$5,046.2	$22.7	$5,109.0	$5.5	$5,114.5
Net earnings	—	—	—	8.3		8.3	0.5	8.8
Other comprehensive income/(loss)					44.3	44.3	—	44.3
Stock-based compensation expense	—	—	144.1	—	—	144.1	—	144.1
Exercise of stock options/vesting of RSUs, including tax benefit of $259.9	14.4	0.1	366.7	—	—	366.8	—	366.8
Sale of common stock, including tax benefit of $0.2	0.3	—	20.4	—	—	20.4	—	20.4
Repurchase of common stock	(10.8)	—	(288.5)	(255.6)	—	(544.1)	—	(544.1)
Cash dividends declared, $0.89 per share	—	—	—	(668.6)	—	(668.6)	—	(668.6)
Noncontrolling interest resulting from divestiture	—	—	—	—	—	—	(3.9)	(3.9)
Balance, September 29, 2013	$753.2	$0.8	$282.1	$4,130.3	$67.0	$4,480.2	$2.1	$4,482.3
Net earnings	—	—	—	2,068.1	—	2,068.1	(0.4)	2,067.7
Other comprehensive income/(loss)					(41.7)	(41.7)	—	(41.7)
Stock-based compensation expense	—	—	185.1	—	—	185.1	—	185.1
Exercise of stock options/vesting of RSUs, including tax benefit of $114.8	6.5	—	154.8	—	—	154.8	—	154.8
Sale of common stock, including tax benefit of $0.2	0.3	—	22.3	—	—	22.3	—	22.3
Repurchase of common stock	(10.5)	(0.1)	(604.9)	(164.8)	—	(769.8)	—	(769.8)
Cash dividends declared, $1.10 per share	—	—	—	(827.0)	—	(827.0)	—	(827.0)
Balance, September 28, 2014	$749.5	$0.7	$39.4	$5,206.6	$25.3	$5,272.0	$1.7	$5,273.7

FINANCIAL STATEMENT ANALYSIS

	Formula	2014	2013
Liquidity			
Working Capital (in millions)	Current Assets - Current Liabilities	$1,130	$94
Current Ratio	Current Assets ÷ Current Liabilities	1.37	1.02
Quick Ratio	(Cash + Short-Term Investments + Accounts Receivable) ÷ Current Liabilities	0.81	0.71
Profitability			
Gross Profit Margin	Gross Profit ÷ Sales Revenue	58%	57%
Net Profit Margin	Net Income ÷ Sales Revenue	13%	0.1%
EBIT (in millions)	Net Income + Interest Expense + Tax Expense	$3,081	($325)
EBIT Percentage to Sales	EBIT ÷ Sales Revenue	19%	-2%
ROE	Net Income ÷ Average Shareholders' Equity	42%	0.2%
ROA	Net Income ÷ Average Total Assets	19%	0.1%
Asset Turnover	Sales Revenue ÷ Average Total Assets	1.48	1.51
Equity Multiplier	Average Total Assets ÷ Average Total Equity	2.28	2.06
ROE (DuPont)	Net Profit Margin x Asset Turnover x Equity Multiplier	42%	0.2%
Operations Management			
Inventory Turnover	Cost of Goods Sold ÷ Average Inventory	6.2	5.4
Inventory Days on Hand	(Average Inventory ÷ Cost of Goods Sold) x 365	58.6	67.3
Days-Sales-Oustanding	(Average Accounts Receivable ÷ Net Credit Sales) x 365	63	62
ART	Net Credit Sales ÷ Average Accounts Receivable	5.8	5.9
Leverage			
D/E Ratio	Total Liabilities ÷ Total Equity	1.04	1.57
Interest Coverage Ratio	EBIT ÷ Sales Revenue	48	-12
Debt-to-Assets Ratio	Total Liabilities ÷ Total Assets	51%	61%
Capital Market			
Book Value per Common Share	(Shareholders' Equity - Preferred Equity) ÷ Number of Common Shares Outstanding	$7.00	$5.95
Dividend Payout Ratio	Dividends Paid in a Year ÷ Net Income	26.3%	4666.7%
EPS	(Net Income - Preferred Dividends) ÷ Weighted Average Number of Common Shares Outstanding	$2.75	$0.01
P/E Ratio	Market Price per Share ÷ Earnings Per Share	27.11	7,650.00

Appendix IV
SUMMARY OF FINANCIAL RATIOS

The following is a guide to some common ratios used to measure the financial performance of a business. Different industries have different benchmarks for each ratio. It is important to understand the trends in a company's performance from period-to-period and the relative performance of a company within its industry for each ratio.

Percentage of Base-Year

$$\frac{\text{New Account Balance}}{\text{Base-Year Account Balance}}$$

Presents the values as percentages of a base-year's balance, usually the earliest year shown.

Percentage Changed since Base-Year

$$\frac{\text{New Account Balance} - \text{Base-Year Account Balance}}{\text{Base-Year Account Balance}}$$

Describes percentage changes between years for line items in comparison to the base-year figure.

Revenue Growth

$$\frac{\text{Year 2 Sales} - \text{Year 1 Sales}}{\text{Year 1 Sales}}$$

Measures the percentage growth of revenues from one year to the next.

Gross Profit Margin

$$\frac{\text{Gross Profit}}{\text{Sales Revenue}}$$

Measures the percentage of revenue remaining to contribute towards operating expenses, after deducting product costs per dollar of revenue. The higher the percentage, the higher the contribution per dollar of revenue.

Net Profit Margin

$$\frac{\text{Net Income}}{\text{Sales Revenue}}$$

Represents the profitability and efficiency of the business. Generally, the higher the percentage, the better because it indicates efficient management and expense control.

EBIT

Net Income + Interest + Tax	EBIT measures the **E**arnings **B**efore **I**nterest and **T**ax.

EBIT Percentage to Sales

$$\frac{\text{EBIT}}{\text{Sales Revenue}}$$	Indicates how efficient the company is at controlling expenses in relation to revenue.

Interest Coverage Ratio

$$\frac{\text{EBIT}}{\text{Interest Expense}}$$	Measures an organization's ability to pay interest owing. Generally, the higher the number the better.

Return on Equity (ROE)

$$\frac{\text{Net Income}}{\text{Average Shareholders' Equity}}$$	Tests the financial return the owners of a business are earning, relative to their investment. Generally, the higher the percentage, the better. Use this ratio to assess risk and reward.

Working Capital

Current Assets − Current Liabilities	Represents the excess dollar amount of current assets available after paying current liabilities.

Current Ratio

$$\frac{\text{Current Assets}}{\text{Current Liabilities}}$$	Measures the ability of the company to pay current debt over the next 12 months (specifically, the number of times current assets can cover current debts). Generally, the higher the number the better. If the ratio is too high (e.g. 4:1), it indicates inefficient use of capital as current assets generally have the lowest returns.

Quick Ratio

$$\frac{\text{Cash + Short-Term Investments + Net Accounts Receivable}}{\text{Current Liabilities}}$$	The number of times the most liquid assets (e.g. cash, short-term investments, and accounts receivable) can cover immediate debts (usually 90 days). Generally, the higher the number the better. If the ratio is too high, it indicates inefficient use of capital (see current ratio).

Debt-to-Equity Ratio

$$\frac{\text{Total Liabilities}}{\text{Total Shareholders' Equity}}$$	Used by lenders to examine their risk relative to the owners' risk. Some debt is good, but too much can cause financial distress.

Debt-to-Assets Ratio

$$\frac{\text{Total Liabilities}}{\text{Total Assets}}$$

Measures how much a company's assets are financed through debt. The higher the ratio, the greater the difficulty a company will have in repaying its creditors.

Days-Sales-Outstanding (DSO)

$$\frac{\text{Average Accounts Receivable}}{\text{Net Credit Sales}} \times 365$$

Calculates the average number of days the A/R is outstanding, and indicates how well it is being managed. Generally, the less days outstanding, the less risk. This ratio is crucial in the service industry. DSO should be compared to similar periods in a cyclical business.

Accounts Receivable Turnover (ART)

$$\frac{\text{Net Credit Sales}}{\text{Average Net Accounts Receivable}}$$

Calculates how many times a business collects its accounts receivable throughout the year. The higher the ratio, the more times per year accounts receivable is being collected.

Inventory Days on Hand

$$\frac{\text{Average Inventory}}{\text{Cost of Goods Sold}} \times 365$$

Calculates the average number of days the current inventory will last, and how well the inventory is being managed. Generally, the lower the inventory days on hand, the less the holding costs (e.g. shrinkage, interest, etc.). Inventory days on hand should be compared to similar periods in a cyclical business.

Inventory Turnover Ratio

$$\frac{\text{Cost of Goods Sold}}{\text{Average Inventory}}$$

Calculates the number of times inventory is replenished within one year. Generally, the lower the inventory turnover, the less times per year inventory is being replenished which results in elevated holding costs. Inventory turnover should be compared to similar periods in a cyclical business.

Return on Assets (ROA)

$$\frac{\text{Net Income}}{\text{Average Total Assets}}$$

Compares the net income earned in a period to the amount of assets used to generate that income. Generally, the higher the percentage, the better.

Assets Turnover

$$\frac{\text{Sales Revenue}}{\text{Average Total Assets}}$$

Tests how efficiently a business utilizes its assets to generate sales.

Earnings Per Share (EPS)

$$\frac{\text{(Net Income – Preferred Dividends)}}{\text{Weighted Average Number of Common Shares Outstanding}}$$

Tests the amount of dollar return a company is making for every outstanding common share. This ratio assesses the profitability of a company.

Book Value per Share

$$\frac{\text{(Shareholder's Equity – Preferred Equity)}}{\text{Number of Common Shares Outstanding}}$$

Determines the value associated with each common share after all debts are paid.

Dividend Payout Ratio

$$\frac{\text{Dividends Paid in a Year}}{\text{Net Income}}$$

Calculates dividends paid as a percentage of net income.

Price-Earnings Ratio

$$\frac{\text{Market Price per Share}}{\text{Earnings per Share}}$$

Provides the investor with a measurement of share price to actual earnings of the corporation. It is sometimes used as an indicator to buy or sell shares.

Note:

The purpose of ratio analysis is to help the reader of financial statements ask the appropriate questions and understand which issues need to be addressed. Keep in mind that no single ratio will be able to provide the complete story. Much like a puzzle, you need all the pieces to see the whole picture.

Appendix V

ASPE vs IFRS

Chapter	Topic	Accounting Standards for Private Enterprises (ASPE)	International Financial Reporting Standards (IFRS)
1	When to use	· Private organization (sole proprietorship, partnership, private corporations) · No plans to become public in the near future · ASPE also used by most competitors	· Public corporation or owned by a public company · Private organization intending to become public in the near future · IFRS already adopted by most competitors · Private enterprises adopting IFRS by choice for other reasons, such as, in anticipation of a bank's requirement for IFRS-based financial statements in loan application or have more access to global markets
	Development status	ASPE may eventually evolve into IFRS in the future	IFRS is positioned to be the global accounting standards for the foreseeable future
	Conceptual framework	· It consists of four fundamental qualitative characteristics including relevance, reliability, understandability and comparability · One of the components of reliability is faithful representation	It consists of two fundamental qualitative characteristics including faithful representation and relevance
	Financial statements	Balance Sheet; Income Statement; Statement of Owners' Equity; Cash Flow Statement	Statement of Financial Position; Statement of Comprehensive Income; Statement of Changes in Equity; Statement of Cash Flows
	Revenue recognition	Companies are allowed to use the percentage-of-completion method as well as the completed-contract method	Companies are allowed to use the percentage-of-completion method; the completed-contract method is not allowed
	Disclosure	Fewer disclosures are required	More disclosures are required
	Constraint	"Benefit versus cost constraint" is the term used	"Cost constraint" is the term used
	Conservatism	It is an underlying principle in the conceptual framework	No mention of this concept anywhere
3	Recording the acquisition of long-term assets	Must always be recorded at cost; allows the cost model only	· Recorded using either the cost model or the revaluation model · Under the revaluation model, assets are revalued periodically to reflect their fair market value
	Cost allocation	The periodic allocation of cost of a long-term asset is called "amortization" or "depreciation"	Only the term "depreciation" is used for cost allocation of a long-term asset
	Impairment tests of property, plant and equipment or intangible assets with finite lives	Only if a company becomes aware of an impairment indication must it conduct impairment tests	A company must actively look for impairment indicators every year, and only conduct impairment tests if indicators exist

Chapter	Topic	Accounting Standards for Private Enterprises (ASPE)	International Financial Reporting Standards (IFRS)
3	Impairment tests of assets such as goodwill	Only if a company becomes aware of an impairment indication must it conduct impairment tests	A company must conduct impairment tests even if there is no indication of impairment
	Reversal of impairment loss	An impairment loss that has been previously recorded can never be reversed	Allows reversal of previously recorded impairments for all tangible and intangible assets, except goodwill
	Presentation of various classes of property, plant and equipment	Reconciliation of various classes is not required	A company must show the reconciliation of the beginning and the ending balances for each class of property, plant and equipment
4	Financial obligation	The financial obligation that will occur if a certain event takes place is referred to as a "contingent liability"	The financial obligation that will occur if a certain event takes place is referred to as a "provision"
	Recording contingent obligations	Recognized as an actual liability when the company determines that the payment is "likely"	Recognized as an actual liability when the company determines that the payment is "more likely than not"
6	Issuing shares in exchange for assets or services	Either the fair value of the goods and services, or the fair value of the shares being issued; whichever value is more easily determined will be used	· Must use the fair value of the goods or services received to record the transaction · If this value is difficult to determine, then the fair value of the shares exchanged should be used
	Number of authorized shares	Not required to disclose in the statement	Number of authorized shares for each class must be presented
7	Other comprehensive income (OCI)/ comprehensive income	· All profit and loss items are included in net income · OCI and comprehensive income are not reported	· Items must be classified as either comprehensive income or net income · OCI must be presented either in a stand-alone statement or as a separate section within the statement
	Presentation of earnings per share (EPS)	Not mentioned	Basic and diluted EPS must be presented on the statement of comprehensive income
	Presentation of expenses	There is no specific rule on how to present the expenses as long as items that are required to be presented are adhered to	Expenses should be classified by either their nature or their function
	Statement for changes in shareholders' equity	· Only changes in retained earnings are presented on the face of the statement · Changes in other equity accounts are presented in the notes	Changes in all equity accounts are presented on the face of the statement

Chapter	Topic	Accounting Standards for Private Enterprises (ASPE)	International Financial Reporting Standards (IFRS)
7	Change in accounting policy	No need to meet the reliability/relevance test	The change is either required by IFRS or it will result in more reliable and relevant information for users of its financial statements
	Listing order of assets, liabilities and equity	· Usually list items from most liquid to least liquid · Liabilities are usually presented before shareholders' equity	· Usually list items from least liquid to most liquid · Shareholders' equity is usually presented before liabilities
	Shareholders' equity section	The accumulated other comprehensive income account does not exist on the balance sheet	Retained earnings and accumulated other comprehensive income are reported separately
8	Amortization of bonds' discounts or premiums	· Either the effective-interest method or other methods such as the straight-line method as long as the results are not significantly different from the effective-interest method · Private companies would mostly choose the effective-interest method	Must use effective-interest method only
9	Debt instruments	All debt instruments are valued at amortized cost	· Only debt instruments that are invested for interest revenue purposes are valued at amortized cost · Debt instruments invested for trading purposes are valued at fair value through profit and loss method
	Strategic investments in equity—no significant influence	· Fair value method · Use cost method if quoted market price is not available	Fair value method
	Strategic investments in equity—significant influence	· Equity or fair value method · Use cost method if quoted market price is not available	Equity method
	Fair value adjustments	Recorded in net income	Recorded in OCI
10	Presentation of interest and dividends	· Interest or dividends received are reported as operating activities · Interest and dividends paid is reported as financing activities	· Interest or dividends received are reported as either operating or investing activities · Interest or dividends received are reported as either operating or financing activities

Notes

GLOSSARY

A

Accounting Standards for Private Enterprises (ASPE) — A set of accounting standards followed by private Canadian enterprises when recording and reporting financial information.

Accounts Payable Sub ledger Report — Presents specific information related to vendors and amounts owing to them.

Accounts Receivable Turnover — It is calculated through dividing a company's net credit sales by the average amount of accounts receivable.

Accounts Receivable Turnover (ART) Ratio — Measures how often during the year a company will collect its entire accounts receivable amount.

Accrual-Based Accounting — This means that transactions must be recorded when they occur, not when cash is paid or received.

Accrued Liability — It is a liability as a result of an expense that is recognized for a current period, but is not paid until the next period.

Accumulated Depreciation — Contra account for a long term asset. It reflects the decrease in value of the long-term asset over time.

Accumulated Other Comprehensive Income (AOCI) — A balance sheet item that presents the total of the other comprehensive income accumulated over time.

Allowance for Doubtful Accounts (AFDA) — An account created to record bad debt in a way that satisfies expense recognition.

Amortized Cost — The final measurement base allowed under IFRS is called amortized cost which is often used to value financial assets and liabilities such as bonds.

Amortizing the Discount — This process of allocating the total cost of borrowing (interest and discount) to the interest expense account over the life of the bonds.

Amortizing the Premium — This process of allocating the total cost of borrowing (interest payment less premium) to the interest expense account over the life of the bonds.

Annuity — A stream of periodic and recurring fixed payments such as interest payments over a period of time.

Articles of Incorporation — A government document filed when a corporation is formed; it contains the operational details of the corporation, including its name, purpose and general objectives.

Asset — Any item that is owned and controlled by a business and expected to provide a future economic benefit, such as cash, accounts receivable, inventory, land and machinery.

Asset Turnover — Measures the ability of a company to generate sales revenue from asset investments—the higher the number, the better. Means how quickly a company converts its total assets, including long-term assets, into revenue.

Authorized Shares — The maximum number of shares that can legally be issued by a company.

Average Cost per Share — The average cost per share is calculated by dividing the book value of the common shares account by the number of common shares issued and outstanding at the transaction date.

B

Bad Debt — An operating expense and related to customers who will never pay their bills.

Bank Overdraft — Financial institution's extension of credit to cover the portion of cash withdrawal that is more than the account balance.

Base Figure — A total dollar amount such as total assets.

Base Year — The earliest year shown and will be the basis for comparison.

Basket Purchase — The same as a lump sum purchase, instead of buying in individually from different vendors, a company may get a good price for a basket of assets by buying them from the same vendor in one transaction.

Bond Issuer — The company that issues the bond.

Bondholder — The investor who purchases the bond.

Book Value per Common Share — A value that indicates what a common share would be worth to common shareholders if the company were to be liquidated (dissolved).

Business Segment — Several different lines of business in a company that serve different types of customers or provide different goods and services.

C

Callable Bonds — Same as redeemable bonds. These bonds give the issuing company the option to buy back the bonds before the stated maturity date.

Capital Deficiency — One or more partners has a debit balance in a capital account

Cash Flow Statement — The preparation of a statement to track the sources and uses of cash in a business in ASPE.

Change in Accounting Estimate — A company's accounting records are based on estimates; Changes in estimates occur, when they turn out to be significantly different from the originally estimated amounts.

Classifying Expenses by Function — Expenses are presented on the statement according to the various functions of the entity such as selling expenses and administrative expenses.

Classifying Expenses by Nature — Expenses are presented on the statement according to their natural classification, such as salary expense, employee benefits, advertising expense, depreciation, and such. Expenses analyzed by nature are not allocated to the different functions of the business.

Common Shares — A type of equity that gives shareholders ownership in the corporation, along with voting rights to elect a board of directors and the potential to receive a share of the company's earnings in the form of dividends.

Comparability — The financial statements of a company must be prepared in a similar way year after year.

Comparative Balance Sheet — A comparative balance sheet is simply a balance sheet that shows the balances for multiple years for easy comparison.

Completeness — Inclusion of all details necessary to understand the true nature of an event. A component of a faithful representation.

Compound Interest — The piling on effect that applying the same interest rate has on an account over a period of time.

Comprehensive Income — The total of net income plus other comprehensive income (or loss).

Concept of Economic Entity — Refers to recording and reporting of business affairs separately from the owners' or shareholders' personal affairs, applies to all kinds of organizations, including sole proprietorships, partnerships and private and public corporations.

Conceptual Framework of Accounting — A framework that provides a common basis for those organizations responsible for setting accounting standards, so that there is little or no risk that identical activities or events might be interpreted differently.

Contingent Liabilities — A financial obligation that will occur only if a certain event takes place.

Contributed Capital — Generally comprised of two sub-categories called share capital and contributed surplus.

Contributed Surplus — Contains additions to shareholders' contributions other than capital raised from the sale of shares.

Controlling Interest — Owing more than 50% of the common shares, controlling how the investee company operates.

Convertible Bonds — Bonds that the bondholders can convert or exchange for a specific number of the company's shares.

Copyright — Exclusive rights of ownership to a person or group that has created something.

Corporation — A legal entity that is separate from its owners.

Cost Constraint — This ensures that the benefits of relevant and faithfully represented financial information exceed the costs of providing that information. It is a standard based on benefits versus costs.

Coupon Bonds — Contain detachable coupons that state the amount and due date of the interest payment. These coupons can be removed and cashed by the holder separately.

Cumulative Feature — A feature allowing some preferred shares the right to be paid the current year's dividends and to accumulate any unpaid dividends from previous years.

Current Liabilities — Obligations expected to be paid within one year of the balance sheet date or the company's normal operating cycle.

Current Ratio — A useful ratio for determining the company's ability to repay its upcoming debts and obligations. The current ratio is calculated by current assets divided by current liabilities.

Customer Loyalty Program — A creative way to retain or attract customers by giving them the rewards that are often in the form of points, store currencies or travel miles.

D

Date of Declaration — The date of declaration is the date on which the board of directors announces (declares) that dividends will be paid to shareholders.

Date of Payment — The date of payment is the date on which the company actually makes the dividend payment to eligible shareholders.

Date of Record — The date of record is the date on which the corporation lists all those who currently hold shares and are therefore eligible to receive dividend payments.

Days-Sales-Outstanding (DSO) — Measures the average number of days that a company takes to collect its receivables.

Debenture Bonds — Unsecured bonds that are backed only by the bondholder's faith in the company's good reputation.

Debt Instruments — Investing excess cash by lending money to someone else for interest income is commonly known as investment in debt instruments (or debt securities).

Debt-to-Assets Ratio — Shows how much debt a company has as a percentage of assets.

Debt-to-Equity Ratio — Assess the balance of debt and equity in a business through dividing total liabilities by total shareholders' equity.

Declining-Balance Method — An Alternative depreciation method developed by the accounting profession.

Depletion — The value of natural resources decreases over time as more natural resources are extracted from the ground. It needs to be accounted for in the books just as depreciation is with property, plant and equipment.

Depreciation — The allocation of an asset's cost over its life span.

Determinable Liabilities — Known liabilities which have a precise value.

Direct Method — Calculates cash flow from operating activities by directly analyzing cash received from sales and collections and directly analyzing cash spent on expenses.

Discontinued Operation — A business segment that is no longer part of the company's regular operating activities.

Discount — When the bond interest rate is lower than the market interest rate, the company sells the bond at a discount.

Dishonoured Note — A note not paid at maturity.

Dividend — A distribution of the corporation's earnings (net income) to shareholders based on the shares that they own.

Dividend Payout Ratio — Percentage of company earnings is paid out to shareholders in dividends.

Dividends in Arrears — With cumulative preferred shares, any unpaid dividends from prior periods are known as dividends in arrears.

Double Taxation — This refers to the situation in which a corporation pays income tax on its earnings and shareholders pay personal income tax on their dividends.

Double-Declining-Balance Method — One of the methods of depreciation where the most commonly used depreciation rate doubles the declining-balance rate of depreciation.

E

Earnings per Share (EPS) — A ratio that indicates the profit earned by each common share. EPS enables shareholders to evaluate the potential return on their investment.

EBIT percentage to sales — Indicates how efficient the company is at controlling expenses in relation to revenue.

Effective Interest Method — The method uses the market interest rate at the date the bonds are issued. The effective interest rate is applied to the amortized cost of the bonds payable and reflects the actual cost of borrowing.

Enhancing Qualitative Characteristics — Characteristics which enhance the usefulness of financial information by distinguishing more-useful information from less-useful information.

Equity — The owners' claim on the assets of a business, representing the assets remaining after deducting all liabilities.

Equity Instruments — Investing excess cash by buying a stake in the ownership of another organization is also known as investment in equity instruments (or equity securities).

Equity Method — The equity method is used to record and report strategic equity investments when the investor owns 20% to 50% of the investee's outstanding common shares.

Estimated Liabilities — Financial obligations that a company cannot exactly quantify.

Expense — A decrease in equity as a result of the costs of products or services used to produce revenue.

F

Face Value — The amount to be paid to the investor upon maturity date; the face value is also sometimes referred to as the bond's par value.

Fair Value — The amount that the asset could be sold for in the open market.

Fair Value Adjustment — Recording of changes in carrying value of the investment due to changes in fair value.

Faithful Representation — The information must capture the true substance of a transaction, and must not be manipulated to throw off the users.

Financing Activities — This component of the cash flow statement tracks cash received from investors and lenders to help run, or finance, the business and cash paid back to the investors and lenders.

Fixed Interest Rate — A rate that remains constant for the entire term of the note.

For-Profit Corporations — Corporations formed for the purpose of generating profits for their shareholders.

Franchise — Contract that allows the franchisee to operate a branch using the franchisor's brand name and business model.

Free Cash Flow — The amount of cash remaining after a business has covered its operating activities and capital expenditures (investing in long-term assets).

Free from Material Error — Estimates and assumptions based on the best available information and reasonably justified. A component of a faithful representation.

Fundamental Qualitative Characteristics — IFRS defines two fundamental qualitative characteristics of relevance and faithful representation that are required to provide useful financial information.

Future Value — The value of the money in the account after a number of years.

G

General Partnership — All partners share the responsibility for the liabilities of the business.

Going Concern Assumption — Assumes that the business will continue to operate into the foreseeable future.

Goods and Services Tax (GST) — A sales tax imposed by the federal government on most transactions between businesses and between businesses and consumers.

Goodwill — A company purchases another company at a cost that is greater than the market value of that company's net assets.

Gross profit margin — Demonstrates the impact of cost of goods sold on the income Statement.

GST Recoverable — The amount of GST that the business spends is usually recorded in a contra liability account.

H

Harmonized Sales Tax (HST) — A sales tax that combines the provincial and federal taxes into one sales tax amount.

Horizontal Analysis — Compares information from one accounting period to another, usually from year to year. This means that you can compare similar line items to see how that item has changed from year to year.

I

Income before Discontinued Operations — Shows the results of the company's operations that are ongoing.

Indirect Method — Analyzes cash flow from operating activities indirectly by starting with accrual based net income, adding or subtracting certain items from the income statement and changes in current assets and current liabilities on the balance sheet.

Instalments — Periodic payments on a note payable.

Intangible Assets — Identifiable assets that have no physical form and largely constitute intellectual property, such as patents and trademarks.

Interest Coverage Ratio — This ratio divides EBIT by interest expense. This ratio measures the extent to which earnings before interest and taxes cover the interest payments that are to be made by the business.

International Financial Reporting Standards (IFRS) — An international set of accounting standards required for public enterprises in Canada when recording and reporting financial information.

Inventory Days on Hand — Same thing as the inventory turnover ratio. Inventory days on hand is equal to the average number of days that it took to turn over inventory during the year.

Inventory Turnover Ratio — The inventory turnover ratio represents the number of times that the company sold its entire inventory.

Investee — The company that issues (sells) the debt or equity to another company.

Investing Activities — This component of the cash flow statement tracks the movement of cash in a business on the basis of the purchases and sales of long-term assets.

Investor — The company that purchases and owns the debt or equity issued by another company.

Issued Shares — Authorized shares sold to shareholders.

L

Lease — A contract between the owner of an asset and another party who uses the asset for a given period of time.

Leverage — Relates to the amount of debt and risk the company has.

Liability — A debt or legal obligation that the business owes and must pay with an outflow of resources.

License — Contract that permits the licensee to use the licensor's product or brand name under specified terms and conditions.

Limited Liability — Shareholders are only liable for the amount that they have invested in the company.

Limited Liability Partnership — Professional partnerships to protect one partner from another partner's negligence.

Limited Partnership — Limited partners only liable for the amount of capital they invest in the business while the general partner has unlimited liability.

Long-Term Debt Instrument — A debt instrument that will take more than 12 months to mature.

Long-Term Investment — An investment held for longer than a year.

Lump Sum Purchase — Instead of buying in individually from different vendors, a company may get a good price for a basket of assets by buying them from the same vendor in one transaction.

M

Market Interest Rate — The interest rate that investors can demand in return for lending their money.

Market Value of Share — In the secondary market, shares are sold at a price known as their market value.

Materiality — The ability of a piece of information to affect a user's decision. A component of relevance.

Maturity Date — The date on which the final payment is due to the investor.

Measurement — An action process that determines an amount to be recorded.

Monetary Unit Assumption — Accounting records be expressed in terms of money in a single currency such as Canadian dollars or Euros.

Money Market Instrument — A short-term debt instrument is usually highly liquid and low-risk.

Mortgage Bonds — Bonds that can be issued when companies put up specific assets as collateral in the event that it defaults on interest or principal repayments.

Mutual Agency — Each partner can authorize contracts and transactions on behalf of the partnership provided the activity is within the scope of the partnership's business.

N

Net Profit Margin — The amount of net profit or loss per dollar of revenue.

Net Realizable Value — The amount of cash that the accounts receivable are likely to turn into, or in other words, the accounts receivable balance net of the AFDA.

Neutrality — Information is free from bias. A component of a faithful representation.

Non-Cumulative Shares — Preferred shares that do not have the right to receive any accumulated unpaid dividends.

Non-current Liabilities — Obligations due beyond one year.

Non-Current Notes Payable — A long-term liability that is due beyond 12 months of the date of issue. They are repayable in periodic payments, such as monthly, quarterly or semi-annually.

Non-determinable Liabilities — The exact amount owing or when it is supposed to be paid is unknown on the date of financial statement issuance.

Non-Strategic Investment — An investor may simply try to generate investment income without intending to establish a long-term relationship with the investee. Such an investment is classified as a non-strategic investment.

No-par value shares — Shares issue with no assigned value.

Note Receivable — It is used to formalize an accounts receivable item and also to extend unusual credit terms to a specific customer.

Notes Payable — A legally binding document that represents money owed to the bank, an individual, corporation or other lender.

Not-For-Profit Corporations — Corporations formed for such purposes as advancing social and environmental causes rather than generating financial returns for their shareholders.

O

Operating Activities — This component of the cash flow statement tracks the movement of cash within a business on the basis of day-to-day activities.

Operating Lease — One form of a lease where the ownership is not transferred to another party over the term of the agreement.

Operating Line of Credit — The maximum loan balance that a business may draw upon at any time without having to visit or request approval from the bank.

Operations Management — It refers to the ability of a company to manage its assets such as inventory and accounts receivable.

Other Comprehensive Income (OCI) — A category of income resulting from transactions that are beyond company owners' or management's control, such as a change in market value of investments.

Other Income (expenses) — Includes items that are not part of the company's regular day-to-day operations.

Outstanding shares — The shares that have already been authorized and issued and are held by shareholders.

P

Par value shares — Shares that are issued with an assigned value.

Partnership — An association of two or more people who jointly own a business, its assets and liabilities, and share in its gains or losses; profits are taxed personally.

Partnership Liquidation — A process takes place when the partners decide to end or sell the business, or if the partnership dissolves due to bankruptcy or other factors.

Patents — A patent gives the inventor the exclusive right to use a product. The cost of the patent is for legal fees or the purchase of rights from someone else.

Payment Terms — A promise to pay for the product or service at a future date.

Percentage-Of-Completion — One method of revenue recognition in which a company can recognize a percentage of revenue for a service that is partially completed.

Preferred shares — A type of share with features that is not available with common shares; they receive preference because dividends must first be paid on them before any dividends are paid on common shares.

Premium — When the bond interest rate is higher than the market interest rate, the company can sell the bond at a premium.

Present Value — Amount needs to be invested today to produce a certain amount in the future.

Price-earnings (P/E) Ratio — As an indicator of company growth and risk, it provides the investor with a measurement of share price to actual earnings of the corporation.

Prior Period Adjustment — Correcting entry that is made to a previous period.

Private Corporation — A corporate form of organization that does not offer its shares to the public. The company's shares are instead owned and exchanged privately.

Profitability — The ability of a company to generate profits.

Promissory Note — The same as a note receivable, it is used to formalize an accounts receivable item and also to extend unusual credit terms to a specific customer.

Prospective Approach — Use of new estimate to adjust records for the current and future periods.

Provincial Sales Tax (PST) — A tax paid by the final consumer of a product.

Public Corporation — A corporate form of organization that trades its shares on a stock exchange.

Q

Quick Ratio — Measures the adequacy of highly liquid assets (including cash, short-term investments and accounts receivable) to cover current liabilities. This ratio that is relevant to the analysis of a business' liquidity.

R

Recognition — An accounting principle that entails including an item on the financial statements.

Recoverable Amount — The asset's market price less costs of disposal, or its future value, whichever is higher.

Redeemable Bonds — Same as callable bonds. These bonds have a feature whereby the company has the right to buy back the bonds before maturity at a set or "call" price.

Registered Bonds — List the bondholders as registered owners who receive regular interest payments on the interest payment dates.

Relevance — The characteristic of relevance is met when the information that may affect a user's decision is present in the financial statements.

Residual Value — The estimated value of the asset at the end of its useful life.

Retained Earnings — The earnings that are kept and accumulated by the company after dividends have been paid to the shareholders.

Retroactive Approach — The approach of changing accounting information on financial statements of prior period.

Return on equity (ROE) — A measure of what the owners are getting out of their investment in the company.

Revenue — Income earned by a business, usually for products or services provided by the business.

Reverse Stock Split — Method of decreasing the number of outstanding shares in a company.

S

Sales Tax — Tax applied by the government to goods or services that are sold.

Salvage Value — The proceeds from selling the scrap at the end of the asset's life less its disposal cost.

Serial Bonds — A set of bonds that mature at different intervals.

Share Capital — Refers to capital raised from the sale of shares and contributed surplus contains other types of additions to shareholders' contributions.

Share Issue Costs — Costs associated with the share issue such as registration fees, legal and accounting fees, regulatory fees and printing of share certificates and other required documentation.

Shareholders — The owners of a corporation.

Shareholders' Equity — In a corporation, the shareholders actually own the company and so owners' equity is called shareholders' equity.

Shares — Units of a corporation's equity issued to raise capital for its day-to-day operations or to invest in property and equipment.

Short-Term Debt Instrument — A debt instrument that will mature within 12 months.

Short-Term Investment — An investment held for less than a year.

Statement of Cash Flows — The preparation of a statement to track the sources and uses of cash in a business in IFRS.

Statement of Changes in Equity — Required under IFRS, this statement reports changes in all equity accounts.

Statement of Comprehensive Income — This statement is equivalent to ASPE's income statement with three additional requirements of reporting the comprehensive income, presentation of expenses by function or by nature and presentation of earnings per share.

Statement of Financial Position — The name of the balance sheet under IFRS.

Statement of Partners' Equity — A statement explaining the changes to the balance of each partner's capital account from the beginning to the end of the year.

Statement of Retained Earnings — Changes in retained earnings are presented on the face of the statement under ASPE.

Stock Dividend — A form of dividends paid in shares in lieu of a cash dividend.

Stock Split — A stock split is an action that increases the number of a corporation's outstanding shares, which in turn decreases the individual price of each share traded on the stock market.

Straight-line Depreciation Method — One of the methods of depreciation that is calculated by taking the total cost of the asset less its expected residual value and then dividing the balance by the number of asset's useful years.

Strategic Investment — An investor may intend to establish a long-term relationship with investee. Such an investment is classified as a strategic investment.

T

Term Bonds — Bonds that mature on a specific date.

Time Value of Money — A basic principle of economics and finance that shows the value of money changes over time.

Timeliness — The promptness with preparing financial information.

Trade name — Grants exclusive rights to a name under which a company or product trades for commercial purposes, even though its legal or technical name might differ.

Trademark — Grants ownership rights for a recognizable symbol or logo.

Trading Investments — When debt or equity securities are purchased with the intention of selling them in the short term at a gain, they are known as trading investments, or trading securities.

Treasury Shares — Reacquired shares brought back to the pool of authorized shares that are allowed to be reissued instead of being retired or cancelled.

U

Understandability — The financial information can be reasonably understood by its users if the users have knowledge of the business and a basic knowledge of accounting.

V

Variable Interest Rate — A rate that fluctuates according to market interest rates.

Verifiability — The ability of financial information to be proven.

Vertical Analysis — Conducted by converting each separate line item in a financial statement into percentage of the base-figure within the specific year.

W

Weighted Average Number of Shares — The number of shares outstanding multiplied by the fraction of the year during which those shares were outstanding.

Working capital — Measure of liquidity that assesses the adequacy of a company's current assets to cover its current liabilities.

INDEX

D

E

K

S

Notes